THE BEST SPORTS WRITING OF PAT JORDAN

The Best
SPORTS
WRITING
of Pat Jordan

INTRODUCED AND SELECTED BY ALEX BELTH

A Karen & Michael Braziller Book
PERSEA BOOKS / NEW YORK

The author wishes to thank the editors of the magazines in which these articles first appeared, sometimes in different or abridged versions or with different titles. The magazines are listed on the first page of the stories they originally published.

Persea Books, Inc.
853 Broadway
New York, NY 10003

Library of Congress Cataloging-in-Publication Data
Jordan, Pat.
The Best sports writing of Pat Jordan / introduced and selected by Alex Belth.
    p. cm.
"A Karen & Michael Braziller Book."
ISBN 978-0-89255-339-6 (hard cover : alk. paper)
1. Sports—United States. I. Belth, Alex. II. Title.

GV704.J67 2008
796'.0973—dc22

2007029412

Designed by Rita Lascaro
First edition
Printed in the United States of America

For Mike Sharp, who began as my researcher and is now my friend;
for Alex Belth, my ideal reader and also now my friend;
and for all the editors who helped make this collection.
—PJ

For my Dad and Mike Fox, who taught me how to
recognize good writing and to appreciate how hard it is to do.
—AB

Contents

Introduction

I HAD BEEN CONDUCTING lengthy interviews with sportswriters for my baseball blog for about six months when, in October 2003, I finally got in touch with Pat Jordan. Pat was on the short list of writers I most wanted to speak with. I had read and loved both of his memoirs: *A False Spring*, the unsentimental account of his three years in the minor leagues in the late 1950s and early 1960, which the *Los Angeles Times* called an "unforgettable book" and the *Kansas City Star* described as "one of the most fabulous failure stories of our time;" and *A Nice Tuesday*, a sequel of sorts, written twenty years later, a book Jordan considers far superior (I liked *A Nice Tuesday* more than *A False Spring* too). Both books are marked by Pat's brutal honesty, particularly when it comes to himself. They are unlike other books written by ex-jocks; literate without being pretentious, insightful without being gossipy. Pat is a writer who happens to have once played baseball, not the other way around. With all due respect to fellow pitchers-turned-writers, Jim Brosnan and Jim Bouton, I don't think that there is any ex-jock who has become a better writer than Pat Jordan.

Most writers are flattered to be interviewed, and Pat was no exception. But unlike other professional journalists who are understandably careful with their words, Pat shot from the hip. During our first conversation, he was caustic and profane and didn't care if he was quoted saying Curt Schilling was a bullshit artist or that Yankee pitcher Jeff Weaver was a wimp. He called women broads without apology. There is nothing P.C. about him. But Pat's cursing is benign, endearing even, in a jocular way, like the banter between Jeff Bridges and John Goodman in *The Big Lebowski*. He's from the old school, that's all. But he is also one of the friendliest writers I've ever met. He is happy to chew the fat, generous with his time and his insights about the craft of writing. After I ran our conversation on my blog, Bronx Banter, I called Pat periodically to say hello and talk about the Yankees. He always sounded happy to hear from me. I was writing my first book at the time and didn't know what I was doing. At one point, I sent him a rough draft of an early chapter and he responded by giving me notes and pointers. Our relationship continued to grow over the next few years.

I was familiar with Pat's magazine profiles, mostly from what I had read in *The New York Times Magazine*. But during the research for the book I was writing, I continued to run across Pat's work. As poignant as I find his memoirs, I'm even more impressed with his journalism. Pat is able to cover a subject and make you feel as if you know it tacitly, sensuously, psychologically—as if you have spent a month among cardsharps or pool sharks, or in a clubhouse of a minor league baseball team.

There isn't another sports writer of Pat's caliber who doesn't already have a "Best of" compilation, maybe because he's never had a best-seller and, unlike many of his peers, he's never parlayed his success at writing into his own TV or radio show. "You know the guy from New Orleans who wrote *Confederacy of Dunces*?" Pat said to me during our first chat. "He was a cult success. I'm a cult failure." Actually, Pat is a writer's writer. He's a dedicated craftsman and something of an anomaly: a working freelance journalist for close to forty years, "The Last Knight of the Freelance," as he mockingly refers to himself.

Pat published his first magazine articles in the late 1960s and has been writing consistently ever since. He worked exclusively for *Sports Illustrated* from 1971 to 1978, and his writing has appeared in the *New York Times*, *The New Yorker, Harpers, Playboy, Men's Journal, Inside Sports, Sport, GQ, Life*, and *The Atlantic Monthly*, as well as *Reader's Digest, People, Women's Wear Daily, Good Housekeeping, AARP, Geo,* and *TV Guide*. He's written about superstar athletes, movie stars, and politicians, as well as no-name hustlers, gym rats, schemers, and has-beens. Pat's writing career began during the age of New Journalism, when lengthy, 10,000-word magazine pieces were commonplace. Unlike the flashy brilliance displayed by writers like Norman Mailer or Tom Wolfe, Pat's style is a throwback to an earlier era. It resembles the prose of Lillian Ross far more than that of Hunter Thompson or Terry Southern. It is classic, formal, and direct—lunchpail, no-frills reporting in the tradition of W. C. Heinz, and *Sport* magazine writers like Ed Linn and Arnold Hano.

Pat is a character in some of his work—a distinct New Journalist technique—but his writing remains lean, the reporting sharp, in spite of this authorial presence. After all, Pat specializes in writing about failures because *he* was a failed ballplayer, and the story of Jordan the failed pitcher has always remained an essential part of his work. "I always thought the guys who failed must be deeper because who ever thinks about success," Pat recalled in an interview with the baseball writer Mike Shannon in the book *Baseball: The Writer's Game*. "When you're success-ful, you don't think about it; you just enjoy it. When you're a failure, you think about it. 'Why did I fail?' Nobody ever thinks, 'Why did I hit fifty home runs?' So my feeling is that failures are more interesting than suc-cesses, and I'd much rather do failures. We have so much in common." Pat brings an insider's understanding to all of the stories he writes, the losers and the winners, the mainstream sports, like baseball and basket-ball, and the marginal ones like poker and beauty competitions. He understands the narcissistic, insular world of athletics and celebrity and taps into the vulnerabilities and fears behind athletes' accomplishments.

I went to visit Pat and his wife Susan in Florida as the Cardinals and Tigers played a dull World Series in the fall of 2006. Pat looked like Buttermaker, the Walter Matthau character from *The Bad News Bears* (though his temperament was closer to that of the young red-ass short-stop, Tanner). White beard, Hawaiian shirt, shorts, and flip-flops. Always smoking a cigar. I already had an idea of what should be included in the book—Pat had sent me roughly seventy sports stories already—but I was in hog heaven when I saw what he had stored in the attic: virtually everything he'd ever written, including notes, drafts, research clippings. Everything. The attic would get so hot in the after-noon that I'd have to go up there in the morning to lug magazines and binders down. But on my second day there, I braved the heat of the afternoon in search of more. I crouched in the attic, dripping with sweat, the smell of pancetta and onions and cigar smoke drifting up from the kitchen below. Pat was cooking one of my favorite dishes, spaghetti Amatriciana. He cursed at me from downstairs, warning me not to screw up the neatly organized folders and bins of material. I hunched over the manuscripts, digging through pile after pile, and hap-pily cursed back.

Eventually, I had read well over one hundred of Pat's sports stories. There are many wonderful pieces that we could not include, but the sto-ries that you have are essential. Pat's *SI* stories have previously been col-lected in three volumes: *Suitors of Spring*, *Broken Patterns*, and *After the*

Sundown. This book features several previously anthologized pieces, but the majority of the work here, including Pat's two most famous stories, on Steve Garvey and Steve Carlton, as well as "Duquesne, P.A.," which was made into *All the Right Moves,* an early Tom Cruise vehicle, is being published in book format for the first time. "A Ridiculous Will," about Bobby Hurley post-car accident, has never been printed anywhere else.

Just as he once possessed a gift for throwing a baseball, Pat has a talent for the revealing detail, scene, and image. In the ideal story, he told me recently, "you want the reader to have an overwhelming impression, a mood or feeling of what the story means, or who the character is without being able to point to any word or phrase or sentence in the story that tells him that. Everything must be under the surface so the reader thinks he discovered the meaning of the story that the writer didn't realize he was making. In this way, the reader feels he contributed to the story as a co-writer."

Pat has the utmost respect for his reader and his craft. He is dogged in his pursuit of *the story*, and, as this collection illustrates, he has the ability to dig beneath the surface to reveal the truths of his subjects— and in the case of these stories, the *collective* truths of those who excel and fail in the arena of competitive sports.

Alex Belth

Author's Note

IN 1968, I WAS A TWENTY-SEVEN-YEAR-OLD ENGLISH TEACHER at an all-girls Catholic High School in Bridgeport, Connecticut, who desperately wanted to be a writer. I just didn't know how to become one. Every night, after my wife and five children went to bed, I walked up a narrow stairway to an attic room, where I had set up a desk and a manual typewriter, sat down, and tried to write. I wrote snippets of dialogue, description, narration, and exposition, all of which existed only as exercises, not complete stories.

Then one day, I read in a local newspaper that Muhammad Ali, who had been deposed of his crown because he had refused to fight in Vietnam, was going to be on a local radio station at six o'clock the following morning. I woke at five, dressed, and hustled down to that radio station in a seedy part of the city. How I convinced him to speak with me I don't know, but as Ali looked out through a plate glass door at the winos and bums sleeping on benches, and his Nation of Islam bodyguards, with their dark sunglasses and narrow bowties, eyed me suspiciously, I conducted my first ever interview.

I spent the next two weeks in my attic turning that interview into my first complete story, using all the exercises I had been practicing. Then I sent the story off to *Boxing Illustrated* magazine. A week later, *Boxing Illustrated's* editor, Lew Esken, called to tell me he would pay me $175 for my Ali piece. I was thrilled but then confused when he added, "I see you're one of those New Journalists."

I didn't know there was such a thing as a New Journalist or an Old Journalist, or what each one was, or why Lew would consider me one or the other, or whether I should be pleased or annoyed at the label he'd put on me after only my first published story. So I asked him what he meant. Lew said, "You know, the New Journalists who use novelistic techniques, like Tom Wolfe and Gay Talese." I had no idea who those two writers were.

The next day I went to my local library to find the "New Journalism" stories of Wolfe and Talese. I read Wolfe's baroque brand of New Journalism and decided his work was too self-indulgent for my taste. Then I read some of Talese's nonfiction stories that he'd later publish in his masterful collection, *Fame and Obscurity*. Now *that* was the kind of writing I wanted to produce! Talese used a novelist's techniques in creating real-life portraits, yet he did it in an artless, objective, and understated way. He didn't do a writer's dance—"Look at *me*!"—but rather receded from his pieces like a wallflower at a party. I had already decided I wanted to write what I thought of as "flat" prose that implied more in the subtext than it explicitly stated, inspired by Hemingway's proverbial iceberg, nine-tenths buried under the ocean. Reading Talese, I saw how it could be done in non-fiction. From that moment on, Talese was my inspiration. I was in awe not only of his technique but also of how hard he worked, how much reporting he did, how long he hung around his subjects just to get that one telling detail that he just dropped in his stories without comment.

Almost forty years later, when Alex Belth said he wanted to compile my stories, he also asked me what writer had most influenced my work. Without a thought, I replied, "Gay Talese. He's the Godfather. The rest of us are just chasing him." Which is a circuitous way of explaining why, with Gay Talese's blessing, we have divided the stories in this collection into two sections: Fame and Obscurity. Not only does it suit certain dichotomies (winners and losers, first place and no place) that have run through my writing for many years, it is also a small homage to the man over whose shoulder I once glanced—and found inspiration—many years ago.

Pat Jordan

THE BEST SPORTS WRITING OF PAT JORDAN

FAME

Roger Clemens
Refuses to Grow Up

(from the *New York Times Magazine*, 2001)

Roger CLEMENS IS *BIG*: 6-4, 240 pounds. He comes from a big state, Texas. He drives a big car, a Chevy Suburban, known as the Texas Cadillac. He lives in a big house, a 16,000-square-foot red-brick mini-castle that is a child's fantasy. There are two or three big-screen TV sets in almost every room. There are video games, a sports memorabilia room, a gym and a movie theater with leather seats and animal heads on the walls, and barely a book anywhere. The mansion sits on three acres in the Houston suburbs and is surrounded by a two-mile running track; an enormous heated swimming pool; a large poolside guest house; and a 7,000-square-foot gymnasium with a basketball court, pitcher's mound, batting cage, bleachers, and a video-game room. It is the kind of house and property that Tom Hanks would have loved in the movie *Big* if he had been a Texas country boy and a major-league pitcher with five Cy Young Awards to his credit instead of a New York City toy-company executive jumping on a trampoline.

Clemens even has a treehouse on his property. It's the size of a North Carolina mountain cabin. It's for his four sons, presumably, all of whom are also big for their ages. Only Clemens's wife is little, about 5-3 and barely one hundred pounds. "I would have liked to have had a little girl," Debbie Clemens says, smiling. "But the boys keep me busy. Roger is my biggest child."

There is a lot that is childlike about Roger Clemens, thirty-eight, both good and bad, which is why the man called "the greatest pitcher of our generation" by his former New York Yankee teammate David Cone has always been an enigma. Fans, the media, and his opponents judge him by adult standards and not surprisingly find him wanting. They tend to view his behavior on the mound as that of an overgrown schoolyard bully. (His longstanding reputation as a headhunter was reinforced last season when he beaned the Mets catcher Mike Piazza and gave him a concussion.) But his teammates say they see him differently. They know him and recognize that, in more muted ways, they are like him—grown men who, longer than most, are still playing a game for boys.

In mid-January, Clemens calls from a Disney cruise he is taking with his wife and sons. He tells me what day he expects me in Houston, where to stay and how to get there from the airport. He tells me where to meet him for dinner that night and gives me directions. Then he gives me his cell-phone number in case I get lost.

Brian McNamee, an assistant strength-and-conditioning coach for the Yankees and Clemens's personal trainer, joins us for dinner. As we get settled at our table, Clemens picks up the menu. "Give me direction—can I have a steak?" he says. McNamee nods. "And potatoes?"

"Dry," McNamee says. He is a sour, taciturn man with a long jaw and narrow eyes and a thin, sinister-looking beard. McNamee's life seems to revolve around the conditioning of Roger Clemens. For his part, Clemens is just as obsessive about his twelve-month-a-year workout routines. One Yankee executive said that if Cone worked as diligently as Clemens, he would still be with the club. When Clemens was with the Red Sox, that team's physician, Arthur Pappas, said, "Roger Clemens's commitment to personal conditioning is unmatched by anyone I've ever known in this business."

Clemens begins training for the season the day after the World Series. He runs, lifts weights, and does agility exercises for five hours a day every day from November to January. Then he begins to throw as well, in preparation for spring training.

"We had a good session today," Clemens says. "Tonight, after dinner, I'll do some weight lifting." Then he tells a story about their run the day before, when he and McNamee came upon a man having a heart attack. "We were doing intervals," Clemens says, "walking fifty yards, then sprinting. We had to stop for this guy who was turning blue. Mac gave him CPR and got his pulse back." He shakes his head. "It makes you think. We were having a good run, too, under our usual time."

A French dilettante once said, "I am such an egotist that if I were to write about a chair I'd find some way to write about myself." Clemens's egotism is more childlike and innocent. He doesn't realize that he sees himself at the center of his small universe, at the center of every story he tells. The man having the heart attack becomes a bit player; the point of the story is the interruption of Clemens's "good run."

Everyone is a bit player in Clemens's universe, even his beloved mother, Bess, who reared him and his five siblings mostly without a father. She left her first husband when Clemens was a baby, and her second husband died when Clemens was nine. Bess has been fighting emphysema for years. "She has her good days and bad," Clemens says. "I only hope she can hang on to see me go into the Hall of Fame."

Clemens assumes everyone's pleasure revolves around him. He says of the Yankee catcher Jorge Posada, "I have so much respect for him that I'd love for him to catch my three hundredth win." (He has 260 wins going into this season.) He says he hates to miss a start because that might deprive his fans, especially young boys, from the pleasure of seeing "the Rocket Man punch out twenty." The Rocket Man is his nickname. He sometimes autographs his book "Rocket Man" or "Roger 'The Rocket' Clemens" and then adds a list of his awards: "Cy Young, '86, '87, '91, '97, '98." He gave his four sons first names beginning with K—Koby, fourteen, Kory, twelve, Kacy, six, Kody, four—because K is the baseball symbol for strikeouts, Clemens's specialty.

Clemens says he got his work ethic from his grandmother, Myrtle, "who made a man of me," and his mother, who worked all day as a secretary and cleaned office buildings at night to support her six children. She took them with her to the offices and "made it fun" for them to help her empty trash cans and do their homework on the desks.

"That's where I got my drive," Clemens says. His mother taught him that hard work was not only a means to an end but also that it could be an end in itself if made fun. Clemens learned to take satisfaction in discipline, in denial, in punishing himself.

"Some guys are scared to see how hard they can push themselves," Clemens says as our steaks arrive. "In spring training, I go to the bullpen between innings to do agility exercises and power sit-ups to exhaust myself, because I know I'm only gonna pitch three innings. I want to be panting in the third inning like I was in the eighth. One game, I worked so hard in the bullpen that when I got back to the mound my legs were so wobbly and exhausted I fell on the mound. The fans laughed."

During the regular season, if Clemens gets knocked out of a game in the third or fourth inning, he'll go to the team's training room to lift weights or ride the stationary bike. When he was in Boston, where he spent twelve years, he would have his wife drive him to the Charles River, and he'd run along it in darkness. One night in Boston, he was taken out in the first inning. He had Debbie drive him to a Little League field, where he threw against a fence for nine imaginary innings.

Clemens has the energy of a hyperactive child. Physical work is his way not only of staying in shape but also of self-medicating. If he doesn't drain himself daily, his energy and emotions spill out in negative ways. In '91, he was charged with assaulting a police officer who was trying to arrest his brother, Gary, in Bayou Mama's Swamp Bar in Houston. (He was later acquitted.) In Boston one year, he fired hamburger rolls at a reporter, who had written something he didn't like, in the clubhouse. Once, he threatened an umpire over a bad call, warning him, "I'm going to find out where you live and come after you this winter." Sometimes he turns an umpire's bad call to his advantage. "The home-plate umpire made a questionable call, and that did it," he once said. "It got me all heated up, and everything started to click. My velocity came back." Clemens is constantly "heated up," hot, his energy and emotions always about to boil over.

McNamee mentions an actor, Clemens's age, he met recently who was in great shape. "He was really buff," he says. Clemens's face gets red. He is thin-skinned about his beefy-looking body. A reporter for the Boston Globe used to call him the Pillsbury Doughboy. He has a spiky crew cut from the fifties over a jowly face, a double chin, and a thick neck. He has the body of a body builder who has gone off his diet.

"Yeah, I know a lot of pitchers who look great in a suit," Clemens says. "But you bump into them, and they shatter like a chandelier."

As a power pitcher nearing forty, Clemens needs to work out to stay strong, not look good. During last year's playoffs and World Series, he proved he still has one of the best fastballs in baseball. Against the Seattle Mariners, he struck out fifteen batters, reaching 98 m.p.h. in the late innings in one of the greatest postseason pitching performances ever. If his waist were trimmer, he might lose the center of gravity that anchors him during the delivery of that fastball.

McNamee is standing at the kitchen counter writing out Clemens's workout routine on this cold, rainy morning. The big kitchen is comfortably lived-in. G.I. Joe action figures on the table. Kids' coloring books. Clothes. Little League baseball uniforms identical to the New York Yankees'. Two Jack Russell terrier puppies are rolling over themselves on the sofa. A cockatiel is squawking in his cage. Clemens is watching the news on TV before he begins his workout. When he hears that Jesse Jackson admitted to having a "love child" with a mistress, Clemens roars. "Awesome!"

When told that Jackson took his mistress to the White House at the same time that he was counseling Clinton on the Monica Lewinsky affair, he breaks out laughing.

"You had me going there for a minute. I almost believed you."

"But it's true."

"Sure it is."

We go upstairs to the gym off his memorabilia room. The stairway walls are covered with photographs of the Clemenses and famous people. Clemens seems to be amazed that a man who came from "country people, homey people" has met so many celebrities. He stops on the stairs and, with a child's wonder, points out pictures of himself and Debbie alongside President Bush the Elder, President Reagan, Gen. Norman Schwarzkopf, and dozens of others.

The hallway at the top of the stairs is lined with baseball bats and balls and caps autographed by players. Some of them are famous, like Pete Rose and Mickey Mantle; some are not. It makes no difference to Clemens. He sees them all in the same way, through the eyes of a fan, a young boy, who can't believe his good fortune.

The glass door to the memorabilia room has two Norman Rockwell etchings: umpires staring at a raindrop and a batter swinging through a pitch. Inside the room is a baseball fan's paradise. Gloves of every color. Baseballs marked with Clemens's achievements. Baseball shirts from Hank Aaron and Nolan Ryan.

Clemens points to the autographs on the shirts. "Every living five-hundred-home-run hitter on Aaron's shirt," he says, "and every living pitcher with three hundred wins on Ryan's. I can get a hundred thousand dollars for them. But I'll never sell this stuff. It's for my boys."

He goes to a glass case and lovingly takes out an old yellowed baseball. He points to a fading, spidery signature—Cy Young. "I keep it out of the light," he says.

McNamee, annoyed, comes into the room and says, "Time to go to work." Clemens goes through a door into a small gym and begins to lift light weights, doing shoulder presses with dumbbells and then leg presses and then stretching exercises while he watches CNN on an overhead TV. Finally, he stops in mid-exercise. He begins a slow pantomime of his pitching motion, like a Little Leaguer trying to remember all the parts. He repeats it over and over.

When Clemens is finished with his preliminary workout, McNamee goes downstairs to see whether the Yankee pitcher Andy Pettitte has arrived yet. Pettitte has been working out with Clemens during the off-season for two years, picking up between three and four miles per hour on his fastball during that time. "Now he can bust one in on three-one," Clemens says, "instead of nibbling."

Through the years, there have been rumblings that Clemens is widely disliked in baseball. "Everyone hates him, except if you have him on your team," says Larry Bowa, a former coach with the Mariners. But there is no indication of strife with the Yankees.

Darrin Fletcher, his former catcher with the Blue Jays, says of playing with Clemens: "Before he came to Toronto, I thought of him as an intimidator, like a gunslinger, rough around the edges. But that's not the same guy I played with. He's friendly. He roots for all the guys. He could easily set himself apart with his accomplishments, but he doesn't."

Clemens walks over to a round table, the top of which is a collage of baseball cards covered by glass, and says with pride: "Debbie made that for me. I help my sons with their homework on it. Aw, I don't know if I'm a strict dad. I got guidelines. If my sons get A's they go to Disney with me and their friends. My oldest son wants to get him a deer if he does well on finals."

Clemens looks up. "I'm trying to be the best dad I can," he says. "Not to break the chain or anything. Not because I grew up without a dad. My mom's been my father figure. Still, I see my teammates' dads come into the clubhouse and give their boys a hug and . . ." His eyes tear up. He blurts out: "I have a big heart. I'm sensitive."

Clemens, Pettitte, McNamee, and the two Jack Russell puppies are running around the track in the early morning rain. The puppies leap up and try to bite Clemens's baggy shorts as he runs. When they finish their run, they walk past the heated pool, steam rising, and go into the gym. The puppies try to slip into the gym, too, but Clemens stops them. He picks them up, kisses them on their snouts, and puts them back outside.

With McNamee shouting instructions, Clemens and Pettitte face each other, hunched over like cave men, and begin running from side to side across the gym floor. "Suck it up!" McNamee shouts. Then he has the two pitchers stand at one end of the gym with a football. On his signal, Clemens runs toward him, tosses him the football, and then backpedals until finally McNamee throws him a pass. Clemens catches it on his fingertips like a tight end and slam dunks it through a lowered basketball basket.

They work like this for an hour. McNamee devises different routines that are both work, and, in a way, fun, like kids' games. Backpedaling and catching the football is fun, but no less of a workout that if Clemens just ran back and forth across the gym without fantasizing, one moment, that he was an N.F.L. tight end and, the next, that he was Shaq stuffing it home.

After their running and some calesthenics, they begin throwing off a wooden mound that's covered with a green rug. Pettitte throws first to McNamee, who is crouched down behind the plate wearing a catcher's mask. Clemens stands outside the safety netting, watching. Pettitte throws with a lefty's smooth, effortless delivery, and still the ball hits McNamee's mitt with an explosion that echoes off the gym wall like thunder. "That's smooth, lefty," Clemens says. He smiles. "It must be nice to be young and throw like that in January."

Now it's Clemens's turn. He begins by soft-tossing it to McNamee. His delivery is nothing like Pettitte's. For Clemens, it's all hard work and grunting, even when soft-tossing. It takes him a long time to build up speed. Finally, after perhaps six or seven minutes, he's grunting hard, and the ball is pounding into McNamee's mitt.

"Your shoulder came out on that one," Pettitte says. Clemens stops and goes through his throwing motion, watching his arm go past his head. He repeats the motion over and over until he's satisfied he has the angle right. Then he begins to throw again. "Drive the ball!" he says to himself and then grunts. The ball explodes into McNamee's mitt. Clemens smiles. "Wow!" he says, "That was super!"

Clemens is a dinosaur, the last of the old-time hardball pitchers. No changeups, slow curveballs, trick pitches. Nothing but hard stuff. Two-seam fastballs that tail in, four-seam fastballs that rise, split-fingered fastballs that sink. He's one of a dying breed of pitchers who defied batters, who challenged them with fastballs up in their eyes, who made every confrontation personal, who never accepted the major-league dictum that hitters "murder fastballs." They do if they're 88 m.p.h. fastballs. No one "murders" 98 m.p.h. fastballs like Clemens's.

"If they did," he says, "I wouldn't be here."

Clemens is famous, or maybe infamous, for his brushback pitches and in particular for his penchant for "doubling up," throwing two brushbacks in a row. Besides hitting Piazza last summer, he sent two pitches at the head of Seattle's Alex Rodriguez in last fall's American League championship series. Many people speculate that Clemens's actions prompted the office of the baseball commissioner, Bud Selig, to issue a memorandum two weeks ago authorizing umpires to eject any pitcher they feel is deliberately throwing at a batter's head. If the memo was aimed at him, though, Clemens is unimpressed.

"This is my eighteenth season," he says. "I'm not going to be concerned by that. I'm the same guy I always was. The same pitcher. I'm relentless. I like to pound guys. Challenge power hitters with my fastball. It gets my blood pumping. I want those big hitters to have to make a split-second decision on a ninety-six-m.p.h. fastball inside at their letters, and they can't. I want to jiggle their eyeballs."

Of brushing back Rodriguez, he says, "Aw, I was just trying to crowd him a little, so I could get him out with a ball away in the late innings." But Lou Piniella, the Seattle manager, had no doubt that Clemens was trying to hit Rodriguez, and according to Clemens, "he threw a fit. The next day I read that I'm a headhunter. Hell, brushback pitches were accepted years ago. Today, it's a federal case.

"Sometimes you're just trying to drive the ball in on a guy, and it gets away from you. You can't worry about it. If a hitter's afraid of getting hit, he shouldn't be in the big leagues. Hell, I gotta stand there on the mound and watch them do their little jig at the plate, digging in and waving their bat. Then they hit a shot off my shins, and they're standing at first base, laughing at me limping around the mound in pain." He utters an obscenity and shakes his head in disgust.

Clemens's most notorious brushback pitch was the one that hit Piazza. Coming to the plate that day, the Mets catcher had seven hits, including three home runs, in his last twelve at bats against Clemens, leading many people—Piazza among them—to label the beaning a deliberate act. Then, a few months later, Clemens faced Piazza again in the World Series in what would become known as "the great bat-throwing incident." Clemens explains the two episodes, which he calls "the deal," this way:

"So here I am pitching against this guy in the World Series I'd hit in the head, and he and his manager had grandstanded about it. Nobody mentioned that the ball hit his wrist first and then his head. Nobody wrote the story that after the inning I went to the clubhouse and asked my trainer to call the Mets clubhouse to see if he was all right. When he called over there, Piazza told him to tell me to go to hell. To me, then, it's over.

"Now, the next time I pitch against this guy, I'm fired up, ready to get it on, what everyone in the country wants to see, me versus this guy. So I throw him a fastball, and he shatters his bat and pieces of it come at me. I fielded what I thought was the ball, and when I realized it was a piece of his bat, I threw it in disgust toward my dugout. I didn't want his bat in my life anymore. And he's halfway to first base, and the bat flies by him. Usually a guy shatters his bat and he goes to the dugout for another bat. Why was he running toward first base?

"After the game, a reporter asked me what I was thinking. I said I thought it was the ball coming back at me. 'You mean when you had the bat in your hand, you thought it was a ball?' No, jerk, not when I had it in my hand. I knew it was a bat then. But by then the story took on a life of its own. Now, I hear someone's trying to get all the pieces of the bat together to auction them off for three million dollars for charity. Am I gonna kiss and make up with Piazza? Aw, I don't know about that."

At noon, McNamee calls a halt to the workout. "The first part of the day is over," he says.

Clemens, drenched with sweat and smiling, says, "We been working while everybody else been sleeping."

Clemens, along with McNamee and Pettitte, drive over to the tony Houstonian Hotel, Club, and Spa to lift weights for a few hours. The men's locker room is carpeted, with dark mahogany lockers and a lounge with overstuffed sofas and armchairs. Male attendants dressed entirely in white cater to the members' needs.

Clemens likes to work out here because he likes to rub elbows with powerful people, including ex-President George Bush. Bush and

Clemens became friends years ago partly because Bush loves baseball and partly because there is something elemental about Clemens that appeals to men of Bush's generation. There is no subterfuge about Clemens, no desire to be P.C., no desire to say anything other than what's on his mind.

When Bush was president, Clemens visited him several times at the White House and at the president's house in Kennebunkport, Me., where they played horseshoes. "He's very competitive about horseshoes," Clemens says. "Once he was gonna play that Russian leader. Who was it? Oh yeah, Gorbachev. And both of them practiced before they met."

Clemens also had an insider's view of the Florida election fiasco. Clemens doesn't know Jeb or George W. Bush that well, he says, but he's close to their brother Neil (best known for his involvement with the failed Silverado Banking, Savings, and Loan), whom he calls "the smartest Bush because he's not in politics." Neil told him he wouldn't believe the conversation between Jeb and George W. Bush on the night of the election. Jeb was crying when he told W. he couldn't hold Florida for his brother. Then, a few hours later, he was elated to tell his brother he had won the state.

After lifting weights at the Houstonian, Clemens and his crew head for his Suburban to go to a Mexican restaurant. He's a little annoyed because "I hit a little bit of a wall on the exercise bike." Pettitte and McNamee are talking golf beside the Suburban. Clemens snaps: "Get in! I'm hungry! I wanna eat!"

Late in the afternoon, back at the mansion, he says, "Wanna see my deer?" He leads the way through the kitchen into the living room, which is being tidied up by two maids. The living room is all white tile and white marble and white Grecian columns, like an expensive mausoleum. Inside his wood-paneled office, Clements points to six mounted deer heads on the wall. Through his office window, I can see a huge shrub that has been manicured into the shape of a Texas longhorn steer. Clemens says that he helped to design his house so that "I never have to leave it if I don't want to."

A few years ago, Clemens said he wanted to retire at thirty-eight. "I'm having too much fun to retire now," he says. "I haven't lost my intensity even though I've done everything I wanted to accomplish." He expects to be elected into the Hall of Fame soon after he retires, and he hopes to win 300 games. "I woulda won three hundred fifty by now if I'd had Rivera closing games for me all my career," he says. Mariano Rivera is the Yankees' magnificent relief pitcher. Clemens loves playing for the Yankees. "I love the history, the legends at spring training, their respect for the game. I get a feeling I don't know how to explain. The players know how to work and how to have fun in N.Y.C. Sometimes they want me to go out with them at night, but I don't. Maybe if I was younger."

Clemens says there are no cliques on the Yankees, as there are on other teams. "I run with everyone," he says. "There's always four different guys eating dinner together every night."

His sense of gratitude toward the team runs deep, for it gave him the opportunity to do the only thing that had eluded him in his career: win a championship. The only way he can repay the Yankees, he says, is to "make money for the coaches and the grounds crew and the clubhouse attendants by getting into the playoffs and World Series. There's a bond there, and it's meaningful. It's important for me to do well in the Series so they get a check that maybe helps them put an addition on their house."

When the Yankees are on the road, Clemens becomes a tourist. Most of the time, he sightsees alone because his younger, single teammates keep late hours. "Guys miss things staying out til two a.m.," he says. He smiles and points to the antlered crew on the wall. "See what chasing women in heat will do to you."

When he finally does retire, Clemens has a child's wish list of things he wants to do that he is prohibited from doing while playing baseball. He wants to go skiing, race a car, and gamble at a casino, because "I never had a taste for it but now I'm ready to put ten thousand dollars on a hand of blackjack."

But as of now, retirement seems a few years off. Clemens is still a pitcher, consumed by his workouts, his pitching, and his diet. Today for lunch, however, he cheated at the Mexican restaurant. He says he ate something "a little fillier," by which he means something rich with fat and carbohydrates.

Clemens has his own personal vocabulary that has often made him the butt of sportswriters' acerbic columns, as if to prove he is less than a brain surgeon. He uses words like "fillier" and "recorrect," and once said of himself, "I'm the goodest guy you can find." Once, a Boston paper infuriated him by running his quotes verbatim for days on end to make him look foolish, which he isn't. He's just what he claims to be, "a country boy" who has spent most of his life playing a child's game. Clemens thinks it's the sportswriters who are the stupid ones.

"My answers to the media are always blasé," he says, "not very informing because they don't ask me the right questions. They ask me, 'How'd you feel tonight?' 'Well,' I say, 'I struck out fifteen, how do you think I felt?'"

Venus & Serena Williams

Breakers West: Where the Kissing Never Stops

(from the *New York Times Magazine*, 1997)

HE PUTTERS ALONG the palm-shaded walkway of the Breakers West tennis club in a little golf cart. Birds chirp sweetly in the palms under a midday sun. The sun is yellow; the sky blue; the palms green. His wife and two daughters walk behind him. His wife is a heavyset black women in an oversized sweatshirt with a cartoon figure on front. She is bouncing a basketball. His daughters are in tennis whites. They are carrying rackets and giggling. He is dressed in tennis whites, too, a big hunched-over black man in his fifties with a grayish beard. He is smoking a thin, brown cigarette and clutching a cellular phone. He putters to a stop at an umbrella-shaded white table in between two green tennis courts. He gets out and greets his guests.

He hugs the two black men in tennis whites—"Brother Brown, Brother Gbedey"—and says, "Hi, Dave," to the white man in blue tennis shorts. He says, "Thank you for joining us today, sir," to the white man in the Hawaiian shirt. He gives him a soul handshake. Then he says, "Brother Brown. Heard you left your tennis stuff in an open car in a white neighborhood." He shakes his head. "Stole it, huh?" He laughs.

Richard Williams likes to play games with white people. He tells white reporters, "Now, don't be intimidated by us. We won't hurt you." He thinks he is throwing them off stride when they interview him about his daughters. Williams is the father, coach, and manager of Serena and Venus, tennis prodigies. They have been prodigies since they were four-and a half years old. Serena, fourteen, is in her first year as a professional tennis prodigy. She recently lost her first pro match badly, 6-1, 6-1, to a girl who said, "I guess I played a celebrity." Venus, fifteen, has been a pro tennis prodigy for two years. She's competed in four tournaments and won none. Still, both girls are very famous for being famous tennis prodigies. Their father, who puts out a newsletter in which he refers to himself as "King Richard," writes in that newsletter, "In the process of taking the tennis courts, there was being born a superstar, Miss Venus and Serena Williams." He refers to them as "champions." He says of Venus, "I don't know anyone who's done what Venus did. She's already made it in tennis. She's head and shoulders above anyone out there. She should be in the top twenty now. She should go right into the Hall of Fame. She's surpassed things needed to be there. She's gonna be there anyway, so why waste time."

Apparently, the Reebok Company agrees with Williams. Reebok has signed to a multimillion-dollar endorsement contract a fifteen-year-old girl, Venus, who has not won a tennis tournament at any level since she was eleven years old. Serena has not won a tournament at any level since she was nine, although her father claims she won forty-six of forty-nine tournaments before then. That computes to almost eleven tournaments a year. Like Venus, Serena has "too many sponsors who want to give her money now," says Williams. He's turned down those sponsors, he says, because too much money might "mess up" his kids. "We have the perfect example in Jennifer Capriati," he says. "They messed up a lot."

Williams uses the Capriatis a lot in explaining his odd behavior toward his daughters' careers. "They said Jennifer's father was a fool" for letting her turn pro at fourteen he says. "She was a great kid at fourteen. At fifteen, she lost her smile. At sixteen, there were problems. She lost it. What happened? I watched her and her family and now I know what to do to make sure that doesn't happen to my kids. I'm sick of looking around tennis and seeing these poor kids making a living for their parents who are prostituting them."

Venus, who is making a living for her parents, agrees with her father. "I learned a lot from Capriati," she says. "She went wrong maybe because she let other people make decisions for her and I'm going to make my own."

One of the reasons why Capriati "went wrong" was that she let her father, Stefano, become her coach. She wasn't the only young female tennis player to fall into this trap. Mary Pierce's father, Jim, coached her for years, with disastrous results both on the court and in their family lives.

Today, Steffi Graf is paying the price for having her father, Peter, not only coach her but also handle all her finances. Graf has even been threatened with arrest by her own government for financial improprieties she claims she had nothing to do with. She claims she was simply a trusting daughter who let her father handle her tennis and financial affairs. Which is the problem with young tennis women when they surrender control of their professional lives to their fathers. They lose their objectivity when their coach is their father. They become merely an extension of his will with no recourse to fight that will, in the way they can an objective, paid coach. How does such a girl say no to daddy?

What precisely Richard Williams learned from the Capriatis is not clear, since he allowed both his daughters to turn pro at fourteen. He even threatened to sue the WTA if it refused to let Serena compete in pro tournaments. Still, he says he is determined to make sure his children don't get "messed up" in tennis. That's why he refused to let them compete in junior tennis tournaments during their formative years. He claims that junior tournaments put too much pressure on children, especially from their parents who "fight, blow-to-blow, over their kids." He cites as an example a little girl who was so frightened to take the court against Venus that Venus "quit the match" so the girl wouldn't have to face her parents screaming, "You let that little nigger whip you!"

Serena says she hasn't played junior tournaments because "I practiced to play on the professional tour level, not the amateur. I feel I'm more than ready to get out here and compete with professionals." Anne Miller, the girl who beat her in her first tournament in five years, doesn't agree. "Maybe she needs to play some junior events to learn how to become match tough," said Miller. "There really is no substitute for the real thing. I felt like a complete veteran compared to her."

Despite the Williams girls' lack of tennis victories, they do *look* like "champions." They are always the most distinctive girls to take the court on those rare occasions when they do take the court. Venus is over six feet tall, very black, very beautiful, very regal, like an African queen. Her cornrowed hair, festooned with white plastic beads that swing wildly and clatter noisily when she plays, make her even more recognizable. Serena is shorter, stockier, less regal but more powerful. If Venus is the queen, Serena is the fierce warrior, though she does share Venus's hairstyle. The hair was their father's idea, one he had when he began sending out brochures to promote his little girls as tennis prodigies.

Tunicia Sheffield, twenty-four, is also a prodigy of Williams's. Sheffield is ranked nine-hundredth in the world. She says, "Mr. Williams has helped me a lot in marketing myself. He told me as a black woman I'm a double minority so I had to use as much as I can to get my foot in the door. He told me it's not about tennis, it's about marketing myself. I should always send out a promotion picture because pictures are better than words. He's very critical of the way Zena Garrison looks. He says she never looks nice. She doesn't have neat hair and her clothes are mismatched. He's gonna give me more marketing skills later, but for now, he says, 'Just be neat.'"

The only skills Williams doesn't help Sheffield with are her tennis skills. He doesn't let her practice with his daughters because, she says, "Mr. Williams doesn't like Serena and Venus to hit with girls. They only hit with men." Hitting only with men in practice is another trademark of the Williams girls. Their father is dismissive of women tennis players, none of whom, he thinks, hits as hard as his daughters. Venus agrees, saying, "I never played anyone [women] who hit harder than me. I don't have any women idols in tennis."

At Breakers West, the Williams girls rarely lose. Their father handpicks their male opponents in the same way Don King, the promoter on trial for insurance fraud, handpicks opponents for his fighters. King is Williams's idol, ever since he picked up the Williams family in a chauffeur-driven limousine and took then to lunch. Williams says, "I wish I was Don King. He's unreal. Class. The most knowledgeable man in the world at making money." While Williams says that there are people who criticize him for associating with King, he says that "they should be more concerned with what we're trying to get from Mr. King. He's the one with the millions."

Williams talks a lot about money. He says he got his girls started in tennis when "I seen this girl play tennis and make more in one tourney than I made in a year. For Venus, tennis was a way of getting money."

Today, Serena is hitting with Gerard Gbedey at one court, and Venus is hitting with David Rineberg at the other. Williams sits under the umbrella under the blue sky and yellow sun and watches his daughters in white. His wife, Oracene, stands under a tree, playing with her basketball. A bird chirps sweetly in a green palm, as if on cue in a Disney cartoon.

Serena moves powerfully on the court, low to the ground, squat, like a pit bull. Venus moves straight up, her long arms like whips driving the ball over the net.

"Serena is awesome," says Williams. "She's gonna be better than Venus." Serena drives Gbedey's serve into the net very powerfully. "That's all right, Serena Williams," says her father.

Serena smiles and runs over to her father. She kisses him on the cheek, and says, "I love you, daddy. You're great."

"I love you, too, Serena Williams. You're great." She runs back to the court.

Venus whips a passing shot past Rineberg's outstretched racquet. The ball is out but Rineberg says nothing. Williams says, "You got Dave's number, Venus Williams."

Venus smiles and runs over to her father. She rubs her nose against his and kisses his cheek. "I love you, daddy," she says.

"I love you too, Venus Williams. You're a great kid." She runs back to the court.

A white family walks past on their way toward another court. The husband is fat; the blond wife is plump; their little boy is dressed in immaculate tennis whites. They all three stare, wide-eyed, at the two black girls in cornrowed hair playing tennis at the Breakers West tennis club in Palm Beach, Florida. The parking lot of the Breakers is filled with Jaguars and Mercedes-Benzes. The grounds are lushly landscaped—royal palms, bougainvillea, and hibiscus—and the courts are immaculate. Lime tennis balls are sprinkled, like Easter eggs, among the lariope and flowers. Williams lets them lie there. He is not impressed with the Breakers. "I don't see no nice life here," he says. "I only see the underprivileged, not the rich peoples. Florida peoples are so laid back. They don't strive to get things. Mosquitoes do more hustling." Williams knows a lot about hustling. He has been hustling all his life. He hustled up discarded tennis balls for his daughters on the public courts of L.A. He slept in old cars in a junk-yard when he was a young man working at Woody's Car Wash, also in L.A. He threw out trash for an old, white doctor when he was a boy from the "poorest family" in the "poorest section" of Shreveport, Louisiana. "I was fifty before I could spell Shreveport," he says. "We were the poorest in the state. We hold the record." He was one of five children, the only son of Julie Williams, a single mother, who supported her brood by picking cotton.

"My mother was my dad, my psychiatrist, my hero, the greatest person who ever lived," says Williams. "She taught me pride, decency, religion, but most of all that the family was the oldest human institution and civilization would disappear when the family went bad. The only mistake she ever made was to marry my father, who didn't care about us."

As a boy, Williams worked many odd jobs before and after school. But still he found time to excel in sports in high school. By his account, he was the "second best basketball player in the state, the best football player in the state, even though some thought Billy Cannon was, and the best golfer in the state. I didn't play tennis. I thought it was a sissy game."

After high school, he moved to Chicago to work on construction jobs. Then, at twenty, he moved to L.A. "because I thought it'd be really nice." He eventually settled in Watts, worked hard like his mother had taught him, started his own security business, and married Oracene, a nurse. They have five daughters (Yetunde, twenty-four; Isha, twenty-three; Lyndrell, seventeen; Venus, fifteen; Serena, fourteen), all of whom he started in tennis and all of whom were talented. Yetunde was "very good," he says. "Isha was awesome. Lyndrell, too. Serena might be the best. But Venus was a champion from the first day."

At the time Venus was four and a half, the Williams family was living in Compton. The only tennis courts available to them were in gang territory. Williams has used that ghetto experience to create the Myth of Venus, Serena, and Richard Williams. He writes in his newsletter, "Venus and Serena was shot at by the gang members while practicing tennis, and the girls hit the ground." ("That's why Venus is so quick," he says.) Mr. Williams was beaten several times by gang members, going home with black eyes, but after about seven months he had earned their respect. He says he became better known as "King Richard, Master and Lord of the Ghettos in Compton, CA." By 1989, Mr. Williams says, he had "helped gang members to go back to high school, underprivileged kids get good grades in school, help parents understand the importance of family and education, helped parents stop prostituting their daughters, and coached seven gang members to getting their G.E.D."

Williams stops talking for a moment. Then he says, "I don't know if I should tell you anymore. I'm gonna write a book about my life in four years. I'd better ask my agent." He flips open his cellular phone and calls his agent. Oracene takes over the coaching.

"Venus, you were late with your racquet," she says.

"Yes, momma."

"Serena, you're too heavy on your feet."

"Yes, momma."

Williams gets off the phone. He loses himself again in his daughters' play. Venus is playing Gbedey now. He's a slim, wiry, quick man on the court. Venus smashes a serve past his outstretched racquet, though the ball is six inches out. Gbedey exclaims, "Shit!"

Oracene, who doesn't talk much about her daughters' careers, said on one occasion, "I was for the girls turning pro at fourteen," and on another "I wanted then to wait until they were sixteen. I worry about them starting out quickly and fizzling out early."

Gbedey hits a passing shot to Venus's left. She strides after the ball, her long legs gobbling up the court, and reaches it easily. She rifles a backhand over the net, handcuffing Gbedey, who flubs it.

Williams calls out, "Way to move, Venus. That's why you're gonna be a superstar." But Venus does not always move so gracefully across the court. She is like a young colt still not grown into her long legs and big feet. At times, her superior height and strength makes up for her lack of finesse on the court. For brief stretches during a match, she can over-power almost anyone with her physical talent. But she can't sustain those blinding stretches because she doesn't have enough tournament experi-ence. At Oakland in 1994, she had Arantxa Sanchez-Vicario down a set, with a service break, before her game fell apart, with Sanchez-Vicario winning, 2-6, 6-3, 6-0. At the Acura Classic this past August, she lost badly in the first round to a relative unknown, 6-4, 6-1. She was described as having "clumsy feet," "an erratic serve toss," and an inabil-ity to hit the ball anywhere except down the middle of the court. She committed twenty-five unforced errors and double-faulted eight times on serve. Still, a *New York Times* reporter described her as looking "spec-tacular" with her white beads and "a white silk vest with a bow in the back." After that debacle, Venus was in tears on the way to her press con-ference. ("Who said that?" says Venus. "I never cry over tennis.") Williams brushed off his daughter's poor performance by saying the only thing she was going to work on the next day was "her education." He said the only reason why she didn't perform well was "she didn't practice much. Her only weakness is she's overconfident."

Williams wants it both ways. He wants to promote his daughter as "a champion," and, when she loses, to trivialize her losses with excuses. She doesn't practice much because, in Venus's own words, "Tennis is just for fun. I'm more interested in myself than in my career." Yet she practices four hours a day, six days a week. "We take off Wednesdays to play basketball," says Williams. But on one given Wednesday, when the Williamses were supposed to be "playing basketball," they were at the Breakers, practicing tennis. This is how Williams hopes to maintain the Myth of Venus and Serena Williams as two uninterested child prodigies of such genius that their stardom is a foregone conclusion. As such, they can be cavalier about their game, since the myth is designed to camouflage their failures. But when she is away from her father, Venus says, "I take tennis very seriously. I care how I play because I have pride in what I do."

On the other court, Serena charges the net on a drop shot from Rineberg and slams it past him. Her father says, "That's a good way to close, Serena. Next time turn more of an angle. You'll sell a lot of tickets that way."

Serena, beaming, says, "Yes, daddy," and runs over to kiss her father. "I love you daddy."

"I love you, too, Serena Williams." She runs back to the court and serves to Rineberg. "Look at that serve!" Williams says. "Did you ever see a fourteen-year-old serve like that? Oh, yes, she's better than Venus. And the only thing that can stop Venus from being number one by eighteen is an accident. Do you know Venus Williams gets more media attention than anyone else in sports except Michael Jordan?"

Despite all of Venus's "media attention," Williams still claims there is "so much racism in America that Americans don't care about black peoples. That's why I plan to promote Venus and Serena in Asia. I don't want to market them in a society that doesn't care about them. Chinese peoples are interested in black peoples." A moment later, he says, "I never thought about marketing my daughters, but I might look at it now." He claims he has never made money off his daughters. Yet a Reebok spokesman, Dave Fogelson, said that Williams was paid a consultancy fee for two years. "Reebok never paid me one penny," says Williams.

Venus is at her father's side. Williams says, "What you want, girl?"

"Nothing, daddy." She bends over and kisses him.

"Thank you, Venus Williams."

"You're welcome, daddy." She runs back to the court.

"My girls know how to be kids," says Williams. He lights another brown cigarette. "They live life as kids." (Venus has said, "I never really had any friends," except for Serena.) Her father says, "Some kids come around and see my daughters don't date, don't do drugs, won't get pregnant, and so they drift off. Still, I won't allow Venus to be a daddy's girl."

Just then, another black girl in a tennis dress comes walking toward Williams. She's pretty, maybe twelve, with a big smile. "Hello, Mr. Williams," she says, and kisses him on the cheek.

"Hello, Angela Carter." He gestures with his head to the white man in the Hawaiian shirt. "Tell him your grades, Angela Carter."

She blushes. "All A's."

Williams smiles and nods, as if he's just proven a point: Education is very important to him. One of his prized possessions is a certificate from Alta Vista Elementary School that certifies Richard Williams as a Very Important Parent. Often, he'll take Venus and Serena to ghetto grammar schools where the girls give motivational speeches. (One of the terms of Venus's contract with Reebok is that she make such appearances.) These appearances are inevitably reported in local newspapers: "Tennis prodigy shares experiences with Lakeland's neglected youth." "Tennis ace serves message to peers." The story that follows quotes Venus: "No matter what you decide to be, you need an education."

Williams says that Venus's appearance at those schools has a profound effect on deprived children. When they see the tall, beautiful, smiling tennis prodigy with the corn-rowed hair and the white tennis outfit, and her loving father, also in tennis clothes, both of them beaming at one another, Venus reaching up to kiss her father, those children can't help being impressed. "One little eleven-year-old girl was pregnant, with gonorrhea, and Venus turned her life around," says Williams. "Now that girl's gonna be a Supreme Court Justice."Education is so important to Williams that for years he refused to entrust their education to schools. He schooled his two daughters at home so that he could be sure they always did "very good in school, extraordinarily well, and I know because I do the grading . . . Venus gets A-pluses."

When Venus and Serena were schooled at home, they had four tutors, not including Williams, his wife, and Lyndrell, he says. (Venus says she had only one tutor.) Williams himself taught Venus about investment, finances, and taxes from the age of five so that by the time she and Serena reached eighteen, "they know how to keep their money. Do you know Phil Nike made over a billion dollars and Bill Gates over twelve billion? That's why I'm trying to get Venus out of tennis. Her goal is to ring the bell at the New York Stock Exchange."

"Venus is back in school now," he says. "But that might be a mistake. I took them out because the things Venus studied, she'd already learned. Maybe I'll check her out of school again and put her in college. But first I'll talk to her psychiatrist to make sure I'm not pushing her too hard." Williams goes on to say he might have Serena quit tennis too, "because she's too bright. I'll just have her work with her lawyers, psychiatrist, and staff."

All of Williams's daughters are talented and brilliant, he says. Yetunde has been in medical school "dealing with hearts, valves, and muscles of the hearts," since she was sixteen, although he will not say what school took her at that age. Isha, twenty-three, was an "awesome" tennis player, who is now in a law school he will not disclose. Lyndrell, seventeen, is a "genius," and Serena is "brilliant." Williams says, "I never say anything derogatory about my kids. I learned that from my mother." He's also said, "I talk to our psychiatrist for advice to keep the love of my children. Every parent does the best they can do."

Oracene says, "It was my idea to teach the girls at home. I never worried about their socialization." Venus, too, "thought it was a good idea to be schooled at home," although, now, she admits that she likes going to a regular school. "I like that I have an exact time to go to school and an exact time to do my homework," she says. "When I was schooled at home, if I woke up and wanted to do my assignments tomorrow, I'd skip them. Maybe I'd learn it in three weeks if I don't want to work that day. If I was tired I didn't have to stay up until nine p.m. to do homework. Now I like to have to do that. The only thing I don't like is if I wake up late now, I have to miss breakfast. That's not what I want." As for friends, now, she says, "How can you make friends in four weeks?"

Williams is talking on his cellular phone again. Oracene produces her own cellular phone and makes a call. Angela Carter is hitting with Morris Brown on a far court. Serena and Venus have teamed up in a doubles match against Rineberg and Gbedey. Williams glances over his shoulder at Carter, and calls out, "Racquet back, Angela Carter."

"Yes, Mr. Williams."

Oracene calls out, "You're draggin' your back foot, Venus." Venus says nothing.

Williams and his wife go back to their phone conversations. The birds are chirping in the green palms in the mid-afternoon sun. Rineberg lobs a ball high into the sun. Venus backpedals. Her big feet get crossed. She staggers a bit before slamming the ball into the net.

"You have to get back quicker, Venus," says Oracene.

"That's all right, Venus," says her father. "That was a great shot."

"Thank you, daddy." Gbedey serves to Venus. She hits a sharp passing shot deep into the corner that Rineberg reaches only with a desperate, flailing swipe of his racquet. His return bounces beyond the end line at Venus's feet. She calls, "Out!" It's a habit she has yet to break in tournaments. "I can't help it," she's said, "I'm used to calling my own shots."

Gbedey and Rineberg take an early lead in sets. They laugh between themselves. The Williams girls look annoyed at this deviation from their father's practices that are scripted in the same way the Harlem Globetrotters' games are scripted against their white patsies, the Washington Generals. Serena, big-bottomed and heavy-legged, stretches for a ball to her left. She misses it.

"That's all right, Serena," says her father. "Great try. Martina didn't become great in a day."

Venus hits Gbedey's next serve into the net. Her eyes shift to the man in the Hawaiian shirt watching her behind dark sunglasses. Again, she looks annoyed. She is not used to playing before an audience. It bothers her. Objective attention. But still, she is a great athlete. She drives the next serve deep into Gbedey's court. The ball bounces up so sharply at his feet that he can't get his racquet on it. It hits him in the chest. Venus smiles and does a little dance.

"Here comes that Wimbledon trophy," says her father. "Let me hold the purse."

Venus runs over to her father and kisses him for maybe the twentieth time this day. "I love you, daddy," she says, and runs back to the court.

"I love you, too, Venus Williams. You're a great kid."

And so it goes. Ad nauseum. Kisses. Praise. The two girls practicing in a vacuum. Not practicing, really, just playing, at their own pace, with no pressure, no real coaching except for an occasional comment from their mother ("Calm down, Venus,") and their father's unqualified praise ("Great shot, Serena Williams). Soon, the two girls' natural athleticism begins to wear down the two slightly built men. When the girls take the lead, they begin to laugh.

"I think we should correct our own mistakes," says Venus. "I don't put pressure on myself or accept it from anyone else."

Williams says, "I don't think I'm protecting Venus from the pressures of life or tennis. I think I'm doing it the right way. I'm making it up as I go along. I don't want my daughters to get beat up like Chris Evert did when she was young."

Chris Evert was coached by her father, Jim, who still coaches tennis at the Holiday Park public courts in Fort Lauderdale. Most of his students these days are housewives swatting at softly hit balls as if they were mosquitoes. Williams has brought his two daughters to Holiday Park a number of times recently to get Everett's appraisal of them.

"I was impressed with Venus," says Evert. "But it's a little early to tell. You have to compete to be able to deal with pressure. Venus has only played three tournaments. That doesn't seem like enough. Competition is very important. The best discipline is learned from tournaments. That's the real test under pressure. But Richard has a different way of doing it. We'll see how it turns out."

Until recently, Rick Macci, of the Inverrary Racquet Club west of Fort Lauderdale, was the Williams girls' coach. They moved from California to Florida to work with him. (Richard Williams denies this.) Macci tutored the girls for three and a half years, thirty hours a week, in the way tennis coaches tutor prodigies. They stand behind them on every shot. They stop play to correct a mistake. They show their students how to shift their feet, raise the racquet for an overhead smash. It's grueling work for both the coach and the student. Two shots and then a pause. A lesson. A practice swing in pantomime without the ball. Another. The sun beating down mercilessly. The student getting frustrated. The coach trying to be patient, remembering he is working with a child who would prefer just to have fun.

"I created Venus's foundation," says Macci. "Then I stopped coaching them. That was Richard's decision. I had given them a scholarship, free housing, meals, and coaching that was worth about two hundred thousand dollars a year." (Williams says, "Macci definitely got paid. No one gave us anything for nothing." Macci laughs. "Richard said that? Well, he likes to keep people off balance. I don't know if I'd call it *lying*.")

When Williams offered Macci a three-year contract to continue coaching his daughters recently, Macci turned it down. "It was not to my best interest," he says. "But it'll be worked out. I put my heart and soul into those girls. I still think Venus could become a top five player by eighteen. She has world-class speed, hands, weapons that supersede her other lacks. She doesn't have a lot of depth. Every little thing has to be addressed with Venus. It has to be done when she's a little girl, not at eighteen. When Richard said he didn't want the girls playing junior tournaments, I thought that was a great idea because Venus and Serena were raw." He laughs. "But I didn't think Venus would go *three years* without playing in a tourney! You get stale and sloppy if you only practice."

At one time or another, Macci has coached the Williams sisters, Mary Pierce, and Jennifer Capriati—all of whom were eventually coached by their fathers. "I've seen a common thread among fathers who coach their daughters," says Macci. "They love them so much they're overprotective. They want to be in charge, take credit. It's unfortunate. Stefano Capriati was a great dad until stardom made him forget what got him there. Jim Pierce wanted to control Mary, and she just wanted him to be her father. Richard is a great dad. As a coach, well, any secretary can tell you to hit the ball higher when you hit it into the net. As for all the kissing, that accelerates only when people are watching."

Williams claims it was Venus's idea for him to be her coach: "I never got a coach for my daughters because it was their decision. I was afraid I'd screw it up. I never learned tennis from no one. The best teacher is yourself. I got Arthur Ashe tapes. Still, it's not a good idea to teach your kids. Tennis breaks up families. It tears them to pieces." He points, as proof, to Jim Pierce's problems with his wife and daughter when he was coaching Mary, currently the third rated pro on tour. When Mary fired her father as her coach a few years ago and signed on with Nick Bollittieri, her father was so incensed he used to heckle her from the stands at tournaments. Finally, he was banned from women's tournaments.

"It's a terrible injustice not to let Mr. Pierce go to his daughter's tournaments," says Williams. "Why, he's done things in tennis never done before. He started Mary at ten, and she was a pro by fourteen. Jim Pierce is one of the greatest human beings I ever met. I respect him more than anyone."

Jim Pierce lives in Delray Beach, Florida, where he waits impatiently for months on end for his daughter to grant him an audience. He keeps her room like a shrine, just as she left it four years ago, strewn with her teddy bears. "I haven't seen her in so long," he says over the telephone. He denies a rumor that Mary sends him money every month. "I wish," he says. "Not a peso, not a penny." If she did, he says, he'd be able to go back into the jewelry business again. He was a jewelry salesman before he became Mary's coach. But right now he could use some money to get back into business.

"Are you interested in buying some pictures of Mary?" he says over the phone. "I've got pictures of her topless, at sixteen, a full-blown woman. How about some of her mother? She's having sex with another man. You won't believe it! How much do you think they're worth? Is there a market for them?"

Jim Pierce, sixty, was born in the south as Bobby Glenn Pearce. He's an ex-marine and ex-con who did five years for attempted robbery. In prison, he was diagnosed as having schizophrenic and paranoid tendencies. After he was released in 1964, he drifted around the country until he was arrested again, in Miami, for possession of stolen property. He jumped bail and fled to Canada, where he reinvented himself as Jim Pierce. He married a Parisian beauty, Yannick Adjani, and they had Mary in 1975. In the early '80s, Pierce plea-bargained his Miami stolen-property charge down to a fine and returned to Florida. He was selling custom jewelry in Hollywood when he realized, Mary, then ten, was a tennis prodigy. She was tall and thin and elegantly athletic, and within two years she was the number-two rated girl in the country, twelve and under.

To understand the difference between Richard Williams as his daughters' coach and Jim Pierce as Mary's coach, it is necessary only to listen to Mary and her father. "He was always very tough," she says. "But the more and more I was winning, the better I was doing, the tougher he got."

"I believe in hard work," Jim Pierce once said. "For seven years, eight hours a day, I hit seven hundred serves at Mary. We used to work until midnight. My son slept by the net. I wouldn't let Mary leave until she got it right. Sure, she cried. So what? I cried, too."

When Mary competed in tournaments at twelve, Pierce could be heard exhorting her on with shouts of, "Mary, kill the bitch!" Finally, he was barred from Florida tournaments for six months. That was only the beginning of Pierce's bizarre behavior which, over the years, would result in numerous banishments, restraining orders, even arrests, and which have brought him to where he is now, living alone in Delray Beach, trying to sell sexually explicit photographs of his ex-wife and daughter.

By seventeen, Mary had had enough of her father's abuse, and fired him as her coach. She signed on with Nick Bolletieri, and she and her mother moved into Bolletieri's tennis camp in Bradenton, Florida. Bolletieri was famous for being Andre Agassi's coach, even though Agassi was not yet regularly winning tournaments. A woman friend of Bollettieri's once told him Agassi was "a fine looking boy, and he has a great game, but the hair has to go." Bolletieri bellowed (his usual speaking voice), "Go? The hair is worth five million dollars a year!" It was a lesson not lost on Richard Williams.

When Bolletieri first began coaching seventeen-year-old Mary Pierce, her father was never far away. He lurked in the shadows, watching, grumbling to himself, grabbing the arm of any passerby to wail in his lisping, southern drawl, "Suddenly I ain't good enough! Everybody's saying, 'Don't work with the father.' Whatever happened to the family? Nobody cares about the family anymore. Listen, Nick's a great guy, he's helped a lot of people, but he's not for Mary's game. He doesn't believe in hard work."

Jim Pierce has small, blue eyes; curly, reddish hair like Harpo Marx; and a redneck's tan. He's a gruff, big-bellied man who tends to dress in the kind of high-waisted shorts worn by football coaches. He looks like a high school football coach and probably would have been more in his element coaching a sixteen-year-old son to be an offensive tackle than he was coaching a sixteen-year-old daughter in tennis. Mary is tall, blonde, regal-looking, with a small-featured face that could have been painted by Botticelli. She moves languorously on the court, back stiff, head up, like a deposed monarch walking past her subjects on her way into exile. In pro tennis circles, she is called "The Body," and for years she has had to fight a reputation for not fulfilling her very considerable potential.

When Jim Pierce talks about his daughter, the injustice she's done him, he keeps poking his finger in his listener's chest for emphasis. He ticks off matches Mary won when she listened to him and those she lost when she didn't. "She struggled like a broken dawg." He once warned her ominously, that if she "stays with Nick she'd better get a button made and put it on her shirt. 'Hi, I'm Mary Pierce! Would you like fries with that burger, sir?'"

Pierce even warned Mary about her mother, who controlled her finances. "I was good enough to put five hundred thousand dollars in Mary's savings account, now I ain't good enough to coach her. Her mother's got her name on that account. When I was young, nobody helped me. I stood on the highway and cried at three o'clock in the morning, not knowing what to do. I gave my life and I gave my money so that my daughter will have money in the bank. All my life I tried to protect Mary from the wolves, and I just hope my wife doesn't become one of them. When we were married, we'd fight like dogs but I slept with my wife every night. When we had sex, the next morning I'd say to my wife, 'Do you like the things we do in bed?' She'd say, 'Yes.' Then I'd say, 'Well, why ain't I good enough to coach Mary, then?'"

When Pierce confronts his daughter, screaming at her about some real or imagined slight, she tends to stare over his shoulder with her cool remove. She blinks once, twice, as if to erase him from her sight. "I'm just tired of it," she says. "He dwells on the shots I miss. Dad's hard to talk to." Finally, he became impossible to deal with, his antics becoming more and more irrational and threatening to his daughter and his soon-to-be ex-wife.

A few years ago, *Sports Illustrated* ran Mary's picture on the cover with the headline: "Why Mary Pierce fears for her life." The reasons were many, beginning with the Women's Tennis Council's decision to ban Jim Pierce from its tournaments in 1993 after he berated her so viciously from the stands during the French Open that she broke down in tears. Since then, Mary and her mother have claimed that Pierce abused them both, physically and emotionally, for years. Yannick accused her ex-husband of trying to steal their passports once and of telling her, "If you leave me, I have nothing to lose. I will kill everybody." He once told Mary, "If you think there was a nut in Waco, you haven't seen anything yet." In Latina, Italy, Pierce got in a fight with one of Mary's bodyguards hired to protect her from her father. Both Pierce and the bodyguard were cut by a knife each claimed the other had wielded. When Mary goes to nightclubs, she is surrounded by bodyguards who give her father's photograph to the nightclub's security staff with the instructions to keep this man away from Mary at all costs.

Since her total estrangement from her father, Mary Pierce has come into her own on the women's tour. She won her first Grand Slam (Australia) last spring and is presently ranked number three on the tour. She has come along way from the distraught young girl who, three years ago, wailed, "I don't know how to play!" She even seems to have found some peace in her life, which she now describes as "fun." She's doing things her father never allowed her to do before: "Eat chocolate cake . . . going to the movies, shopping with my girlfriends, talking to my friends on the phone." (When she was a teenager at Bolletieri's, she was schooled at home, like the Williams girls, and claimed she had no friends.) "I'm feeling good inside," she says.

Pierce has come to acknowledge the benefits, hard-won as they might have been, that came from her father's coaching. "He pushed me hard every day," she's said. "He gave me a tough mental attitude to keep fighting. I worked with my dad for eight years. I don't reckon it was bad. I mean your coach shouldn't be so nice but you shouldn't be so mean, either. There's a happy medium where you have to know when to push a girl or a boy, and when not to." (Françoise Durr, the former pro, says that Mary can thank her father for her "killer instinct" on the court.)

Mary has even made her peace with her father, a separate peace that may be only in her mind's eye. "He's my father," she says. "I love him. I have him in my thoughts. I just want to establish a relationship with him as father and daughter, not as a tennis coach. But it will take time."

After practice, Venus Williams walks across the court to the shaded bleachers and sits down to talk. Her mother follows her and sits a few rows below, chaperoning her daughter's conversation. Her father sits across the court under a shaded umbrella, smoking his brown cigarette, talking into his cellular phone in the late, sunny afternoon of a South Florida day.

"What are my flaws on the court?" Venus says. She slaps her head. "Think, Venus! There are two things I have to work hard at, but I can't remember what they are."

Venus says she doesn't think she's hurting her tennis development by not playing many tournaments. "My father said I'd play six this year, then five, now it's three. I don't know about that. I disagree with my father sometimes, but I don't get angry. I'm only a kid here. I try to keep positive thoughts. I don't worry about pressure because I'm not exposed to it. It's crossed my mind I might not be great by eighteen, but I don't dwell on it. Like when I lost my dog. I got over it. It's something I couldn't do anything about." Suddenly, she looks annoyed. "Do I fear failure?" she says. "I don't want to answer that."

Venus doesn't like to dwell on unpleasant possibilities, not only because she's self-assured but because she's solipsistic. She's been raised only to see herself through uncritical eyes. The world, her small world, does revolve around her for the moment. It's a world as artfully drawn in primary colors as any Disney cartoon. The blue sky. The yellow sun. The green palms. The chirping birds. The pretty black girls in tennis whites. The loving father.

"Aren't you gonna ask the hated question?" she says. Then she asks it, "Why do you and your dad get along so well? I don't answer that any- more."

Venus gets up, steps past her mother, whom she hasn't kissed this day, and walks across the court to her father. He looks up smiling. She bends over and kisses him on the cheek.

"I love you, daddy," she says.

"I love you, too, Venus Williams."

Greg Louganis

The Fanciest Diver

(from *Gentleman's Quarterly*, 1988)

·

His NATURAL FATHER abandoned him, and his adoptive father fought him. He despised his first coach, dominated his second, feared his third, respects his fourth. He formed an almost worshipful relationship with one of the most powerful agents in Hollywood, a much older man. He fired one manager, is in litigation with another, and now lives with his third in a house tucked high into the hills of Malibu, overlooking the Pacific Ocean. They are both in their late twenties, handsome, with jet-black hair and trim, muscular bodies. Although they are not really much alike, they look uncannily alike. They are mirror images of each other, not in the way of brothers, nor in the way of couples who over the years have come to resemble each other, but in the way of certain people who gravitate to their mirror image because of the pleasure it gives to see themselves in another.

He is wearing only bikini briefs as he stands, shivering, at the edge of the high board, thirty feet above the Mission Bay pool on a cold, blustery fall day in Boca Raton. Below, the parents and their children who have come to see his diving exhibition look up expectantly. A strong wind blows him back from the edge of the board. A mother's voice cries out, "My God! He should call it off!"

He sets himself again at the edge of the board, his legs pressed together, his arms tight to his sides. At five feet nine, 160 pounds, he has an almost perfectly muscled body. His shoulders, arms, chest, abdominals are all exquisitely defined. Only his legs are out of proportion. Too large, too muscular almost, the legs of a dancer. His body is far superior to that of a merely well-conditioned athlete. It is a work of art, like Michelangelo's *David*, and as with *David*, people gawk at it without shame. High-school girls send him letters, begging him to take them to their prom. One fourteen-year-old girl wrote him that her parents had given her permission to sleep with him. Another fan sent him a bouquet of roses with a note that read, simply, "I watched you wash your car the other day." A man sent him money to correspond with him. Another wrote to ask his permission to masturbate over his picture.

He owes much of his success to this body, not only to its strength and grace but, as *Time* once said, to the fact that "he takes the lead in any competition simply by putting on swim trunks." It is an edge he does not need. He is unquestionably the greatest diver of his age and, quite likely, any age. He won a silver medal at the 1976 Olympics at the age of sixteen. He won two gold medals at the 1984 Olympics. He has won nine world championships and forty-three United States titles. He is the only diver ever in national and international competition to receive seven perfect scores of ten points on one dive, and he is the only diver to score over 700 points in a single Olympic event (710.91, 1984, platform).

He won the James E. Sullivan Award for the best amateur athlete in the United States in 1984, and the Jesse Owens Award for the best amateur athlete in the world in 1987. Yet, despite his sustained excellence over twelve years, a remarkable span of time for an amateur athlete, he is relatively unknown in his native country, compared with other amateur athletes whose successes were merely the pop of a flashbulb. After Mary Lou Retton, a short, chunky, modestly attractive girl, won a gold medal in gymnastics at the 1984 Olympics, she became a celebrity. She had no previous or future successes and, in fact, would probably not even have won her medals if the Soviet Bloc had not boycotted the Los Angeles Olympics. Yet over a period of two years, she made millions of dollars endorsing various products and eventually became the first woman athlete to appear on a box of Wheaties, the Breakfast of Champions.

Wheaties never offered to put *his* photo on the box. Kathryn Newton, a Wheaties spokesperson, says that Mary Lou Retton's appeal to Wheaties was greater than his at the time, according to three criteria the company uses to pick an athlete for its box front: the individual's breadth of appeal to the public in his or her sport, a connection to championship, and a wholesomeness in the athlete's off-the-field lifestyle. He complains that despite his successes, he landed only one endorsement deal for a nationally known product, Speedo swim wear. He was reduced, like a struggling starlet, to promoting gym equipment and clothes for a regional merchant in Kansas, Nebraska and Minnesota. He says his lack of recognition stems from his successes being in a minor sport, yet swimmer Steve Lundquist was signed to endorse Sasson products, and gymnast Mitch Gaylord starred in a movie, got his own talk show and was signed to endorse Soloflex bodybuilding machines. When a Soloflex executive was asked why the diver with the body like *David* was not asked to promote Soloflex, she reportedly said, "What's his name again?"

Now he springs high into the winds and hangs, suspended, for an interminable moment. His secret: His incredible leg strength allows him to leap higher off a board than any other diver and to hang in the air longer before descending. He jackknifes his body, fingers touching toes, and finally begins to fall. His exceptional upper body strength lets him contort into such positions more gracefully than other divers and to control those positions longer. As he falls, he unfolds himself until he is perfectly straight and his arms are outstretched like wings. His plummeting body picks up speed. He moves his arms fluidly toward his head until they form a perfect line with his body. He hits the water like an arrow, with a sharp crack and a barely noticeable splash. He surfaces to applause and shakes his head so that his glistening black hair is slicked back just so. He glances, worried, at his coach, who's kneeling by the pool. His coach nods. He says of his diver, "He fills the space [of a dive] the way you'd fill a painting."

Greg Louganis emerges from the water, smiling. The dazzling smile of a dark-skinned, handsome man who could be of Greek descent, like the man who raised him, if not for his slightly flared, hooked nose. Greg's natural father, whom he's never met, was Samoan. "Samoan! Gahd!" Louganis says. "All I can think of is fat linebackers. I'd like to lop off my Samoan nose." He claims that none of his diving talent can be traced to his Samoan heritage. The only thing he credits his ancestry with, other than his nose, is a weight problem. "I have this fear of fat because of my Samoan heritage," he says. "I have to constantly starve myself. I go to the grocery store and just look at the food I can't eat. Sometimes I dream about food. When I wake up, I swear that I ate it. But the hunger pains are still there. Sometimes they feel good. The pains make me feel thinner."

He shivers in the cold, hugs himself, and walks toward a small, heated whirlpool to get warm. He likes to refer to himself as "just a jock," but despite his body and physical talent, there is nothing about him of the typical jock. When he emerges from the pool after a dive, he walks in quick little steps, his shoulders tight, his elbows pressed to his sides, his hands crossed at his chest as if holding something very dear to him.

Greg Louganis is dancing in an empty room with mirrored walls. He is wearing a tank top and skintight spandex shorts. He twirls on his toes, then races across the room and leaps into the air to the sounds of the Turtles singing, "Me and you, and you and me, no matter how they toss the dice, it had to be. . . ." He freezes, pointed on his toes, counts one, two, three.

He is practicing for his world dance premiere in Indianapolis. It is a move both he and his manager, Jim Babbitt, feel is necessary at this point in Louganis's career. They have decided to "market" Louganis as something other than a "jock," since his jock image has not earned him the kind of lucrative endorsements he and Babbitt had hoped for after twelve years of unparalleled success in diving. Louganis is a particular favorite in Indianapolis because the U.S. Diving association is based there and he won two gold medals there at last summer's Pan American Games, and they are counting on the Hoosiers' misty-eyed goodwill toward Greg to carry over to his dancing. When Babbitt is asked why Louganis's premiere isn't going to be held in a high-visibility city such as New York or Los Angeles, where Greg lives, he says, "I wouldn't throw him to the wolves."

Finally, Louganis is comfortable with dance because, he says, "movement is my area of success. Dance is just a different kind of movement than diving. Besides, I was a dancer before I was a diver." (A few months later, *Dance Magazine*'s critic would say of the Indianapolis premiere, "If I did not know of Louganis's athletic fame, or had not seen the concert's promotion, I would have presumed [the troupe] had simply added another talented dancer to its ranks.")

When Greg was eighteen months old, his mother took him to his older sister's dance class. Greg was so enchanted he toddled onto the floor and became a regular member of the class. At the age of three, he was starring in his class musical. He wore a top hat and carried a cane. When the curtain came down to applause, Greg refused to leave the stage.

"I'd always loved dancing," Louganis says as he takes a break from his practice. He wipes sweat from his brow with a towel, then wraps the towel around his neck, like a yoke, and holds each end. "But as I got older, I became ashamed of my dancing. It was a sissy sport."

Louganis and his manager both know that he is too old, at twenty-eight, to begin a serious dancing career. But they feel that his dance premiere will show people in the arts and advertising that Greg has talents other than diving that are "marketable." They would love to land Louganis a job as a spokesperson for a high-visibility product, the kind Brooke Shields had with Calvin Klein jeans. They claim to have already turned down two such major offers—one from André champagne, the other from a Las Vegas gambling casino—because they wouldn't present Greg in the proper "image."

Since no solid spokesperson jobs have yet appeared, Louganis and Babbitt have also set their sights on landing Greg roles in feature films. He studied drama in college and has already read for parts in two movies, *Spaceballs* and *Prince Valium*. He didn't land either, although he claims both films' directors were "favorably impressed that I wasn't just another jock turned actor." Greg says he has turned down a number of "jock" roles in minor movies and also a part in Neil Simon's *Brighton Beach Memoirs*, on Broadway.

So far, the only movie Louganis *has* appeared in is a teen flick called *Dirty Laundry*, not to be confused with the highly successful *Dirty Dancing*. The movie, which features Sonny Bono, the redoubtable Palm Springs mayoral candidate, skipped theaters and went straight to video.

"Those who've seen it say I'm the best thing in it," Louganis says. "I play a womanizing beach bum who doesn't wear a whole lot of clothes. I didn't want to do it, but Jim argued me into it. He said nobody had a tape of anything I've done." Then he adds with a smile, "Jim's not sure how to market me yet. I'm just *there!*"

Jim Babbitt is twenty-nine. He has a psychology degree from the University of California at Irvine, where he met Greg in 1983. Louganis was already a famous athlete, and Babbitt was on the rowing team. They had in common, among other things, unhappy childhoods. Babbitt was one of twelve children, nine brothers and three sisters. His parents divorced when he was two, and he was raised in Phoenix as a Roman Catholic and in Cerritos, California, as a Mormon. He was already pretty much on his own by the time he entered high school. Babbitt and

Louganis became friends at Irvine. Greg confided in Jim that he was never happy with any of his managers or his agent, none of whom seemed to be doing much for his career. Jim convinced Greg that he could do more for him as his manager for less of a percentage than Greg was giving the others. As proof, he booked Greg on a Christian TV talk show. "It was the first interview I ever got paid for," Greg says. "Imagine! Someone paying to hear me speak."

Babbitt became Greg's manager in 1985. Greg was Jim's first client, and today he is still his only client.

"The problem with Greg," says Babbitt, "is, what do you do with him?" Babbitt claims that Louganis's Q-rating, his recognition factor with the public, is highest among fourteen-year-old girls. Fourteen-year-old girls don't spend money on the kind of products a twenty-eight-year-old man might promote, and, furthermore, those girls are fans of Greg's because of his beauty, not his diving talent. That's why Babbitt is trying to create a market for Greg's beauty, a market that will support Greg's $400,000 Malibu home—"the only thing I own," says Greg. Babbitt has brought out a Greg Louganis poster that has much in common with most of the other Hollywood beefcake and cheesecake pinups. It features Louganis, his black hair slicked back, wearing only his dazzling smile and a Speedo bathing suit.

Until Babbitt creates that new market for Louganis, though, Greg is dividing his time between South Florida, where he lives the spartan life of an athlete training for the Olympic Games, and Malibu, where he lives the life of a minor celebrity whose days are filled with guest appearances at Boys Club events and promotions for the Chevrolet dealer who has lent him a Corvette. Louganis is used to compartmentalizing his life; it is a habit from his youth. But lately, his life of guest appearances has begun to take a toll on his diving. Last spring, for the first time in nine years, Louganis finished second at the U.S. Diving Indoor Championship in all three events, the one-meter, three-meter and platform. His coach was less than pleased with his performance. Louganis, however, didn't seem to be overly concerned.

He continues training in his normal fashion, diving for two hours in the morning and two in the afternoon. Later, he works out with weights, does aerobic and abdominal exercises, somersaults and special diving exercises, jumping back and forth from a platform to the floor. He says that he has only recently begun to lift weights, and credits his muscular body not to any specific set of exercises but to the dancing, tumbling, gymnastics, and diving he's done.

"Even now, I'm still not in control of my diving," Greg says in the dance studio. "I get disoriented in a dive and lose the water. It's terrifying. But after the nationals, I realized I was doing too much. I made a decision to cut back on my appearances and concentrate on my diving for the Olympics. Pretty soon, my body will just do what it's supposed to do when I leave the board. After the Olympics, I'd like to quit diving for a while and concentrate on my appearances and my acting. If things don't take off for me, maybe I'll come back for the ninety-two Olympics. Diving has been my only distinction in life, but I'm not afraid to leave it."

Ron O'Brien, Louganis's diving coach at the Mission Bay Aquatic Training Center in Boca Raton, thinks Greg would be foolish to leave diving now. "He can sustain himself as a world-famous athlete for maybe ten more years," O'Brien says. "He's one of a kind in his field. His problem is he's trying to do too much right now. He can't train right in L.A. There are too many distractions."

In L.A., O'Brien says, "Greg is under Jim's thumb. Jim is a very dominant person in their dealings." In Boca Raton, Ron O'Brien is the dominant person in Greg's life. O'Brien is short, slight and boyish-looking at fifty. He has been Louganis's coach since 1978, when Greg was turned over to him by Dr. Sammy Lee, his coach from age thirteen to eighteen. At the time, O'Brien was the diving coach at the Mission Viejo facility outside San Diego. Once he moved to Mission Bay, Greg followed. O'Brien is a brusque, taciturn man who seems to have little interest in anything but his diving team and little patience with anyone who does not share his devotion to the sport. He is, Greg says, a master technician when it comes to diving.

"Ron would have me dive for the next ten years," says Greg, "but I can't see myself doing that. He likes to control the lives of his divers. If he feels my acting is getting in the way of my training, he'll tell Jim. He'll get on me about my appearances. But the funny thing is, if I had my way, I'd do all the appearances for free." (Babbitt claims Louganis gets up to $10,000 per.) "It's just that Jim wants a career for me other than diving. I'm just not a driven type, you know. I let other people do that for me. Now Jim is driven for me to make a living so I can support the house."

Greg's house dominates his conversation. Often, it is the reference point from which he begins and ends all discussion of his diving or his acting. He found that house through the assistance of a renowned Hollywood agent named Stan Kamen, who represented, among others, Joan Collins, Barbra Streisand, Walter Matthau, and Warren Beatty before dying two years ago at sixty of lymphoma.

"He took care of me," Louganis says of Kamen. "He saw me in the 'eighty-four Olympics and told me I could become a big star. He'd invite us up to his house and then go with us to look at real estate. He was incredible. I often think, Where would I be if he was still here? We got very close. Then, when he got sick, he started distancing himself from me so I wouldn't be hurt. I miss him. I still carry his address with me."

He was born without a name in San Diego, and he did not have a name for the first nine months of his life. His mother was Welsh-Irish-English. She was five feet four, blonde, blue-eyed. When he talks about his mother, Louganis seems fascinated by these minor details. Of his father, he says only that he was a "full Samoan: I think he played basketball." His mother and father were both fifteen. They were unmarried high-school kids, with no prospects of supporting an infant son. His father wanted to raise him as a brother, but his mother convinced him it would be best to put him up for adoption.

Frances Louganis, a tall, lanky strawberry blonde from Mount Pleasant, Texas, and Peter Louganis, a tough, swarthy Greek who owned a tuna-fishing company on the docks of San Diego, were married for five childless years before they adopted a daughter they named Despina and then a son. When Pete Louganis brought home his nine-month-old boy, he showed him to his wife and smiled. "He's walking already," he said. He named his son Gregorios Efthimios Louganis and told his wife, with pride, that he would raise him just as he had been raised, "from the old school."

As a child, Greg was timid, scrawny, and afraid of heights. He also stuttered. When he tried to tell his mother what he wanted to eat, he couldn't get the words out. His sister got in the habit of finishing his sentences for him, a habit Greg found comforting but one his mother constantly tried to break. "Despina only wanted to help," Greg says. "I could visualize the word but I couldn't get it out. Despina would say, 'Greg wants potato chips, Ma.'"

He always loved gymnastics and, after he had conquered his fear of heights, diving. His mother sat by their backyard pool and watched, first with fear and then in amazement, at her son's daring acrobatics off the diving board. "As long as there was water under me," Greg says, "I didn't fear heights." He did, however, fear his father. Pete Louganis was a gruff, stubborn, heavy-drinking man who was unable to see that his attempts to raise his son as he had been raised went against the boy's grain. When he took his son to a local boys' club and made him wrestle, Greg hated it. "Greg hated all contact sports," his mother said.

When Greg entered grammar school, he stuttered so badly that he was put in a speech-therapy class. He conquered his stuttering by the third grade, but by then a new problem had surfaced. He could not read properly. His classmates laughed at him when he read the sentence "God saw a dog" as "Dog was a god." His teachers thought he was retarded. His classmates called him "stupid," and because his smooth skin tanned beautifully in the Southern California sun, they called him "nigger," too. Although his parents had told him early on that he was adopted, that they had *chosen* him, they had never told him of his Samoan ancestry. At home, he pored over maps of Africa to see where his "ancestors" had come from.

Like most children, he learned to compensate for his handicaps by circumventing them. He offered to erase the blackboards for his teachers, to close the curtains, empty the wastepaper baskets, anything that would ensure that he would not be called on to read. So now his classmates added the taunts of "teacher's pet" and—because of his involvement in dance, tumbling, and diving, sports that even he called "less than macho"—"sissy." They beat him up with such regularity that he often arrived home with new bruises. He'd tell his mother he'd fallen.

Years later, when he would return to his hometown as a famous Olympic athlete, mothers of his former classmates would come up to him and say, "Remember? You and my son used to be friends." He would smile and say nothing. "I remember who beat me up," he says.

By his early teens, he though of himself as a "freak," and a "wimp," and he resolved by a sheer act of will to do something about it. He decided to outsmart the bullies who were abusing him by ingratiating himself. He became what he calls "a trained seal for them." He told them to bet their lunch money with other kids that he could do, say, a particularly difficult backward flip. After he had performed his trick, his new friends split their winnings with him. They were tough, stringy-haired teenagers whose lives were destined to end in jobs pumping gas and in drunk-driving charges and maybe even thirty-day jail terms for aggravated assault. He smoked cigarettes with them and pilfered cheap beer and wine.

"I didn't want to be different," he says. "I wanted to be like everyone else. So I learned the advantage of role-playing. I kept all my lives separate. I learned to keep my dancing and my diving classes separate from my drinking friends, and my drinking from my dance and diving friends. It was bizarre, really. No wonder why I'm schizo."

Around his thirteenth birthday, he found himself in juvenile hall. That night, he had gotten into a fistfight with his father. After they were separated, he went into his room and lay down. When he woke, two policemen were standing over his bed. They handcuffed him and took him away. In juvenile hall, he was told by a counselor that "I was going through this whole thing that if my natural parents couldn't love me, no one could," he says. "I saw kids there whose parents really didn't love them, and I began to realize how lucky I was. After that, I got closer to my mom." For the first time, he expressed interest in his natural parents. His mother took him to the adoption agency, where he learned a few basic facts about them. When the possibility of meeting them was discussed, he went home to think about it, deciding finally against it. From that moment on, he says, "Frances and Pete were my parents."

Shortly after that, he came under the influence of Dr. Sammy Lee, his third diving coach. He had already had some diving successes, particularly at the Junior Olympics in Colorado Springs, where Lee first saw him dive, but his diving did not seem to be progressing at a pace with his exceptional talent. He despised his first diving coach at age ten, "a hideous person who was always screaming at me." His second coach, John Anders, was a less strident man who tried to teach him that "diving should be like poetry." That's how Greg approached his dives, as performance, not competition. He visualized each dive as if it were some ideal work of art, an aesthetically prescribed pattern in the air into which he had only to fit his body. It was not unlike Michelangelo's attitude toward art. When asked how he could have conceived *David* in that block of marble, Michelangelo replied that *David* was already there and he had only to free him.

When Lee became his coach, he didn't talk to Greg about art. "I told him, 'That S.O.B judge just screwed you, Greg. Now stick it to him on your next dive,'" Lee says. "But Greg would just put his head down and say, 'Gee, Dr. Lee, if I got angry, I couldn't do it.'"

Lee, a physician of Korean ancestry, is a short fireplug of a man with a drill-sergeant crew cut. He won Olympic diving medals for the United States in 1948 and 1952, and when reporters questioned him about his Korean background, he would bristle. "That always pissed me off," he says. "I was born in Fresno and raised in L.A. That's like asking Ernie Banks about Africa."

The first time Lee saw the ten-year-old Greg dive, he turned to his son and said, "There's the greatest diver in the history of diving if he gets the right coach." A few years later, after one of Lee's divers had beaten Greg in a competition, Pete Louganis approached him. The following week, Pete turned his son over to Sammy Lee. The first day Lee coached Greg, he told him to do a tuck dive. Greg said he couldn't do tuck dives. Lee said, "Either do it or get your ass outta here." Greg did the dive and nailed it.

"There was a lot of chicken in Greg then," says Lee. "He was young and sensitive, and he feared me. I was hot-tempered. I had a tough attitude with most kids, but with Greg I couldn't say things that might hurt him. I was more like a father to him. When he told me how he had been discriminated against because he was Samoan, I told him how I suffered discrimination because I was Korean. Tears came to his eyes. But you know, that boy has become the greatest diver ever in this sport. Why, when I went to China, they asked me if I knew the secret to Greg Louganis. I told them, 'Nobody knows the secret to Greg Louganis.'"

Sammy Lee was Greg's coach when he won his silver medal at the 1976 Olympics; a few years later, due to time and job constraints, he turned Greg over to his present coach, Ron O'Brien. "He's tough," Lee says of O'Brien. "My kind of guy."

SOUTH FLORIDA

Louganis, in spandex shorts and a tank top, is sitting on the edge of a bed in an apartment in Fort Lauderdale, watching the ballet *Romeo and Juliet* on television, mesmerized by the dancing of Alessandra Ferri.

He is talking, hesitantly, about his college days in Florida. "I majored in theater at the University of Miami in nineteen seventy-eight," he says. Then, after a long silence, he continues. "I grew up here," he says. "I got in touch with myself here." He says that Miami was the first place he lived where he wasn't identified by his diving successes. He liked the anonymity of being just another drama student. He could get on his bike and pedal anywhere without being recognized, without people making demands on him. He made sure that his theater friends knew nothing of his diving, and that his diving friends knew nothing of his theater activities. "I drew a line to keep them all from getting close," he says. "I appeared to be open with them, but I was always hiding." He smiles. "It was my comfort zone."

When pressed as to what this means, he smiles, stares at the television, and says nothing. It is a habit of his to talk intimately up to a point and then cryptically let his conversation drop off in silence. When asked what caused that fight with his father when he was thirteen, he just says, "Something dumb." His comfort zone.

There is a sad sweetness about Greg Louganis. It is not exactly innocence but rather reticence. An incredible remove, almost a blankness. He is never totally *there*. Even when he talks about his painful past, he does so without emotion, like an abused child in court reciting unspeakable acts he does not yet comprehend. And like a child, Greg is both suspicious and trusting because he doubts his ability to know things. He is suspicious of the most innocuous questions and trusting of the most idiotic statements. As a child, he believed he was a "nigger," he says, because he was afraid to find out what he really was. He also believed he was an alcoholic during his teenage years because his adoptive father was a heavy drinker. "I felt I had a problem," he says, "because I recognized aspects of my father in me. I used alcohol as an escape to avoid my problem. I didn't like myself a lot. . . . Oh, it was just personal things." He smiles, is silent. His comfort zone.

Greg stopped drinking and smoking on his own at twenty-three, but when he announced to the world two years ago that he had once been an alcoholic, coaches Lee and O'Brien scoffed at the possibility. "I believe he exaggerated his drinking," says O'Brien, "but Greg believes he was an alcoholic."

That belief reveals an almost childlike literalness, a desire to see things in black and white. He has defined himself as a "jock" because he competes in sports, as "retarded" because his teachers labeled him as such, as a "nigger" because his classmates said he was. It was not until he came to Miami that he began to free himself from all these stigmas. It began with a term paper he wrote. He came across the word "dyslexia" and realized the learning disability had been the cause of his reading problems. It helped open up his world.

After Louganis left Miami in 1980, he transferred to the University of California at Irvine. It was in Southern California that he had what he calls "an emotional crisis." He confronted "something in myself I didn't like very much," and after the confrontation was resolved, he claims, he made his peace with himself. Shortly afterward, he bought his house in Malibu and found himself a new manager.

SOUTHERN CALIFORNIA

Frances Louganis lives in a mobile-home park near San Diego that is bounded by a golf course, a parking lot, a grammar school, and a junk-yard. She has lived there alone since her divorce from Pete Louganis four years ago. "Greg blames Pete for the divorce," Frances says, "but I told him it takes two." She is sitting on a sofa in the living room of her huge, spotless mobile home. She is a tall, trim, pleasant woman of sixty, dressed in gabardine slacks and a brown silk blouse. She describes her-self as "just a little farm girl from Texas" in that coquettish way of south-ern women who know they are much more.

"I hardly see Greg anymore. I'm just a Texas farm girl, and I don't feel comfortable with Greg's friends in Los Angeles." She smiles. "I can't even get through to Greg on the phone. Jim says Greg's not allowed to answer the phone. Once I tried to get a message to Greg that a man he had been close to was dying of cancer, but I don't know if he ever got it. Greg seems to pick these people who talk for him. He never talks when he's around Jim. I think Jim is stagnating Greg. He should be much farther along in his career than he is. Jim wants to market Greg as handsome, but what good is that? I don't think Jim is doing much of anything for Greg, really. Of course, Jim is not about to turn Greg loose. Greg just won't listen to people like Ron O'Brien who tell him about Jim. How long will it last? Oh, you mean the relationship between Jim and Greg? I hope until tomorrow." She laughs, then stops herself, as if considering that she really shouldn't be saying such things while knowing full well that she is saying precisely what she has wanted to say for years.

Pete Louganis's voice on the telephone is gruff and annoyed. He says, "You talked to my wife. What you got from her is the same thing you'd get from me." He hangs up. Frances Louganis says of her former hus-band, "He can't stand Jim." When Greg found out that Frances and Pete were dating again, Greg said, "Isn't that cute."

*   *   *

Louganis is in the spacious, airy living room of his Malibu home. He is quiet, his head down, autographing his posters while Babbitt greets their visitor. Louganis does not look up. Babbitt gives the visitor a tour of that house. He points out the Sullivan trophy and the Owens trophy. He points out the teddy bear that Greg named Gar and took with him to interviews during the '84 Olympics. He points out Louganis's bedroom and the weightroom, filled with gleaming chrome dumbbells, and the second bedroom, which has a stuffed Mickey Mouse doll propped up on the bed. He walks out onto the deck of the beautiful redwood home, perched high on a hill overlooking the Pacific Ocean. Below the deck, the ground has been hollowed out for Greg's swimming pool. Babbitt makes a sweeping gesture with his arm to encompass all the expensive homes dotting the valley and the beachfront below.

"Barbra Streisand lives around here," he says. "And Ali McGraw, Adnan Khasoggi, David Letterman, and Johnny Carson." He smiles, a handsome man in a denim shirt and jeans who cannot believe his good fortune. At twenty-nine, he is moving, if only on the edges, in a world of famous and powerful people. He likes to tell intimate stories about these people, as if to solidify his place among them. He gossips about two actresses and a female singer who were involved in a heated love triangle. One of the actresses punched out her lover on the set of a movie. "Now the studio is trying to marry off the actress who got punched," Babbitt says, "so they can save her career." He smiles. Babbitt is a young man to whom power is a new and sometimes giddy aphrodisiac. He is not always sure how to use it. When he senses he has power over someone, he can be curt, dismissive, the kind of man who can loudly berate a girl in a theater ticket booth by snapping, "Don't you know who I am? I'm Greg Louganis's agent!" When the tables are turned on him, he becomes almost obsequious, smiling, sweating. His behavior seems dictated solely by power. His and others.

"I kinda call the shots for Greg," he says. "It's my job to sell him."

When their visitor leaves, Babbitt smiles and shakes hands. Louganis is still autographing his posters. He does not look up.

SOUTH FLORIDA

"I've heard some rumors, too," Louganis says with a smile. He is standing at the far end of the Mission Bay pool, where he has just won yet another meaningless diving competition in preparation for the Summer

Olympics, still seven months away. He won in his typical style. He entered the final round tied with another diver, then nailed his last dive to earn a slim victory and a smattering of applause from the handful of spectators and other divers on this cool, sunny day in Boca Raton. He accepted a small medal, standing with the second- and third-place finishers on little boxes, and waved to his fans. Now he is talking to a visitor while the spectators and other divers drift off.

"I heard rumors that I lived with the president of a movie studio in Hollywood," Louganis says, "I'm flattered, but I swear I only met the man three or four times in my life. I wouldn't recognize him if I passed him on the street." He flashes his dazzling smile. "But I hope he never hears that. I'd love to work for him some day."

He laughs. He seems truly at ease here, in contrast to his taciturnity in Malibu. Then he adds, "Besides, even if it was true, I wouldn't kiss and tell. My sexual preference is no issue. It's nobody's business. I would never say whether I slept with men or women. I'm just old-fashioned. I want to keep my sexuality private. I'm very satisfied with what I am. I'm at peace with myself.

"You know, I've been approached by a man who claims to be my natural father, but I don't care to meet him. I have wonderful parents in Pete and Frances. I've come to grips with the fact that they did the best job they could for me at the time. No, I wouldn't change anything in my life, even if I could. Except, of course, to have more financial success. I saw Mary Lou Retton on Ted Koppel's *Nightline* recently, and she was complaining that she wasn't prepared to be thrust into the limelight after the eighty-four Olympics. I don't feel sorry for her. She's made five million! Give me her problems, please!" Louganis laughs again, just as three blonde girls, each about ten years old, come up to him, giggling. One of them has a camera.

"Can we take your picture with your father?" the girl with the camera says. The visitor groans out loud. Louganis throws back his head and laughs uproariously. The girls look confused.

When he stops laughing, he says, "He's not my father. But sure, I'll take a picture with you." Each of the girls poses in turn with Louganis while another snaps their picture. In a stiff, bashful way, he puts his arm around their shoulders. When all three have had their picture taken, they thank him, then scurry off in that deliriously happy way of young girls. Greg follows them with his eyes. He is smiling.

"Aren't they cute?" he says. "I'd love to adopt them."

*   *   *

Louganis and Babbitt, both in black tuxedos, stand in the ornate lobby of the Gusman Center for the Performing Arts in Miami. They greet the men in formal wear and the women in glitzy evening gowns, welcoming them to a benefit performance for the U.S. Olympic Committee—the Miami Orchestra featuring Phyllis Diller on the piano. Before the concert begins, Greg will come out onstage to say a few words of thanks. But that is still minutes away. In the meantime, it is Louganis's job to greet the guests. He shakes hands with a little bow and then looks up, smiling. Babbitt stands beside him and introduces each of the guests. Now it's a silver-haired man with a blonde woman in a very low cut white dress who might be his daughter, save for the way she clings to his arm. Louganis greets people, one after another, until, off to his left, he sees some friends. He makes a move toward them and calls out. Babbitt grabs his arm and pulls him back. Chastened, Louganis smiles at the next guests, a younger man with an older woman who's wearing a fan of peacock feathers as a headdress. The woman clings to Greg's arm while her escort raises a camera to take their picture. Babbitt puts his hands on Greg's shoulders and turns him toward the camera. Then Babbitt takes a single step backward, out of the camera's range, until after the flash, when he steps forward again, leans over and whispers into Greg's ear.

Ron O'Brien is seated behind his desk in his office at Mission Bay. The windows behind him look out onto the pool and the diving boards. The front of his desk is lined with trophies his teams have won in various events over the years. Otherwise, his desk is neat and clean, tidy in the manner of the man sitting behind it.

"Sammy [Lee] was more of a surrogate father for Greg," O'Brien says. "I'm more of a coach-friend. I helped him with his growing-up problems. When I first met Greg, he didn't offer much in the way of conversation. As a famous athlete, he was isolated from normal relationships. Greg's not a multi-directed person. He's one-dimensional. A little thing can upset him for the day. I have to keep hammering at him until he tells me. He doesn't like surprises, so Jim directs where Greg goes and what he does. Jim's an aggressive guy. He moved into the picture slowly. Sometimes he does dominate the conversation when he's around Greg." O'Brien smiles—not a smile, really, just a slight upturn of the corners of his thin lips. "I try not to let him dominate the conversation with me and Greg."

O'Brien ponders a question. His thin smile broadens slightly. Finally, he says, "No, I wouldn't say that. No, never, not to the point where I'd want to punch Jim out." Then O'Brien's smile becomes almost gleeful, and he says, "But I can certainly relate to that."

O'Brien stands up. A worried look crosses his face. He walks out from behind his desk and over to the far wall, where a poster-size photograph of Greg Louganis hangs. O'Brien stares at it for a long moment, and then, with the slightest tap of his forefinger, he aligns the picture.

Steve & Cyndi Garvey

Trouble in Paradise

(from *Inside Sports*, 1980)

THIS IS A STORY about Southern California and baseball, and sex, and fame, and wealth, and beauty, and the American Dream. It is a story about a famous athlete and his beautiful wife and the life they live in that rarefied atmosphere in which few of us will ever breathe. And yet, despite its uncommon trappings, it is not an uncommon story. It is simply a love story about men and women who marry when young, when they are merely tintypes of one another and their lives together are spread out before them like some preordained feast. It is a story about husbands who go off to work, and wives who become mothers, and the ordinary lives they slip into along the way—lives that are satisfyingly simple. It is a story about people who change over the years, who grow older in different ways, who become different people from who they once were, and how this is really no one's fault. Finally, this is a story about people who have slept together in a familiar bed for so many years that it is a profound shock to them when they wake one morning to discover they are sleeping alongside of someone they no longer recognize.

THE HOUSE

The house is decorated in a style common to people who have the resources for instant gratification but who have yet to grow into a style of their own. The young wife did not have the style, or the patience, to coordinate every detail (the plaid wallpaper with the print sofa), which might have taken years, and so she merely hired the right decorator to whom she could entrust the ten-room house while she and her husband were away. When they returned, the empty house had been filled with things. There was a color television set in every room, and two in the family room. There were LeRoy Neiman prints on the wall of the library. There was a pool table in the den, a few balls scattered across the felt as if to imply a game in progress. There were plants everywhere: hanging plants in hand-painted pots, floor plants in wicker baskets, wall plants in elephant horns, plants with spidery tendrils, plants with cactuslike trunks, and plants with rubbery-looking leaves as large as the blade of a shovel. There were three bars done in a Mediterranian style but no liquor bottles, since neither the wife nor the husband drinks. There were four bathrooms done in Italian marble, with gold-plated fixtures and a toilet, which, when flushed, spewed forth royal blue Sani-Flush. There was an art book or a high-end magazine (*Architectural Digest, Paintings by Norman Rockwell, Paintings by Vincent van Gogh, Celebrity Houses*) in every bathroom, and on every coffee table and end table in the house, and there were three such books on the massive glass-and-chrome coffee table in the living room, each book arranged casually atop the other, just a bit off-center. There were oriental rugs, too, and inlaid tiles, and matching white linen sofas, and a brick fireplace with a large gold fan in front of it. The fan was so large, in fact, that it obscured the fireplace it was meant to adorn. There was a cut-glass sherry decanter ringed by tulip-shaped, long-stemmed glasses on a silver tray on the bar in the library. The decanter was a third filled with an amber liquid, and it was arranged on the bar in such a way that, on sunny days, the light through the window would reflect off the cut-glass in a rainbow of colors. Soft music floated through the house from unseen speakers.

The children's bedroom overflowed with stuffed animals of every pastel hue. Pinks and yellows and baby blues littered the beds, spilled onto the floor, rose, in a miasma of color, to the ceiling. The master bedroom was done entirely in white. There was a telephone in each of the dressing rooms off the master bath. There was a sauna. There were photographs in the bedroom hallway. Photographs of husband and wife and children. Photographs of the husband and wife. Photographs of the children, two young girls with windblown hair—one blonde, one dark. Photographs of the blonde daughter, laughing, with an upraised can of soda. There were more photographs downstairs: The husband in a baseball uniform, holding two small American flags in each hand and smiling at the camera. The wife in profile, her blonde hair as unreal in its perfection as that of a Breck girl. The wife getting out of a car. *Posed* getting out of a car, the car door opened, the wife smiling as she points one leg out of the car, her silky dress hiked past her thigh. The husband in uniform again, the wife beside him, holding a baby in her arms, the microphone, homeplate, and, unseen, thousands of adoring fans. There were dozens of such photographs, and more. Photographs of the husband swinging a bat, throwing a ball, sliding into homeplate, posing with other baseball stars, posing with actors, actresses, politicians, and presidents.

All the photographs were the same. Stylized. Posed. Perfect exposures without a blemish. They were the photographs of an unseen portrait photographer, who had spent weeks following the family, taking snaps, developing them at his studio, discarding hundreds of possibilities before finally selecting those snaps from which he would let the wife choose.

There were mementos, too. In glass cases. World Series rings. Golden Gloves. Bronzed spikes. Metal sculptures. Framed magazine covers. Civic awards from the Israeli government. From the Junior Chamber of Commerce. From charities. The husband contributed his time and energy to this charity and that. The husband was one of the ten outstanding young men in America in 1977. The husband was a Guardian of Freedom.

All the mementos were the same. Recent. Expensive-looking. Freshly minted reminders of the husband's past, as if, for this family, there was no past worth recalling other than the husband's and no past more distant than that of a few years ago.

Everything in this house looked the same. Unblemished. Freshly minted. Disposable. Objects with no *real* past. Objects that could be replaced instantly with enough money. There were no rotting gray baby shoes of a revered grandmother. There were no brown-tinted photographs of some stern great-uncle in a high-button collar, his slicked-down hair parted in the middle. There were no off-focus photographs, poorly but lovingly taken by a young husband with his first Polaroid camera. There was none of that faintly shabby, comfortably worn feel of a house filled up in stages over the years as the family prospered and grew. This was a house in which most of its objects seemed to have been purchased at once, and, if they were replaced, it was not because they had been broken, but because someone had had a whim to change a mood, to redecorate. This house was stuffed with such things. There was no unused space. It was as if, for this family, all these expensive-looking objects were needed to fill in the gaps in their unformed natures.

Outside, the house and its surroundings are typical of a certain kind of affluent Southern California architecture and landscaping. Stucco walls. Orange Mission tile roof. Greenhouse plants and flowers. Grass the color of forest green and laid down in sod strips that could be rolled up like a carpet and replaced when the strips died in the Southern California heat. There is the obligatory swimming pool, reached through sliding glass doors in the den. There are floodlights aimed at the house. And a sprinkler system. The sprinklers are aimed at the house, too, not at the grass, because this is the San Fernando Valley, the land of brush fires, a land without trees, with only tall, dried grasses that flame up in the summer, a land once so uninhabitable that only coyotes and rabbits and rattlesnakes thrived.

The house sits at the end of a dead-end street on a bluff overlooking the valley and the community of Calabasas Park. Below in the valley lies a spotless, geometrically laid-out community of similar houses, of streets with vaguely European names (Park Capri, Park Siena, Park Vicente), of schools and shopping centers and country clubs and a man-made lake. All of it looks as if it sprang up, full-blown, only yesterday, without the benefit of a past, a *real* past, a past more distant than a few years ago. It is not the kind of community in which people go from birth to death without leaving. People move into Calabasas when they become suddenly affluent, and then, after a few years and an amicable divorce, they move back to Los Angeles thirty miles south.

THE WIFE

The wife is thirty years old. She is tall and thin. She has long blonde hair. She is pretty. Conventionally pretty. Pretty in the manner of a Miss America contestant. Undistinguished. Lacquered. She embellishes that look to give it distinction—bleached hair, heavy make up—but her efforts only underline its *lack* of distinction. It is a look thought glamorous in certain regions of this country, and despite her protestations to the contrary ("I don't try to look this way. I just always was glamorous."), it is not a look acquired without effort. She claims her looks are a burden. "As a kid, they made me shy. People reacted to me in a negative way because of them. I always wanted my personality to overcome my looks, but it was difficult for people to get past them." Her ambivalence is not uncommon among women who have been pretty all their lives. They have taken satisfaction from their looks for so long that even when they wish to break the habit, it is not easy. "Men bother me on planes," she says. "Businessmen. Sometimes I leave first class and go back to coach to read in peace. Sometimes, though, if they're only trying to be polite, if they say something like they like my profile, well, then I *have* to stay and talk to them."

She was born in Detroit of Czechoslovakian ancestry. Her father was an air force colonel who dragged his family back and forth across the country. She attended more grammar schools than she can remember, and four high schools before she finally graduated from one in Washington State. She learned early how to forgo a social life in favor of academic achievement. She learned also how to be alone. "I'm still not comfortable in group situations," she says. She describes her parents as "harmonious opposites." Her father was very strict with her, more strict than he was with her two brothers. "Still, I loved him," she says. "But I identified with my mother. She kept the family together. She made a home wherever we were. And even though she taught me domestic skills, I've always felt she wanted me to *be* something. To achieve. She was not a career woman herself. She could have been, I think, if she hadn't followed my father all over. When I was a little girl, I told my father I would never marry a man who was gone all the time."

She met her husband at a dance at Michigan State, where she was a freshman, he a sophomore and a professional baseball player. Although he was then in the minor leagues, he was one of those golden youths for whom major league stardom had already been predicted. It was merely a matter of time.

"He was different from anyone I'd ever met," she says. "He was a gentleman. He was not all over my body the minute I saw him. He seemed so *stable*. Maybe it was because of my childhood, but it was terrific to talk to someone who knew what he wanted to do. He'd already signed then. He was so *directed*, you know, to be a baseball star."

They dated for two and one half years, during which time he *did* become a major league star—he was the National League's Most Valuable Player at the age of twenty-four—and their relationship reached a point where, as she puts it, "either we married or it died. I'd never thought of marrying a baseball player. I wasn't even a fan, and then suddenly I was the wife of a major leaguer. The wife of a star."

For the first time in her life, the wife, always a pretty woman, became visible in relation to someone else—her husband. It was exciting. She would walk down the ramp leading to her seat with the other wives at the stadium, and fans would turn in admiration. Children, even grown men, begged her for her autograph. When her husband came to bat, he always paused a minute in the on-deck circle and looked for her in the stands. The camera quickly panned to her (she was easy to spot, with her long blonde hair). She cheered her husband on. He hit a home run, or a double, or a single, and in a way, she had shared in it.

"The high point of my day was going to the ballpark," she says. "Soon my entire satisfaction was in my husband's career, *his* day-to-day achievements. Some of the wives tear their hair out during the games. I watched one wife unravel the entire hem of her dress. Another tore her nails off. I wasn't that bad. I wasn't that team-oriented. Until my husband came to bat, I would read a book to pass the time. I made sure the book was in my lap so no one would notice."

In her early twenties, she became used to living her life in the public eye, in that rarefied atmosphere of adulation and deference and instant gratification so familiar to famous athletes, politicians, actors, and rock stars, who, after a while, see it all as their birthright. Her husband bought her a baby blue Cadillac with a vanity license plate—"CYNDI N6" (her name, his uniform number). Her husband took her with him when he was a guest on a television talk show. While she waited in the wings, he took his place beside Johnny or Dinah or Merv or Mike. Wearing a three-piece suit, his thumbs hooked into his vest pockets, looking for all the world like a young Southern entrepreneur, the husband could not contain himself. He waited for an opening—forced it, even—and then began to tell Johnny or Dinah or Merv or Mike about his wife: how intelligent she was (3.8 grade average in sociology), how beautiful she was (a model), how talented (a dancer), what a great wife she was (she inspired him to hit home runs), what a great mother she was (for by then they had two daughters), and, finally, how much he loved her. The audience applauded. (At home, unseen, more than one ordinary housewife groaned at his effusiveness.) Then the husband, hinting broadly, told his host that his wife was waiting for him off-stage. The host invariably took the bait. *Well, let's bring her out!* She slipped through the curtain onto the stage. The audience applauded again, applauded as resoundingly as if she had been a famous actress or singer and not merely the wife of a baseball star. As she walked across the stage toward her husband, he beamed.

The husband took her with him everywhere, and always, it seemed, it was a public occasion recorded by the media. She went to banquets when he gave a speech or received yet another award. There were mostly men at these banquets, older men, baseball executives, Rotarians, and they were all charmed by the wife. "They always said the same thing," says the wife. "'Oh, isn't she lovely!' They said it to my husband. In front of me. 'Lovely' became my middle name." She went with her husband to charity functions, too, and political fund raisers (for even then the husband harbored distant political ambitions) in which she and her husband were as celebrated as the politicians seeking office. "When we walked in," says the wife, "the crowd parted for us as if we were royalty."

Their public perceived them as a handsome, loving couple. And nice. Nice in that bland, middle American conception of niceness. ("If you can't say something nice about someone, then it's best not to say anything at all.") It seemed almost irrelevant that, despite their image, they *were* nice, truly nice to those who got to know them. The media, in which, increasingly, they seemed to live their lives, began referring to them as baseball's perfect couple. The blonde wife with the perfect smile (so what if, picture after picture, it was the *same* smile and her hair seemed a solid piece?). The handsome husband with the blow-dried hair (so what if he looked a bit *too* boyish and his hair was done at Jon Peters's salon in Beverly Hills). They signed on with the William Morris Agency. Endorsements began to pour in: Pepsi ("As soon as I get to my seat at the stadium," says the wife, "I order a Coke. . . . Oh, I mean Pepsi!"), Jack LaLanne (the husband and wife exercising, smiling, not a drop of sweat anywhere, and the wife, curiously, appearing taller than the husband), Mattel (the makers of, among other things, Ken and Barbie dolls. After they signed with Mattel, the media began to refer to the couple, not without a touch of sarcasm, as "the Ken and Barbie dolls of baseball." The sarcasm escaped the wife, at first: "I was so flattered," she says. "I only wish I had . . ."—modest pause—". . . as much on top as she does.").

Soon their public image began to work against them. No one could be *that* perfect! No couple could be *that* much in love! No life was *that* simple! ("But it was," says the wife. "It *was* simple. We were just young and in love and we did a lot of charitable work.") Her husband began to have trouble with his teammates, who felt he was receiving a disproportionate share of publicity. Worse, they felt he courted it. (More than once, he was heard saying to a magazine writer, "Will this be a cover story?") His image grated on them. They questioned its sincerity. How could someone, a baseball player, a star, on whose time the public had made unfair demands, be so nice to *everyone?* Before every home game, he went out of his way to say hello to two little old ladies in the stands. "They've come to every game," he says, and then adds with all humility, "They just wouldn't feel right unless I said hello. It makes their day."

There was a much publicized locker room fight with a teammate. Punches were thrown. They grappled on the floor. Their teammates had to pry them apart. Afterwards, there were televised apologies. The husband began to crack. In an emotional speech, he told the audience he was defending his wife's honor. He refused to elaborate.

The bad feeling that some teammates harbored against the husband spilled over onto the wife. The other wives complained that she was too often with her husband, especially on those public occasions when the media were present. They told her she had never paid her dues in the minor leagues as they had, as if this were the wife's fault. They complained that a woman's magazine photo layout of the team wives carried a disproportionate number of photos of the wife. They threatened to withdraw their approval of the layout unless the imbalance was rectified. They complained, finally, that too often during a game the television camera panned over the wives and focused on the wife.

"It wasn't my fault," says the wife. "It was just that my hair made it easy for the camera man to pick me out. And *I* didn't tell the magazine to use more pictures of me than the others. It was *their* decision. A few of the wives—and I want to emphasize this point, I've only had trouble with a few of them—maybe were not as pretty as I am, and maybe they didn't have a vehicle like I did—" meaning the husband—"I began to sit off by myself at games. Why not? I'd always felt their conversation was so trivial, anyway. I mean, those few I didn't get along with. They spent hours talking about makeup. I would go wild. They said I was a snob for not sitting with them, so I went upstairs to the Stadium Club. I watched the game from behind a glass partition.

"I phased out of baseball three years ago. I don't see the wives much anymore. I don't have to ask them about their kids or their husbands or anything. I only went to eight games last year. It wasn't any one big thing, it was just that a season came along and I said, that's it. I don't go to banquets anymore with my husband, either. I told him I couldn't take it. I wanted to scream! All those men talking baseball. I was just a 'lovely,' that's all. I promised myself I wouldn't do that anymore. My husband says I don't want to participate in any part of his life now. He gets invitations that say, Oh, and your wife can come, too. She can sit on the dais with you. Of course, she isn't gonna do shit, but so what? I wouldn't go. There would always be this empty place beside my husband with my name tag and my name spelled wrong. I hate that. But that's the way it was. . . . I don't go with my husband to talk shows either. I'll only go if I have a vehicle of my own. I can sing, you know. I can dance. I can talk. I can chew gum."

The wife was twenty-nine years old. Life was no longer simple. She took a job.

THE JOB

The chef is smoking a long cigar while plucking the feathers from a dead chicken. The lady from Adopt-a-Dog is sitting on stool with two whimpering puppies and a towel on her lap. The male model is smoothing the sides of his hair with the flat of his palms. The housewife, who lost her husband to her best friend and wrote a book about it, is talking to an actress whose career was based on her talent for marrying a succession of men, each more wealthy than the last. The actress, a plump little blonde, is telling the housewife how she has managed to retain her taut facial skin without benefit of a facelift. She throws her hair forward, over her face, and points behind her ears. "You see, dahlink," she says. "Not even a scar."

Suddenly, there is a call for quiet on the set. The director, a slim black man with a gold earring in one pierced ear, begins counting down, out loud, from ten. "Nine . . . eight . . . seven . . . ." Behind him, a New York commercial actress is telling a bearded man about her network coffee commercial. "You see this," she says, pointing to her face. "This is the face that launched a thousand coffee cups." The director whirls around on his heels, plants his hands on his hips, and snaps, "Quiet, LOVE! If you please!" He returns to his counting. The battery of cameras begins to move forward, toward the talk show host, a dapper man in a pinstriped suit, who is sitting on a large sofa. Sitting beside him is the wife, the show's co-host. The director points at the host and nods with great exaggeration. The host begins his monologue. The wife smiles at the camera. She is sitting up very straight, legs crossed, hands folded in her lap, leaning slightly toward the host. Every so often she interjects a comment. The host responds without looking at her. She smiles at the camera. The host goes on. From the shadows, the New York actress whispers to the bearded man. "It's a regional look," she says of the wife. "It would never play in New York."

The wife is wearing a teal blue Qiana pajama suit with white high-heeled shoes. The suit is belted at the waist with a large cloth flower. There is a string of pearls around her long, tanned neck. Her blonde hair is pulled back into a pony tail revealing a pair of oversized bulb earrings. Her hair is pulled back so tightly from the sides of her face, stretching the skin, that her face looks gaunt. She is too thin. Her thin arms appear as sticks protruding from her sleeveless blouse. On the television screen she appears as only slim, but in person she looks emaciated. There are deep lines, parentheses, on either side of her wide mouth, as if from too much smiling, or too severe a diet, or maybe just from an inner tension that is finally beginning to show in her face.

The host is telling a funny story directly into the camera. The wife adds a word here and there, no more than a phrase. She punctuates her words with a taut smile, a laugh, a flutter of eyelids, a gesture of her hands, all of which seem a bit out of sync with her words. She smiles too broadly, too often, too late. The host finishes his story and she laughs, laying a hand on his arm and leaning against his shoulder. The host begins another story. The wife listens, smiles. She initiates nothing, ventures nothing, seems content only to react to his lead, as if all her life she has been only an appendage of men.

As the host is finishing his monologue, the wife interrupts him with a truly funny comment of her own. The camera crew breaks into laughter. The host turns his head towards her, simultaneously pulling away from her as if her touch carried contagion. "What the hell do you know?" he says, only half-kidding. "You've only been doing this show for a year. I've been doing it for five years." She smiles at him, as a dutiful wife would a husband who has chastized her in front of guests. Unseen by the camera, she kicks him in the shins.

"Oh, jeez," says the New York actress to the bearded man. "No wonder she doesn't have much confidence. He won't give her a break. He's a real cunt."

Before the commercial break, the host introduces the day's guests. The camera pans to each of them at various parts of the set. The chef at the kitchen set. The Adopt-a-Dog lady on the stool. The blonde actress and the housewife-author. The male model in a jogging suit. The model looks properly macho into the camera, a snarl on his lips, and then, when the camera leaves him, he dashes off, like the athlete he is supposed to be, toward a makeshift dressing room in the shadows. A male attendant is leaning against the dressing room wall. As the model dashes inside, the attendant disdainfully peels off after him.

During the commercial break, the wife takes a sip from a mug of coffee. When she returns it to the coffee table in front of her, it is smudged with lipstick. She climbs down from the elevated sofa set and goes over to the Adopt-a-Dog lady and sits on a stool beside her. She smiles at the lady and pets the whimpering puppies with a wary hand. The director hands her a towel. She lays it across her lap and reluctantly takes the two puppies. She is holding them stiffly in her lap when the camera returns to her. She smiles into the camera as she begins to interview the Adopt-a-Dog lady. She gives the audience a number to call if anyone of them wishes to adopt one of the puppies. As she finishes her interview, she looks suddenly startled. She looks down at the puppies in her lap. She shakes her head and rolls her eyes heavenward. The camera crew breaks into laughter. The Adopt-a-Dog lady blushes. The wife forces a smile into the camera as it pans away from her for another commercial break. The wife, with a forced smile, dries her lap with the towel and goes back to the sofa set with the host to wait for the camera's return. The host points at her soiled lap and laughs. She says nothing, smiles at him, and sits stiffly waiting for the camera to return. When it does, and the host begins to introduce the next guest, the male model, who is now in a white summer suit, the wife takes the wet towel in her lap and lays it gently over the host's shoulder. . . .

After the segment with the model, the wife goes over to the kitchen set with the chef. She is replaced at the sofa set by the housewife-author and the blonde actress. The blonde actress stops at the foot of the elevated set, her arms held out from her sides like wings, and says, "Dahlinks, somebody please give me a step up." The director holds her under her outstretched arms and helps her up. Soon the camera pans back to the sofa and the host begins interviewing the housewife-author, who is plugging her book, and the blonde actress, who is plugging a line of cosmetic jewlery. Waiting at the kitchen set, unseen by the camera, the wife is laughing softly with the chef. He is a robust, barrel-chested man with a van Dyke beard and slicked-back hair that curls up at the nape of his neck. He tells the wife something with a lascivious grin, flourishing his cigar for emphasis. Laughing, she brushes lint off his navy blazer and straightens the handkerchief drooping from his coat pocket. At the sofa set the housewife-author is telling the host about her experiences. "The problem with most women," she says, "is that their self-esteem is always tied up with a man."

Finally, the camera pans to the wife and she introduces the chef. He drops his cigar and steps on it as he greets her and the audience with a booming, good-natured voice. He resembles an 1890s circus strongman. He says he is going to teach the wife how to prepare a chicken for stew. He hands her a potholder glove. She looks at it, holds it up to the camera with a thumb and forefinger as if it were rancid. "What's this?" she says. "I haven't been in a kitchen in three years." The chef roars with laughter. The wife shrugs, slips on the potholder. She is no longer studied, seems very much at ease now, and confident with the chef. Perhaps it is because she is freed from the tyranny of the host, or perhaps it is merely because the chef is such a good-natured, sexually robust man, and the wife is so obviously attracted to such men.

The chef holds up the plucked chicken by the neck. It is a ridiculous sight. He pinches it in various places, slaps it a few times to the delight of everyone on the set. "You know," he says to the wife, "I used to be a geek in the circus." The wife laughs, a truly genuine laugh, and as she does she slides her arm around his back and clings to him. . . .

At the close of the show, the camera pans back to the host who announces tomorrow's guests. The wife stays to talk to the chef. From the shadows, the New York actress says to the bearded man, "You know, she *could* make it in New York. If I was a casting director, and she came to me for a job, I'd tell her to go home, wash her face, cut her hair, get some sleep, gain fifteen pounds, and *then* come back and read some copy. Oh, and of course, she'd have to get over whatever it is that's making her so drawn and tense."

THE HOTEL

The two producers have taken off their suit coats and silk shirts in the morning heat as they sit by the hotel pool playing cards and talking business into telephones. They pause in their business dealings only to acknowledge each other's play of cards with a nod and a flourish of their long cigars. They are in their sixties, distinguished-looking men, in that typically Southern California manner: Tanned. White-haired. Mustachioed. Vigorous-looking, with the faint muscle tone of older men who train daily with chromium-plated weights. They are wearing gold medallions around their necks that are partially obscured by the white foliage on their chests.

The pool, like the pink stucco hotel beside it, is camouflaged from the street by palm trees and dark, tropical vegetation, as are most of the pools belonging to the mansions on this residential street of millionaires.

The pool boy circles the pool, laying white towels over the arm of each deck chair. A woman is swimming laps. She swims from one end of the pool to the other and back again. She swims with a maddening precision, altering her stroke only to lift her head from the water for a breath before plunging on. The pool boy is oblivious to the woman in the pool. He is wearing white tennis shorts, and he moves with a ponderous, thick-legged slowness. He is blonde but no longer youthful, and his body has not aged well as it has taken on flesh. He stops to hand a towel to an actress reclining on a chaise lounge reading a script. She is wearing dark glasses, a string bikini, and satin short-shorts. She accepts the towel with a languidly raised hand without taking her eyes from her script. She resembles, faintly, Jane Fonda, only in a more conventional way, with less of Fonda's distinct, big-jawed prettiness. A few chairs away, a party of men in bathing suits is seated around an awninged table, finishing their breakfast. One of them is the son of the wealthiest man in the world. A few years ago the son was kidnapped and held for ransom in Italy, and after he had been released there was talk that he had engineered his own abduction to bilk his father out of millions. Every so often, one of the men at the table glances over at the actress. Finally, the youngest-looking man, red-haired and freckled, with part of an ear missing, leans forward and whispers to one of his friends. The friend gets up and goes over to the actress. He is wearing Bermuda shorts and white patent-leather loafers without socks. He hovers over the actress for a long moment, waiting for her to acknowledge him. She does so only after she has finished a page of her script. He smiles at her and says something. She looks at him wearily, closes her eyes behind her dark glasses as if to erase him from sight, and, without speaking, returns to her script. The man utters a curse and returns to his friends. The actress does not look up from her script again for a long while, and when she finally does, the men have gone. Only the remnants of their breakfast remains. Two hummingbirds are hovering over the plates, pecking at the morsels of food.

The maitre d' sighs, snaps up the menus he has just deposited on the table near the service bar and leads the wife and her gentleman companion to another table in the center of the nearly deserted hotel restaurant.

"Will *this* do, Madam?" he says.

"Yes. Thank you very much," says the wife, smiling. They sit down. After the maitre d' leaves, the wife says, "Well, I just don't care. I will not be seated near the service bar." Her companion nods. He is a tall man, in his forties, with a salt-and-pepper beard. He unbuttons the cuffs of his silk shirt and is about to roll them back when the wife says, "Oh, let me do it. I think it looks sooo sexy." She rolls back the cuffs twice, smiling at the man as she does so. It is the smile of a coquette. Of someone who thinks she is being sexy. Of someone who is *trying* to be sexy. Of someone who has read too many of the wrong women's magazines. It implies nothing, is merely a dessert filled with empty calories. Falsely satisfying, yet without substance. She knows, and she assumes her companion knows, that her flirtation is meant to lead nowhere. She is the wife of a star and can afford such a luxury. She is used to flirting without having to deliver on it. It is safe. Most men are gratified by it, by her merely laying a hand on their arm, a small blessing for which they are grateful.

Her companion asks how she manages to put up with the talk show host. She smiles and says, "You mean Bozo? Oh, he's my big bad brother. He's always teasing me, but I can put up with it because I don't need it. The show, I mean. They told him the show would be a lot better if he'd do less. But he won't. Actually, he's good for me. There's a lot of give and take, and I have to hold my own against a very strong man. Viewers like the way we bicker back and forth. It's like a husband and wife bickering over coffee in the morning. The funny thing is, we really like each other. I mean, he was in a bad mood today because he didn't get a commercial he auditioned for last night. That's all. He took it out on me, but that's the way it is. Still, I really do like him. And I love the atmosphere of the set. It's kinda like a baseball locker room, only on a higher intellectual level, don't you think? Oh, that's dumb to say. I've never been in a locker room."

A waiter comes to take their order and then leaves. The room is filled now, with voices and the clatter of silverware against porcelain. The people at tables in the middle of the room are talking to one another, while those at the more prestigious booths along the walls are talking into telephones. The telephones are green, hospital green, their wires a faded pink. Everything in this hotel-lounge, which is famous for its movie star clientele, is done in pink or green. Napkins (green). Tablecloths (pink). Rubber plants (green). Carnations (pink, their stems green). Leather booths (green). The telephones are green and pink. A woman in a turban is seated alongside a man at a booth. The man is eating while the woman is talking into a telephone. The man says something to the woman. She puts a finger into the ear nearest the man so she can better hear the voice coming through the telephone. The man sighs disgustedly and pours heavy cream over strawberries in a silver dish. He sprinkles powdered sugar over the cream. At another booth, two men in dark suits are talking very loudly into telephones in order to be heard over the chatter of the three young blonde women interspersed between them. The men are leaning back in the booths, away from the women, who are leaning forward over the table, chattering gaily.

"Actually, this show is my kindergarten," says the wife. "I'm working, learning, and some day I'll graduate. I'll be all right. I'm not twenty-two anymore. I'm no little nymphet. But I'm no ballsy career woman either. I'm just trying to balance a career with being a wife and mother. I have all this energy and nowhere to channel it. Now I have a voice of my own. I'm gonna do something with my life. Maybe I'll do news, or straight acting, or a talk show. Whatever, I won't go through life wondering what I might have been.... Would I like a career in New York? You mean, if my husband was traded to New York? Oh, you mean just me." She laughs, as if embarrassed. "I can't answer that right now. The way things are...."

After the waiter brings their food, the wife is quiet for a long moment. She picks at her food. Finally, she looks up and says in a flat voice devoid of emotion, "When I married my husband, I had no idea it would lead to a career of my own. I never intended to be anything but a wife and mother until a few years ago. I was bored, so I took a job. I know my husband wants me to be happy and fulfilled, and if this job does it, then that's what he wants for me. In the long run, my career might even be bigger than my husband's." She laughs again, as if contemplating a fantasy. "You know, a woman in her thirties needs mobility to grow," she continues. "When she gets into something she's hard pressed to give it up, even for a man. I know in my own case, if I was single now, I'd be a hard person to marry. But still . . . my career doesn't fill the void of not having my husband home during the baseball season. He's gone ninety-two days out of the summer, and during the off-season, he's very active in business. He's got to take advantage of his peak earning years as a ballplayer. He's got to capitalize on his success now. Of course, he only endorses products he uses. But God, sometimes, I wish I could cuddle with someone. I have to have someone to talk to at night. Baseball is a tough sport for a wife. A baseball wife can't work at a conventional job, like teaching, or else she'll never see her husband. Baseball doesn't leave much time to be together, unless the wife goes to the park and sits in the stands and cheers her husband on. I don't do that anymore. I'm sick of baseball. It's fun for guys, but it's a watching sport for girls . . . Jeez, when there's no man in your house you can really go nuts. . . .

"The wife of a baseball player must see that baseball is his main thing. I have to be a constant support for my husband. If I'm angry at him when he leaves his house for the stadium, I feel guilty maybe he won't do well. Of course, he always *does* do well." (She says this not with pride, but with sarcasm.) "At first I channeled all my energy into him. Now he calls home, and I'm not there. A baseball wife either lives her life around her husband's career or else she gets frustrated and this affects their marriage. A lot of us discover a need for our own identity at thirty, but we're so used to thinking in terms of a man, we think all we need to get rid of the frustration is a different man. We trade up, we think. It's a halfway measure. If the new man's an athlete, we'll outgrow him, too."

Throughout her monologue, the wife is speaking in a brusque, nasal voice that sounds almost whiny except that there is no self-pity behind it. Her voice is perfectly flat, objective, punctuated here and there by quick smiles and brittle laughter that seem rarely to correspond with the words she is speaking. In fact, her words contain none of the nuances of felt emotion.

"Of course, baseball leaves the wives a lot of time to develop," she continues. "The men are gone so much of the time. It's one of the advantages, if that's what you want. If you don't, you're lonely. I'm both. And wives left alone tend to take charge. But charge of what? You think, great. I've got a famous husband, a big house, a career, everything, but what good is it? Go try to sleep with it. There's always a dark moment when you want to make love to someone and there's no one there, so you go stumbling around an empty house talking to yourself. . . .

"The off-season's no better when your husband is like mine, with a lot of outside business interests. You try to fulfill social obligations, go to dinners, shows, friends' homes, and still you're alone. You end up talking about a ghost person. You know, baseball wives are told how lucky we are, and we're not ungrateful for the good things, but . . . it's just that sometimes you crave good conversation, a laugh, and in baseball these things aren't there for women. If a woman shows a baseball player too much in a non-sexual way, he doesn't know what to make of her. That's why I love older men. They can appreciate you. They're their own men. They aren't still growing up. I mean, I always wonder, am I gonna go through life knowing only baseball players? They're so shy around real women. They're nice guys, but I don't have much to say to many of them. Is that what a hero is? Of course not. I wouldn't want my child to look at baseball players or any athletes as heroes. It's such a limited endeavor. You train so hard, for what?

"My feelings about baseball must sound trite to fans who see players as heroes making so much money. I mean, I don't want to sound ungrateful. As Chico Vasquez on *Saturday Night Live* says, 'Baseball been berry, berry good to me.' And it has. I've got security. How do you complain? The average fan is gonna read this and say, 'What the hell does she have to be frustrated about? Hollywood must have turned her head.' But they don't know. Do you want to hear a baseball story? A real baseball story?

"The other day my daughter fell out of a tree and broke her wrist. My husband and I rushed her to the hospital. While she was in the operating room I had to fill out a questionaire for a nurse. When I said my husband's occupation was 'baseball player', she asked, for what team? I told her. Then she asked, what position? I got so pissed off, I shoved the paper at my husband and told him to deal with her, she was obviously more interested in him than our daughter. Now there's another woman who's gonna think I'm just the stuck-up wife of a star.

"Anyway, just before they set my daughter's wrist, my husband had to leave to go to the stadium. He couldn't wait. That's the clearest vision of when the game comes first. Before anything. It's so cut-and-dried with him. I got furious. It's always been like that. Another time I had a baby while he was playing in the World Series. When they wheeled me back from the delivery room—I'm just coming out of the anesthesia—the nurse is putting on the TV. 'I thought you'd like to watch your husband playing in the World Series,' she says. I screamed at her to shut it off. Hell, he didn't come to watch me. I could have died in childbirth and my man wouldn't have been there. The burden is always on the wife's shoulders. Her man is never there. You can't even make love to your husband when you want to. You've got to wait for an off-day. What if you get your period? What if you don't feel like it then? How often can you put that aside? Do you think a marriage can survive that? I need to be cuddled, tested, talked to, made love to, and if I don't have those things I turn into a stone princess. I'm very sexual-looking, but I can be like ice when I'm near someone who doesn't give off a sexual aura. I'm much more sexual than my husband. I need a man more than he needs a woman. And I want a man when I want one. That's my ideal fantasy love. I love men. Men who are their own man. I don't want a man who's still growing up. My husband is the same person now that he was when I first met him. On exactly the same emotional level. He's so goal-oriented. He wants to be a senator. Ten years from now I'll be a senator's wife. Isn't that funny? When he wants something he puts blinders on. That's why he's so successful. He's disciplined and controlled. He's never loose. He can't be mussed. We play tennis, and after a few minutes, I'm a mess. He doesn't have one hair on his head out of place. It's not that he tries to be that way, he just is. He's neat. Everything about him is neat. He's the pinnacle of what everyone should be. Really, isn't that awful? It makes life so boring. His image has been carried over on to me. We look alike, so people think we are alike. But what have I ever done to make people think I'm so cherry pie? I'm not like him at all. I'm street smart. Emotional. Sensitive. I mean, he edits his thoughts. I can't. It drives him nuts. I'm so uncontrollable he's afraid of what I'm gonna say. I've been misquoted so often. I get so angry when I'm thrown into an article about him without my being talked to. He didn't tell me you were doing a story on me, because he wasn't sure I'd agree to it. When I found out, that old feeling clicked in me. I thought he set me up for it so I couldn't refuse. He's still reverberating from my wrath over the last story. Old news about the wives all hating me. A lot of Ken and Barbie shit. I told my husband, thanks a lot. Now what are you gonna do about this? He said there would come a time. I said, when? My husband's been in this town for twelve years, and if people respected him as a man, they'd respect his wife, too."

When the wife and her companion finally get up to leave, the maitre d' comes over to them. He apologizes to the wife for not having recognized her earlier. He is ashamed of himself, he says. Why, he watches her on television every morning. She forgives him with a smile and then brushes his cheek with hers, her lips puckered into a kiss that caresses the air.

THE HUSBAND

The husband, dressed in a white baseball uniform with royal blue letters and red numerals, goes to the refrigerator in the clubhouse and withdraws a bottle of Diet Pepsi. He does not bother to ask his guest, a bearded man in jeans, if he wants a soda, too. The husband scoops up some ice into a plastic cup and then pours the soda over the ice in such a way, the cup tilted at just the right angle, that the foam will not overflow the cup. Satisfied, he scissors his hair off his forehead and hands the cup to his guest.

In person, the husband does not look so boyishly soft as he does on television. He looks more rugged, manly, but in a Hollywood way, with a handsomely lined face. He is too handsome to be a long-distance truck driver and not nearly scuffed enough to be a rodeo cowboy. Yet his face has more character than one might expect, certainly more than that of the messianic Jim Jones, whom he closely resembles.

The husband is sitting on a sofa in a small room off the clubhouse, watching a video tape of himself batting in a game. He stares at his image through narrowed eyes. Without taking his eyes off his image, he tells the man running the video tape to replay it. His image back-tracks like that in an old-time comedy movie. Then it goes forward again, slower. He watches himself swing the bat. He fouls off the ball. Still without taking his eyes off his image, the husband says, "Not that far off. Yes. Not that far. Maybe move back in the box a bit." He speaks in a soft, droning, almost hypnotic voice, and it is not clear whether he is talking to anyone else in the room, or merely to himself. His image swings again. The husband says, "Hmmm. That's it. That's a training guide right there." He nods his head and smiles. It is a small smile. Smug, almost. The smile of a man who is so obviously satisfied with himself in a world of the dissatisfied.

The husband hops up the dugout steps onto the field and breaks into a trot towards firstbase while, around him, his teammates are taking pre-game batting practice. He moves precisely, with a textbook stride, almost in slow motion. He is conscious of the way he runs and of the fact that he is being watched. His pumping arms are properly bent into L's at his sides, and held away from his body a bit, like wings, as if to keep his shirt from wrinkling. He resembles a man trotting to catch a bus in a new silk shirt on a hot day.

A fan in the stands calls out his name. Without breaking stride, the husband glances back over his shoulder and bestows a blessing. He smiles. It is an odd smile, both humble and smug, and it is the same smile he shows in every newspaper and magazine photograph of himself. It is automatic, perfected, the smile of a man who is used to smiling often in public, even when the occasion does not demand it, just as a foreigner smiles too readily at things he does not understand.

Standing at first base, the husband takes groundballs during batting practice. He moves deftly around the bag, scooping up balls with studied nonchalance and then pausing a moment to examine each ball. He looks for scuff marks or caked dirt which might cause the next groundball to take a bad hop. If he finds a blemish he either tosses the ball into the dugout or else scrapes off the dirt with his fingernail before lobbing it back to his coach. He sets himself again in a classic first baseman's pose, and waits for the next ball. He moves to his right, bends low and spears the ball. He moves with a certain stiffness, as if he has yet to loosen aching muscles. His are the movements of a man with a single-focus concentration, a man for whom nothing—running, picking up a ball, smiling—is natural and everything is learned.

The husband trots over to the batting cage to take his swings. There is a crowd of people around the cage. Teammates. Opposing players in orange and black uniforms. Photographers with cameras slung around their necks. Reporters with tape recorders and steno pads. Television announcers wearing patchwork sports jackets and white patent leather loafers. The husband shakes hands with an opposing black player and jokes, "No social-ism before a game." It is a malapropism. He means socializing. He allows each writer a few moments for an interview; he poses for photographers; he stands for an interview with a television sportscaster. He greets every-one around the cage with good cheer and a smile. ("You *should* say some-thing nice to everyone," he has said.) It is the same smile for each. Only his compliments vary. They are personal to each man. He asks one man what kind of gas mileage he is getting with his new car. He congratulates another on his daughter's acceptance into a prestigious college. He compliments a third on a book he has written. ("I gave it to my wife," he says. "She read it *three* times.") Each person is slightly taken aback by the husband's knowl-edge of their personal affairs; and then flattered that he, a star, has taken the time to bestow a blessing; and finally disturbed, although they are not sure why. It is as if, like a good politician, he has memorized the voluminous file cards his advance men have accumulated on the personal lives of each con-stituent he is about to meet at a fund raiser.

Twenty minutes before the game is to begin, the husband is seated by his locker in the clubhouse. Around him, his teammates joke amongst them-selves, ignoring him. ("I don't understand how he does it," says the wife. "His locker is between those of two players he doesn't get along with." "It's not so hard," says the husband. "You have to learn to live with thirty play-ers because you've got to play together.") He tells a sportswriter it would be best to conduct the interview in the concrete runway where they can have some "privacy." They go out to the runway and sit on uniform trunks. Before the writer can even ask a question, the husband begins the interview in his soft, droning voice. A star, he is used to being interviewed. Immediately, he steers the interview in the direction in which he wishes it to go. He talks about his children. How he sent them to a Catholic school to get a Catholic base. How difficult it is for him to function like other fathers. Still, despite the burden of his stardom, his daughters are very well-adjusted. He and his wife *try* to be like other parents, he says, and then, "I can be a silly daddy, too, you know." He looks down and flutters his eyelids as he speaks. It is meant to be a humble gesture, The Emperor Without Clothes, but it comes off only as contrived. Self-conscious in the extreme.

"I always try to do what I feel like doing," he continues. "I'm not act-ing. This is not a concentrated effort. I am the same as I was ten years ago. Everyone has their own space and they have to decide how they want to use it. It's natural to me to say hello to everyone. To wave to those little old ladies who haven't missed a game. I look forward to seeing them. In life, you're either a people person or a private person. I'm a people person. I like dealing with groups of people. I think I can get along with banker's sons and blacks from the ghettos. When I retire, I'd like to go into politics."

He talks for a few more minutes about his political ambitions, and then he begins to talk about his wife. Her 3.95 grade point average in college. Her energy. Her deep insight. Her talent for interviewing. The speed with which she mastered her talk show format. "It amazes me," he says, truly amazed, and he goes on. He can't stop. About his wife, he is compulsive.

It is Band Day at the stadium. A few minutes before the game is to begin, a dozen or so colorfully uniformed high school bands assemble in front of a small conductor's platform at the pitcher's mound. The public address announcer introduces the guest conductor. It is Lawrence Welk! The fans applaud. Welk, smiling, wearing a powder blue blazer, white slacks, and shoes, leaps out of the home team dugout as agilely as any young player. He walks briskly towards the pitcher's mound. His hair is slicked back into a stiff pompadour, and he looks remarkably fit for a man in his seventies. The public address announcer calls attention to this fact: "Isn't he amazing, folks, seventy-seven years young!" Welk breaks into a trot. The fans applaud louder. Welk starts to run, as fast as a seventy-seven-year-old man in patent leather loafers can run on slick grass. When he reaches the pitcher's mound, he is exhausted but still smiling. Two men grip him by each elbow and propel him up the platform.

There is something disturbing about Lawrence Welk's vitality, about his *show* of vitality—at seventy-seven. It is not enough for him to be remarkably fit at that age—an age when most men are tending a lone orange tree behind their mobile home in St. Petersburg, Florida—he is compelled to *show* us how fit he is—at seventy-seven. He intends to remind people of what they will never be, to remind them of how dissatisfied they should be in the face of his obvious satisfaction with what *he* is. He is gloating in the same way many people feel that the husband is gloating over the successes of his life—his wife, his children, his talent, his image, his future. To make matters worse, the husband is satisfied with himself so soon, at thirty-one! He seems so positive he is the best he can be that he strives only to protect the delicate balance of his perfect life without ever questioning the worth of what he's created. It is an enviable state, and those who have not reached it resent him for implying that this is their failure. But he doesn't. Unlike Welk, the husband does not intend to rub our noses in his perfection. He is merely a simple man who has worked very hard at being what he thinks he should be, and now he is single-mindedly compelled to maintain the standards he has set for himself.

THE PROBLEM

"My husband is a very warm, gentle, understanding, considerate... father. His controlled traits pay off with our children," she says.

The wife, dressed in a peach-colored velour jogging suit, is sitting cross-legged on the print sofa in the den of her house. A bearded man in jeans is sitting in a chair beside her. He is leaning toward her, his elbows on his knees, his hands folded in front of him. There is a tape recorder on the coffee table in front of her, the microphone aimed at her. She does not look at the microphone as she speaks, nor does she look at the man to her left. She stares straight ahead, through unseeing eyes, as she speaks in her brusque, whiny, yet absolutely unemotional voice.

"We don't talk baseball or my show anymore," she says. "Just the children. We're not good in certain areas. I'm not as affectionate as I used to be and he, he's so jumbled up in his career and his outside interests. When I say, 'Let's talk about it,' he says, 'Whoa! Is this gonna be the same old stuff? How unhappy you are?' I say, 'Oh, forget it, then!' Maybe relationships are just bound to deteriorate gradually, I don't know. Don't get me wrong, we're not serving papers, or anything. It's just... I wonder, are marriages ideal anymore? I mean, I'm out here in the land of fantasy and I see relationships come and go and I don't know whether or not it's worth it to cash in on something stable in order to find something more fulfilling. That's why I want to try everything to make this thing work. During the off-season we're going to Europe. I really hope in the next year my husband can develop to keep my interest. I want to see if what I fell in love with is still there.

"Sometimes, though, I feel I'm banging my head against the wall. I'm trying to get him to see other possibilities, that the way he sees things is not the only way. But he's so satisfied with the way he is. He's stayed the same all these years. He does everything the way people wish they could do them. He can't break that mold. It's really him. He's a nice guy. He gives and all, but... ah, I want electricity, a spark, some idiosyncrasy.... Now catch this act. It was so stupid. A few days ago we had three hours to ourselves. We're driving in the car. He says to me, 'Where do you want to go to eat?' I mean, I'd love my man to say, 'I'm taking you here and then back home to make love.' Now, I could have said that, but it wouldn't be the same. I want him to be smart enough to arrange his meetings around me. I don't want him to have to be told. I don't want to teach him anymore. Oh, he tries, but he can't be something he's not. He has no interests other than baseball. He doesn't understand music, or art. Those LeRoy Neiman prints? They all look alike to me. And he's not a sexual guy. Sometimes he teases me. He walks around the house with this great body, and when I try to focus love and attention on it, it's not there. I'm a girl who needs a regular sex life. . . . I've reached the point where I don't care anymore. Then again, maybe it's me? Maybe it's not his problem, but mine? Maybe I haven't told him exactly what I want? Maybe this will pass and I'm just going through a cycle? Sometimes I think I'm distorted, that what I want can never be. I told my husband he should have married another girl. I don't want to sell him short. I don't want to downgrade him; he has no choice because of the structures of this sport. When we have our little fights, I say, 'How do you fight with a sport?' How do you do that?

"I'm open now, because I'm angry. I'm tired of that Ken and Barbie shit. I never questioned before. I was always busy with the children. The suburbs drove me nuts. I had to get out. That's why I went back to work. Maybe my job will be a way out. I don't want to give up what I've got unless I can go to something else. I don't want to drag my kids around during my indecision. If I can tolerate it, if I can live within the confines of this marriage, I'll stay. I'm not wanting for anything. It's convenient . . . No, it's not even that. That's not enough. Maybe some miracle happens to help you make up your mind? Sometimes I wonder if I met someone would a relationship develop? I haven't had any affairs yet, but I wonder what it would be like. Someone who's his own man. I'm untapped. No one touches me. There's no mentor in my life. Someone to tell me to shut up. I get so depressed. I have too much time to think. What am I doing here? Life is going on around me and I'm not participating. My security is to go out and then come back. I can't keep doing this. Everyone tells me how lucky I am. If I divorced my husband I'd have to get out of town. He's a god here. Where would I go without my husband? Do you know what a price it is to be told that? A real kick. I mean, just because he doesn't beat me or anything, it doesn't mean . . ."

She falls silent for a moment. She is still staring straight ahead. Throughout her monologue, the tone in her voice has remained constant. Brusque. Unemotional. Confusing to her listener. How can she reveal such intimacies without the nuances of felt emotion? Does she feel nothing? Or is it simply that there is some strange lack in her, some inability to communicate her deepest emotions in conventional ways? She does not cry. Her voice does not falter. Her expression never varies. In fact, at times she flashes her brittle smile precisely at that moment one expects her to cry. She reveals everything—trivialities and intimacies—on the same note. It is the single note of a public persona, of one who is used to smiling in front of a camera, or the public, no matter what the mood of the moment may be. It is as if her nature had been formed in some charm school where she was taught always to smile, to be nice, to express herself in a pleasant way. Now, at thirty, when she is feeling unpleasant emotions, she knows of no other way to express them. It is her curse. She will always be misread. She will always appear to be cool, aloof, unfeeling, no matter how deeply she feels. She is like her husband. Their style will always be misconstrued as a lack of substance.

She begins again. "Sometimes, half-kiddingly, I say to my husband, 'If I ever left you, would you always be my good friend?' He says, 'No,' and then a little later, 'Okay.' He's like a brother to me. What I'm hoping—if I don't get involved with a lover somewhere—is that . . . I'm going to have to . . ." She falls silent again. She is still staring straight ahead. Her face still has that perfectly composed look, only now she is trying very hard not to cry. She forces back her tears with a weak laugh and a brittle smile before she can continue. ". . . We'll have to be good friends for a while . . . maybe we can . . . I mean, sometimes, I'll catch a vignette, it's like I'm wearing three-D glasses, and suddenly I'll see something we're doing together, and it's all right again. Maybe we're at a show, or playing tennis, and I'll say to myself, 'Oh, that's it! That's fine!' But then it goes away and a few nights later I'm sitting home alone, crying, thinking, is this the future for me? To gut it out . . ."

THE COUPLE

It is dusk in Calabasas Park. The bearded man walks up to the front door of the house on the bluff at the end of Park Vicente and rings the door bell. The husband appears, smiling, and welcomes him inside. The husband is wearing a V-neck sweater and gray slacks. He leads the bearded man to the family room where he has been watching television. They sit down on a sofa, and after a few words of small talk, the husband returns his attention to the television. He is now watching a program whose premise, in imitation of the Superstars competition, is to find the best bar bouncer and the best belly-flop diver in the country. A huge black man, Mr. T, who claims he is Leon Spinks's former bodyguard, is the last contestant in the bouncer competition. Mr. T has a shaved head, a goatee, and a ring through his nose. A bell rings and he dives over a fake bar, picks up a dummy, and heaves it, head first, through a plate glass window. Then Mr. T crashes through a door, splintering it, and rings a bell. His time is recorded and he is judged the winner. He is interviewed by Bruce Jenner.

After a commmercial, during which the husband is still silent, the belly flop championships begin. A man in a straw boater and a tuxedo climbs up onto a diving board and leaps off into a pool. He lands with a splat on his stomach. The audience around the pool cheers wildly. The next contestant, a man in a red T-shirt, dives off the board and as he is suspended in mid-air, his arms outstretched like wings, he bursts into flames. The flames are doused when he hits the water. The bearded man can't keep from laughing at this. The husband looks at him for a moment, and only then does he smile.

The wife appears, holding the daughter with the broken wrist. The daughter, a beautiful blonde child with pouting lips, is sobbing with pain. The husband says to the bearded man, "Well, let's get the interview over. We can do it in my office." But before he can rise, his wife snaps at him.

"Oh, Garvey, you make me sick," she says. "Stay right there!" She goes over to the television set and turns it off. "Did you offer him a drink at least?"

The husband jumps up and asks the bearded man if he would like a Pepsi. He goes to the kitchen to get one. While he is gone, the wife says, "Sometimes, he just. . . . I mean, he leaves the dumb TV on when you're here. I hate that. And then he pulls that interview shit." She shakes her head.

When the husband returns with the Pepsi, the wife hands him their daughter for a few moments. The husband is very careful in the way he holds his daughter. While his wife and the bearded man talk, he soothes his daughter with his voice. Soon her eyes fill with sleep. He gently presses her head to his chest. Finally, the wife tells the bearded man she had best put her daughter to bed and then get to bed herself in order to get up in time for tomorrow morning's show. The husband hands her the child, and the wife and child go upstairs. The husband looks down at his sweater. His sweater is wrinkled from the warmth of his daughter's body. With the palms of both hands, he smooths away the wrinkles and then sits back on the sofa.

"This is the first year she's been out working," says the husband. "She's sacrificed a lot for my career. I'd like her to have a job of more importance than mine, not so much for her to be a success but so she'll be happy. I love the woman very deeply. I have this sense of injustice because of what I do. It's been draining to her. You see her now in a period of frustration. The things she's told you, she's told you out of emotion. Deep down she knows there's nothing I can do about my job. She used to do a lot of things with me, but now she doesn't have time because of her job. I do things alone or else I try to fit my schedule into hers.

"We're not so different from most people, really. People would see that if they just didn't take into account our appearance. We're just two people who love each other and who have gone through a lot... I hope... maybe... it's just a cycle she's going through... What do you think?"

When the bearded man tells the husband what he wants to hear, the husband smiles. It is unlike his other smile. It is a smile of absolute vulnerability. The husband is genuinely infatuated with his wife, in the same way a porcelain collector is infatuated with an exquisite piece—a ballerina poised on one toe as she is about to pirouette. He has loved her in the same way for ten years, and now that that is no longer enough for her, he is confused.

Finally, the bearded man gets up to leave. The husband shakes his hand at the door and tells him he is sure he and his wife will resolve their difficulties. The bearded man says he is sure they will, too. The husband opens the front door and the bearded man steps outside into the darkness. It is night, now, and strangely quiet. There is not even the sound of crickets in the hot stillness of this arid land that was not meant for human habitation. The bearded man gets into his car, and as he pulls out of the driveway, he sees the husband, a silhouette, framed in the doorway by the light at his back. The silhouette waves once, and then turns its back and closes the door.

Efren Reyes

The Magician

(from *The Atlantic Monthly*, 2005)

IT WAS BITTERLY COLD at midnight on January 15, and the lobby of
the Executive West Hotel near the Louisville, Kentucky, airport was
crowded with men and a few women, all waiting anxiously for the guest
of honor. The Executive West is a convention hotel, although the men
in the lobby didn't look like conventioners in cheap suits with
nametags. They were a disparate crowd. Big-bellied men with trucker's
caps and ZZ Top beards. Rawboned men wearing cowboy hats, jeans,
and pointy-toed boots. College kids in University of Louisville T-shirts.
Bald little men who resembled Wallace Shawn. Professorial types with
pipes. Gaunt men with gunslingers' waxed and curled mustaches.
Round Samoan youths with combs stuck in their frizzed-out hair.
Latinos and blacks wearing Sean John gear. Skinny slackers with goat-
ees, computer nerds with horn-rimmed eyeglasses, punk Filipino kids
with earrings and spiky, dyed-red hair.

The only thing that all these people had in common was that they carried, slung over their shoulders like arrow quivers, long, cylindrical cases.

A man in a yellow windbreaker came through the front door and
walked toward the registration desk. There was a murmur from the
crowd. Everyone stared at him: a small, brown man of forty-nine. He
had slit-like eyes, a wispy, Fu Manchu mustache and no front teeth. He
wore a soiled T-shirt and wrinkled, baggy jeans. He moved hunched
over, eyes lowered, like one of those invisible men from the underbelly
of society. A migrant worker picking cabbage in North Carolina. A jan-
itor cleaning up the kitchen in a fast food restaurant at closing time. A
homeless man foraging for bottles and aluminum cans in a dumpster.

The crowd formed around him. Men flipped open their cell phones and called their friends: "He's here!" They introduced him to their girl-friends with deference reserved for celebrities. The man looked embar-rassed. Another man thrust his cell phone at him and said, "Please say hello to my son, he's been waiting up all night." He mumbled a few words in broken English. Then the hotel clerk asked him his name. He said, "Reyes." Someone called out, "Just put down 'The Magician.'"

Efren Reyes, forty-nine, was born in poverty the fifth of nine chil-dren, in a dusty little town without electricity or running water in the Philippines. Often, as a child, he had nothing to eat, so, at five, his par-ents sent him to live with his uncle, who owned a pool hall in Manila. He cleaned up the pool hall and watched. He was fascinated by the way the players made the balls move around the table and fall into pockets, and, more importantly, by the way money changed hands after a game. At night he slept on a pool table and dreamt of shots. He mastered the game in his head before he finally picked up a cuestick at the age of eight. He stood on three boxes to shoot, two hours in the morning and two hours at night. At nine he played his first money game and won $100. He sent $90 home to his family and kept $10. At twelve, he was the best pool shooter in Manila. His Chinese friends waited for him in the pool hall after school, handed him his cuestick when he walked in the door, and backed him in gambling games. He was already the best pool shooter in the Philippines when he quit school at fifteen. By his twenties, no one in the Philippines would play him, so he toured Asia. He wrote down the names of the best pool shooters in the world in a book and beat them one by one. He became a legend. People who had seen him play recounted the impossible shots he had made. They called him a genius, the greatest pool shooter who had ever played the game. Even people who had never seen him play had heard of The Magician.

In 1985, a small, brown man with slit-like eyes and a wispy Fu Manchu mustache entered Red's Pool Hall in Houston, Texas. He said his name was Caesar Morales, from the Philippines, and offered to play all corners. Over the next twenty-one days, he played all of the best pool shooters in the States, and won $81,000. The players he beat argued amongst themselves as to who was the better pool shooter, Caesar Morales or the legendary Efren Reyes. They were astonished to learn, shortly before he returned to the Philippines, that Morales and Reyes were one and the same.

Over the next eighteen years, Reyes would win every major pool title and tournament in the world. He won the Champion of Champions, the Challenge of Champions, the World Pool League Championship. He was named the Player of the Year in '95 and was a World Champion in '99. He won the most lucrative prize money in all of pool: $160,000 in Japan, $100,000 in Hong Kong, and $50,000 in a host of other tournaments. The Philippine Jaycees named him an "Outstanding Filipino," and the Philippine government awarded him the Philippine Legion of Honor. He endorsed McDonalds Restaurants and Puyat Sporting Goods and San Miguel beer. The first thing visitors see when they enter the Manila airport is a life-sized poster of Efren Reyes. His closest friend today is Fernando Poe, Jr., who is running for president of the Philippines.

Reyes and about six hundred other pool shooters, mostly men, had come to the Executive West to compete in the Derby City Classic pool tournament over ten days and three events for prize money totaling almost $80,000. They practiced on the seven practice tables off the Boozeseller Bar and played their games on the twenty-eight tournament tables in a huge conference room down a long hallway. The first few days were devoted to nine-ball bank games in which the object ball must hit at least one cushion before being pocketed. This would be followed by a few days of one-pocket games, in which players pick a corner pocket into which he must deposit all his balls, and, finally, a few days of nine-ball games, in which the balls must be pocketed in order, one to nine, with only the nine ball being the money ball. The winners and high finishers of each game would be eligible for the overall best-in-tourney-player prize of $20,000.

The Derby City Classic is not like most other tournaments or even those matches seen on ESPN, with their referees in black tuxedos and a ring of polite, hushed fans. The DCC is a gambler's event: The players are less interested in tournament matches that end at midnight than they are at the gambling games that run from midnight until seven a.m., and the games of craps and Texas Hold 'Em poker that run twenty-four hours a day in the hotel rooms. Indeed, gambling is the only itch worth scratching. If Jenna Jameson, the porn star, was lying naked on satin sheets in room 416, and there was a game of Texas Hold 'Em in room 418, Jameson would spend a solitary night.

"We're a subculture, like computer nerds," said a twenty-five-year-old Asian American man staring at the Reyes check-in. "Only with us, it's gambling. I graduated from the University of St. Louis with an engineering degree. Now I play Texas Hold 'Em. No girls, no drugs, no booze, just gambling. One of our regulars is seventeen."

The DCC is ten days of hustling pool, cards, dice, for men with names like Shannon the Canon, the Scorpion, Scott the Shot, Kid Delicious, Spanish Mike, Goose, the Hurricane, Kid Confidence, the Killer Pixie, and Piggy Banks, and a few women with names like the Black Widow and Ming. None of the men wore pinchback suits and none of the women were scarlet, although Ming (a Japanese version of Gina Gershon) and the Black Widow (a.k.a. Jeanette Lee, of Korean ancestry) were certainly gorgeous. Yet they, too, were obsessed with gambling and pool.

Spanish Mike, Reyes's backer in gambling games, is having breakfast in the hotel restaurant. He is a big-bellied man of seventy, from Philly by way of Puerto Rico. "Efren is a poor loser," he says. "When he plays for money his eyes get like a snake's. That's his strength, the money. And his knowledge. Sometimes I don't see a shot, but I see his eyes going fast and I know he sees one. Efren is a genius. But very shy. Except when he sings karaoke." (His favorite song is Engelbert Humperdinck's "The Way It Used to Be.")

Ming is sleeping on the sofa in the lobby. She played nine-ball all night and into the morning. Behind her, there is a lot of action on the practice tables off the bar. A crowd has formed around one table. "Jack" Frost, in his twenties, with a big hoop earring, is playing one-pocket for $350 a game against Ronnie Allen, a portly old man in a silk shirt. Allen is drinking from a plastic cup and playing to the crowd. "We got a sayin' in Oklahoma," he slurs, grinning, winking. "I need one ball, he needs 'em all." "Jack" Frost is silent, unsmiling.

The hallway leading to the conference room is lined with vendors' tables: cuestick dealers like Joss, Lucasi, Guido Orlandi; a man in a Florida Gators' T-shirt trying to hustle up a three-card monte game; a man selling candied nuts; two men playing poker; a man giving away copies of *Inside Pool* magazine. The snack bar at the end of the hall across from the conference room is doing a brisk business. Sandwiches, fudge brownies, beer, bourbon. The hallway is packed with players eating, drinking, and smoking cigarettes. A teenaged girl with a cuestick case slung over her shoulder is smoking a cigarette and drinking from a bottle of beer. It's eleven a.m. Behind her, a masseuse has set up her tables for players with aching muscles after a night of shooting nine-ball.

She has put up a No Smoking sign over her table. Behind her, three men smoking cigarettes are pitching pennies at a wall.

There is tournament action on all twenty-eight tables in the conference room. Spectators drift from table to table, watching the action, or sit on folding chairs against the walls. Scott the Shot, the tourney emcee, is talking into his microphone. "All starting times are approximate," he says. "If the schedules on the wall read ten a.m., it could be five p.m. Approximate means within twenty-four hours." Scott the Shot is fifty-six, with a spiky gray crewcut, a silver suit, and a cartoon tie of Bugs Bunny playing pool.

Ming, in black silk pants, is flouncing around coquettishly at table 13. The Black Widow is practicing with her husband, George Breedlove, on table 25. She is wearing a tight black sweater with a rhinestone black widow spider on her chest. Earl "The Pearl" Strickland is playing on table 4. He's a long, lean North Carolinian who was considered the best nine-ball player of the 1990s. Now he's hit a dry spell that has made him paranoid and neurotic. He has a reputation for arguing with referees and fans, who, he says, "laugh at me." Johnny Archer, a.k.a. the Scorpion, is playing on table 10. He's a hunched over, sinister-looking man with his black goatee. He was voted Player of the Decade in the '90s. Ralf Souquet, a trim, bald little man who resembles Tweety Bird, is playing on table 9. He's thirty-five, from Germany, and the current World Pool Association World nine-ball champion.

The Magician is playing a twenty-one-year-old youth from Ohio on table 8. This is the youth's first tournament "and I drew the number one player in the world," he says, trying not to hyperventilate. It doesn't help him that Reyes has drawn a small crowd that applauds his masterful shots and laughs at his self-deprecation. Reyes smiles when he misses a shot, scratches his head, slumps down in his chair between shots, and hangs his head as if he were the most pitiful pool shooter in the world. This is not an act. His friends from the Philippines say that he is a "simple, humble guy," who's somewhat astonished by his fame.

Scott the Shot says into his mic, "Max, we got some football action here." Then, he adds, "What does a professional pool player have in common with a medium sized pizza?" He pauses for effect. "Neither can feed a family of four." Laughter. But it's a truism. The best players in the world barely earn over $100,000 a year from tournaments. That's why they like to play gambling games.

Every great pool player possesses three talents to a varying degree: the ability to make shots; the ability to control the cueball to set up the next shot (called playing position); and the intelligence to read the balls spread out on a table to determine the order of his shots. All great pool players are brilliant men who have chosen to focus their considerable brainpower on what some might call an inconsequential game.

Beyond these shared talents, players have distinct approaches and techniques. Souquet plays a maddeningly slow and methodical game meant to disrupt the rhythm of his opponent. Archer plays a cautious and precise game, preferring to rely on pinpoint position to avoid difficult shots. Strickland is an explosive shot-maker who can be unbeatable when he is in "high gear," according to Scott the Shot.

Reyes plays a fast, flamboyant game marked by three extraordinary traits: his control of the cueball to make seemingly impossible shots; his ability to read the layout of a table eight or even nine shots ahead (three is more typical); and finally—simply—his genius. Reyes sees what lesser mortals don't, remote possibilities that to him are realities. He looks at balls spread out on a pool table and sees a deceptively simple shot that is obvious to no one else, or a convolutedly complex shot that is unfathomable to anyone else. His genius is not merely intelligence or acquired knowledge. Reyes has the ability to intuit beyond his intelligence and knowledge. He sees what he never saw before and never learned. His genius is not unlike that of Michelangelo, who looked in a block of marble and saw in it *David*.

"Efren has more imagination and creativity than the rest of us," says Archer. "We're more basic. He takes one glance and sees it all. He knows things we don't. A few times he's taken a shot I couldn't even envision until after he made it, and I saw it was an easier shot than I'd thought."

"Three times a game he'll take shots I don't see," says Souquet. "He's in a different league than the rest of us. He's the greatest player who ever lived. But he's beatable. I'm his worst opponent because I throw off his rhythm. I play by the book. He does wild stuff I wouldn't do, shots I would never take. I like to play Efren because he's fun. I consider him a friend. But I wouldn't play him in a gambling game. No one in the world will unless he gives them a spot." (A "spot" is a handicap in pool parlance, the advantage a better player will give a lesser player to entice him into a game. A typical spot from Reyes to a lesser player in, say, one pocket would be nine-to-six: Reyes would have to make nine balls in a rack to win and his opponent only six.)

Scott the Shot announces, "The Scorpion's a winner on table Adam and Eve." More laughter.

Six years ago in Hong Kong, Reyes played Strickland in a winner-take-all gambling match for $100,000. The first player to win 120 nine-ball games pocketed the money. They played six hours a day for four days. Toward the end of the fourth day, Strickland was ahead, 118 games to 117, when Reyes ran out the last three games to win the match. "He's the best I've ever seen," Strickland says. "The luckiest, too. The fans love him and disrespect me."

A few years before that match Reyes beat Strickland in a nine-ball game in Reno, Nevada, with what has become known as The Shot.

"It was the greatest shot ever made in pool," says Archer. "Efren's cueball was hidden behind the nine so he couldn't hit the object ball, the eight. It was a no-escape shot. But Efren hit the cueball off three rails before it cut in the eight *and* gave him perfect position for the nine."

Reyes wins his match easily and leaves the conference room as Scott the Shot announces, "What's a pool player without a girlfriend?" Pause. "Homeless." Laughter.

Reyes moves quickly through the hallway crowd before his fans can recognize him. He's embarrassed by their adulation. When he gets to the indoor swimming pool, he sits down at a table and begins to talk in his heavy Tagalog accent. "I now like be famous," he says. "But not morning when fans call me sleeping." He smiles his elfin, mischievous smile, his slitlike eyes closing.

Reyes has two kinds of fans. Pool aficionados who worship his genius and Filipinos who worship *him*. When he plays throughout Asia and the Middle East, he stays in fancy hotels, many of which are staffed by Filipino waitresses, maids, janitors, nurses. They see him as one of their own who had pulled himself up from poverty to become world famous. After his matches, they bring him his favorite Filipino dishes of fried fish and chicken and rice. He takes them out with him to karaoke bars where he sings and buys them drinks.

The best part of his fame, Reyes says, is that it brought him a part in a Filipino martial arts movie called *Pakners*. "I beat up a bad guy with a cuestick," he says, giggling. "I never fight in my life. Now I want to fight in movie again."

With his fame came money beyond his wildest dreams, he says. "As kid I have no dreams," he says. "Pool just sport. I never thought make money with pool. Now, I like my kids finish school and family be good." (He has a wife, Susan, and three children, ages ten, eighteen, and twenty, living in a country town in the Philippines called Angeles City.) "I support all my family, my wife's family. Forty-four, but more kids coming." He smiles his guileless smile. "I give just to family. I don't want anything to me."

His life today in Angeles City is not much different from the life he saw around him as a child: a simple life in a dusty little town. There were few amusements for the poor. Pool was one. It was cheap, and it didn't need a lot of space or expensive equipment. (Reyes still uses the $10 cuestick from his youth. Most players have cuesticks that cost upwards of $2,000.) In fact, that's why most of the great pool players come from small, sleepy towns, whether in America or the Philippines. Pool was a way to kill all that dead time, it was a way to express one's personality, and it was a means to money.

These days, in Angeles City, Reyes patters around his house and front porch in flip-flops, shorts, and a T-shirt. Chickens and fighting cocks peck around his front yard and waddle onto his porch and through the house. Efren's house is a meeting place for all of the neighborhood's children, his relatives, and his cronies. They drink beer all day, play cards or mah-jongg, have hot-soup-eating contests, and hold cockfights. Reyes rarely plays pool at home. But he does play chess, a newfound passion of his. He learned chess the same way he learned pool: in his head.

"I watch first," he says, "then play. If he beat me once I learn the way he beat me and never again. If you remember the way they play you learn easy." He smiles his squinting smile. "But I not do chess tournament because I not master and don't think I win." Then he adds, not smiling now, "I have to win." That's why he gambles only on pool, a game he knows he is the best in the world at.

His famous opponents are "good pocketers—better than me," he says. "But not see the shots I see. I see everything, even hard shots to get through. I learn hard shots from bad players. A good player plays simple shots. A bad player always takes trick shots. Sometimes they make them and I see and learn." (Ralf Souquet says, "Efren is the only player I know who does this, watches weak players to learn new shots.")

Reyes points to his slitlike eyes and says, "I see spin on ball and know way it moves. A lot of spin hard to read for others, not me." Phil Hill, the former Formula One race car champion, once said that what separated great race car drivers from ordinary people was their ability to see in more frames per second than the ordinary. Ted Williams, one of the greatest baseball hitters who ever lived, said that the secret to hitting a baseball was his ability to see the spin on a pitched ball so he could determine whether it was a fastball or a curveball.

Reyes says the turning point in his career came in 1985 when he came to the States to hustle American players as Cesar Morales. Although he did win $81,000, it was a Pyrrhic victory. His Filipino backers cheated him out of his share, and his cover as Morales was blown, as everyone in the pool world now knew who Efren Reyes was.

"I try not to show my speed in 'eighty-five," he says, "so I can always hustle." He shrugs. "But hard to hustle after that. I have to give spot now. Even player like Johnny Archer who can beat me in tournament won't play me even up in gambling games. Everybody, they smart. I get no side games. Can't get any action because everyone knows me, so I play tournaments. But I like to hustle most. In hustling game if you play long enough best player win."

Reyes says the only player he fears today in nine-ball is Strickland, the man he beat for $100,000 in '97. "But many young players are good now," he says. "Archer, Ralf. Mika Immonen from Finland. It a young man's game now. My game only fifty percent of when I younger." It's an axiom in pool that a player's best years are between his twenty-fifth and thirty-fifth birthday. After that, the eyes begin to go, and then, with aches and pains, the stroke, and finally, said Spanish Mike at breakfast, wiggling his fingers, "the nerves go."

The Black Widow steps into the hallway and is besieged by her fans. She gives them autographs, poses for pictures, and chats with them. Jeanette Lee is the most famous pool player in the world, because of her talent (she is rated number four on the women's tour), her beauty (she is tall and lean, with cupid-bow lips and straight black hair that falls to the small of her back), and her infectious personality. Lee has worked hard at her Black Widow persona, which is why she's famous even among people who know little about pool. Reyes is famous only among pool aficionados.

It takes Lee and Breedlove fifteen minutes to navigate their way through her fans to a table in the restaurant for lunch. Lee orders a hamburger and french fries, then says, "I got educated by Efren. We all did." (Efren beat her easily in a nine-ball exhibition in the Philippines a few years ago.) "But I love him. I don't think he has a single enemy."

A black woman is standing by Lee's table. "Could you come to our table and take a picture with us?" she says. Lee says yes, after she eats lunch.

When the woman leaves, Lee says, "Efren is the only player who makes pros' jaws drop. What we see as a risky shot isn't risky to him. He's got all this creativity and spaciousness."

Breedlove says, "I saw him take a shot once that no pro would." He begins diagramming the shot on a piece of paper. "It's a trick shot," he says, "But he made it." It tells you something, he says, that no pro will ever play Efren in a game without a spot.

"If Efren has a flaw," says Lee, "it's his attitude." She pauses, trying to get her words right. "It's not a matter of courage . . . it's just . . . Efren's weakness is he doesn't . . . want. I mean, you take someone from a rough background and some become arrogant when they make it, and some become like Efren. He reminds you of a simpler self we'd like to be. That's why people love him. He's content with what he is. He lacks drive. I grew up in a rough background in Flatbush, New York. I was the only yellow person in a black neighborhood of drugs and sex. I grew up wanting to be someone. I had this passion. Efren, well, he . . ."

(There is an old Italian expression, "How many chickens can you eat?" Reyes already has more chickens than he ever dreamed of.)

Late in the afternoon, Reyes is practicing on table 1, while around him there is tournament action on the twenty-seven other tables. A slight, boyish youth in baggy hip-hop clothes is watching him. He is brown like Reyes, but he has spiked hair that is dyed red. He is Alex Pagulayan, the Killer Pixie, also from the Philippines. Pagulayan and other young pros like Corey Deuel and Scott "Jack" Frost look to Reyes for pool knowledge the way young students might look to an aged and revered professor.

Reyes points out the lay of the balls and takes a shot. Pagulayan nods. Kid Confidence comes over to the table waving a beer bottle. He begins barking at Efren, who looks up, smiling.

"I'll play you any game you want," says Kid Confidence. He has a splotchy, drinker's face, a bulbous nose, no upper teeth, and a tiny paunch. If he were heavier and older he'd resemble W. C. Fields. "But I'm catchin' the break no matter what." Reyes looks amused. "Now make the game," says Kid Confidence.

"I could be the fish," says Reyes, in a child's light voice that is barely audible.

"I'll play you nine-six . . . awright . . . eight-six and the break."

Reyes, grinning, shakes his head, no. It would be giving Kid Confidence too much of a spot, what in pool parlance is called a trap.

Kid Confidence takes a swig from his beer and continues to bark at Reyes as he practices. His name is Keith McCready, and at one time he was a great nine-ball player. Now he begins drinking beer at nine a.m. McCready is famous in the pool world for the bit part he had in the Tom Cruise movie, *The Color of Money*. He hustled Cruise in a game and then turned to him and said, "It's a nightmare, isn't it? It just keeps getting worse and worse." Now he's comic relief at the tournaments he enters.

"Efren makes no sense to me," he says. "He always tries to lock it up. I'm not afraid of him. You just gotta stay in long enough to take him down. But he won't allow that. He won't take chances with his own money. If he bet his own money, I'd play for five thousand dollars and his game might change."

At midnight, Reyes is sitting on a chair watching his countryman, Jose Parica, play a nine-ball bank tournament game. Parica is a small, round man of fifty-four who now lives in L.A. He was the first great Filipino pool player to come to the States, and yet, despite his considerable skills, he never became as famous and beloved as Reyes. It's left him a little bitter.

"Efren owes me a lot," says Parica. "I was first here. But I'm underrated because I'm a build-up person. I talk a lot, and Efren is quiet. People like that." Parica says the story of Reyes's poverty as a child was good for his image in the states. "My father owned pool halls and a transportation company," says Parica. "I was born with a silver spoon. I more richer now. I have a one-point-five million dollar house in L.A. He lives in Angeles City. I can beat him seventy percent of the time. I a position player. Efren does magic show. When Efren under pressure with me he comes up short."

Scott the Shot announces a game between two Japanese players, then adds, "You come all the way from Tokyo just to play each other?"

Corey Deuel comes up to Reyes with his dinner and a chessboard. They go off to look for privacy to eat and play chess. They walk over to the main table that is surrounded by chairs banked up eight rows high, overlooked by TV cameras. They sit down on the first row of chairs and lay out the chessboard. Reyes opens his food and masticates a fried egg while they play chess. Reyes wins the first game and giggles as Deuel knocks over his king. A crowd begins to form around them. First a few people, then a few more, until by their fourth game they are being watched by a crowd of twenty.

When Deuel wins his first game against Reyes, at two a.m., he jumps up and down and claps. The spectators laugh. Reyes grins and scratches his head in disbelief. When Reyes wins the next game, he laughs like a child and taps Deuel on the head.

Deuel is a youth of twenty-five, nondescript except for his catlike eyes. When he was fifteen and a pool protégé of Spanish Mike in Philadelphia, Reyes came to town to give an exhibition. The emcee pulled the teenager out of the audience to play Reyes, and Deuel beat him.

"I stuck it to him using his fancy shots to rub it in," says Deuel. "Efren just laughed. Spanish Mike told me I'd never get any action anymore."

Deuel has the confidence of youth. He says, "Efren is the most creative, a lot of tricky stuff, but he needs it too often. He has to do fancy shots because he doesn't play good position. That's his only weakness, shooting all those tough shots. But he's a real good clutch player for all the cheese." He grimaces when asked about playing Reyes in chess. "Aw, he beats me to death."

Like most young pool shooters, Deuel is brilliant but unlearned, with little knowledge of the world outside of pool. He claims not to know of two of Philly's most famous sons. "Wilt Chamberlain?" he says, "Didn't he play sports? That other guy... Dick Clark? I never heard of him."

The following afternoon, Reyes is playing a nine-ball bank tournament game on table 2 against Steve Hasty, a bald Kentuckian wearing thick-lensed eyeglasses. Kentucky is the bank pool capital of the world, but the game is not very popular anywhere else. Reyes doesn't like it. "No action," he says. It's a game of very little strategy and a lot of trick bank shots that are often missed, drawing out each game. The best bank pool shooters bang the balls hard. Reyes is known for his delicate touch.

With a small crowd watching, Reyes loses his first game, 5-2. He wins the second game, 5-0, with a series of soft banks in which the object ball barely makes it into the pocket. His opponent, banging the balls hard, wins the third game, 5-2. Someone in the crowd says, "That guy's hangin' in there like a hair on a biscuit."

Reyes wins the fourth game by banking in five balls in succession, but he quickly falls behind, 4-1, in the fifth and deciding game. His opponent takes a deep breath, goes over to a bag, sprinkles baby powder on his hands, exhales, lines up his shot, and banks in the game-winning ball. He shakes hands with Reyes and goes out into the crowded hallway.

"I was a nervous wreck," says Hasty, who works in a printing factory. "The whole match was a blur. The biggest moment of my life and I don't remember any of it."

At four p.m., Scott the Shot relinquishes his mic and goes to the Boozeseller for a drink. The bar is dark and empty. A desultory band is playing covers of '50s rock songs. Scott the Shot orders a frozen margarita to soothe his sore throat. He takes a sip, then says, "Efren is an absolute genius. The greatest who ever lived. You go dig up the best players of all time, put 'em in a room with Efren for twenty-four hours, and he'll have all the money."

He orders another margarita. Then he says, wide-eyed, "Did you hear about The Shot? In Reno, against Strickland. I can still see it in slow motion. The ball rolling toward the pocket, the crowd coming up out of their chairs, all those faces astonished, even Strickland coming out of his chair, smiling, clapping his hands as the ball rolled into the pocket to beat him." Scott the Shot shakes his head. He has witnessed a moment in history that to him surpasses any other such moment in sport.

"Jeanette Lee was there," he says. "She was sobbing for breath, she was so overcome."

Scott the Shot says the only player in the world that scares Reyes is Strickland. "Efren doesn't like to play Early when he's in high gear," says Scott. "But Earl's crazy. I deal with him, my stomach churns. I deal with Efren," he smiles a blissed-out smile, "and I have inner peace. Efren is a rare individual. Fair, honest, loyal, truthful. Did he tell you about the earthquake in Angeles City? Efren fed the whole town out of his pocket."

Scott the Shot finishes his margarita and stands up. "Imagine," he says, in wonder. "Efren Reyes is alive and well in my own time. It's like Babe Ruth. You think I don't love it?"

Scott the Shot works his way back to the crowded hallway outside the conference room. Before he enters, a man bursts through the door and shouts, "Efren's got a game!" The crowd surges toward the door, pouring into the conference room where already the spectators inside are leaving the games they are watching and hurrying toward table 25 as if they were in a fire drill. The crowd of people stands four and five rows deep. The people in the back rows stand on chairs, boxes, anything they can find.

Reyes is shooting one-pocket for $500 a game against Ricky Byrd, a pool hall owner from Alabama. Reyes has given him a dangerous spot, 9-3, which means he must pocket nine balls before Byrd pockets three in order to win.

The crowd watches in rapt silence as Reyes wins the first game. Byrd digs into his pants pocket, pulls out a wad of hundred-dollar bills fastened with an elastic, peels off five bills, and hands then to Reyes.

When Reyes loses game two, he hands Byrd $500. Byrd hands the money to a big, light-skinned black man with a stubble of beard, standing against the wall. The man is wearing a Phillies baseball cap on backwards, a T-shirt, and gray sweatpants. Sitting beside him is Spanish Mike, watching the action through tinted shades.

The men in the crowd are talking on their cell phones, giving their friends a play-by-play of the action.

Reyes wins game six and seven to go ahead by one game. Then Byrd wins the next four games. Grinning, he says to Reyes, "Efren, want me to get you a stick?" Reyes is sitting on a chair against the wall. He doesn't get up for the next game. One of the fans says into his cell phone, "Efren's in a trap." Finally, Reyes shakes his head, no. He quits. A small man steps out of the crowd and says to Byrd, "Play Efren nine-four."

Byrd shakes his head, no. The crowd mutters, people call out, "Play him nine-four." But Byrd refuses to diminish his spot.

Finally, Byrd turns toward the burly man in the Phillies cap and points at him. "Let Efren play Cliff," he says. "I'll put up five dimes on Cliff if Efren plays him eight-seven."

All eyes turn toward Reyes, sitting on his chair. He rises off his chair and says, "I play."

The crowd erupts. People are yelling into their cell phones, "Efren's playin' Cliff for five dimes!" Men start shouting, "I'll take five nickels of that action!" "I'll take a dime!" Dozens of men are waving fistfuls of bills at the little man. He goes through the crowd, collecting bills, writing down names on a piece of paper. He collects maybe $20,000 in side bets. Meanwhile, Spanish Mike digs into his pocket and produces a wad of bills. He counts out $5,000 and hands it to the little man. Byrd does the same. The game is set. Five thousand dollars, winner take all. Reyes must pocket eight balls a rack to win, and Cliff only seven. The first man to win eight games pockets the cash.

The crowd surges away from table 25 toward table 4 in the center of the room. People rush to the folding chairs along the wall to grab a seat. The other players in tournament games, Lee, Souquet, Strickland, look up from their shots at the crowd surging past them. "Jack" Frost, Corey Deuel, and the Killer Pixie set up chairs close to the table, too, but a few feet away from the others.

The first game begins before a crowd of over four hundred fans all sitting on one side of the room. If the room were a ship at sea it would capsize. The series of games lasts six hours of unbelievable tension and skill. No one leaves his or her seat even to go to the bathroom. They are witnesses to a game of a lifetime between two men who are rated the best one-pocket players in the world but have rarely played each other.

Cliff Joyner, in his early forties, is from Houston. He is rated the number two (one-A, some might say) one-pocket player in the world. Reyes is number one at a game that may be the most cerebral game in sport. One-pocket pool is to all other pool games what chess is to checkers. Except that one-pocket requires skills and a level of genius most chessmasters don't even approach.

Despite his gruff appearance and bulk, Joyner plays a game every bit as nuanced and delicate as Reyes. He studies the table, then taps the cueball so it is hidden behind a another ball, leaving Reyes without a shot. This is called a safety. Joyner's strategy is to play a series of safeties against Reyes, hoping he'll become frustrated and take a wild shot that will leave Joyner with an open table he can easily run out. But Reyes doesn't take the bait. He plays Joyner safety after safety, too. Reyes knows his advantage is his genius. He waits. He studies every one of Joyner's safeties to see if he can find a shot in them that Joyner, and every other pool player in the world, cannot even conceive of. In this way, the two men nibble away at each other, safety after safety, then a shot, a pocketed ball, more safeties, each man winning a game, losing a game, the games going on and on for agonizing minutes, the crowd silent, holding their collective breath, until finally the two men are tied at six games each.

Reyes wins the thirteenth game to go ahead, 7-6. Joyner begins the fourteenth game by pocketing four balls in a row. Then he plays Reyes a weak safety, a mistake, and Reyes pockets seven balls in a row before he finds himself without a shot. He plays Joyner safe. Joyner returns the favor and plays Reyes an impossible safety that is rewarded by applause from the fans.

Reyes studies the balls. Deuel, "Jack" Frost, and the Killer Pixie hunch over, staring at the table, whispering to each other. They are trying to find a shot for Reyes, but there is none.

Reyes's cueball is against the rail next to a corner pocket. The object ball is against the rail a few inches away on the other side of the same pocket. To win, Reyes must pocket the object ball in the corner pocket at the far end of the table. But that is impossible. So he aims his cuestick at the cueball to play a safety. But he hits the cueball too hard, and both the object ball and the cueball go spinning around the table, hitting one cushion after another in what is such a terrible mistake that a collective groan comes up from the audience. The path of the two balls crosses in the middle of the table. The cueball heads for another rail while the object ball is moving on a 45-degree angle and it suddenly dawns on the audience where it is moving toward and the four hundred fans rise out of their seats screaming as the object ball rolls slowly toward Reyes's pocket and drops in.

There is pandemonium everywhere: people shouting, applauding, yelling into their cell phones, while Reyes makes a little punch of the air with his fist, then sits down and hangs his head. He has just won $5,000 on a shot that no one but he could ever see, and that rivals The Shot he once made against Strickland. This is why he is called The Magician.

Wilt Chamberlain
Wilt in Winter
(from *Philadelphia* Magazine, 1997)

H E CHALLENGED a Russian athlete to a vodka-drinking contest, Arnold Schwarzenegger to a weight-lifting contest. He challenged the world's fastest man to a foot race, Bobby Fischer, the chess champion, to a game of dominoes. He challenged Dan Gurney, the former race car driver, to a car race across America. He challenged the co-author of his autobiography to name the state with the most cities having over 250,000 in population. He plays bridge with old ladies who have blue-rinsed hair and smell of talcum powder. When he plays a bad hand, they say, "Wiltie, this isn't basketball." He says, "I know, ma'am."

"I love games," he says. "Sometimes, I'll be stopped at a light in my Bentley. I'll see another stoplight a mile ahead. I'll try to hold my breath until I get to it." He smiles. "Just to test myself."

Wilt's directions to his house high in the hills over Los Angeles are exact. Seven-tenths of a mile here, two-tenths of a mile there, purple gates, push the intercom buzzer. He's standing by the garage, waiting.

"I'm sorry I wasn't ready," he says. "I was in the sh-sh-sh-shower."

"I'm early."

"I know, I expected you to be early." He smiles. A huge man in a T-shirt and sweatpants and bare feet. A habit from his youth. His father would take him from Philly back to the family farm in Virginia during the summer. He loved to feel the red mud between his toes.

He enters the garage and points out, "My new toy. The first one in eight years." A black Mercedes-Benz SL600.

"Where's your sports car?"

"It's in the other ga-ga-garage. I'll show it to you later."

The most striking thing about Wilt Chamberlain on first meeting is not his size or his bare feet, but his stutter. He has been battling it all his life. Maybe that's why he talks so compulsively. He's afraid if he dares to pause, that stutter will overwhelm him, mute him.

Wilt, at sixty, looks the same. Small, round head. Pointed Trekkie ears. Goatee. Though he's heavier through the middle. Older, balding. But still BIG. Seven feet, one and 1/16 inches tall. The greatest basketball player ever to play the game. In this, the NBA's fiftieth anniversary, it's instructive to remember how Chamberlain dominated his sport like no other basketball player before or since, as Babe Ruth changed the game of baseball in the 1920s. Thirty-five years ago this month, Wilt scored one hundred points in a single game. The next highest total is seventy-eight—Wilt. That same year he *averaged* fifty points a game for an entire eighty-game season. Michael Jordan has scored fifty or more points in a game three dozen times in his entire *career*. Wilt led the NBA in field-goal percentage nine seasons, one year making more than 70 percent of his shots. Today, 60 percent will lead the league. He averaged twenty-three rebounds a game for his career. Today, Dennis Rodman is considered a god because he grabs fifteen a contest. Wilt is the only center ever to lead the NBA in assists.

He was a champion volleyball player well into his forties. In track and field, his personal bests in the decathlon are better than those of Bob Mathias, who won two Olympic gold medals in the event. Even into his fifties, he was approached by NBA teams to return as a backup center.

Wilt was always bigger than life, mythic. The rules of basketball were changed three times solely to cut him down to mortal size. But nothing did. Yet no matter what he accomplished, it was never enough. People always expected more from him because he made it look so easy.

His teams won two NBA championships but lost a playoff series five other times in the final game. He was called "selfish" because he scored too many points, had too many rebounds, too many assists. He was accused of lusting after statistics in lieu of winning. People always focused more on his flaws and failures (that foul shooting!) than on his talents and successes. He was doomed always to fall below people's expectations because he had set those expectations so high himself. He was the world's most famous underachiever. People came to games just to root against him, the NBA's wrestling villain. He was called a "whiner" because when his teams lost, he blamed the referees, his teammates, and bad luck. He once claimed that TWA had a vendetta against him because the airline delayed a flight *he* was on.

Mostly, though, Wilton Norman Chamberlain was called "loser." The most gifted and famous "loser" in sports.

He claims he outrank the Russian athlete, outlifted Arnold, and "demolished" Bobby Fischer in dominoes. The only reason Dan Gurney beat his cross-country driving record was that Gurney had a co-driver and Wilt drove alone. The only reason he lost the race to the world's fastest human was that it was a sprint, not a distance race. He's a world-class bridge player who always beats the blue-haired ladies. When his co-author correctly named the state with the most cities having over 250,000 in population (California; ten), Wilt insisted he name all the cities. Even when he *loses*, *knows* he's lost, he refuses to accept it.

It is ironic that the world's greatest "loser" has a compulsion to be the best at everything. His idol is Leonardo Da Vinci. Wilt largely designed his own house. He designed his own sports car. He's written three books, the last two by himself because he didn't want a co-writer "to over-influence what I had to say." His new book, self-published, is called *Who's Running the Asylum*, and it deals with the foibles of modern-day athletes. His second book was sprinkled with his thoughts—he called them "Wiltisms" ("Greed, envy, and fear are the cause of much human behavior. Too much."), which he compared to the sayings of Confucius. In it, he also writes that he is very "introspective" and "funny" and that he has bigger biceps that Arnold and the highest vertical leap of any athlete and that he once squared off against a rhinoceros and scared the rhino off.

"People say it's egotism," he says, sitting on an ottoman in his living room. "They say, 'What the fuck isn't he the greatest at?' But I'm not bragging, I've done all these things." He did them, he says, "because all my life I've been trying to get people to see me as something other than a basketball player. I wanted them to see *me*. That's my egotism. I was tired of people talking about my height as the only reason I did good at basketball. It's like men of color who want to get an education to show blacks are not dumb. It's why I love games. If I win, they can't say it's because I'm seven feet tall."

So he spent his life setting up artificial challenges for himself to prove he could be the best at everything, thereby diminishing the very thing he *was* the best at. He deliberately diffused his concentration to gratify his psychic needs at the expense of the game that made him famous in the first place. (Of the free-throw shooting, he says, "It's a stigma in my life. I lost focus on the foul line. It was fear. I just wanted to get off.")

It exhausted him. "Being Wilt was tiring," he says. "A chore."

Wilt was born and raised in a West Philadelphia rowhouse, into a family of nine brothers and sisters. His father was the neighborhood handyman, and Wilt followed suit at an early age. As a child, he hustled around delivering papers, washing windows, cleaning cellars, unloading milk crates, and scavenging junk to sell. He even sold watermelons, going up and down the streets shouting, "Watermelon man!"

He says he was fortunate to be raised as he was. He learned the value of hard work early, and "was blessed with roots. Race was never mentioned in my house. I went to Catholic and Baptist churches and Jewish synagogues all over Philadelphia."

In his second autobiography, Wilt includes a photograph of his fourth-grade class. The students, mostly black, are posed against a red-brick school. The girls are seated in front, their hands folded demurely over their skirts. The shorter boys stand in the second row; taller boys and their white teacher stand in the third row. In the middle of that row stands Wilt, already more than six feet tall, almost two feet taller than any other student, and a foot taller than the teacher.

His first sports love was track. "It was primal with me," he says. "You know, the fastest guy gets the meat." He competed in the Penn relays, but by the time he was in seventh grade had already turned his attention to basketball. As a freshman at Overbrook High School, he was more than 6 foot 8 inches tall. Before he left for school each day, his mother admonished him to make sure he tip his hat and give up his seat on the El to any woman standing. He'd sit there, on the El, in mental torment, hoping no woman would stand near him. When one did one day, he says, "I wanted to hide. I didn't want people to look at me." He'd wait until the next stop. If she didn't get off, he'd stand up, and up, and up, and give the woman his seat with a little tip of his snap-brim hat while everyone around him gawked.

By the time he graduated from Overbrook, headed for the University of Kansas on scholarship, Wilt, by then seven feet tall, had already begun to feel the sting of the failure label. In his sophomore year at K.U., his team lost the NCAA Championship to underdog North Carolina in triple overtime by one point. Then, after a brief stint with the Harlem

Globetrotters, Wilt entered the NBA, where his teams (Philadelphia and Los Angeles) seemingly always lost in the seventh game to the Boston Celtics and their stellar center, Bill Russell, who would forever, in people's minds, be identified as Chamberlain's nemesis.

"That's when people really started calling me 'loser,'" he says.

He gets up from the ottoman and lowers the sound on the TV, where he has been watching a football playoff game. He sits back down and continues talking. He tells a story about Red Auerbach, the legendary Celtics coach, who once said that Wilt and Russell both played such great defense that neither one would score more than twenty-five points against the other. Wilt laughs and says, "Red was half right." Then he tries to explain for what must be the umpteenth time why his teams never won as many NBA championships as people thought they should. He can't control himself. He is constantly flashing back to some long-forgotten moment in the past that *he* can never forget.

"We [the 76ers] were up on the Celtics three-one in the 'sixty-eight championships," he says. "Then Dr. King got assassinated. I held a team meeting and said we should postpone the playoffs. The players agreed. We didn't play again for a week, and during that time Billy Cunningham and Hal Greener both got hurt in practice. When we finally played the Celtics again, I passed off to the open man, but no one could make a shot. I got blamed for the loss because I didn't shoot enough. But I had four guys on me—I always did when I played the Celtics. Just look at the pictures in my book. It would have been wrong for me not to give up the ball."

Suddenly, he stops. "I'm sorry," he says. "Can I get you something to drink? Something to eat?"

"No, that's all right."

"Are you sure?"

"Yes."

When Wilt and Russell appeared on a TV program recently honoring them as two of the greatest NBA players of all time, they were a study in contrasts. Russell appeared professorial with his suit and tie and glasses, his graying hair and goatee. He was soft-spoken, modest, almost deferential as he described how he would have Thanksgiving dinner with Wilt, "and then he'd go out and beat the hell out of me" in a game. Russell giggled. Wilt wore a tight black T-shirt to set off his gold chains. His goatee was suspiciously black. He spoke loudly, brashly, gesturing with his arms. When Russell complained that he didn't score much because his teams didn't have plays for him, Wilt snapped, "Are you saying that otherwise you would have scored fifty?"

Russell has always been self-deprecatingly humble in public. When he commented on TV recently about a game Shaquille O'Neal had played, he said, "Shaq was great." Wilt said, "Shaq played awful." Then added, "I don't know how you cannot be controversial. I'm just being Wilt."

Throughout the '60s, when they competed against each other, Russell was always the fan favorite because "he was the blue-collar guy," says Wilt. "He rebounded, played defense, but didn't score. I was the brash black guy stealing the white guys' thunder by scoring. The press always pitted me against Russell because we were black. They created a confrontation that was both real and mythical. Russ was the underdog because he was under seven feet. He was unselfish because he didn't score. I was the selfish gunner. But if a guy's a shooter, he's supposed to shoot. You get paid to do what you do best."

There were other reasons why the fans and press rooted for Russell, Wilt believes. At the time, Russell was married to a black woman with two daughters ("He gave them African names," says Wilt. "Boo-boo-waa-waa, whatever"), and as a black man in what was then a white man's game, he "seemed to know his place," says Wilt. "They thought I didn't know where I belonged, that I was treading on sacred ground. I went out with white girls."

But the real Russell was much more harsh than his image, and the real Wilt was less brash and arrogant than he was almost childishly naïve. When Russell found out Wilt was making $100,000 one year, he secretly demanded that the Celtics pay him $100,001.

"I was outside Boston Garden with him one night after a game," says Wilt. "The same fans throwing things at me during the game were now asking for my autograph. While I signed, Russ walked by them and said, 'Get the fuck outta my way.'"

Russell not only conned the public, Wilt says, but conned him, too. All the years Wilt thought they were friends despite their on-court rivalry, Russell had been bad-mouthing him behind his back, Wilt learned from others. Russell once said, "What it's all about is winning and losing, and he [Wilt] has done a lot of losing."

"To Russ, winning at basketball was everything," says Wilt. "It was a test of his manhood. I looked at basketball as a game, not a life-and-death struggle. There are too many other beautiful things in life—food cars, girls, friends, the beach, freedom . . . Bill is a shallower man for all his basketball triumphs."

Race was itself another, more fundamental conflict between the two. Russell was a militant black man during the '60s who, for the most part, kept his politics under wraps. Wilt considered himself first a human being, then an American, and lastly a black man. Many of his friends were white, especially his girlfriends. ("It's strange," says Wilt, "I was always identified as being with white girls, but Russ's second wife is white, and so is Kareem [Abdul-Jabbar]'s.")

"I had problems with Russ and Jim Brown and Kareem," says Wilt. "They were racist problems. Jim was very militant, and when Kareem became a Muslim he refused to talk to me anymore. I never looked at Russ that way for a long time, even though I always knew he was a racist. But now I know, absolutely, my problems with Russ were racial."

Wilt was never black enough for the militants of the '60s and '70s. He admits he was never a racial pioneer. He didn't consider scholarships to Southern schools if he found out he'd be the first black to play there. And if he couldn't avoid racism, he dealt with it in his own way. When a white teammate, Tom Meschery, refused to double date with him, Wilt confronted him outside their locker room. Meschery broke down and cried for forgiveness, which Wilt gave.

"I'm not bitter," says Wilt. "Why should I be? When I was a boy in Virginia, my father and I would take our cows to graze on a white woman's property. She'd tell us, 'Make sure and take some peaches, now.' When I worked at Kutsher's in the Catskills in high school, they were like my second family. They'd sneak me milk with a meat meal, which wasn't kosher, because they said I was a growing boy. Now how can I be bitter when I have so many friends of different colors?" For Wilt, it seems the glass was always half full.

It took him thirty-six hours to drive across the country; he can hold his breath for four and a half minutes; he's calculated he's spent two years of his life signing autographs; and he believes most men lose interest in a woman after thirteen months.

"That's totally factual," he says about the last. It's factual, he says, because *he* came to that number, and because "numbers never lie. Numbers are magical to me. They're real. You can't fudge numbers. Two always equals two." That's why he believes so fervently that the points he scored in his NBA career are proof of his absolute greatness above all other players.

"My signature was that I was the greatest scorer ever," he says. "Points are the standard in sports. Steals and blocked shots may or may not lead to points. A rebound only matters if it leads to two points. Points are the most important thing in sports."

The number he's most identified with these days, for better or worse, is 20,000. He claimed in his second book that during his first 55 years he had sex with 20,000 different women. (He rated them on a scale of one to twenty.) Coming out around the same time as Magic Johnson's announcement that he was HIV-positive after sleeping around, it proved an unfortunate claim at best.

"My editor told me to put more sex in the book," Wilt says. "But I didn't mean to reduce women to numbers. At the time, I wasn't married—" he still isn't, never has been—"wasn't engaged, and I'm not gay. I was just trying to say I had known a *lot* of women. But if I had to do it all over again, I'd emphasize more that it would have been better for me to have one woman a thousand times. It's my sorrow. It embarrasses me. I wasn't bragging that I was a great lover, a Don Juan. Actually, if you look at it, you can say that I had so many women once because I was such a bad lover they never came back a second time." He laughs.

Wilt has always been outside of—some might say out of touch with—the mores of conventional society, not to mention politically correct society. In the '60s, when it was unconventional for a black man to date white women, he did. In the '90s, when it was no longer fashionable, he bragged about his female conquests, flaunted his wolf-fur coat, claimed black women were not sophisticated enough for him, said blacks could accomplish anything they wanted as long as they worked hard, and conspicuously flaunted his wealth.

In the mid '80s, Wilt hired the man who designed the James Bond cars to build a special sports car for him. He thought the car would cost $100,000, about the same as a Ferrari would have. Eleven years later, the car sits in his garage, still unfinished. It has cost him $1.5 million so far. Wilt doesn't like to talk much about that car now. He'd prefer to talk about his house, a house he designed twenty-six years ago.

It sits on a mountain off Mulholland Drive, north of L.A., commanding a panoramic view of the city all the way to the ocean. It looks like a futuristically designed church of some quasi-religious sect: a towering A-frame with a 55-foot chimney. The walls are made of glass, the floor stone, the ceiling stained glass because Wilt has always felt comfortable in a church. The house has no right angles, only triangles, because "I believe in pyramid energy," he says. The A-frame is held up by 80-foot metal beams in concrete. The front door weighs 2,200 pounds. The swimming pool begins in the living room and meanders outside. Small ponds all around the house are stocked with fish. The ponds are backlit, and whenever Wilt has a guest, he makes a point of putting on the lights.

There is a sunken bath in his bedroom, with a statue of a naked woman in it. Above his huge bed, the glass ceiling opens at the press of a button to reveal the sky. Wilt likes to open that skylight whenever he is "entertaining a lady."

The toilet in his bathroom is more than a foot higher than most— normal-size men have to urinate up, not down.

The living area on the first floor is decorated in browns and beiges and imitation animal skins, leopard and jaguar, made of Ultrasuede. The skins are tossed around the room, over sofas and easy chairs and even over the twelve chairs around his dining-room table. Above the table hangs a 27-foot-tall cut-glass chandelier that looks like a stalactite from a Superman movie.

The imitation animal skins are soiled; the sofa is stained; the metal plate on the front door is peeling off; and the windows that are the walls of the house are dirty. "Birds fly into the windows and kill themselves," says Wilt. "Hawks and eagles. It's not their fault. I keep the windows dirty so they can see them."

It is a house of a '70s bachelor who has taken to heart too many of Hugh Hefner's *Playboy* columns. Even Hef by now is married with two young children. But Wilt has lived that *Playboy* philosophy far longer than most because he is Wilt and it is difficult for him to admit he was ever wrong.

"I'd like to think I am happy," he says, sitting again in his spacious living room with the stained glass rising all the way to the pointed ceiling. "Maybe I did use my wealth selfishly. I made more money than it's proper for anyone to make. I'll be sad if I die with just a few toys." (Wilt made his money early in his career and invested wisely in Arabian horses, a nightclub, the stock market, and "land all over the world.")

"I like to believe I've changed," he says. "I know blacks have had problems in life that prevented them from achieving. Before, I took it for granted that everyone could accomplish what I have. Now I realize I've been blessed. I know I'm still selfish. But I'm working on it. I do a lot of thinking."

Wilt Chamberlain, unmarried, without children, thinks alone in his empty house with no one to edit him. He thinks that dining-room tables should be built taller so that the tabletop reaches just below a person's chin. That way the diner won't have to raise his fork as far, thus diminishing his chances of spilling food. Wilt also wonders why rearview mirrors come with the disclaimer that the distance between the car and the object in the mirror is distorted. Why not have a mirror that accurately reflects that distance? Some of the things Wilt thinks about make a kind of skewed sense, some of them are merely obvious, some of them show genuine insight, and some of them are just the silly musings of a man who's spent too much time alone. A man who has come to believe that everything he thinks, from the frivolous to the truly weighty, has the same value because *he* thinks it. That's why Wilt has set up his life in such a way that he is responsible to no one but himself, the ultimate solipsist.

"Being lonely is a state of mind," he says. "I cook for myself. I work out hard." He picks up a hundred-pound dumbbell. "Go ahead, try to lift it."

He'd rather go to a girls' volleyball game than a Lakers game because he can be relatively anonymous among the few hundred fans. When he goes to the U.S. Open tennis tournament, he prefers the back courts rather than center court where the celebrities like to be seen. He writes until late at night, sometimes while watching two and three basketball games on TV. He rarely goes to bed before five a.m. A good life, he says.

"I made this dynamite pasta the other day," he says. "Scallops, mussels, wine, cream cheese. I ate by myself. It was wonderful. I called my secretary and said, 'I wish you were here to have some of this. I'll probably never make it right again.'"

Still, he thinks it might be time to share his pasta with someone. "It'd be nice to find a lady," he says. "But I demand so much. Maybe now I can accept the fact that she might not be the greatest cook."

His problem, he says, is that he prefers people in the abstract more than in the reality. "I do love people," he says. "I just can't take them in big doses. Living alone, I get a sense of who I am. Most stars today travel with an entourage that wouldn't tell them the right goddamned time of day. Look at Michael Jordan! I know a lot of ladies he calls. He goes to clubs with an entourage, and when he sees a lady he likes, he sends a friend over to get her. He goes with an entourage for cover. I just go out alone. If I saw a blonde, I'd go over to her myself, and everyone in the club would see me." (David Falk, Jordan's agent, says, "It's not appropriate for Michael to respond to everyone's uninformed opinion.")

Wilt is particularly critical of today's sports stars, who he thinks are selfish, overpraised, overpaid, and more concerned with being celebrities than athletes. "These guys make ten times what we made, but they don't have fun. We had fun."

The problem, he says, begins with sports announcers who fawn over today's stars "like car salesmen trying to sell a product. They never say how great guys from the past were, but only that today's stars are the greatest so they can get the fans to come and see them. I'm sick of hearing how Jordan and Shaq are the greatest."

Wilt is particularly annoyed with Jordan, because Jordan is the only NBA player with a higher career scoring average than his. It hurt Wilt's feelings the night he heard an announcer say that Jordan had scored more than forty points 240 times and was the greatest scorer in NBA history. Bill Walton, the co-announcer, said, "Yeah, but Wilt averaged fifty points a game for a whole season. Can you imagine?"

"The other goddamned announcer didn't say a thing," says Wilt. "Listen, I'm not a big fan of Michael Jordan's, because he never led the league in field-goal percentage. If you take the dunk out of his game, his percentage will be even lower. Oscar Robertson shot forty-eight percent and *he* never dunked the ball. When Jordan goes to the basket, the waters part. Did you ever see Jordan knocked to the floor? How can you let him go to the basket like that and not knock him on his ass? Because jobs depend on Michael Jordan, that's why. Look at those gambling stories. Did he really get suspended from the NBA [when he temporarily retired]? The media stay away from that because their jobs depend on him."

Wilt is annoyed at Shaquille O'Neal because, he says, he was asked to appear in one of Shaq's movies gratis. "What's Shaq making, fifty million on that movie, and they wanted me to do it for nothing? On my birthday! The balls of these people!" But it's more than that. Wilt doesn't feel that Shaq, overrated and overweight, should be mentioned in the same breath as players like himself and Russell.

"Look," says Wilt. "The Lakers claim Shaq weighs three hundred pounds when he really weighs three-forty. He's not in shape. That's why the Lakers lose in the last quarter when Shaq gets no points. That's why Orlando got rid of him."

Once Wilt gains a full head of steam, he is like that rhinoceros he once faced down. He can't stop himself, flailing his arms, cutting down everyone in his path.

"Do you know when Kenny Anderson was with the New Jersey Nets he refused to tie his shoelaces in practice?" says Wilt. "And his coach couldn't do anything about it. And what about Rodman and Deion Sanders? They epitomize all the wrong things. And yet they get endorsements, and guys like Jerry Rice and Barry Sanders don't. Rice epitomizes professionalism and Sanders is the most unaffected, nicest superstar. I mean, Darryl Strawberry hits a home run and the fans cheer. Are they cheering for the home run or because he beat his wife that night? You know, there'll come a time when some great athlete is on death row, scheduled to be executed, and the owner of his team will call the governor. 'Do you think you can hold off the execution until Monday?' he'll ask. 'So we can use him in the Superbowl Sunday?'"

One of the reasons more militant blacks like Russell, Brown and Abdul-Jabbar have disparaged Wilt is because he's not afraid to criticize other black stars for what he feels are their weaknesses. He says Mike Tyson is "a wonderful warrior" who'd do better for himself if he'd get rid of men like Don King. He never thought Muhammad Ali was as smart as people claimed, but that Ali was just a puppet who mouthed the Muslim party line he'd been taught. Now that Ali is suffering from Parkinson's disease, Wilt feels it is a crime to trot him out "in public the way he is. I remember when Joe Louis was in a wheelchair and Ali pointed at him and said *he'd* never end up like Louis." As for Abdul-Jabbar, Wilt claims, "I raised him in high school. I took him by the hand to UCLA and then he became a Muslim and turned on me.

"I saw Kareem some years ago. His contract with the Lakers had run out. He said to me, 'Do you believe no one will give me an offer?' I thought, Yeah, I believe it. But I told him to go back to the Lakers, who knew his style of play. A new team would want him to get twenty rebounds a game when he couldn't. When Kareem came into the league he said he'd only play four years. But he played for twenty. You had to get a pitchfork to drag the S.O.B. out." Wilt feels Abdul-Jabbar stayed in the NBA as long as he did only to break Wilt's career scoring record, which he did.

Wilt says he's so bluntly candid because, "If I believe something, I have to set the record straight. I'm not looking for recognition only for Wilt but for others, too. For Jerry West and Oscar and Elgin Baylor." But mostly he's always trying to set the record straight about himself. He has always felt abused by the fans, the press, other players. He has the sensitivity of a child to personal slights. And as with a child, those slights bring him to anger. And why not? He thinks all the critical abuse he took during his career diminished it.

"I never played as good in the pros as I did in high school," he says. "I did stuff in high school I couldn't do as a center in the pros. I fell into what people wanted of me. When they said I was selfish for scoring too much, I stopped doing it. The media imposed on me a need for assists, defense, and rebounds, so I gave up the ball to my teammates to make everyone happier. I totally let myself be conned into it. It was a total con job. I coulda led the league in scoring for fourteen years instead of seven. I diminished my own career to appease people. They say I became a great defender, but that's bullshit. I always played great defense, but my offense obscured it. When I stopped shooting, they said I finally learned to play defense."

In Wilt's first seven years in the NBA, he averaged almost forty points per game, but his teams won no NBA championships, while Russell's Celtics won all seven. Over Wilt's last seven years, when he barely managed to score twenty points per game, two of his teams, the '66-67 Philadelphia 76ers and the '71-72 LA Lakers, won an NBA title. Wilt doesn't think there's a cause-and-effect relationship between his decreased scoring and his team's successes. Maybe it's because he never saw his career in terms of his team's success in the first place. He always thought in terms of his own numbers, and, as Wilt likes to say, numbers never lie.

Reluctantly, he goes down to his garage to show off his self-designed sports car, the one he's been working on for more that a decade. He takes off the protective covering to reveal a low-slung yellow vehicle that looks like a cross between a Ferrari and a Ford GT-40.

"Go ahead, sit in it," he says. The seat is so low and pushed so far back for Wilt's legs that an ordinary man can barely see over the steering wheel. When the clutch is depressed, however, it sinks to the floor.

"The clutch doesn't work."

He grimaces. "I know. I've only driven it a few times. It's still not finished." He shakes his head in disgust. "I hate to even talk about it. It shows how selfish I am." But it bothers him even more that his $1.5 million car doesn't work than that people might think he's been extravagant to spend so much on what he calls "a toy."

"Whatever you do," he says, "don't tell anyone about the car." But even as he says this, he knows it is a futile request. So he adds, "You can tell them it'll do two hundred forty m.p.h., the fastest street car in the world."

Alberto Tomba

The Italian Prince

(from *Special Reports*, 1988)

THE OLD ITALIAN WOMAN smiles and nods to the photograph on the wall inside the only bar in town. Setting a round of espresso coffees on our table, she says, "Alberto è forte." *Alberto is the greatest.*

We are in the village of Castel de Britti, a collection of salmon-colored adobe villas perched on a cliffside in the central Italian Apennine Mountains, twelve miles south of Bologna. The four of us—Kirk, our translator; his friend, Mima; my wife, Susan; and I—have an afternoon appointment with the man in the eight-by-ten black-and-white photograph hung on the tavern wall. Mima, a Florentine high school teacher in her thirties, is smitten by the likeness.

"Oh, he's so sexy-looking," she says. "I can't wait to meet him." Her eyes fix on the image of the dark, handsome, curly-haired man who looks much older than twenty-two.

La Bomba Tomba. The Beast. Media heartthrob. Self-proclaimed messiah of skiing. Winner of two Olympic gold medals. Possibly the best slalom skier ever, according to skiing legend Ingemar Stenmark, who should know. And the embodiment of the mythological Italian stud.

The Italians, in a legendary adulation of great lovers, relish Alberto Tomba stories that portray him as a womanizer even when they are embellished. Once, when the secretary of the Italian basketball league called Tomba's home and Tomba's father said he didn't know where his son was, the secretary smiled and said, "He's probably racing his Ferrari around Italy with a beautiful woman at his side." The truth, he later learned, was that Tomba was in military training. And his car is a more modest BMW.

Still, the paparazzi follow his sexual exploits throughout his native land—on beaches with bikini-clad girls and in the fashionable bars along Via Veneto in Rome. He is Italy's prodigal son. A man so idolized in his own country that Italians are dumbfounded as to why any woman would spurn him. Ever. Even if that woman was Katarina Witt, the aloof East German princess of skating, who at the Olympic Games in Calgary coolly turned down a date with the dazzling Italian prince of skiing.

The old woman in the bar gives us directions to the Tomba home nearby. Alberto Tomba lives with his parents in a restored sixteenth-century villa, which sits alone on a hilltop above Castel de Britti. The villa was built by Cardinal Pizzaro. In those days it was not uncommon for a cardinal's dealings to be more financial than spiritual, and so Cardinal Pizzaro's home was a businessman's villa.

It still is. Franco Tomba, Alberto's father, is the owner of an exclusive men's clothing store in Bologna that he renamed Minarelli de Alberto Tomba, following his son's Olympic triumphs. The store has been passed down through three generations of Tombas. Presumably, when Tomba retires from the sport of skiing, he plans to work in his father's business alongside his older brother, Marco.

From the village, we follow a narrow road that snakes uphill for about a mile. Bordering the road is a white wall on which someone has spray-painted ALBERTO IS THE CONQUEROR OF THE WHITE WORLD. We come to an electronically controlled wrought-iron gate that opens onto a narrow driveway leading past new BMWs and Mercedeses to a sprawling villa perched on a hill overlooking the valley. A beautiful, black-haired woman—Tomba's mother—sits under the shade of a tree, sipping a drink. His father, Franco, meets us with his half-dozen dogs and leads us to the backyard, where we sit at a circular lawn table shaded by an umbrella.

Tomba's twelve-year-old sister and her cousin are playing tennis on the family courts above us. His pack of dogs romp across the vast grounds, chasing one another through the perfectly manicured, labyrinthine gardens before stopping, tongues hanging, to drink from the circular fountain with the marble cupid spouting water at its center.

Franco says that his son is inside the villa, sleeping off the effects of too much wine after his cousin's morning wedding. While we wait, Franco questions us with furrowed brows about what kind of article will be written about his son. He is a wiry little man with small eyes and a big nose who is less muscular and handsome than his son.

Tomba appears minutes later, rubbing sleep from his eyes. Dressed in a plum-colored polo shirt and jeans, he is unshaven, a serious, almost dour-looking boy who seems to have nothing in common with the gregarious hero of last year's Winter Olympic Games. Still, he is unfailingly polite. He offers drinks and calls to his mother to come meet us. His brother, Marco, a tall, pale man, appears briefly, dressed in a shirt and tie, hurrying around the side of the villa. Tomba calls to him, too, but Marco acts as if he does not hear.

Tomba's father, puffing his pipe, stands beside his son's chair as if to protect him from my questions, beginning with one on the skater. Tomba listens, nods, looks down at his hands, scratches his nose. "Katarina," he says, "she is a *bella donna*, but . . ." He shrugs. "Between us, there was *niente*." Franco nods.

It was not a perfect match. Katarina Witt is cool and calculating. A slightly built East German figure skater with an actress's smile and so much makeup on her face that it muddies her considerable beauty. Tomba is rich, brawny, and famous. A dark, husky boy with the rugged good looks of a much older man—until he smiles. A gregarious smile. Guileless. And sexy, too.

"I am a beast," Tomba told the world at the 1988 Winter Olympic Games in Calgary. "I am the new messiah of skiing. I can do whatever I want." And he did. He won a gold medal in the slalom and another in the giant slalom despite the fact that he approached the games as if they were a toga party in *Animal House*. He stuffed ice cubes down the backs of other athletes; threw spitballs at them during team meals; tried to sneak out of his team's training camp to party the night before his first competition; drank a half liter of wine only hours before he was to compete; and then, only moments before he was slated to leave the starting gate, telephoned his sister in Bologna to tell her he was having a ball.

That night, after winning his first gold medal, he sprayed champagne at a victory celebration to the fans' cheers of "Tomba! Tomba! Tomba!" which, in Italian, means "tomb." A misnomer, if there ever was one.

There is nothing funereal about Alberto Tomba. He approached the Olympic Games as just another event to be enjoyed for sport. Which did not sit well with the other competitors. Stern Germans, Swiss, and northern Italians, they accused him of trying to distract them at the starting gate with his constant chatter.

Even his coach complained that he seemed not to take the games seriously. He did not like to train, said his coach. Which was why, despite his considerable promise, he did not win a World Cup race in two years. Then, the November before the Olympics, he won his first World Cup event, and then his next seven of nine to become the world champion.

His coach, Joseph Messner, attributed this string of victories to a weight-lifting regimen Tomba had finally agreed to undergo only after he realized that the muscles would transform his baby-fat, 200-pound body into a rock-hard, 190-pound physique. Tomba saw the change would not only benefit his skiing but also attract the attention of the girls on the beaches at Rimini on the Adriatic, where he likes to drive in his black BMW with his name printed in block letters on each door. He liked the weight lifting, said Messner, "because in summer he can go to the beach and make a muscle. Before, he would agree that he had to train harder, but two days later he would forget."

Messner described Tomba as a natural athlete who doesn't think too much. Which is why skiing comes easily to him, says former Italian skiing star Erwin Stricker. "To be a good racer, you must be brainless or be able to turn off the brain," Stricker said two months before Tomba's Olympic victories. "For that reason, Tomba will win a lot of races."

It is likely the same reason that, at twenty-two, Tomba has yet to earn the school degree most Italian males get at eighteen, why he doesn't like books, and why he refuses to learn English. And also why he chose to enter the Carabinieri, a paramilitary force whose members are the butt of Italian jokes because of their supposed ignorance. In the custom of Italian sports figures, Tomba joined the Carabinieri because it is noted for its great skiers. As with other Carabinieri skiers, his military duty is to excel in his sport.

Still, despite his skiing successes, the tough little East German figure skater was not swept off her feet when Tomba brought her a rose on the eve of her greatest triumph. She had no intentions of sharing the moment with anyone, least of all this burly puppy dog who offered to give her one of his two Olympic gold medals if she did not win one of her own. She told him, in effect, to take a hike.

Nonetheless, four months after his Olympic triumphs, Tomba received a phone call from Witt. She was in Milan, she said, and wondered if he would like to drive up from Bologna to show her around Italy. This time, he told *her* to take a hike.

"Now we are even," he says. By then, he was no longer just the carefree flirt he had been at the games. He seemed to have already grown bored of his image.

Tomba's mother appears with wine and orange juice for her son's guests. Maria Grazia Tomba appears to be in her mid-forties, a bosomy, dark-skinned woman in jeans and a halter top.

When her son was a teenager, his mother forbade him to compete in downhill skiing because she thought it too dangerous. Tomba is not ashamed to admit that that is why he does not compete in the downhill even today. "I even worry when Alberto goes down the slopes in the slalom," Maria says. "But I still want him to be first because all Italy is watching him."

After pouring the wine, she excuses herself to sit in front, under the shade of a tree, and enjoy her drink. She does not involve herself much in her son's career. She leaves that to her husband.

Franco dotes on his younger son in the way of a Little League father, nodding, frowning, smiling at his every word. Tomba first gravitated to skiing partly because he did not like soccer. ("It was too tough," he says) and partly because his father, a skier, insisted that his son become a skier, too.

Often Franco answers for his son. Tomba falls silent, grows fidgety, his attention wandering like that of a young boy surrounded by adults. He appears uncomfortable around adults, even when two of them are attractive older women, one of whom, Mima, could not wait to meet her country's newest sex symbol. Tomba barely notices her. He addresses only the men of the group, complaining of excessive media attention.

"The first two, three times it was fun," he says. "But no more. Too much publicity. Too many demands from the public. My neck is weighted down by gold medals."

Tomba says that much of his public image stems from his being Bolognese. To fathom that, it is necessary to understand that, even today, in the twentieth century, Italy is virtually a country of city-states, each inhabited by people with stereotyped images. Romans are arrogant. Neapolitans are thieves. Milanese are money-hungry. And Bolognese are carefree.

"I am different from other skiers," he says. "They are too serious. They like to keep apart. Everybody in the world is interesting to me. It doesn't bother my concentration to be friendly. Five minutes before a race I am laughing. The other skiers don't even smile. They say I laugh to throw off their concentration. But that is not so. I am just a happy man. I come from Bologna. Bolognese love to drink wine and party. Bolognese are happy people."

Not only is Tomba Bolognese, but he is also a *rich* Bolognese, in marked contrast to most other Italian skiers, who are poor boys from the north.

"They were closed to me," he says of his northern compatriots. "They are half German and they gave me a hard time for being Bolognese. I felt isolated. But now there is no problem." He smiles his boyish smile. "Now they try to emulate me."

Despite the adulation, Tomba says he has no intentions of pursuing a skiing career much longer. He may ski in the 1992 Olympics, but only if he can keep his weight down. Unlike many Olympic athletes, he does not need the money his fame will bring him. He has no plans for promoting products or turning to an acting career.

Besides, he says, tugging on the roll of fat at his waist, it is hard to maintain an Olympic level of perfection for four years. "I let my training go sometimes," he says with a shrug.

Right now, he has more practical goals, such as fulfilling his obligations with his Carabinieri regiment in Rome. The Carabinieri's lackluster reputation apparently does not bother Tomba. Despite his outrageous behavior at the Olympic Games, he shows no signs of developing a star's ego. His fame is simply an offshoot of his natural flamboyance.

"I never thought I would be famous," he says. "Now that I am, I don't like it. Nothing in my life has changed since the Olympics. I wouldn't let it. I could party every night if I wanted to, but I don't."

He makes a disgusted sound with his mouth. "Girls?" he says. "*Aiie*, girls!" He makes a backhand toss of his hand as if to imply that his reputation as a ladies' man is exaggerated.

And yet he makes a great production out of his attraction to girls. When he mentions that his girlfriend is napping inside the villa, he lowers his voice conspiratorially and says, "But I have many girlfriends, you know."

Finally, Mima, who has sat silently since our arrival, is unable to control herself any longer. She smiles flirtatiously and says she has seen a picture of him dressed in only a towel in an Italian scandal magazine. Tomba puts his head down, embarrassed. Before he can answer, his father says, "The photographer had no right. He caught Alberto coming out of the shower. Now the photographer is in trouble with the Carabinieri. I told the Carabinieri to get him."

Tomba nods like a chastened boy. Mima's face drops, and she sinks in her chair. She stares at Tomba as if studying him the way she would one of her students. The same boy, presumably, that Katarina Witt saw at Calgary. A boy dominated by his father.

Tomba excuses himself to go inside for some of his posters to sign for us. "He's just like most Italian boys his age," Mima whispers. "Pampered. Good-looking. But still a boy."

I follow him into the villa. He is in the family dining room, where he keeps his posters and skiing equipment. It is a beautifully restored room with a rose-colored marble floor littered with skis, boots, helmets, poles, unopened boxes, just as any teenage boy's room might be. The dining room table groans under the weight of thousands of Alberto Tomba posters. They show him smiling in his ski uniform—a dark, rugged, handsome man-child with thick black brows and the look of mature sexuality so marked in contrast to his guileless smile. Tomba spreads out a poster on the table and bends over it.

"Who is it for?" he asks.

"My niece," I say.

He looks up with a leer. "Is she pretty?"

"She's only twelve."

"Is she pretty, though?" he asks, as if he had not heard me. Then he writes, "For Christina. With one perfect kiss. Love, Alberto."

While he prints laboriously, a painting on the far wall comes into focus. A fat, pink, naked, deliriously happy cherub with wine-stained lips. Bacchus.

How the Boston Bruins Flaunt Their Muscles

(from *Sport* Magazine, 1970)

WHEN I WAS FIRST MARRIED I took my wife to a shabby French restaurant for supper. The waiter, a sullen old man with a clip-on bowtie, served our courses quickly and sloppily. At one point he reached across the table and handed my wife her soup dish rather than walking around and depositing it. When he swept our dishes away after the main course he accidentally picked up my wife's gloves and dropped them on the floor. When he returned he stepped on them. By the time dessert rolled around I was thoroughly intimidated, and my voice was a quaking whisper when I asked if he would please translate an item on the menu. He muttered something in French to himself, then growled at me:

"If Monsieur can't read the menu then he doesn't belong here."

I have been too terrified to enter a French restaurant ever since. And when I traveled to Boston Garden recently to watch the Bruins play hockey, I could not help recalling that waiter and restaurant of years ago.

Boston Garden is a dark, cold, concrete tomb. Its echoing corridors smell of cigar smoke and stale beer. It is the kind of arena where people instinctively reach to their back pockets when jostled in a crowd. The Garden's shadowy runways are patrolled by sour-faced ushers in stiff red uniforms who seem to get more pleasure from pushing people out of the aisles than leading them to their seats. But no matter how gruff the ushers might be, and no matter how much dampness is seeping up through the seats, you could not sell even your soul for a seat in that Garden when the Bruins are playing hockey.

Bruins fans do not come to their Garden for comfort. Nor do they come after a fine dinner and cocktails like New York Ranger fans go to their Garden. Instead, Boston fans come after an argument with their wives, their dinners pushed aside in anger. They come not to complement a good day but in one last angry attempt to "get even" with another in a long line of very bad days.

The Bruins are very much at home in their Garden. "Of course other teams don't like to come here much," says their young coach Harry Sinden. Then he adds with a small, catlike grin, "Especially the goalies."

The Boston Bruins are not an especially big hockey team. When they arrive for a game carrying their thin attache cases, they look more like grim businessmen than athletes. It is only after they apply layer upon layer of padding and long stiff gloves, then lace on their skates and finally grab their curved sticks that they take on the proportions one expects from the "biggest and baddest" of all National Hockey League teams.

On this Saturday night, December 6, the Bruins are playing the Chicago Black Hawks of Bobby Hull and Stan Mikita. When the Hawks take the ice for their pre-game warmups, the Boston fans greet them with silence. When the Bruins appear there is a deafening roar.

After their warmups, as the two teams skate silently past each other toward their respective dressing rooms, the Bruins' John McKenzie casually drops his stick into the oncoming path of Chicago's Gilles Marotte. The stick glances of Marotte's shoulder, and Marotte whirls around just as McKenzie, a smile on his face, disappears through the runway. "Thatta baby, Pie," yells a Boston fan. "Give that jerk a taste of what's to come." There is a scattering of applause for McKenzie, as if the right wing had just made a fine play.

Even before the game begins the crowd is tense with excitement. On almost the first play the Bruins' Garnet Bailey checks Marotte against the corner boards. When the action moves away from the two men, Bailey gives Marotte a quick jab in the gut with his stick. Marotte skates furiously after him and shoves Bailey from behind. The referee catches Marotte and gives him a two-minute penalty for roughing.

"Oh, jeez, Marotte, but that was a smart play!" yells a fan. Other fans begin to laugh. "You're a real marshmallow, Marotte! A real marshmallow!"

While Marotte is sitting out his penalty the Bruins score their first power play goal. A few minutes later the Bruins' Don Awrey checks

Dennis Hull against the boards. As he pushes off from Hull he smacks him across the jaw with his elbows. The Boston fans take offense at Awrey's tactics.

"The stick, Awrey! Hit 'em with the damned stick!" There is a chorus of, "The stick! The stick!" and then a few boos for Awrey.

Amid similar shouts of encouragement from their fans, the Boston Bruins proceed to deflower the Chicago Black Hawks until by the beginning of the second period they have fashioned a 3-0 lead. They accomplish their intimidation in small ways: an elbow in the ribs here, a wildly swung stick there, a grabbed shirt, and even, on occasion, a straight body check.

Mostly the Bruins work over the younger Chicago players like Marotte (24), Ray McKay (23), and Keith Magnuson (22). They are particularly hard on the boyish, red-haired Magnuson because only a few weeks ago he had a fight with the Bruins' Bobby Orr in Chicago. "Magnuson was pushing too many people around," says Derek Sanderson, the Bruins' young defenseman. "So when the game gets out of hand it's time to settle old grudges."

The Bruins wrap up the game quickly and then settle their grudge with Magnuson while the fans hoot them on with a chorus of "Hit Megason, hit Megason, that chapped-lipped S.O.B.!"

Wayne Cashman spears Magnuson with a stick. Bailey elbows him in the face and the two men scuffle briefly. Phil Esposito smashes him with a body check from Magnuson's blind side. Finally, Johnny Bucyk body-checks Magnuson with such force that Magnuson's stick is splintered over the ice. Magnuson is so dazed he just stands in the middle of the ice before he remembers to go to his bench for a new stick.

The Bruins do not have to be so rough with McKay, a tall, stringy defenseman who played at Dallas last year. By the third period McKay has been easily intimidated. He has so receded from the action that the fans are beginning to call him Lamont Cranston, The Shadow. Later Sanderson will say, with pride: "One night I ripped McKay's shirt right off his back. Then I threw it in the stands. I did it for effect. You know what I mean?"

With less than a minute left in the game, the Bruins are leading, 6-1. There is a meaningless faceoff by their net. As the players line up around the circle, Awrey sneaks behind Eric Nesterenko, slides his stick between Nesterenko's legs, and tries to trip him. Nesterenko and Awrey trade a few feeble punches before the referee breaks it up. Shortly afterwards the clock runs out. "Even when you've got a big lead," says Awrey, "you've got to take a run at him. Let him know you'll be waiting for him next time out. Sort of give him something to think about between games."

Bobby Orr, the Bruins' soft-spoken, priceless young talent, does not talk about the Bruins' style of play in the same tone as Sanderson and Awrey. Not that he can't be every bit as intimidating on the ice as Sanderson and Awrey. But when Bobby describes the Bruins' style of play, he speaks in terms of "finesse" and "forechecking" rather than "evening grudges."

"The Bruins aren't going to finesse a team to death like the Rangers and the Canadiens," he says. "We try to . . ." and here he searches for just the right word, ". . . try to wear them down physically. We play a tough forechecking game mostly, in the hope that we can get other teams to play our game."

The Bruins' coach Sinden is not so diplomatic as Bobby Orr. "Sure we try to intimidate other clubs. We've been doing it the last few years. I admit it's a conscious effort, but you've got to understand that intimidation is a big part of the NHL."

Sinden stops for a minute, then continues in his low, nasal monotone. "Listen, for nine years the Bruins were the laughingstock of the NHL. Now, for the past few years we've come up with some tough young players and we're trying to win back our self-respect. No one laughs at the Bruins anymore, do they?"

Sinden does admit, however, that the Bruins' roughhousing doesn't apply to every player on every team they meet. "There are some guys you leave alone," he says. "You don't want to wake them up because they play better when mad."

"You mean like Hull and Mikita?"

Sinden smiles that small smile of his and says, "Let's just say, 'some guys,' and let it go it at that."

Although the Bruins' barroom style has carried them out of the NHL cellar, it has not yet deposited them at the top of the league. Harry Sinden doesn't think it ever will, at least not by itself.

"We need more than intimidation to win this league," he says. "You don't see Montreal pushing people around, and they win every year. In the past the only way we could make our presence felt and get fans into the Garden was by playing hard. Now I think our talent has matured. We can forget about foolish penalties and just play hockey. Besides," and now he is all innocence, "we're not really any tougher than any other team in this league." His wide eyes and curious grin also tell me something. They're saying: "Believe that last sentence and you'll believe anything."

The next night the Bruins play the Minnesota North Stars, a young, physically tough team much in the style of the Bruins. The North Stars, who don't talk as much about their roughness (or lack of it) as the Bruins do, are currently leading the NHL in penalty minutes.

The Bruins set out to intimidate the North Stars just as they'd done the night before with the Hawks. The only difference is that Minnesota doesn't scare easily. Nor do they explode emotionally. Instead, they trade stick for stick, punch for punch, although it is obvious that their tactics are more in defense than in any attempt to intimidate the Bruins. (As Harry Sinden says, "No one tries to intimidate the Bruins in Boston.")

One Minnesota player, Dan O'Shea, is particularly rough on Sanderson. A few times he high-sticks Derek, and once he gets caught for a two-minute penalty. The Boston fans seem amazed that anyone would dare to use the same tactics as their beloved Bruins. "That O'Shea is emotionally disturbed," says a woman beside me, shaking her head in disbelief.

O'Shea finally angers Sanderson, who gets caught for a foolish penalty that allows the North Stars to score their first goal on a power play. By the middle of the second period the Bruins see that the North Stars refuse to be intimidated and change tactics. The roughness ebbs slightly and both teams concentrate more on moving the puck.

But just moving the puck puts the "finesse-less" Bruins at a disadvantage. "Look at that, look at that!" screams a fan in horror. "A behind-the-back pass. They can't even pass it straight and they gotta try fancy moves like that." He slaps his head with his palm and groans.

The only isolated act of Bruin intimidation occurs when Bobby Orr gets hurt. Jean-Paul Parise and Orr are chasing a free puck when Parise slips and falls into Orr, smashing him head first into the boards. Orr is momentarily unconscious, and a woman cries out, "Oh my God, they've killed Bobby!"

But Orr soon limps off the ice amidst a great cheer from the Bruins' fans. Someone says the referees are letting the game get out of hand. A few others agree. "Those North Stars are just dirty hockey players," says another fan incredulously, the same fan who implored Awrey to hit Hull with his stick the night before.

Almost immediately after Orr's injury, McKenzie whacks Minnesota's Tom Williams in the back with his stick. Williams goes down in pain, but the North Stars do not come to his defense, and there is no scuffling. It's almost as if Minnesota expected the Bruins to retaliate and are glad it is finally over. The fans, meanwhile, are cheering McKenzie.

"I was swinging for the puck," McKenzie will say after the game, but Sinden's not so sure. "I wouldn't say I told Pie to get to Williams," the coach says, "but then again I wouldn't say the incident wasn't premeditated, either. Even if Orr's injury was an accident there are some things you can't let go by."

The game concludes uneventfully with the North Stars earning a much-deserved 2-2 tie, something of a moral victory for a visiting team in the Garden. "Big Bad Bruins my eye!" says a woman getting up from her seat. "They played like a bunch of fairies out there."

After the game it occurs to me that the Bruins are not as rough as they would like people to believe. They are like that waiter in the French restaurant, masters at irritation and intimidation rather than violent hatchet-men. At least that's what they had become this season. They seemed far more brutalizing the year before, when they were led into battle by violent defenseman Teddy Green. I ask Sinden now if Green's absence has an effect on the Bruins' growing reluctance to raise out-and-out hell.

"We miss Green," says Sinden, tight-lipped. "If there's such a thing as a policeman in the league, then we had the captain of the force."

Green was out, of course, as the result of a violent stick fight between him and Wayne Maki. It happened in an exhibition game between St. Louis and Boston this past fall. Green struck first; Maki retaliated by smashing Green over the head, almost killing him. Green was given last rites by the Catholic Church, and even though he lived, he has a steel plate in his head, and his speech and movements have been impaired; he may never be quite right again. He keeps insisting, however, that he will be playing before the season's over.

Sinden does not like to talk about the Green injury. Neither do the other Bruins, but they do so anyway, perhaps as catharsis. "Teddy was a damned tough guy," Bobby Orr says slowly. "Damned tough! And he almost died. Don't you think for a minute that didn't start a lot of guys thinking. I don't think anyone will ever be so quick to raise his stick after that. As for myself, I don't like sticks. I drop mine whenever I see trouble coming."

I tell Bobby what John Pierson, a former Bruin player, had said about the recent rash of stick-swinging fights. "Once it starts everybody panics," Pierson had said. "No one wants to be the first guy to drop his stick in a fight."

"I don't know about that," Orr says now. "I drop mine right away. If a guy hits me with his stick, his day will come soon enough and he knows it."

Sanderson, the Bruins' shaggy-haired, broodingly handsome, tough defenseman, was Teddy Green's roommate before his injury. Derek, who admits to having been greatly influenced by Green, prides himself on his ability to handle his fists. "I get a kick out of beating someone in a fight," he will say. Or: "What I like about the Bruins is if you fight one of us you've gotta fight us all." Or: "If you let someone in this league think you're a coward, you won't last long." And then, like all the other Bruins, Derek finally concludes with: "To tell you the truth, we're not that tough. We're no tougher than any other team in the league." He smiles at me and winks.

All the façade and pretense melt away, though, when he remembers the night Teddy Green almost died. He speaks more softly now, almost with wonder that such a thing could happen to such a tough human being.

"Maki was scared to death of Teddy," Sanderson says. "He hit him from behind, *whack!* over the back of the head." He pauses a second. "Teddy's face was all bashed in on one side. Just like it had collapsed. There was blood all over the ice. It was the worst thing I ever saw."

I ask if the Green incident hadn't affected his style of play.

"Not a bit," he says sharply. "You can't let an injury bother you. I still wouldn't think twice about raising my stick in a fight."

When I leave Sanderson he's talking to teammate Phil Esposito. "Remember how Teddy looked that night," he is saying. Esposito is staring at the floor, nodding his head slowly.

The next day I talk to Stan Mikita about violence, the Bruins, and Teddy Green. Stan, an articulate, pleasant man of twenty-nine, has gone from one extreme to the other in his career: from an admittedly dirty player to a winner of the Lady Byng Award for sportsmanship.

"When you first come into the league everyone's taking a shot at you, so you've got to prove you can take it and dish it out," says Mikita. "But some guys seem to go out of their way to show how tough they are, especially in front of a crowd. There's a little bit of the ham in all of us. We get in front of those screaming fans and it brings out the sadist in us. We do things we'd never otherwise do, and before you know it you're swinging a stick at someone's head. I don't think anyone plans to swing a stick. It just happens. Look at Teddy; after he got hurt he admitted in the papers that all the years he'd swung his stick it never occurred to him that he could actually hurt someone. You swing the stick a few times and don't hit anyone, then pretty soon it gets easier and easier and you forget how dangerous it is.

"The only time you remember is when you hear that sickening thud. Then you get sick to your stomach. No one gets any satisfaction from it, I'll tell you. All you get is this sick feeling and a guy's life is almost ruined. . . ."

On a rainy Wednesday evening, December 10, the Boston Bruins arrive at the plush Madison Square Garden Center for a home-and-home series with the New York Rangers. The Rangers are currently riding a fourteen game streak without a loss.

"They're plenty tough," says Bobby Orr. He holds up his thumb and points to it. "The last time we played them a guy bit me. No kidding! It got infected. Can you imagine that?"

This is somewhat ironic, because the Bruins seldom had trouble with the slick-skating but mild-mannered Rangers when Teddy Green was in the lineup.

"They hated him here," says Orr. "One night they put a bounty on his head. 'Wanted, Dead or Alive,' it read." He shakes his head.

The Bruins begin the game with Bailey, Awrey, McKenzie, and Sanderson all taking quick shots at the Rangers' fleet Rod Gilbert. Gilbert takes it for a while, then blows up and charges into Bailey. He gets a two-minute penalty and the Bruins promptly score on a power play for a 1-0 lead.

Then the Rangers settle down. They concentrate on moving the puck and keeping clear of the tougher but more ponderous Bruins. They are just too fast for the Bruins and by the beginning of the third period they have a 4-2 lead. The Bruins look listless and they are beginning to huff and puff like the proverbial big bad wolf. But they can't seem to blow anyone's house down tonight. Their goalie, Gerry Cheevers, typifies their frustration when, in the closing minutes, he moves out of his goal to take a swing at the Rangers' Dave Balon. The Bruins are tagged with a two-minute penalty and ten seconds later New York's Jean Ratelle scores the Ranger's fifth and final goal.

"The secret to beating them," Gilbert says later in the Rangers' dressing room, "is not to lose your cool. You can't let them get you mad or scared." Then Gilbert says a strange thing. "You know, I don't think the Bruins are any tougher than most of the other teams we play."

His coach, Emile "The Cat" Francis, agrees with him. "There's a big difference between a really tough player and a clutch-and-grabber. Stan Mikita is a guy I'd hate to get in a fight with. And although the Boston players are aggressive, they're more irritating than anything else. As long as you don't lose your head and you make them play your game, you're all right. Most of the time it's not the instigators who get caught, it's the guys who try to retaliate."

"You mean like in the Maki-Green incident."

"Oh, I didn't see that," he says. "But that could have been the case."

Francis admitted that he thought the Bruins missed Teddy Green even more than they cared to admit. "He wasn't just a tough guy. He was a talented defenseman who could bring that puck out from behind his net. People lost sight of his talent because he had this reputation as 'Tough Teddy.' That made him even more valuable. Teams underestimated his talent and he made better use of it."

Later, in the Bruins' dressing room, Gerry Cheevers agrees with Francis. "Sure we miss Teddy," he says. "The Rangers skate and skate and skate you to death. Teddy would have slowed them down. Just his reputation alone would have done it. That helps a lot, you know, a team's reputation. The other clubs worry about you then."

The following night in the safe, shadowy confines of Boston Garden, the Bruins meet the Rangers again. "I don't think tonight's game will be much different," says Francis wistfully. The Bruins' fans crush his hopes from the opening face off, however. "Chop his damned head off!" screams a woman in the upper balcony, as McKenzie takes a swipe at Gilber.

In five minutes there are three separate fights. They are not vicious affairs, and as Bobby Orr says, everyone is very quick to drop his stick before they begin their swinging. The third fight lasts almost five minutes, and the biggest damage is done to Orr's shirt, which is stretched out of shape.

Although the Rangers more than hold their own in these shirt-pulling affairs, they seem mentally drained by the Bruins' repeated harassments. Early in the second period, the Rangers seem content to ice the puck into Boston territory and then wait as the Bruins doggedly return the puck to their net. After repeatedly crashing the New York net the Bruins finally gain their 2-1 lead.

In the closing minutes of the game the Bruins are hit with two quick, unpremeditated penalties that give the Rangers a last life. On the second penalty call the arena erupts in mayhem. Fans begin throwing popcorn bags and beer cups down on the ice. The game is halted while the referees try to restore order and clean the ice. In the upper balcony two young boys are fighting. One of them is trying to push the other over the bannister. The fans are cheering wildly for the boys while the players watch from below with a curious detachment.

"What are they fighting for?" I ask a fan alongside of me. "Everybody in this place must be a Bruin fan."

"They fight to fight," he says. "They get all worked up over the game so they fight, that's all."

Order is restored eventually, the ice is cleared, and the Bruins stave off the last New York effort. During the final minute all the 14, 831 fans are standing, screaming, and stamping their feet until the building seems to be shaking loose from its foundation.

In the Bruins' dressing room after the game Sanderson is saying that the Rangers "backed off" tonight. "We'll take them yet," he says. "They've already had their winning streak. We're just about due for ours."

In another corner Awrey is saying how much the Bruins' fans mean to them. "There's a little bit of the homer in all of us," he smiles. "That's why we need a few fights like that. That fans get going and then we pick up momentum. The fans lift us right up with them."

And it almost makes them forget about Teddy Green.

Carlton Fisk

Conversations
with the Dinosaur

(from *Men's Journal*, 1993)

"THEY'RE SO DELICATE," he says. "They let you know if they're not happy. If I don't give them the attention they demand, I feel bad. So I come home from work at two a.m. and get to know them. I crossbreed them. Once they're pollinated—*poof!*—the flower dies. The pod begins to swell." He cups his big hands close together, then farther and farther apart. "They get stretch marks, then nine months later they flower." He smiles. A big, muscular man—six feet two, 235 pounds, dressed in a muscle shirt, sweat pants, and Nike sneakers—he is sitting hunched forward in a booth in a restaurant southwest of Chicago. "The beauty of orchids awes me," he says. He looks up with a scowl. A businessman is smiling down at him.

"I know this is unprofessional," the intruder says.

"Yes, it is. *Very!*"

The man hands him a Chicago White Sox T-shirt. "Could you sign this?"

"You just happened to have it with you, huh?" He scrawls his name across it, then thrusts it at the man. The man backs off, grinning, and is gone. "I *hate* that!" Carlton Fisk says. "Sometimes I just wanna scream, 'What the fuck do you want?'"

Fisk, the forty-five-year-old catcher for the White Sox ("I hate *that*, too! Being defined by my age, not my talent"), is angry at a lot of things. Autograph hounds. People who want to know too much about him ("Why the fuck should I tell them?"). Store clerks who can't make proper change ("And we wonder why the Japanese are killing us!"). The paperboy who tosses his morning paper on his snow-covered driveway instead of his front porch. ("The next morning, I was waiting for him. I told him, 'Do it right, or don't deliver it again.'") Drivers who litter, which is why his Ford Bronco looks as if he's been sleeping and eating in it for weeks ("I *never* throw anything out the window"). Friends whose girlfriends pose for cheesecake photographs ("Look at her!"). Country and western music that's so maudlin it propels people to commit suicide ("All that 'My dog died' shit. It just drags me down"). People who treat dogs as if they were people ("Dogs aren't supposed to eat omelets. They're supposed to eat dog food, mice, chipmunks. Like my wife's terrier. But he's like fifteen years old. He doesn't have the fire anymore, like a lot of us. But hey, we're still valuable").

Most of all, though, Fisk is angry at the way the game he's played most of his life has evolved. He's angry at fans who worship players as rich and famous personalities rather than as ballplayers. ("More fans know Bo Jackson from his Nike ads than as a baseball player!") He's angry at the sportswriters who created a rivalry between him and the late Yankee catcher Thurman Munson ("I was tall and handsome, and he was squat and ugly and in the dirt all the time. I was in the dirt, too, but I looked cleaner") and sportswriters who don't use tape recorders. ("They make you slow down, repeat yourself; you lose your train of thought.") He's angry because the game is no longer a game but a business ("There's no fun in it, no soul, just money. Older players used the game as a motivating factor; now it's the dollar sign"). He's angry at the game's use of computers, which can tell what pitch an opposing player hit off a pitcher three months ago but can't tell that a catcher "feels" that same pitcher will get the batter out that day. He's angry at players in general who are immature and coddled, while he's never been "stroked," never gotten "respect," always had to "motivate myself," and he's angry at players in particular who are lazy or "stupid," like Nolan Ryan ("His priority was not to win but to strike out as many as he could, to make batters look foolish"), or merely "selfish," like Deion Sanders of the Braves. ("Me! Me! Me! I! I! I! His selfishness *offends* me!")

Three years ago Fisk was catching when Sanders hit a pop fly to the infield. Sanders stood at the plate and watched. Fisk shouted at him, "Run the fucker out, you piece of shit!" Today, Fisk laughs. "He was offended. I don't know why." The next time Sanders came to bat, he said to Fisk, "The days of slavery are over." Fisk was so enraged that Sanders was trying to turn his righteous anger into a racial incident that he ripped off his mask and lashed into Sanders as both benches emptied. "There's a right way and a wrong way to play this game," Fisk says, then adds, "You know, later he stuck it up my ass. He ran down three balls I hit that shoulda been doubles." He smiles.

Fisk is even angry at himself for the way he mishandled Ferguson Jenkins when he pitched for the Red Sox. ("I did him a disservice. I never felt I called the game right for him. I . . . ah . . . I don't know. We coulda had a lot of fun.") But he is angriest at the managers and front-office executives of the two teams he's played for, the White Sox and the Red Sox. He once threw a batting helmet at a Red Sox manager who questioned his pitch calling, and he once kicked down the door of a Red Sox general manager who questioned his team loyalty. Fisk says his present manager, Gene Lamont, is "not in control of the team." Both organizations have always seen Fisk as an irascible character, who is sometimes more trouble than he's worth. The White Sox media staff warns writers that Fisk can be "difficult, moody," and this past February team owner Jerry Reinsdorf was quoted in a Chicago newspaper as saying Fisk was a "prima donna" who acts "like a baby" and "doesn't like anybody and is always unhappy." Fisk responded by saying that Reinsdorf must have made those comments when looking in a mirror, then admitted, "I do have a reputation as a grouch."

What made Fisk particularly grouchy in February was that the White Sox had offered him a minor-league contract with the promise of a spot on the major-league roster. It was an affront to his pride after a twenty-one-year major-league career of such sustained excellence (he leads all catchers with 351 career home runs—a team-record 213 of them with the White Sox—and is one of only three to amass more than 1,000 runs and RBI) that he has been an All Star eleven times and is a shoo-in for the Hall of Fame when he retires. That is, if he retires. At forty-five, with no intention of retiring, Fisk feels he has retained most of his catching skills (he is regularly one of the top fielding catchers in the league, and Sox pitchers generally have a lower ERA with Fisk catching than with anyone else) and his batting skills (at forty-three, he hit 18 home runs with 74 RBI).

He also still has the competitive fire he had as a rookie, in 1972, when he screamed at Red Sox teammates Carl Yastrzemski and Reggie Smith for not hustling. Referring to young catchers, he says: "These guys couldn't take the job away from me. No one challenges me. I see myself as a torch to show younger players you can transcend age through your work ethic.

I'm unique in my commitment. I set standards—one hundred forty games a year, power, defense, handling pitchers—that other catchers can't maintain."

In his mind's eye, Fisk is still a young catcher. He takes pride not in his age but in his accomplishments. In fact, he rails against his age the way Dylan Thomas railed against the night, because Fisk hates the fact that his age qualifies his achievements. He angrily plucks at the white hairs in his beard, which is why he is usually so clean-shaven. He refuses to get eyeglasses. "I used to autograph baseballs by propping them on my chest," he says. "Now I have to prop them on my lap to see them. It's a pain in the ass."

And finally, Fisk still has the hard, muscular body of a man half his age, which, ironically, he never had when he *was* half his age. Like many baseball players of his generation, Fisk had always relied on the game to keep him in shape, until he suffered a debilitating knee injury in 1974. After both knees were reconstructed, his doctor told him he would never play again and would probably walk with a limp. Fisk refused to accept the diagnosis. He joined a gym and began to rehabilitate his knees with a regimen of lightweight exercises. He did leg extensions and leg curls and lots of running until, as he puts it, "I overcame the injury."

Then, in 1984, he suffered another serious injury—pulled muscles deep in his stomach. That winter, he turned to the gym again, only this time with a personal trainer named Phil Clausson. According to Fisk, "Phil pounded the piss out of me," with a daily three-hour regimen of heavyweight lifting that was so exhausting that Fisk used to call his then manager, Tony LaRussa, to say he was too tired to make it home. "He's a tough man," says LaRussa, "both physically and mentally."

There was nothing unique about Claussen's program—it was the same kind of weight-lifting routine used by football players, track athletes and bodybuilders for years—other than that it had rarely been tried by baseball catchers, especially one of Fisk's advanced age, thirty-six. For years it was thought that weight lifting would make ballplayers muscle-bound, restricting their movements, so coaches stressed running to build endurance and flexibility and stretching exercises to enhance mobility. But since all those movements are similar to those a player perfoms during a game, essentially what the coaches were doing was further tearing down their players' muscles. "Just playing a sport does a lot to break down the body," says Pete Shmock, the Seattle

Mariners' strength and conditioning coach. What players needed were exercises that *complemented* their playing movements (i.e., exercises that build muscles, not stretch them). Furthermore, players of Fisk's generation had never exercised much during the winter. They were too busy scrambling for another job in an era when the best players were paid $100,000 a season, as opposed to the $5 million a season many get today. The advent of huge salaries in the eighties has afforded players the luxury of spending the off-season hunting, playing golf, or exercising. The result is that most of today's players, at least the conscientious ones, are arriving at spring training *in* shape rather than having to work themselves into shape.

The cornerstone of Claussen's routine for Fisk rested on heavyweight squatting exercises. A catcher's legs suffer a terrible beating from the constant squatting and standing behind the plate hundreds of times per game, day after day, which tears down the muscles, tendons, and joints of the legs. Fisk, like most catchers, thought that squatting in a gym with heavy weights would only further tear down his legs. But the reverse was true. Squatting with heavy weights strengthened his legs, tightening the muscles and tendons around his joints.

Twice a week, Fisk lifted weights for his shoulders and back, his arms, and especially his legs. He also performed hundreds of sit-ups every day to strengthen his stomach muscles. Claussen even changed Fisk's ballplayers' diet (heavy on fats and red meat), putting him on a diet high in complex carbohydrates (beans, pasta, rice), fruits and vegetables, and, for protein, chicken and fish instead of red meat. Since Fisk didn't drink much hard liquor, he had only to switch from regular beer to light beer. But while he's not a smoker, he has never been able to give up his remaining vice: chewing tobacco.

"It was grim," Fisk says of the regimen, but he did it. It was so grim, in fact, that after former teammate Jerry Remy worked out with Fisk for only one day, he quit. "Why does anyone want to go through such humiliation?" Remy said. (And even though Yastrzemski had one of the best baseball years of his life after working out all winter with a personal trainer, he sat out the next winter. When Fisk asked why, Yaz just said, "Too hard.")

By the end of the winter of '84, Fisk had recovered from his stomach injury, and his thirty-seven-year-old physique had responded dramatically to his regimen. He more than doubled his strength (he began squatting with 135 pounds and finished with 315 pounds) and added 30 pounds of muscle to his frame. Even his features seemed changed. Today he has the unlined face of a thirty-year-old ("Dorian Gray," he says, laughing). But most important, his weight lifting jumpstarted his career a second time. He hit 37 home runs and batted in 107 runs in 1985, one of the many years, he says, when the White Sox had assumed he was washed up. "My legs were never tired all season," he says.

What made Fisk's phenomenal year even more astonishing and revolutionary was that he achieved it while he continued to lift weights during the season, something few baseball players had ever done. He would finish a game by eleven, rest in the clubhouse for twenty minutes, then, when everyone had gone, trudge into the team's weight room (by then, most clubs had weight rooms) and begin his lonely, exhausting routine of squats. What he had just torn down during the game, his legs, he methodially rebuilt after the game. Then, barely able to walk, he went home at 2:00 a.m., to his orchids.

Fisk's routine hasn't changed much over the past nine years. He tends to lift lighter weights (275 pounds) when squatting now, an accomodation to his age and to needing more rest between bouts of lifting so that his muscles can rebuild themselves. Still, his is a routine that would devastate most younger players. It has allowed him to play his game far beyond an age when most catchers have long since retired. It has even brought him some belated TV fame, with a Nike commercial. "It's only thirty seconds," he says. "I'm doing sit-ups in a run-down warehouse. As I walk away, I say: 'I didn't have to do this to stay competitive before. But hey, I'm not forty anymore.'" It's also brought him the respect of his peers. "He's so deserving," says Jeff Torborg, the former White Sox manager and present Mets manager. "He works so hard."

What it hasn't brought him, however, is the respect he feels he deserves from the White Sox. Although he will probably go down in baseball history as the premier catcher in the game after he breaks Bob Boone's games-caught record of 2,225 this season (he needs 25), the White Sox, according to Fisk, have indicated that this will be his last, after a '92 season dominated again by a serious injury. ("The one knock on Carlton," says another former White Sox manager, Jim Fregosi, "was always that he was brittle, because of all his injuries.")

"I hurt a tendon in my foot in 'ninety-two," says Fisk, "and I didn't play much [.229 average, three home runs in 62 games]. The doctor said it could have happened to anyone in his twenties. When you're hurt at twenty, they say it's because you play with 'reckless abandon.' When you're hurt at forty-four, they say it's age. Like at the end of 'ninety-one: I had three foul tips off my shoulder. I got hit in the eye and tore off a fingernail. I wasn't productive the last few weeks. After the season, our GM says, 'The scouts said you look tired.' I told him about the injuries, but he just said *tired*. Then they announce on the radio a few weeks ago that this is my last season, that I'd agreed to my own contractual eulogy. They just assumed if I break the games-caught record, I'll quit. But that's not my determining factor. I never said this was my last year. If I did, my energies would dissolve as I got to the end. I'd like to quit when I'm no value to the team. When *I* decide I'm no value. Just because I no longer play like a Hall of Famer doesn't mean I have no value. I can still contribute. It pisses me off everyone else is determining when I'm done. The more they do, the more I'll play. If they said they needed me another year, I might have retired five years ago." He laughs.

Despite recent changes in the game, baseball is still a conservatively run sport-business. In baseball, things are done a certain way because they have always been done that way. Philosophies are espoused not because they are thought out but because they have been inherited from the game's past. This has been the cause of much of Fisk's frustration with the game today. Although on the one hand he's a throwback to a certain kind of old-fashioned, hard-nosed ballplayer (he says there are only a few such dinosaurs left—George Brett, Paul Molitor, Dave Winfield, Robin Yount. "What happens when we're gone?"), on the other hand he's a very modern man who'se not afraid to confront boundaries with innovative ideas that he claims the game refuses to consider. It makes him angry.

"For years, the organization has presented obstacles to me," he says. "It motivated me to overcome them. The last few years, that's been deflating. Why do I have to prove this again?"

What he has to prove again is that baseball's perception of aging needs to be brought in line with many sports physiologists' new definition of aging. Dr. Lawrence Lamb, a sports physician, has reported that an athlete can continue to grow and build muscle into his fifties and that often the only thing that deteriorates in older athletes is their will and desire to work out as hard as they did in their youth. Dr. Bill Evans of Tufts University, who works with NHL and NFL players, says: "[Muscles] don't really decline during an athlete's career. They decline only because an athlete doesn't work at it." Kay Porter, a Eugene, Oregon, sports psychologist who has studied aging, says: "Societally, there is a difference in what we perceive as being older. [Older athletes] are helping to form that new image of aging. They just keep playing, and nobody's telling them they have to stop."

"Everything that happens to me is attributed to age," says Fisk. "They perceive players by their age without really evaluating them they way they would a younger player. But I think I'm realistic in what I can do at forty-five."

One of baseball's problems with Fisk is that the game rarely had to confront a catcher still playing at his advanced age. There are no prototypes to compare Fisk to, so the game falls back on clichés of its past. Furthermore, baseball is not used to a mature, intelligent man like Fisk verbalizing his thoughts in a way that challenges its clichés and in a way most young players can't. In fact, Fisk is such a thorn in the side of the White Sox organization that the team's coaches have forbidden him to work with the younger catchers or to contribute much to pregame team meetings.

"Hey, I caught a long time," he says, "and I'm pretty friggin' good at what I do. I've been there before, so I *know*. Yet they told me to stay away from the younger catchers because I do things differently. Before a game, the pitchers and catchers go over the opposition with our coaches. They told me not to get involved because my answers are too long. I said, 'It's your loss.' They don't want to deal with a guy like me verbalizing. They view me as a threat to their job. So they try to suppress you. They're afraid I might expose something."

A few weeks before the opening of spring training this past February, Fisk still hadn't signed his White Sox contract ("I will," he said, "but it won't be pleasant." He eventually did sign, on February 24, for a guaranteed $650,000, which could reach $1.1 million if he plays at least ninety games), and yet on a freezing, snowy day he was still driving to his gym to work out with weights. He drove past snow-covered fields in the farmland southwest of Chicago, where he lives with his wife, Linda, and their three children, daughters Courtney, seventeen, and Carlyn, twenty-two, and son, Casey, twenty-one. "We're country people," he says. He was raised on a farm in rural New Hampshire, surrounded by land not much different than this.

"The difference is in the people," he says. "These people are soft. Not like New Englanders. New Englanders won't prevent you from doing something—they just make sure you don't enjoy it."

Fisk's childhood was anything but soft. He was one of six children of Cecil and Leona Fisk of Charlestown, New Hampshire, population 4,300, a town, he says, without a movie theater, a stoplight, or blacks but with three churches.

His father made only $6,000 a year working in a machine company and supplemented that by raising cows for milk and chickens for food. All the Fisk children had chores. They spread manure, cleaned the yard, and if they didn't finish their chores, there was no TV that night. If Carlton (called Pudge because of his childhood plumpness, a name that still sticks to him) wanted spending money, he had to deliver newspapers, mow lawns, shovel snow, and later, as a teen, lay pipes for the sewer department and pour concrete for a contractor. It was the kind of rural life a lot of kids lived and didn't think that what they were living was particularly deprived. "I never had a drink," says Fisk, "and I didn't know anything about sex."

In high school, Fisk shone not only in baseball but also in basketball, once scoring forty points and grabbing thirty-six rebounds in a state tournament game. After the game, the only thing that his father said to him was: "You missed four foul shots."

"Compliments from my father were few and far between," says Fisk. "It was a motivating factor, but I didn't know it then. I always thought I coulda done better. I never got a pat on the back. My father didn't tolerate people who didn't bust their butts. . . . I have never been close to him, really."

Fisk got a basketball scholarship to the University of New Hampshire, where one day in the cafeteria line he met his future wife, Linda Foust ("She was sucking a lemon," he says); they have been married twenty-three years. After a one-year stint with the army reserves, Fisk left college early to sign a contract with the Red Sox, where he thought he would play the rest of his baseball life. He became a New England hero after his dramatic twelfth-inning game-winning home run in game six of the 1975 World Series against the Cincinnati Reds. "That was so early in my career," he says, "it was like another lifetime ago. Looking back, it's like it didn't happen to me."

He was twenty-seven, and five years later he'd become such an annoyance to the Red Sox, demanding they renegotiate his contract, that they let him go as a free agent. Already, they assumed that at thirty-two he was on the decline as a catcher. But he didn't decline, he just kept playing year after year at a high level of excellence, in good part because he had set standards for himself few ballplayers ever have, standards he learned from his hardscrabble background far removed from the modern world, which no longer seems to value them.

When Fisk speaks, he speaks mostly in aphorisms, like a modern-day Francis Bacon. He says things like "Success has no shortcuts, only a high price of pain and humiliation"; "Going back to the past isn't the future"; "Do it right, or don't do it at all"; "A lot of things you sacrifice, you never get back"; "Loyalty is a two-way street"; and "I have a lot of pride. I can't tolerate mediocrity."

Fisk's three children have inherited a lot of their father's personality and standards, as he inherited those of his father. Carlyn, a star volleyball player at the University of Illinois-Chicago, says, "I don't smile a lot, like my father doesn't." Her coach calls her quiet, difficult to get to know, competitive. "Oh, my goodness, yes," says Casey, a baseball player at Illinois State. "We're all competive." Carlyn says, "I always wanted to be the one about whom they say, 'You know, she really hustled.'"

Casey captured the Fisk work ethic once in a poem that ended: "When you bust your butt and dreams come true/Is when you'll have your fun."

Carlton Fisk is busting his butt and having fun at a gym near his home in Lockport, Illinois.

"Come on, you fuck!" says a bodybuilder wearing a HOMICIDE SQUAD T-shirt (WHEN YOUR DAY ENDS, OUR DAY BEGINS). "*Drive that weight!*"

Fisk, looking like a water buffalo with a metal bar and 275 pounds of weight across the back of his shoulders, squats down, then drives up again, over and over, under the watchful eyes of his trainer, Claussen.

"He's an exceptional athlete," says Claussen, 36, bald, with a droopy bloodhound's face. "He has more dedication and discipline than anyone I know. Others can benefit from him." Fisk squats. "Eight," says Claussen. "Four more." Then Claussen gestures with his arm to encompass the gym. "It's a good place to work."

The gym is, indeed, almost empty at 3:00 p.m. Two heavy women in sweatsuits are doing triceps push-downs. A few compact bodybuilders are doing bench presses on the chipped and peeling benches. There are the inevitable posters of professional bodybuilders on the wall, but, strangely, they are from another era. Sergio Oliva, "the Myth," from the sixties. Boyer Coe, Franco Columbo, Lou Ferrigno and Mike Mentzer, from the seventies. "The Carlton Fisk room," says a bodybuilder, pointing to the posters of the old-timers. "There's no Spandex here."

Fisk lays the weight bar on the rack and backs off, sweating and breathing heavily. Under the harsh fluorescent lights, his face looks older, the pale skin sagging under the eyes and jowls. It is the high-cheekboned, flat-featured face of a Native American, except it is so white. Fisk steps away from the squat rack and folds his arms across his chest like a warrior.

"People mistake me for Tom Seaver," he says. "When they used to mistake Seaver for me and ask him for *my* autograph, Tom would scream, 'No fuckin' way!'" He laughs. "That was great for my image. You know, I caught his three-hundreth victory." He shakes his head in admiration. "He taught me a lot. An awareness that there are things other than physical talent important in this game. He knew his limitations. When to quit. I only know my limitations when I run right into them."

Fisk walks back to the squat rack with that erect, slow, arrogant walk that has become his trademark. He bends under the bar, hoists the weight on his shoulders, steps back and begins squatting again. A blond woman who looks to be in her thirties stops to watch. She is plain-looking, dressed in a floppy sweatshirt.

"I can't pinch Pudge's ass 'cause you're here," she says to me, watching Fisk squat. "I got a picture of Pudge in my attic."

"Does it look like Dorian Gray?"

"Naw."

Fisk backs off from the squat rack again. "Hi, Charlotte," he says to the blonde. "You're still my favorite. You're the best." She blushes and flings her hand at his compliment. "Hey, Charlotte, wouldn't you want to know at thirty what you know now?"

"No. At eighteen." Fisk laughs. Charlotte walks off in a heavy-footed, plowman's way and goes over to another weight bench. Fisk follows her with his eyes.

"You know, she's in her forties. I like older women who have a commitment to their bodies."

"Come on, Pudge," says Claussen. "Another set." Fisk walks to the rack.

Fisk likes women in that old-fashioned, fifties sort of way, when women were a mystery so men tended to treat them all, pretty or plain, with a certain romantic, sexual gallantry. "In my day you either liked a woman as a girlfriend," he says, "or you didn't know them. We were never *friends* with a woman. That's why I never see a woman without *something*. There are qualities in every woman."

Fisk is still squatting. "Pause now," Claussen says when Fisk has squatted, his behind parallel to the floor. Claussen counts, one, two, three, four, then says, "Drive it up!" Fisk explodes upward until he is standing on shaky legs. "That's specifically for catchers," says Claussen.

Again, Fisk backs away from the squat rack. Again, he is breathing heavily, his face drenched with sweat, but he is smiling. There is nothing of the grouch about him now.

He actually seems happy, as he often is when doing physical labor. "I could never smoke," he says. "It's hard enough for me now. When I first came up, half the team smoked; now very few do. A lot of the guys drank then, too. It was a badge of courage to go drinking, then come in the next day and play the game in the bag. I couldn't do it. Then players began to smoke dope, do coke, and now they're back to booze. But it's still not the same. We used to have fun in the clubhouse. We had clothing wars. I remember once when Yaz, Gary Peters, and Luis Aparicio had a *war*. Aparicio always wore suits. Yaz dressed like Columbo, in an old trench coat. And Peters dressed somewhere in between. They began by cutting up each other's ties. Then cutting the toes off each other's socks. Nailing each other's shoes to the floor. Finally, one day, they threw lighter fluid in Yaz's locker, and then—*poof!*—the locker was on fire. It was unbelievable."

It is 6:00 p.m. The gym is packed with weight lifters now. After three hours, Fisk is still working out. He gets up off the leg-curl machine and looks around at the crowded gym. He sees a black bodybuilder working out. "You know, I never saw a black in New Hampshire. The first time was in the army reserves." He makes a surprised face, points, and shouts out, "There's one now! A black person!" The bodybuilder comes over to him.

"Mr. Fisk, I once met you when I was a kid. My father was a minister," he says and shakes Fisk's hand, then looks him up and down in that professionally appraising way that bodybuilders have. "You're looking good, man. Real good."

Thirty minutes later, Fisk is winding down by running on a treadmill in a room filled with treadmills and other runners, all watching the television set high on the wall. Sweat is pouring off Fisk's body as he runs, going nowhere. He talks between gasps of breath.

"I was never a fan," he says. "I have no friends in the game. No one knows me. I didn't want to reveal myself and give them an edge. I still like to keep it that way. But people had misconceptions about me. Once, Chili Davis and I went on a Nike tour. Afterward, he said, 'I'm glad I got to know you.' I had misconceptions about him, too. I thought he was surly, but he's soft as a grape. I'm more mature now. I appreciate my opponents for the way they play the game; before, I just thought about getting them out."

It is dark in the parking lot as Fisk, still wearing his sweat-soaked clothes, walks toward his Bronco on this cold winter night. "I useta write it all down," he says. "Pages and pages of all those pounds I lifted. Very impressive." Then he remembers something an old-time southern Red Sox scout once told him. "I was in the minors, catching on a hot summer day in South Carolina, complaining about the heat," he says. "His name was Mace Brown. He comes up to me in the dugout and says," Fisk mimics Brown's southern drawl, "'Carlton, I wanna tell ya somethin' my daddy tole me. I know it's a hot day, son, but if ya hadn'ta wanted ta work, ya oughtn'ta hired out.'" Fisk laughs. "Every time I sweat and work, I remember that. 'If ya hadn'ta wanted ta work, ya oughtn'ta hired out.'" Then, apropos of nothing, he adds: "Hey, wanna go to Hooters for a beer? The scenery's not that good—hell, my twenty-two-year-old daughter's got a better body than those waitresses. Aw, maybe I'm just getting old."

Driving to Hooters, a restaurant famous for its chicken wings and pretty, scantily clad waitresses, Fisk calls his wife on his mobile phone. Before she answers, he says: "Linda's flexible. Actually, she isn't. If I don't call to tell her I'm going out for a beer, she'll yell at me. If I do call, she'll yell. So why call, huh?" Linda answers the phone. He tells her he's going to a restaurant with a friend. After a pause, he says, "No, I did not show off my body. In fact, he was yawning at the gym. You know, just two old guys." He listens a moment, then says, "No, I said *yawning*, not *gagging*."

"Do you like old men?" says Fisk. We are seated at a table in Hooters, looking up at a twenty-two-year-old waitress in a T-shirt and tight orange satin shorts.

She smiles down at us and nods.

"How old do ya like 'em?" I ask. "We got the full spectrum here—forties or fifties."

The waitress says, very seriously, "I once dated a guy who was thirty." Fisk and I laugh. "Thirty! Jeez, did he walk with a cane?"

After we place our order—a pitcher of beer and, for Fisk, a chicken-breast sandwich—Fisk leans over the table and says: "The most remarkable thing about my career *is* my career. I beat the odds. I came from a small town. I only played ten games a year in high school. And I became successful at the highest level. But I had to give up things. My kids are grown and gone. I was consumed by the game to a fault. I didn't want to take my wife out to eat, or mow the lawn, because it would distract me from the mental approach to the game."

The waitress returns with the food. She is blushing. "Someone told me to ask if your name is Carlton," she says.

"Naw," Fisk says. "Tell 'em they're mistaken." When she is gone, Fisk says: "I have no friends. The game hasn't offered me the chances. Aw, maybe it has, and I just didn't see them. I guess I missed opportunities because I was suspicious of people's motives. My New England heritage. I wanted to keep my family real. Never dwell on being a big leaguer. There were parts of my life people didn't need to know."

"Excuse me, Mr. Fisk?" A man in his thirties is standing at the table. "Can I bother you for an autograph?"

Fisk glares up at him. "*What?*" he screams.

The man blinks, once, twice, but holds his ground. "I asked for an autograph," he says.

"Why?"

"Because I admire you," the man says.

Fisk takes the paper from the man and signs it. The man thanks him but still stands there. "I just wanted to tell you how much enjoyment you've given me watching you play."

"Well, I appreciate that," Fisk says. He's no longer the grouch now. He likes the way the man has held his ground in the face of Fisk's bellowing. It took a certain kind of courage, and courage is something he respects. Sometimes it seems as if Fisk's grouchiness is merely his way of testing people's mettle. When they back off, he dismisses them. When they fight back, he admires them. That's why he likes his gym so much. No one there cuts him any slack. He's just another jock working out, and everyone treats him that way: "Come on, you fuck, don't quit now!" He likes being treated that way a lot more than he likes being treated as a baseball star, because after all these years, Fisk still sees himself merely as a working man. He values physical labor, which is what catching is all about. Playing every day with broken fingers and bruised shins and never complaining.

"I played a lot of games injured and in a recuperative state," he says. "And I never asked for a day off. It's the nature of the job. You've got to be talented to produce at seventy percent. But still, it frustrates me I didn't play more games. With my physical injuries and organizational obstacles, I missed almost five years."

That's why Fisk has such contempt for baseball's front-office executives. They are the men who sit behind desks and push paper and tell him they know how he feels ("How the hell do they know? They've never been in the war before"). Which is why he has no plans, once he retires, to become a manager, many of whom he calls puppets. He'd have to defer to those front-office people, he says, adding: "I'm not much of an ass kisser. Still, I know a lot about this game, a lot I don't think they know." He goes quiet, takes a bite of his sandwich, then looks up and says softly: "I'm afraid to leave the game because I'm afraid there's nothing out there for me. I have no burning desire to do anything else. Baseball has been so much of my life. Will anything else be that rewarding? Aw, maybe I missed opportunities over the years. I never thought about it. Hey, I'm not the brightest guy in the world, I know that. Maybe when I'm done, something will present itself. Ya know, I always thought I'd like to repair cars for a living."

He takes a drink of beer and is quiet for a long while. This talk about leaving baseball has disturbed him. So he does the only thing he knows how to do to change his mood. He begins talking about his game. His World Series home run. Leron Lee's slide into home plate in 1974 that destroyed his knees. Bucky Dent's home run that beat the Red Sox in the 1978 A.L. East divisional playoff. "I wanted to reach out and grab that pitch before it reached the plate," he says.

It is late now. A couple of pitchers of beer have been consumed. Fisk is talking animatedly about his nemesis, Nolan Ryan, whom he calls the most intimidating pitcher he has ever seen.

"I mean, guys say big leaguers hit fastballs, but not ninety-eight-m.p.h. fastballs!" he says. "He was devastating. I mean, his curveball was ninety-five m.p.h. I useta stand up there thinking, 'Hey, he's an old dude, I'm an old dude, let's get it on.' But then he'd throw that curveball at my head, and I'd say, 'I know it's a curveball, I know it's a curveball, but what if it isn't?'" Fisk jumps up and assumes a batting stance right there in the restaurant. Behind him, people are staring, but he doesn't notice them. He waves an imaginary bat and says, "I only got five hits off him in my life, and after one, a single, he kept throwing to first base—not to pick me *off* but to *hurt* me, he was so pissed off. Another time, he fired a fastball at my bat and then helmet, and it went flying all the way to the backstop. I called timeout. I mean, I couldn't stand there, my legs were shaking, I was *hyperventilating*! I walked over to our third-base coach, Don Zimmer. He said, 'Pudge, I got no sign on.' I said, 'I know. I just ain't ready to hit.' He said, 'I don't blame ya.' Just what I needed. So I go back to the batter's box"—Fisk assumes his stance again, waving his imaginary bat—"and I'm in an uncontrollable state of anxiety. Then Nolan fires a curveball at my head, and I know it's a curveball, but I can't help myself." He begins to wiggle his ass, then pulls his leg away from an imaginary plate and takes a feeble swing. Strike three. Behind him there is applause from the other diners. Fisk is aware of them for the first time. He sits down, embarrassed. A man comes up to him with a smile.

"I didn't want to bother you," the man says, "but I just had to thank you for that performance. I'll never forget it."

Deion Sanders
The Two Faces of Prime Time
(from *Special Reports*, 1989)

W HEN HE WAS FIVE YEARS OLD, he lived with his mother in a low-income housing project in Fort Myers, Florida. It was a neighborhood of drug dealers and pimps, addicts and prostitutes—and young women, like his mother, who were trying to raise their sons as best they could without a man around.

He was small and skinny for his age. His size made him shy, silent, and fearful. He worried about fights with bigger boys, and most of all, he worried about going to jail—like some of the older boys in his neighborhood. He suffered from migraine headaches, brought on occasionally by hunger but mostly by stress. When he began to play sports, he placed such importance on them—on sports as a way *out*—that sometimes he had to miss his team's crucial games because the pain was so bad that he couldn't get out of bed.

The headaches were a condition inherited from his grandmother, his mother, and his father, who had left home when he was a year old. He would come home from school with a migraine and sit on the doorstep and cry. Most days, however, he just came home from school, went to his room, and watched television for hours.

"He was a very sensitive boy," says his mother, rocking slowly in her chair on a hot day in Fort Myers. The living room of her six-room frame house is overrun with mementos of her son's career: trophies everywhere, plaques, awards, magazine covers, photographs. There are pictures of her son in a New York Yankees uniform, in a Florida State football uniform, in a tuxedo, in a shiny black sweatsuit with dark sunglasses and gold chains dangling from his neck. In the baseball photographs he has assumed a bored look, in the football photographs a threatening look, and in the others a grin that rings false. Except for one.

"That's his real smile," says his stepfather, a big, dark, tough-looking man with a sweet smile. He sits in a straight-backed chair and listens to his wife of fourteen years.

"He always had a ball in his hand," says his mother. "When he was in Little League, he felt bad because I had to go to all his games alone. He was embarrassed that his father was never there. I always sacrificed for my son. He loved nice clothes even then. I always bought him the best. I worked two jobs to buy him seventy-dollar shoes. Lord, he was lazy. He never worked but one time, at Hardee's. Lasted two weeks. He said, 'Mama, work is a bummer.'"

She seems lost in her big chair, a tiny woman who looks more like a teenager than a forty-two-year-old mother of three. She talks in an off-hand way, as if not really thinking much about what she is saying—which could not be further from the truth. She is a woman whose slightness, whose beauty, whose easy demeanor belie her strength.

Her gruff-looking husband always defers to her when she is speaking. He sits there, nodding, smiling, until she stops and he can add a word or two.

"Deion used to cry when he lost a game," he says. Then he falls silent as she goes on.

"Girls had to call him. He never volunteered nothing. You had to drag it out of him. That's the real Deion. Even at college, he was quiet. He called me every day. He'd say, 'Mama, should I do this?' Then he started to get loud. On the football field, all you could hear was Deion. He got into his gold jewelry, too, and sunglasses and sweatsuits, like drug dealers do. I told him, 'Deion, I can't stand all that gold. And you talk too much. All that Prime Time stuff. You can cool it now. You already sold yourself.'"

Deion is Deion Sanders, twenty-two, one of the most gifted athletes of his day: "Neon" Deion to the press; "Prime Time" to himself. Like many self-anointed media personalities, he refers to himself in the third-person singular, as in "Now, Prime Time wakes up every mornin' and says to the mirror, 'Mirror, mirror on the wall, who's the flashiest, best-dressed of them all?' And every mornin' the mirror says, 'You, Prime Time.'"

Sanders, this year's first-round draft pick of the Atlanta Falcons, is justifiably proud. His stardom spans four sports and almost ten years. As a high school senior, he averaged more than twenty-four points per game for his basketball team, was offered a $75,000 baseball bonus by the Kansas City Royals, turned it down because he demanded $90,000, and instead accepted a football scholarship to Florida State University, where he began to fashion his own legend with both his talent and his mouth.

"He could be one of the greatest cornerbacks ever to come into this game," said former Washington Redskins general manager Bobby Beathard during Sanders's senior year in college.

At FSU, Sanders was a two-time All-America defensive back; a winner of the Jim Thorpe Award, given to the best defensive back in college football each year; an Olympic-caliber track star; and, in his senior year, an outfielder in the farm system of the New York Yankees who had signed a $60,000 bonus contract. Once, while playing a baseball game, he left the diamond, ran to the nearby track field to finish one leg of his school's relay race, and then ran back to the baseball field to deliver his team's winning hit.

In football, Sanders returned a punt 100 yards for a touchdown in his freshman year, set a school record for tackles, and regaled sportswriters and broadcasters with outrageous comments:

"I made everybody's All-America, including Betty Crocker's."

"I'm a punt returner, the best cornerback you'll ever get, and an entertainer."

Asked once if he had ever visited the NFL Hall of Fame, he replied, "No, but I heard they already dusted off a place for me in there."

And when he signed the baseball contract while still at FSU, he excused his poor grades by saying, "I don't want to ever see another math book. I learned a lot about math. I used to know how to add and subtract. Now I know how to square my money."

On the field, he harangued opponents with incessant chatter, in one game telling wide receiver Dale Dawkins of the University of Miami, "Dale, we're out in front of sixty thousand people in the Orange Bowl, and you run this ugly pattern I got to follow. Man, that's embarrassing to the both of us."

After the NFL draft, Sanders said that he would be happy to play for the Atlanta team, which had suffered six consecutive losing seasons. "If we win after I come, I get all the credit."

In choosing Sanders, the Falcons satisfied his demand that he play in a warm climate. "If Detroit [Lions] had picked me, I would have asked for so much money, they'd have had to put me on layaway."

By then he was already bargaining for his own television show in Atlanta; he had designed a logo, a lightning bolt, to use on his own line of men's sportswear; he owned two cars, a black Chrysler convertible and a black BMW M3, both with PRIME TIME vanity plates and a sign in the rear window that read MILLIONAIRE. He shelled out $108 for haircuts, and he adorned himself in a Mr. T starter kit of gold jewelry on his fingers and wrists and around his neck. One piece, a pendant, is a dollar sign the size of a golf ball.

He accomplished much of this though the manufacturing of his own image as Neon Deion/Prime Time—in spite of the fact that he had not yet signed an NFL contract and early in his second year of professional baseball was struggling with a .250 batting average for the Albany-Colonie Yankees of the Class AA Eastern League.

He had also left FSU without a degree. He admits he's no Einstein, and besides, as he noted just after his first-round draft selection, "I've got a lottery ticket. I've just got to cash it in."

Sanders, of course, is hardly the first athlete with an outrageous image. Self-aggrandizement has played a key role in the career of other athletes such as Joe Namath and Muhammad Ali, Sanders's idol. "He was the greatest, the way he promoted himself," he says of the Champ.

What makes Sanders different from his idol, however, is that the Prime Time of outrageous one-liners and dress bears only the slightest resemblance to the real Deion Sanders.

Sanders is grumpy, sullen, in a foul mood. It's two months before he is to report to the Falcons' training camp, and he has been trapped for two days in a Ramada Inn in Hagerstown, Maryland, because his baseball team has been rained out on successive nights.

Sanders, who is still weeks away from being called up to the majors, doesn't like minor-league life. He doesn't like the long hours spent riding buses (in college, he used to take a stretch limousine to games); the middle-class hotels (when he can, he pays his own money to check into a Hilton while his teammates stay at a Holiday Inn); or the food (whenever possible, he and teammate Kevin Mmahat take a cab to a restaurant while the others eat Domino's pizza in their rooms).

In fact, Sanders is so conscious of his image that he tries to hide from his teammates any signs that he is content with the life they lead. Once, running to catch a team bus, he was clutching a paper bag to his chest.

He tripped, spilling the contents of the bag on the ground: a Happy Meal from McDonald's. Prime Time was humiliated when one of the other players yelled out the bus window, "A Happy Meal! Man, that's no way for a millionaire to eat!"

But Sanders is not yet a millionaire. Still, he is a lot better off than his minor-league teammates. They average about $2,000 a month in salary; Sanders is making $60,000 for five weeks of baseball and will earn another $300,000 over the next two years if he stays with the Yankees. He will become a millionaire when he signs the football contract, any day now. The fact that the contract is still pending, though, is another reason that he is in a foul mood.

Still another reason is that a print journalist has dragged him from his bed, which he is sharing with his girlfriend, a graduate of Florida A&M with a psychology degree, whom he refers to only as "Baby." Sanders doesn't much like print journalists. They pry too much into his life. He would prefer to be interviewed by television journalists. A quick thirty-second sound bite, of which he is the master. Prime Time, in his shades and chains, grins at the camera and says something outrageous, and it's over.

Dressed in a red, white, and blue satin sweatsuit, Sanders slumps in a chair at the motel's indoor pool, which reeks of chlorine. He mumbles an incoherent greeting. A Sanders ploy. When unsure of himself, or annoyed, he affects a slurry *sotto voce* designed to mask his words and discourage questions.

"I almost never let people get close to me," he says. "I don't trust too many people."

He is without his trademark shades and gold chains. "I'm saving them for Atlanta," he says. After grumbling about being dragged from his bed at noon, Sanders admits that he also doesn't like baseball. "I'm just using it as leverage for football," he says. "You got to calm yourself down for baseball. I don't like to hit. I just like to get on base and run. In football I don't have any weaknesses. I can make an instant impact. Take control. Baseball is boring to me because I'm not dominating in it."

Buck Showalter, the Albany manager, says that Sanders has all the tools to become an "impact player" in the big leagues. He can run, throw, and field, and he will learn to hit after he gets enough minor-league batting experience. "But I don't know if he has the temperament for baseball," Showalter says. "It's an everyday grind. Who can say whether Deion can stand up to it with football in his background?"

Another reason Sanders doesn't like baseball is that it is a reflective sport, not an emotional one. Baseball usually doesn't take kindly to players with the loud image of Prime Time. And Sanders's image means a lot to him.

"Prime Time never been one to be like nobody else," he says. "Prime Time isn't acting out there; he's doing what he feels. I just gotta be me. Having fun. Being Prime Time releases my frustrations.

"When I'm talking to another team's player on the field, I'm not being mean or cursing. I don't curse. I'm just saying things in humor, to make the other guy think. I say things like 'Boy, you gonna go to Arena football, playing like that. Maybe I can give you a job driving my car someday.'

"That kind of thing makes players think, you know. It gives me an advantage. And the things I say to the press after the game are just things I feel. I like what I said about Detroit putting me on layaway. I thought about that one ahead of time. It was the truth, though. That's the point. I think I say things that are obvious but in a clever way.

"Some people come down on me because they see this black kid talking, dressed in black leather with a lot of gold jewelry and a cellular phone to his ear, and they think it ain't right. They think I'm a drug dealer or something. But that's why I am Prime Time, to show young kids you don't have to be a drug dealer to have jewelry and nice things. It gives them something to shoot for."

Prime Time's flamboyant dress occasionally attracts trouble. In his senior year at FSU, he was arrested in a Fort Myers mall for causing a disturbance in a jewelry shop. Sanders claims that the woman who waited on him assumed he was a drug dealer because of his clothing, and an altercation followed. She accused him of hitting her, and he had to be restrained by three cops and spend a night in jail.

"I was trying to be very polite to her," he says. "But she wouldn't listen. She started cussing me. Man, those are the kinds of things that sour you. That was the first time I was ever in trouble. Man, she said I tried to steal a pair of twenty-dollar earrings! Me! Prime Time! Why, I always have a thousand dollars in my pocket."

When Sanders and his girlfriend, who resembles Florence Griffith Joyner, enter the Ramada Inn restaurant at nine p.m., everyone stares. Sanders is dressed in a stonewashed jacket and jeans, dark shades, and gold chains. He sucks on a toothpick and sips from a can of orange soda. As the hostess leads his party to the table, he hands the empty soda can to Baby.

Sanders doesn't speak when the waitress takes his order. He glances at his girlfriend, and she mumbles an order for him: "He'll have a shrimp cocktail, two fried-shrimp dinners, and a Coke."

Baby talks so quietly that the waitress asks her three times to repeat the order. The waitress leaves, and Sanders finally speaks. "I'm in the process of buying a Mercedes-Benz," he says. "560SEC. Black with palomino leather. Black is my color, you know. I like nice things. When I was a boy, I told my mama I was determined to have nice things in life. She said, 'Boy, you think money grows on trees.' I say, 'It do on television, Mama.'" He laughs for the first time that day.

When the food arrives, he picks at it desultorily until Baby takes over for him. She peels the shrimp and hands it to him, telling the waitress, "He'll have another Coke."

Halfway through the meal, Kevin Mmahat joins them. Mmahat is a big, handsome white pitcher from New Orleans. The moment he sits down, Sanders opens up and becomes more articulate and energetic. Mmahat kids him about a blind date Sanders had in college.

"Man, she had a 'ten' voice," says Sanders, "but she must have weighed two hundred fifty pounds."

"She looked," Mmahat says, "like she was dipped in Hershey chocolate—twice." Everyone laughs.

Sanders gets along well with his baseball teammates. He keeps a low profile in the clubhouse and on the field. He is often thoughtful of his fellow players. When he left the team for a few days to meet with his agent in Chicago during the NFL draft, he made a point of returning with something for each player: an Atlanta Falcons hat and shirt. And when there weren't enough shirts and hats to go around, he organized a lottery so that no one would feel left out.

"My first impression of Deion," says Mmahat, "was that he was a gifted athlete who wasn't particularly flamboyant. He wasn't wearing all his gold, so I asked him where it was. He said he left it home for football.

"He's just marketing himself, that's all. He'll get what he wants a lot quicker in football than in baseball as Prime Time. The only problem is, sometimes your image gets so magnified by the media that it becomes bigger than you are."

Now Baby complains to Mmahat that Sanders has been in a bad

mood ever since she arrived in Hagerstown from Albany. "I drive all this way to see him, and he's a beast," she says.

"Oh, Baby," says Sanders, "you know the bus ride does that to me. Once I get in the limelight in Atlanta, I'll be all right."

Baby is only the second steady girlfriend Sanders has ever had. His first was his high school sweetheart. They began going together in the tenth grade. When Sanders was at FSU, he told reporters, he was homesick every day for his sweetheart. She was a simple, old-fashioned girl. She didn't like it, though, when Sanders started developing his Prime Time image, and they broke up more than a year ago.

Sanders is still protective of his former girlfriend, which is why he doesn't talk much about his new love. "My old girlfriend is still in the broken-heart stage," he says. "I don't want her to be reading about Baby in the newspapers."

He is just as solicitous of his mother. When he got his $60,000 Yankee bonus, he put it in a joint bank account with her and told her to take whatever money she needed. But she often refused. "It didn't feel right," she says. Sanders then bought his mother a new black Mercedes 560 SL for her birthday and promised to buy her a million-dollar house once he gets his football money.

"A lot of guys in sports say they're gonna repay their mothers for what they did for them," he says, "but you never can. You can only pay them back a little bit. That's been the most rewarding thing for me. My mother's been like a sister to me all my life."

Sanders's mother, Constance Knight, rocks in her chair and smiles at the mention of her son's thoughtfulness. "I want Deion to get everything he couldn't afford as a boy," she says. "When he took me to the Mercedes dealer to pick out a car, I told him I liked this little black one. Then I saw the price! He said, 'Mama, don't you be looking at that price tag. That's my business.' He brought that car from Tallahassee to Henderson Street on a flatbed truck for my birthday. He said, 'I don't want no one to be drivin' that car first but my mama.'"

Her husband, Willie, interjects: "I thank God for that boy," he says. "I pray so hard that someday he will hit a home run in Yankee Stadium or score a touchdown for Atlanta."

"The only thing I worry about with Deion," Sanders's mother continues, "is that the wrong people be latching on to him. I tell him to be careful now that he's out there in the big world. I don't approve of his new girlfriend. Where has she been all this time? His old girlfriend, now, was like a member of the family. She just didn't like it when Deion became Prime Time. She's an old-fashioned girl. She didn't like that flashy stuff. He tried to tell her that was how he was gonna make it, but she still didn't like it. She could be stubborn! She was selfish with me when I first met her until Deion told her, 'My mama comes first all the time,' and after that, we were all right.

"Deion never even told me about his new girlfriend. I had to find it out through other people. Now, when a boy can't bring his girl home to his mama, you know she must be trash.

"She's crowding him. I call her his maid. She doesn't work or do anything but travel with him. She's got it made. She makes him think he needs her cause he's so busy now that he's Prime Time. She cuts his food! I can't stand that! Like he can't take care of himself. I told him I raised him to cut his own food and to take care of himself. He told me, 'She's got a degree in psychology.' I say, 'Yeah, and she's using it all on you.' Deion says, 'Mama, you're just jealous.' I told him I don't think it's that. I just want things to be right for him."

The telephone rings. Knight gets out of her chair slowly and drifts over toward the phone. She passes a window that looks out on her driveway. Parked there is a black Mercedes with a license plate that reads MOMSDREAM.

Constance Knight picks up the phone and says, "Hello." Then after a short pause, she says, "Yes, baby. This is your mama."

Whitey Herzog

King Rat

(from the *Los Angeles Times Magazine*, 1992)

THE WHITE RAT TELLS JOKES. Sexist jokes about the spinster and the foul-mouthed parrot. Racist jokes about the black dude in the elevator. Redneck jokes about the gay cowboy in the bar. He sits there, in the dugout, chewing tobacco, spitting into a plastic bottle, talking. He is surrounded by young baseball players. They look down at him and smile. He is sixty years old, a pugnacious-looking man from another time and place. He has a bristly, rust-colored crewcut; a bullet-shaped head; a jutting jaw; a big, hard belly; and, curiously, a child's bottled-up energy. He rocks back and forth as he talks. He reaches out to touch a player on the arm, the shoulder, anywhere, just to make contact, to draw them closer. "And so," he says, "this cowboy looks up from the bar and says, 'Moo moo, Buckaroo!'" The players laugh, shake their heads. "That's funny, Rat." Then they trot off to batting practice.

It is a hot afternoon in the desert: Yuma, Arizona, spring training home of the San Diego Padres, who, this day, are playing the California Angels in the first exhibition game of the spring. The stands are filled with older men and women not unlike the White Rat: retirees from small towns far to the north. Yuma is where night watchmen go to retire, after forty years, with a company watch and a new mobile home, because they can't afford Phoenix. They live in a trailer park, eat the early bird special at Jack and Rosie's, visit the old territorial prison on the hill out by the railroad tracks, take weekend trips to Mexicali over the border, and then, when spring training begins, they put on their good knit golf shirt, their Sunday polyester pants, fill a thermos with iced tea, and go to the Ray Kroc Baseball Complex off Desert Hills Drive to watch a game. Between innings they stop by to chat with the White Rat who, dressed like them, is now sitting in the stands along the first-base line. They go up to him smiling, a little nervous, but familiar, as they would with an old friend, someone like themselves but more successful, who might not remember them now.

"Hi, Whitey," says a big man wearing a trucker's cap. "My cousin Claude met you at a Little League banquet in Festus. Remember?"

Whitey looks up into the sun, shades his eyes with the flat of his hand like an Indian scout. "Sure do," he says, but he doesn't. "Festus, south of St. Louis."

The man smiles, crouches down like a football coach beside Whitey. "We seen you lotsa times with the Cardinals," he says. "You did some job with them."

"Well, thank you." Whitey spits tobacco juice into his bottle.

The man nods, grins, is silent for a moment as he thinks of something else to say to cement his friendship with his idol. He blurts out, "Say, Whitey, why didn't you sign Winfield?"

"Tried to," says Whitey. "But you know how it is today. The whole damned deal is money."

The man shakes his head in despair at the greed of baseball players. Then he says, "Say, Whitey, you like to fish, dontcha? Well, there's this river up in Alaska . . ."

"I'll be sure to try it." Whitey turns back to the field now to watch a young pitcher for the Angels. The man in the trucker's cap senses his time is up.

"Before I leave you alone, Whitey," he says, "could you sign this for my grandson?" He hands Whitey a pencil and scrap of paper torn from a brown bag.

Whitey looks at it, then signs his name. A big, sprawling *W*, and then a smaller *h-i-t-e-y*. then a big, sprawling *H*, a curlicue, and nothing, as if embarrassed by his last name.

The man looks at the scrap of paper, and says, "Thanks a bunch, Whitey. And good luck this year."

When he's gone, Whitey says, "Aw, it don't bother me. Signing autographs. I enjoy it that everybody recognizes me. I played fourteen years and never signed an autograph. I got a lotta catchin' up to do since I impersonated a player." He laughs, then says, "I'll tell ya what bothers me. Every guy's got the best damned river to fish in. When you go there the fish ain't there. Where'd they go? Shoot, the last time I fished in Alaska the only thing I caught was mosquitoes. They were so big they could stand on their hind legs and screw a turkey." Which reminds him of a sexist joke. He tells it, then says, "I should be careful today, huh? Can't go around tellin' my secretary she's got a cute ass or else I'll never become a Supreme Court judge." He laughs again, then gets serious, as he always does when he talks baseball. "You know, Winfield built this big house in Anaheim. You'd think he'd want to stay there. We offered him three million a year, but he turned it down to go with the Twins." Whitey just shakes his head. Three million dollars! Such figures were beyond his comprehension when he was a teenager digging graves for a funeral parlor and sweeping up a brewery for spare change. Those days are behind him now. He's the vice president of the California Angels. He signed with the Angels because of his long friendship with "the Cowboy," as he refers to Angels' owner Gene Autry. "I wanted to bring the Cowboy a world championship," Whitey says. "He always helped me out when I needed money."

Last summer, Autry called his good friend Whitey Herzog, who had quit his job as manager of the St. Louis Cardinals in mid-season after ten years with the club, and pleaded with him to help straighten out the Angels organization. For years, the Angels, who finished seventh in the American League West last year, had the reputation of trading off their talented young players and spending large amounts of cash foolishly on free agents who seldom produced for them. ("They never had a plan," Herzog says.) Whitey listened to Autry and told him he had planned to spend the rest of the year playing golf and fishing. Then Autry made him an offer he couldn't refuse. Whitey called his financial advisor, who told him he didn't need Autry's money, but if he took it he would be able to retire at sixty-two with $25,000 a month, tax-free, for life.

"I can't ever spend that much money in my lifetime," Herzog told his advisor, then signed with the Angels anyway. It was a challenge, he said, "to make the Angels one of the better organizations on the field, with their fans, and in their farm system." Then he said he felt the organization had been unfairly blamed for its bad trades and free agent signings in the past. He signed a contract on September 16, 1991, as vice president in charge of player personnel. His primary duties would be to evaluate talent, both the Angels' and other teams', and suggest trades and free signings. Since the '91 season was almost over, and since Herzog knew little about the Angels, he would have to wait until well into the '92 season before he was familiar with the organization. "I ain't gonna do anything rash," he said, referring to trades, "just because I'm here." The Angels' senior vice president, Dan O'Brien, says Herzog has carte blanche when it comes to making trades and signing free agents. "If he wants to do something, he can," says O'Brien. "We have no expectations he's gonna turn it around immediately." Richard Brown, the Angels' president, says, "I didn't hire Whitey to overrule him on baseball decisions."

By the time Herzog reached Yuma for the first exhibition game of the spring, he *was* familiar enough with the way the organization was being run to say, "One of our big problems is that some of the dickheads we got working for us think we're competing with the Dodgers, and we're not." Then he adds, in disbelief, "You know what the hell's really wrong with the Angels? Some people don't get to work until ten a.m., West Coast time. Everyone in New York is out to lunch by then. When the Angels go to lunch at noon, the New Yorkers are just getting back from lunch. By the time the Angels get back from lunch it's six p.m. in New York and everyone there has gone home. How the hell can you make a deal? You'd think that they would get to work at seven a.m., wouldn't ya?"

On the surface it would appear, Dorrel Norman Elvert "Whitey" Herzog is a typical product of his background and his age. He was born in 1931 and raised in one of those small, pinched, hardscrabble Midwestern towns so often delineated in the short stories of Sherwood Anderson. It was the kind of town where people were more apt to remember a successful son's failures than his successes. When Herzog returned to his hometown as a major league baseball player in the '50s, people would say to him, "Your brother Herman was a better player than you." Herzog would snap back, "Why don't you tell *him?*" He's carrying mail right here in town."

New Athens, Illinois, population 1,400, lies forty miles west of St. Louis. Sixty years ago, as it is today, New Athens was a farming and coal-mining town with two lumber mills, strip mines, a foundry, a brewery, and sixteen bars. Its inhabitants, mostly descendants of German immigrants, were neat, clean, orderly, punctual, hard-working (and hard-drinking) people who, inexplicably and proudly, referred to themselves as hard-headed Dutchmen. They saw the daily sameness of their lives as comforting, not confining. A day in the mines. Shots and beers on the way home. Checkers on Saturdays at the barber shop. The big Sunday dinner. Laundry on Monday. The same week month after month, year after year. They sat on the same bar stools, alongside the same people, who said the same things. To an outsider, or maybe even a townsperson with a different psyche, the sameness of those lives might seem maddening. When Herzog passed through that town with an army baseball team in 1953, the bus stopped for the players to eat lunch. Herzog, who had left the town five years before, took his teammates on a tour. He told then who would be sitting where in which bar at what time, and they were. "And unless they're dead," Herzog would write in his autobiography, *White Rat*, thirty-four years later, "that's where they are right now."

Herzog is reticent about his parents. He says only that his mother worked hard in a shoe factory and was so fanatically strict about cleanliness that he preferred to stay away from home as long as possible, playing sports and working in the brewery, where he learned to drink beer, like his father. Edgar Herzog worked at the Mound City Brewery where he had the distinction of never missing a day of work. The only thing Herzog remembers his father telling him about his job was that he made sure to "be there early and give them a good day's work, so when it comes time to lay someone off, it'll be the other guy."

If to an outsider Herzog's childhood sounds parched and devoid of affection, he glosses over these deficiencies and points out the positive things he learned: how to make his own bed, a habit he retains to this day; the value of a dollar; hard work, order, punctuality, and self-reliance. He learned how to entertain himself, he says, to make his own life. He talks disparagingly about kids today, who wouldn't think of playing Little League baseball unless they had the best uniforms, the best equipment, hot dogs, their parents cheering them on in the stands. Herzog and his friends played baseball endlessly, in open fields, by themselves. Their parents had no interest in games. They worked too hard.

"But I really think we had it better," Herzog says. "For kids today, everything is organized. I don't see kids having much fun."

Herzog is proud of his New Athens values and claims there is still a lot of New Athens in him today. When he meets a couple for dinner in Yuma, he is fifteen minutes early. When they arrive, only ten minutes early, Herzog is pacing back and forth in front of his car. He tells them he's worried because he doesn't have a sports jacket. "Do you think it will be all right?" he says. "In Yuma?" says the man. Inside the restaurant, most of the customers are wearing jeans and T-shirts. The hostess tell Herzog's party it'll be ten more minutes. "But our reservations are for seven," he says, almost panicky. When they are all finally seated, he checks his watch again. Fifteen minutes late. He fidgets, says, "My kids, they're always late. I don't know how they hold a job." Then he adds proudly, "But they all got their masters degree."

His three grown children were raised differently than he was. When asked how he was raised, Herzog does not answer. Was he close to his father? He looks pained. "What do ya mean?" he says, angrily. "Every kid is close to his father, isn't he?" He calms himself, looks down, and says, "We were poor. Dad drank a lot. Women did the work. He never talked to me. The fucking Germans are like that. The only time my father asked me if I needed money was when he knew I had it. I supported myself since the seventh grade."

In high school, Herzog was a star athlete in baseball and basketball and, despite his considerable intelligence, a terrible student. He used to skip school and hitchhike to St. Louis to watch the Cardinals play. "Anything to get out and see the world," he says. He got his wish when he graduated from high school and signed a $1,500 contract with the New York Yankees to play in their minor league system. "More money than Mickey Mantle got," he says, smiling. They were both centerfielders, which was only part of Herzog's problems during his seventeen-year playing career. He was a good outfielder who always hustled but couldn't hit a curveball. While Mantle was hitting fifty home rums a year for the Yankees, Herzog managed to hit only sixty-five home runs during his entire career, in the minors and the majors combined. (He spent two of those years, '53-'54, in the army where he was given an IQ test. He scored 140. "Aw, they were simple questions," he says. "Who couldn't answer them?") It was in the army that he learned to lead. "I was twenty-one," he says, "and in charge of other people." It began to dawn on him that there was a way of life beyond New Athens. "I didn't have to do things everyone else did in New Athens," he says.

Herzog never made more than $18,000 a year as a player. (He says sarcastically that if he was playing today he'd probably only make $250,000 a year as a utility man.) During the off-season, he supported his wife, Mary-Lou, his childhood sweetheart, and their growing family, by working in a bakery, a brewery, as a laborer, and for a brick and pipe company. They lived in a trailer that Herzog dragged from town to town until 1958, when he attended a technical engineering school so he could learn how to build their first house, which he did.

Herzog never did play a game for the Yankees (he was a bit player with Washington, Kansas City, Baltimore, and Detroit from '56 to '63, with a lifetime .257 batting average), although he did play with the club during spring training. One spring, he got his nickname because of his resemblance to Yankee pitcher Bob (The White Rat) Kuzava. He also became Yankee manager Casey Stengel's pet that spring. "He took a liking to me," says Herzog. "I was his Boo Boo." When asked why, he looks annoyed, as he often does when asked introspective questions. ("Why do I like to ski?" he snaps. "What do ya mean? I just like it.") Finally, he says, "Casey said I was a great leader. I don't know why. He just did."

Stengel was the first of a number of older baseball men who "took a liking" to Herzog and helped further his career. They saw in him a younger man with an old man's values, something of themselves. He had an old man's reverence for the value of money. He bought his wife a Mercedes-Benz six years ago, and they so pampered that expensive car that today it has only 16,000 miles on it. Herzog respected his team's owners' money, too. "I never signed a big salary player," he says, "unless I traded a big one to keep in the budget." He was also one of the few managers who thought it his job to put fans in the seats to pay those salaries, which was why he was always accessible to the press. Older men, like Stengel, appreciated his New Athens work ethic, and he, in turn, respected them. They were like fathers to him. Stengel. His grandfather. His father-in-law, who lived with him for a while and used to drink beer at the games and second-guess his renowned son-in-law. Herzog smiles and says, "He'd get beered up by the fifth inning. When I brought in a pitcher who gave up a home run, he'd tell me at home, 'You're not so goddamned smart!' I'd say, 'Elmer, why didn't you come down to the dugout and tell me what to do?'" Gussie Bush, the Cardinals' owner, was the first man to trust Herzog's judgment and innovative theories, which is why Herzog called him "the greatest owner I ever worked for." When Bush died last year, Herzog lost heart. He quit to work for another old man he respected, the eighty-four-year-old Autry. Herzog immediately found himself in the middle of a contract squabble between the Autrys—the Cowboy and his wife, Jackie—and the Angels' power hitting firstbaseman, Wally Joyner. Herzog's first impulse was to side with his player. When the squabble reached an impasse, however, he did what most of the working men in New Athens learned to do. He said the bottom line was, "I work for the Autrys."

Herzog's respect for older men has a lot of New Athens in it. It is the respect of a working man for his boss. It comes from a great distance in the mind's eye. Herzog sees himself fingering his hat in his hand, at one end of a vast expanse of office where his boss sits behind a burnished mahogany desk. "Yes, sir," he says, and backs out the door. Which is why today, as an older man himself, Herzog seems to enjoy more the company of younger men, his players. He greets them all by name, with a smile, a slap on the back, a dirty joke, and then, serious now, *sotto voce*, a solicitous inquiry into a wife's pregnancy. The players' faces light up when talking to the White Rat. He is more like them than he is like a front office man. He is still physical (he can't talk to people without touching them), still profane, raunchy, like a jock. After his recent cataract operation, he told his wife, "I got a new eye, a hearing aid, and now if I could only get a pump for my dick, I'd be O.K."

"I want them to be my friends," he says of players. "Yet respect me as a person, too." He's quick to mention that whenever newspapers conduct polls to find the manager players would most like to play for, his name usually tops the list. Who wouldn't like to play for the White Rat? A man grown younger with the years while others around him have aged. "Talk about a man who enjoys life," said Kansas City Royals public relations man Dean Vogelaar. "I've never seen anybody who can go as hard, twenty-four hours a day, like Whitey."

Casey Stengel was in his twilight years when Herzog first met him that spring in the fifties. He was the Yankees' flamboyant, eccentric manager, already famous as an astute judge of talent and character. He saw things in his players other managers might have missed. He had a reputation for taking modestly talented players, like Billy Martin, and talking them into exceeding the limits of their talent. He spent a lot of time talking with his pet Rat, in whom the old man glimpsed a latent intelligence even Herzog was not then quite aware of. Stengel talked mostly baseball, the intricacies of the game, as if sensing even then Herzog's future lay not on the field, but in the dugout or front office. He impressed upon Herzog the importance of the media in a manager's career. Stengel was the first manager to foresee the power the media would attain in sports. He spent hours in the dugout before a game, regaling sportswriters with stories. He passed that lesson on to Herzog, who never forgot it.

"Stengel taught me how to control an interview," Herzog says today. "Spend a lotta time answering their first question so they don't get a chance to ask another." He laughs, then says, "But I enjoy writers. They work hard today. But they can create controversies. We had just as many players who were assholes when I played as there are now. But the media didn't write about that stuff then." He admires sportswriters, he says, because he sees in them the same love of the game he has. He doesn't have the same feeling toward TV sportscasters, however. He calls them an expletive: "You don't see 'em all year, then during the World Series they want an interview right now." Like the local TV sportscaster who approached him as he left the dugout in Yuma to go into the stands. "Whitey, can I have a few minutes?" the man says. Herzog glares at him. "Why dontcha ask McIlvaine?" (Joe McIlvaine is the Padres' general manager.) Then, he notices the man has two withered arms. "Awright!" Herzog says. He sits in a chair in front of the home plate screen, facing a camera, and sullenly answers questions. When the interview is over, he says, "During one World Series the baseball commissioner told me 'The Today Show' was sending a limousine to pick me up at five-thirty a.m. I said, 'If I get up at five-thirty a.m., I'm goin' fishin.'" He smiles. "And I did."

Stengel may have taught Herzog how to handle the press, but he could not talk him into rising above his talent. On April Fool's Day, 1955, he traded him to the Washington Senators but not before telling him, "If you have a good year, I'll get you back." Herzog never did.

When he was released by the Detroit Tigers in 1963, after an undistinguished career, Herzog said, "We can't all be Mickey Mantle, can we?" And then, "It's a tough thing for a ballplayer to come to grips with the limit of his talent." It was something he never forgot. (Years later, when he had to release thirty-six players himself, he tossed and turned in bed the night before, got up, prowled the house, was unable to sleep.) His first job outside of baseball during the winter of '63 was as a construction foreman in Kansas City. One afternoon, his boss told him to lay off twenty men based on seniority, not performance. He told his boss, "I don't need a business where you have to fire the good guys and keep the dogs," and quit.

Herzog began looking for another job under the assumption his destiny was to live out an ordinary working man's life like his New Athens peers. But then Charlie Finley, the owner of the Kansas City A's, offered him a major league coaching job. Herzog grabbed it. His destiny now, it seemed, was that of a marginal baseball man, a coach who owes his career to a kindly owner or manager precisely because he threatens no one. Managers pick coaches from among their friends who are less famous than themselves. Managers take their coaches with them from team to team when they're fired and rehired as long as that coach is loyal, hard-working, not too bright, and grateful for his job, which often is as mind-numbingly boring as the jobs in New Athens. Coaches hit groundballs to infielders until their hands are callused. They give a false good cheer—"Atta boy, pick it up, good kid!" They drink late into the night with their manager. They listen to his monologues without disagreeing. They cover for him with his wife when the manager takes a woman to his hotel room on the road. They are Sancho Panzas, carrying not a lance but a fungo bat. But that was not Herzog's destiny. He took his coaching duties so seriously at KC that Finley called him the "best coach" in baseball. If so, Herzog said, then why are you paying me less money than coaches like Luke Appling and Eddie Lopat? He already knew the answer. The latter two were more famous than he. When Finley refused to give Herzog a raise, Herzog told him "to get your donkey to coach third base," and quit. ("I never worried about a job," Herzog says today. "I always had confidence in myself.")

Herzog wasn't out of work long. The Yankees hired him as a minor league manager in '65, then the Mets hired him as their third base coach in '66. He became the team's director of development in '67 and was responsible for bringing along such Mets stars as Tom Seaver, Nolan Ryan, Gary Gentry, Tug McGraw, and Jon Matlack. Along the way, he made friends with New York sportswriters, who promised him that someday they would help make him a manager. When the Mets won the '69 World Series, their manager, Gil Hodges, told Herzog, "Every time I asked you about a player, you told me right about him." The Mets promised Herzog he would be their manager when Hodges stepped down. When Hodges died suddenly of a heart attack in '72, the Mets hired the more famous Yogi Berra to manage the team. Herzog quit the team and was immediately hired by owner Bob Short to manage his Texas Rangers. Herzog called his first press conference as a manager and said, "This is the worst excuse for a big league club I ever saw." He was both candid, as always, and right. (Herzog's blunt honesty is legendary in baseball. He once told a manager he "traded his best pitcher for a sack of garbage." At other times he called the Oakland Coliseum "a graveyard with lights" and Candlestick Park "a toilet bowl with the lid up." When a writer whose baseball knowledge Herzog respected once claimed Nolan Ryan was an overrated pitcher because of his mediocre won-loss record, Herzog glared at him. "I thought you knew something," he said. "But you're just stupid.")

The Rangers were in sixth place in mid-season when Herzog was fired and replaced by the more famous Billy Martin. It must have galled him, always being passed over for men more famous but not necessarily more talented than himself. People always underestimated him, which may be why he has a penchant for tooting his own horn. He is quick to claim he was the best third base coach, the best manager, the best player development man—though not the best player—to anyone who asks. Milwaukee GM Harry Dalton once said, "Whitey doesn't care whether people like what he says or not. With him, I think it's 'I think, therefore I am.'" But Herzog's braggadocio is understandable, and he is justifiably proud of his accomplishments, achieved in spite of his background and undistinguished playing career. "You know," he says, "I went to South Korea a few years ago and everyone recognized me." And then, smiling, he adds, "I'm so well known I couldn't get laid if I wanted to."

Herzog was managing again in Kansas City beginning in 1975. He won three division titles and finished second once in four years, before he switched over to the Cardinals. He managed there for nine full seasons, winning three pennants and one World Series, and periodically also served as the Cardinals' general manager. He was named Manager of the Year three times and the Executive of the Year twice, as well as Manager of the 1980s by *Sports Illustrated*.

"The White Rat" is a misnomer for White Herzog. His hair is not white but orange. There is nothing ratlike about him. He is not secretive, underhanded, or untrustworthy like, say, Billy Martin, who, he says, "lied to everyone. Even his friends." Herzog is honest to a fault. He says he convinced the Angels to sign lefty pitcher Mark Langston to a long-term contract because he knew the pitcher wanted to stay in Southern California to further his wife's acting career. "But she ain't that pretty," says Herzog. Of another Angel, Junior Felix, Herzog says, "He's a dog. Always has been. They say he's got talent, but a lotta players got talent." Todd Worrell, his ace relief pitcher at St. Louis, was "a pussy," according to Herzog, until he married a tough-minded woman Herzog calls a "bulldog." He is not afraid to speak his mind about born-again Christians in the clubhouse, either, despite their growing power. "Those ministers don't want to help the players," he says, "they just wanna use them." He remembers one born-again player, catcher Darryl Porter, who was a reformed drug addict. "He hit into four double plays one game," says Herzog, "and when I asked him what was wrong, he said, 'Oh, Rat! The Lord'll take care of it.' I said, 'Darryl, the Lord don't know nuthin' about hittin',' and then traded him." Herzog is not even afraid to criticize his beloved Cowboy, when it comes to the Angels. "The Angels have never been a factor with Latin American players," he says, "because the Cowboy always wanted California boys." He raises his eyebrows and waits for his listener to get the picture. California boys. Blonde, blue-eyed, *white*. Then he goes on, "The Cowboy'd say, 'That kid's from Southern Cal, why didn't we draft him?'" Herzog shakes his head.

A year ago, Herzog had a much publicized fight with Bobby Bonilla's agent. The agent used the Angels in a bidding war to get higher offers from other teams without telling Herzog that Bonilla had no intention of signing with him. Herzog was furious, not because the agent used the Angels, but because he didn't tell Herzog he was using them. "That S.O.B. lied to me," Herzog said. "If he'da asked me not to withdraw our offer so he could use it with other teams I woulda said, 'The offer's there for you,' But he didn't *ask* me!" Herzog vowed never to deal with that agent again and then just as quickly began bargaining with him over the services of another client, Danny Tartabull. "He wanted a five-year contract for Tartabull," says Herzog. "But at KC, Tartabull had a five-year contract and he only played good his first and last year. So I offered him a three-year contract. I figured this way he'll only have one bad year for us."

Herzog is not afraid to talk openly to sportswriters because he feels he has an unspoken bond with them. He'll tell them the truth, or 'no comment', and they'll use what he tells them in a way that won't hurt him. He told one sportswriter that he fired a former coach of his because he was giving his players "greenies," or amphetamines. He mentions the coach's name, then looks the writer in the eye, and says, "Now, you gotta be careful about that."

One morning in Yuma, the Padres-Angels game was rained out. Herzog wandered over to the press room to wait out the rain. He sat at a corner table with an old friend, Kenny Parker, a scout, while around them sportswriters and TV sportscasters filled up the room.

Parker is in his fifties, a pink-faced man with white hair, a Deep South drawl, and a riverboat gambler's straw hat. He reminds Herzog of the time they got drunk in a hotel room in Mississippi. Herzog laughs, then tells Parker a joke about the guy who got killed by a car in front of his friends. The friends decided to send their most sensitive cohort to break the news to the man's wife. The sensitive man knocks on the door. The wife opens it. "You the widow Jones?" the man says. "I'm not a widow," she says. "The hell you ain't!" says the man. Parker laughs so hard his face turns crimson. When he stops, he looks around, as if for eavesdroppers. He leans forward to whisper in Herzog's ear. Herzog nods, then says, "No, I think he can still play." Parker says, "Thanks, Whitey."

Before the rain stops and Herzog leaves, he and Parker will be interrupted a number of times during their conversations. The men are mostly old-time scouts. They stand respectfully in front of Herzog as if waiting for an audience. He greets them all with a smile, as if he remembers them. They lean down to whisper in his ear. Herzog shakes his head. "I don't know," he says. "He's got a bad attitude." The men nod, "Thanks, Whitey," and leave.

Parker says baseball men are always picking Herzog's brain, not only because he's such a great judge of talent but because, in the words of one of them, "Whitey don't lie. If you're horseshit, he tells you to your face." Frank Cashen, the Mets, GM, once said, "Whitey Herzog is the best judge of talent I ever saw." Other have called him the most talented baseball man of his age. The most innovative. A baseball genius. A man not tied to his background and age but who has risen above both. His genius lies simply in his ability to see the obvious, then act on it, no matter if it had never been done before in baseball. ("I did things against the grain because the way things have been done in baseball don't mean shit," Herzog says.)

Herzog questions everything. Why do pitchers run lazy windsprints in the outfield? "It don't do them no good," he says. Why do Arizona state police give speeding tickets to cars on long, straight, deserted desert roads. "It don't make sense," he says. "Give 'em tickets around Phoenix where all the accidents occur." Why do managers insist that players not drink at the bar in the hotel where the team stays on road trips? "I never understood that," Herzog says. It only forced the players to spread out at different bars where they were more inclined to get in trouble. It was safer to keep them together in the hotel bar where they were staying, so, Herzog says, "I gave my players the hotel bar and I found another one."

Herzog was the first manager in baseball to tailor his team to the realities of artificial turf. During his years with the Cardinals he was saddled with mediocre starting pitchers and punchless hitters. He simply adjusted by relying heavily on his relief pitchers and by building his offense around speed and defense, which perfectly suited the fast artificial turf of Bush Stadium. A typical Cardinal rally would produce a run on a walk, a stolen base, a sacrifice bunt, and a sacrifice fly. Whitey Ball. (In '82, the Cardinals hit only 67 home runs all season, then went on to beat the Milwaukee Brewers, who had hit 216 home runs, in the World Series.)

When the Cardinals were picked to finish last in their division one season and then finished first, Peters said, "They're not that good, but damn if they don't keep getting it out for Whitey."

The White Rat tells stories. Baseball stories about people. The minor league pitcher called up to the Mets one year. He went home first to get his good sport coat for the Big Apple. "He got syphilis," Whitey says, "and never pitched again." He shakes his head in shared pain, a pugnacious-looking man sitting in the sun in Yuma along the firstbase line, watching a baseball game. He tells another story about his good friend, Roger Maris, who died young. Whitey went to the funeral with Billy Martin and Mickey Mantle. The wind-chill factor was 30 degrees below zero at the cemetery. They stood there shivering, Herzog and Martin and Mantle, who'd been drunk and crying for three days over Maris's death. Finally Mantle said, "If I'd known I'd live this long I'd have taken better care of myself." Herzog, remembering that moment, smiles, and says, "Mickey's father died young from working in the mines, and Mickey always thought he'd die young, too. So he drank."

Lance Parrish, the Angels' veteran catcher, walks past Whitey's seat on his way toward the bullpen to warm up the next pitcher. He smiles and waves to Whitey. Whitey stares after him, a big, lumbering man at the end of his career.

"Now that bothers me," Whitey says. "Lance is on the last year of his contract, and if I sit him on the bench to play [rookie catcher] John Orton, he won't put up any numbers to bargain with next year. But this year I want to give the kids an opportunity to play. The Angels never did that before. They just signed free agents. But you gotta find out about these young kids. I wanna get some goddamned answers. We got Tony Perez's kid in the minors and he can play. We got this pitcher, Paul Swingle, he's got the best arm in camp. He used to be an outfielder until they made him into a relief pitcher." Whitey opens the Angels' press guide to check Swingle's statistics. "Look here!" he says. "Eighty-eight innings in three years. I wanna know why he wasn't pitchin' two hundred innings a year, to get some experience, and *then* put him in the bullpen."

Whitey stares down toward the bullpen. Parrish, sweating in the heat, warms up the next pitcher. "He's a good person," Whitey says. "He's been good for baseball. Goddamn, I worry about him!"

One reason why Whitey wants to see if his young players can play is that the usual avenues for building teams, trades and free agent signings, are closed to him. The Angels won't spend millions on free agents any-more because of financial trouble, according to Jackie Autry, who has been running the team for the past two years. She claims the team lost $3.6 million last year and will probably lose $8.5 million this season. "By August we'll be twenty-one million dollars in debt," she said, and if their financial prospects don't improve she may sell the team. As for trades, the Angels don't have much talent that anyone wants. They lost Dave Winfield and Joyner, most of their home run and RBI production, and they failed to sign anyone to replace them. The only players on the Angels any team would want are its three left-handed pitchers, Langston, Chuck Finley, and Jim Abbott, and their ace reliever, Bryan Harvey. But unlike most baseball men, Whitey doesn't believe in trading an ace pitcher for an everyday player, no matter how good he is. That doesn't mean he won't make trades, however. He's a master at finding players with isolated skills who fill a need on the kind of club Herzog and the Angels' manager, Buck Rodgers, are trying to build. Good pitching, speed, and good defense. It's Herzog's concept for a team in the nineties, and he's one of the few baseball men who always builds his teams around a concept, a plan, not superstars. He feels the days of simply building a team by buy-ing or trading for superstars is over. It's too risky, too expensive, often counterproductive (teams loaded with superstars are often less than the sum of their parts), and it goes against the grain of his New Athens work ethic. That doesn't mean he's averse to *keeping* the superstars his clubs already have. Take Jim Abbott, the Angels' eighteen-game winner last year, for instance. He made under $400,00 last year, and the Angels promptly signed him to a $1.8 million one-year contract. Herzog thought that was foolish. He thought the Angels should have signed Abbott to a long term contract for a lot more money.

"If they signed Abbott to a long term contract when he's making only three hundred forty thousand," Whitey says, "then the Angels are essentially negotiating from that figure. Next year, when his contract's up, they'll have to negotiate from one-point-eight million. They were afraid he'd hurt his arm and they'd be saddled with a long term contract. So what? Get an insurance policy. The time to sign him to a long term contract is *before* he has a big year. You got to stay ahead of the hounds."

Herzog also doesn't believe in the Angels' policy of waiting until the season is over before negotiating with a player whose contract is up. "I'm not sure you can wait until a player is in his 'walk year' before getting it resolved," he says. What he means is that it is often cheaper to sign a player in mid-season before other teams begin sniffing around him, dropping hints about what they would play for his services.

Because of the intricacies and risks involved in trading for, buying, and signing superstars to long term, multi-million dollar contracts, Herzog prefers instead to pursue players with isolated skills who are undervalued by their own teams. (A slick-fielding, weak-hitting shortstop, say, who will anchor a shaky infield, which is just what a team of strong pitchers like the Angels needs.) In a way, Herzog is an artist at what he does. Not a contemporary artist who relies on bold strokes and primary colors (i.e., superstars) but rather an old master who prefers more subtle strokes and a finer brush dabbed with an infinite variety of secondary colors to fill up his canvas.

"I'll follow a guy from team to team," says Whitey, "and look for things, then grab him. I like to get a guy after a bad year. Hell, you can't touch him after a good year." Besides, Whitey says, if you continually steal another team's stars, soon nobody will want to tangle with you. "The secret to trading," he says, "is making trades that help the other club, too."

Whitey also isn't afraid to trade for other teams' headaches. When Joaquín Andújar pitched for manager Bill Virdon at Houston, he drove the placid Virdon to distraction. "What's his problem?" Whitey asked Virdon. "He wants to pitch every day," said Virdon. I can live with that, Whitey thought, and traded for Andújar. When Whitey went out to the mound to take out Andjular, he says, "I didn't tell him he was horseshit,

I'd tell him, 'Great job, Joaquin! You're pitching Tuesday.' He'd smile and say, 'Okay, Skip,' and walk off the mound."

Whitey smiles at the simplicity of his solution to the Andújar problem. It was so obvious—the secret to his success—that he must wonder why others hadn't thought of it. Then, remembering Andújar, he says, with affection, "He was wacky, ya know, but he had a heart of gold. I called him the other day. Just to talk to him. He lives in the Dominican Republic. Maybe he could do some scouting for us down there."

Although Whitey often traded for problem players, he just as often got rid of his own problem players when he saw they were disrupting the delicate balance of his team. And that's always what his teams are—delicately balanced. He got rid of John Mayberry and Gary Templeton (whom he called "the most talented player I ever saw") because they wouldn't hustle. He traded off Lonnie Smith after *repeated* drug problems, and finally Andújar, himself.

"A leopard can't change his spots," Whitey says. He mentions Steve Howe and Pascual Perez, two Yankee pitchers. Howe was arrested on drug charges this past winter and Perez was banned from baseball for failing a drug test during training. "Now that's bad management," he says. "It's not only talent. You got to find his personality, too." Whitey is a master at getting inside his players' psyches. He told the Mets that Nolan Ryan was lazy until he adopted Tom Seaver's work habits, and that Tug McGraw was too hyper to become a starting pitcher. "Hell, he wouldn't sleep all night if he knew he was gonna start he next day," Whitey says. So the Mets made McGraw a reliever, and he became one of the best in the game.

The game is in the late innings now. A lazy, spring training kind of game in the hot desert sun. A lot of delays. Pitching changes. Fans growing restless, looking over their shoulder at the White Rat. They still go up to him between innings.

"Hey, Whitey! Remember me?" says a man with a sunburned face. "I was in Korea with you."

"Sure do," says Whitey. The man hands him a beer, crouches down to talk awhile, then leaves. Whitey hides the beer under his seat. In a way, he's still an old-fashioned man, conscious of his image in public. He may curse, tell raunchy jokes, but never around people he doesn't know.

"Whitey, can I have your autograph?" says a teenaged boy with stringy hair. He hands him a baseball. Whitey notices all the other signatures on it.

"Whataya gonna do, sell it?" he says, and signs.

"Wow!" the boy says. "Right on the sweet spot!" It is that spot always reserved for the biggest stars on a team. Joe DiMaggio. Ted Williams. "Whitey, what do ya think of McIlvaine?" the boy says.

Whitey glares at him. "None of your damned business!" he says, and turns back to the action on the field. He sits there, rocking back and forth, touching his companion on the arm to make a point, commenting, questioning, remembering a life lived in the game he loves.

"One year with the Yankees," he says, "Don Larsen got drunk and ran his car into a tree at five a.m. When he called Stengel, Casey said, 'Good. Stay there.'"

Abbott, the one-armed pitcher, lines a foul ball down the first base line. "Pretty good swing for a one-armed man," Whitey says. Then, "If he gets a hit off this pitcher I'd release the S.O.B." The Padres' catcher Dan Bilardello goes out to talk to his pitcher, Greg Harris. "I like Harris," Whitey says. "Don't know how he can still brush his teeth, though, the way the Padres used him. Now Bilardello, he's never had much of a career, but he always keeps popping up in the bigs. He's the only guy I know who ever lost in arbitration at one hundred forty thousand." (The major league minimum salary is $100,000.) Whitey laughs at something he remembers about Bilardello. "I read the other day where he was in the batting cage and the coach says, 'Man on third, two outs, Dan, whataya do?' He stepped out of the cage and said, 'They always pinch hit for me.'"

Apropos of nothing, Whitey blurts out, "Ya know what the two most amazing stats in baseball are? Ted Williams hit four hundred against Herb Score, and Nolan Ryan pitched one hundred seventy consecutive innings without losing the lead after the seventh inning. I never did think Nolan would make it in New York, ya know? He needed a relaxed atmosphere. Some guys can't play in certain cities." Such intangibles are what Whitey looks for when he makes a trade.

When the Angels score a run on a groundball single, a stolen base, and two fly balls, Whitey says, "Helluva rally! If I was our manager, I'd tell 'em, 'There's our run, boys, now hold 'em.'" Then he answers a question before it's asked. "I ain't here to manage the Angels." He raises his eyebrows, then adds, "But it ain't written in stone I won't manage the Rhode Island Reds or some Korean team. I was a good manager, ya know. You can check it out. But today a manager doesn't control his destiny. That would bother me."

*   *   *

After the game, Whitey stops off at the hotel bar, where the team is staying, to unwind. He has a few drinks, explains again why he always gave his players the hotel bar. He thinks a lot about his players, their needs, fears, dreams. Still, today's ballplayers confuse him.

"They're programmed to deal with failure," he says. "Not success. They're always talkin' about pressure. Pressure! I'll tell you what pressure is! A guy who's got to put food on the table for his family."

He drains his drink and orders another. When it comes, he holds up the glass and says, "Drinks are like a woman's breasts. One ain't enough, and three are too many." He takes a sip and settles back into his chair. Comfortable. A sixty-year-old man from a small, pinched town and a parched background who has risen above it all, who's achieved fame, wealth, success—the good life beyond his wildest dreams. He can play golf and go fishing whenever he wants to. He can watch four different baseball games on his four TVs. He can buy his brother a pet Vietnamese pig as a joke. ("He's got all this pig shit," Whitey says. "Ashtrays and stuff. So I said, 'You like pigs, huh? Let's see if you like this one!' And damned if he don't.")

Suddenly he lurches forward, his elbows planted on the table. "You know what I don't understand? One year I made six thousand dollars as a player and had to buy my own tickets to the game for my family. Today, you got players making two million a year and they want five hundred free tickets." He shakes his head in disbelief. "I just don't understand it," he says. "I never saw so many unhappy millionaires in my life."

Sylvester Stallone

The Noble Turtle

(from *Premiere*, 2006)

THE COYOTES ARE RESTLESS. They roam in packs among the gated mansions in the mountains of Beverly Hills. They kill cats and dogs, and attack children. "They're not afraid of anything," the man says. Not his two monstrous, snarling lion sculptures that flank his electronically controlled driveway gate that leads to his Mediterranean villa, which is the color of salmon flesh. Not his many pseudo Greco-Roman statues of overly muscled gods that are planted around his property. They are not even afraid of him, though he is even more muscular than those gods.

"Yeah, I got a gun," he says. "But you can't kill them. PETA." He's standing on his back lawn in the late morning sunlight, staring out at the drab dusty-green hills of Hollywood. "So I bought a dog. A Chattahoochee cur." He grimaces. "I couldn't get a *black-tongued* cur." He looks down at Spooky, wagging his tail. Spooky is a mottled gray-black-white adolescent male with the pale eyes of a blind prophet and a goofy grin. "Spooky could kill one or two," he says, "but a pack of coyotes would tear him up." So he keeps Spooky in a wire dog crate on the grass.

Sylvester Stallone, at sixty, is too busy to kill coyotes. Or maybe he doesn't have the interest. There are too many of them. Let them roam. He has more important things to worry about: A new movie, premiering in December, *Rocky VI*. Stallone, as Rocky, has been climbing into a boxing ring for almost thirty years, ever since the original *Rocky*, in 1976, won three Oscars, among them one for Best Picture. *Rocky* earned over $117 million and instantly made Stallone a wealthy and famous man. His next three *Rocky*s earned an average of $110 million, but by the time *Rocky V* was made, fifteen years ago, Stallone's fans had lost their enthusiasm for Rocky Balboa. That film earned a mere $41 million, and it was assumed, by most people, that a stake had been driven into the heart of the *Rocky* franchise and, not coincidentally, of Stallone's career as well. But Stallone, who describes his latest *Rocky* as being about a man who "goes against common sense," and has more "will" than "skill," refused to let Rocky die and has resurrected his alter ego for one last fight.

"I wanted to show I had balls at sixty," he says. "So they couldn't write me off." He says *Rocky V* failed because it was too depressing. "Too much egotism, all that underbelly of Rocky's life. People don't want to see a character they love on his downside. No one wants to see Superman on a drinking binge." So he created, in *Rocky VI*, a character who "wins his peace of mind, who deals with the frustrations of his youth as an old man, without screaming, the only way he knows how. Through his body. Rocky has always been a guy who's about giving and receiving pain, purging old pain with new." '

Rocky, like Stallone, has always been less a cerebral character than a character who "listens to his gut," says Stallone. "Just 'cause society says I'm old doesn't mean I *am*. I'm pursuing happiness even if it makes the people around me unhappy. Sure, I made wrong turns in my life, but I want one more shot to go out on my terms. People said my time had come and gone. No one believed in this project. The producers of the previous *Rocky*s said they had no interest: 'Never! Never! Rocky's dead.' But that's what movies are about. Going against unbelievable skepticism. It's about raging, blind optimism."

When Stallone talks about his latest *Rocky*, he does so with the same raging enthusiasm he always has. He talks about his camera techniques—he stars *and* directs—and how the fight scenes are so much more authentic than in the previous *Rocky*s, which were all cartoonish *Bams!*, *Pows!*, and comically distorted facial reactions. He calls those techniques "tricks" he doesn't use in *Rocky VI*. Even the characters are more realistic, he says. "Local color from Philly. This one girl I saw on the street in front of a drug rehab. A real fallen angel. I stopped the car and said, 'You wanna be in a movie?' She said, 'I don't know about no fuckin' movie.' I said, 'Perfect.' "

Stallone describes a lot of the characters in *Rocky VI* as "nineteen-to-twenty-year-old hard bitten druggies who don't know who I am. 'I heard you was good once,' they tell Rocky. 'Buy us a drink.' In one scene they call a woman I'm with a whore, so I slammed this kid up against a car. It awakened new emotions in me." He means in Rocky. Or does he?

Stallone is not unaware that his latest *Rocky* might be met with cynicism and derision. Already, before the movie's release, Stallone and his alter ego have become the butt of Hollywood jokes. David Letterman imagined some *Rocky VI* dialogue along the lines of, "Yo, Adrian, got my Lipitor?" The *Miami Herald* claimed that *Rocky VI* was "irrefutable proof that mankind has officially run out of ideas." It was suggested that Rocky's opponent would be Alan Alda.

When he told his wife, Jennifer Flavin, he was planning another *Rocky*, she said, "Why to do want to expose yourself to humiliation?" He replied, "I know I'm not what I used to be. But I'd rather do something badly I love than feel bad because I didn't do something I love."

Stallone hasn't had a hit movie in ten years and hasn't been in a movie in eight. During that long dry spell he busied himself with a host of trivial interests. He wrote a fitness book. He came out with a line of vitamin and dietary supplements called Instone. (His protein pudding tastes like glue.) He hosted a reality boxing series on television, "The Contender." He published a lifestyle magazine, *Sly* ("Everyone just calls him Sly," says his publicist) for men between the ages of thirty-five and fifty-five, with the help of American Media, Inc., the tabloid publisher of the *National Enquirer* and *Star*. A spokesman for AMI said, "Sly approached us and we thought it was cool. He's the ultimate guy. He wasn't afraid to talk about his mistakes and Botox. He financed part of it and AMI the rest. We'll publish three to six issues at least." *Sly* lasted three issues.

Such ventures were a sad comedown for an actor whose five *Rocky* movies and three *Rambo* movies, all written or co-written by Sly, grossed over $2 billion in the '70s to the '90s and made him, at $25 million a picture, the highest paid actor of his day. And then, in the '90s, people stopped coming to his movies. He says he has nobody to blame but himself. "I became arrogant," he says. So with nothing to do with his life, he busied himself with other pursuits, all of which had to do with his body, which was always more currency than his acting. *Sly*, for example, was a *Maxim* for rich old guys still chasing youth. Its tone was steam-room Rat Pack. Sly was on the first cover, showing his good side, his muscular and vascular right arm, not his smaller, smoother left.

Inside there were a lot of buff male models hawking hair, skin, diet, testosterone, and sex enhancement products along with articles about slowing down Father Time, "growing old gracefully" (eat more peaches, raspberries, curry, whey, and almonds), and maintaining better erections (ingest pills such as Tribulus Terrestris, Eurycoma longifoliaJack, and Potency Wood). The subject of sex figured prominently in *Sly*. There was advice on how to get women in bed ("Make her feel beautiful") and how to catch a cheating wife (buy a semen detection kit).

Sly was filled with consumer advice for men who had spent so many years chasing money that now, in their fifties and sixties, they didn't know how to spend it. *Sly* told them about the best TVs, cigars, wine, beers, cars, fight movies (his *Rocky* movies were modestly excluded), and vacations. Amsterdam was a great vacation destination because prostitution is legal there. Park City, Utah, was great for skiing, although the Sundance Independent Film Festival is "packed with indie film snobs, Hollywood moneymen, and Robert Redford acolytes. Attend at your own peril."

To break up all the shilling for products and places and his other ventures (Instone, "The Contender"), Sly conducted interviews with an odd mix of celebrities, most over fifty. His Q&A with actor Ray Liotta revealed that Liotta wished he'd had smoother skin. His dialogue with James Caan revealed that Caan was still playing Sonny Corleone in real life. (He called Stallone "a schmuck.") His Q&A with author Jackie Collins revealed the nugget that Paris Hilton had read all of Collins's books—or at least listened to them on tape—which was why Collins considered Hilton "like, one of my heroines." Finally, there was a Q&A with porn star Jenna Jameson who said that she learned at fifteen "that I didn't have to open my mouth" (she meant in conversation) to get boys to chase her, "because I was really good at [sex]." Good enough to make a fortune out of sex, but not to be too jaded about it to lose her modesty. When Wesley Snipes once asked her if she liked anal sex, she was insulted.

Sly also included in his first issue excerpts from his *Rocky VI* script, which, he said then, even the actors hadn't seen. The script was as revelatory about Stallone as all his movies have been. It opens with Rocky and Paulie at Adrian's grave. Paulie tells Rocky, "rememberin' stuff don't feel so good," and "Ya can't change nuthin'." Another character tells his fighter about respect: "You ain't gonna get it, 'cause once people have made up their minds about who a man is, it really ain't ever changin' much," which is why "self respect . . . that's the only kinda respect that means a damn thing." His fighter responds, "Ya'll put a label on an' when that label's on, it don't come off—no matter what the hell I do."

The excerpt ends with Rocky telling a woman, "one second they like ya, next second you're a bum." (Joe Roth, the producer of *Rocky VI*, along with MGM and Sony, says he was drawn to the project because the sixty-year-old Rocky was a man "desperate to not make a third act of his life go in anonymity." Talia Shire, who plays Rocky's wife and dies in *Rocky VI*, said, "Sylvester is always putting issues from his own life into his movies.")

Sprinkled throughout *Sly* were Stallone's aphorisms on how to live an ideal life: Be the predator, not the food source. Follow your passion, not money. Be a champion of your dreams. Stallone, as an actor and a person, has always been about dreams. The dreams of the inadequate, underap-preciated, sensitive victim who, against all odds, becomes a champion.

Sly and I are driving down a hill to his gym, The Compound, in Beverly Hills. We come to a single-file construction site on the road. Sly motions to the two women in the SUV facing us to move past his Mercedes. The SUV moves slowly so as not to nick Sly's car. He says, "Women don't have spatial relations. They can't parallel park." When the SUV passes us, the women gawk at Sly. It's one of his problems as an actor. He can't hide from himself. He's so physically identifiable as Sylvester Stallone, even now at sixty, that no matter what character he plays, the audience sees only Stallone the star or, more accurately, Stallone as Rocky. When he went to Dodgers Stadium one night, the fans saluted him with shouts of "Yo! Rocky!" Publicly, Sly has com-plained for years that his fans refuse to accept him as any character other than Rocky or Rambo. Yet his good friend, the actor James Caan, says, "Sly became the very thing he dreaded. He wants to be an actor but he doesn't know if he can. It's sad, he can't walk away from what made him or he'll disappoint his fans." Caan pauses, then adds, "Ya know, the greatest luxury in life is to fall on your face. Some guys won't take the chance. They stay in their comfort zone."

Today, Sly says he has made his peace with the burden of his recogni-tion, but still, he thinks that's part of the reason why for so long he didn't have a career in movies. Sly's problem is that he still looks like the

Sly of *Rocky* years, with his black hair and distinctively droopy features that look less wrinkled than they do melted, like hot wax.

"People think I dye my hair," he says, "but it's just good genes." His father Frank, in his eighties, recently married a woman forty-five years his junior. She has Tourette's syndrome. When she visits the three young daughters Sly has with Flavin, his third wife and a former beautician, she coos to the children, then shouts out obscenities. "I said, 'Jeez, dad,'" says Sly, "'She's scarin' the kids.'"

Sly describes his father as "a frustrated singer" and his mother Jackie as "a bon vivant." (She's been married many times.) Both parents spent more time pursuing their own dreams than worrying about their son's when he was a child. His father was especially hard on him. He told Sly that his brain "was dormant." When he tried to teach Sly how to drive a nail in with a hammer with one stroke and Sly took three, he berated him. Sly snapped at him, "I'm not gonna hammer nails like you, get it?" His mother ridiculed his attempts to be a football player, which she called "pathetic." Sly says she was and still is a tough woman who once had a gym called Barbarella's and once promoted women's wrestling.

"She's taking trapeze lessons now," he says. He looks at me with a bemused smile. "According to her, she's only sixty-one. I was a tough birth."

Sly is only half kidding. When he was born a forceps nicked a facial nerve, which paralyzed the left side of his face, caused an eyelid to droop, and eventually slurred his speech. As a boy, his peers tormented him. So he withdrew and "spent my time day dreaming" of super-heroes. His stepfather Tony Filiti once said, "He always fantasized about being the world's greatest. He just wasn't sure at what." When a skinny, thirteen-year-old Sly saw his first Steve Reeves movie, he had an "epiphany" and began lifting weights to sculpt his body. But no matter how muscled his body became, he says it was just a veneer that hid a psyche filled with "inadequacies." He said, "Once you've been born an underdog, you always identify with that character." Sly's sense of his own victimhood is both justified and self-pitying. He's been abused, like most people, and blessed, like few. But he glosses over the blessings, preferring to pick at the scabs left by his parents, the critics, the press, his brother. One time, Sly invited his brother, Frank Jr., whom he supports financially, over to his house to watch the Super Bowl. Frank said, "Any celebrities gonna be there?" Sly shouted, "I'm your brother! I'm gonna be there!"

The critics, too, have not been kind to Sly after his first success, *Rocky* which earned Sly 10 percent of its $225 million gross. Once he became rich, Sly was determined to prove he was a versatile actor in a way that would define his career. He took on projects (*F.I.S.T., Paradise Alley, Rhinestone, Oscar, Stop! Or My Mom Will Shoot*) that required dramatic or comedic talents he didn't have. When they failed, he reflexively churned out another *Rocky* or *Rambo*, which were what his fans and Hollywood moneymen expected from him. Warner Brothers producer Mark Canton once said that he didn't know what he'd do if Sly ever approached him with an offbeat, intellectual role, but that he hoped he wouldn't "have to cross that particular bridge."

The critics savaged Sly on two fronts. They accused him of trying to repeat his *Rocky* and *Rambo* successes with increasingly schlocky and mindless, violent versions of the originals and also of trying to stretch himself in dramatic and comedic roles he had no talent for. He was cartoonishly anguished when he tried to play drama and inexpressively unfunny when he tried to play comedy. Stallone was confused. (He has always been more intuitively bright than intellectually bright.) He was being savaged for trying to repeat his successes *and*, at the same time, for trying to distance himself from them. He felt abused, hurt by injustice. (Despite his physical bulk, Sly has always been more sensitive than macho.) He felt he was being underappreciated for his efforts when he should have felt grateful for being overcompensated for them. The critics and his fans stereotyped him as Rocky or Rambo, and wouldn't accept him as any other character. But the truth was, that as an actor, Stallone's limited range found its fulfillment in Rocky and Rambo and nowhere else, except for one other role that, in a sense, was the real highlight of his career.

Sly is working out with his trainer, Gunnar Peterson, also Jennifer Lopez's trainer, in The Compound, which looks like the living room of a Beverly Hills mansion except that it is decorated with expensive black weightlifting machines. I ask Gunnar whatever happened to dirty iron gyms.

"Not in 90210," he says.

Sly works out manically hard, supersetting from one machine to another without a rest, his face contorted in Rocky pain as he heaves heavy weights over his head. His body is massively muscled and vascular, which, he says, while he works out, "Definitely hurt me in movies. My private life butted heads with my professional life. Exercise is my salvation, my discipline. Aarrggh!" He hoists a weight. "The best roles come and go."

The best role Sly ever played was the only one in which his body wasn't chiseled. He gained fifty pounds to play Freddy Heflin, a fat, simple-minded sheriff who was bossed around by a gang of corrupt New York City cops in the 1997 movie, *Cop Land*. Sly perfectly captured Freddy's hunched-over, shambling, plodding movements and his innocent psyche which he knew was being corrupted.

In *Cop Land*, Robert De Niro plays a police detective investigating the corrupt cops, who are led by Harvey Keitel, Freddy Heflin's friend. De Niro asks Heflin to help him put Keitel and his gang away for good. Freddy hesitates at first, out of a misguided sense of loyalty to Keitel. When he finally realizes that his hesitation is more about cowardice than loyalty, he musters the courage to go to De Niro and tell him he's ready to help him.

De Niro says, "I offered you a chance to be a cop and you blew it."

Freddy says, "It took me awhile to be a cop."

"What? You finally wake up from your slumber? It's too late."

Sly finally takes a rest from his workout and begins shadow boxing. "Freddy," he says with his twisted smile. "A noble turtle. The bravest character I ever played. He knew he was gonna lose but he still did what's right. He was my proudest achievement. An ego saver. I took scale for that, ya know. The other actors were taken care of. But I wanted to get in the ring with all those great actors I'd been barred from. And go one-on-one with them." He stops shadow boxing and ticks off names of co-actors in *Cop Land*. "DeNiro, Keitel, Liotta, Peter Berg, Annabella Sciorra...." He stops. "I thought it was odd no more roles like that were presented to me." He shrugs. "My image." *Cop Land* came late in his career and his image was chiseled in granite by then even despite his brilliant performance as a "noble turtle," who had more in common with the real Stallone than Rocky or Rambo ever had.

Sly goes back to his workout, grunting and grimacing cartoonishly. It's a revelation! He's not overacting in Rocky or Rambo! He's just exhibiting his normal facial expressions. I mention to him an old Hollywood adage that every actress is more than just a woman; every actor is less than just a man.

Breathing heavily, soaked with sweat, Sly says, "That's true. Acting is a feminine profession. Women are better at it emotionally and hormonally."

Gunnar interrupts him. "You don't want to say that to him, Sly."

Sly looks confused. "I didn't mean all actors are, like, gay," he says. "I just meant women are more sensitive, which makes them better performers than men." Curiously, Sly could be talking about himself. He is more sensitive than combative, even if that sensitivity is often manifested in self-pity.

After his workout, Sly and I get back into his Mercedes and head up the hill to his villa. He talks mostly about sports as we drive: the Lakers, the Super Bowl, Philadelphia sports fans. (Sly went to school in Philadelphia, where the original *Rocky* was filmed.) "Ya think Philly sports fans are loyal to McNab—" Donovan McNab, the Eagles' quarterback—"or to the team, or to Philly? Where is it?"

The inside of Sly's home is decorated in a style best described as Renaissance Baroque. More classical statues of muscled gods. Huge wall paintings of gods and goddesses. Heavy, antique wooden furniture and lots of reds and burgundy velvets. He grabs two cigars from his humidor and leads me to his office. He shows me pairs of boxing gloves once worn by Rocky Marciano, Muhammad Ali, and Max Schmeling; the requisite celebrity photos on the wall (Sly with this actor and that athlete and that politician); the covers of various publications he's been on: *Newsweek,* the *New York Post* with a headline that reads: "Do It Yourself Film Wins Oscar." Then he shows me a photograph of himself standing high above Lincoln Financial Field prior to the Eagles' 2004 NFC Championship game. The stadium is packed with over 68,000 fans, all screaming for "Rocky!" amidst a crescendo of fireworks.

Sly grins and shakes his head. "I can't blend in anywhere," he says. But in the photo he's wearing a football jersey with "Stallone" printed on the back. Sly is a hero in Philly, mostly among the city's blue-collar workers, who saw in *Rocky* a metaphor for their own lives. In fact, Sly is so worshipped in Philly, he says he's thinking of moving back to the City of Brotherly Love. It's a reflexive habit of his, always moving closer to worship. When he made a film with Sharon Stone in Miami Beach, *The Assassin,* he was so well received there he was given the key to the city. Soon afterwards Sly pulled up stakes in L.A., where his key to the city had been figuratively revoked, and moved to Miami.

When Stallone commissioned a statue of himself as Rocky in 1983, he gave it to the city of Philadelphia and asked that it be erected on the top steps of the Philadelphia Museum of Art (MOA), where he triumphantly raised his arms in *Rocky*. The city's Art Commission turned down his offer because they said the overly muscled statue was a movie prop, not art, and then shipped the statue to the sports arena, The Spectrum. (A Boxing Hall of Fame executive once complained that there was a statue of Rocky in Philadelphia, but no statue of Joe Frazier, the Philadelphia-born former World Heavyweight Champion.) Recently, the MOA reconsidered its earlier rebuke, and in September 2006, Sly will return to Philly for a ceremony returning the statue of Rocky to its rightful spot in Philly lore, on the top steps of the museum.

Actually, there were three Rocky statues made. One of them came up for auction on eBay. Asking price, $5 million. When there were no takers, the price was dropped to $3 million, then to $1 million, and then $750,000, and then finally the owner asked Sly to buy it. He refused.

"It would be self-glorification to the point where even *I* can't do it," he says with an embarrassed smile.

We sit down beside each other on a sofa, light up our cigars, and he begins to talk about his life in that easy, honest way of men who no longer have anything to hide. Still, despite his features contorted in laughter or annoyance, there is about him a curious remove. He exhibits emotion through his features, but no deeper. He once said that as an underdog he learned to control his emotions. He says he gets up at 5:45 a.m., does some stretching, then rouses his daughters for their "extra curricular activities." Five minutes of billiards, Spanish language TV, piano, golf, soccer, "to give them focus before they go to school." Sly is obsessed with time. It's running out, he says, so he crams as much into a day as he can. Sly paints and writes, lifts weights, acts when he can, and works on his new projects of the moment. He once said that his desire to cram so much into his life was "a sickness, an obsession . . . always driving, driving. . . . "

"I expected my magazine to be met with skepticism," he says, "but at least I got my philosophy out," He thinks critics, like those coyotes, attacked his magazine because it was his, not because it was a shallow effort.

Sly works in his office until noon, then, "I go into a daydream state," he says. "I think of things to do." He doesn't go to clubs anymore, but he still has friends in the business. Caan. Kurt Russell. Liotta. Mickey Rourke, Arnold Schwarzenegger. The kind of men one would expect to be his friends. "Lately," he says, "I'm trying to develop relationships away from the acting community. Industrialists. Publishers." He is as ploddingly methodical about these friendships as he was about everything he ever wanted to accomplish in life.

In high school in Pennsylvania, he says, "I was inept at sports, especially football, so I carried a football in my hands for a year." By a sheer act of will he made himself into a decent enough player to make his high school team. "The sad part was," he says, "we were oh-for-ten."

When he attended the University of Miami, he says that he "auditioned" (an actor's verb, not an athlete's) for the football team as a running back. "They put me in the backfield and told me to run off tackle. I saw this skinny linebacker behind the defensive line, named Hendricks..."—it was Ted Hendricks, future NFL Hall of Famer— "... So I ran off tackle and he hit me so hard he almost broke my neck. I bounced off the ground..." Sly bounces off the sofa "... and said, 'Okay! Which way to the Drama Department?" He walks quickly across his office, laughing, then returns to the sofa.

After he left UM (he never graduated), Sly went to New York City and began to make the rounds of casting offices as an actor. "With my slurring voice and droopy eyelid," he says, "I was told at each stop, 'Maybe you oughtta rethink if you have something else you want to do." Sly laughs. "So I took a test and found out I was suited to be an assistant electrician. Not even an electrician! Not even full voltage!" He takes a puff of his cigar, then adds seriously, "You can either buckle under and wallow in your misery or look for another avenue into the business. So I began to write film scripts," which he once described as being "drenched with nihilism." His first script was "Cry Full, Whisper Empty in the Same Breath," about a rock singer who couldn't stop eating bananas.

Ever methodical, Sly got a job as an usher at a little-attended movie theater so he could study films. Obscure Indian films he'd watch forty times, then go back to his "fleabag" apartment and try to rewrite the dialogue. "I was lonely," he says, "no female relationships, nothing." He got his first break when a friend asked him to be his sounding board when he read for a part in the movie, *The Lords of Flatbush.*

"I got the part and he didn't," says Sly. "He wouldn't talk to me for two years." He also contributed a bit of dialogue and got his first writing credit, which encouraged him to think of himself as a screenwriter. So he bought a $40 Pontiac "with two-tone rust" and drove across the country with his new wife, Sasha, and his bull mastiff "packed in ice."

His car blew up on Hollywood Boulevard ("I'm not kidding!") and he had to walk to the apartment of a friend, Henry Winkler, who had been in *The Lords of Flatbush*.

"I asked him for help," says Sly, "and then I got a place far out in the San Fernando Valley and worked on my scripts."

After he received a little encouragement over a few of his scripts, he sat down and in 86 hours wrote *Rocky*. By then he had learned that, "If you wanna make money, you have to write heroic stories . . . So now I'll write about raging optimism. Flip, flop. Flip, flop." When he finished the script, he says, "I knew this was it!" Producers Irwin Winkler and Robert Chartoff offered to buy his script if they could hire Ryan O'Neal to play Rocky. At the time, Sly had $106 to his name, but still he refused to sell, even when the producers offered him $360,000.

"I wanted one chance to sink or swim," he says. "I knew there'd never be a part like that for me again. I was raw, but so was *Rocky*. If someone else received accolades for *Rocky* I woulda jumped off a bridge. I woulda sold out and *Rocky's* not about sellin' out. Ya know, so many opportunities are blown by people taking the short end . . . including myself." Finally, the producers gave in, signing Sly to play Rocky for $600 a week and 10 percent of the profits. But first they inserted a morals clause in the contract. "I was terrified when filming began," says Sly, "that they'd look for an excuse to fire me." He shakes his head at the memory of his courageous self. "I don't know if I'd have the guts to do that today." He smiles. "Ya know, you fear losing a lifestyle you didn't have when you were poor."

Rocky made film history, the little film that could. "I hit a grand slam the first time up," says Sly. "Where do I go now?" Where he went after *Rocky* became the story of his career, and his frustration. He signed succeeding contracts that were more and more lucrative under the condition that he would repeat *Rocky's* success, and later, *Rambo's*.

Although the critics have been relatively gentle with Sly's *Rocky*s, they have been vicious with his *Rambo*s. They accused Sly of promulgating a right-wing, war-mongering agenda in the form of a crazed ex-soldier, Rambo, who destroyed everyone and everything in his path. Stallone defends himself against those charges by saying that he's essentially apolitical. He says, "*Rambo* met with a lot of opposition compared to, say, *Platoon*. But it's always been a male fantasy to fight a war you have control over. Is that liberal or conservative?" Arnold Schwarzenegger was accused of the same right-wing philosophy in his violent movies. In fact, Sly and Arnold have a lot in common. Both are probably centrist Republicans, but Arnold has more savvy. "Arnold understands in L.A. you can't be dogmatic," says Sly. "He knows if you don't bend, you break." Arnold also always had a goal that his film career would be a stepping stone to another career, which indeed it has been. For Sly, his film career has been the be-all and end-all of his life. He has never had Arnold's egotistical vision of himself. Sly wanted to conquer the film world. Arnold wants to conquer the entire world. (Recently, as governor, Arnold presented Sly with a Certificate of Recognition, a sort of attendance award for filming *Rocky VI* in L.A.)

In between his blockbusters, *Rocky* and *Rambo*, Sly tried to prove he was a versatile actor by playing a variety of off beat parts in a series of films that were flops.

"When I followed *Rocky* with *F.I.S.T.* [which flopped], I realized I was cast as Rocky forever. I took it the wrong way and shouldn't have worked so hard against it. You can't be better than you are as an actor. I can't play Shakespeare." He pauses a moment. "But still, I always thought I had a sensitive side, ya know, like Lennie in *Of Mice and Men*." Which was why, in between his Rockys and Rambos, Sly tried to play characters 180 degrees removed from those two characters. He admits now that was a mistake. "I shoulda just gradually evolved as an actor over the years, like Clint Eastwood. But Rocky took away my opportunity to build to a peak."

Sly's and Eastwood's acting styles and careers are mirror opposites. As an actor, Eastwood was Hemingway to Sly's Faulkner. Eastwood was a minimalist on screen, Sly was a baroque maximalist. Eastwood began his career as a non-verbal actor in spaghetti westerns made in Spain and then became a brutal, taciturn cop in *Dirty Harry*, who evolved over his career into a taciturn but sensitive tough guy (*Unforgiven*) and then into a man whose sensitivity was expressed by his silences in *The Bridges of Madison County* and his recent hit, *Million Dollar Baby*. Eastwood never shied away from playing himself, over and over. He just refined that self over the years, chipping the stone from a sharp-edged image until it became smooth and graceful and aesthetically pleasing. Sly tried to flee from his image, then, after failure, returned to it without ever refining it.

I tell Sly that Eastwood should send him a bouquet of roses for paving the way for his *Million Dollar Baby*, the plot of which is based on

Rocky. But Sly says, "Aw, I'd like to take credit for it, but all fight movies have the same plot. A guy doesn't drop out of Harvard to become a pug." He says Eastwood was lucky to be able to take each of his small successes and build on them film after film because his fans, and Hollywood money, didn't put demands on him based on great expectations. "Clint was smart," says Sly. "He never went too far from his tight-lipped character. He delivered the kind of performance people could rely on. I went to extremes. I couldn't break my persona. Also, Clint controlled his destiny by directing his movies."

Eastwood wasn't tempted by big money early in his career because he wasn't offered it. Sly was. "Big money does corrupt," he says. "In the late eighties I had opportunities . . . maybe I didn't capitalize on. I vacillated between money-fame-power-personal achievement. Fame is addictive, but money comes first. I had opportunities to break financial barriers in the industry. It became a competition in the eighties and nineties because for the first time actors' salaries were being published in magazines and on TV. It was an agents' game. 'I got my guy twenty-two, twenty-three, twenty-four, twenty-five million.' And the projects suffered. Today it's more about fame. Johnny Depp and Leonardo DiCaprio make a big money film, then they do a serious film for little money to add to their caché and refurbish their fame. Their body of work adds to their fame. In my day, it was simply who got the most money."

During those years when Sly was getting "the most money," he says he developed a heightened "sense of false superiority . . . an aura of invincibility. I thought I could make anything work. I pontificated on every subject—capital punishment—I didn't know anything about. I was full of anger, too, for being taken for granted. I was antagonistic to the press. I though I was a victim, the butt end of a joke. People said, 'He made his bed and sold his soul to the devil and now he has to pay.' I really don't have any defense." He shakes his head and looks pained. "I look back and I *hate* that man!"

One of the major problems with "living in the time of your own legend," he says, was that his deteriorating personal life was on display to the world. His first marriage to Sasha began to fall apart when she gave birth to their autistic son, Seargoeh, in 1976. Like most mothers in such a situation, Sasha began to devote much of her life to her son while, she said, her husband "didn't have time" for him. They began to drift apart and were finally divorced about the time that Sly received in the mail a photograph of a six-foot, two-inch, statuesque Swedish blonde named Brigitte Nielsen.

Sly laughs. "No, she wasn't nude. It was just a modeling shot." Their tempestuous relationship and marriage and acrimonious divorce (Nielsen ran off with her blonde secretary and $2 million of Sly's money) was such fodder for the paparazzi and gossip columnists that Sly described it as "some rolling carnival of horrors put on public display to be mocked. My marriage to her rates with the riddle of the Sphinxes. I fell madly in love with an ideal of physical perfection."

Recently Nielsen has fallen on hard times. She was reduced to starring in the VH-1 reality TV show, "The Surreal Life," with her supposed paramour, Flavor Flav. They made an odd couple, the six-foot-two-inch Amazon blonde and the five-foot-eight-inch black man with gold-capped teeth. Their shenanigans, most of which seemed to be played out under the influence of alcohol, were described in the press as being almost too painful to watch. One night in bed, though, Sly and his wife, Jennifer Flavin, did watch in disbelief. Flavin sat up in bed and turned to her husband. "What were you *thinking*?" she said.

Sly stifles an embarrassed laugh. "I told her, 'We get what we deserve at the time.' I just wanted a little girl to stay home and make soup.'"

I say, "Like Joe DiMaggio wanted from Marilyn Monroe. She said life with him was boring."

"Being married to me is boring, too." Then he adds, "I feel sorry for Brigitte. Ya know she speaks five languages. Jesus, watching her on that show is an out-of-body experience."

Like most movie stars, Sly has an ambivalent attitude toward the press. He says, "I expect the inconveniences of my fans, it's part of the job. But the paparazzi." I mention that when he was in bed with American Media he didn't have to worry about that anymore. He laughs, "Yeah, my master plan." Then he tells a story about actor Edward G. Robinson. "Ya know, he hated autograph-seekers. But he said he never really understood real fear until one day he walked across a hotel lobby and no once recognized him. Actors. Some people think we feel more than ordinary people." He shakes his head no. "We just need more. We're like a bottomless pit that needs to be filled."

By the '90s, when Stallone's star was falling in Hollywood, the tabloids that once clamored for his interviews now began writing stories titled, "Alone with Stallone," and "The Forgotten Stallone." He was portrayed as an outcast in Hollywood, where, he says, "people didn't return my phone calls. It had been a roller-coaster ride and I couldn't get off." So he and his young wife, Flavin, pulled up stakes and moved to Miami in '96 because "it was exotic and cutting edge." But once ensconced in a mansion on Biscayne Bay, Sly realized, "I had nothing in common with these people. All I did was watch mosquitoes fly off with dogs. Jennifer was getting agoraphobic. She wouldn't leave the house. I felt like a foreigner. I was losing touch with my L.A. friendships, my career momentum. In L.A. I belonged to a network, like a campus. You have to be available even if you're Sylvester Stallone." So he moved back to L.A. and now lives on a mountain top in Beverly Hills with the coyotes closing in and not even Spooky to keep them at bay.

"I'm thinking I might move to Santa Barbara," he says. "L.A. is a town for the young."

His female assistant pokes her head through the doorway and points to her wristwatch. I get up to leave, but before I do, I ask Sly if I can see his paintings.

"Sure," he says. He leads me upstairs where his huge paintings line the hallway walls. They are done in an abstract style, thick with paint, mostly reds and blacks, and even thicker with angst. He points to one, "When you put your head above the clouds, they shoot at it." Then another. "I was angry then." And another. It's the painting of a man, his bloody, droopy features all melting like hot wax. "That was a painful period in my life."

But like all pain, it has subsided with time and age. Sly is not so angst-driven these days. He's made his peace with his frustrations. Instead of picking at the scab of all those dramatic roles he never played, he has accepted the fact that "I was lucky to deliver someone, Rocky, who endured. When you're young, ya know, you don't wanna be stereotyped. Now, I say, it's who I am."

Sly even feels a kind of vindication in having created a believable universe and beloved hero as his life's work. He is not unlike J. K. Rowling, the author of the Harry Potter novels. After Rowling writes her last Potter novel she might switch gears and write a serious adult novel that could be met with critical derision from a public that will accept her only as the Harry Potter novelist. But that won't alter her life's accomplishment. Sly understands that now.

"When I die," he says, "I know I'll be remembered as this left-handed boxer, Rocky Balboa." It does not even matter whether *Rocky VI* is a hit or a flop, he says, because, either way, "It won't do my career much good. People will always say that's all I can do as an actor. So I'll retire. I'd like to direct movies now. Arnold told me it was silly for men our age to put on makeup and shoot bad guys. That's not me anymore. It's almost a relief, ya know, to retire. Rocky was fuckin' killing me."

Phil Hill

Of Memory, Death, and the Automobile

(excerpted in *Sports Illustrated*, 1976)

"... all stories, if continued far enough, end in death ..."
—Ernest Hemingway, *Death in the Afternoon*

PART ONE

PHILIP TOLL HILL is a forty-nine-year-old businessman with a vivid, if selective, memory. He can recall the exact make, model, color, year, and gear-shift pattern of every automobile he has ever been in, and he can recall the minutest details of every funeral he has ever attended. He remembers, for instance, that at the age of eight he and some friends were driven home from a birthday party in a green, 1933 Chevrolet sedan whose gear-shift had a wide, sloppy neutral and a spongy feeling when the gears were changed. He remembers the feel of that gear-shift because he had been permitted to sit beside the driver and shift gears only after he had paid each of his friends twenty-five cents for the privilege. His friends were, at first, disbelieving of his request and offer, and then, when he made good, they began to laugh at him. He remembers being oblivious to their derision at the moment but much later feeling, for the first time, that his fascination with the automobile, which he could trace back almost to his first conscious memory at the age of two, might somehow be unnatural. About the only things he cannot remember from that childhood incident are the names of the driver and his friends.

Hill remembers another moment in his life when, at the age of twenty-four, he stood over a casket and scrutinized his mother's features. He grew suddenly agitated, disturbed, not by something he had felt but by something he had seen. He summoned the undertaker.

"Those aren't my mother's lips," he said. "This is not the way they were." Then, in precise detail, he described exactly how his mother had painted her lips in life so that the undertaker could repaint them accordingly in death.

Hill can remember such details because for a good many years and almost to the exclusion of all else, his life had been devoted to (some might say, obsessed with) the mastering of death and the automobile. He has owned, driven, raced, and restored more automobiles, and he has attended more funerals, confronted and contemplated death more often, than would a hundred ordinary men. His obsession with the automobile came first and led, inadvertently, to a career as a racing car driver out of which grew his obsession with death.

Throughout the 1950s and early '60s, Phil Hill was the most successful American racing car driver in the world and was, and still is, the only American ever to win the Formula One World Driving Championship, the most prestigious of all racing championships. He began his career as a mechanic for a racer of midget cars in and around his hometown of Santa Monica, California; graduated to driving himself with the purchase of a British MG-TC sports roadster in 1947; won his first competitive event, a three-lap trophy dash at Carrell Speedway in Gardenia, California, in 1949; and won his first major United States sports car race on November 4, 1950, at Pebble Beach, California. He was twenty-three years old. He drove a new XK–120 Jaguar, only a few of which had been imported to the United States for such famous and wealthy people as Clark Gable and Gary Cooper. Hill had journeyed to England specifically to purchase his car and then brought it back to the States in the ship's hold of the *Queen Mary*. At the time, the XK–120 was considered to be the ultimate in boulevard sports cars. It was long and low and hump-fendered and, generally as sleek-looking as its namesake, but by the time Hill finished punishing it around the 1.8 mile Pebble Beach course, it had been rendered merely another mud-splattered, dented, brakeless, and clutchless racing relic. Hill's driving technique at the time consisted of simply plowing his car into every turn faster than it was capable of navigating, bracing himself for the impact as the car bounced off the protective bales of hay that lined each curve, and then furiously jerking the steering wheel until the car straightened out again and proceeded down the straightaway with his foot nailed to the accelerator pedal. It was a technique, Hill admits today, without fear or style. Over the next eleven years, however, that technique would evolve into one of consummate and meticulous skill nurtured by an increasingly heightened and almost paranoid fear of death.

Hill built a reputation as the premier sports car racer in the United States during the early '50s, and then went to Europe where he enhanced that reputation as a driver for the legendary Enzo Ferrari and his racing team. Still driving sports cars, Hill became the most successful sports car and endurance racer in the world. He won the Grand Prix of Sweden and the Messina Five Hours of Sicily in 1956; the Grand Prix of Venezuela and the Nassau Governor's Cup of the Bahamas in 1957; and in 1958, when he was voted the Sports Car Driver of the Year, he won the Twelve Hours of Buenos Aires, the Twelve Hours of Sebring, and the Twenty-four Hours of Le Mans, the latter the most prestigious of all endurance races and one which Hill would eventually win three times. Finally, in the fall of 1958, Hill was promoted to Ferrari's Formula One team. The Formula One car was and still is the ultimate racing automobile and in fact is less an automobile in any conventional sense of the word that it is an out-and-out racing machine whose sole purpose is to go quicker around corners and faster down straightaways (upwards of 195 mph) than any internal-combustion automobile in existence. From above it looks like a cockroach. The engine and driver are encased in an aluminum shell shaped like a football. The car's frame and axles are nothing more than metal tubes of the lightest possible weight. The front and rear wheel axles jut out from the cylindrical body like the spindly legs of a cockroach, and they terminate in oversized black tires, which in Hill's day were tall and narrow but today are low and fat.

After two years of modest success as a Formula One driver, Hill became the first American in thirty-nine years to win a major Formula One event, the Grand Prix of Europe at Monza, Italy. The following year he won the Grand Prix of Belgium and Italy, finished second in the Grand Prix of Monaco and Europe to amass enough points to become the first and only American ever to win the Formula One World Driving Championship. Hill could attribute his victory to a number of factors, some within his control but just as many beyond it.

In 1961, Phil Hill may not have been the fastest racing car driver in the world—that distinction belonged to Sterling Moss—but he was the best. Whereas Moss had a talent for driving the fastest laps and sometimes even the fastest races, he also had a penchant for disastrous crashes (he was hospitalized numerous times, once for a period of six months) and for pun-ishing his car beyond its breaking point. Moss led a great many more races than he ever finished, while Hill finished the extraordinary total of 80 per-cent of the races he started. He had the self-discipline and restraint to avoid taking unnecessary chances. ("He drives more with his head than his foot," the renowned American driver Briggs Cunningham once said.) Hill was never in a major accident that led him to be hospitalized, nor did he have a reputation for breaking his cars. He was a perfectionist regard-ing both the cars he drove and the tracks over which he drove them. Before each race he drove the track in a sedan at five miles an hour. Often he stopped along the way, got out and picked up wet leaves on the track. He made a mental note of every natural and man-made oddity of the track—of every tree whose overhanging branches might drip morning dew, of every building which might create cross-winds that would lighten his car at high speeds. He was equally fastidious about the preparation of his car, and, in fact, on the night before he won the World Championship, he forced his Ferrari mechanics to install a new engine in his car simply because it didn't sound right. The mechanics grumbled at the prospect of working through the night, accused the driver of being a typically tem-peramental, spoiled driver. Finally, at Enzo Ferrari's order, the mechanics acquiesced. When they finished installing the new engine the folllowing morning only minutes before the start of the race, they began to examine the extracted engine. They discovered a broken valve spring in one cylin-der, which would have forced Hill to retire early from the race and would have prevented him from becoming the World Champion.

More important to Hill's driving than his self-discipline, his perfec-tionism, or his physical attributes (e.g., his exceptional reflexes and eye-sight) was that ability, which passes for genius in any field, of intuiting beyond experience. He saw things before they happened. For example, while other drivers suddenly found themselves *in* crash situations and had to resort to every bit of skill to extricate themselves, Hill anticipated such situations before they developed and then drove around them. It was such an intuition that saved his life in 1955, when, as co-driver with Umberto Maglioli, in the Twenty-four Hours of Le Mans, he was stand-ing on a bench in the pit area waiting for Maglioli to come in and turn the car over to him. "I had this extra sense," says Hill, "that always warned me something was going wrong before it happened. It stayed with me all the years I was racing. I'd always worked out what I was going to do if a car got loose in the pitts; I was very conscious of self-preservation in those days. Anyway, when the cars came down the straight-away that passed the pits, I heard this unfamiliar sound . . . ptt . . . ptt . . . pttt. . . . So I didn't think, I just jumped backward off the counter and crouched down."

What happened next has been called racing's darkest day. The driver of a Mercedes 300SLR lost control of his car, which hurtled into a crowd of spectators at over one hundred mph. The car disintegrated, sending pieces of metal and even the still buzzing engine deeper into the crowd. Eighty-five people were killed that day, and over one hundred fifty injured, and, although nearby he could see a *gendarme* lying on the tracks without his legs, Phil Hill was unscratched.

There were other reasons for Hill's World Championship. He was lucky, as all racers must be to survive. Also, his Ferrari was the fastest, if not the best handling, of all Formula One cars that year. (The best handling car was the Lotus of Sterling Moss.) Furthermore, it was rumored that Il Commendatore, Enzo Ferrari himself, had decreed that Hill should become this year's World Champion in order to coincide with Ferrari's upcoming assault on the American automobile market. This decree simply meant that Hill was to be given every possible advantage over other drivers in the Ferrari stable. It seems that the Grand Prix racing circuit, despite its surface gloss, is not so unlike the sanitation men's union of New York City. There is a seniority system, whether spoken or unspoken, that determines which of two front-running team drivers should cross the finish line first. At times on the track, a younger driver will defer to his senior teammate, will actually slow down his car and wave ahead his trailing teammate so that he can take the checkered flag. Hill performed such a courtesy himself in 1958, when, comfortably leading at Casablanca, he slowed down to allow teammate Mike Hawthorne to cross the finish line first. Hawthorne's victory in that race ensured him of the World Championship over Sterling Moss, an American. The margin was a single point, 42 to 41.

When Hill signed on with Ferrari in 1955, he was the ninth driver on a nine-man team. By 1961, he and Count Wolfgang von Trips were Ferrari's two senior drivers: all but two of his teammates had been killed in various crashes. Von Trips himself was killed early on in the very race, the Grand Prix of Italy, in which Hill won his World Championship. In fact, in that race von Trips lost not only his life but also that year's World

Championship, as at the time of his crash he was leading his teammate for the title, 33 points to 29. By the fall of 1961, most of the great Formula One drivers of the 1950s had already been killed on the track, twenty of them in races in which Hill himself was competing.

For years Hill had accepted the deaths of his contemporaries on the track as the inevitability of their profession. His attitude had been not unlike that of most racers ("It's just another funeral") although whether this stoicism was truly felt or merely a façade was not clear even to him. But now, during the winter of 1961, when he should have been savoring the fruits of his World Championship, he found himself obsessed with the attrition rate of his fellow drivers, without whose deaths he might never have become World Champion, and with the growing realization of his own mortality. He wondered for the first time, "How many funerals can you go to?" Within three years he would retire from Grand Prix racing without ever again having approached his '61 successes. He returned to the less dangerous sports car racing for a few years and then in 1967 he retired from automobile racing altogether. He was forty years old. His retirement was unlike that of most racers, in that it was not brought about by a serious and debilitating injury such as those suffered by Fangio and Moss, nor was it brought about by the onslaught of age since many racers continue to drive through their forties. Furthermore, unlike most ex-drivers, he retained no contact with his former profession, either as an owner or builder of race cars, but simply disappeared completely from the racing scene. His disappearance had been voluntary and, many racers and fans alike felt, premature. It had been brought about by a number of reasons both internal and external, but most of all because, according to Hill, "I had a premonition that I was ultimately going to kill myself, and more than anything at that time, I did not want to be dead."

In retirement, Philip Toll Hill is drawn back daily to the past. Apropos of nothing, he will exclaim, "I just flashed to Lisbon in 'fifty-nine. I can see Graham Hill in front of me when suddenly he starts to spin. He's sideways and I nail him broadside. I bang my nose on the steering wheel and the next thing I know these police are dragging me out of the car, then carrying me across the track. Out of the corner of my eye I see Graham get out of his car by himself. Later that night he was very upset with me because I never asked him how he was. I told him he didn't ask me how

I was! It was not his responsibility, he said, since I hit him. 'Hell,' I said, 'It was *your* fault!' Anyway, looking back, maybe he was right." He shrugs.

Hill flashes back not only to the remembered past of his own experience, but also to a dimly remembered past beyond that, to a past filled with the history of all human experience that, he feels, is inherited by each new generation. He calls this past alternately "our subliminal inheritance" and "the continuity of spirit." He lives with his wife and three children in an old Spanish-Mediterranean house in a quiet neighborhood in Santa Monica, California. The house is surrounded by newer homes, but in 1929, when he first entered it with his parents, it was one of only two houses on the street. "The rest was prairie," he says. Hill has preserved that house exactly as he remembered it forty-seven years ago, when he was a two-year-old child. Its exterior walls are a cream-colored stucco and its roof consists of orange tubular tiles. Inside, the house is all white plaster walls, exposed beams, and darkly wooded floors. When Hill lived in that house as a child it was meticulously kept by servants, and the only brightness he remembers in it were the colorful mosaic tiles embedded in the stairwells leading to the second floor. Now the house is comfortably rumpled, filled to overflowing with his children's plastic toys and stuffed animals and with the many ancient artifacts of his own fascination. A perfectly restored Mills violin lies under a glass case. An old bible is split open on a book stand. Other books, mostly ancient volumes with leather bindings, embossed gold letters, and gilt-edged pages of stained parchment, are stacked in bookcases along the walls and propped on coffee tables. One wall is lined from floor to ceiling with age-faded cardboard containers that house the remnants of his once vast collection of player piano rolls. Standing side by side are his two player pianos, perfectly restored, their polished chestnut gleaming under dark beams. The past seems everywhere. It is in the smell of worn leathers and in the burnished haze emitted by dark and polished woods that give each room the grainy textured look of an old brown-tinted photograph.

He withdraws a small volume, props up his bifocals, which hang from a black band around his neck. He is nearsighted and yet can read distant highway signs at night. He is wealthy and yet dresses in a nondescript way—plaid shirt, inexpensive corduroy jeans. He is almost fifty, with a creased and worried face, and yet, curiously enough, resembles a young boy. He has tousled, sandy-colored hair; a prominent forehead; bright blue eyes; small features; and a knobby chin. He looks slight in stature, has the large upper torso and short legs of a small boy, and yet, like a small boy, indignantly claims otherwise. "I am *not* small! I am five-ten, an average height." He is very quick and eager and even in repose seems to be scurrying in confusion to keep pace with his enthusiasms. In short, he has the exuberance of a child, which invariably prompts his teenaged stepdaughter to smile maternally at him and say, to his utter confusion, "Phil is just sooo cute!"

He holds the book at a stiff arm's length and peers down his nose as he turns the pages. The pages rustle like leaves. Each is protected by a smoky interleaving made over a century ago by compressing dried reeds. The book is an inheritance from his grandmother whose Dutch ancestors settled in New York State in 1640. It is dated 1837 and contains poems, stories, letters, exhortations, and drawings, all penned by a variety of hands in tiny but elaborate script whose lines are as fine and faint as if drawn with the strand of a single hair. The inks used were once bright reds and greens and blues but have now faded to pale rose and umber and olive, and what was once the color of grapes is now brown. He pauses at a page on which is rendered in the minutest of details, the drawing of a peacock. Its every feather is more finely delineated than is every blade of grass in an Andrew Wyeth painting.

"Can you imagine?" he says. "The time it must have taken! Whoever did it must have sat around a fire for hours each night just drawing these feathers. What kind of life enabled someone to devote so much time to something like this?"

He replaces the slim volume and then withdraws a piano roll from the wall and inserts it into one of his player pianos. The keys begin to move and the room is filled with "The Enchanted Nymph," by Mischa Levitski. He listens but seems less enthralled by the music than he does by the moving keys being struck by an invisible hand. "A minor piece," he says. "Not one of his best. I got interested in restoring player pianos partly because of the music but most of all because I wanted it to seem as if the musician was right here in the same room, through all those years, playing just for me."

The only part of the house that has undergone extensive alterations through the years is the garage, which has progressively grown until it has now almost entirely devoured his backyard in order to accommodate his many restored antique automobiles. His collection has grown so large, in fact, that he has been forced to quarter many of his cars in neighbors' garages. Only a few favorites remain at home, each car meticulously and painstakingly restored to a state far superior to that when it was new. There is a silver 1947 MG-TC, identical to the one in which he captured his first racing trophy. There is a 1931 Pierce Arrow Lebaron Town Car, which he purchased from film star Harold Lloyd. "Come here!" he says. "You've got to see it! You'll love it! It gives you such a feel for the thirties. See how plush the rear seat upholstery is! Now look at the driver's seat. Black leather. It's very stark, but durable. It was done that way on purpose. It was a deliberate attempt to degrade the chauffeur, to remind him by the starkness of his domain of his inferior station in life."

He stops beside a black 1918 Packard Twin Six Fleetwood Town Car, reaches inside to the dashboard, and flicks on the head lamps. There is an audible *poof* and then a thin whisper of smoke as the gas-operated lamps are ignited. The flames flicker and dance inside their glass cases. "I just flashed," he says. "My wife and I and Dan Guerney and his wife are driving through the desert on our way to Palm Springs. Dan was at the wheel when we got into a bit of a dice with a lady in a Mustang who wanted to pass us. Dan went berserk, and all the way through the desert we diced with that lady in my nineteen eighteen Packard."

Hill has a particular fondness for that Packard because it has been in his family since it was new and before he was born. It is the first automobile in his conscious memory, and so it is that car that he associates with many childhood memories and with the igniting of his passion for the automobile. As a youth during the depression, he remembers being driven to school by a chauffeur in that Packard. He remembers the humiliation he felt upon pulling up to his school and waiting while the chauffeur got out and opened the door for him. He inherited that Packard from his aunt before she died in 1959, and it was the first car he ever restored. He had been sports car racing for almost five years, when, in 1953, he began to suffer severe stomach pains that were diagnosed as an ulcer. Under doctor's orders, he quit racing for a year and, to pass time, began to restore the old Packard. When he finished the restoration a year later, his ulcer had subsided and he was determined to resume his racing career at all costs and to its ultimate conclusion. During those ensuing racing years, he continued to purchase and restore old cars as a hobby. A few years after he left racing, his hobby had become a very lucrative business, one that he still operates today out of a surprisingly modest garage in downtown Santa Monica. The concrete building is painted a dull mustard color, and its windows are painted gray so that nothing inside is visible from the street. There is no sign over the door to indicate the building's owners (Hill and Vaughn) or their enterprise (The Restoration of Antique Cars). The only form of address to be found are the numbers 1428 above the garage door. Inside, the garage is clean and brightly lighted. Its employees are mostly young men in their late twenties, except for the two owners (Ken Vaughn is fifty-four) and their upholsterer, an elderly Italian with whom Hill invariably stops to pass time in his native language. Hill speaks Italian and French fluently and a number of other foreign languages haltingly.

There are about a dozen cars in various states of restoration. Each restoration varies, but a typical one might take from one to two years at a cost to the car's owner of over $75,000. The restorers, unlike one's neighborhood garage mechanic, quote no estimates. They rely simply on the trust of their customers to whom they send an itemized bill each month. For instance, in one corner of the garage there is a wine-and-buff colored 1931 Packard Eight with 79,000 miles on its odometer and the nameplate of its original purchaser—Princess Jacqueline Broglie—implanted in its walnut dashboard. The car, virtually completed at a cost of almost $50,000 and two years of labor, is in a state so pristine that before it leaves the shop Phil Hill himself (he does much of the work on each car and has calloused hands to show for it) will wipe any remnants of dust off the waxed engine. What is holding up its delivery to its owner, a Santa Monica ophthalmologist, is an almost inaudible squeak in its dashboard that has driven Hill to the point of distraction. "It should not be there!" he says. If necessary he will take the entire dashboard apart again to discover the source of that squeak.

In another part of the garage there is an Offenhauser engine being assembled by a pale, thin young man wearing bifocals. The young man is sitting on a stool under a bright conical light measuring the distance from each of the engine's exhaust ports with a micrometer. He works with the same deliberate care and precision as would Dr. Christian Barnard preparing for a heart transplant.

Laid out on four boxes near the Offenhauser is the completely stripped frame of a 1927 Packard. The frame has just been sprayed with a coat of purple enamel paint, which is the frame's original color. The car's clutch and pressure plate have also just been painted purple. Every screw and bolt and color in a Hill-restored car is original with each car. There are no anachronisms. Once, admiring an old car at an antique car show, Hill grew agitated at the sight of a screw that was not indiginous to that car's history. He lost all interest in the car. He will either purchase his antique parts at a junkyard, an auction, an antique car show, such as the one held at Hershey, Pennsylvania, each year; or, if necessary, he will have that part reproduced in his own machine shop at a cost that is often hundreds of times more expensive than was the original.

"I'm a perfectionist," says Hill. "But most of all every car I restore must be pretty damned sound mechanically. I can't bear something that's all wrong. All my cars must first run right, like they were intended to. I use all my old cars." Hill remembers specifically a night when he and his wife went to a party at the home of movie director John Frankenheimer. They grew bored and left early. On their way home they stopped to eat at a drive-in hamburger stand. The parking lot was filled with teenagers in souped-up, chrome-wheeled Mustangs, Corvettes, and Camaros. Hill was dressed in a black tuxedo; his wife wore a mink stole. They parked and, like the teenagers around them, ate their hamburgers in their car which just happened to be a 1918 Packard Twin 6 Fleetwood Town Car. Unlike those teenagers, however, they did not adjourn to the backseat to make out.

"I have this tremendous acquisitive streak that just won't quit," says Hill. "I love to go to old car shows and just mill around all those bolts and nuts—the parts, not the people—and search for maybe an old bumper or a carburator I need. It's a symbolic search. I have a collecting passion to have things no one else has. It's as if, by possessing it, you have a certain distinction even if that worth is artificial. Over the years, though, my old car passions have changed. Now I can go to another collector's house and enjoy his car without envying it in an evil way.

"But mostly," he adds, "I restore old cars because it is a great chunk of what I can do well. I love rebuilding old cars. I get a tremendous gratification from taking something in a state of decay and forming it back into the thing it was meant to be. I'm so tuned in to the historical aspect of restoring old cars that it's as if I was in on the birth of the automobile, as if, by restoring an old car, I lived in another time."

Hill's acquisitiveness, then, is not sterile. It is not merely a desire to possess by osmosis the past that lies beyond his experience but rather to share in that past by contributing to it. He gets less pleasure from possessing a restored car than he does from restoring one. But since his restorations are invariably superior to their original state, what he considers to be a restoring of the past is actually a perfecting of it. He puts the past into a more perfect order than it ever was for the same reason that a writer puts order into the chaos of reality, so that, in retrospect, it can be more easily understood. Because if Hill's acquisitiveness is overshadowed by anything in his life, it is by his compulsive, almost uncontrollable inquisitiveness. More than anything, he wants to understand. Years ago that inquisitiveness was channeled almost solely into his fathoming of the automobile and, later, racing and, finally, death. But today his mind is a prism of diffracted light. His curiosity shoots everywhere, to the serious as well as the trivial. Through the prism of his every sentence flash a dozen disjointed curiosities, "Why is that? What does that mean? Who could do such a thing?" He disassembles his wife's hairdryer for no other reason than to see how it works. Disenchanted by its cheap construction, he leaves it in shambles and she is forced to pay to have it put back together again. At night, he reads himself to sleep with medical books, not because he is sick or a hypochondriac but simply because he is curious about the workings of his body. Passing a newspaper vending machine, he is caught by the headlines. He stoops down to read of a young father who murdered his child and then kept the body in the trunk of his car for twelve days. "Who could do that?" says Hill, not with a self-satisfied emotional disgust but with a true, cold, intellectual curiosity. "What kind of man could do that?"

Today, Philip Toll Hill is most inquisitive about himself. He is firmly committed to the principle that the unexamined life is not worth living. He wonders daily, "Why did I do that?" His day was ruined recently when a man whose intelligence he respected told him that "there must be something wrong with me that I like Glenn Miller. What can't I see?" Hill often tries to understand himself by returning to the past, partly to that past beyond his experience, but mostly to that past within it, the past of his childhood. Daily, he flashes back, painstakingly reconstructing each memory down to its minutest detail so that he can more satisfactorily understand that past, himself, and, most of all, the reason why a man of his intelligence devoted so great a chunk of his life to an endeavor, automobile racing, that he now calls "meaningless" and whose practitioners he characterizes as "insane."

PART TWO

"I have been accused of having a fabulous memory," says Philip Toll Hill, a forty-nine-year-old restorer of antique automobiles and the only American ever to win a Formula One World Driving Championship. "I can remember the day the rabbits got loose in the yard. I was precisely three and one-quarter years of age. I cannot eat asparagus because I remember the day I ate asparagus and went off to nursery school. As a teenager I used to stand on street corners with my friends and identify the year, make, and model of every automobile that went by. I can still remember those cars. For years I could talk endlessly about such things, as if by remembering them I was implying that I knew everything about my childhood, as if I was remembering my childhood. I suspect such a memory now. It is an excuse for blotting out one's real childhood, one's overall impression of that childhood, which, for me now, is one of confusion, fear, and chaos."

Hill's early years were filled with privilege and deprivation. At a period in history, the thirties, when most Americans were struggling merely to subsist, his childhood in an old, Spanish-Mediterranean house in the suburbs of Santa Monica, California, was peopled by servants, chauffeurs, music tutors, and an indulgent aunt who bought him his first automobile when he was twelve years old. He was deprived, however, in less tangible ways. Like many offspring of wealthy parents in those days, his life seemed nothing more than a succession of taboos and restrictions meant to protect him from the physical injury and social deficiencies associated with the lives of the poor. He could not play any of the usual sports, baseball or football, and to this day harbors a fear of catching a thrown ball; and he could not date at the same age as his less affluent contemporaries. He says of his youth, "We well-to-do kids were terribly envious of the others. The kids from poor families seemed to have freedom denied us. We'd been sheltered while they roamed free."

One year, for instance, Hill was taken out of school and tutored privately because his mother had heard of a polio epidemic she did not want her son exposed to. Such pampering would eventually produce a youth both withdrawn and introverted, and one terribly deficient in forming even the most rudimentary social relationships, a deficiency that would remain with him through much of his adult life. "Maybe it's me," he says today. "I'm standoffish. I don't see something in myself that makes people misread me."

But those privileges and restrictions were not viewed only as protective devices by the wealthy parents of that day. They were viewed mainly as proof of parental affection by people who viewed such affection not as an emotion felt and expressed in private but as a public display that existed only when expressed in visible terms. For the rich, affection had to be seen to exist, seen especially by the poor to whom it was intended as proof that the latter were deficient, not only in their material possessions but also in their filial devotion. The rich degraded the poor even in their parenthood just as they degraded their chauffeurs in their limousines by appointing their own rear-seats with the plushest upholstery and the driver's seat in stark, durable leather.

Hill's mother, Lela Long Hill, born in 1896, was a descendant of French farmers who left their native country in 1812 and settled in St. Louis, Missouri. She was, according to Hill, an austere, pampered, domineering woman of marked contradictions. She was a fervid religionist who wrote and published religious tracts and hymns such as "Jesus Is the Sweetest Name I Know" and who contributed great sums of money to Billy Graham's evangelical crusades. Often, she forced her young son to stand with her in the rear of a revival tent for upwards of twelve hours listening to the fiery admonitions of some backwoods preacher. On the other hand, in her youth she was said to have had a "serious" flirtation with a famous Cleveland Indian baseball player whose name her family has conveniently forgotten. She also wrote a frivolous ragtime tune called "Down at Miami's Beaches" that she penned during what would later prove to have been an atypical but memorable and idyllic honeymoon in Miami with her dashing, ex-navy lieutenant husband.

Hill's father was a serious man whose Dutch ancestors came to the New World in 1640 and settled in Schenectady, New York. He attended Union College in Schenectady, as had every male member of the Hill line since the school's inception in the late 1700s. The line was broken, however, by his son who, in an act of rebellion, enrolled at USC in 1944. After leaving the Navy after World War I, Hill's father alternately served as the city editor of the *Schenectady Gazette*, a sales manager for the Mack Truck Company in Miami, and finally, from 1935 until his death in 1951, as postmaster for the city of Santa Monica. Hill remembers his father as "an unloving man" whose only admonition to his son upon sending him off to Hollywood Military School was to be "a good little soldier." His father also trained him to greet women with a bow and a click of his heels, a habit he has yet to break and that still causes him great humiliation. ("Jesus, but I can't stop! It's a damned reflex!")

"We always had a considerable amount of regimentation around the house," says Hill. "Our father believed in a strict upbringing, and we were carefully disciplined. My mother liked to sleep late, and my brother, sister, and I were trained to tiptoe until it was time for her to be up. A buzzer rang, which announced to the help that she was awake. Then we could play. I called my father 'sir' and we could never seem to establish any kind of really close relationship. Whenever I did some small act of rebellion, he would force me to stand at attention while he lectured me on respect. 'I'll teach you to respect me,' he would say. I would be silent, but all the time I was standing there I would think to myself, 'I won't ever respect you! You can't make me respect you!'"

Hill and his siblings particularly dreaded the call to dinner at "the big table," where the children were forced to eat in silence, heads lowered in shame, while around them servants hovered in silence and their parents raged. Each night at dinner, Lela Long Hill and Philip Toll Hill, Sr., savaged each other across the length of the table. Their bitterness may have surfaced in disagreements over politics (she was a Republican, he a Democrat) and religion, but its wellspring was simply in the dissipation of their marriage. More than one night, the senior Hill would come home drunk and strike his wife in the presence of the children. His son remembers in particular a night when he was fourteen. His father was about to strike his mother, when he intervened and pushed him away. "It was the first time I ever struck my father," says Hill. "I had this feeling of power over him, finally. I remember it was a good feeling."

Hill's rebellion was not confined only to his father but would surface in response to his mother, too, only much later in life. When she was on her deathbed, she pleaded with her twenty-four-year-old son that he be baptized as her dying wish. Remembering all those years of her religious sermons to her, he refused.

The only real affection Hill remembers in his childhood came from his aged, divorced aunt, Mrs. Helen Grassi. She was something of a recluse, he says, always feeling poorly and remaining in bed throughout the day while her servants ran the house. Her only source of satisfaction seemed to come from spoiling her nephew. She encouraged his interest in cars, beginning with her own 1918 Packard, which she let him drive at the age of nine, and continuing on through a used Model-T Ford, which she bought him in 1939 for $40, an extravagant amount to spend on a twelve-year-old at the time. By that point, Hill had already been fascinated by automobiles for ten years. He could identify on sight the make, model, and year of every car made in America to that time. After school, while classmates played sports, he walked through junkyards, hypnotized by rusted wrecks. His fascination with the automobile was less an act of rebellion against his parents, whose attitude toward his passion was more of indifference than disapproval, than it was a genuine obsession.

"Ever since I can remember," he says today, "I have expressed myself via the automobile. It is difficult to explain why kids freak out over the things they do. It would seem to me that, unless a person had pretty powerful feelings of inadequacy, he wouldn't have the need to turn on to such a symbolic little deal. I guess I sensed at an early age that I was in an insane environment and that my only escape was in something that had structure, that made sense. I listened to all those arguments, explosions, and then was told that everything was perfect. I was never free to express myself, to say, 'Hey, wait a minute, everything around here is all screwed up!' Instead, I was led to believe that there was something wrong with me, that I was a fool to see things that way. It wasn't until the car thing that I felt any worth. Cars gave me worth. As a kid driver I could do something important—and correctly—that no one else my age could do. I was known as the kid who could drive. I could take cars apart, too, and put the nuts and bolts back together again so that the thing would work. And when it worked they could not prove me wrong. It was ultimately fathomable. I could understand the workings of cars, which made sense, in a way I could never understand the workings of people, which did not make sense. People have intangibles and cars don't. Cars are easy to master; they hold no threat; and, if you're careful, they can't hurt you like people can."

To retain his distinctness, Phil Hill had to constantly remain a step ahead of his contemporaries. He was the first of his age group to learn how to drive, and later, when others followed, he outstripped them again by his daring on the city streets of Santa Monica. "I became Phil Hill, 'the gutsy driver,'" he says. In military school, he formed a friendship with George Hearst, the grandson of publisher William Randolph Hearst, whose family had a dirt track on their vast estate in Santa

Monica Canyon. After school each day, Hill and George Hearst would go there and stage impromptu, two-car races. For Hill it was only a short evolutionary step from such larking to the more serious and organized automobile racing that would dominate his life from the late '40s to the late '60s.

"As a young sports-car racer in California, I was a nutcase," says Hill. "I was driven. My own worst enemy. I drove on instinct, not intellect. In practice I would go out and immediately go too fast and have to sort of scramble around. Then I'd progressively slow down, or what seemed like slowing down, because in fact I was going faster the whole time. I'd arrange it so that I'd have to react to danger rather than doing a heady job. I literally did not think about the possible dangers. The things I did badly I conveniently forgot about. Somebody would say, 'Now, about that time you went down the escape road,' and I would reply, 'What do you mean? I didn't go down any escape road,' and really believe what I was saying.

"At the time, I never thought about why I was racing. I just had these greedy little needs that were not being fulfilled at home and could be fulfilled by racing. My parents, by the way, were apprehensive about it, but they did not object. They felt it was just a phase I was going through. I really loved those early days. It was such a simple life. People were not so serious then, and there was less pressure. It was something I was totally devoted to because it was something I could do so well, do better than most, in fact. And, like all sports, it gave you answers right away. You either won or lost, and you knew it immediately. Winning is a happy experience in any sport. But because those victories are only symbolic they have to be repeated daily or else their satisfaction fades. And there *is* a particularly great thrill in getting into a fresh, beautiful racing car on a particularly beautiful day and beginning practice on a circuit that hasn't yet been soiled by rain or patches of oil. All doubts, all anxieties, all memories of past painful struggles fade away before the magic of this occasional purity, and I am at one with the car."

By 1953, Hill had progressed to a high level of international racing competition that brought an abrupt and traumatic end to those simple and idyllic sports car days of his youth. He was suddenly forced to confront the dangers around him. At the Carrera Panamerican, a five-day marathon race in Mexico, a driver was killed before his eyes, and a few months later at the Twenty-four Hours of Le Mans, Tom Cole, an American driver, was also killed. Hill began to brood about these deaths and he could no longer avoid the fact that he was now involved in a sport in which people were crashing and dying around him. He developed serious anxieties, which manifested in a stomach ulcer so severe he could eat only baby food. Finally, in 1954, he was forced to quit racing under doctor's orders. He returned to Santa Monica, where, with his brother, he took to restoring his aunt's old Packard. It was a restful preoccupation, which lasted a year, during which time his ulcer subsided. He decided to return to racing again, this time determined to pursue his career to its ultimate conclusion. He returned, however, with a new respect for the hazards of his sport, which both greatly affected his attitude toward racing and his style of performance in it. He became ambivalent toward a sport, which, on an instinctive level, he could do so well and took such pleasure in, and on the other hand, which he increasingly began to realize, on an intellectual level, was destructive and without meaning. For years, this ambivalence was not consciously realized. It surfaced, however, in subliminal ways, such as in Hill's increasingly paranoid anxieties about the preparation of his cars, which, to satisfy him, had to achieve an impossible level of perfection. Hill's driving style also changed drastically from one of reckless instinct to one of meticulous intellectual discipline. In order to rationalize continuing to race, he had formed the conclusion that a driver affects his odds in relation to the dangers of his sport to such a high degree that he could learn to drive on the edge of disaster without ever breaching that line. Over the next few years, Hill's new discipline became evident in his success in endurance sports car events like the Twenty-four Hours of Le Mans. "I was always a much better endurance driver than Formula One driver," he says today. "I had the discipline to pace myself in long distance events that other drivers didn't. Some guys could never stop from getting into dices early in an endurance race. The minute someone was alongside of them, they started to sprint and burned themselves out. I had the patience to hold back."

After years of sports car success, Hill finally became a Formula One driver for Enzo Ferrari in 1958. But by 1961, his repressed anxieties about the dangers of his sport would surface dramatically. These anxieties surfaced for a number of reasons. A Formula One car is nothing more than spindly axles and frame, an aluminum cockpit, and a powerful engine. It is the fastest and best handling of all racing machines but also the flimsiest. "You don't become tuned in to the subtle dangers of those little cars until you have had some time in them," says Hill. "Compared with the bulkier [enclosed bodied] sports cars, they seem fantastically easy to drive, but they bite you in a far more serious way. You can lose control of them so fast it's incredible."

Furthermore, after the depletion of Ferrari's Formula One ranks through tragic deaths, Hill found himself and Count Wolfgang von Trips the two senior Ferrari drivers with the best opportunity to win a world title. Hill became obsessed with that possibility partly from a competitive urge to excel and partly from a desire to get approval from a man, Enzo Ferrari, whom he described on one hand as "cold, a hard bastard whose only ambition in life was to build the greatest racing machine ever" and on the other hand as "a man I respected, and from whom I wanted more than anything affection and for him to be a good daddy to me." To Hill it seemed he had miraculously been given another opportunity to restore the past, to perfect a relationship with his own father that in reality had been disastrous. In fact, Hill's eight-year relationship with Il Commendatore was every bit as chaotic as had been his relationship with his father. Hill was repulsed by Ferrari's "pompous, patrician superiority," so similar to his father's, and by Ferrari's disdainful attitude toward his drivers. "The drivers rarely saw him," says Hill. "Usually at the start of the season there would be a message that Mr. Ferrari wanted you to stop by and say hello. I still see clearly those dark offices as I waited, waited for my audience. In later years I saw many instances of Ferrari's mastery in putting even the most important visitors off balance with long heel-coolings in those dim chambers. You would wait the standard half hour or so, and then be shown in for a light bantering exchange. '*Come vai*? How's your love life?' That sort of thing. And Ferrari's language could be x-ratedly blunt. Maybe it was the incongruity of that Roman-coin face uttering such words that surprised me. But to this day I do not know whether we were just tools tolerated as necessary evils in his grand scheme of things. When one of us did win, it was as if Ferrari felt the victory was doubly his—he had managed to build a car that was not only better than all the other cars but that was also good enough to foil even his driver's natural destructiveness."

Hill's relationship with Ferrari was both ambivalent and one-sided. Because of his own psychic needs, Hill seemed to be constantly trying to create an affection in himself for a man who, on certain levels, he detested, and then to wrest from that same man a reciprocal affection that either he did not feel or else was simply incapable of expressing. Often during those eight years, Hill contemplated quitting the Ferrari team, usually after one of Il Commandatore's tongue-lashings over the breaking of a car or what he saw as an inadequate driving performance. For years, however, Hill could not make that break. "It would be like rebelling against your own father," he said. (It wasn't until 1962 that Hill and Ferrari severed their relationship amidst mutual recriminations. Ferrari accused Hill of becoming an overly cautious driver and yet of breaking too many cars, while Hill accused Ferrari of saddling him with a deficient automobile. Both accusations may have been justified. For years the two men did not speak. Hill was haunted by a nightmare in which Ferrari, shrunken to the size of a small doll, angrily berated Hill for betraying him. The nightmare was finally put to rest recently when the two men had an amiable reconciliation.)

Hill admits he would have found a much more "rational milieu" in the Lotus racing camp of Colin Chapman, a cool, efficient Briton with flowing gray hair and a Bengal Lancer's mustache. At the time, Chapman had a reputation for being his sport's most innovative designer. He may have been, in fact, too innovative in his attempts to make a racing machine of the lightest possible construction (in contrast to Ferrari, whose cars were always of a sturdy, oftentimes bulky construction), as his cars often literally fell apart in the driver's hands. One driver of a Lotus attempted a sharp turn and snapped off the steering, while another heard a 'thunk' and looked back to see his car's fuel tank sitting on the track. There was a time during those years, says Hill, when members of the racing fraternity felt that Chapman was morally negligent regarding the safety of his drivers, although over the years his concepts of design have become widely accepted and copied. Hill's decision not to join the Lotus team, however, had nothing to do with the delicate construction of a Chapman car, which, in fact, Hill has always insisted would have helped him become a more successful Formula One driver. His decision to remain with Ferrari was based partly on his fascination with that passionate, almost infantile Italian temperament so similar to his own and in marked contrast to the coolness of the British, whom Hill describes as affecting "that bloody, R.A.F., stiff-upper-lip crap." Hill realized that Chapman would never fulfill his psychic needs in the way

Ferrari might. Even when that Hill-Ferrari relationship did not meet Hill's expectations, he could reconcile himself to the knowledge that "a demanding, accusing, unforgiving father" was better than none.

Hill was not the only Ferrari driver to identify so closely with Il Commendatore. To a lesser degree, almost every driver in the Ferrari stable saw their leader as a father figure. Ferrari sensed this and used his drivers' childlike need for his approval to prod them on to greater efforts. The results were sometimes tragic. There was a high attrition rate among Ferrari team drivers. Says Hill, "There was, though, something about the ambience at Ferrari that did, indeed, seem to spur drivers to their death. Perhaps it was the intense sibling-rivalry atmosphere Ferrari fostered, his failure to rank the drivers and his fickleness with favorites. Luigi Musso died at Rheims while striving to protect his fair-haired-boy status against the encroaching popularity of the Englishmen, Peter Collins and Mike Hawthorne. And Collins, a firm favorite while he was living in the little hotel within earshot of the factory, began to get a Ferrari cold shoulder when he married Louise King and went to live on a boat in Monte Carlo. Peter was dead within the year. Time and again I felt myself bristling as Ferrari used Richie Ginther and Dan Guerney to needle me. And certainly Trips and I were locked in direct combat."

Ferrari fueled the rivalry between his two senior drivers, Hill and Count Wolfgang von Trips, by refusing to name either man his team captain during the '61 season. He merely sat back expectantly and watched them fight it out for the World Championship, which, in either case, would be his, too. The results were predictable. The two drivers constantly embroiled themselves in games of one-upmanship. For example, going into the French Grand Prix at Rheims, Hill was leading von Trips for the championship, nineteen points to eighteen. He was also noticeably faster during that race's practice, which, he admits, "gave me a guilty surge of pleasure." Von Trips complained to Ferrari that Hill had been given a faster car. He wanted Hill to drive his car in practice to prove that it was slower. Says Hill, "I didn't really want to. After all, it might *not* be running right and they *might* fix it so that it would be faster than mine." Hill acquiesced only when he heard that there was an oil spill on the track, which he could use as an excuse if von Trips's car was noticeably slower than his own. Once on the track, he discovered, however, that the oil spill was negligible and certainly not enough to influence his driving and so, he says, "I really let it all hang out. I flew. When

I came into the pits, Trips was the picture of gloom. I said, 'I'm sorry I wasn't able to turn on a good one with all that damn oil all over, but it doesn't feel half bad to tell you the truth.'" Hill's time in von Trips's car had been almost a second faster than von Trips's time, and there was no further talk about Hill having a faster car.

Like Hill, von Trips wanted more than anything to become the first man of his nationality to win a Formula One Championship. It would help placate his parents, who had always looked with foreboding on his racing career, he said. They did not think it the proper endeavor for a German nobleman who could trace his lineage back four centuries, and whose family still lived in its ancestral home, the 850–year-old Hemmersbach castle.

Von Trips, with his angular, almost gaunt, aristocrat's face, was the archetype for the wealthy, careless, ephemeral, and slightly decadent play-boy one so often associates with European automobile racers. And although he identified strongly with his image as a racer and was serious about it and his career, he nevertheless lived a swinger's life that was in marked contrast to the brooding Phil Hill's. "When I am away from the track, I forget about racing," said von Trips. "But Phil, he just hangs around Modena"—the home of Ferrari and his factories. "He has no home over here. He just hangs around hotels all the time. It must make him sick."

Von Trips's driving style was as careless as his lifestyle. He was described in the *New York Times* in 1961 as being the kind of racer who could "never control his impetuousness early in races," and who at times was "slightly inaccurate" when trying to maneuver his car on a track. He had a long history of crashing on the first or second lap of a race, that same article went on. He had crashed on the first lap of his first tryout at Monza in 1956, and again at Monza on the first lap of the 1958 Grand Prix. He crashed on the second lap of the Grand Prix of Monaco in 1959 and also on the first lap of two successive Targo Florios. His compatri-ots called him "Count von Crash," a nickname he did not find totally disconcerting.

Hill, on the other hand, lived the life of a recluse at the little Reale Hotel in Modena. He breakfasted alone and in the afternoon often could be seen prowling through the Ferrari factory scrutinizing the produc-tion of each new racing machine. His interests outside of racing had broadened over the years, but they were essentially solitary ones—fine wines, classical music, restored player pianos and antique automobiles, and, on occasion, dinner with a beautiful woman. (At thirty-four, he was still a bachelor.) And all of his interests, like his driving style, were spare, disciplined, and thoroughly thought-out. He was one of the safest racing car drivers ever because he left nothing to chance. He thoroughly intellectualized every aspect of his sport, which, in the summer of 1961, had brought him to the point at which he had begun to intellectualize and express openly his ambivalence about it. He talked about his fear of death and his increasing awareness that what he was doing was meaningless in the scheme of things. Such expressions had always been taboo among his fellow drivers. To become successful, it seems, a racing car driver must develop a blinkered view of life for the same reason a race horse must be blinkered; to focus all his concentration and energies on a single endeavor, his sport, the perfection of which is the primary goal of any professional athlete. (As Pete Rose, for example, has said, "I live for two hundred hits a year.")

Without this single-focus view, it would be difficult for an athlete to rationalize devoting his life to the mastering of a game. Everything has value, even a game, but an athlete can't question whether that value is proportionate to the time and energy expended, to the exclusion of other worthy endeavors, and to the dangers he must endure in perfecting his sport. The moment an athlete questions whether the former is worth the latter is the moment his concentration is shattered. For most athletes, such a moment results in a diminution of success and ultimately in failure, which for a racing car driver can be terminal. In short, the moment a racing car driver first contemplates death—the *possibility* of death—in his sport, the more likely its actuality becomes. Graham Hill, a British racer for twenty years, knew how to avoid such diffusion of concentration. He said, "I don't think about it. I don't want to think about it. I just want to bloody well get on with it." Hill, his American counterpart, found that in the summer of 1961 he could no longer sustain such an attitude. He had lost his single-minded devotion to his sport, feared that soon his concentration would be shattered completely, which would result finally in his death.

"I felt I was most single-minded about racing in 1960," says Hill. "Although I finished third for the World Title, I have always felt that was my best driving year. The following year, I had found satisfactions other than in racing—my piano rolls, for example—and I was not putting as much of my inner self into racing. I was a much better driver than Trips, but I have always felt I backed into the title in 'sixty-one. I was aware, by then, that I was no longer as gung-ho as my colleagues. I was wondering what the hell I was doing as a racing driver. I had been to too many races and to too many funerals, and a battle was mounting within me. There was an inner drive to excel, but there was also a tremendous desire to stay alive and in one piece. Some drivers never entertain that conflict. They go right through their entire careers without a hint of it. I think Wolfgang von Trips was one of them. He was tremendously turned on by everything about racing. The driving, the adoration. His inner image of himself seemed to be as a racing hero. I had always hated the notoriety and I never thought much about the money. Racing had always been just a compulsive turn-on with me. But now as I look back I find it hard to believe that anyone doing something as irrational as gambling so openly with his life can be totally free of conflict. What you do, of course, as a driver is either quit or accept the risk and then forget about it. The danger comes, I think, in taking caution with you in the car, chewing at your instinctive responses. Doubt must be left in the pit along with your spare goggles and street shoes, or it can kill you.

"But here's another thing about racers. Their machine can always take a large part of the blame for their failure. How do you know when a driver, suddenly uncomfortable about dangers, doesn't subconsciously arrange for his machine to have mechanical failures? I've seen drivers like Tony Brooks, for instance, a man with marvelous technical ability and a marvelous machine, whose machines always seemed to break the year they decided to quit. Brooks's wife had been chipping away at him—'Tony, we've been going to too many funerals!'—and all the while he tried to explain that those guys had died because their cars were destined to break or the guy did this or that wrong, or countless other rational explanations. The following year, however, when Brooks announced this would be his last year, *his* car was plagued with mechanical failure. Nothing serious, but just stuff that wouldn't let his car work. I don't think it was the car but his unconscious desire to break the car to protect himself."

Because Hill had begun to encroach on areas his fellow drivers did not want to contemplate, they began to call him "Hamlet in a helmet," a term not of admiration but of ridicule for that gloomy, introspective and ultimately doomed Dane. "Whenever I got the least bit serious, they'd turn off," says Hill. "I'm not sure today I wasn't deliberately antagonistic. I was possibly deliberately putting myself at odds with them and their attitude toward their sport as if to reaffirm my own emerging attitude. It was like my growing interest in piano rolls. I was immersed in them, which took away some of my concentration from racing. I think I did it deliberately in preparation of quitting. It was the same with my racing colleagues. I was painting myself into a corner with them so that I would be forced into an action, quitting racing, that I was still ambivalent toward."

On September 10, 1961, at Monza, Italy, prior to the running of the Grand Prix of Italy, Count Wolfgang von Trips was leading his teammate, Phil Hill, for the World Championship, thirty-three points to twenty-nine. The margin was so close, however, that a victory for either man in that race would ensure him of the title. The race began uneventfully on a warm, hazy Sunday afternoon with a brisk southerly breeze fluttering the dozens of banners lining the track and swaying the branches of the thousands of trees covering what had once been a Royal Italian Hunting Preserve, but that had been a race track since 1922. Midway through the second lap of the race, von Trips attempted to pass Jimmy Clark in a Lotus at a speed of about 150 mph. He misjudged the distance between the two cars, nudged Clark's car with his own, and lunged out of control up an embankment, through a wire restraining fence and into a crowd of spectators. Fourteen spectators were killed and twenty-five injured. Von Trips was also killed. Hill, still on the circuit, was aware that von Trips had crashed but was ignorant of the extent of the damage, and so he continued to drive his race. He had learned to avoid letting such events intrude upon his race concentration years earlier, in 1955, when at the Twenty-four Hours of Le Mans, he saw a Mercedes-Benz plunge into a crowd, killing 85 people. For a number of laps during that race, he drove as in a dream, clouded by absurdity of what he was then doing. Suddenly a white Mercedes flashed by. The car was being driven by Sterling Moss, then only twenty-three years old but already a cold, hard, clear-headed professional who had learned early to perform business as usual in the face of even total disaster. It was a lesson Hill would not forget, and so at Monza in 1961, despite von Trips's crash, he drove an almost flawless race to victory and the World Championship.

Hill received the news of von Trips's death at the same moment he was being awarded he victory laurels. He began to cry. "Every racing car driver who has been around for any length of time has had to cope with the deaths of other drivers," said Hill. "I was saddened by his death and I felt terribly sorry for his parents, who had wanted him to quit racing, but I was not shattered. Does that make sense?"

And yet, the death of Count Wolfgang von Trips would eventually affect Phil Hill and the course of his career in a way no other racing death would. It affected him not because of any emotional attachment between him and Trips ("We were never really friends") or because it had tainted his World Championship, but because it was the one death during the course of his career that he would not be permitted to forget. He had learned, by then, that one's despair over the death of a compatriot would always be diminished with the passing of time. Time wove each solitary death into the entire fabric of such deaths until it was no longer singularly distinguishable and tragic. In the case of von Trips's death, time would only heighten Hill's despair and firm up his resolve to quit racing.

"My defenses were equal to the shock of his death," says Hill. "They were strained to the utmost, however, by the ordeal of his funeral. There were three separate services. The first was held in the Trips castle near Cologne. Richie Ginther and I had traveled from Modena to serve as pallbearers. A funeral Mass was said at the castle and then a procession formed outside. It was raining, yet none of us wore raincoats or carried umbrellas. We walked a mile to the Trips's church. The pace was set by an old, old woman, all dressed in black and carrying a symbolic brass lantern. There was a band, also dressed in black, which played Chopin's funeral march. The casket was carried on Trips's personal Ferrari sports car, an open model, which, of course, had to be driven very slowly.

"At the church an interminable Mass was sung. Then the procession re-formed to go to the cemetery, perhaps another mile away. It was raining harder than ever. The Trips family chapel is situated on a knoll in the cemetery. The procession stopped at the foot of the knoll, eight of us clambered up the rise, slipping and sliding on the muddy earth with the very heavy casket. The last service was held and poor Trips was finally entombed. I have never experienced anything so profoundly mournful as that day."

PART THREE

During the first five years of his retirement from automobile racing, Philip Toll Hill, the only American ever to win a World Driving

Championship, continued to live the kind of solitary, almost reclusive life he had grown accustomed to over his first thirty-nine years. Except for a maid and a manservant, whom he had inherited from fellow racer Carroll Shelby, Hill lived alone in what had once been his parents' old Spanish-Mediterranean-style house in a quiet suburb of Santa Monica, California. Each day began as the last. His manservant, whose name was Coakley, would knock once on his bedroom door and, without waiting for a response, would enter the room carrying a sterling silver tea service, depositing it beside the bed on which Hill slept. Coakley would then say, "Good morning," and move to the window. With a vigorous flourish, he'd rip open the curtains, whose rustle invariably caused Hill to squint toward Coakley through a single, malevolent eye. Coakley would look out at the morning, sigh, and no matter what the weather—sun, rain, or smog—make the same detached response, "Well, Mahster, another dull day," and depart.

If Hill's life, now totally divorced from racing, was no longer as sensually stimulating as it once was, still it was not inactive. Each day he immersed himself in a hundred preoccupations, some of which, like his piano rolls and antique automobiles, he had pursued while racing, others of which he came to only after racing, and all of which were completely self-absorbed, if more than a bit sterile.

Three times a week he underwent vigorous routines of weightlifting and calisthenics so that even today, at forty-nine, he retains the muscular chest and arms and trim waist not only of a much younger man but of a much younger man who lifts weights. He became an omnivorous reader of everything from medical books to novels to articles on extrasensory perception, heredity, the continuity of human experience, human behavior, and dying. His education was at times ploddingly slow and at other times so breathtakingly swift, the resulting ideas forming in leaps and bounds, that he felt "trippy." He formulated labyrinthine theories of his own on such topics as sleep ("an impossible reconciliation can exist in one's mind that will somehow, not only be smoothed over, but made rational by sleep") and life ("a continual bleeding off of frustrations which ultimately evolves away from those frustrations") and, naturally, death. He decided that death was not a journey to nothingness but rather a transcendence to a new state in which the dead become part of the cosmic unity of all creation, past, present, and future.

Hill pursued his new interests with a fervor similar to that with which he had pursued racing. He did not rest until he had mastered each one, although his pursuit was now less a compulsiveness of the possessed than the zeal of the convert—a fine distinction, to be sure, between madman and saint. Unlike his pursuit of racing, his new interests were not attached to any single-mindedness. In fact, he seemed to jump from interest to interest in midstream as if in a panic that he was on the verge of drowning in lost time. Always, however, he returned, sometimes by the most circuitous of routes, to each interest and perfected it. His satisfactions had been perceptibly altered too. They were no longer merely the negative "bleeding off of frustrations" but were now the more positive delight and fulfilled wonder of a child. His most fascinating new toy was introspection. He used it unsparingly on himself ("Obviously I gravitated to the mastering of things instead of people because I always failed so miserably with the latter") in the hope that finally, with enough time and distance, he would come to an understanding of his past self and his obsession with automobile racing.

"If racers have one thing in common," says Phil Hill, "it is their gut-level desire to race. It is a blinding compulsion that transcends everything else. A racer digs getting into his machine and making it go faster than the last time. For him, that is the only real going anywhere. He is turned on by the action, but most of all by the possibility that he is doing something that could kill him. Most racers I know had unhappy childhoods. Their lives were chaotic. Racing was an outlet for pent-up aggressions of people who have always felt their lives—and they themselves—were inadequate. They try to put order into their lives by taking something dangerous, potentially chaotic, and imposing their order on it. It gives them worth. A racer believes he can make his deadly machine safe. He is playing God. A racer has all the qualities of other athletes, but he believes he has one more. He is one of the blessed. His sport *must* be deadly so that in competing and surviving his skill takes on mystical qualities. The best way to anger a racer is to tell him his skill is just reflexes, eyes, his ability to see at one hundred frames per second while the rest of humanity sees at fifty frames. They don't want to hear that. They want to hear that they have a power that transcends anything the rest of mortals have. They can prove they are one of the blessed by racing, by winning, but most of all, by surviving. It says something they want to hear about themselves. I have seen guys whose whole appearance was elevated by racing. Little, mousy, endomorphic guys, who took on heroic stature. Lance Reventlow, for example, was a soft guy, a weakling. It stuck out a mile. He looked like he had been brought up by a bunch of women. And yet, by racing, he became heroic. You feel almost God-like when you beat death. The cliché is that racers have a death-wish. They are trying to kill themselves. Nothing could be farther from the truth. The only racer I ever met who had a death-wish was Pedro Rodriguez. Most racers are more afraid of dying than anyone else. I remember sitting in restaurant once near a plate glass window that was rippling from a strong wind. The racers were the first ones to flee the window before it shattered. They are always the first ones to flee an accident on the track. They don't want to die, they just want the possibility of death. It is their way of reaffirming life, reaffirming *their* life, that they *are* alive. Without racing they don't feel they are really alive. Of course, this is not rational. The best way to stay alive is to not race at all. I could never say that until I quit racing.

"The fans are like racers, too. They don't come to see anyone get killed. They come to see this confrontation with death, the accident, the fiery crash, and then the racer walking away unharmed. It satisfies their animal bloodlust on one hand and their moral humanitarianism on the other. They are not only applauding the racer walking away, but they are applauding themselves for having such a noble satisfaction in wanting the racer to be unhurt. But the only way they or the racer can understand this whole drama is to see, over and over again, its manifestation in a crash. And if a racer ever does die, well, he chooses the way he goes, which is more than most of us can say. Death is not the worst thing in one's life. Take that poor girl, the Quinlan girl they are keeping alive with all those machines. A racer believes the quality of life is a hell of a lot more important than anything else. The problem with racing is, if you do it long enough and survive, your awareness of death becomes heightened. This causes you to lose your concentration, become less an instictive driver than a too-conscious one, which invariably slows you down and makes you more susceptible to death. It's not age and fading reflexes that slow down older racers but this heightened awareness, which they can't escape. I left racing because I could see where I was ultimately heading. I was symbolically playing over the same script in an erotic sort of way every weekend. I realized there was never going to be an ultimate gratification other than merely the avoidance of death. It occurred to me that I was not reaffirming that quality of my life just by avoiding the negative. I had also begun to feel some self-worth beyond racing and I no longer had to hear the things racing was telling me. But I had to fight to stay away. For a long while, I had to cut myself off from all aspects of it, lashing out against it to make sure I would never go back. Now that I can go to a race every once in a while, I have to defend my position for quitting to racing people who always felt I quit too soon. A lot of racers feel as I did, but they couldn't make the break. Take Mark Donaghue. He was always ambivalent towards it. He quit and then came back because he couldn't reconcile his feeling that he wasn't doing anything worthwhile with his compulsion to race. If I could have talked to him I might have saved him. I had gone through the same thing. I know. I only met Mark a few times, but I remember him vividly. He was the saddest person I have ever met."

On June 5, 1971, Philip Toll Hill married Alma Varanowski in a quiet ceremony in a church near his Santa Monica home. The bride was a thirty-three-year-old divorcee with an eleven-year-old daughter. The bridegroom, heretofore a confirmed bachelor, was forty-four and had a manservant (who would shortly be given his notice). Hill says of that wedding, "I never thought I'd get married. I had seen what happened to my parents so why should I jump into a pot of boiling oil? Besides, I had never really dug any one woman until I met my wife. Even then I fought marrying her. I'd invent a thousand little reasons for not getting married."

Hill's decision to marry finally was influenced to some extent by a number of the reasons that usually influence such a decision but more so by an incident at once so familiar to Hill and yet so incomparable to any previous experience that he can remember it to this day down to its most minute details.

"Alma's father had died," says Hill, "and they had the funeral in their house. They live in Phoenix, Arizona. They had fled their home in Germany and the Nazis after the Second World War. During the war they had all been displaced persons. They were always being shipped off somewhere, and to this day Alma has a terror of railroad stations. When they finally escaped to Arizona they lived a kind of pioneer life. Her father built this small house piece by piece with his own hands. You could see where he added a room here and then later added a bathroom, and so on. It was a simple, beautiful house. At the funeral, Alma's mother, they call her 'Mitti,' sat by her husband's casket while mourners passed by. They were mostly these big, tough, truck-driver types her husband had worked with. They were crying, these rough-looking men, and *she* was consoling *them!* She hugged and kissed these guys, and I remember amid the tears there was laughter, too. It was all so foreign to me. She threw her arms around me and kissed me. I hugged her and kissed her, too. Then I couldn't believe I had done it. It was something I would never do. My family never touched, never expressed emotion or affection like that. Funerals were dark, cloaked things in our family. People huddled in silence behind dark curtains. But here is the thing I will never forget. The casket was open, you see. You could see him, lying right there beside his wife as if he were just sleeping, and all the while Mitti was greeting mourners she was absentmindedly stroking his forehead, soothing him in a way I will never forget."

Sitting across from her husband at breakfast one morning recently, Alma Hill, a tall, striking blonde with a hearty, expansive nature, is telling stories about her husband's bachelor lifestyle. She speaks in that precise, clipped English of one for whom it is a second language. "Oh, it really was a scream!" she says. "I could never get past his servant, poor old Coakley. I used to call Philip at home when we were dating and Coakley would answer the phone. He always said the same thing. 'I shall see if the Mahster is indisposed,' Can you imagine!" Alma and her guest laugh, while her husband looks embarrassed at this remembrance of his past lifestyle. Then, finally, he too begins to laugh.

"Marriage was quite traumatic for Philip," she continues. "After all those years alone he acquired not only a wife but a daughter, too. I was very worried about how my daughter, Jennifer, and Philip would get along. My fears lasted until the morning after our wedding. Without knocking, Jennifer walked right into the bedroom with two cups of coffee and sat down on the bed. She handed one cup to Philip, and when I reached for the other, she began to sip from it. Well, I tell you, she just made herself at home, sitting there sipping coffee and talking to Phil as if he were *her* husband. She has adored him ever since. He is an excellent father, really, to Jennifer and to our two small children, Vanessa, who is almost four, and Derek, who is one year old. He is very strict but loving, too, and he never talks down to the children. I remember once, though, he lost his temper. Vanessa was crying and he started to shake her and scream at her. He completely lost control of himself and then suddenly he stopped. He had flashed to his own father and he was terrified that he would be like him. It *was* hard on Phil, after all those years. When we had Derek he decided that the house had got too small and so he was going to sell off his piano rolls to make room. He really didn't have to sell them, but he was determined to. It was a symbolic thing with him."

"I had spent those years acquiring those piano rolls and studying the mechanism of player pianos," says Hill. "I had a reputation for having the finest collection of rolls in the world—eighty-seven hundred of them. When a record company wanted to tape-record those rolls, I refused to let them take the pianos out of the house because it might disturb their delicate mechanism. But when the new baby came, I got this offer from someone and I impulsively sold them. I worked late into the night cataloguing them before the new owner took them and then one night I got this terrible panic. It was like racing—I was painting myself into a corner—so I couldn't go back."

"I really cried when he sold them," says his wife. "He was deliberately giving up a part of his life for us."

"All my life I have been a 'thing' person," says Hill. "My wife is a 'people' person. I have been trying to learn from her. I remember recently I saw that picture in the newspaper of that poor Boston woman falling off the fire escape with a young child. The photographer caught them in mid air and then when they landed. She was killed. For days I was devastated by that picture. It was so terrible, and then it dawned on me that years ago I never would have felt a thing. I would not have let myself feel anything. You can't let yourself be sensitive to death when you are a racer. If you do you will never be able to keep it all straight in your head when you are on the rack."

"I look at all those old pictures of my husband when he was a race car driver," says his wife, "and he looks so different now. The others, like Dan Guerney and Graham Hill, they look the same. Oh, they look older now, but basically you can recognize them from those old pictures because they are the same person. They are still in racing. Philip is not. He has undergone a psychic change that has changed the way he looks. My husband has worked very hard to remake himself into another person. But in some ways he can't. I don't think he will ever be able to divorce himself from other guys like Dan or Graham, or move from this house and his cars. No matter how unpleasant his past may have been, he will always have to keep a part of it with him in his memory. My mother used to have a saying, 'No matter what,' she said, 'you can not cut blood.'"

Both Dan Guerney, a native Southern Californian, and Graham Hill, a native Englishman, are younger racing contemporaries of Phil Hill. They were driving Formula One cars when Phil Hill won his World Championship in 1961, and they were still driving ten years later. Guerney retired from driving in 1972 without ever having won a World Championship despite the fact that he has been considered by many knowledgeable racing people to be America's most talented race car driver ever. Graham Hill, on the other hand, retired from driving this past summer after almost twenty-one years of competition during which he was twice a World Champion. Both men have retained their racing identities through, what was for each, a painful retirement that was softened only by their transition from driver, to owner and builder of cars, and trainer of younger drivers.

Dan Guerney is forty-five years old. In photographs and from a slight distance, he looks to be a much younger man—looks to be, in fact, the same man he was ten years ago. He is a big, hulking blonde, with hair-less Nordic skin and broad features that break spontaneously into a brilliant smile. He has eyes like Paul Newman, an unreal blue, and like Newman's they are opaque, reflect no images. He is a vigorous-looking man, also in that Nordic way—skiing out of the Alps, zigzagging down the slopes until he comes to a slicing halt in a spray of snow at your feet, flipping up his goggles, and flashing that brilliant smile. It is only up close or when he moves, however, that that image is shattered. He has a soft body, without definition, and when he walks, from behind he looks like a prehistoric man. His thick arms swing pendulously at his sides and his shoulders are hunched forward, rising and falling in slow rhythm with his nodding head as he navigates each plodding step with the utmost concentration. His every movement, in fact, even the chewing of food, seems to require from Guerney an almost painful, single-minded concentration, one that grows more heightened with each passing day, until finally one day in the future, one envisions, he will be completely immobile under the oppressive weight of that concentration.

Whenever Guerney bids farewell to someone he has not enjoyed talking to, he flashes that brilliant smile, and, as it dissolves into his jaw, says very quickly, "Good-bye and fuckyouverymuch." He has been described, even by friends, as being a "cold, hard, charming man." He is single-mindedly devoted to automobile racing, and seems to have little left of his personality to waste on other amenities. He is the owner, builder, and chief mechanic for the Eagle Racing Team of Santa Ana. He *is* the Eagle Racing Team. Before each race, he takes his young protégé-driver, Vern Schuppan, on a tour of the track. Schuppan, Nordic-looking like Guerney, only smaller, sits behind his mentor on a motorcycle that sags under their combined weight. Schuppan wraps his arms around Guerney's thick waist and they roar off, with Schuppan listening carefully as Guerney points out various oddities of the track and tells his driver how he expects him to run the race.

If anyone should know how to navigate a race course, says Phil Hill, it is Dan Guerney. "He was a marvelous driver," says Hill. "Really beautiful. But he had a reputation for over-tinkering with his cars. He could never leave well enough alone. It was his ego coming out. Without it he might have become World Champion, too. Dan and I still see each other socially, and sometimes at races. Every once in a while before a race, he'll call me and say, 'Phil, we're down twenty-five horsepower with only a week to go!' I say, 'That's too bad, Dan.' And he says, 'But we were down sixty horsepower a month ago,' and hangs up. It was very difficult for Dan to retire from driving, he identified with it so much. He has always been more famous with racing people in this country than I have. He has the gung-ho, red-blooded, All-American he-man image that racing fans can identify with. They look at me and hear the things I say and don't know what the hell to make of me. Even now, Dan still gets the urge to go back to driving. You can always tell. He'll start complaining about his young drivers. 'The kid doesn't have it, Phil. He's just not putting out for me. I don't think he'll ever cut it.' Pretty soon I'll get a call from his wife, Evie, who is frantic. 'Please, Phil, you've got to do something! Dan's getting into a very dangerous frame of mind again!' I usually can talk him out of it. But then, a year later, maybe Swede Savage gets killed—not injured, mind you, not just smashed up, but killed—and then the next thing you hear is that Dan Guerney was seen taking a few laps at Riverside."

If Dan Gurney's retirement from active racing was a wrenching and painful experience for him—it still is, in fact—then Graham Hill's retirement this past summer was a traumatic experience that he would never come to grips with. At forty-five, he was older than Guerney when he retired, and so was more firmly rooted in the patterns of his last twenty years. And those patterns had been of infinitely greater success than what Guerney or most racers had ever experienced. Graham Hill was twice a World Champion and missed a third championship by a single point. Furthermore, he had given more to racing than most racers, both in body and spirit. The former had been crushed innumerable times in near-fatal accidents and then hastily (and oftentimes inadequately) patched together, but the latter was never crushed; he was indomitable, in fact. Graham Hill gave to and received more from racing than did almost any racer in history. He competed in over 700 races in his career, and in 176 World Championship Grand Prix, which is 125 more than the legendary Juan Fangio. More than any racer, Graham Hill identified with his image as a racer—*was*, in fact, that image. He was born in poverty in London; was apprenticed for five years to S. Smith and Sons, Ltd., an instrument firm; spent two years stoking coal in the boiler room of a ship in the Royal Navy; spent some time on the welfare rolls; and, finally, upon seeing an advertisement in the April 24, 1953, issue of *Autosport* magazine, became a race car driver at the age of twenty-four. The advertisement stated that for five cents per lap, anyone could drive a Cooper 500cc around the Brands Hatch race track. Graham Hill drove that car around Brands Hatch four times and has been involved in automobile racing in some capacity ever since.

Graham Hill speaks with a jaunty, aristocrat's accent. He has dined regularly with Prince Rainier and Princess Grace of Monaco and has been to Buckingham Palace to chat with the Queen. He wears a scarf around his neck when racing. He has long, swept-back silvery hair that curls up at the nape of his neck. He has a high forehead, grim eyes, an aquiline nose, and a trim mustache over a lipless mouth. His jaw juts forward belligerently. He looks as if, at any moment, he should come swooping out of the clouds in his Sopwith Carmel in hot pursuit of the Red Baron. He is, in fact, the archetype for that stiff-upper-lipped R.A.F. "bloody well get on with it" racer that Phil Hill always finds so disconcerting. Whether Graham Hill's raffishness is merely a persona he assumed after he became a racer, or whether it is an aspect of his personality that finds a natural outlet in racing is not clear. It is clear, however, that he lived that image to its fullest. After his legs had been crushed one year, he appeared in a bar hobbling on two canes. He stood painfully talking to friends. They offered him a seat. He declined gallantly and stood for another half hour before hobbling out. A few days later he had to be carried by his crew and placed gently into his racing car, which he drove to sixth place at the Grand Prix of South Africa.

More than anything, it was this image that sustained Graham Hill and its loss that he dreaded. Once he had retired, he seemed hard-pressed to sustain an interest in the cars he was building and the drivers he was coaching. He would go to each Grand Prix and be seen standing stiffly beside his Embacy Racing van, his arms perfectly still at his sides, his hands cupped toward his legs. He was always dressed impeccably, maybe in a navy double-breasted blazer and cream-colored slacks. His legs were extremely bowed and when he walked he hobbled painfully left and right. He was like a cowboy who had been in the saddle too long. Mostly, it was too painful for Graham to move, so he would just stand there beside his van while spectators streamed past, pointed him out, called his name, smiled. He would raise his right hand slowly from his side and then with a brief, tight smile, a simultaneous dip of the head, he would make a single wave of the hand. It was a gesture in slow motion: the hand, palm out, moving from left to right across his vision as if wiping away forever a faded image. The gesture was exhausting. The hand fell back to his side. Often, a young woman would be standing near. She would be smiling, too, sometimes at the crowd and sometimes at Graham Hill. She seldom spoke to him, seemed in awe of him, really, and he rarely said a word to her.

"I don't see Graham as often as I do Dan," said Phil Hill not long ago, "although we were on a radio talk show together recently. It was held at this horrid pseudo-Australian restaurant in Long Beach that looked like something out of *Death in Venice*. All these decayed potted palms and oriental waiters from Hong Kong and the Philippines. Anyway, Graham and I were on with a young British driver named Jackie Oliver—an obnoxious little guy with a little man's ego. He treated me like this decayed old driver who doesn't understand today's racing—gumball tires and airfoils and all. He looks at me and says, 'But you don't understand, Phil. You only had little wings then. We have big wings today.' Maybe he's right. Maybe I am the way people see me. 'Poor old Phil who's lost without racing.' It is a bit of fakery for me to talk about gumball tires. Such things don't apply to my world anymore.

"Anyway, during the program the master of ceremonies asked Graham why he recently retired from driving. Graham looks at him and says in his very best 'jolly good show' tone, 'I gave up racing for the younger fellows, actually. Like my protégé Tony Brise. I didn't want to show him up. It would be awkward if I went out and battered his time, wouldn't it?' What bullshit! Graham had lost it all by then. He was always starting last on the grid and then slowing down all the younger drivers on the tracks. He had had so many accidents his legs were all busted up and put back together wrong, or maybe just put back together too quickly because he was always in a sweat to get back in a car before he should have. And besides, he was old now, in his forties, and even with that R.A.F. attitude of his, he couldn't avoid facing the fact that for him dying was a very real possibility now. It was degrading to Graham to see him struggling those last years, and, so, when he finally quit four months ago, we all breathed a sigh of relief for him.

"Just before the program ended, the emcee asked Graham what was the most important ingredient for a race care driver to have. Graham made this very dramatic pause and then said in his most raffish tone, 'Well, actually, I think the most important ingredient for a young racer is to have a good old competitive spirit.' Competitive spirit? Bullshit! Competitive spirit isn't an ingredient. It's a symptom."

Whenever Phil Hill is in Graham Hill's company, he defers to him as one would a superior. He addresses Graham in Italian as "due volta campione"—two-time champion—while referring to himself as "una volta campione." However, Phil Hill cannot keep from grinning even as he defers to Graham, nor can he excise from his voice a faint, mocking tone of condescension. Graham, delighting in Phil's deference, nevertheless senses something is amiss. His head inclines away from Phil and he looks down at him as would a lepidopterist scrutinizing a strange and mutated specimen whose markings and patterns he has yet to fathom. Phil Hill would be the first to admit to his ambivalent feelings toward both Graham Hill and Dan Guerney. On an objective and intellectual level, Hill can not hide his distaste for their attitudes and pursuits, once so similar to his own, but on a more primitive and instinctive level he finds himself drawn to such men for a number of reasons. His attraction to them is partly that of the reformed alcoholic to the bottle, which he keeps unopened on his bureau to reaffirm his resolve. Occasional exposure to such contemporaries invariably helps Phil Hill to bring into sharper focus his own divergent and evolving attitude. Also, with the passing of time and the hardening of his own new attitudes, he is less fearful of relapse by association. On a more positive level, however, Phil Hill is a more tolerant man than he once was as a possessed young perfectionist. He is more charitable to the foibles of his fellow man and can say of people like Enzo Ferrari, of whom he was once so critical, "I no longer try to separate the good and the bad in him. I accept him whole, recognizing that, as in many people of genius, his great virtues are the other face of his faults. I now have a more rounded appreciation of him."

No matter what has transpired over the years, there is still a part of Phil Hill that identifies with Ferrari and Graham Hill and Dan Guerney, and it is not a part of him that he can cut out. "Graham always called me 'fratello'— brother. I care deeply about what Dan and Graham think of me. I want their respect." Phil Hill is afraid that he may have lost that respect over the years, that it has been tarnished by his premature retirement and the ferocity with which he has lashed out against racing and its drivers. He seems intent upon restoring that past image just as he has successfully restored much of his life. He goes to races again. He can be seen circulating amongst racing people around whom he is deferential, almost obsequious, as if consigned in their presence to a purgatory of mea culpas for past transgressions. They view him warily, as a distrustful curio ("I wonder what brings a guy like Phil out of the woodwork?") whose behavior cannot be predicted. He is careful not to offend, worries about his image as World Champion, because, ironically enough, Phil Hill has again become proud of his racing accomplishments. He feels they may have a greater worth than he has given them credit for when he was in the process of quitting racing. Of course, at that time, if his retirement was to be successful, he *had* to denigrate those accomplishments. Now, secure, he can accept them for what they are: remarkable achievements whose ultimate worth will always be open to his questioning. Hill realizes now that no matter what he believes on a rational level, no matter what even he *wills* himself to believe, there will always be a certain part of his nature and his past that he can never deny. At best, he can understand and control that part of himself, but he can never excise it, because in the long run he has truly come to understand that one cannot cut blood.

On September 28, 1975, a blazing hot Sunday afternoon in Long Beach, California, Phil Hill, Dan Guerney, and Graham Hill are sitting in

Guerney's pick up truck trying to negotiate their way through a throng of spectators who press against the slowly moving truck for a closer look at three of racing's most famous retirees. All three men are wearing their metallic-looking racing suits. Their helmets rest on their laps. Phil and Guerney are wearing racing shoes, which look like bowling shoes, while Graham is wearing brown shoes and argyle socks. Occasionally, they wave out at their fans as they make their way to Ocean Boulevard, which is the starting line for a race course that has been laid out through the streets of Long Beach, and where 30,000 fans and three identical Toyota Celica sedans are waiting for them. All three men have agreed to stage a three-lap match in those Toyotas as a promotional gimmick prior to the first running of the Long Beach Grand Prix for Formula 5000 cars. (An F5000 car is identical to a Formula One car, except that it uses a heavier, big-block American engine instead of a lighter, small-block European engine.)

Of the three, only Phil Hill is apprehensive. Guerney seems less preoccupied with racing his Toyota than he is with his F5000 car, which is entered in the Long Beach Grand Prix. Graham Hill seems not to be worried about anything, seems merely distracted as he stares out the window at the spectators he does not even see.

"I asked the Toyota mechanic if he bled the breaks," says Phil. "He says, 'Don't worry about the breaks, they should last three laps.' I started screaming, 'Jesus Christ, they should last three laps? What the hell does that mean? I'm driving the goddamned thing, you know. More guys have got killed in this type of thing.'"

Guerney laughs and says, "Come on Phil, don't worry. Remember what Ferrari used to say, 'Not to worry. You get in-a, you drive-a, you win-a.'"

"But I don't want to win," says Phil. "I just don't want to stuff it or finish last and make an ass of myself. Jesus, I should never have agreed to do this thing."

"Well, then, why did you?" says Guerney.

"I'll be damned if I know. I don't know why. I only know we're gonna make fools of ourselves, that's all."

Without turning his head from the window, Graham says, "Just one more time, Philip, that's all."

"Oh, that's all right for you to say, Graham," says Phil. "You've only been retired a few months, and Dan, Jesus, he's been goddamned practicing at Riverside. I'm an old man, for Christ's sake."

"Oh, Philip, you are not an old man," says Graham. "You are an old lady. You are an old lady, exactly as you were years ago."

"Yes, I am," says Phil, winking to a friend beside him. "I haven't changed a goddamned bit, Graham, and I'm proud of it, too."

When the truck reaches the starting line on Ocean Boulevard, there are 30,000 spectators waiting to greet the three men. Graham says, "Well, chaps, I am simply going to put on my helmet, crawl out on all fours, and hide behind a tire." The truck stops, and the three men all get out to thunderous applause and the calling of their names. For a few minutes they pose for photographs for dozens of photographers. One, a pretty woman with large, blue-tinted sunglasses, is crouching at Graham's feet, snapping photograph after photograph while cooing to herself, "Oh, he's such a dreamboat!" Dan Guerney is, by far, the crowd favorite. His name is constantly being called out and he turns smiling to wave. Phil is signing autographs on the back of LBGP programs. He looks at one such program, which carries a brief biography of him. He says, "Jesus Christ, Graham, will you look at this! It mentions how I finished third at Monaco in 'sixty-one. I finished second in 'sixty-two. Why the hell didn't they mention *that*?"

All three men pose for one last picture. They stand side by side with their arms around each other's shoulders. Phil is in the middle. He is dwarfed by the other two, who are well over six feet tall. He looks oddly incongruous amongst them. Their racing suits are sleek-fitting and streamlined while his is so old fashioned and baggy that he looks as if he must have shrunk over the years, diminished in size from the man who once wore that suit. It is held together in spots with masking tape. Phil stands very stiffly in his suit, the way Graham stands in street clothes. The photographer asks the three men to put on their racing helmets. Even Phil's helmet is a relic. It looks like a beekeeper's hat, or a polo cap. It has a small peak and a colorless Plexiglas visor that covers only his eyes, like the windshield of an old MG-TC. Inside the helmet is printed the following: "Herbert and Johnson, 38 New Bond Street, London, West, By appointment hatters to the late King George VI." There is a picture of an antelope and a Latin inscription, *Nunquam Non Paratus*—never unprepared. The helmets of Guerney and Graham Hill are more modern. They have dark blue-tinted Plexiglas visors that cover their entire faces, concealing their identities, like spacemen.

The picture is taken finally and the three men get into their Toyotas. They start their cars, whose open exhausts sound, according to Phil, "like a farting cow. Jesus, what I wouldn't give for the sound of a Ferrari right now."

The cars take off amid the hoots and cheers and laughter of the spectators who find it humorous to see three such famous Formula One drivers hunched over the steering wheels of these tiny cars that will not reach a top speed of 110 mph.

The race is uneventful. Phil's fears are unfounded, as all three men conspire to cross the finish line in unison. When they return to the starting line, the F5000 cars are already staggered on the grid in preparation for the first running of the Grand Prix. When Phil and Dan and Graham emerge from their Toyotas, they are given a brief cheer, but already the spectators' attention has turned to the sleek, low F5000 cars, which will reach speeds of upwards of 175 mph as they race through the city streets of Long Beach. The course runs past the baroque, old-age hotels on Ocean Boulevard and the porno movie theaters, now featuring *Sodom and Gomorrah*, and then along Shoreline Drive, which runs parallel to the Pacific Bay Harbor, in which is anchored the Queen Mary, which once brought Phil Hill and his new XK–120 Jaguar back to America to begin his racing career twenty-six years ago. It is now old and seedy, an amusement attraction and hotel, the hull of which filled with sand to keep it solidly anchored in the harbor.

Guerney hurries over to his F5000 car on the grid. He crouches down to give Vern Schuppan, his driver, one last bit of advice. Graham Hill simply vanishes. Phil Hill takes off his helmet and begins the long walk back to the paddock area where he will change back into his street clothes. He is sweating profusely and extremely agitated as he walks alongside the F5000 cars on his left. The spectators, separated by a wire, are on his right. Occasionally, as someone points him out, calls his name, the phrase, "World Champion" can be heard. Phil is oblivious to all. He is walking furiously and talking with passionate intensity. "Jesus, I'm glad it's over! You know, I wasn't kidding! You could get killed in this type of thing! I remember Mike Hawthorne, Christ, he was on the way to an awards banquet and his car hit a tree! He was killed instantly! He had only retired six months before!"

Phil is passing car after car on the starting grid. The drivers all look the same. Encased in their small cockpits, they are perfectly still. Their hands are stretched out before them, gripping a tiny steering wheel. They stare straight ahead, oblivious to the mechanics hovering over them for last second preparations. Their eyes are the only parts of their faces that are visible behind their visors. The turtleneck sweaters they wear under their racing suits are are pulled up over their mouths like outlaw masks so that, in the case of a crash, they will not breathe in flames. Their eyes are strangely blank, wide, and glassy, as if unseeing of everything before them except for some private vision.

"It's just like I thought," says Phil Hill. "It's the kind of thing you don't want to do. I'm afraid I might like it, and I could never just race a little, you know what I mean? It's like an alcoholic taking one drink. It's possible to rid oneself of the psychopathic aspects of drinking and drink normally again, but it's not worth the chance." Hill's voice is strangely loud now, because suddenly there is silence. The spectators are standing in the bleachers, and others are pressing against the wire fence that separates them from the racers. A man in a powder blue blazer and white slacks is walking between the F5000 cars toward the first car on the grid. He is carrying starting flags in either hand.

"It's like when I went to Europe," says Hill, his voice uncommonly loud now amid the silence and stillness. "I had been married only a few months, and so I went over to Europe to be with the guys. I lived a bachelor life again, and when I came back home to Alma, all of a sudden, I couldn't sleep anymore. I was up at three a.m., looking for things to do. I had the case of the shakes, this terrible panic that I was really married and that it was all over for me. Who the hell wants to go fifty-five miles per hour for the rest of his life?"

Hill is alongside of the first car on the starting grid now. He is about five feet from it, but he does not even notice the car, sponsored by the Theodora Racing Team, or its driver, who is staring straight ahead, perfectly still, like all the others. The driver is Tony Brise, the twenty-three-year-old protégé of Graham Hill. On December 8, 1975, Brise will be sitting alongside of Graham Hill in his light airplane that will crash on a golf course outside of London, killing them both.

Tom Seaver & Pat Jordan

The Best of Friends

(from *People*, the *New York Times*, and
Newsday Sunday Magazine, 1978–1988)

PROLOGUE

TOM SEAVER and I are friends. Not best friends. Not *intimate* friends. Just friends. We used to live only a few miles from each other. I would call him now and then, when he was pitching badly, to give him advice.

"Tom, you're throwing too many breaking balls."

"You really think so?" And then, "What the fuck do you know?"

We have a lot in common, Tom and me. We are both in our early forties. Big men. Six-one, two hundred pounds. We are both athletes. Pitchers. Bonus babies. Tom signed with the Mets for a $50,000 bonus when he was twenty. I signed with the Braves for a $50,000 bonus when I was eighteen. We both threw hard. I threw harder, of course, but Tom will never admit to that. He had better control than me (at least *I* will admit to *that*) and a longer career. His lasted twenty years. In the *major* leagues. Mine lasted three years. In the *minor* leagues. The *low* minor leagues. And then out. Back home to Connecticut. At twenty-one. Married. Lugging bricks and mortar up a rickety scaffold for a Lithuanian mason.

Over the years, I passed through all those stages most people do in the course of their ordinary lives, while watching, from a distance, Tom Seaver pass through the stages of his *extra*ordinary life. His *extra*ordinary career. *My* career! That was *my* life he was living! Why him? Why not me?

I

Tom Seaver and I are playing basketball at the Greenwich Y. One-on-one. It is November of '71. We are both in our late twenties. There is no one else in the small gym. Just the two of us, banging against one another with such force that the red brick walls echo with the smack of flesh against flesh. The walls are perilously close to the baseline underneath the basket. We drive to the hoop, shoot, and then raise our hands, palms out, to cushion the shock as we hit the wall.

Tom has the ball close to the hoop. He fakes. I go up. As I come down, he goes up, his shoulder clipping my jaw, rattling my senses. Swish.

"You all right?" he says, without interest. He walks back to half court with the ball.

"Sure." I smile at him. When his back is turned, I open my mouth and move my jaw around to see if it is still attached.

We have been playing for hours. We are both drenched with sweat, our faces red and swollen from exhaustion and the fierceness of our competition. Tom is only an adequate basketball player. Strong, straight moves. Without grace—clumsy, in fact, which is to his advantage. It excuses his blatant fouls. But he has strong hands, like a vise, and once he gets close to the hoop he is unstoppable. His basic move is to back in towards the hoop, left-right-left-right, until he is close enough to throw a short jump shot. I am a much better shooter than Tom. He gets furious when I dribble the ball nonchalantly beyond the top of the key and then suddenly go up for a twenty-foot jump shot. Swish. When I try to get closer to the hoop than the top of the key, he slows me down with a shoulder to the gut. When he backs in to the hoop, bent over double, his behind sticking into my gut, I thrust my hips against his behind to stop him. Whack. He pushes backward with his behind. I whack at him with my hips. He pushes. I whack. Push. Whack. Push. Whack. We must look like two crazy queers. Finally, he goes up for a jumper. I slap the ball back into his face. It bounces high in the air. He leaps for it, comes down with it, goes up again, this time with the top of his head aimed at my jaw. Clunk. I go backpedaling into the brick wall. Swish. He grins, blood trickling down from his nose.

"You all right?" he says again, walking back to half court with the ball.

"Sure. Want me to get some tissue for your nose?" He glares over his shoulder. I smile.

We go on like this, evenly matched, for hours. Finally, after too many games to count, we agree that the winner of the next game wins the day. We are bruised and scraped, our T-shirts speckled with dried blood, our knees and elbows raw. There is a pulsating welt on the side of my forehead. Tom's nose is swollen a flaming pink, like a pig's, and the dried blood caked above his upper lip looks like Hitler's mustache. The next basket wins. Tom has the ball at the top of the key. He is dribbling around to catch his breath. I am crouched over, waiting for Tom to set himself and begin backing in toward the basket. But he surprises me. He takes a dribble and is by me before I recover and follow him. Just as he is about to go up for a lay up and I am about to push him with both hands, I see the wall in front of him, and then, in my mind's eye, I see him slamming into that wall, hear the sickening sound of his arm breaking—crack!—against the bricks. Tom Seaver's arm! Jesus, God! I drop my hands. He lays the ball in.

It is raining. We are driving back to Tom's house in my car. An old Corvette with a T-top roof that rattles. And leaks. The car is painted gold. When Tom sees it, he laughs.

"Jesus, why didn't you buy a Porsche?" he says.

"I did. And a Ferrari. This is just my knockaround car, you know."

"No, seriously. Why didn't you?"

I look across at him. "Because I'm not Tom Seaver, that's why."

"That's a fact." Rain is seeping through the T-top that rattles. Tom looks up. Water drops onto his brow. He blinks, wipes off the water with the back of his hand. He shakes his head. "It leaks."

"No shit." I am hunched forward over the steering wheel, wiping off the fogged window with my bare hand.

"Put on the defroster," he says. I glare at him. "*That*, too?" he says, and he begins to laugh in that high-pitched, girlish way of his.

"You know, I let you win that last game," I say.

"You did, huh?" He raises his eyebrows.

"Yep. I was afraid I might hurt you if I pushed you into the wall."

He looks over at me, his eyebrows still raised, a faint smile on his lips. "Bullshit, Jordan. You never let anyone win at anything in your whole life. You *always* have to win."

"I let you win today," I say. "I mean, you're Tom Seaver. A big fucking star. I coulda broke your arm." He doesn't answer. "You know what else?" I say. "I threw harder than you, too."

"In your dreams," he says.

"No, I did, Tom! I did! I just didn't know where it was going." We both laugh.

Tom is right, though. I *do* have to win every game. I have to perfect *every*thing. It exhausts me. At the end of a day I have nothing left.

Tom hoards his energy, is selective about his perfectionism. He refuses to waste it on things on which he places little value. Or on things he feels are beyond his comprehension. His reach never exceeds his grasp. "Innocence!" he says. "Whoever thinks about it?" To analyze such things would be a waste of energy. Not because he couldn't fathom them, because in most cases he could. If he expended his energy. Energy, he has decided, should be used for his pitching. Nothing else exists but the batter seen through a narrow tunnel. My concentration is fractured light, darting everywhere with a will of its own. On the mound, concentrating on the batter, *trying* to concentrate on the batter, I begin my pump, raise my left leg, pivot sideways to the batter, see off in the stands a pretty girl in a summer dress, a farmer in bib overalls, a child of three, and, overhead, a brilliant sun. These things blind me.

Tom and I are sitting in the living room of his farm house, drinking beer. He is not in a good mood today. He is having contract problems with the Mets, squabbling with Bob Scheffing, the General Manager, over money. But he makes an effort to overcome his bad mood for my benefit. He begins to tell a funny story. It is about Dick Schaap, the sportswriter-television newscaster, and one of his ex-wives. Tom and Nancy Seaver were friends of the Schaaps, lived only a few miles down the road from them in an exclusive part of Greenwich, Connecticut. Big, old, white colonial houses with expansive front lawns. Tom and Nancy went to dinner at the Schaaps one night. The meal was served by a maid. Schaap's wife entertained the Seavers with stories of her previous love affairs. Dick was silent. Tom and Nancy looked down at their plates. The maid entered with a huge rib roast. Everyone began to eat. An hour later everyone was stuffed. Tom sat back and lighted a cigar. There was still over half of the rib roast left on the table. Schaap's wife summoned the maid with a little bell. Mrs. Schaap told her to dispose of the remaining rib roast. The maid picked up the silver tray with the rib roast on it and carried it into the kitchen. She left the door open. Tom began to laugh at something Dick said, and then, out of the corner of his eye, through the haze of his cigar smoke, he saw the maid about to dump the rib roast into a garbage pail.

"Stop!" he cried. Everyone looked at him. The maid stared through the doorway. "Jesus, don't throw that away," Tom said. Then, to Mrs.

Schaap, he said, "If you're not gonna use that rib roast, I'll take it home." And he did.

"Can you imagine?" Tom says, recounting that story to me in the living room. "That roast fed my family for a week!" He shakes his head.

The screen door of the farmhouse springs open, slaps shut. Nancy enters the living room with an armful of packages. Boxes, not groceries. Designer boxes. She is blonde, pretty, with a brilliant smile that reveals nothing. She has been portrayed in women's magazines as being a typical baseball star's wife. Blonde, cute, wifely. It is an image she does not work at dispelling. Yet she seems less cute than she does interestingly attractive. She is not thin-lipped and falsely bright-eyed like most stars' wives, although her hair is bleached a too-bright blonde.

"Hello, boys," she says in a lazy, lilting, breathless way that seems vaguely southern. "I've been shopping."

"Really," Tom says. Then, to me. "You know, shopping is Nancy's very most favorite thing in the world." He nods, grinning. "No kidding!"

Nancy, still smiling brilliantly, says, "Now, Thomas, you know that's not true. My *very* most favorite thing in the world is sitting in the sun for eight hours a day. Shopping is only my *second* very most favorite thing in the whole world."

Tom, glancing sideways at me, raises his eyebrows. "Do you believe it?" he says.

Still smiling, Nancy says, "By the way, Thomas. Did Mr. Scheffing call today?"

II

The following spring, March of '72, Tom and I are standing behind the batting cage at home plate at the Mets' training stadium, Al Lang Field, in St. Petersburg, Florida. The Mets are taking batting practice, while the Cardinals, their opponents for today's game, are warming up along the sidelines. We are watching Ed Kranepool take his cuts. Easy Ed. A big, soft man with an effortless, left-handed swing. He lofts long flyball after long flyball to the rightfield wall. A few pitchers hang by the wall, leaning up against it, making little leaps to snare each of Kranepool's drives.

Tom shakes his head and spits tobacco juice through the screen. "Do you know he hit twenty balls to the warning track last year? Twenty fucking balls! Another ten feet and they would have been home runs. I know I'd find the strength somewhere to hit those balls another ten feet." We are both watching Easy Ed swing. He lofts another lazy flyball. Tom looks over at me. "I mean, if you don't think baseball is a big deal, don't do it. But if you do it, do it right!"

An umpire joins us behind the batting cage. A trim, little man with a cherub's dark, syrupy face in a crisply-pressed uniform. He watches batting practice for a few minutes and then says something to Tom. They talk, while I lose myself in the rhythm of batting practice. Out of the corner of my eye I catch the umpire staring at me. He is still talking to Tom but he is looking past him to me. Finally, I recognize him. Terry Tatta. He was an umpire in the Midwest League when I pitched there in 1960. Then, I was a madman on the mound. Screaming, red-faced, when Terry missed a pitch. "You asshole!" I shouted as I stalked toward the plate. He came out from behind the catcher with his mask tucked under his armpit. He held his hands, palms out, as if to halt traffic. "Take it easy, Pat! Take it easy! It was a good two inches off the plate." I wouldn't stop. He let me rage on for a moment, knew, like most Italians, that it meant nothing, was directed not at him but at my own frustrations. He smiled. "Are you finished?" I felt foolish. Put my head down. He tossed me a new ball. "Come on," he said. "Show me what you got."

And now, here we were, twelve years later. He was a Triple-A umpire now, on the verge of becoming a major-league umpire. And me? I had been out of baseball for ten years. Me! With a fastball better than Seaver's!

Terry leans across Tom and says to me. "Don't I know you? You look awful familiar."

I smile. "Yeah, Terry, you know me. The Midwest League, nineteen sixty."

A big smile spreads across his cherubic face. "Pat! Jesus Christ! How are you doing?" And then, without thinking, he turns to Tom and says, "Tom, you shoulda seen this guy. They shoulda made a law against him. He could bring it like you only dreamed you could."

Naturally, Tom accuses me of staging that little scene. I swear I didn't, but he won't believe me. Still, that's not the point. The point is I *could* bring it faster than Tom. I always could. In Little League. In high school. Tom never had the luxury of *my* blinding talent in his youth. "I never threw hard then," he says. "I was aware of my physical limitations at fourteen. I had to adjust."

Pitching became for Tom, at fourteen, not a physical activity, but a mental one. He learned how it felt to be shelled unmercifully one inning and then have to walk out to the mound to begin the next. "It's a terrible feeling," he says. "You want to quit. You feel it's hopeless. You have to force yourself to start again. Some guys can't do that. They're always fighting things beyond their control."

Tom Seaver learned, earlier than most, to deal solely within the framework of his limitations. To *circumvent* those limitations. Unlike me. I raged against my limitations, and in the process, my very real talent suffered.

III

Tom is not pitching well. It is early summer of '74 and he has won only three games while losing five. I saw him pitch last night on television. He reminded me of myself years ago, in the minor leagues. He still had his great fastball, but he threw as if he had forgotten everything he knew about pitching, except throwing the ball with as much effort as possible. I called him the next day at his house.

"Now you know how I felt on the mound," I said.

"Yeah," Tom said. "I can understand, now. I was just throwing. I knew what I was doing wrong even while I was doing it. But I couldn't make myself stop. I just got angrier and angrier and then I got afraid."

"You're still throwing as hard as ever."

"Oh, that's no problem. It's my concentration I'm worried about. Not my fastball."

"Don't worry," I said. "It'll come. Just remember who you are. You're Tom Seaver. The fucking greatest." He laughed. "Just keep reminding yourself. 'I'm Tom Seaver, not Pat Jordan. I'm Tom Seaver, not Pat Jordan. I'm Tom Seaver, not Pat Jordan.'"

Still laughing, he said, "Thank God for that." And then he invited me to his house the next afternoon for lunch. "We can talk about it," he said.

I drove to his old farmhouse in Greenwich in my old Corvette. I see Tom sitting alone in the shadows on the porch of his colonial home. He is working a crossword puzzle in the *New York Times*. He draws on a long cigar. Pauses. Leans back in his wicker chair. Exhales to the sky, savoring the silence. It is broken only by the sound of a screen door springing open, then slapping shut. A small black dog emerges from the house. The dog sits beside Tom. Absentmindedly, he begins to scratch behind its ears. I get out of my car. It is noon of a sunny day. A softly undulating, neatly trimmed lawn surrounds the house on three sides. It is bordered by thick foliage and tall trees that cast shadows on the lawn and that completely obliterate from view the three houses that border Tom's.

He gets up to greet me. I comment on the seclusion. He smiles.

"They're there," he says, with a sweep of his arm toward the other houses. "But I can't see 'em. We're pretty safe here." Then gesturing toward the eighteenth fairway, he adds, "And nobody's gonna build on *that*."

After the 1969 season, when he won twenty-five games and his league's Cy Young Award, and his team, the Mets, won the World Series, Tom and Nancy took a brief fling at being public personalities. They appeared frequently on television talk shows. Were rumored to be about to host their own television show. Were the subjects of numerous magazine articles, which invariably billed them as "The Perfect All-American Couple." Were willing, it seemed, to advertise any and everything, including themselves, whom they offered to prospective advertisers in a New York newspaper ad that referred to them as "American as Apple Pie."

Within a year, the Seavers' fling at being public personalities began to backfire. New York baseball writers began to take too much pleasure in Tom's infrequent failures on the mound. And Nancy became the object of a number of harshly critical magazine articles. One, in particular, in a women's magazine, helped foster her growing image as a typical, cute, blonde baseball wife. She had gone to lunch with the woman writer of that piece and she had spent that lunch being cute. When the dessert arrived she was quoted as saying, "Hello, dessert." And when its remnants were removed she was quoted as saying, "Good-bye, dessert."

In 1970, Tom had a mediocre season. Mediocre for him, anyway. He won eighteen games, lost twelve, and within a year he and Nancy had left their New York City apartment and their public visiblity for the seclusion and serenity of Greenwich, Connecticut There, Tom deliberately began to cultivate, along with the flowers in his garden, a studied "dullness" that freed him from public scrutiny, and, kept his mind uncluttered, his energies untapped, his concentration intense, for that which he called "the most important thing I do in my life. Pitch."

Over the next three years, his pitching flourished with his garden. He posted two twenty-victory seasons and won his second Cy Young Award in 1973. His successes on the mound came so consistently that they actually became boring to baseball fans who routinely expected from him only greatness. Unwittingly, Tom began to play his fans' demand for perfection by informing them through interviews that he, too, expected greatness from himself; that he, in fact, expected to become the greatest pitcher who had ever lived.

During the first three months of the '74 season, Tom is not routinely great, but only mediocre. For the first time in his career, he is greeted with boos as he walks to the mound to start each game at Shea Stadium. The boos grow louder with each home run he surrenders and become almost deafening when, with head lowered, he walks off the mound in the middle of the inning. The rapaciousness with which his fans now greet his failures is almost beyond comprehension, since Tom, unlike, say, Pete Rose, does little to court their antagonism. At times it can be truly frightening. One night I drove with him to Shea. He parked his car in the Mets' players lot behind the rightfield bullpen, where he was recognized by thirty or so fans standing behind the screen that separated them from the players. They began to shout that he is overpaid. Washed-up. A bum. Their shouts became obscenity-laced, grew more and more hysterical until finally it appeared as if they were going to physically attack him. They gripped the wire screen with their fingers and shook it. The screen rattled in waves.

"Can you imagine that?" Tom says, recalling that scene to me now on the porch of his colonial home. "That's got to be sick! One night it got so bad I charged the fence. They all scattered." He grins at the remembrance of that scene.

"What would you have done if you got to them?" I say.

He shrugs, still grinning, looks at his watch. Time for lunch, he says. I follow him into the house. He hands me a beer from the refrigerator and takes one for himself. We sip our beers while Tom assembles the ingredients for our lunch. Two tomatoes. Two cucumbers. Two ears of corn. Some fresh mushrooms. One T-bone steak and one huge filet mignon. He brings the steaks outside and lays them on a smoking charcoal grill. He returns to the kitchen and arranges the vegetables on a wooden chopping block under a conical light. He begins slicing the mushrooms first. He works neatly and with great concentration. When he speaks now, he invariably stops working and looks up. When he goes back to work he does not speak.

When everything is sliced he arranges the cucumbers, mushrooms, and tomatoes on two separate plates. He spreads them all out precisely as a card player would a deck of cards, each slice overlapping the next just so. He looks at the plates and is satisfied.

"Oh, Christ!" he says. "I forgot the steaks!" He runs outside to turn the steaks on the grill. "They're okay," he calls through the door. "They're not burnt. Jesus! I forgot all about them."

When Tom returns to the kitchen, he says, "All in all, this has been a very frustrating period for me. For a while I just didn't want to talk about it. I didn't want to talk to anyone. After one of my losses to Chicago, I was so mad I wouldn't talk to the writers after the game. The next day one writer comes up to me and says, 'If you lose your next game are you gonna talk to us?' Christ, can you imagine that! He thought I planned such things. Like I'd already made that decision before I pitched! It was just an emotional thing. No matter how hard I try to discipline my emotions, sometimes I can't. I've kicked over my share of water coolers and trash cans and training tables. I'm not *that* calculating!"

As with those rabid fans, it seems the New York sportswriters are deriving more than a bit of satisfaction from Tom's present failures. They seem too eager to hint that, at twenty-nine, he will never again be the kind of dominating pitcher he once was. "Times have changed," wrote one writer. "There were times when Tom Seaver would pitch a shut-out and talk about how he should not have given up three hits." The writer goes on to say that Seaver has lower expectations now, that like the rest of us he no longer expects to be perfect but is happy just not to lose a modestly pitched game.

There *is* something about Tom Seaver that gives rise to envy in the rest of us. But it is not envy for his success, or his talent, or his money, or his lifestyle. It is envy for the obvious satisfaction he derives from these things. He too glibly articulates that satisfaction in a world of inarticulate people. He is too self-content in a world of discontented people. His standards are too lofty in a world whose people cannot meet their most minimal standards. His life is too orderly and disciplined in a world whose people's lives daily border on chaos. He is too simplistically rational about such endeavors as pitching a baseball, while around him most people are rendered irrational by life's more momentous complexities. He too easily funnels his concentration on any single, simple task of the moment, while around him are people whose concentration is diffused, rendered impotent by a thousand overwhelming tasks.

*   *   *

Tom and I are standing over the grill outside. He checks his watch and then forks the two steaks onto plates. He gives me the huge filet. He laughs. "That's the biggest fucking filet I ever saw." We carry our plates to a glass-topped table on the porch and sit down. Before he begins to eat, he says, "If people get pleasure out of knocking me, what can you say about them? I really don't care what people say about me. In my own mind I don't consider myself a public figure. I don't read the newspapers anymore. I mean, you can't control what they write about you, so why bother? I feel no pressure from the fans or anyone. I don't live in their world. I live in my own world. The real world."

IV

It is the late spring of 1982. Tom Seaver and I are sitting in the bright sunshine on the redwood deck of Tom's condominium, which is located only a few yards from the third tee of the Jack Nicklaus Golf Course in Mason, Ohio, a suburb thirty minutes from Cincinnati. Through a line of trees we see a steady parade of golf carts. They putt-putt up the fairways in agonizing slow-motion. I am reminded of those little carts in the television serial *The Prisoner*, with Patrick McGoohan. The golf carts are occupied by men in pastel sweaters and brilliant checked or plaid pants.

I have taken off my shirt. I'm sprawled, half-sitting, half-lying, in my chair, my eyes closed, my face to the sun. Tom, a wad of chewing tobacco in his cheek, is hunched over a sea of flower pots. He is wearing a plaid shirt and chino pants, and he is planting, with great concentration, geraniums, begonias, violets, and impatiens into clay plots. We spent the better part of the morning at a nursery where Tom meticulously searched out just the right flowers for those pots.

"This is a joy to me," he says. He kneads the dirt with his bare hands. "My daughters will love all the colors," he says. He spits tobacco juice into a pot as he plants a begonia. "I put in a rusty nail," he says. "The iron is good for the soil." He glances, sideways, at me and grins. "You really give a shit, huh?"

Without opening my eyes, I nod, "That's all right, Tom. Keep talking. I don't mind humoring you." Tom grunts an obscenity and continues planting. Nancy and their two daughters will not arrive from their Greenwich home until school gets out in a few weeks. Until then, Tom is leading the life of the bachelor. He doesn't like it. He likes it even less when he is not pitching well, and so far this season, his sixth with the Reds, he isn't.

Tom Seaver is thirty-seven years old, and he is in the twilight of a career against which all future careers will be judged. He has won 20 games in a season five times during a fifteen-year major league career that includes 259 victories, 3,788 innings, 3,075 strikeouts, 54 shutouts, and a lifetime earned run average of 2.60. He has averaged over 17 victories a season and has won the Cy Young Award three times. Last year he was 14-2 in a strike-shortened season and almost certainly would have won his fourth Cy Young Award (which would have been a record) if the Dodgers' Fernando Valenzuela had not won it for reasons having little to do with his pitching. Tom Seaver was the best pitcher in his league last year, bar none. But such things do not bother Tom. Nor does he worry about being underpaid. He earns about $400,000 a year while teammate Tom Hume, with a lifetime 39-37 record, makes almost $600,000 per year. Nor does Tom worry about winning 40 more games to become one of the handful of pitchers to win 300 games in a career.

"If I don't get it, I don't get it," Tom says. "It's good to have goals, but sometimes you lose sight of what the initial enjoyment is if you worry too much about goals. It's like the other night. I was driving home from the ballpark, listening to the radio, when they had this interview with an oboist for the Minneapolis Symphony Orchestra. He was retiring, and they asked him if he had any advice for young musicians. He said, 'Remember, no matter how long you work, don't forget what made you do it: love for music.'"

Tom glances up and nods to make his point. Then he looks out through the trees to the third tee. He sees three young Reds' teammates about to tee off. Tom jumps up. "Watch this!" he says. He sneaks over behind a tree. He peeks out like a comic book villain as one of the players is methodically teeing up his drive. Seaver waits until the player is in his downswing and then he lets out a blood-curdling scream. The player tops the ball and it rolls a few dozen yards into the line of trees before it stops. Seaver is roaring with laughter. He goes over to the players. They talk and laugh with an athlete's kind of boyish camaraderie that knows no age limit.

Tom is at ease with teammates in a way few stars are. He truly likes them. The rookies, the veterans, the farmboys, the jocks, the big city dudes, the intellectuals. He likes them all. He is amused, not annoyed, by natures that differ from his own. Tom and I are opposing tintypes. The hot-tempered Italian writer. The phlegmatic WASP pitcher. Sometimes, when I say something to him, about innocence, say, or some other abstract subject, he cocks his head like a confused puppy and gives me a tiny grin. Not a condescending grin. Not a grin that says 'What a fool!' But more a grin that says, 'That's Pat, all right.' He judges no one.

While Tom is talking to his teammates I go inside to make a phone call. Laid out across the dining room table is a mammoth puzzle of minute pieces. The pieces, when fit together, will make up a serene country landscape. I see Tom suddenly in my mind's eye, late at night, alone, after a bad game, hunched over that puzzle, fitting piece after piece together with that infinite patience of his, as if each piece were a pitch in his vast career.

While I'm talking on the phone I notice a newspaper headline taped on the refrigerator door. It reads: "Seaver Throws Erratic Shut-Out At Astros, 4-0." It is precisely the kind of thing Tom would find amusing. I have a quotation from Joan Didion, the writer, taped over my desk. It reads: "Writers are always selling somebody out."

When I return to the deck, the players are far up the fairway and Tom is talking to the next door neighbor. A tall, silver-haired man with a farmer's tanned and leathery skin. The man is saying to Tom, "She's been losing weight. I don't know. All we can do is wait for the tests and cry."

"Yeah, well you gotta cut that out pretty damned quick," Tom says. The old man looks down at his feet. He nods weakly and then walks back to his condominium. Tom shakes his head in disgust. Almost fury. "Jeez, it'll break my kids' hearts. She baby-sits for them. They love her."

At 5:45 p.m. the Reds' clubhouse is filled with players in various states of undress. Only Caesar Cedeno is totally naked. He walks back and forth across the carpeted floor as if to draw attention to his body. Unlike most players he is not fat around the middle. He has a lean, tightly muscled body that is the color of bitter chocolate. He is wearing almost as many gold chains around his neck as Mr. T does. He is also hung, in locker room parlance. He nods to Tom as he passes. Tom looks sideways at me. He raises his eyebrows. "Tells you something about a guy, huh?" Then he goes over to the clubhouse stereo system to put on a tape he recently bought. It is of Alberta Hunter, an eighty-seven-year-old black singer who began her career at age twelve, singing in Chicago saloons. Soon her scratchy, sexy voice fills the clubhouse. Tom goes to his locker, undresses, and puts on his longjohns. He sits down on a three-legged stool and begins working a crossword puzzle in the *New York Times*.

"Listen to her," Tom says. "Isn't she great? She quit singing for twenty-four years and just recently went back to it. She's singing at the Cookery in Greenwich Village." He sticks a wad of chewing tobacco in his mouth and pores over the crossword puzzle.

Alex Trevino, the Reds' catcher, stops by Seaver's locker to discuss the way they will pitch to a certain Houston batter. "He likes the ball away from him," Trevino says.

Tom, serious now, shakes his head. "No, Alex. I think he likes it inside. He turns his wrists over."

"No. Away, Tom."

Tom shakes his head, no. "I don't think so, Alex."

When Trevino leaves, Tom says, "You know, I was reading the *Sporting News* the other day and I thought I was leading the league." He grins. "Then I realized I was reading the paper upside down."

Tom stops suddenly, cocks an ear to Alberta Hunter. She is singing, "Get your hand off it. It's too delicate for you. I'm saving it. I'm talkin' about my big red rose." Tom screams out, "She's eighty-seven fucking years old! Do you believe it! She's full of life!" His teammates break into laughter.

At exactly 7:05 pm—the game will start in twenty-five minutes—Tom finishes his crossword puzzle and puts on his uniform. "Time to go to work," he says.

I watch him warm up in the bullpen. His motion is still the same. Seaver's motion. A conscious, painstaking, meticulous creation. The pump, the kick, the release, the grunt, the little hop at the end to square himself off against the batter. It is a perfectly compact, powerful motion, but without grace. Unlike mine. I had a big, easy, effortless-seeming motion that seemed too graceful for a man my size. I loved the aesthetics of my motion. Maybe too much. Tom knew, long before I did, that it was perfection, not grace, that really mattered.

He pitches a strong if atypical game for the Tom Seaver people remember back in New York when he pitched for the Mets. He no longer has that good, strikeout fastball, but he still has a decent sinking fastball, and his intelligence, and above all, that doggedness. He *never* quits! He gets the Astros to hit routine ground balls for six innings before they finally push across a run in the seventh. But still, he gets out of the inning with a 3-1 lead. He does not return for the eighth. I am waiting for him when he reaches the clubhouse. I extend my hand.

"Thanks," he says, as we shake hands. He is keyed up, as nervous as any young boy in Little League. Still! After all these years! It is amazing. "I didn't have anything warming up," he says. "But when I got out there I didn't force it. Patience. That's what Gil Hodges always preached. Patience." Tom's uniform is drenched with sweat and he is breathing heavily as he talks. His eyes are almost glassy as if he were on a drug. It is then, at that moment, standing alone with him in the deserted Cincinnati clubhouse, that I admire Tom Seaver as much as any man I have ever met. Over the years I have learned things from him I can never hope to repay him for.

Tom goes to his locker, strips down to his shorts. The trainer wraps an ice pack around his right shoulder. When the trainer is finished Tom hurries into the players' lounge and calls Nancy in Greenwich. She picks up the phone on the first ring. They talk a long time while Tom sips from a can of beer. He is sitting on a leather sofa. His head is inclining toward his left shoulder, toward the telephone receiver. I watch him through the doorway. He nods as Nancy talks. Then he says something. She responds. He smiles.

V

It is winter. The stone walls of the old cellar are cold. Tom Seaver has a virus, and still, dripping sweat, he is throwing baseball after baseball into a net while his dog, Penny, watches. It is Tom's day to throw. He is forty years old. Throwing baseballs into a net in the cold cellar of his home in Greenwich, Connecticut. He picks a ball from a blue bucket. Pumps. Delivers with a grunt. The ball hits the net high and bounces back to Tom. He fields it with a swipe of his glove like a young boy.

The cellar belongs to a huge old barn Tom and Nancy bought a few years ago, down the road from their previous home near the golf course. They have converted the barn, at great expense, into a luxurious home. It is filled with slabs of sunlight even in winter, and vast open spaces, and green plants. The house is sparingly decorated with antique furniture, original paintings, delicate china, and children's toys tossed comfortably about the den off the kitchen.

"The antiques are Nancy's things," Tom says to me, between pitches. "The paintings are mine. I don't know much about art, just what I like.

When we first moved a few years ago, there were bats living in the rafters." He laughs. "They used to fly down when we ate dinner. We couldn't even smoke them out. They're gone now."

Penny scampers off and Tom begins his delivery. In mid-motion, he pauses, says to me, "They say you get past thirty-five and you lose your velocity. But last year I could still bring it in the nineties when I had to." He fires. The ball hits the net low and outside to a righthanded batter. "I threw that ball pretty good, huh?" He snares the rebounding ball. "Velocity's only one thing. Then there's location and movement of the ball. You can still determine the latter two no matter how old you get. And you can always learn to change speeds. I've got a great change-up now. Wanna see?" He throws again, and despite his considerable arm speed, the ball moves more slowly towards the net. "Not bad, eh?" He smiles, snares the rebound with a swipe of his glove. "My ego doesn't get in the way," he says. "I don't have to strike out batters with a fastball any-more. I wish I had a better curveball, though." He stops, puts his hands on his hips. "You know, I never intellectually understood why it works. A curveball, I mean."

After a quick shower, Tom, dressed in a plaid shirt, chino slacks, and house slippers, goes into his office at the far end of the house. His winter days in Greenwich always follow a certain routine. He wakes, works around the house—*putters* is the word for it—as if he were a much older man, before returning to his office to take care of business matters. Tom *is* a putterer. Recently, he trimmed his wine cellar with oak taken from the barn. It was gouged and nicked by horse's hooves. Tom stripped the wood and refinished it. He likes to rub his hands over the dark, glistening wood. "This is beautiful stuff," he says. "It's gorgeous. I love it."

Tom leans back in his chair, props his feet on his desk in his den that is filled with photographs of his wife and two daughters, and begins flip-ping through the *Baseball Encyclopedia*. He comes to some statistics about Sandy Koufax, the ex-Dodger great. "Jeez, he had great stats," Tom says. He sounds like any baseball fan in mid-winter in the north. He reads off Koufax's stats with great admiration.

"I'm satisfied with my career," he says. "I've been consistent. That's the kind of thing I admire. I have no disappointments except for maybe all that time I've wasted in airports and hotels and locker rooms. I pass the time reading and playing bridge. Do you know the books of Robert Ludlum?" I nod. "I can read him in the clubhouse. Can you imagine?

With all that noise?" He smiles. "I just keep turning the pages." He makes a dramatic pause, looks at me very earnestly and says, "Maybe you should try to write books like Ludlam?"

"Fuck you, Thomas."

"Just a suggestion," he says. "Now, John Fowles, him I can't read at all. Some of his sentences are one hundred fifty words long! I'll bet you love *him*, now, don't you?"

"Yep."

"I thought so."

"Why do you like to play bridge?" I say.

"It's a fascinating game."

"Why is it fascinating?"

Tom looks at me, bemused. "It just is."

"But why?"

"Why? Why? Why? It's always, 'Why?' with you. That's sick! I don't know why! I don't even *think* about why!"

I shake my head at him as a father would at a young boy. Tom makes a sound of disgust with his mouth and waves the back of his hand at me. I ask him what he would like to do with his life when he retires.

"Manage."

"What about pitching coach?"

"Nope. No control. I've got to have control."

"What if no one asks you to manage?"

"Then maybe broadcasting, or maybe we'll just take a year off and travel. The family. We'll go to the Masters and the Kentucky Derby and the Indianapolis Five Hundred. All those things I've never seen. And maybe to Europe. I've thought too about going to Georgia and just hunting and fishing and maybe painting for the rest of my life. But I don't think that's realistic. I've got no talent for painting. I have to do something that's rewarding. A challenge. That's my biggest concern. If I have any fears at all, it's that I won't ever find something as challenging as pitching. That would be horrible. But I'm sure I'll find something. It's out there. I just don't know what it will be yet."

Tom pauses for a moment. Reflecting. Something he doesn't like to do. It bothers him. The thought of the unknown. Then he says, "I guess I shouldn't say 'fear.' I don't 'fear' it. I know I'll find it."

When it's time for me to leave Tom walks me to the front door. He takes my coat out of the closet and helps me on with it. Nancy appears, smiling, from the living room. She has let her hair, once bleached bright blonde, grow back to its more natural sandy color. She *looks* more natural than she did years ago when I first met her. They have both aged well. Especially Nancy. She comes toward me and shakes my hand.

"Was Thomas a good boy today?" she says.

"About usual," I say.

Nancy shakes her head in despair. "He wasn't in a very good mood. *People* magazine wants to do a photo layout of us, isn't that right, Thomas, and *People* is not one of Thomas's favorite magazines."

"The last time they sent a photographer to the house," Tom says, "he tried to get me and Nancy to pose lying on our bed. Shit, this time maybe he'll want us in a hot tub, sipping champagne."

Nancy smiles at me. "Better he should get you in the shower, Thomas. With a Stroh's beer in your hand and a cigar stub clenched between your teeth."

I laugh, but Tom just shakes his head in disgust at the thought of this impending invasion of his privacy. He would not even have volunteered to do this piece for *People* if the writer had not been a friend of his who desperately needed the money.

As I am about to leave, I notice a beautiful, smoothly aged, well-rounded antique breakfront. I mention it to Nancy. She laughs and pats her behind.

"It is smooth and well-rounded, isn't it, Thomas," she says. He glares at her. She looks back to me and says, "Thomas loves smooth, well-rounded things. Don't you, Thomas?" He looks mortified. Nancy smiles at him. Finally, he smiles, too. She goes over to him and offers up the side of her face for a kiss.

OBSCURITY

Gregory "Toe" Nash

No Joy in Sorrento:
A Baseball Myth Strikes Out

(from *Harper's*, 2004)

THE MYTH IS: He walked out of a sugarcane field with a bat over his shoulder, an unknown, eighteen-year-old man-boy, 6-6, 240 pounds, with chiseled muscles and a talent as prodigious as Babe Ruth's.

He was born in the sugarcane fields of Sorrento in northwestern Louisiana. His feet were so big his aunt Nora nicknamed him "Toe," or maybe it was his grandmother. He learned to hit a baseball by swinging a broomstick handle at beer-bottle caps tossed to him by his father. When he was twelve a professional scout saw him strike out seventeen of twenty-one batters and hit two home runs, one left-handed, one right-handed, in a Little League game. He quit school at thirteen because it was "boring," and then disappeared. He lived in a trailer with "friends" and cut sugarcane for a living. By fourteen, he was playing in the semi-pro Sugar Cane League on hardscrabble fields littered with collard-green plants and oil drums. He played with much older men, migrant workers and washed-up ballplayers of distant repute, who called him "Hit Man." When he was eighteen, the scout who had seen him at twelve tracked him down and saw him hit two 400-foot home runs, one lefty, one righty, and throw 93-mph fastballs. The scout spirited him off to a Tampa Bay Devil Rays tryout where he hit ten home runs lefty and ten home runs righty. Tampa general manager Chuck LaMar told the media that "Toe" Nash had "Mark McGwire power and a Doc Gooden arm." Tampa's scouting director at the time, Dan Jennings, said he was a "monster... like something out of the old Negro leagues. 'Toe' Nash is Babe Ruth." LaMar added that Nash's life should be "an inspiration to all young men." Then he signed Nash for a $30,000 bonus in September 2000, and a few months later, in January 2001, the Myth of Toe Nash was born.

The Myth was started by Benny Latino, thirty-four, a part-time scout from Hammond, Louisiana, who said that discovering Toe was "the pinnacle of my short career." Then he introduced Toe to Larry Reynolds, a California sports agent, who came to represent Toe. Larry Reynolds told Toe he was living a fairy tale and then introduced him to his brother, Harold, a former major leaguer who is now an ESPN commentator. Harold invited Toe to live with him in California, where he introduced him to famous big leaguers like Tony Gwynn, Eric Davis, and Shawn Green. Harold said he would help Nash get his GED because he was a "good kid. I'll be a father figure, a big brother, a place to live." Then he introduced Nash to Peter Gammons, an ESPN-TV commentator and writer, who wrote a story about Nash on the Internet on January 11, 2001, titled "Devil Rays Find The Natural in the Cane Fields." Gammons compared Nash to the mythical Roy Hobbs in Bernard Malamud's novel *The Natural*. His story had more than 3 million hits, and soon The Myth was picked up by newspapers throughout North America. Oprah Winfrey was interested in his story. Paramount, New Line Cinema, and Disney wanted to make a movie of his life. CBS-News profiled him. There· was talk of $3 million. Gammons was approached to write a book about Nash. After playing in only fourteen games after Little League, and before he played his first professional game, Nash's baseball card was selling for $9.99; he once made $10,000 in two hours signing his cards.

Those stories posed more questions than they answered. His grandmother or his aunt? Why had ESPN got the location of Sorrento wrong? How could Nash strike out seventeen of twenty-one batters in a Little League game when Little League games were only six innings? Why was he allowed to quit school at thirteen, and who were the "friends" he lived with? Many of the writers who wrote about The Myth of Toe Nash never actually went to Louisiana to report on it. They just took the word of people—scouts, agents, general managers—who had a vested interest in promoting The Myth. If Toe Nash really was living a fairy tale, and if his talent really was as prodigious as Babe Ruth's and Roy Hobbs's, I wanted to find out for myself. So over the next ten months I went to Louisiana twice and interviewed everyone involved in the Myth of Toe Nash.

I first flew to New Orleans in mid-February of 2002. I spent five days driving from one small southeastern Louisiana town to another (Hammond, Sorrento, Gonzales, Donaldsonville, Napoleonville, Thibodaux). I drove mostly on two-lane blacktops past rusted-out trailers and cars on cinder blocks, vast fields of sugarcane, swampy bayous, and an occasional plantation mansion set back off the road and shaded by the weepy moss of live oaks. I interviewed people in law offices, sheriff's departments, jails, restaurants, strip malls, trailer parks, gas stations, and in the bleachers of ballparks. Sometimes, driving from one interview to another, I talked to people in California and Florida via my cell phone. Here is what I learned.

Gregory "Toe" Nash was born around the sugarcane fields of Sorrento, population 1,300, a depressed little town of poor whites and poorer blacks living mostly in trailers in *southeastern* (not northwestern) Louisiana. His mother was a drug addict who abandoned Nash and his little sister to his father, Charles Payton, when Nash was thirteen. Shortly afterward, Nash was expelled from two schools, once for fighting and then for threatening a teacher with a knife. He was called "a delinquent" with "no ambition" and "a follower." At sixteen, he moved into a trailer, but with a forty-one-year-old woman, a two-time divorcée and mother of numerous children named Charlene, who had a few aliases—Suttle, Potter—and so many bogus addresses that even the local D.A. didn't know where she really lived. (Last year she was a witness in a murder case.) At eighteen, Toe's body was less chiseled with muscle than marbled with baby fat. He never cut sugarcane, though he did mow his uncle's lawn a few times until he quit because his uncle was too strict with him. The baseball fields he played on were well manicured, and he wasn't unknown to professional baseball. The Pittsburgh Pirates scouted him but decided not to sign him when they discovered his long rap sheet at the Ascension Parish sheriff's office in Gonzales, Louisiana, where he was known as "a criminal, a bad citizen."

Chuck LaMar told me, "The scouting department was aware of *some* trouble but didn't know all the details. I didn't know about his probation." LaMar did admit, though, that Tampa Bay had agreed to monitor Nash's strict probation (no drugs, liquor, weapons, or criminal friends) if he agreed to be on his best behavior "and not embarrass the organization."

Once Nash's past surfaced in late January 2001, everyone who had a vested interest in The Myth rallied around him. His crimes were described as mere bumps in the road, minor offenses committed by a man-boy described as innocent, naïve, trusting, a simple country kid who got lost in airports and was astonished to find out that he could order a pizza over the phone.

Harold Reynolds claimed Nash had "a great personality, fun to be around. He just got caught up with the wrong crowd. You're not dealing with a kid who's a gang member caught in drive-bys."

Jennings, now a vice president of player personnel with the Florida Marlins, said, "After the Gammons story it took on a life of its own. It was a feel-good story. He's a good kid who made some bad choices. Baseball will give him a second chance, because there are two sides to every story."

Toe Nash began his first pro season at Princeton, West Virginia, in the Class A Rookie Appalachian League, where "he was a model citizen," said Jennings. He arrived there already famous. People clamored for his autograph. They fed him dinner, braided his hair, drove him to the mall, loaned him money.

Roy and Ruby Beasley were his host family in Princeton. Ruby told me, "We took him out to eat, on a picnic, to the mall, to church. He was very quiet. Greg was a follower. He wasn't very mature. He was more like a child that depended on us. I told my husband that if he goes back to Louisiana, he'll get into trouble again."

After Nash's first season, in which he batted a mediocre .240, with eight home runs and twenty-nine RBIs in forty-seven games, he returned to Sorrento, where on January 21, 2002, he was arrested for robbery and the forcible rape of a fifteen-year-old white girl.

"He's a street kid who had some potential and squandered it," said Tony Bacala, an Ascension Parish sheriff's deputy. "He surrendered his baseball career to crime." Bacala sat behind his desk leafing through Nash's arrest reports. "Somebody's got their hands full."

Nash was arrested for the first time on March 17, 2000, for driving without a license and possession of marijuana. He told the arresting officer he didn't know his address, Social Security number, or driver's license, and said, "I don't have nothing." In plain view was a bag of marijuana.

Thirteen days later, Nash and a friend, Dalacy Bureau, were arrested for beating up a youth named Chris Oncale and stealing $200 from him. Nash told the arresting officers, "We kicked his ass because he was talking shit." Dalacy Bureau took the $200 from Oncale and gave Nash twenty.

One day later, Nash was arrested for theft and simple battery and damage to property in a fight with Charlene in her trailer. When she asked him to leave her trailer, he punched her fifteen-year-old daughter, stole Charlene's purse, and broke two windows in her car.

Less than a month later, on April 19, 2000, Nash was driving with Charlene when they were stopped for a traffic violation. The officer found marijuana in one of Nash's socks and Valium in the other. He also discovered that there was an outstanding warrant on Nash for missing his court date in the Oncale beating. In November of the same year, Nash was arrested again on a marijuana charge.

On January 30, 2001, Nash was charged with simple battery when he and Charlene, who described their relationship as "loving," got into a fight. She threw a light bulb at him, and Nash banged her head against a wall. He claimed she came at him with a knife because she was angry he was leaving her to go off to play baseball, but there was no mention of a knife in the arrest report.

On February 18, 2001, Nash was arrested for a misdemeanor possession of alcohol by a minor, shortly before he was to go to spring training. The Ascension Parish D.A., Anthony Falterman, agreed to release Nash to Tampa Bay if Nash promised to leave the state, and Tampa agreed to supervise his probation, which the team did. Nash spent the following months until September in West Virginia. He then returned to Sorrento, where he was arrested for robbery and forcible rape on January 21, 2002, again shortly before he would go to spring training with Tampa Bay. There were questions about the fifteen-year-old girl's testimony (Nash admitted he had sex with her but claimed it was consensual and that "I didn't know how old she was"), so the assistant D.A., Robin O'Bannon, reduced the charges to carnal knowledge of a minor, and Nash pleaded guilty. He was sentenced to seventeen months in the Ascension Parish jail in Donaldsonville and served half that time, which covered the entire 2002 baseball season. When he was released from jail, Tampa Bay had cut him and he was signed by the Cincinnati Reds in the winter of 2002. One month later, on January 14, 2003, Nash was arrested for second-degree battery of his white friend James Eric Thomas, who, Nash claimed, had called him a "nigger." He was jailed again and denied bail when it was discovered he had "absconded from supervision" by failing to report to his parole officer. (Nash has spent two years in jail since he turned eighteen.) If he were found guilty of either charge he would be forced to serve ten years in jail for violating his carnal knowledge parole. That hearing was scheduled for March 19, at which time Nash would learn whether he would spend his next years wearing an orange prison jumpsuit or a baseball uniform. Even before that hearing, the Reds had had enough of "Toe" Nash and released him in February before he had ever played an inning for the organization.

Benny Latino lives in Hammond, northeast of Gonzales, where he runs a construction company that restores houses. I met him across the street from Southeastern Louisiana University at noon, and we went for lunch at a nearby restaurant. He's a good-looking man with a wispy, reddish goatee and sunglasses perched insouciantly on his forehead. After only a few minutes talking to Latino it became clear that he dreaded this interview. After he signed Nash, which "changed our lives," he was made a full-time scout. Then, after Nash's crimes were exposed, Tampa Bay made him the fall guy for failing to inform the team of Nash's past.

"I didn't know any of the trouble he's got in," said Latino, as we ate our po'boy sandwiches. "I mean, it wasn't like I could go to his high school and check on him. Oh, I'd heard some things, but I was told it wasn't a big deal. When I was with the kid he seemed fine."

Latino described Nash as having "limited life experience. He had no problems in West Virginia, 'cause he's not smart enough to get in trouble on his own. If that girl flashed him her I.D., I don't think he could read it. I'm sure he didn't know statutory-rape laws. He's the kind of kid you've gotta pick him up and take him everywhere he's supposed to be."

Latino claimed that the Reynolds brothers "dropped the ball" with Nash every time they let him leave California to return to Sorrento. He pointed out that the rape occurred two days before Nash was scheduled to return to California, and this January's aggravated-battery charge came three days before he was supposed to return to California. The Reynolds brothers, he said, had high plans for Nash, but he was too much to baby-sit for all the time. Then, when they found out there was no movie deal after the rape charge, "they dropped him, because their big payday was gone. Everyone had their own motives with Toe. Even the

D.A. [Anthony Falterman]. He's friends with Hot Rod [John "Hot Rod" Williams, a former NBA basketball player and Nash's uncle], and Hot Rod delivers the black vote. This is still Louisiana, you know."

Latino claimed that Williams convinced Falterman to release Nash on probation to Tampa Bay because of their friendship, and that it was Williams who discovered problems with the rape victim's testimony and cast a shadow over her claims.

"You gotta talk to Hot Rod," Latino said, picking up his cell phone. He got Hot Rod and told him I'd be driving down to Sorrento in an hour. Then he hung up. "Hot Rod's a good guy," he said. And then he told me he thought many of Nash's problems stemmed from The Myth. He wished he'd never told Gammons about Toe Nash and the sugarcane fields. Latino looked pained. "The kid had so much raw ability. All he needed was a hundred twenty games a year for four years." Then he brightened. "I got this other kid now, the fastest kid in the Sugar Cane League. I met him in the parking lot one night after a game. His friends were betting whether he could jump over a car. I said, 'I'll take forty of that action.' And he did it. I signed him for twenty-three thousand, and he's in the Sally League now." He looked at me. "He's a hulluva story."

Hot Rod Williams was waiting for me by the baseball stadium he built in Sorrento for his team, the Williams All Stars, which Nash played for in the Sugar Cane League. It's a beautiful field that reportedly cost Williams a million dollars. He's known for giving back to the community where he grew up. He had invested the money he made in the NBA in a construction company. While his men were repairing the road alongside the field, Williams and I sat in the stands behind home plate and talked. Williams is a handsome man, six-foot-eleven, with a beard, who resembles a black George Clooney. He talked exuberantly.

"Greg's a good kid but easily led," he said. "He has a man's body, but he's a child inside. The friends he follows let him use their cars so he'll be beholden to them. One of them's in jail with him for shooting a kid in the back with a shotgun, killing him." He shook his head. "I try to help the boy, get him outta jail, tell him he can do whatever he wants to do, but he just stopped. He lost his space, ya know? Gave up on life." When Nash was about to sign with Tampa, Williams offered him the services of his lawyer and his agent, "but the boy went behind my back and signed with Larry Reynolds. He's got power of attorney over Greg's money. Where'd it go?

I'm the one bailed Greg outta jail. Larry sent a check, but it bounced."
(Reynolds denies this.) "Him and Harold washed their hands of Greg.
They don't even return my calls. Everyone wanted to jump on the band-
wagon too fast—the book deal, the movie—and then after the rape
charge they distanced themselves from him, and I'm still here."

William's account was not entirely accurate. It was Larry Reynolds
who hired a high-priced, high-profile New Orleans defense attorney
named Arthur Lemann III to fight Nash's rape charge. Williams said that
was one of Nash's problems. He should have a local lawyer.

"Lemann didn't do nuthin'," Williams said. "I found out about the
girl's past, that she said two other guys done the same thing to her, and
I told Lemann."

When Williams finally caught a breath, I told him that I wanted to
interview Nash in jail, but the warden wouldn't allow any media in the
jail. Williams jumped up. "We'll see about that," he said. He went over to
his crew and came back with a short, portly, sweet-looking black man
who could pass for a beardless Santa Claus. "This here's his daddy,
Charles," Williams said. Charles Payton smiled and turned his face away,
a painfully shy man. He has worked for Williams for the last nineteen
years. "His daddy will get you in the jail tomorrow," Williams said.

I asked Payton a few questions about his son. He gave me a sideways smile and mumbled, "I tried to talk to him. He say, 'Yes, Daddy,'
and do what he want. I let him go his own way. I couldn't get him rid
of his friends."

I asked Payton what happened to his son's $30,000. "I don't know. I
ain't seen none of it."

Before I left, Williams introduced me to Cedric Robertson, twenty-
three, a centerfielder in the Tampa organization. We walked out to the tall
tree behind the right-field fence. Robertson, a college graduate from
Texas, said, "Tampa sent me to Hot Rod because he's the guy got Toe
together. I'd heard about this legend, how he hits the ball four hundred
feet lefty or righty, and I wanted to compare myself to him. The first time
I saw him he hit a ball over that tree. I found out the legend was true."

The next morning at ten, I went to the Lemann law offices in a restored
old building on a cobblestoned street in New Orleans. While I sat in the
waiting room, the receptionist brought me a book written by Arthur
Lemann III, titled *Hail to the Dragon Slayer*. In it Lemann recounts his

privileged childhood on a sugarcane plantation in Donaldsonville, and then his most famous cases. He has defended more than a few Louisiana senators and governors, the Mafia Don Carlos Marcello, and a priest accused of trafficking in child pornography. Lemann got the priest acquitted by recounting his own sexual exploits when he was thirteen to laughter in the courtroom. My cell phone rang. It was Larry Reynolds, who hadn't returned my calls in a week until he discovered that I was in Louisiana and that Nash was in jail again.

"That boy is trying everyone's patience," said Reynolds. "I don't know why I should even bother if the boy doesn't have a career." He asked me if the D.A. would let Nash loose to play baseball. I told him I didn't know. "Then I can't have any plans for the kid until I hear what the D.A. will do," he said. "I can't tell teams he'll stay outta trouble. I already got burned."

After Reynolds hung up, a boyish-looking man, slightly rumpled, without a jacket or tie, came into the room and introduced himself to me as Arthur Lemann, Nash's lawyer. Larry Reynolds may have thought he had hired Lemann III, but it was Lemann's son, Larry Lemann IV, who handled Nash's case.

We went into the conference room and sat at a long table. Lemann IV produced his files on the rape case and said, "I first met Toe in jail. He didn't trust me. He's a chameleon. He can be quiet or menacing, a thug with his friends. He had a long rap sheet. His fee to retain us was twenty-five thousand dollars. Most of his bonus went to us. But he didn't care. Money's not real to him. He's immature. He just doesn't care about right or wrong or think of consequences. I'm not even sure he wants to be a baseball player."

Then, without looking at his files, Lemann IV told me about the rape case. "She asked him to autograph her arm," Lemann IV said. She didn't accuse Nash of rape on her first visit to the police station. After she filed rape charges, "Hot Rod did what he could," said Lemann IV. "He told me the girl accused two other guys of rape too. Hot Rod's a political player, you know. He makes contributions. The charge was reduced to carnal knowledge, and he admitted he knew she wasn't of age."

Before I left, Lemann IV gave me copies of his rape-case files. I asked if he would represent Nash at his March 19 hearing.

"He's already used up his retainer," he said, "but I might do the revocations hearing." He smiled. "But I'll think twice about handling his next case."

I drove west out of New Orleans to Thibodaux to talk to the man who would ultimately determine whether Nash would ever played baseball again: his parole officer, Craig Berteau. His office was in a strip mall off St. Mary Street. The receptionist asked me if I was on parole with Officer Berteau. I said, "Not yet."

Berteau came into the lobby and led me down a hall to his tiny office. He sat behind his desk and I sat across from him. I told him what the receptionist had asked. He smiled, a slim, small man with the slicked-back hair and pencil-thin mustache of a riverboat gambler.

"My business cards are all over the parish," he said. "Nobody wants to admit they know me." I asked him about Nash's revocation hearing. He grimaced. "Aw, I can't talk about that. Let's just say he seemed mild-mannered and polite." That's how all the adults who come into contact with Nash describe him, even the officers who have arrested him. Berteau did agree to describe the hearing process, however. "The judge has the final say. I'll give him the facts. What I think. Sometimes the judge will ask for my recommendation, but he don't have to follow it." In Nash's case, Berteau's recommendation will take into account whether he will leave Sorrento, where he will reside, and with whom, and whether that person will supervise his probation. Berteau assumes that person will be one of the Reynolds brothers. If the Reynolds brothers do not present a detailed plan for supervision of Nash at the March 19 hearing, then it is a foregone conclusion that Nash will spend the next ten years in jail.

I left Thibodaux at noon and drove north to Sorrento, where Charles Payton, dressed in his best jeans and a clean shirt, was waiting for me beside Williams's baseball stadium. We drove in silence to the Donaldsonville jail, a small, square, white brick building surrounded on all sides by a wire fence topped with razor wire.

Inside, Payton asked the officer behind a glass partition if he could talk to his son. A few minutes later, the warden, Bobby Weber, came out of a door. "I told you I can't allow no media to talk to him," he said. I pleaded my case. Weber looked at Payton. "Well, if it's awright with you, Mr. Payton?" Payton nodded.

We went into a narrow room with chairs and a telephone by each cubicle on either side of a glass partition. I saw the bottom half of an orange prison jumpsuit moving past the cubicles. Toe Nash sat down across from me. He was a huge, handsome kid with braided hair. We talked to each other through the telephone. I asked him first about his pro-baseball season.

"It was tougher than I thought," he said. "[St. Louis Cardinals pitcher] Rick Ankiel struck me out three or four times." Then he said the toughest part of his season in West Virginia was living up to his myth. "I wish I coulda just played a few years like everyone else before that stuff."

Then Nash described life in jail. "We play basketball outside. Cards, dominoes. The loser got to do sit-ups. A good bit of my friends is here. The new guys ask me questions 'cause they read about me in the papers. But, shit, I wanna get out." He hung his head.

When I asked if his problems were caused by his friends, he showed a flash of anger. "It's not like anybody controls me. I can't blame no one else. I just wanna play ball so I can help my daddy and little sister. I ain't never had no money before." I glanced at his father, who'd told me he hadn't seen a penny of his son's $30,000.

"All my money's in a bank in L.A.," he said. "With Larry, whenever I need it."

Our time was almost up, so I let his father talk to him. Payton didn't say much to his son, just mumbled a few words, nodded, and we left.

On the morning of my third day I drove north to the D.A.'s office, in a Gonzales strip mall, to talk with Assistant D.A. Robin O'Bannon, who handled the rape case. Lemann IV had described her as "tough but fair."

O'Bannon is a vivacious blonde who had canceled our last meeting because she had to watch the last episode of *The Bachelorette*, which she described as "very funny." She sat behind a desk piled high with papers and said Nash was a "little hood that didn't appreciate the opportunity that was given to him." She said he was lucky to get his rape charge reduced to carnal knowledge when the girl's credibility came into question. "I didn't believe we could prove a rape beyond reasonable doubt," she said. "But I do believe Nash raped her. Now the girl and her parents hate me."

I asked her if she believed Nash's problem was that he was afraid to leave Sorrento. She exclaimed, "Oh, puhleeze! He got in trouble because he's afraid to go away and play baseball for thirty thousand dollars?"

Before I left Gonzales I stopped for gas. I remembered that someone familiar with the case had told me everyone dumped on the girl because she was poor white trash. I pulled out Lemann IV's files and began to read the arrest report:

At midnight of January 21, 2002, Nash, Bureau, and Thomas, known as "Money," went to the house of a seventeen-year-old girl in Donaldsonville. Bureau and Nash took turns having sex with the girl, and the other one carted off her father's safe, a Kentwood water jug filled with coins, and a CZ-Czechoslovakian semi-automatic pistol. At about 3:00 A.M., at a house in Gonzales, the alleged victim and two white male friends were drinking. One of the males called Toe for marijuana. When Nash, Bureau, and Thomas arrived they brought in the safe and the Kentwood jug. They told the girl they had pulled a "lick" in Donaldsonville. While the three were trying to crack the safe, the girl went into the bathroom. A few minutes later, she claimed, Nash and Bureau broke down the door and raped her. In her written statement to the police, in a child's big, round, printed letters, she wrote,

> We were all chillin hanging around talking and stuff. . . . I sat my drink down to go to the restroom then I went back to the livingroom someone told me that delacy and toe put something in my drink. I didn't believe them so I finished it off. 20 minutes later I went back to the bathroom. This time I heard a knock . . . and delacy he said Are we going to faxx or not When I said no toe forced hiself on top of me. When he done . . . delacy got on and he did the samething. After that was over Toe put his you know what in my butt and he keep saying it feeled good huh. I told them a bunch of times to stop but they did not. They just continue. After everything was over delacy, toe, and Eric left. That they were going to hurt me and family members if I was not quit. End.

The problem with the rape victim's testimony was that she did not give it to deputies when she was first interviewed at the police station. The girl and her mother left, then returned a few minutes later, and then the girl told an officer she'd had sex with Nash and Bureau. When asked if she was forced, the girl said, "I can't remember."

On the page after the arrest report there was a petition from the court that claimed the rape victim as a thirteen-year-old had been an ungovernable child and a truant. In the middle of that petition was the girl's name, and her address in Gonzales. I called the operator and got the number. Her father answered. I told him who I was and what I was doing.

"A story on that fucking nigger," he said. Then he insisted I talk to his daughter, who was now sixteen and living with a boy. He gave me her number and I called her. She had the light voice of a child. "Yes, sir," she said, "my daddy told me to talk to you." She gave me directions to her trailer and I drove there. She lived at the end of a street lined with ramshackle trailers and rusted-out cars. There were four rusted-out "vehicles," as she called them, on her front lawn, and a number of mangy-looking pit bulls prowling around as well. The girl was sitting on the deck in front of the trailer, drinking a Pepsi. A boy, maybe eighteen, skinny, with a shaved head, was sprawled in a chair behind her. I climbed up onto the deck and introduced myself. I asked the boy who he was. He replied, sullenly, "I'm the one lives here."

I sat down across from the girl, who was pale and pretty and small, and asked her if she would mind recounting the night of the rape. She began to talk without emotion:

"I didn't know him before that night," she said. "Except as a known drug dealer. I thought he would just come to my house, we'd pay for the weed, and he'd leave. My older brother was passed out, and my younger brother was asleep. I had a glass of Bacardi and took two Valiums. After I done took them, Toe and Dalacy put something in my drink. I went to the bathroom to throw it up and they broke the door off the frame. Toe told me, 'This is the way a bitch is supposed to be treated,' all kinda stuff like that. Then they held me down with a hand over my mouth so I couldn't scream. First Dalacy did it, then Toe. I was bleeding real bad after it." When she was examined at a hospital the next day, doctors had discovered anal tears.

"Toe had a gun he said he got in Donaldsonville. I seen it. He threatened to kill my little brother if I told. The next day I didn't tell the police 'cause I was scared. My mother made me go back and tell 'em when I told her about the bleeding. But nobody believed me. Everybody said I was lyin', even my own defense attorney [Assistant D.A. O'Bannon], because Toe was a famous baseball star."

After she finished her story, I thanked her and went to my car. Just before I pulled out of the driveway she came over to my window. She asked me for proof that I was a reporter. I showed her a letter that satisfied her. Then I remembered something that Lemann IV had told me.

I said, "If you didn't know Toe was a famous baseball player, then why did you ask him to autograph your arm?"

"I didn't," she said. "He autographed my butt after he, you know. He wrote on it, 'Toe Nash, Fuck Number 24.'"

It was already hot and sunny at 9:00 A.M. on March 19, outside the Ascension Parish Courthouse, a nineteenth-century red-brick building shaded by live oaks in the sleepy little town of Donaldsonville along the banks of the Mississippi River. Donaldsonville has a high, grassy levee to hold back the river, a small park with a gazebo, a number of partially restored antebellum Colonial and Victorian houses, and the Railroad Café, where black women wearing white aprons serve oyster po'boy sandwiches and sugary, homemade pralines.

The second-floor courtroom of Judge Alvin Turner, Jr. was already packed to overflowing. Spectators sat on worn wooden benches and stood along the walls. Lawyers with wavy, silvery hair hustled back and forth with sheaves of paper. A number of beefy officers in blue stood guard over the twenty or so prisoners in orange jumpsuits who sat, handcuffed together, in two rows of long benches like church pews. Most of the prisoners waved and smiled at friends and family. They pantomimed instructions. Nash sat in the second row, his jaw in the palm of his hand as if he were bored, or sleepy, or maybe just anxious to get back to jail for lunch. When his case was called, he had to be told to stand up.

For the next thirty minutes, O'Bannon and Berteau argued their case *sotto voce* to the judge, while Lemann IV stood between them looking bewildered. ("He had no clue what was going on," Berteau said later.) Nash stared at the floor, shifted his weight, then sat down. O'Bannon glared at him. "Please stand, Mr. Nash!" she said. He stood up again. He seemed unaware that a lot of people had an interest in his life, even if he didn't.

Judge Turner's decision was that Nash could be released *only* to Larry Reynolds's supervision in California, or else Nash would have to remain in jail where, almost certainly, his carnal-knowledge probation would be revoked and he'd go to jail for ten years.

The next afternoon I called Larry Reynolds and asked him what his plans for Nash were. "Well," he said, "we're in the process of making arrangements to get the situation handled." I told him the judge wouldn't let Nash out of jail unless Reynolds supervised his probation. Reynolds blurted out, "Hell, I'm not takin' responsibility for no parole."

In June of 2003, Toe Nash was released from jail. He boarded a flight for Ontario, California, where he was met by the twenty-six-year-old college student and mother of two small children with whom he would live. She was a close friend of Larry Reynolds, whom she referred to as "my uncle." For a number of reasons, she pleaded with me not to use her real name, so I will call her simply Mary.

Mary was majoring in early childhood studies at a community college and worked in the business office of her church. She lived in what she described as an "affluent condo in a drug- and crime-free zone that is right next to a golf course."

She had first met Nash during one of his stays with Larry Reynolds. She described him then as "a very sweet, sweet guy when he was around Larry. We became friends, then our relationship turned romantic." When Nash was arrested on his carnal-knowledge charge, Mary said, "He told me he loved me and that he was innocent."

While Nash was incarcerated, said Mary, they communicated through letters, which led her to believe he was still a "nice guy." When she learned that Nash could be released from jail after a May hearing only if someone in California took him in and monitored his behavior, and that Larry Reynolds refused to be responsible for Nash, she called the judge and then wrote him a letter stating that Nash could live with her and that she would provide a stable environment. She assured the judge that "he would never hurt anyone again." Mary is an articulate woman, and the judge was so impressed with her letter that he released Nash to her care in June.

Shortly after Nash moved in with Mary, she realized he was "a totally different person than the one I'd met." Although she didn't know it at first, Nash began a sexual affair with Mary's twenty-six-year-old neighbor only days after he'd arrived. He started coming home late at night, and when Mary questioned him, "he would become violent and force himself on me. When I went to work, he'd sit on my front porch drinking and smoking and talking on the phone all day to his friends in Louisiana. He ran up a thousand-dollar phone bill, and my phone was disconnected. I told him he'd promised to get a job and go to church with me, but he never did."

When Mary had minor surgery on her hand, the doctor gave her a prescription for Vicodin. Nash stole the pills and swallowed sixteen of them. When he started to come down from the effects he became violent and "threw" Mary around in front of her children. Then, about a month after Nash moved in with Mary, he came home at 1:00 A.M. after having sex with her neighbor. When Mary confronted him about this and told him he wasn't adhering to his curfew, "he absolutely beat me up," she said. "He grabbed my hair and shoved my face into the ground. He ripped my small braids out of my head. I was crying when he lifted my denim skirt over my head and rammed his fingers inside me, both places. He was laughing, like it turned him on. 'This is what you want, bitch,' he said. That's when I called Jennifer and told her to come and pick him up."

Jennifer Marisnick is the director of marketing for Reynolds Sports Management. She is in her late thirties, married, with three sons. According to Mary, when Jennifer came to pick up Nash and Mary told her what Nash had done to her, Jennifer warned Mary not to tell anyone. She told Mary no one would believe her, they'd just think Mary was jealous of Nash's relationship with Mary's neighbor, and that Mary made up her accusations to get even. Besides, Jennifer told Mary, it would ruin her friendship with her "uncle," Larry Reynolds.

"To keep me quiet," Mary said, "Larry gave me five hundred dollars. They said they'd pay my expenses, but they never did. They really used me."

Months passed and Mary did nothing, while Nash lived in a trailer on Jennifer's property. "She told me Toe was a perfect angel," said Mary. "But he always is an 'angel' with adults." Mary said that Nash seduced adults with his soft-spoken deference, his humility, his ineffectualness, his ability to parrot back to adults what he knew they wanted to hear. But with his peers he was aggressive, violent, and sexually abusive.

When Mary began cleaning out her old phone numbers in October she came across mine. I had called her in late June to ask if Nash was living with her. She had just "kicked him out" but was too frightened to tell me this. Now she decided to call and tell me what had happened because "he's gonna hurt someone else if I don't," she said. "He turned out to be exactly what he was accused of. Exceptionally violent. He's got sexual hang-ups. It's pretty grotesque what he did to me. He should absolutely be in jail."

After speaking with Mary, I called Jennifer at Reynolds Sports Management. She told me Nash had gone directly from Louisiana in

June to live with her. "He was fabulous," she said. "He went to school every day, worked out with the high school coaches. Of course, I had to take him to school, because he didn't know how to use the bus system." Jennifer insisted Nash had never lived with anyone but her and her family since he was released from jail in June and that "I was not aware he ever got into any trouble [out here]."

In late August, Nash told Jennifer he was "homesick" and uncomfortable living with her. "My husband and I ran a tight ship," she told me. "Very structured. He had to do chores. Toe began to cry. He said he just wanted to go home, and he didn't want to play baseball anymore. He was uncomfortable with the media attention. I was very disappointed, because at the time some major-league teams were interested in him. It's a sad story. He's a product of his environment, and he has no deep drive to change." Before she hung up, Jennifer beseeched me not to write anything negative about Toe Nash. She claimed he was just a good kid who had been misled by his peers.

On September 2, Jennifer called Berteau and told him Nash was returning to Sorrento because he was "homesick for his family." Nash arrived on September 4 and immediately went to the home of a friend Berteau described as "a hoodlum." Because Nash was still on probation for his carnal-knowledge conviction, he was required to report to Berteau the moment he set foot in Louisiana. When he didn't, Berteau had him picked up on September 5 and transported back to the Ascension Parish jail.

He remained in jail until his next hearing, on December 15, at which time the judge released him and reinstated his parole, which meant he had to report to Berteau. A few months ago I called Berteau and asked how Nash was doing. He told me that Nash was fulfilling the dictates of his probation. He was still in Ascension Parish, of course, but living with his father now and playing with the Hot Rod Williams All Stars in the Sugar Cane League. At twenty-two, he had more in common with his older, more world-weary teammates than with the eighteen-year-old phenom he used to be. He certainly was no longer a myth.

Frank Viera

The Pork

(from Yankee Magazine, 1988)

Porky. THE PORK. FLORINDO. FLO. He hasn't changed. After all these years. I smile as he comes toward me. Pigeon-toed. Bow-legged. Like he was carrying a barrel between his knees. He takes short, bouncy, pigeon-toed steps, his shoulders hunching forward, shifting left-right, like a fighter warming up in his corner. That's the way he played. Like a fighter, always overmatched. I remind myself again to call him Frank. Fifteen years ago I saw him at a college game.

"Pork! How's it going?"

He looked up, pained, and gave me a little sideways turn of his head as if to fend off light. "Jeez, Pat! Come on! It's Frank, now."

For him, maybe. For Frank Viera. Mr. Viera. Coach Viera. But not for us. Who'd seen him play. The Pork. At the Boys' Club gym. The old Brass Armory. Madison Square Garden. Anywhere there was a game. Sometimes two. In the same day. He scored 106 points one day. Fifty in the afternoon, before he got loose, and then 56 at night, after an hour's drive in a sweat-soaked uniform. Nobody stopped the Pork. I saw him score 65 one night. Seventy-two the next, 77 the night after that. He scored 27 against Sihugo Green and the Knicks, and claimed it was an off-night. He scored 28 in a half against Hot Rod Hundley and the Lakers. He scored 55 against Goose Tatum's All-Stars, and the next night they roughed him up pretty good. He outscored Wilt. Head-to-head in the Catskills. All the old Jews laughing in the stands, laying bets, even money, that the spic would outscore the schvartze. And he did. Thirty-eight to thirty-three. Wilt was furious. He hung back one time, under Porky's basket, and waited. The play had moved to the other end of the court. Porky stole the ball, came back over half-court alone, saw Wilt waiting for him, lowered his head, and went straight at him. To the right of the foul line Porky went up, off the wrong foot, for a hook shot. Wilt leaped at him, his arms outstretched like wings. In midair, Porky spun from right to left, his hand with the ball swooping down in an arc and then up again, under Wilt's arms. He layed the ball high off the corner of the backboard, gave it a little cueball spin. Good. And a foul. Nobody stopped the Pork. Not Wilt. Not Sihugo. Not Hot Rod. Not even Topsy. Topsy DelGobbo had a nice game. He could play. Smooth. Maybe too smooth. Slick, really. He never sweated. A south-paw with a second-rate crooner's good looks and a spotlessly pressed uniform. He wore blindingly white sweat socks that reached almost to his knees. But he gave Porky fits. Made him work. The joke was Topsy used to meet Porky at the ticket window at the old Brass Armory. Porky would push through the big brass doors looking always a little rumpled, carrying his leather satchel with his stuff, his uniforms, dozens of them for all the different teams he played on, all of them wrinkled and stiff with sweat, his sneakers dirty and scuffed, his sweat socks gray and wilted. And there was Topsy. Smiling. Waiting. Looking almost starched in his uniform. Porky would give him that pained, sideways turn of his head and walk right past him. Topsy followed him down to the locker room, watched him dress, followed him back upstairs onto the court, watched him warm-up, followed him to the circle for the center jump, never taking his eyes off Porky. Topsy's sole purpose in a game was to stay less than a foot away from Porky's face. He didn't care about the action behind him, a blown whistle, time-out, half-time. He cared only about Porky. He stayed face-to-face with him like a sandwich board and he had to be pulled away from Porky during a time out. Nobody shadowed Porky like Topsy. He dogged him, really, smiling up into Porky's face. Topsy, impassively smiling. Porky, waving his arms, screaming in that shrill, little-girl's voice of his, "Gimme the ball! Gimme the ball! Gimme the fucking ball!" Every once in a while Topsy would have a good game against Porky, a *nice* game, really, good enough at the whistle to receive a standing ovation from the crowd for holding Porky under fifty.

Like I said, Porky was the first guy ever to outscore Wilt in a game. It was in the late fifties, in the Catskills in the summer. After the game they posed Porky with Wilt for a photograph. They stood side by side. It was a comical picture. Wilt, unsmiling, stood with his hands behind his back. Porky, smiling at the camera, thrust out his big, melon-like jaw. Wilt and the Pork. Wilt, seven-foot-one, with legs like palm trees. Porky, with his bowed legs. And his barrel chest. And that jutting jaw. Porky. The Pork. Flo. Florinda Viera. A Portuguese immigrant from Bridgeport, Connecticut. Five feet, five and one-half inches tall. The top of his head was level with Wilt's waist.

He still looks the same, approaching fifty, as he walks toward me across the parking lot. Slicked-back, black hair. Dark skin with a faint olive tint. An even darker stubble, a shadow, around his jaw. That jaw! Like a watermelon. Joe Palooka's jaw. Only he wasn't anything like Joe Palooka. Not pale. Not blond. Not amiable. Not modest. Porky was dark and fierce and possessed, like a demon, a Tasmanian devil on the court. And off. He ran to Danbury on a dare—from Bridgeport, thirty miles away. He was in a car with some friends, just cruising. They drove past the jail and the North End Boys' Club when somebody told him, kiddingly, that Topsy DelGobbo was in better shape. "He don't look like shit at the end of a game like you do, Pork."

"What?" he screamed. "Stop the fucking car!" Porky got out, still in his street clothes, his hard-soled shoes, and began to run. His friends followed beside him in their car. They drove slowly down Madison Avenue, past Pacelli's Italian Bakery, past Yurdin's Hardware, past Frank's Market, the Rodeph Shalom, St. Margaret's Shrine. Drivers honked their horns and cursed as they swerved out to pass. When they reached Route 58 in Easton, Porky picked up the pace. He ran past the reservoir and the pine trees and the old colonial houses, and when he reached the city limits of Danbury he sprinted the last few yards just to rub it in, and then turned around and offered to run back again to Bridgeport.

"Awright! Awright!" His friends said. "Get in the fucking car awready!"

Porky is wearing black shoes, dark slacks, and a nylon navy windbreaker with the name of his college stenciled on it in white. New Haven College. Thirty miles from Bridgeport. Porky has been a teacher and a coach here since 1962. A college professor. With tenure and an academic chair. Porky Viera. That's why he changed his name, legally, from Florindo to Frank about fifteen years ago. That's why he asked his friends to stop calling him Porky. It was an embarrassment to him, to Frank Viera, the professor and the coach. He wanted to distance himself from that twenty-two-year-old Porky who ran to Danbury on a dare. His boss at New Haven College told him to wear a tie, to stop saying "fuck" every other word, and to get rid of that ridiculous nickname. So Porky did it, went even farther than that. He changed his given name. On the day it was announced in the Bridgeport newspapers that Florindo Viera, better known to area sports fans as Porky Viera, once the highest scoring college basketball player in the nation in his freshman year (1953-54), had legally changed his first name to Frank, the laughter of his old cronies could be heard all the way to New Haven. "Who does he think he's kidding?" said one. "He'll never be anything but the Pork."

"Jesus, but I didn't show my face for weeks," Porky says. "I was so fucking embarrassed."

The irony of all this was that Porky had been hired at New Haven College as only the assistant basketball coach and, as a sop, the head baseball coach, a game he had always played well, almost as well as basketball. The head basketball coach used Porky to recruit players all the while promising him that in a few years, when he retired, Porky would take over the reins. But that coach held on for so long that Porky lost interest in the job and concentrated all his energies instead on his baseball team. Today he is one of the most successful college baseball coaches in the country. He leads all active coaches in victories, 552, against 130 losses. His teams have appeared in nine national tournaments, twenty-two post-season tournaments, and thirty-five of his players have signed professional contracts. A number of those players have reached the major leagues, the most famous being Atlanta Braves relief pitcher Steve Bedrosian.

Porky, coming towards me, smiles. He is wearing narrow black sunglasses circa 1955, and he is smoking a cigar. He waves the cigar in greeting. The cigar looks huge in his stubby little fingers. Porky always had tiny hands and feet, like a girl's. A basketball in his hands looked like a beachball in the hands of a gnomelike child. He could never even think of palming a basketball, nor could he shoot one-handed like most basketball players, who spread their fingers over the ball, gripped it firmly, and propelled it with their fingertips. When the ball left their hands their fingers would be spread wide as if they were about to cop a feel from Dolly Parton. Alas, Porky's small hands couldn't encompass the breast of an eighth-grade girl. So he adjusted. He held the ball softly in his hand, his fingers pressed together so that his hand looked like a solid piece, like a seal's flipper. He shot the ball with a downward flip of his wrist—limp wristed, some might say. His feet, too, were too small for a basketball player. On top of that, he was so bow-legged that his short legs looked as if they had been deformed in his mother's womb. To compensate, he had to take quick little steps just to maintain his balance. He looked like a man in shorts scurrying over hot coals. And still, in spite of all these deficiencies, he was the greatest scorer in college basketball history. During his four years at Quinnipiac College in New Haven, Connecticut, he averaged thirty-three points per game. He once began a game by missing his first ten shots and ended it with sixty-eight points.

Porky throws up his hands in mock disgust. "Jesus Christ!" he says in that shrill voice of his. "What the fuck happened to you? You look like a fucking bandit with that beard." He throws an arm over my shoulders and gives me a hug. Porky. The Pork. Still the same. After all these years. I remind myself, again.

"It goes with the image . . . Frank. I'm a writer now."

"Image, my ass. And cut that Frank shit. I dropped that awhile ago."

I smile. "Awright, Pork."

He looks at me. "How much money am I gonna get for this book?" I smile again, shake my head, no. "What? No fucking money?" He nods. "All right, I'll take a lunch." I shrug, pull out the insides of my empty pants pockets. Porky gives me that pained, little sideways turn of his head. "Aw, man. Not even lunch. I'm the Pork. The fucking greatest." He exhales a deep breath and shakes his head in despair. "All right, come on you cheap bastard, I'll buy you a coffee."

Walking back to his car, he says, "It wasn't me. Frank Viera. I wish I never did it, but I did. That asshole made me, but still I shouldn't have done it. It sucked. I was the Pork. I couldn't change that. But it made me uncomfortable at college. I was trying to be something different. For a while there I didn't want to be Porky Viera, but now it don't bother me." He glances, sideways at me. He is smiling. "Why should it, eh? The Pork was the greatest. Nobody stopped the Pork. He invented shots. I showed Wilt shots he never saw before or since."

Driving to the diner, Porky talks. And talks. And talks. Without guile. In that high-pitched, little girl's voice of his. "I thought it was all p.r. in college. Me, being short. *Ernie* was short. I could see *that*. He was five-three, for chrissakes. But I never thought *I* was fucking short. I never *played* short. I played like everybody else was short and I was ten feet tall.

Shit, I never realized I was short until a few years ago. Me and the wife were dressing to go out to dinner. I had on boxer shorts and black socks. I look in the mirror at myself and see that the socks went all the way up to my knees. I turned to the old lady and said, 'Jeez, hon! They were right all those years. I ain't got any fucking legs.'"

Porky was born and raised in the Italian ghetto, only a few blocks from where I was born and raised near Nannygoat Park. His was only one of five Portuguese families in the city at the time. 1935. In those days in the ghetto, there was a lot of prejudice. Most of it was directed at the city's newest ethnic arrivals, which in 1935 happened to be the Italians. The Italians took great pains to find an ethnic group that *they* could be prejudiced against. They looked for an ethnic group that someday might pose a real threat to their social position in the city. They didn't bother with the few blacks in the city, who were so far down the social ladder they posed a threat to no one. Then the Portuguese arrived. All five families. The Portuguese settled in the Italian ghetto because they thought they had more in common with that ethnic group than with any other in the city. They were right. They both had Mediterranean-type cultures. Patriarchal. Catholic. Macho. They were both swarthy races easily identifiable as immigrants in the city. Still, this made no difference to the Italians who began to direct their prejudice toward the newly arrived Portuguese. They called them Portuguese bastards. The Italian boys called the few Portuguese boys, like Florindo Viera, little Portuguese bastards. Then it became little Portee bastards. Finally, after Florindo Viera had scuffled in the dust with enough Italian boys, after he had blackened enough eyes, split enough lips, he finally earned their respect. He became Portee. Then Porky. The Pork. Still, he didn't stop. He was so conditioned to defend his honor that, now, he saw imagined slights everywhere. His older brother, Gus, took matters in hand. In fact, he took Porky in hand and dragged him to the city's Boys' Club. "I gotta direct that energy of yours somewhere else," he told his brother. He took him to the gym, pointed out other boys his age playing basketball. "See that kid," he said, pointing to a handsome little Italian boy who was a few years older than Porky and a couple of inches shorter. "If that kid can play this game," Gus said, "so can you." He pushed his little brother onto the court.

"Jeez, Gus was a good guy," Porky says as we drive through New Haven. "If it hadn't a been for Gus, I don't know how I woulda turned out." In his youth, Florinda Viera hung out with some tough guys. More than a few of them have served long stretches in the state prison for armed bank robbery, drug dealing, loan sharking, racketeering, and murder. One, in particular, murdered two of his wives. He grew up with Porky. Played basketball with him, briefly, at the Boys' Club. Then he quit, drifted out onto the city streets. If Gus hadn't found an outlet for Porky's anger and aggressions he, too, might have been doomed to a life of violence on the city's streets.

Porky looks over at me. "He died, you know. Gus. A few months ago." He looks back to the road. "Heart attack." He shakes his head once, and smiles. A pained smile. Through wincing eyes. "He was a real gentleman, Gus."

"I know, Pork." I remembered Gus. He was a big man, bigger than Pork, with a gentle, flat-featured face. When I was a kid, I saw him pitch when I played in the Senior City League, a tough semi-pro league for ex-minor leaguers, ex-big leaguers even, a few college stars, and only rarely a high school player. I was just coming up then. The new high school hot shot in a neatly pressed uniform. My parents came to all my games. I pitched a one-hitter the first time out. I fanned fourteen. I was only fifteen years old. Gus was much older—in his thirties, a bricklayer. He came to the park in his work clothes. He was covered with white lime and gray dust from head to toe. He changed into his uniform in his car, and then, after a ten-hour workday of laying blocks and bricks, he took the mound for his team, the Lenox A.A. He still threw the ball pretty well. He had a nice motion, fluid. I used to study him from the bench. The way he wore his uniform just so. The way he tugged the bill of his cap, his pinky finger raised. The way he hitched up his pants with both hands after a good pitch. He rarely spoke, Gus. He just smiled at compliments from his teammates as he walked off the mound. When the opposition ragged him or when his teammates made an error behind him, he put his head down, landscaped the dirt near the rubber with his toe. He waited for the ball again, tugged his cap once with that pinky finger raised.

"You know who that little fucker was?" Porky says, his voice high-pitched and enthusiastic once again. "Ernie Petruciano." Porky shakes his head and smiles. "You know, it's funny. I spent most of my youth fighting Italians, and the rest of my life hanging with them. Ernie was my first friend. Now, Ernie was short. Even I could see that. We played together for twelve years, through grammar school, high school, and college, and he was still only five-three in college. Imagine! One game in college we scored sixty-eight points between us. When I first met him at the Boys' Club he was way ahead of me in talent. He was already the star of the eighty-five-pounders. Yet, from the first, he subordinated his game to mine. To this day, I don't know why he stepped aside for me. I was his closest friend, and yet I never really knew him. He wasn't anything like me. He was a loner. Quiet. Shy. He had a baby face. I always looked older than him. The only thing we had in common was we were both obsessed with basketball. And we were both short. Well, he was short, anyway. We never fucked with anything that would get in the way of basketball. I was fortunate to have Ernie all those years. He helped make me the Pork. You know, he was the only player I ever feared. It was all psychological. He being the star first, and then older than me. I only played against him once, in an All-Star game. It was the worst game I ever played in my life. He held me to twenty-one points."

In their youth, Porky and Ernie were the stars of the Boys' Club's eighty-five-pound team that would play other eighty-five-pounders between the halves of NBA games in Madison Square Garden and Boston Garden. Porky's first trip to Madison Square Garden was Ernie's seventh, which led Porky to believe that Ernie was a lot older than the twelve years he claimed.

"I always thought somebody forged Ernie's birth certificate somewhere along the way," Porky says. "He looked so young, who knew how old he was in high school?"

Those eighty-five-pounder games were played before an NBA crowd of thousands. Lowered baskets were brought out at half-time. New referees. The players warmed up quickly and the games began. They lasted only eight minutes, but still Porky managed to score as many as fourteen points during that brief span. It was his first success in basketball. The next day he saw his name in the local newspaper. "I got a feeling of pride that's never left," he says. "It's driven me for forty years." Porky grew so obsessed with basketball that in grammar school he would plead with his teachers to let him out of class so he could go to the gym and shoot baskets. To put him in his place, one teacher told him that if he could do fifty minutes of sit-ups, without stopping, then he'd let him out of class to shoot baskets. "I did it," Porky says. "Without stopping. I had scabs all over my lower back. Still, I got to shoot for an hour."

Porky and Ernie went to Central High School in Bridgeport. It was a tough, inner city school, whose student body in those days, 1953, was made up almost entirely of tough Irish and Italian teenagers. There were few blacks at the school. The Hilltoppers, as they were called, since the school was on a hill, had one of the best high school basketball teams in New England. Their coach was a crusty old Irishman named Eddie Reilly who had last played the game when the ball had laces and every basket was followed by a center jump. His success as a coach rested on his being smart enough to know what he knew and what he didn't. He knew his boys, their background, their temperament, and how to motivate each one individually. He knew also that the game he'd once played was passing him by. It was no longer played by sturdy, pale-skinned, Celts with Germanic-sounding names and handlebar mustaches. It was no longer a slow game of methodical plays and crisp, two-handed bounce passes that seemed to go on forever before a player broke free for a lay-up. It was now being played by dark-skinned, wild-eyed youths with flying black hair and vowels at the end of their last names. DelBianco. Patruciano. Viera. They raced up and down the court at breakneck speed and their baskets more often resulted from instinctive moves and shots rather than methodical plays. They were reinventing the game as art, not science. Eddie Reilly knew he did not know how to coach this kind of basketball, so he became a Rousseauean coach: "That coach was best who coached the least." Nobody coached less than Eddie Reilly. At practices, he would take all the basketballs out of a canvas bag, toss them onto the court to his waiting players, and leave the gym.

The Hilltoppers played their games in the basement of their school. It was a makeshift, low-ceilinged gym with even lower-hanging water pipes and steel girders. The players learned to adjust. They fired their shots as if on a clothesline. Porky made check marks on the gym floor to indicate how high he could afford to arch each shot in order to clear a hanging pipe or girder. "I'd come down court," he says, "with my eyes on the floor looking for check marks. When I came to one I went up for a certain type of shot."

In Porky's freshman year, the Hilltoppers were the number one rated team in Connecticut. They played before screaming, overflowing crowds in their tiny gym. "I bombed out," says Porky. "I was awed by the crowds. I just wasn't ready like Ernie and the Globe." The Globe was a portly Italian named Ron DelBianco, who, along with Ernie, became one of

Porky's closest friends. Porky was determined to join them on the start-ing team his sophomore year. He spent the summer at the Boys' Club. He practiced his unorthodox shots an average of eight hours a day in the summer heat which reached over one hundred degrees in the gym. He was the Hilltopper's sixth man in his sophomore year, when the team won the New England High School Basketball Championship in Boston Garden. The players were greeted by over ten thousand fans when their bus returned to Central High School. Again, Porky spent a summer at the Boys' Club. His hours of practice began to pay off in his junior year when he averaged 16.5 points per game, was named to All-State and All-New England teams. His team lost in the New England semi-finals by one point. It was assumed by local fans that Porky would probably hit the magical 20–point-per-game mark in his senior year, a feat accom-plished by few players in that era when high school teams rarely sur-passed 50 points in a game. He was fulfilling those expectations early in the season when his team traveled to nearby Norwalk. He had a phe-nomenal game, hitting 41 points to break the old state record of 32. From then on he went on a tear, scoring over 30 points in thirteen of his last fifteen games.

"It all started then," he says. "Each game was standing room only. Then the games were being sold at six o'clock for an eight o'clock game. One game I scored twenty-five points and there were headlines in the local paper. 'Porky held to Twenty-Five.'" For the rest of his basketball playing career—ten years—fans would show up to his games routinely expecting him to score thirty-five or so points, an average game, for the Pork, while hoping for an exceptional game from him: a forty-pointer, fifty maybe, sixty.

Few colleges bothered to recruit Porky or Ernie after they were grad-uated from high school for a number of reasons. The most obvious had to do with their height—or rather, their lack of it. Porky was 5-5 1/2, and Ernie was 5-3. Bob Cousy, the former Holy Cross star, was consid-ered short in college basketball circles and he was 6-1. It was felt that Porky and Ernie were just *too* short to successfully make the transition from high school to college basketball. Even those few coaches who were willing to gamble on one short but talented player were not insane enough to gamble on two. And Porky and Ernie would not be sepa-rated. They told every coach who came around that they were a pack-age deal. Ironically, more coaches were interested in Ernie than in

Porky. They felt Ernie's game could adapt to college play in a way Porky's couldn't. Ernie was a point guard. A playmaker. He came down the court dribbling the ball as if on a string, like a yo-yo, and no one could take it away from him. Ernie was the master of the blindsided pass. A magician. A master of deceit. Standing straight up, looking left, he flipped the ball underhanded off his right hip, like a pickpocket discarding a wallet, into Porky's greedy hands. He performed his magic with a minimum of motion. He played a calm, soothing game that always seemed to be less than it was. He picked off opponent's passes like a pigeon picks off breadcrumbs. Quick, quicker than the eye could follow. He never forced a shot, but he never missed an open one. He set up at the top of the key, dribbling with one hand, eyeing the opposition. When they fell back to clog up the foul lane against Porky's threat, Ernie took a two-handed set shot, swish, and began backpedaling on defense, his head lowered, as if embarrassed. He lulled the opposition to sleep. They always underestimated his ability. Unlike Porky, the whirling dervish who seemed to scream, "Come and get me! Here I am!" He played the game only at full speed: leading a fastbreak or weaving in and out of the opposition, trying to get free, to pick off the two and three defenders hounding him, all the while waving his hands and screaming, "Gimme the ball! Gimme the ball!" That was the only way to stop the Pork. Keep the ball out of his hands. Once he touched leather it was all over. Nobody in their right mind ever left Porky free for a shot. Besides, he wouldn't let them. He preferred to draw them to him, and then beat them. They tugged at his shirt to slow him down. Tried to trip him. Hooked their elbows into his, like a couple dating. Swatted at him in despair. Knocked him, finally, to the floor in frustration. He bounced up like a Shmoo. Was off again. Waving his hands, screaming, "Gimme the ball! Gimme the fucking ball!"

Ernie receded from the game. Grew smaller than he was. Smaller and smaller until he was insignificant to the naked eye. Porky dominated the game, grew larger than he was, larger and larger until his presence on the court eclipsed all else. The very game itself. Only the Pork existed, frenzied, exorcising his private demons. All else vanished. Which was why most college coaches were not so hot to have him on their team. He was too much the center of the action. He could never subordinate his game to that of a team's. There *was* no team when Porky played. No game. No final score. Nothing but the Pork. When Porky played, no one ever came to see the game. They came to see Porky's game, the game he had patented during all those hours at the Boys' Club. It was like no other game before or since, and Porky was not about to throw away that invention on some college coach who didn't have the imagination to appreciate it, who wanted to make Porky a playmaking guard. The thought was ludicrous to anyone who'd seen him play. Who tells the Pork to pass? Someone who lectures the Pope on sin. The Pork was uncoachable, they said, and they were right. Nobody had ever coached Porky and nobody ever would.

Enter Toofy Maroon. His real name. An Arab, in his fifties, bald, with a sheik's nose, and a low-slung, white clay meerschaum hanging precariously from his fat lower lip. Toofy was the head basketball coach at Quinnipiac College, a small school in New Haven. Not bad in basketball. Respectable, always above .500, but going nowhere. Even its students had trouble spelling the school name (some long-forgotten tribe of New England). But Toofy had ambitions. And a degree in journalism and public relations. He took one look at Porky and Ernie. Five-five-and-a-half and 5-3, respectively, and gave them a four-year free ride. Then he gave them the ball. He sat back in his folding chair on the sidelines and smiled. Toofy, in his navy blazer and repp tie and pressed charcoal-gray slacks. He crossed his legs in a feminine way, held the bowl of his meerschaum with one hand, and puffed. Porky averaged thirty-eight points per game in his freshman year. He was the highest scoring college or professional basketball player in the country. At 5-5 1/2. The AP began to carry Quinnipiac box scores—carried them for four years alongside box scores for Kentucky, UCLA, Ohio State.

"Those were great years," says Porky. "Glorious years." We are sitting in a diner having coffee. "I got to experience things at Quinnipiac that none of those pro cocksuckers would ever understand. They missed out for all their fucking money. They never felt the things I did. When I stepped onto the court I had this feeling that no one could stop me. I invented the box-and-one in college. I always felt I could wear down anyone trying to guard me. I had too much energy for anyone. They stayed with me for a while, but somewhere along the way I'd demoralize them. I'd miss a few shots and they'd smile and think they were getting the job down, and then boom, I'd hit ten straight and they'd quit. I made them quit. The only guy who ever gave me fits was Joe

O'Brien from Assumption College. He wouldn't quit. He just kept trying for forty minutes. He didn't care about anyone else but me. He
kept me under my average every game. I think my best against Joe was
twenty-seven points."

Before Porky began his sophomore year at Quinnipiac, Ernie
Petruciano was drafted into the army. The year was 1954. The Korean
War. Porky went into a slump the next two years. A slump for Porky, no
one else. He averaged 29 points per game in his sophomore year and 30
points per game in his junior year. He rebounded in his senior year with
a 35–point-per-game average, missing out on the nation's scoring
championship by .001 of a point per game. But still, with Ernie gone,
much of the fun had been taken out of Porky's game.

"It wasn't the same without Ernie," he says, sipping coffee. "We'd been
together since we were kids. We knew each other's game. No matter who
was checking me Ernie could always get me the ball." To get some fun
back in his game, Porky began spending more and more time at the
Boys' Club gym, playing ferocious, three-man games at half-court. He'd
practice with Quinnipiac from two until five p.m., and then drive to the
Boys' Club and play on into the night.

"Those three-man games became even more important to me than
the Quinnipiac games," Porky says. "I was the fastest gun in the west.
Guys came from all over the city to challenge me. Sixty, seventy guys
waiting to play. To beat the Pork. To stuff him. Shit, I was fucking ruth-
less in those games. I'd knock people over. I'd kick over lockers if I lost.
They had to hold me back. There were so many three-man teams waiting to play that if your team lost you had to wait for hours to get back
on the court. Once you got the court it was a war to keep it. People
thought I was crazy. They'd say, 'Pork, you're leading the nation in scoring and you're killing yourself at three-man games at the Boys' Club. You
could get hurt!' I didn't care. I wouldn't give up those three-man games
for anything. It was the purest basketball you could play. I loved it. The
guys eyeballing me, waitin' to get a shot at the Pork. The pressure was
great. And the talent! Shiiit! A few years later I played in the East-West
College All-Star game in Madison Square Garden. You know, a lot of All-
Americans. Guys like Charlie Tyra, who went right to the NBA. At practice one day I told 'em. 'You guys ain't shit. I can go to the Boys' Club
right now and round up five guys who'll beat the shit outta all of ya.'"
Porky shakes his head for emphasis and smiles. He raises his eyebrows

and looks sideways at me. "Wasn't that the truth, Pat? The Boys' Club was where it was at. Shit, you should know. You were there."

I was fourteen years old when I asked my father to drive me back to the ghetto. It was the fall of my freshman year of high school and I wanted to learn to play basketball. Even then, the mid-fifties, basketball was a city game and the only place in the city to really learn the game was at the North End Boys' Club in the heart of the Italian ghetto where I was born. All the best basketball players in the city congregated there from the fall to the spring and some, like Porky, even played on through the hot summer months since there were no baseball diamonds in the ghetto. Baseball was a suburban game and the athletes I was now living near played basketball only as an off-season sport in between their more serious pursuits—baseball or football. (Indeed, this was precisely why the game of basketball was invented by Dr. James Naismith of Springfield College in Springfield, Massachusetts.) The suburban athletes I grew up with thought of basketball as an outdoor game. It was played on the driveways of their homes where their fathers had nailed up a backboard and a basket over the garage. Those driveways, where we played pick-up games, were narrow and littered with obstacles—a little sister's doll, a younger brother's tricycle, a father's station wagon. We learned to play a confined game. We seldom dribbled the ball over the uneven pavement; we seldom drove towards the basket for fear of slamming into garage doors; what we did instead was take long, stationary jump shots that barely cleared the low branches of a spreading maple tree. Often, we had an audience: girls our own age, future cheerleaders, who sat, cross-legged, on the lawn and cheered their favorite player. The driveway where we played the most often, because it was the widest and had the best backboard and net, belonged to a father who had three daughters and no sons. We thought that strange, although obviously he didn't. Over the years each of those daughters would end up going steady with one of the best basketball players in the neighborhood.

Quite soon I grew dissatisfied with those confining games played under the shade of a maple tree amid falling red and gold leaves in the autumn. I began driving recklessly towards the basket, slamming into the garage doors, leaping, elbows out, for a rebound. I began to put off my cooler, more phlegmatic cohorts, who, unlike myself, did not trace their ancestry back to Nannygoat Park or even farther back, to the docks of Naples. They were mostly Yankees of English and Scottish ancestry, and they played a gentleman's game of polite "excuse me's" whenever they so much as breathed on an opponent. I played like a wild man, slapping wrists, climbing players' backs for a rebound, growing more and more wild-eyed and red-faced with each basket. Only one player ever responded to my fury in kind. She was a girl, a few years older than I, who dressed and talked like the boys and had nothing at all in common with the girls sitting cross-legged on the lawn. She had short hair, cut like Mamie Eisenhower's, a reddish face, slitlike eyes, and she played every bit as furiously as I did. In fact, one day when I knocked her into the garage doors, almost shattering a window, she set off after me. She chased me around the maple tree and then we stopped on opposite sides of the tree, feinting one another left-then-right, right-then-left, and then I took off for the street with her in pursuit. I ran down the street until I came to the river, a small stream, really. I ran through the shallow water, my sneaks and pant legs getting soaked, and up into the woods on the other side. She stopped at the river and swore at me. I laughed at her. I thought it was all so funny. A girl! Chasing me! What could I have done but run? If it had been one of the boys I would have stood my ground.

She was one of the best athletes in town—male or female—and I'm sure, if she'd had the opportunity, she would have made the boys' high school basketball team with ease. But the year was 1954 and so she played instead on the girl's slow-pitch softball team and hated every minute of it. "They throw like girls!" she once told me, which made perfect sense to both of us. She threw like the guys, with a big, loose-limbed overhand motion rather than with a girl's tentative little short-armed flip, like throwing darts. I met her years later when she was in her thirties. She was with her girlfriend who was a star on a woman's professional fast-pitch softball team. She looked the same. The same short hair and bangs. The same men's clothes. Gant shirt with a button-down collar, the shirt worn outside of her men's slacks. Penny loafers with thin white socks folded over at the ankle. She has the same, swaggering, shoulder-shifting walk of an athlete. The same red face, only puffier now, almost swollen-looking, like an athlete who had somehow dissipated a career through excess.

Her behavior that day, when she chased me down the street, must have humiliated her in some way. It must have underscored for her the fact that she was a duck out of water. She did not belong with those girls sitting cross-legged on the lawn, or on their softball team, nor did she belong with us boys on the basketball court. The other boys deferred to her, made only feeble attempts at blocking her shots, which she hated; and I, I treated her on the court just like one of the guys, which confused her then. Soon she stopped showing up at those games and left them entirely to the boys.

Those games meant so much to me. I took them seriously, unlike my friends. When I was the captain of my team I picked only the worst players for my side—Richie Greenberg in his crewneck sweater, pressed chinos, and white buckskin shoes. The others thought I was crazy, but there was a method to my madness. With a lousy supporting cast, I was always the star, and furthermore, I had an added incentive to win. I knew even then it was no fun winning when you were supposed to. I played like a man possessed, and when we won, which was often, it was not only a sweet satisfaction for me, but also for Richie Greenberg who might otherwise never experience such triumphs over the truly talented players like Doug Holmquist and Richie Perkins.

Eventually, those boys began avoiding me. When they saw me coming they disbanded the game, told me they'd been playing for hours, they had to go home for lunch. I went back to my house. One day I drove to the store with my mother. When we passed that driveway I saw the boys reconvening only moments after they had told me they had to go home. It was then that I asked my father to drive me to the North End Boys' Club in the ghetto. My mother did not like the idea. "It's too rough for Patty," she said. My father said, "It's about time. That place will make a man of him."

The North End Boys' Club was a low, flat, brick building that looked like a warehouse. It sat on a scruffy, grassless patch of ground across the street from the high walls of the county jail and, a little to the left, a white, wood building that was Pacelli's Italian Bakery. Every Saturday and Sunday morning at nine o'clock, my father would drive me there. I waited outside with the other boys my age until the club opened. Across the street, behind barbed wire, I could see the prisoners in khaki work clothes. They were hoeing and watering the long rows of prison vegetables. There was a long line of people at Pacelli's. The line curved out the door and around the corner. They were mostly Italian immigrants from the neighborhood,

as we had once been, although there were also a few people from the suburbs, like us now, who would never even think of buying bread anyplace
other than Pacelli's no matter how far from the ghetto they had moved.
The smell of hot-baked Italian bread and grinders wafting across the
street made my mouth water. I had to fight back the urge to get in line
and buy a grinder, because I knew if I did I would be late for the morning games. Then it might be hours before I was chosen for a team. I
remained where I was, with the other boys, who were nothing at all like
my friends in the suburbs. Nor were they much like me. They were city
kids, short, dark, scruffy. They were wild and wise in ways I wasn't. Louie
Piazza. Joe Troiano. Nicky D'Amato. Babe Cabral. Richie Belzer. They
looked me up and down as we waited. I stood a little apart from them, so
obviously a suburban kid. They wore dark gabardine slacks, ripped at the
knees and too short for them. They wore black high-topped Keds with
navy dress socks. I wore white Converse sneakers with fluffy white sweat
socks. I had gym shorts under my jeans, and I carried a gym bag, too, with
neatly folded towels in it, and a change of clothes and underwear for after
my shower. Those boys never showered at the club, never changed their
clothes before or after our games. They just played basketball all day and
into the night in their gabardine pants and then, when the club closed at
10 p.m., they went out into the night in their sweaty clothes. I'd follow
them outside and watch as they pushed and jostled one another on their
way to the candy store down the street. I stood under the street light in
front of the club, dressed in my fresh clothes, and watched them go off
while I waited for my father to pick me up. I wondered what they did so
late at night, without their parents knowing. It excited me, the thought of
hanging around outside a candy store until midnight. The city darkness.
Their camaraderie. The thrill of it. But I never went with them to the
candy store, never went with them across the street to yell at the prisoners behind the bars in the jail, never tried, like Louie did one night, to
scale the barbed wire fence of the jail. Half way up the fence he began rattling the wire in imitation of a caged gorilla. I never did anything with
those boys other than play basketball in the gym. We knew each other
only on the court, although years later when we were men we would hear
about one another. I heard that Babe Cabral, one of the few blacks at the
club, had married a white girl. Louie Piazza was somehow involved in a
beauty contest. Then I heard he'd become a hairdresser. Then I heard
Babe had taken to racing cars, both at the track and on the city's streets.

Then I heard a rumor that Joe Troiano had done some time. Armed robbery in L.A., I heard. Richie Belzer was in L.A., too, and New York City. He was a television comedian now. On the Alan Thicke show. On HBO. I saw him one night. Richie, one of the few Jews at the club when I was a kid. He had that same thin, pock-marked, hatchet face. The same thick eyeglasses he was perpetually cleaning sweat from in the gym, only now they were tinted, with gold frames. The same swept-back black hair which always seemed oily when we were kids but now looked manicured and blow-dried. In the club, Richie had this frenetic energy. He never shut up, was always trying to make us laugh. "For chrissakes, Richie, shut the fuck up and play the game!" Now, on TV, he was much cooler, laid back, really, not so funny as he was as a kid. Too stylized now. Controlled.

In the suburbs I played a distinctively physical game that put off my friends. Not so at the North End Boys' Club. What I thought was rough, the guys at the club took for granted. Of course you climbed an opponents back for a rebound! Of course you pushed an opponent with your elbows when he drove to the hoop! Of course you lowered your shoulder and slammed sideways into an opponent setting a pick! Of course you tugged an opponent's shirt to slow him down! Of course you hooked your elbows around an opponent's arm under the hoop to keep him from jumping! Of course you planted your hand in the small of an opponent's back and pushed when he tried to back into the hoop! You did all these things and more at the Boys' Club, and anyone who called a foul was a "pussy." "No blood, no foul," was the rule. And you cheated, too. Any way you could. You fought over every ball that went out of bounds. "I never touched it! It nicked your shirt! I saw it! I swear!" The game was stopped. Curses thrown back and forth. Players threatened to quit, called your bluff by stomping off to the lockerroom. You shot around for a while until they returned and you knew you had them. The matter was settled with matching foul shots. The game resumed. Until the next controversy and you lied again. Another argument. Foul shots. The game resumed. Anyone who didn't cheat in those games was worse than a pussy. Was a jerk. I loved it all. The pushing, the shoving, the arguments, the absolute fierceness with which every moment of those games was filled.

We held the court, uninterrupted throughout the day. At supper time, when our feet were so blistered we could barely walk, we hobbled across the street to Pacelli's. We bought glazed donuts and jelly donuts and hot grinders. We consumed them with a quart of milk on the way back to the club. We couldn't wait to get back, even though, for us, for all intents and purposes, play was over. We hurried back to watch the big boys play. To watch Porky play. To study his game. To hope against hope that someone on his team (but never Porky) would sprain an ankle and one of the younger boys would be pressed into action. We stood with our backs against the tiled gym wall, one leg bent, one sneakered foot planted against the wall, and watched. We watched for hours, watched only Porky, no one else, and when one of those games was over and the big boys went to the water fountain, we hurried onto the court, took a few quick shots, and then hurried off as they began their next game.

Porky had the purest of games, despite his unorthodox shots. A high, arching, two-handed set shot. A fade-away jump shot held behind his head and flung high into the air. A straight-to-the-basket, hard driving lay up in which the ball hit the backboard with a variety of spins. A driving hook shot which Porky fired from low off his right hip with terrific backspin. When the ball hit high off the right side of the backboard it spun, as if on a magnet, into the hoop.

Porky stood at the edge of the half-court circle, facing the basket and his defender. He held the ball in both hands, low to the floor. He faked the defender back with his left foot and, if the defender fell for it, Porky pulled back and fired his two-handed set shot. Swish. If the defender was checking him too tightly, Porky would take a long first step, hooking his left leg around the defender's left leg so that the defender could not move until Porky was by him, and then all he could do was follow. If the defender was still in the front of him on a drive, Porky would stop on a dime, jump, fade backwards so that his body was at a 45–degree angle with the floor, and loft his behind-the-head jump shot. Swish. If the defender forced him to the right of the basket on the drive, Porky would leap, hang suspended in the air, the defender to his left, between him and the basket, and fire his patented hook shot from low off his right hip. The ball would hit the high, right-hand corner of the backboard with ferocious backspin that would carry it into the hoop. He was uncheckable. There was no defense to which Porky did not have an offensive reaction. Often, he could adjust his offensive reactions in mid-shot. A hook shot became, in midair, a spinning, swooping, underhanded lay-up. No one stepped to the Pork. Only a slim, quick, seven-foot Buddha with eight hands stood a chance.

We watched from the sidelines in amazement, but to no avail. No one could copy Porky's game. Those who tried failed miserably. It was said at the Boys' Club that Porky Viera ruined more young basketball players than any player before or since. Even my father, who knew little about basketball, would tell me, "Don't ever try to copy Florindo's shots. Just copy his intensity."

Late one night at the club, I stood along the wall with the others my age, fourteen, and watched Porky play. His team was tied at fourteen-all in a fifteen-point game. One of his players went up for a shot, missed, and came down hard on his ankle. He limped off the court. Porky screamed at him, "Where the fuck you going?" The player waved his hand in disgust at Porky. He sat down on the sidelines and took off his sneaker. His ankle was swollen to the size of a softball. He massaged his swollen ankle. Porky came over to him, still screaming, "It's nothing! It's nothing! You can still play!" The player shook his head, no, and grimaced in pain. Porky flung the back of his hand at him, looked around, wild-eyed, and grabbed me by the shirt. "Come on! You take his place!" He half dragged me onto the court. I was terrified. Porky said to me, "We only need one basket, kid. You get the ball, you give it to me. Understand?" I nodded. The play began. Players cut back and forth, jostled one another, banged me around like a ten-pin until I was disoriented, stood blinking, stupidly, at the top of the keyhole. Someone took a shot. The ball hit the rim, everyone leaped. The ball bounced high in the air, straight toward me. I caught it, dumbfounded, blinked again, adjusted it in my hands, and jumped. Just as I was about to release a picture perfect jump shot, I heard this shrill scream, "No! You fucking asshole!", and, out of the corner of my eye I saw Porky, my *teammate,* leaping at me, his hands outspread to block *my* shot. The ball left my hand a split-second before Porky knocked me on my ass to the floor. Seated on the floor, my legs outspread like a child, I watched the flight of the ball. Swish. I jumped up, smiling, reached out my hand for Porky to slap it in congratulation. He knocked my hand away with the back of his hand.

"What the fuck's the matter with you?" he screamed.

"But, Porky. We won. I made it."

"Made it! Made it! What are you fucking crazy?" He was poking his finger into my chest repeatedly. "Nobody takes the last shot on Porky's team! Nobody but Porky! Do you fucking understand?"

I put my head down and nodded.

Later, in the locker room, when the gym was closing, I went up to Porky and apologized. "That's all right, kid," he said. He was bent over, unlacing his sneakers. I wanted to keep on talking to him, to Porky, my teammate now, and so I asked him a serious question.

"Pork," I said, "I was wondering. Before a game, you know, how do you get loose?" He looked up sideways at me. "I mean, warm up," I added.

"Get loose, kid?" he said. "Shit, I whack off in the locker room, that's how I get loose."

After that, whenever Porky was short a player he would always pick me for his team. He'd grab me by the shirt and yank me onto the court with a smile on his face. "I like this kid," he'd say to the other guys. "He's got balls. Like this." He held up the basketball in both hands. Then he told them what I had done. They looked at me in disbelief. I turned red in the face. They pointed at me and shook their heads and laughed.

Porky and I are sitting in the diner, drinking coffee, when I remind him of our first meeting at the Boys' Club years ago. He smiles, shakes his head.

"I believe it," he says. "That's the way I was then. Crazy."

He was finishing his senior year at Quinnipiac at the time, and he was the nation's leading scorer again. He was averaging 35 points per game, though he would lose the nation's scoring championship by .001 of a point to someone named Kent Hammond. When the season was over Porky was one of a handful of players picked to play in the East-West College All-Star game at Madison Square Garden. It was his one opportunity to show NBA scouts he could play his game against major college competition. But it was not to be. He hurt his leg in practice and he never appeared in that game. It was one of his (and our—his fans') biggest disappointments. Porky returned to Bridgeport, signed on with the Savoy A.A. in the Connecticut Professional Basketball League and waited for NBA scouts to call. But they never did. Only the Harlem Globetrotters offered him a contract. To play with their perennial patsies, the Washington Generals. Porky's role was to be a foil for the Trotters, on a team that was supposed to lose their every game. He turned the Trotters down. "I couldn't play like that," he says. "The Pork, taking a dive every night. I wouldn't do that for any money." Porky learned years later that the Minneapolis Lakers had approached his college coach, Toofie Maroon, and asked him if Porky would be interested in trying out for the team. When Toofie learned that the Lakers planned not to use Porky much, but just to bill him, like a sideshow freak, as the world's smallest pro basketball player, he turned down the Laker offer without ever telling Porky.

"I harbor no resentment toward Toofie for that, "Porky says. "He was right. I couldn't play a game like that either. I wasn't small, don't forget, not in my mind. I was the fucking Pork. The greatest."

For the next five years Porky played in the Connecticut Pro League and on a host of semi-pro teams whose sole purpose, it seemed, was to serve as a showcase for Porky's scoring talents. Weekend tournaments would seemingly be organized overnight, just so that Porky could round up seven of his friends into a team for which he did all the shooting. These pick-up teams always had the same character. A good passing guard and three clumsy, bull-like rebounders who never let the ball leave their hands unless it was in Porky's direction. Porky would score fifty, sixty, seventy points almost every time out, and the fans would leave the gym satisfied. Most of the time, though, his competition was fat, out-of-shape ex-collegians of little known repute, but occasionally, as in the Connecticut Pro League, he faced stiff competition. Topsy DelGobbo and the Hartford Knights. Harry Bosley and Bobby Knight of the all-black Milford Chiefs. Bill Spivey and "Black" Jack Molinas, All-Americans out of Kentucky who were banned from the NBA for fixing college games. An occasional NBA team that would pass through Bridgeport before or after their season. On those Sunday afternoons, when Porky faced stiff competition, the tiny, old Brass Armory would be filled to overflowing with his fans. Families in their Sunday best fresh from Mass. Boys in short pants, little girls in starched dresses, older brothers looking awkward in their suits. And their parents. All of them milling around the armory entrance waiting, like Topsy, for Porky to arrive.

Those games were a war for Porky. Topsy and Harry Bosley (with his shaved head), and "Black" Jack Molinas (with his scowl) never saw themselves as foils for Porky's exploits. They hounded him throughout the game, roughed him up when they could, the fans yelling to the referee to open his eyes. He worked for his points in those games, and he got them. Never less than thirty, as much as sixty. And always, his defender got an ovation just for giving Porky a decent match-up. And then, five years after he graduated from college, Porky quit the game.

"I'd had enough," Porky says. "Have ball, will travel. It was vaudeville. The Savoys. The Viera All-Stars. We'd play anywhere there was a game. Nobody cared who won. They came to see the Pork ring up points. It wasn't even basketball anymore. So I quit. I always felt I should have been given at least a chance to play in the NBA. Jeez, I was the best shot-maker ever. I was never too short to score points—against anyone. But the rap against me was I was too short on defense. They said those big NBA guards would just take me to the hoop and beat me up. But I never had the chance to find out if they would. . . . It wasn't hard for me to quit. I'd had my glory years in college. It was a stage of life I'll never forget. I wouldn't trade those years with Ernie for anything, not even an NBA career. Then I got the job at New Haven and a few years later I got my basketball referee's license. I'm a good referee, you know. I've worked the NIT, the Holiday Festival, all the big college games, and wherever I've worked I kept the game sacred. I never let those kids tarnish the game when I'm refereeing. Nobody gets away with shit when Porky's on the court. I refereed the way I played. For the game, not the fame."

David Williams

Is This Man the Future of Poker?

(from *Playboy*, 2005)

Brittany DEWALD is in another snit. "I'm cold!" Nothing. Her
boyfriend, David Williams, is sitting on the sofa playing online poker on
his laptop for $1,600 a pot. His friend Minh Huynh is sitting at a table
behind him playing online poker on another computer in Williams's loft
apartment, which is high-ceilinged, cold, dark, and cavernous, with barren gray concrete walls and exposed pipes and air ducts. There is nothing on the walls—no prints, photographs, or mirrors. The only
furniture in the room is a black sofa, a matching love seat, a coffee table
with a small photograph of a Chihuahua, a computer table with
Williams's collection of *Playboy* magazines stacked chronologically
under it and a sixty-inch flat-screen television showing the finals of the
2004 World Series of Poker on ESPN.

It is nine p.m. in Dallas, and the only light in the room comes from
the TV and the eerie cyber-blue computer glow reflecting on the faces of
Williams and Huynh. Williams is twenty-four and lean, with a wispy
goatee, a head of tight black curls and creamy, coffee-colored skin. He
looks vaguely black, vaguely Middle Eastern. Huynh is thirty-two and
from Vietnam. Very heavy, with a jowly face and thick-lensed eyeglasses,
Huynh is a loquacious, funny, acerbic fat man. Williams is laconic, spare
with his words and emotions. He looks like NBA star Tim Duncan, were
Duncan to dress like a slacker in baggy T-shirts, jeans, and sneakers. Like
Duncan, Williams has the eyes-lowered, self-deprecating slouch of a
supremely confident man. Williams and Huynh have been playing poker
for more than four hours now.

"I'm cold," DeWald says.

"Yes!" says Williams. "A seven-hundred-thirty-five-dollar pot."

Huynh glances at the World Series of Poker (WSOP) on TV. "That Eskimo Clark is an old-timer. Traveled around to underground clubs, got raided by the cops or hijacked and couldn't go to the cops. Poker is mainstream now." He goes back to his computer. "Jesus Christ!"

"Fuck!" says Williams. "A set of threes." He glances at the TV. "Scotty Nguyen can drink Michelob all night long."

"I'm cold," DeWald says.

"Then put some clothes on," Huynh responds.

DeWald pouts. "This is a fucking man pit. There's too much estrogen in here."

"You mean testosterone," says Williams.

"Whatever. It's a boring lifestyle." DeWald, twenty, flops down on the love seat beside me. A beautiful, curvaceous redhead with white skin and hazel eyes, she's wearing a low-cut, short camisole that exposes her plump breasts and navel ring. Her tiny miniskirt barely covers her ass. She flips through one of Williams's *Playboy*s. Williams reads the magazine from cover to cover each month, but says he passes over the nude photographs because he doesn't think the models exist.

"Where are these girls?" he asks. "They don't go to the grocery store. They should be human, but I never see them."

"I plan to have a body like Pamela Anderson's," says DeWald.

"Great," says Williams. "Let the world know how shallow David Williams's girlfriend is."

"My mother had a boob job."

"She had six kids. It was time." Then, after another winning pot, he says, "I'm up two thousand, seven hundred ninety-three dollars now."

I ask DeWald if she plays poker. "I'm learning," she says. "The object is to win all the money. I play only very, very low limit."

"That's because you're so bad," says Williams.

"Asshole!" Then to me, "I don't have the attention span for poker. Everyone in my family has A.D.D. I hate to lose. One game, I put all of my money in the pot and lost, and I cried."

"There's no crying in poker," says Huynh.

"I was pissed. I'm a woman, and I'm emotional. One game, this guy took all his girlfriend's money and didn't give it back."

"Daniel Negreanu once bluffed his girlfriend out of a pot," says Huynh.

"It's common courtesy not to browbeat your girlfriend," says DeWald.

"It's common courtesy to the table not to soft-play your girlfriend," says Huynh.

Williams and Huynh glance at the WSOP on TV while their fingers move across their computer keys. They seem not to have to look at the computer screens, as if they're playing by osmosis.

ESPN is broadcasting twenty-two weeks of the 2004 WSOP (the previous year the network aired just seven episodes), which took place at Binion's Horseshoe Casino in Las Vegas. More than 2,500 players— 1,700 more than in 2003—put down a $10,000 entry fee for the chance to win the $5 million first prize, the $3.5 million second prize or the diminishing amounts for other top finishers. Most important to professional poker players, they also competed for the diamond-encrusted gold bracelet that proclaims the recipient the best poker player in the world.

Texas Hold 'Em, heavily featured at the WSOP, is one of the simplest yet most challenging of all poker games, which is why the WSOP title is the most prestigious. Players must have an uncanny instinct for reading their opponents' two down cards, a mathematical bent in figuring out the percentage of drawing a card they need, an innate ability to read an opponent's "tells"—his mannerisms when looking at his cards or preparing a bet—and the guts of a burglar in knowing when to try to bluff an opponent out of his superior hand by raising large amounts of money until he folds. That is why the game has made TV stars out of a disparate group of men and a few women, who have little in common except their poker skills. Those players fall easily into two groups: old-time poker players who cut their teeth on illicit cash games (in which they bet their own money) and the newer breed of players, younger and more intelligent, who cut their teeth on online video games, then graduated to card games like Magic: The Gathering (a sort of Pokémon game for pre-adults), and finally to online poker before venturing into live cash games and then the WSOP.

"Williams and guys like Negreanu are the new breed," Huynh tells me. "Many of them started with Magic and then went to online poker. Williams is so smart. You can't beat him. When he was sixteen I saw him push his last two thousand dollars into a pot. You can't teach that."

Williams was fifteen when he met Huynh at a Magic tournament. Williams describes Magic as an analytical card game with features of chess, bridge, and poker. The artwork has a fantasy element—goblins and knights—but he says the game is nothing like Dungeons and Dragons. It's played mostly by teenagers and people in their early twenties. "Most of them are not very social," Williams says. "All they do is bitch about Magic."

Huynh says the David Williams he met "was smart and mature, and he wanted to learn from me." By the age of sixteen Williams was already one of the best Magic players in the world. He traveled to the Netherlands, Aruba, Singapore, and Paris for money tournaments and won as much as $45,000 in a year. During his Magic days Williams made an assortment of friends around the world who remain his friends today: Huynh; Neil Reeves, now twenty-six, from Arkansas; and Noah Boeken, now twenty-three, from the Netherlands.

Williams's Magic friends "are so dorky," says DeWald. "They're nothing like David. They're kind of nerdy."

"Yeah," says Williams, "and they're all earning deep six figures playing poker."

By the time Williams turned seventeen, Magic was less of a challenge for him. His Magic friends on the Internet told him about the new big thing online. "I was intrigued by poker," says Williams. "Huynh helped me out and then got me into some illicit games. I didn't play any games that would hurt me."

"Williams went in with $500 and didn't stop until he'd won $5,000," says Huynh. "He figured the game out and in three months was better than I was."

Williams read every book he could find on poker, every issue of *Card Player* magazine from cover to cover and within a few years began to make a living at the game, which he'd play online and in illicit cash games in underground Dallas clubs. When Reeves moved there a year ago, Williams taught him the game, and the three men would go to clubs to play poker for up to thirty hours straight.

"David has no fear," says Reeves, who describes himself as a fat, ugly white guy. "He looks at chips as chips, not money. He introduced me to underground poker games. They're like a spiderweb, and now I'm making more money than at anything else I could do, maybe eighty-two to eighty-six thousand this year."

Williams's attraction to Reeves, and to all his Magic and poker friends, says Reeves, "is that we're all extremely smart and don't want to work nine to five. It's the most intelligent collection of scumbags I've ever met. It's an alternative lifestyle."

By the time Williams, who describes himself as smart and lazy, turned twenty-one, he was playing poker for a living and making between $50,000 and $100,000 a year at it. He finally decided it was time to play in the biggest game of his life, the World Series of Poker. The day before he went to Vegas he won an online tournament, which paid his $10,000 WSOP entry fee. "I had no expectations," he says. "I thought of it as a learning experience."

"There's a big difference between a cash player and a tournament player," says Huynh. "There's less pressure in a tournament, because you can lose only your qualifying fee. In cash games, I used to lose two months' salary in just one game. Vietnamese gamble out of all proportion to our salaries. We'll bet a third of our week's salary on a pot. Man, poker brings out the worst in people. After a bad loss, a miserable bastard will be an even more miserable bastard."

"I played nothing but cash games before the WSOP," Williams says. "In those, if you lose, you go into your pocket for more money. In a tournament, if you lose, you're out, so players are more cautious."

"Live poker games are more artful," says Huynh. "A lot of bluffs and skill. They're more fun than online games."

"But I can make five times more online," Williams insists.

"Yeah," says Huynh, "but online games aren't art, just math. I have notes on almost a thousand online players. I see a weak player in a game, and I jump in. I play four online games at a time, two hundred fifty hands an hour. You can play only thirty-five live hands an hour. I play online eight hours a day. It's like going to work. I make more than a hundred thousand dollars a year."

Reeves says he prefers live games because he can play the player, not the cards: "I look for tells. David is the best face-to-face player."

Williams says he got into a zone at the WSOP. "I was gaining talents like I was possessed," he says. "I could read a guy's body language. If he looked at his cards and tensed his shoulders, he had a good hand. It meant he was thinking. If he relaxed and looked around, he had nothing."

DeWald speaks up: "Poker is such a huge part of our life and relationship. David's on his laptop eighteen hours a day. I get jealous. 'Don't you wanna sleep or eat?' I ask him. I try to sleep, but guys are hollering over a pot at three a.m. I wake up at nine, and guys are sleeping over or still playing."

"She says I'm the lamest," says Williams. "I don't drink, do drugs, jog, work out, go to clubs, dance, nothing. I send her out to the grocery store. I play poker."

"We're opposites," says DeWald. "David chills and cools. I'm energetic. I love roller-coasters."

"Why do something that makes you sick?" Williams asks.

"I wanna skydive next." I notice that DeWald has a pierced tongue with a silver barbell in it. I ask her about it. "It's just something to play with when I'm bored," she says.

"I told her it's time to take it out," says Williams. "You're an adult now. When adults have those things there's something wrong with them."

DeWald screams at him. "There's nothing wrong with me! Look at you—it took you six months to buy a sofa. We had nothing but a TV. You said you'd buy a car with your WSOP money, but you won't get one by Christmas."

Williams shrugs. "I don't like to spend money."

At 10 P.M. Williams starts making telephone calls, looking for an illicit cash game. When he finds one, Huynh, Williams and I get up to leave.

"I thought you were taking me out to dinner," DeWald says.

"Tomorrow night," he says. She storms out of the living room and goes upstairs to their bedroom.

Williams, Huynh and I drive north out of Dallas to a Steak 'n Shake for dinner, then on to the poker game. Williams tells us about his WSOP experiences. He says he entered the WSOP because he's a perfectionist with a strong desire to be the best at anything he does. At the age of six he had to beat his mother at video games. In grammar school he had to have perfect grades. When he once got a 95, he confronted his teacher about his five missing points. "I always wanted to beat the game," he says, "find the secret no one else knew."

Because he was a WSOP unknown, Williams felt little pressure. At first he played cautiously, but on his second day he was only up $2,000. Disgusted with himself, he started playing faster and looser. In one game he pushed in all his chips when he had two jacks, not knowing that his opponent had two aces. He got his third jack on the flop and won, he says, "because you have to be lucky to win. And lucky to dodge the other guy's luck. You have to be focused and emotionless. You can't let a bad beat affect your mind. That's always been my nature. Brittany says I never cry or get angry. I don't, because I accept reality. Getting mad doesn't

change it, so why expend the energy? Maybe that's good for personal relationships, but it's bad for poker. That's how I reconcile my perfectionism
with fate. I call it the law of probability. Nothing's guaranteed. To be a
great player you have to accept that."

Williams moved steadily through the field for a week until he finally
found himself, on the day before the finals, in tenth position. That
night's game would stop only when nine players were left for the final
table the next day. Williams desperately wanted to be at that final table.
If he made it, he would be the youngest player ever and the first black
player (his mother is African American, his father from Iran) at a final
table; most poker players are white, Asian, or Middle Eastern men. But
Williams had the lowest stack of chips of any of the ten players at his
table, which put him at a distinct disadvantage. So he played cautiously,
dropping out of hand after hand to protect his short stack.

"I'm sitting there like a pussy," he says. "Scared, hoping I can make the
final table. But even if I made it, with no chips I'd be the first one out. I
wasn't playing tough. Finally I said to myself, 'Be a man. If it's meant to
be it's meant to be.'" So when he drew an ace and a queen (his opponent
had two tens), Williams put all his chips into the pot. When the subsequent three cards, called the flop, didn't improve his hand, he began to
pack his things. He new friend Marcel Luske, now fifty-one and one of
the best poker players in Europe, put his arm around Williams and said,
"Relax. The next card will be an ace."

"I don't believe in voodoo," says Williams, "but the next card was an
ace, and I moved to the final table with enough chips to protect myself.
It was amazing how Marcel in his heart wanted me to win. He loves to
teach, and I love to learn. It was a real moment for me."

Williams describes the WSOP finals as the best poker played by the
most boring players. "There was no chatter," he says. "It was too tense
for that. That's the appeal of poker. It's like reality TV. You can drop in
on it at any moment and find drama—highs and lows that are captured
in a moment."

At the final table one player after another went bust until only
Williams and a Connecticut lawyer named Greg "Fossilman" Raymer
remained. They played a few hands, one or the other dropping out
quickly to conserve his chips. Then Williams decided again to play it fast
and loose. He pushed in $300,000 in chips while holding only an ace and
a four. His opponent had a pair of eights. "I didn't think he had a pair,

says Williams, because he didn't look at it too long. A pair of eights, you got to stop and think."

The flop was two-four-five, so now Williams had two fours to Raymer's pair of eights. Raymer immediately raised $1.6 million. Williams called instantly. "I'm a quick thinker," he says. "I went with my gut. People say I should have slowed down."

The turn came up a two, which gave Raymer two pairs, his pocket eights and the community-card twos. Williams also had two pairs, fours and twos. Before the river Raymer bet $2.5 million, and Williams called him. The river came up another two, which gave both men a full house, but Raymer's was higher because of his eights. Raymer pushed in all his chips, and Williams, certain Raymer didn't have a pair of down cards, pushed in all of his. When they turned their cards over, Raymer was the new champion. Williams, who was $3.5 million richer, had still finished second, which tormented him. "Nothing hurts like busting out of your first big one," he says. "I think about that final hand every day. So close to being the champion. Winning was so much more important to me than the money. If first paid three-point-five million and second five million, I still would have liked to win. I don't know if I'll ever get it out of my head."

Williams was so disheartened by his second-place finish that he ordered takeout food and ate it in his room. But the next day his new fame hit him. A lot of young actors, including Tobey Maguire and Ben Affleck, are poker aficionados. Williams met Maguire, who began to call him Number Two. (Williams solidified this nickname four months after the WSOP when he finished second in a World Poker Tour event in Atlantic City, winning $600,000.)

"I said, 'Who are you?'" Williams says. "He said, 'Tobey Maguire.' I said, 'What do you do?' He said, 'I'm an actor.' I said, 'Really. What movies have you been in?' He said, '*Spider-Man*.' I said, 'Oh.'"

Weeks later Maguire beat him in a cash game. "I could see sadness in his eyes that he beat me," says Williams.

Veteran players began to offer Williams a seat in their million-dollar cash games, but he'd decline. He had already gone to dinner with enough veteran players who told him about players' "leaks"—a poker player's vice that leaks money. It could be drugs, booze, women or other forms of gambling. Phil Ivey, the young black player who favors NBA jerseys, is "the greatest player in the game," says Williams. But he has a leak. He likes to gamble. He once lost $250,000 in a poker game he actually won. Between hands he made proposition bets of thousands of dollars on the color of his next card. "Guys pointed out players who won millions in poker and are now broke because they had a leak," Williams continues. "Most leaks are gambling. Poker players are challenge seekers. It's not enough to beat someone in poker. They have to beat the unbeatable next. Craps. Roulette. Anything."

One poker player bet $500,000 that he could drink twenty-three beers in twenty-three hours. Another bet $10,000 that Howard Lederer, a confirmed vegetarian, couldn't eat a hamburger. He did, and the bettor was annoyed that Lederer didn't throw up. Another player bet an opponent $30,000 that he couldn't live in Des Moines for thirty days. Another bet his opponent $10,000 that he couldn't float in the ocean for twenty hours.

Once he returned to Dallas, Williams made only one purchase, a $25,000 Rolex wristwatch. He gave his mother $50,000 and paid off her bills. He also promised he'd pay off her $125,000 mortgage. Shirley Williams, forty-nine, has been a Delta flight attendant for twenty-six years. "My mother's a great woman," says Williams, "but she never saved for retirement. Now I can do it for her if I don't blow it. If she doesn't want to work, I'll support her. If she ever needs anything, she can have it. But Mom's not good with money. She lives paycheck to paycheck. I didn't think it was good to give her half a million dollars and turn her loose. I got her a thousand dollar line of credit for online poker, and it's already gone."

When Williams was back home in Dallas, he went to see a financial advisor. He sat in a conference room around an oval mahogany table and discussed his finances, how to minimize taxes and how to invest his millions with a man named Kent, who was dressed in a suit and tie. Williams wore his usual slacker's outfit—oversize T-shirt, ripped baggy jeans, sneakers. He told Kent, "I want to do the right thing with my money, something productive like owning a company so I won't ever have to work nine to five for anyone. I'd like to invest so that by the age of thirty I have ten million, but I know my goals conflict with my conservative nature. There's a trade-off between risk and reward. I don't like to gamble." Then he produced all the meticulously kept records—his expenses, poker losses, etc.—he has maintained over the years, ever since he decided to live off his poker earnings.

"Living off poker is not dependable," Williams points out. "It's the only job where you can come home with less money than you started with. You can't make ten thousand one night, spend it on a six-thousand-dollar TV, and the next month be struggling for cash."

At the end of his financial meeting, Williams learned he could pay off his mother's mortgage without paying an extra gift tax. He also learned that if he declared himself a professional gambler to the IRS he could deduct his losses and expenses. "So it's settled," Kent said. "You're a professional gambler." He laughed and added, "Now all your family will be coming out of the woodwork."

"I have only my mother," says Williams. "I never knew my father."

We pull off the highway north of Dallas at 11 P.M. and drive east past a flat, barren stretch of land until we come to a strip mall and a Steak 'n Shake. We order hamburgers and shakes from a thin, pale waiter.

While we're eating our burgers, Williams says, "After the WSOP I was invited to play in a tournament in L.A. I was the first player out. Just as I got up, one of the guys from the WSOP came by and asked if I was just starting. I told him no, I'd already been eliminated before most of the players had even registered." Williams shakes his head. "After the WSOP, guys told me you lose your confidence. You're afraid to play again because you don't want to be embarrassed. They told me to expect a dry spell."

His cell phone rings, and he answers it. He listens for a moment, then says into the phone, "If you're gonna pay that kind of money to have your car detailed, make sure you look the car over before you pay the guy and he leaves." He listens again, then adds, "I love you, Mom," and hangs up.

"Her car is always filthy," he says to me. "Like anything I do, I'm cautious. I take my time, look into it." He smiles, something he rarely does, and says, "My mother and I have more of a brother-sister relationship."

After we finish dinner, Williams makes an attempt to pay the bill. I tell him the magazine will pay for it. Even before he won $3.5 million at the WSOP, Williams often paid the bill for his friends, much to DeWald's dismay. "Why do you always have to pay?" she'd ask. "It's in my nature," he'd respond. But after the WSOP, Williams found that his friends, including Reeves, were insulted when he tried to pay their dinner bill.

"I'm a man," Reeves told him. "I can pay my own check. Just because you won some money, you're not paying for my meals for the rest of my life. I'm your friend."

Williams shrugs. "I picked my friends right. On their character. We make sure we help each other out."

Williams surrounds himself with men who are older than he is, yet he seems older than his years. He has a gravitas and a sadness about him. Williams likes the company of men and only tolerates the company of women. That's part of his attraction to poker.

"It's a guy thing," says Huynh. "I love my wife and two kids, but I've left them to play poker with the guys for seventy-two hours straight." When Huynh plays poker, he's no longer just a fat guy. He's a player. He has personality and a kind of power. When Williams plays poker, he's no longer "the lamest" or "lazy." He's sharp, focused, a man to be respected and reckoned with. Poker defines these men. It brings out their repressed personalities, which they keep hidden during those few hours a day when they are not playing poker.

We drive east at midnight past desolate countryside. We go down a side street and come to an industrial strip mall that should be deserted, but more than twenty cars are in the parking lot.

Williams goes up to one of the mall doors and knocks. Someone opens the door, Williams tells him who he is, the door opens, and we step inside. The front room looks like a shabby office space for an auto body shop or a tile company, except on the wall is a little sign that reads, WE ARE A POKER DEALER'S SCHOOL. SOMETIMES WE PLAY POKER AFTER CLASS. On another wall is a copy of a check made out to the Dallas Police Department.

The owner of the club greets Williams and Huynh and tells them a game awaits in the back room. Williams and Huynh go down a corridor while I ask the club owner about the check on the wall. He smiles and says, "Every little bit helps." I ask him if the neighbors get suspicious with so many cars in his lot at midnight. "They haven't so far," he says.

Williams and Huynh stand around a poker table crowded with about ten men, all of whom are in their twenties or thirties. They all look like Williams—baseball caps on backwards, baggy T-shirts, jeans—except they are all white. They look up at him and smile. "Come on, David!" They make room for Williams and Huynh at the table, and someone says, "So tell me, David, how many new friends you got? Broke friends, I mean." Everyone laughs while Williams and Huynh buy chips.

It's obvious that the players genuinely like Williams because, as he puts it, "I'm one of their own in their eyes. They're proud of me. I give them hope. If I can do it, they can do it. And here I am, playing right alongside them."

Williams, no longer lame, comes alive while playing Texas Hold 'Em in a dingy strip mall club with his friends, laughing, joking, cursing a bad hand. I stand behind Williams and watch a few hands before he moves a chair close to him and invites me to sit. Every time he gets his down cards, he curls them back at the edges, cupping his hands around them so only I can see them. Despite his curious remove, Williams is unfailingly polite and helpful to me, as he is to everyone. "He's reliable," says Huynh, "and he always returns his calls." When Williams makes an appointment to meet me and he's five minutes late, he apologizes profusely. When he has his financial meeting, he makes a point of having me sit in, even though he's discussing his most intimate finances. As long as I'm in Dallas to see him, he says, "I'm available to you whenever you want me."

Williams looks at his down cards, two eights, and pushes a big stack of chips into the pot. His opponent has two jacks but is scared off by Williams's assertive play. He folds his better hand. Williams hugs his chips toward him. He stacks them lovingly, fingers them, almost caressing them like small loved ones. It's as if he has a romance with his chips, the way most players do, needing the tactile sensation of them for reassurance. The more chips they have, the more they can feel between their fingers, the more confident they become.

Williams has the beginnings of a straight: five-six-seven-eight. He pushes in $300 in chips. Only the man beside him, a twenty-five-year-old wearing a red baseball cap, is still in the hand. He has a pair of queens. He stares at Williams, trying to read him and determine if he's bluffing. Williams goes cold, blank, devoid of expression. He lets his opponent stare at him for long moments, until finally his opponent folds his hand—the winning hand had he stayed in the game. Williams pulls in his beloved chips.

We drive back to Dallas at six in the morning. Williams has won $600 and is as exhilarated as if he'd just won the WSOP. It's not the money but the six hours with friends that makes him animated. Huynh was a big loser, but he doesn't care. He'll just go online tonight and win it all back. The money is almost irrelevant to Huynh and Williams. It's just a means to keep score. The action is what motivates them. They're using their brains, skill, and, most of all, character in a game that proves their manhood—if to no one but themselves.

I ask Williams about the player with two queens whom he bluffed out of a pot. "I could tell by his body language that he didn't like it when I bet his queens," he says. "I could see his fear. He's a weak player."

The following morning I meet Shirley Williams and her daughter, Tina, David's half-sister, for breakfast at Denny's. Shirley arrives heavily made up and wearing a pair of short shorts and high heels that show off her fine brown legs. She is one of those women pushing fifty who still think of themselves as younger; in Shirley's case, she does look much younger than her age. She's still very pretty, with skin much darker than her son's. Although Williams says he has a brother-sister relationship with his mother, it's more complex than that. Williams is protective of his mother, much like an older brother. He's always complaining about her "acting like a kid" and being "too emotional" and not as responsible as she should be with her money. Williams has no concept of women except as people who need to be protected from themselves. When he saw his mother at the WSOP talking too long to a man, he went over to her and demanded, "Who was that?"

At breakfast I ask Shirley if David is like his father. "I don't know," she says. "I only knew him for a few months. David always resented that he had no father. He thought his father left him. I explained to him that his father didn't know I was pregnant. When he was a child he always said, 'I wish I had a daddy.' One day I said, 'Okay, I'll put you up for adoption,' and he cried, 'No, no, Mommy, I want to be with you.' That was mean of me, I know."

When Williams was a child and his mother would leave to fly with Delta for two or three days at a time, he would stay with his grandparents. When his mother returned, she would be home for four days at a time, which Williams thought was "cool." They'd play Scrabble and video games, bickering over them like two kids. "I always loved games," says Shirley. "I played Atari when David was in my stomach." Shirley got her love of dominoes from her father, a dominoes player. "Nobody could ever beat him," says Williams.

"David was forced to grow up early," says his mother. "When he was twelve he got bored with his grandparents' house when I'd be gone, so he stayed at home alone. The first time, I cried." Williams would make his breakfast and then catch the school bus. When he'd come home he'd do his homework. "I never had a party or got into trouble," he says. "I couldn't let my mother down. She put her trust in me. I would only have made it harder on her." When his mother was home, she hosted card games at the house. Williams would fix the drinks and serve the food. It was at about this time that Shirley asked her son if he wanted to find his father. He said no.

In school Williams was so much smarter than his peers that he fin-ished his work early, got bored, and began to cause trouble. Shirley says she had him tested and found out how smart he was. "So I enrolled him in a magnet school for gifted children," she says.

The school was in a bad neighborhood, says Shirley, "yet David got along with both types of kids."

"Socially I hung with the cool kids, a few deadbeats, but I had a dark side," says Williams. "I was a closet nerd. I'd go home and watch the Science Channel, but I could never tell my friends about the properties of chemicals. I adapted, like a chameleon. It was a mixed neighborhood, but my friends didn't think of me as black. I was just David. I didn't fit into any stereotypes. Some kids said, 'You don't act black.' I hated that term, the gold-chain stereotypes. I told them they were ignorant. You can't act a race."

Williams got his first job at the age of fourteen to help out his mother. When he was fifteen he doctored his birth certificate so he could work at Wendy's. Then he began playing Magic for cash prizes, entering tour-naments around the world and becoming part of the nerdy subculture Magic attracts. (One year, he was disqualified from a tournament for cheating, which he adamantly denies doing. Wiliams was accused of having a marked or bent card in his hand. He was automatically disqual-ified despite his claim that the marked card was a meaningless one, akin to a deuce in a poker hand of three kings.) When, at the age of seven-teen, he turned his attention to poker, Shirley never worried about him in those games because, she says, "He was always respectful. Always, 'Yes, ma'am' and 'I love you, Ma.' And he was always so calm."

Williams finished his last two years of high school by taking classes at the University of North Texas. When he graduated, he had a 1,550 SAT score and was considered a college junior. He chose Princeton because an article in *U.S. News & World Report* claimed it was the number one school in the country. But Williams hated Princeton—the cold weather, his more privileged classmates, and the fact that he had to work in the cafeteria serving them. He was so depressed and lonely that he was admitted to the infirmary before Shirley finally told him to come home. He returned to Dallas and eventually entered Southern Methodist University, where he has a year to go to get his economics degree. Williams has a 4.0 grade point average at SMU, but his overall college GPA is 3.9 because of his grades at Princeton. "That point nine really gets me," he says. "No matter what I do

I'll never be able to get it back. I'm obsessive about my grades. I guess I'm stuck in the anal stage."

I ask Shirley about the money her son gave her. "I knew David would help me out financially if he won the WSOP," she says. "But that's my son's money. I want to keep working. He's only twenty-four. Maybe I don't know how much money that is. It's got to last him a lifetime."

After breakfast Shirley and Tina take out their makeup cases. Then mother and daughter stare into their mirrors and apply fresh makeup before they drive to Williams's apartment for the afternoon. Before they leave I ask Tina, who is pretty like her mother, if she and David are close. "Not too close," she says. "He's not home very much. But my girlfriends think he's cute." David has said of Tina, "She was born when I was eight. I struggled for attention because I'd been the only kid. I'm not always there for her now, but I ask about her grades."

It is late afternoon in Williams's apartment. He's curled up on the love seat, sleeping in his clothes. His mother is watching a soap opera on TV. Williams stirs, wakes, and sits up. He looks at his mother and says, "Quality entertainment, huh?"

"David, why don't you give me more money for my online account?" she says.

"Because you'll burn it up." He puts his computer on his lap and turns it on, and within minutes he's playing poker.

After Shirley and Tina leave, I ask him where DeWald is. "She's mad at me. She went to her mother's." Then, his eyes still fixed on the computer screen, his fingers playing over the keys, he adds, "Maybe I was meant to live alone." Williams is a curious case. Despite his obvious affection and concern for his mother, and even for DeWald, he talks about them without emotion. The only time he reveals emotion is when he talks about his beloved Chihuahua, which died recently. "I was holding him and dropped him onto the floor," Williams says hesitantly. "He hit his head and died. I didn't get another dog because it would be unfair to him. It's like if your wife dies. It's hard to remarry."

Williams met DeWald when she was seventeen. "She was goofy and hyper," he says, "but I never thought about it. We're opposites. She's emotional, illogical, and whiny. I'm her out for everything, like I'm her father."

A few days ago DeWald came home late after a night out and damaged her cell phone. She called Williams, who was in Vegas, and told him her cell phone didn't work and she wanted a new one. He told her he couldn't do anything about it until the following Monday. "But what if I get a flat tire and someone tries to kill me?" she said. "People got flat tires before cell phones and weren't killed," Williams responded.

When Williams went to the WSOP, he didn't want DeWald to go with him, because he felt he couldn't give her the attention she would need. But she showed up and stood behind him, saying, "Come on, baby, give me a smile." Williams told her to be quiet; this was his moment. "I was on the verge of winning three-point-five million," he says. She stormed off, crying, and Williams had to go look for her. "I'm trying to get her some counseling," he says. Reeves, for one, doesn't think she needs it. "She's basically a child," he says. "David doesn't respect her. He's always complaining about her. I told him to get rid of her or shut up."

"David's pretty honorable," says Huynh. "He'll never break up with Brittany unless it becomes intolerable. Something's holding him back. He never had a father figure, you know. Maybe he doesn't know women."

Williams's fingers are playing his computer keys as if he were a concert pianist. I ask him if he ever played sports. "I wasn't raised to play sports," he says without looking up. "Maybe I wouldn't have been a nerd and would have been into basketball if I'd had a male influence." Still, Williams has never had any desire to find his father. "I wouldn't acknowledge him if he showed up," he says.

He pauses a moment after winning a pot and adds, "Things are what they are. I don't have any insecurities. I accept things. I don't mean this as a knock on my mother or grandparents, but there's no person I look up to. I am who I am."

Just then DeWald comes through the door. She moves silently through the apartment without acknowledgment from Williams. With a rare, faint smile he says, "I can't wait for the WSOP next year. It's so fun. Like poker summer camp." His fingers play over the keys. "A set of jacks," he mutters to himself. Then, without looking up from his laptop, he says, "Baby, wanna go out to dinner tonight?"

DeWald looks at him. "What about my cell phone?"

Pete Rose, Jr.

War of the Roses

(from *Gentleman's Quarterly*, 1989)

"What'd I learn from my dad?" he says. "You mean, like a father-and-son talk?" He tugs on the bill of his baseball cap and sprawls back on the sofa. A nice-looking boy of nineteen. With a red crew cut, brown eyes, and freckles. He is dressed in a gray T-shirt, jeans, and high-top sneakers. A perfectly ordinary boy of his time. Born and raised near a river in the Midwest, he could pass for the Tom Sawyer of his age, if, like Tom, he still had boyhood illusions.... *He tosses a scuffed baseball to his dad. His dog leaps at the ball suspended for eternity in a cloudless sky. His dad looks up with his kind face. His sister, pouting on the porch, dresses her doll. His mom, smiling at her boys, stands at the screen door with two glasses of cold lemonade.*

He stops fidgeting with his cap and stares at the ceiling. Finally he says, "My dad told me to hit the ball where it's pitched." That's it. In a flat voice, devoid of emotion. He knows precisely what he's saying. The nuance of it. "That's all I remember," he says and sits up on the sofa in a barren room in a West Palm Beach, Florida, apartment complex. A minor-league-baseball player's apartment. A few pieces of cheap Danish-modern furniture. A half-eaten bowl of Froot Loops on the table. A crumpled Fritos bag on the sofa. A pair of baseball spikes and sweat socks on the floor. A copy of *Playboy*. A new, leathery-smelling glove in an open box. A photograph of his girlfriend beside an unmade bed.

"We don't talk like that," he says. "You know what I mean? I never hugged or kissed my dad. If I did, he'd think I was a sissy. You know, queer. My relationship with him is more player-manager. Sometimes he gives me a high-five."

He is at that age when most boys lose their illusions, against their will. It is a scary time for boys who want desperately to hang on to the fathomable verities of their boyhood, even as they are about to become men. "If I work hard, then everything will fall into place," he says "I never thought, 'What if I make the big leagues?' It never crossed my mind I wouldn't.... I hope I room with two blacks, so people won't think I'm a rich kid.... My dream is to have my mom and dad in the stands watching me play.... I see myself at bat in a Cincinnati uniform in the ninth inning of a playoff game, with a runner on third and the score tied...."

He looks down at the rug as he speaks. A curiously passionless boy for his age. Without conviction even for the illusions he mouths. Which is why he's no Tom Sawyer. He is, rather, a Huck Finn who's seen the world earlier than most and found it wanting. The loss of his illusions at such an early age was a kind of premature theft of his boyhood. It has left him partially empty, filled only with a vague sadness, suspicion, and fear. Even when he smiles or laughs, it always comes from his mouth and never his eyes. Still, like Huck, he has not lost his generous heart.

"I'm a lot like my dad," he says. "I like fast cars, the ponies, clothes, and baseball. I hustle like him. I'm a better fielder than he is, but I'm not as good a hitter yet. If he's got size-sixteen shoes, then I'm only a size four now. It'll be tough to fill them, but I'm gonna try to be better than my dad. It's hard for me, though. People never see me. When they come to see me play, they expect to see my dad. That's why I never run to first base on a walk. I want to be my own person.

"In some ways, I guess, I'm not much like my dad. We're not alike inside. I show more emotion than he does. When he used to kiss my mom or my sister, it hurt me. I wish he could kiss me. I wish he'd made time for me when I was growing up. If he'd been around, I'd be a lot like him now. But he wasn't, so I'm not. I don't see him much now. He said he'd try to see me play here in West Palm, but I know that means he won't come. Even if I wanted to call him, I don't have his telephone number. I have to call his agent, and he tells my dad I want to talk to him. We don't get in touch unless my dad wants to. Still, I love him. He's my dad."

His dad, Peter Edward Rose, currently the manager of the Cincinnati Reds, is the greatest singles hitter in the history of baseball. "I *live* for two hundred hits a year," he once said. He became baseball's all-time hits leader, surpassing time-honored legend Ty Cobb, when he got his

4,192nd hit on September 11, 1985. He holds a .303 lifetime batting average and more than thirty major and National League records; has played in sixteen All-Star games and thirty-four World Series games; was named Sportsman of the Year in 1975 by *Sports Illustrated* and National League Player of the Decade for the Seventies by *The Sporting News*. He accepted that accolade as his right, saying, *"I'm* the Player of the Decade, not [Hank] Aaron."

He is guaranteed first-round selection to the Hall of Fame, his last and greatest achievement, when he becomes eligible for that honor five years after his retirement from the game he has played so much longer than most. Forty-eight years old this month, he has yet to retire officially from baseball, although he has not played in two years. He prefers, instead, a state of limbo from which, at any moment, he might rouse himself to play again, to continue his avaricious pursuit of hits, games, wins, awards, honors. Despite his pride in his achievements ("I'm the biggest winner in history," he has said), they seem to have left him unsatiated. He still has that glutton's gleam in his eye for more and more and more of what he has devoted his life to at great cost, not necessarily to himself but to those who love him. His daughter once said, "We'll all be happy when he becomes the best of all time, because he sure had to give up a lot to get it."

His accomplishments in the game have rewarded him handsomely. He has made millions of dollars from his salaries as player and manager, now $500,000 a year ("And I never even went to college," he's said); from an as-told-to autobiography he coauthored, called, simply, *The Pete Rose Story* ("I never read it"); and from the dozens of products he has endorsed over the years: Aqua Velva, Jockey, Geritol, Swanson TV dinners, Gekimen noodles, Mountain Dew, Zenith, Mizuno, Grecian Formula and his own soft drink called, again, simply, Pete. He has also merchandised, at various times, T-shirts, key chains, hats, posters, and gold and silver coins, all with either his name or his likeness on them. Most of the money he has made, it seems, he has spent on himself. He buys expensive clothes and even more expensive cars. He owns three Porsches, a Rolls-Royce, and several other fine machines. He has also been known to indulge his gambling appetite at dog and horse tracks around the country. He was once rumored to have lost $13,000 at a single day at the track, and on another occasion he received a dead fish in the mail as a warning to pay a gambling debt he was refusing to acknowledge. "He said he was Pete Rose, and he didn't have to pay no gambling debts," his ex-wife says. But the wise guys he owed didn't see it that way.

He has been married twice and fathered three children (possibly four, according to a Tampa woman, who filed a paternity suit against him in 1979; Rose didn't contest the suit), and he has a reputation as a ladies' man. His attitude toward his women is not much different from that toward his gambling debts, and he is notoriously cavalier about his adulteries.

His present wife, Carol, thirty-four, is a former barmaid and Philadelphia Eagles cheerleader who tends to dress in leopard-skin capri pants and was once described by a friend as "looking like a lonely go-go dancer." He was attracted to her because she had, according to another friend, "the prettiest butt in Cincinnati," and also because she was almost fifteen years younger than him. He likes young women, he's said, "because they make me feel so young." He feels the same about baseball and money, which may explain his avaricious pursuit of all three.

Of all the products he has endorsed over the years, the one people most identify him with is Wheaties, "The Breakfast of Champions." It perfectly fits his fans' perception of him. The athlete from an ordinary background, who achieved great success not from an abundance of talent but from an abundance of boyish desire and hard work. He played his game the way young boys played it when Norman Rockwell was painting covers for the *Saturday Evening Post*. He slid headfirst into third base. He ran to first on a walk. His uniform was perpetually caked with dirt and ripped from his fearless style of play. His fans read into that style of play a host of qualities—courage, discipline, desire, perseverance—that have little to do with him or his success. The secret is much simpler than that. He devoted his life to one thing—baseball—at the exclusion of almost everything else.

"All I am is an American boy," he said in his forties, "who knew what he could do and what he couldn't do and did it for a long, long period of time."

"Pete hits the ball on the ground more consistently than any player I ever saw," explains Tom Seaver. "Some of those ground balls are bound to get through for hits."

"What would I do in that situation?" the son says. "With a runner on third in the playoffs?" He does not hesitate. "I'd hit a single to center field."

*   *   *

In the summer of 1988, Peter Edward Rose, Jr., (known as Little Pete and Petey) led his Cincinnati American Legion team to the Legion World Series Championship. Around the same time, he was drafted in the twelfth round by the Baltimore Orioles as a third baseman. Petey was crushed. He thought he should have been drafted higher, but most of all, he had dreamed of being drafted by his father's team, the Reds. On the night of the draft, Petey and his mother, Karolyn, sat in their living room with twenty-six baseball caps, one for each major-league team, and waited to see which one Petey would wear. Their celebration turned to despair as Petey was bypassed in round after round. Finally, he fled the house in anger, only to discover the next day he had been drafted 295th overall.

Petey claimed most teams bypassed him in deference to his father's team, which they assumed would draft him. John Cox, the Reds' director of scouting, said that was foolish speculation. In the opinion of most clubs, he said, Petey was a twelfth-round choice. The scouts' criticisms of the son were the same as those leveled at the father years ago. He was slow afoot, his throwing arm was only adequate, and he didn't hit for power. But according to Len Johnston, the Oriole's scouting coordinator, "We waited to see what Cincinnati would do. I don't think Pete's old man had enough balls to sign his own kid. If it was my kid, I'd break my neck to sign him for my team. I don't think the old man wanted to."

(Despite repeated requests, Pete Rose declined to be interviewed about this or anything else in this article.)

When Petey finally overcame his disillusionment, he signed with the Orioles, received a $21,000 bonus and in early fall was promptly dispatched to the team's winter-league club in West Palm Beach. There he would get special instruction with other young prospects in preparation for his first spring training in March. He arrived at West Palm boyishly happy. Reporters clustered around him constantly. He told them that he "loved the game because it's fun" and that he was happy with his famous name, even if it did put extra pressure on him. "It'd be a lot easier for me if my name was Smith," he said. When he walked into his clubhouse, he said, "I got a big cold chill when I saw a locker with my name on it . . . my *own* locker."

For someone so young, he handled himself remarkably well in interviews. He had spent a lifetime watching his father be interviewed and, on occasion, being interviewed himself. ("I'll bet your friends envy you having such a famous dad, eh, Petey?") Now it was his turn to talk solely about himself, but nobody seemed to be listening. When he appeared on a Fort Lauderdale TV sports show one night, the host, smiling, said he guessed Petey owed a lot of his talent to his famous dad. Petey said, "My mom has been the main influence in my career." The host, still smiling, continued to talk about his famous dad while Petey, flushed, stared at his hands in his lap.

The father never did come to West Palm to see his son play, although he indicated he was proud of his son for following in his footsteps. "He and I put a lot of hours into preparation," the father said. "I'll live and die with every at bat he takes in the minors. That's my blood."

When little Pete was a boy, he says, he had no sense of growing up with a famous father, except on those rare occasions when his father took him to the stadium. They were usually Father and Son days, or All-Star or World Series games, when there would be a host of reporters and photographers present. Petey would be dressed in a fitted uniform, with hat, spikes and glove, a miniature of his father. "I went first-class from the age of five," he says. He would be photographed playing pepper with his dad, swinging a too-heavy bat at his dad's underhand tosses and sitting beside him on the dugout bench. He was a silent little boy, with scared eyes that squinted into the photographers' flashbulbs. After the game, still in his uniform, Petey would get into his father's black limousine for the ride home. His face was barely visible pressed against the limo's blacked out-window.

At home, his father rarely played catch with him on the lawn. And even when he did, those catches bore not the slightest resemblance to the kinds Norman Rockwell captured on his *Saturday Evening Post* covers. The leaping dog. The sister pouting. The mom with lemonade. They were less "catches" between a father and son on a sunny afternoon than they were fierce "workouts." Baseball for an adult, not a child. Pete rarely praised his small son's efforts to please him, to be like him, because he always assumed a certain adult level of competency from Petey that he could never deliver. Pete did not understand how to "play" with children, nor did he bother to try. He did not take a father's delight in his children, because his mind was always on his concerns. *His* career, *his* desires, *his* single-minded pursuit of *his* boyhood dreams. He sustained those dreams over the years of his son's childhood. Ultimately, they are what robbed his son of his own dreams.

Pete Rose took even less interest in his daughter's attempts to please him. He tried to discourage her from playing baseball, even though Fawn, five years older than Petey, was a better ballplayer than her brother. "Some people don't even know I have a sister," Petey says. "But Fawn was a bitch in baseball. Dad didn't want her to play because she was better than the boys. One day he hit a pop fly that hit a tree branch and came down and broke Fawn's nose. When she cried, Dad called her a sissy."

Pete had trouble relating to his daughter for a number of reasons, not the least of which was that she is a girl. (An irony is that Pete now has to work for a very tough-minded woman, Reds owner Marge Schott.) Fawn is also very bright, honest, and, like him, stubborn. Karolyn likes to say that "Fawn always did favor Big Pete," but that description doesn't sit well with Fawn. "I love my dad," she says, "but I don't respect him." Fawn's relationship with her father has always been confrontational, in contrast to Petey's worshipful childhood view of his father. She was never afraid to question him to his face on his lack of interest in her and her brother. She was probably one of the few people in his life who ever had the courage to question him. But he had trouble dealing with her for another reason, too. Fawn has always had a serious weight problem. It embarrassed Pete. When he was taking his son to the track one day, Karolyn asked why he wasn't taking Fawn, too. Pete said she was too fat and he would be ashamed to be seen with her. Fawn heard him from another room.

Karolyn Engelhardt Rose was the perfect baseball wife. Not only did she subordinate her life to her husband's career, but she actually seemed to relish that subordination. Whenever Karolyn asked her husband to do some small chore around the house, to mow the lawn, say, his response was always the same: "What if I get hurt?" Then he would go to his room, where he spent long hours watching sporting events on television. His wife would bring him sodas and chips throughout the day.

When he spent lavishly on himself, on his clothes and cars ("It's *my* money, not yours," he would tell her), she did not question him. She merely saved pennies by shopping for the rest of the family at Kmart. It was not only her wifely duty, it was her higher calling, because Karolyn was her husband's biggest fan. When he came home depressed by a hitting slump, she would console him with advice. "I think you're crouching too much," she said once. His response: "How many home runs have you hit, anyway?" At the ballpark, she was his most visible fan. Whenever Pete Rose came to bat at Riverfront Stadium, the television cameras would immediately pan to his wife in the stands. Karolyn was a beautiful woman, with luxuriant chestnut-colored hair, a raspy cigarette smoker's voice, and a body so voluptuous she was once detained at the stadium gate by a security cop who thought she was Morgana Roberts, the Kissing Bandit. Eventually the Reds' camera crew was given instructions not to focus in on Karolyn so often, because some of the team's more straightlaced fans were complaining about her heaving breasts.

Karolyn had a kind of celebrity of her own in Cincinnati (she had her own radio program), attributable not only to her husband's fame but also to her own good-natured, vivacious personality. She drew people to her, especially men, in the same way tough-talking waitresses at truck stops have their legions of fans. She was honest and earthy, and more than one man had a crush on her, even if she did not see any man but her husband. When Karolyn and Pete went to parties, which they rarely did, Karolyn, as much as Pete, would be surrounded by admirers. That annoyed her husband, and soon he would drag her home.

Still, Karolyn Rose accepted her subservient role because she was proud to be part of her husband's career. She even accepted the fact of her husband's many girlfriends. She had known about them almost from the first year of their marriage, in 1964. She conceded them as part of the lot of a baseball wife—*if* Pete followed the rules of that game. He could have his girls while on the road, if he was discreet about them. When the Tampa woman filed the paternity suit against Pete, Karolyn described it as "nothing." "It happens," she says. "I handled it." Nor did Karolyn complain when she was hospitalized with a blood clot and Pete never bothered to visit her. "I didn't get flowers, and I didn't get a call or anything," she once said. "But I accepted it because he was busy playing baseball, and they were trying to win a pennant." But his teammates' wives became furious, for by then Pete had begun to flaunt his affairs in a way that even Karolyn could no longer ignore. He started giving Karolyn's game tickets to his girlfriends. He flew them with him on the team plane and began to squire them around openly in Cincinnati. He acted as if now that he was Pete Rose, the greatest singles hitter in base-ball, the conventional rules of morality, even baseball morality, did not apply to him.

One time, Karolyn was driving home when she saw her own red Porsche being driven by Carol Woliung, who would become Pete's second wife. She turned around and followed the Porsche until she caught up with it at a stoplight. She jumped out of her car, tapped on the window of the Porsche and, when Carol rolled it down, punched her in the face. When the police arrived, Carol claimed the car was a gift from her fiancé, the famous baseball player Pete Rose. Karolyn, who was still married to Pete, told the officer to check the car's registration. It was registered to Karolyn Rose. While Carol found another way home, Karolyn drove to the stadium to confront her husband. He refused to come out of the clubhouse.

Another time, when Fawn and Petey were old enough to understand their father's affairs and be crushed by them, Karolyn took them to a banquet in Cincinnati honoring their father. The children burst into tears when they saw Pete's brother escorting Carol to a table. Petey was nine when his father asked him one day if he wanted to go to the track with him. Petey left the house thrilled to be out with his father. When he returned home, he was curiously silent, until his mother asked him if he'd had a good time. Petey, with the innocence of a child, responded, "We had lunch with dad's girlfriend." Even today Petey refuses to talk about that moment when he lost his boyhood innocence. He just shakes his head and says, "I don't want to say nothing about Carol."

Karolyn Rose filed for divorce a few months later, in 1979. "I divorced Big Pete because he was flaunting his women, and I had to protect the kids," she says, "not because I didn't love him anymore."

The divorce didn't seem to bother Big Pete much. He got four hits in one game against the Mets soon after the couple separated. He justified his adulteries by saying, "If a guy doesn't like women, he's queer, so if you want me to say, no, I'm not queer, then I'm not queer." He justified his divorce by saying, "I guess if I have an all-American image, I should go through a divorce, because that's what Americans do." Then he said that he had no sympathy for his wife of sixteen years, because "she ain't a ballplayer's wife anymore, is she? . . . I'm happy the way it is. What do I need a wife for? As far as being lonely, baseball is my substitute."

Finally, he said, jokingly, that the secret to dispatching wives was simple: "Hey, just give her a million dollars and tell her to hit the road."

After their divorce, as parents often do, Pete and Karolyn used their son as a conduit for their transactions with each other. Petey was the go-between for communicating anger, in Pete's case, and heartbreak, in Karolyn's. She sent her son off to visit his father with the hope that seeing him would remind Pete of the family life he was missing. Karolyn always harbored fantasies that Pete would return to her one day. Almost a decade later, she still does. "Every January twenty-fifth, our wedding anniversary, I set an extra plate for Big Pete," she says. "I still believe he'll come home someday. Is that stupid?"

But Pete didn't miss family life with Karolyn. The only thing Pete was reminded of when he saw his son was his ex-wife. He cut short his son's visits, never asked him to sleep overnight, and finally made those visits fewer and farther between. "I see my son as much as I want," Pete said. Petey was confused and hurt and angry. He blamed his mother for the loss of his father.

"I got mad at Mom 'cause Dad was gone," Petey says. "Then one day she sat me down and told me that me and Fawn were her whole life now. Since then, she's been Mom and Dad for me."

Petey grew so attached to his mother (he was almost a mama's boy, says Fawn) that he would cry when she left the house. He was terrified that she would leave him, too. When she got a job as a barmaid at a shot-and-a-beer bar in Cincinnati called the Wagon Wheel, Petey would call her, crying, late at night to make sure she was going to come home.

Petey grew up over the next decade in the new house his mother bought after the divorce. They moved their things in the Rolls-Royce Karolyn got in the divorce settlement. ("Just like the Beverly Hillbillies," she says.) "I hate that car," says Fawn. Karolyn rarely drives the Rolls anymore. She keeps it in storage. Still, she can't bear to sell it, since it's one of the few reminders she has left of her days as Mrs. Pete Rose. (She may have to sell the car eventually, though, since her $50,000 a year alimony will expire in 1995.)

The house is big and empty, except for furniture and necessities. It is virtually devoid of family mementos, since the only ones Karolyn ever had in her houses were her husband's plaques and trophies. She seems not to know how to fill her house with signs of a new life. Or maybe she is simply disinclined, too, until her husband comes home. She fills that house instead with people. It has become a kind of way station for the troubled in Cincinnati. Throughout the day and night, her house is filled with boys and girls moving about, rummaging through the refrigerator, watching TV, sleeping in one of the spare bedrooms, while Karolyn labors in the kitchen, cooking a twenty-pound turkey for whoever appears at the dinner table.

She adopted a black high-school friend of Petey's after his parents split up. Petey likes to tell people he has "a brother who's a lot smarter than me. He's gonna get a college scholarship." Then he adds, with a grin, "He's black." Petey and Larry Canady are a lot alike, except that Larry doesn't play sports. They both like to spend long hours watching movies on television in their room. Often, they entertain Karolyn by acting out parts from such movies as *Slap Shot* and *Used Cars*, or, in Petey's case, doing a parody of his father. It is a good imitation, especially when he acts out his father's middle-aged attempt to spike his hair with gel or wear his double-knit suit with flared-legged trousers. "You know the kind I mean," he'll say, "with the real tight pants, so you can see Dad's wad of bills bulging in the front pocket." Petey struggles, mimicking his father, to get his hand into his pocket while Larry laughs.

Karolyn also took in a local doctor and his family for a few months while they were waiting for their home to be built. And she took in the wife and two sons of Pete's old Reds teammate Tommy Helms after their marriage broke up. Karolyn gave up her own bedroom to Rita Helms, while she slept on the sofa in the family room. Rita and her sons stayed for six months.

Karolyn thinks nothing of giving up her bed to guests. She will work all night at the Wagon Wheel, where she fancies herself a kind of Carla on *Cheers*, and arrive home exhausted at 4 A.M. She will flop down on the couch and then bolt awake two hours later to take her guests to the airport on a freezing winter's morning. Before she lets them into her car, she warms it up for them. She drives in darkness, talking herself awake until they get to the Ohio River, where they have to wait for the ferry to transport the car to the other side. Karolyn sees a flock of ducks on the river. She castigates herself for being thoughtless. "Oh, I should have remembered to bring them bread," she says.

During the years when Petey's relationship with his father grew more and more strained, Pete and Carol had a son, Tyler, now four. (The boy is named for the object of Roses greatest quest, Ty Cobb.) Petey became jealous of the attention his father bestowed on his new son. "He took Tyler to King's Island amusement park," Petey says, "so I asked him why he never took us when we were kids."

Petey thought that now that he was becoming a man, his father would want to get closer to him, but just the opposite happened. Pete seemed to feel threatened by Petey's emerging manhood in the face of his own fading career. As Petey forged his own identity as an athlete (despite heavy abuse from fans, who reminded him constantly he was not his father), Pete tried to undermine his son's achievements. When Petey had trouble making his team one year, his father told him to quit baseball. "I thought that was kinda strange," says Karolyn, "since Big Pete never quit anything in his life." Another time, Pete told his son that when Tyler grew up, he would be a better baseball player than Petey. And finally, just before Petey was drafted, his father told him that maybe it would be better for him to go to college than to play professional baseball. When Petey insisted on giving pro ball a try, his father then suggested that he change his name to make it easier on him.

"That really hurt Petey," says Fawn. "I've always thought Dad was jealous of Petey. He doesn't want another Pete Rose in baseball. Besides, Dad's not playing anymore and Petey is. Petey has the only thing Dad doesn't have now. Youth."

Fawn is sitting at a table at the Wagon Wheel late at night while her mother works. The Wheel is filled with blue-collar couples drinking their shots and beers while listening to fifties rock-and-roll songs played by a disc jockey. There is a poster of Pete Rose, Jr. in an Orioles uniform, on the wall behind Fawn. She glances over her shoulder at her mother, who is smoking a long cigar, tossing back drinks, and laughing with her customers. At forty-seven, Karolyn Rose doesn't look much like the curvy woman in the BIG RED MACHINE T-shirt anymore. She has gained a lot of weight in the years since her divorce. Pete told her she was eating herself to death.

"I wish Mom wouldn't smoke," Fawn says. "Or drink. She doesn't need to be here. The owners take advantage of her because she's so good-hearted. They don't pay her hardly anything. People use her. All those people around our house. It bothers me. She just does it to take the place of Dad."

Fawn Rose is twenty-four now, and recently got her degree in psychology at Thomas More College in Kentucky. She says the first person she wants to psychoanalyze is her father. "He's unique," she says. "My father is the world's worst father."

Fawn is a pretty girl, but vastly overweight. In a way, she is trapped in her body. It defines her in the eyes of people who cannot see the woman beyond it. Friends of her mother are always asking writers doing stories on Petey to "mention Fawny in the story, won't you! Nobody ever mentions poor Fawny."

"Petey was kind of a brat when he was a boy," Fawn says. "He got more attention from Dad than I did. Dad never took me anywhere. He was more comfortable with Petey. He only talked sports with us. He talked down to Petey a lot, and it hurt Petey. He's very sensitive. Still, sometimes I wish Dad was hard on me like he was on Petey."

Karolyn Rose is dancing now. Her face is flushed as she works up a sweat on the dance floor. The long cigar is still clenched between her teeth.

"Mom's not healthy about Petey's baseball career," Fawn says. "Baseball is an obsession with her. Sometimes I think she's ignorant about it. I think she uses Petey to show up Dad, now that he's not playing and Petey is. The only thing Petey has is baseball. He'll never get away from it. But I don't know if he's driven toward it like Dad. He used to look up to Dad but not anymore. When Dad's agent, Reuven Katz, found out that Petey was being interviewed for an article, he warned him not to say anything bad about his father. Petey told him that he was going to tell the truth, like his dad had taught him.

"We never thought of ourselves as children of a famous man. He was just Dad. Sometimes I even denied I was Pete Rose's daughter when people asked me. But then I felt guilty. I would still like to have a normal father-daughter relationship with him, if there is such a thing. I want him to give me away someday when I get married. I will never understand why he never had any time for us. We didn't expect anything from him except to just like us. All we ever did was love him and want him to love us back. Sometimes I think he will come back someday, and when I do, I hope Mom won't take him back. She devoted her whole life to him, and all he ever did was shit on her."

Karolyn Rose is sitting high up in the stands behind home plate a few minutes before her son will take the field for his first professional baseball game. It is a cool, sunny fall day in West Palm Beach. The stadium is almost deserted except for a few older men, scouts, with radar guns behind the home-plate screen, and a few young girls higher up, the girl-friends of players.

Petey, in his Orioles uniform, stands beside the dugout squinting up into the bright sunlight. He scans the home-plate bleachers for his mother, as he always does. "The hardest thing in the world to me," he says, "will be to look into the stands someday and not see Mom there. She's always come to my games, cheering me on, picking me up when I'm down, yelling at me to keep my ass down on grounders."

When he spots his mother, he smiles and waves. Karolyn waves back and yells, "Go get 'em, Goog!" just before he runs onto the field with his teammates.

"That's always been his nickname," Karolyn says, without taking her eyes from her son at third base. "So people won't know who his father is."

Karolyn is dressed in bermuda shorts and a sweater she hugs to herself. She is heavily made up, with long red fingernails and lots of gold jewelry dangling from her wrists and on her fingers. She is compulsively popping sunflower seeds into her mouth, shelling them with her teeth and spitting out the shells while she talks.

"I look at Little Pete and I can't believe it," she says. He is hunched over third base in that simian pose of his father's, waiting for the batter to swing. "It's funny how time repeats itself," Karolyn says. "Except now I'm a mother and not a wife. You know, baseball must be a calling from God, I think. Little Pete has it in his blood just like his father. Big Pete's first love was always baseball. He used to say he had this much ability . . ." (she holds the thumb and forefinger of her left hand about an inch apart) ". . . and this much desire." (Now she spreads both arms wide.") She keeps her arms spread wide and adds, "I think Petey has the same desire as Big Pete, only more ability. He has more compassion for people, too."

All the while Karolyn is talking, she keeps her eyes glued to her son in the field. When he handles a routine grounder and throws the runner out, she starts tapping the arm of the man beside her. "See that!" she says. "See that!"

The game unfolds on this lazy day while Karolyn rocks nervously in her seat, popping the sunflower seeds into her mouth, rummaging through her purse for Kleenex, sipping from a can of Coke, and talking. "Big Pete had to fight for respect in baseball," she says. "Baseball never thought he was that great. Now Big Pete is the greatest. He doesn't think anyone will ever break his record. It's an awful pressure on Little Pete. I told him he can't live through his father any more than his father can live through him. It's over."

When Petey steps up to hit, his mother stops talking for a moment. Unlike his switch-hitting father, Petey bats left-handed and, at six feet one and a half inches and 190 pounds, is taller and slighter. He stands at the plate with his feet primly close together and his bat held high above his head. He holds the bat very still, almost delicately. His stance is almost the exact opposite of his father's squat, spread-out attack. Big Pete was intense, coiled anger, at the plate. He used to grind the bat handle in his hands until his knuckles were white, and wave the barrel menacingly at the pitcher.

Petey hits a soft curving liner to the left fielder to retire the side. Karolyn begins to talk again, now about the good old days when she was a ballplayer's wife and Pete was struggling to make the major leagues in his rookie year, and how he came home from practice with blisters on all his fingers, and later when pennants were won or lost and her husband had batting streaks or slumps, and how once a broken thumb kept him out of the lineup for so long that she had to hide his uniform to keep him from playing.

"I miss those days," she says. "It's the one thing I have that no one can take away from me. Going to spring training with Little Pete will bring back memories."

Len Johnston, the Orioles' scouting coordinator, stops by to say hello to Karolyn. He tells her Petey is looking good, progressing nicely. He's slotted to play in Frederick, Maryland, in the Carolina League come spring. Karolyn thanks him and then says, "Big Pete will be coming to see Petey play soon. He'll want all his stats." Johnston tells her they don't keep statistics in the winter league. Karolyn just shakes her head and says, "Big Pete'll want to see him."

(At the end of the season, Johnston offers this assessment of Petey as a ballplayer: "He played against three- and four-year minor-league veterans, and at first the pitching was too hard for him. It affected his fielding. He got down on himself. But he came on strong near the end. Made a little bat contact, and his fielding improved. His running is still below average, and so is his throwing, and he needs a quicker bat. His strength is that he always hustles and wants extra work. Nothing about him reminded us of his father, except he wants to play.")

When Johnston leaves, Karolyn says, "It'll really hit Big Pete when he sees his son in uniform. I still love him, you know. I've never dated since our divorce. I refused to accept the annulment papers from the priest. I told him, in my eyes and the eyes of the Church, I'll always be married to Pete Rose. I just don't know him anymore."

The batter hits a sharp grounder to Pete Rose, Jr. at third base. He bobbles the ball for a split second, then throws it to first on a bounce. The runner is safe. Petey hangs his head and kicks the dirt.

"Don't get disgusted with yourself, Goog!" his mother yells.

It is an attitude, self-disgust, his father was not familiar with. They are not much alike, father and son. The son has more talent than his dad at the same age. But that is not saying much. His father didn't become the greatest singles hitter in baseball history because of natural talent. He succeeded because he had an angry intensity and a chest-puffing arrogance, both of which are defined in baseball by the word "heart." The son lacks his father's heart, in a baseball sense, but in another sense he has his own heart, which, although admirable in life, doesn't count for much in the game he's playing.

"It's time to go to the yard," he says, sitting on the sofa in his minor-league-baseball player's apartment. An ordinary-looking boy of his time. But before he goes, he says, "You know, I love my dad. I just don't want to be like him. Whatever money I make is gonna be my wife's too. I'm gonna take my sons to the stadium all the time. I'd like to get to the point in my career when people will just see me as Pete Rose, not Pete Rose's son. And then, after I retire, they'll come to see my son play, too. They'll say, 'Oh, shit, here's Pete Rose at the plate. Ya know, his father played ball, too.'

Duquesne, PA

(from *Geo*, 1980)

THE DARKS AND LIGHTS are muted, the texture grainy, as if the photograph, dated 1921, had been taken through a dusty lens. Facing the camera, a line of football players stand on a grassy knoll. Behind them loom the smokestacks of the steel mill glimpsed in the valley below. Beyond the mill is the river and, beyond that, the mountain on the opposite side of the valley.

The players are wearing coarse woolen jerseys and padded pants that end below the knee, exposing thick striped socks. Their arms are folded behind their backs, and they stare sternly at the camera. They are pale young men, with the high, slanting cheekbones and narrowed eyes of Central European immigrants. Some have slicked-down hair, parted in the middle. Others have waxed mustaches. Suspended above their heads, like soft, shapeless halos, are clouds of smoke billowing up from the smokestacks. As the smoke drifts away, it becomes a palpable haze that settles over everything—the mountain, the river, the mill, the players, the very lens of the camera.

"That's Albert Gedman, my husband's father," says Mrs. Bernie Gedman, pointing to one of the players in the photograph. "He was the first Gedman to play football in Duquesne. It was originally Gedminus or Gedmanus—I'm not sure which—before the family came to America. They're part Lithuanian, Hungarian, German, and Slovak. My maiden name is Asmonga. Hungarian."

She is sitting at her dining room table, drinking coffee and smoking a cigarette. Spread out before her on the table are dozens of mementos of the Gedman's family's sixty-year-long association with football in

Duquesne, a steel-mill town five miles southeast of Pittsburgh. Mrs. Gedman is in her forties. Her pretty face has a decidedly Old World cast, as do so many faces in Duquesne. She is dressed in flannel pajamas and an old bathrobe. She is without makeup. Her short, frosted hair is uncombed, as if she had just been roused from sleep. The impression is further heightened by the languid, almost sensual way she habitually moves and speaks.

"When Albert Gedman was a boy," she says, "the foreign element in town—mostly Central European—would not let their children play football. They had no time for sports. Everyone had to go to work. Albert Gedman and some others were the exceptions. He played semi-pro football in his spare time and worked in the mill forty-two years. He'd come home from work, sit in his easy chair, open the paper, and fall asleep before he turned the first page. Hard work is a way of life for us. My husband is a plasterer. He works seven days a week, ten hours a day."

"He'd work eight days a week if he could," says Debbie, her twenty-four-year-old daughter, who has just entered the room. She is carrying a pot of coffee, from which she refills her mother's cup. Like her mother, she moves unhurriedly—a pale, thin girl in sweatpants and a floppy sweatshirt.

Mrs. Gedman nods in agreement. "He feels better when he works," she says. "Even after he had open-heart surgery, he couldn't wait to get back to work. All the Gedman's have had heart trouble, you know." She rummages through the scrapbooks, snapshots, plaques and yellowed newspaper clippings on the table until she finally produces one of the many articles written about Albert Gedman's five sons. Three of them— Dennis, Wayne, and Gene—died in middle age of heart attacks (Wayne on the sidelines of Duquesne Stadium while coaching a junior varsity football game); and the other two—Bernie and Ronnie—have had open-heart surgery. All excelled at football in high school. Wayne went on to play at Arizona State University. Gene was by far the most famous of the Gedmans. A five-foot-ten, 220-pound halfback with the handsome, square-jawed face of a matinee idol, he was the Most Valuable Player at Indiana in his junior and senior years, 1951 and 1952. He went on to star with the Detroit Lions in the National Football League before a knee injury ended his career in 1958. Gene had to sue the team for disability payments and eventually, in 1964, won a $16,500 judgment. It was the first such case in NFL history. After that award, according to

Mrs. Gedman, Gene was blackballed from coaching in the NFL, so he became a minor league football coach in Grand Rapids, Michigan.

"Oh, Gene was a handsome man," says Mrs. Gedman as she searches for a bubble gum card with a picture of Gene in a Lions uniform on it. Debbie finds the card and hands it to her mother. Gene appears in a stylized, almost balletic pose that no running back could ever execute so gracefully in a game. Balanced on his right foot—the left leg bent at the knee and raised so high it almost touches his jaw—his body is slanted away from an imaginary tackler about to be stiff-armed.

"They nicknamed him the Baron because he was such a dapper dresser," says Mrs. Gedman. "I remember when he was at Duquesne High School, he used to run the river road every morning at five o'clock. After he left Duquesne, he never came back but once. When he was with the Lions, he gave the town a party for all it had done for him. He rented Paule's Lookout restaurant and invited hundreds of people.

"He died at forty-two. He had high cholesterol, but he always defied it. Whenever he'd come to our house for dinner, he'd demand that I put real butter on the table. Oh, the Gedmans were tough men! Their environment made them tough. Kids in Duquesne grow up hungry, you see. They know there's no free ride in life. They either make it in football or go to work in the mill. Parents now have a different attitude than in Albert Gedman's day. They encourage their sons to play football. A lot of them even keep their boys out of kindergarten an extra year, so they'll be more mature when they're seniors in high school. But still, fathers in Duquesne don't have time to play ball in the backyard with their sons. The boys have to do it on their own. If they don't, they end up like most everybody else in Duquesne. They graduate high school, get a loan from the credit union, buy a fancy car, get married, and go to work in the mill for forty years."

As Mrs. Gedman talks, her thirteen-year-old daughter, Veronica, arrives home from school for lunch. Without disturbing her mother, she makes herself a fried bologna sandwich and sits at the table to eat and to listen. Debbie, meanwhile, goes upstairs to get some mementos of the football career of her nineteen-year-old brother, Jeff, who starred at Duquesne High and is now on football scholarship at Indiana University.

"We have seven kids," says Mrs. Gedman, "and none of them have ever been babied. If I'm not here, they make their own supper. Maybe it's just the way of our kind of people. When Debbie went to live in New

York for a while, we didn't try to stop her. It was good for her to learn how to pay her own bills, all those wonderful things her father and I went through to make a life."

Debbie returns with her brother's plaques, photos, and scrapbooks and hands them to her mother. Mrs. Gedman holds up a picture of her son in a tuxedo. He is a handsome youth with curly black hair, but he looks too slight to play football at a Big Ten college. He stands only five-foot-ten and weighs 175 pounds.

"We kept Jeff out of school for a year to help him mature for football," says Mrs. Gedman. "It was Kop's idea, really. Kopolovich. He was the old coach. He's gone now. He was a harsh disciplinarian, and he knew his football, whatever else you want to say about him. After Kop left, they hired a young guy named Mazza. He wasn't from here. He wasn't tough enough for the kids. After Kop, they were used to being disciplined. The team had won twenty straight under Kop and then five straight under Mazza before they lost a game. After that, the town fired him. The new coach is Janusek. He's supposed to be tough. People here respect his background. He comes from Duquesne."

South of Duquesne, in the predawn darkness, the river road is a narrow, winding, pitted two-lane blacktop bordered to the west by a granite cliff to the east by scruffy bush and the Monongahela River. From the direction of the town, dump trucks filled with hot slag rumble by. Steam from the slag spills over the sides of the trucks like swamp moss. Long after the trucks have passed, the steam still hovers low to the road, so that visibility is all but nonexistent.

Around a sharp curve, the road suddenly widens into a four-lane highway. There is a sign: "Welcome to Duquesne, a Growing City." The town rises in layers up a steep hill to the west. To the east, the McKeesport-Duquesne bridge spans the Monongahela River. Up ahead in the darkness, alongside the river, is the steel mill. It is visible only as a dark mass, a series of shapes illuminated here and there by an orange glow: a length of massive pipe, part of a huge cylinder, a steel girder, a few yards of overhead walkway suspended in the night, a long steel-sided building, a short stretch of railroad tracks. A low-lying mist flecked with greenish-orange surrounds the mill like a moat, clings to the sides of buildings and furnaces, climbs the towering smokestacks like some eerie, growing thing.

At a luncheonette nearby, steelworkers sit on stools at the counter and drink coffee from mugs. Some eat doughnuts. No one orders eggs, and there is little talk. The waitress who dispenses the coffee places a paper napkin under each mug. She is a pert young woman with a head of tight brown curls and even tighter-fitting jeans. She greets each man by name in a little girl's voice and punctuates her greeting with a smile, the warm yet oddly blank and indiscriminate smile of the innocent. The men smile back and look down at their coffee. Their eyes glaze over. Other workers stand behind them and wait for a free stool. Someone is playing the pinball machine in the corner. Others watch in silence. The dimly lighted room is musty with the odor of work clothes.

The bell over the door jingles, and another steelworker comes in out of the darkness. He goes to the cash register and buys chewing tobacco from an old man. Money is exchanged wordlessly. The cash register rings. The room is filled with men, and yet it is strangely still. Quiet is savored before the onslaught of the mill.

In the emerging daylight, the mill becomes visible as a series of huge rectangular buildings, blast furnaces, smokestacks and cylindrical towers, with railroad cars and dump trucks parked alongside, all seen through a haze of dust and smoke and burning graphite. The mill runs along the river for about a mile, the entire length of the city of Duquesne. At the far edge of town stands a corrugated steel structure resembling an airport hangar with the words "United States Steel— Duquesne Plant" stenciled in blue on its side. Farther along are piles of finished steel billets, stacked like logs, and another hangarlike building, then railroad tracks and the mill's main entrance. Beyond are the huge blast furnaces, each with attendant cylindrical stoves. An overhead walkway leads from the mill and across the road to the city. Finally, at the eastern end of town near the McKeesport-Duquesne bridge, there are more railroad tracks.

The flow of work at the mill follows the flow of the river. Railroad cars bring iron ore to the mill under the bridge. The ore is deposited into the furnaces, which are heated to almost three thousand degrees by the air from the stoves. When the ore is molten, it is transferred to the corrugated steel building, where it is poured into huge vats and purified. The impurities are scooped off the top like cream, and when they harden, they become chunks of slag, which are loaded onto trucks and carried away. The purified steel is poured into torpedo-shaped ladles on flatbed railroad cars and sent to the next building, the rolling mill. Here the hardening metal is shaped into long billets and put on rollers to be cooled by water, shaped further, then cut to size and finally stacked outside.

The mill fills the valley. To the east, across the river, rises a hill of scraggly brush. To the west, across the river road, rises the city of Duquesne, population 10,000, down from the 30,000 of forty years ago.

At nine a.m., Nick Medich, carrying a cardboard box filled with old newspapers under one arm, comes out of the Avenue News, turns his back on the incessant pounding of the steel mill below and begins the long climb up Grand Avenue, the steep hill that is the main street of Duquesne. Grant, like all the east-west roads in the city, is paved with yellow brick and leads directly to the steel mill.

The day is overcast, misty with precipitation, and hazy, as always, with the smoke from the mill. Nick moves ponderously up the hill with the aid of a cane. He is a massive, swollen old man with fierce little blue eyes. He is wearing a plaid jacket, a fisherman's hat with a pink daisy hanging from the band, and black hard-soled shoes. His shoes are unlaced, his ankles swollen, and he is wearing no socks. With each step, Nick bends forward at the waist, as if leaning into a head wind.

At Sally's Fashions, a woman in her fifties is staring at the mannequin in the display window. The mannequin is modeling an imitation cheetah coat, hat, gloves, and scarf. The woman is wearing a kerchief, a cloth coat, white ankle socks, and brown tie-shoes. Nick passes the woman and then passes Novack's bar and Honey's bar and the Kandy Kitchen and Irene's diner. In the display window of Dorman's appliance store sits a white enamel washtub with a hand-operated wringer-dryer. The Salkovitz dress shop has orange cellophane covering its windows to keep the clothes from being faded by a sun that only rarely breaks through the city's haze. The alleyway alongside Soltesez's market is sided with asbestos shaped like bricks and adorned with dozens of faded and ripped advertisements for Old Golds, Philip Morris, Chesterfield, and Mission orange soda. A large number of storefronts along Grant Avenue are boarded up, and many of the town's row houses, glimpsed on the side streets, are for sale.

When old Nick reaches Shrager and Donovan real estate, he stops for a breath. He is wheezing badly. Three high school girls walk by. They are wearing heavy makeup and baggy jeans tucked into cowboy boots. A flatbed truck with "United States Steel" painted on its side lumbers down the hill toward the mill. Three young workers are sitting in its bed drinking beer. When they see the girls, they begin to hoot and whistle. The girls ignore them. Nick chuckles to himself, wheezes again, and decides to rest on the bench at the bus stop, where two men, evidently not natives of Duquesne, are already sitting.

"You two sports gonna buy this town or what?" he says as he sits down. "Ha! You oughtta sell it instead, only it ain't worth nothin'." The men laugh. Nick sticks a wad of chewing tobacco into his mouth. He is leaning forward, his elbows on his knees. Looking straight ahead, Nick says, "Shit, I'm carryin' too much weight. Use' ta be, when I was two-forty, nobody could beat me up this damn hill. Now I'm all swollen up with water." He spits tobacco juice into the street.

"I been trying to get into the old home, but you got to know the god-damned President," he says. "Hell, I'm entitled. Hell, maybe I ain't enti-tled to a goddamned thing except a hole in the ground. And maybe not even that."

He is silent for a while, staring straight ahead through tiny, firece eyes The two men, amused, ask him if he has ever worked in the steel mill. Nick begins to curse, then says, "Everybody in this town worked in that mill one time or another." He points down toward Grant Avenue to the mill entrance. "There use' ta be homes where the mill is now. They called it Castle Garden. It was mostly for the old-timers from the old country. They'd be processed at this circular stadium, you know, like Ellis Island. They'd start at the top and see the doctor, than go to the dentist on the next level, and so on until they worked their way down. In those days, they use' ta cast every six hours. Then they built more furnaces and began to cast every hour. They had to bus in black people to work in the mill. Use' ta feed 'em on benches, like in army barracks. I was only a kid. I'd sneak in amongst 'em, and they'd feed me scraps. Now they'd prob-ably hang me." Nick shakes his head sadly. "They tore the guts outta this town when they built that goddamned mill," he says. "Everything's changed. It's every dog for himself."

Nick rises with difficulty, picks up his cardboard box and his cane. He spits one last time and then turns his back on his audience and the mill and resumes the long hike up Grant Avenue. He reaches the Polish Alliance Club. Then the Gallagher Pharmacy. Babe's bar. The Lithuanian Club. The Linda Files Beauty Salon. F. Capristo's barbershop. Sam

Markida's tailor shop. The Laundromat. The Moose. Bost's bar. Danny Simak's bar. Then he is at the top of the hill and gone.

By 2:45 P.M., as they do every afternoon, cars begin to arrive at the foot of Grant Avenue, across the river from the mill entrance. They sit along the street with their motors running, occupied mostly by women waiting for their men to get off the 7:00–3:00 shift. (There are two other shifts at the mill: 3:00 P.M. to 11:00 P.M. and 11:00 P.M. to 7:00 A.M. The mill is in operation every minute of every day of each year.) A few minutes before 3:00 P.M., workers are lined up at the mill entrance and, farther down the river road, on the overhead walkway. When the whistle blows, the men break into a dogtrot. They dodge traffic across the river road, some running toward their cars, others heading up Grant Avenue and slowing to a walk. They walk in groups—the old, the young, the black, the white—each man carrying a black lunchbox. Each group stops at its favorite bar at the foot of the avenue. More than one steelworker has been known to drink his way all the way to the top, stopping at Novack's and Babe's and Bost's and Danny Simak's before he heads for home.

Over at Duquesne High School at about the same time, while the players are running wind sprints across a mud-soaked field, Fran Janusek, the football coach, stands on the sidelines with a clipboard tucked into the back of his sweatpants and spits tobacco juice into the wind. "This town likes a strong, disciplined team," he says. "We play hard and we live hard. Last year, the coach was a little lax. He got fired and I took over. I had graduated from Duquesne High School in 'sixty-seven and Edinboro State College in 'seventy-four. It took me eight years to get through college. You learn not to quit. I worked in the mill during the summers. The first time I ever was in a mill I was scared to death. These ladles as big as four steam shovels were pouring white-hot steel into a vat. I was fortunate. I got a job as an inspector-marker. There were some bad ones, though. Some guys'd sweep out the flues in the blast furnaces. It was backbreaking, dirty and hot, especially in the summer. It'd be ninety degrees outside, and it's so hot in the furnaces you got to wear long johns and three sets of clothes to keep from dehydrating. They only let you stay down there for ten minutes at a time or else you'll die."

Fran Janusek is thirty-one years old, stands five-foot-five, and weighs 150 pounds, the same weight he carried in college when he went head-to-head with 230-pound defensive linemen. He is a round-shouldered man with thinning hair, a prominent forehead, intense, unblinking eyes, and a scar on his upper lip. There are some little men whose toughness is a posture. Others, like Janusek, must exert a great effort to control their hysteria.

Janusek's assistant coaches—John Kuster, Jan Komorowski, and Ed Kachur—have divided the team into offensive and defensive units and are running them through plays they will use tomorrow night against General Braddock High School from nearby Braddock, Pennsylvania. His cheek puffed out with chewing tobacco, Janusek stands behind the action and watches. The team is 5-0 so far on the season and is ranked ninth in the Western Pennsylvania Interscholastic Athletic League (WPIAL) Class A Division. In five games, Duquesne has surrendered only one touchdown, and Braddock, despite being a Class AA team to Duquesne's Class A, is the underdog. Duquesne, with an enrollment of 470, often must compete against teams from bigger schools—Braddock has an enrollment of 2,000.

Still, the team has more than held its own over the years. Under its former coach, Mike "Kop" Kopolovich, Duquesne—then a school of 900 students—once defeated a team from a school with 3,600 students. Kopolovich is a legend in Duquesne, for both the teams he produced and the way he produced them. His teams won seven conference titles in ten years, six of them in a seven-year stretch. He had undefeated teams in 1968, 1969, 1976 and 1977. His 1976 and 1977 teams won twenty straight games, and at the start of the 1978 season, under new coach Frank Mazza, Duquesne stretched the winning streak to twenty-five. Those twenty-five victories were one short of the state record. In Kop's day, it was not uncommon to find 10,000 people at a Friday night game.

"It was no fun to play under Kop," says Janusek as he watches his team drill. "You feared him. Maybe Friday night's game was fun, but Monday's practice wasn't. When you did something wrong, he smacked you on the helmet or the face. It didn't bother you, really, because he humiliated everyone like that. One practice I did something wrong and he screamed at me. He pushed me in the facemask and knocked me on my ass. What'd I do? I got up and waited for what else was comin'. That's the way we was brought up. He was an authority figure. When you leave this area, you can't do that kind of thing. Kop went across the bridge to McKeesport High, and they wouldn't tolerate his stuff."

Duquesne's two practice teams are bent over the football now, waiting for the snap. Their pants are splattered with mud. The two units consist of eight blacks and fourteen whites. The quarterback, Terrance Pitts, is black; so are two of the running backs, Kirk Neal and Darwin Short. The fullback, Ken Bitkowski, and the tight end, Steve Adams, are white. The races seem to mix naturally. As one white player puts it, "Why not? We're all from the same environment. We're all poor. We all been to the same schools for years. We all been chasin' the same girls. We do everything together. We got the same interests. The main thing for us is to play football and get out."

Pitts takes the snap and drops back to pass. His offensive line breaks down, and before he can get off the pass, he is swamped by the defense. Komorowski blows a whistle and begins screaming hysterically at the offensive team, "You mothers! You stupid mothers! You're nothing but a bunch of mothers!" The players put their heads down and wait for his tirade to subside. When it does, he diagrams the play for them again and tells them to run it one more time.

Janusk, watching on the sidelines, does not say a word. His hands are tucked into the back pockets of his sweatpants. He leans forward and spits tobacco juice. "We'll keep 'em here all night, Coach," Komorowski says to him, "until they get it right."

The team runs the play again. Pitts goes back to pass, only this time he has plenty of protection, coming mostly from a six-foot-one, 230-pound lineman named Phil Madgic. Madgic is using his elbows like fists to batter his defensive opponent about the helmet. He is growling and snapping like a rabid dog. Pitts completes the pass, and Komorowski whistles the play dead. Madgic and his opponent are still going at it, however. Squatting like a sumo wrestler, Madgic is growling and laughing with glee as he keeps battering his opponent with his elbows. The coaches are smiling. The players look embarassed. Finally, the coaches call Madgic off. Smiling with an insane gleam in his eyes, he walks back to the huddle. He moves delicately for a big man, splayfooted, on the balls of his feet, like a woman protecting the hem of her gown from puddles. His opponent goes back to the defensive unit. His eyes are wide and frightened, like a hurt boxer's. He is near tears.

"All summer long, that boy's been saying he wants Madgic," says Janusek. "Well, now he's got him. He's got him every damn day."

Sitting in a booth at Joe's luncheonette for a seven A.M. breakfast, Phil Madgic is surrounded by steelworkers having one last cup of coffee before running to the early morning shift at the mill. "Football's a way out," he says. "Without a football scholarship, college is a little shaky for me. I'd probably have to go to work in the mill. It's the first time in my life I've felt pressure. One of my friends was a National Honor Society student, but he didn't like school, so he just went to the mill."

Phil Madgic is of Slovakian, Polish, and Croatian heritage. He has a high-cheekboned, narrow-eyed, heart-shaped face and a heavy body. Despite his bulk, however, and his ferocity on the football field, there is a certain delicacy about him. When he smiles, his lips curl up into his cheeks to give him an even more pronounced heart shape. He speaks in a very soft voice, and he punctuates his words with a flutter of his eyelids and a little, pained, sideways gesture with his head.

"My father operates a train in the mill. It takes steel from the blast furnace to the basic oxygen furnace. He played football at Duquesne; so did my three brothers. Ever since I was a little kid, it seems, I was watching them practice and waiting for the day I would play at Duquesne. My father held me out of kindergarten for a year so I'd be more mature when I played for Kop." Madgic smiles at the mention of his former coach. Then he says, "Kop was a complex man. He knew what he wanted and how to get it. He was hard, man. He'd physically push you around. You never hit back, though. He hit you to make you a man. He made us scared to lose. He was a perfectionist. If we ran a play wrong, we'd run it over and over until we got it right, or until Kop just walked off the field. I liked playing for him. He was the best coach Duquesne ever had. The parents never complained about his treatment of us, either.

"Kop left because he wanted more money than the town was willing to give him. The next coach was Mazza. He was a bullshitter. He played up to the townspeople. At school functions, he'd dance with the cheerleaders and the sisters and mothers of the players. When it came to game time, he didn't have no plays. Mr. Janusek, now, he's a lot like Kop. A modern Kop. It's a nice discipline. He don't have to bat us around. But he's strict, too. He has bed checks, and he rides the streets at night to make sure we're at home. Kop, now he used to have the police look for us on the night before a game. If he caught you out, he'd either pull you out of the game or else make you run the gauntlet on Monday afternoon. He'd line up the eleven best hitters on the team and make you run at each one. You couldn't drop the ball or else you had to start all over again. You'd get hit, run at the next man, get hit, get up, and so on. The last three or four guys were tough. They'd hit you at will. I seen guys with tears in their eyes."

On the morning of game day, Friday, Mrs. Judy Adams, wife of the police chief and president of the Duquesne High School Football Mothers Club, is sitting on the edge of the sofa in her immaculate living room, which is furnished with imitation colonial pine. The house is famous in Duquesne as the one in which Albert Gedman raised his five football-playing sons. Today, the red-brick façade is partially obscured by a bed sheet. On it, spraypainted in red, is an exhortation to her son: "You're Super-Fine #89! Let's Go Stevie!" Similar signs can be found on the homes of all the Duquesne players on the day of a game. Kickoff tonight is at 7:00 P.M.

Mrs. Adams is a youthful-looking woman in her thirties with a wide, Slavic face. She looks too youthful, in fact, to be the mother of four children, the eldest, Stephen, an eighteen-year-old high school senior. As president of the Mothers Club, she recruits women to work in the concession stand during games, to bake things for sales, to run raffles and to raise funds for the team's annual banquet. She says of her job, "It's hard to get mothers to join. They don't want to miss seeing their sons play while they're in the concession stand. Pat Monroe's mother died, and she'll never see him play again.

"Football is very important to us, you see. It gets the kids scholarships, thank God! They start learning when they're very young. When Kop was here, he had a hand in all the football programs in town, all the way down to Pee Wees. When a boy got to high school, he'd already been exposed to Kop's ways for years. Kop told us to keep Stevie out of school a year, so we had him repeat the eight grade. Everybody knows why we did it. Kop wanted mature boys on his team. He was rough on them. He wouldn't let them ride home for lunch: they had to walk. On the days before a game, the mothers would feed their boys high-carbohydrate diets—pancakes, macaroni, *haluski*—and most of them would throw up after walking uphill to school. Kop said it made them tough, and everybody in Duquesne put up with him."

Noontime at Babe's bar, halfway up Grant Avenue. The place is filled with businessmen, teachers from the high school, construction workers in thigh-high rubber boots, steelworkers with dirty faces and hard hats, and Babe's regulars—old-timers who have retired from the mill to spend their days beneath their porkpie hats drinking shots of Calvert's and Iron City beer. Babe's is a clean, well-lighted place. Its walls are panelled in light pine, and its bar is decorated with neatly printed signs ("Homemade Hot Sausage Patties," "French Fried Smelts") and hand-carved plaques of an owl, an eagle, a wolf, and a fox.

Gladys, the cook and waitress, is in the tiny kitchen of the bar frying smelts and fish; Curly, the bartender, is busy pouring drinks and showing his customers a dirty birthday card he has received; Charles "Babe" Cardemone, the owner, is counting out change for a $50 bill to a loquacious customer. "For two more dollars, you can buy the damned joint," says Babe, twirling rosary beads hanging from his pants pocket.

At the bar, the bus driver for the football team is talking to a stranger. "Kop was somethin' else," he says. "Many a night, I seen the lights on at the field after ten P.M., and practice started at four P.M. I remember one game, the Dukes was winning easily when the other team had gotten close to scoring a meaningless touchdown. Kop calls time, walks out on the field, says something to his defense, and walks off. The other team never scored. Later I heard from the kids that Kop said if the other team scored he wouldn't stop on the way home so they could eat."

When the local news appears on the television set over the bar, no one bothers to watch it. A feature story about steel-mill towns is headlined. It is titled "The Plight of the Ghost Towns," and the gist of it is that steel-mill towns are dying because of foreign competition. Suddenly, the image flickers, the lights dim, and everything goes black in Babe's bar. Nobody seems upset. A man calls out—it is Babe—"Where's Gladys? I want Gladys." Another calls out "I got seconds." The lights flicker back on again, and Gladys, sitting on a high stool between the bar and the kitchen, is grinning a gap-toothed smile and blushing.

A little later in Novack's bar, a man and a woman enter laughing. They are both wearing jeans, down vests, and light-blue tinted sunglasses. The woman tosses the long hair off her face and slides into a booth. None of the steelworkers at the bar bothers to look up.

"Brandy would be nice, babe," she says to the man in a New England accent. "If they have it." She looks around, then leans toward the man and says in a stage whisper, "It's another world, isn't it? It's like something out of *McCabe and Mrs. Miller*."

The man goes up to the bar and asks for two brandies. The bartender just squints at him. "Brandy?" the man repeats. The bartender turns and studies the stacked bottles in front of the mirror. Then, breaking into a smile, he reaches for a bottle of brandy, holds it up to the light, blows the dust off it, and shows it to the man.

"We got brandy," he says, as if proud of his discovery. "We got lots of brandy. How do you want it?"

"In shot glasses," the man says. The bartender pours the drinks, and the man hands him a five-dollar bill. The bartender returns $4.10. The man leaves a dollar and a dime on the bar and brings the drinks back to the booth. Before he has a chance to sit down, one of the steelworkers taps him on the shoulder. There is a smile on his grimy face. He hands the man the dollar and the dime and says, "You forgot these."

At three P.M., sunlight slanting through a window highlights the cheerleaders practicing in the hallways of Duquesne High. Their bodies in the shadows, they kick their legs high in the sunlight to the music of the Jackson Five. The girls are expertly made-up and wear short-skirted red-and-white uniforms. Presently, they head upstairs, past deserted classrooms, to the auditorium, where the students are assembled for a pep rally for tonight's game against General Braddock. The girls form a conga line and high-step into the auditorium toward the stage to the cheers and applause of the audience.

Onstage, they are joined by the school's majorettes (in Dallas Cowgirl-style white boots and shorts), the junior varsity cheerleaders (wearing red jumpers and white blouses), the color guard (young girls carrying white toy rifles), the drill team (young girls holding large flags), the band (wearing street clothes), the coaches (wearing red windbreakers), athletic director Jack Proksa (a Michael Moriarty lookalike in a short-sleeved white shirt and a tie), and, finally, the football team (in jeans and their red game jerseys). The cheerleaders, in the front row, go into a routine. The students join in. The band begins to play. The color guard presents arms. The drill team raises its flags. The players manage to assume various states of sprawl while standing. The coaches look dutifully serious. The students chant and sing and clap their hands, and suddenly it becomes apparent that there are more people onstage, more students who have an active part in the football program, than there are in the audience.

When the room is finally quiet, Proksa takes the microphone. He makes a few announcements and then exhorts the students to come out tonight and support the Dukes. The students listen respectfully. In the back row, a few boys are slouching in their seats. A tough-looking man in a red sport coat comes up from behind. He stands alongside the boys and glares at them. Immediately, they sit up. Behind the boys, standing in the shadows against the rear wall, is a woman wearing a kerchief, a cloth coat, socks, and tie shoes, and she is smiling toward the stage with a mother's pride.

After the rally, all the players walk down the hill to St. Joseph's Church to pray for success in tonight's game. They walk singly and in pairs. They are mostly silent. Inside the church, each player in turn kneels at the altar, lowers his head until it almost touches the floor, and prays.

An hour before game time, the Duquesne locker room is unusually quiet. The players, dressed only in shoulder pads and shorts, are sprawled about the room, their eyes closed in either sleep or meditation. John Kuster, one of the assistant coaches, is kneeling before a boy lying on a bench and whispering in his ear. In the cramped trainer's room, which smells of analgesic balm, assistant coach Ed Kachur, wearing a butcher's apron, is taping a player's ankle. Beside him, Phil Madgic is spooning honey out of a jar with a tongue depressor and swallowing it in globs. A player near Madgic is pulling on a pair of women's panty hose and complaining about the cold, damp weather.

"Oh man, it ain't cold," says Madgic with a pained expression. "It's nice. This is the way football is supposed to be played."

In the coaches' room, Fran Janusek and Jan Komorowski are sitting in folding chairs, huddled over a clipboard. While they are talking, the officials for the game, overweight men in zebra-striped uniforms, enter, say a few words to the coaches, and proceed through to the field. By now, most of the players are dressed in their red-and-white uniforms. When Janusek enters the locker room, the players stand around him. He tells them that if they win the coin toss, they should choose to kick toward the muddy end of the field. Madgic raises his hand in disagreement. He says he thinks it would be better to receive against the wind, before the field gets even more muddy. Janusek snaps at him. Why? Madgic doesn't falter. He explains his reasons, and finally Janusek accepts them and tells his captains to receive if they win the toss. The players form a huge huddle, leaning toward Janusek in the center, and pray. Then each boy in turn says his own prayer for the team. Madgic says, "Please, Lord, let everybody stay healthy." When the prayers are done, the players leap up, shouting, clapping their hands, while Komorowski yells, "Let's send these mothers back where they came from."

Before 1,500 enthusiastic fans, mostly students, the Dukes play a sloppy, dispirited first half. The field is so muddy that their running backs slip and slide all over it, and quarterback Terry Pitts can't grip the wet ball firmly enough to pass effectively. Both teams lose the ball often. Still, through the dogged pursuit of Madgic on defense, and after two acrobatic pass receptions by Steve Adams, the Dukes manage to go into the locker room at halftime with a 14-0 lead.

Exhausted and caked with mud, the players sit on the locker room benches with their heads down. Most of them have played both offense and defense so far. Janusek is pacing back and forth in the center of the room. He is seething. Finally, he loses control. He begins to scream at his players. "I can't take any more of this goddamned shit! You son-of-a-bitch bastards are embarrassing the whole town!" There is a wild look in his eyes. He storms out of the room. Komorowski takes over, as he has done during much of the first half. It was he who called most of the plays on the sidelines and substituted players, while Janusek stood stoically beside him in the mud. Now Komorowski goes to the blackboard on the wall and begins diagramming plays. The boys cluster around him. He speaks softly, in a laid-back, macho way, as if he's underplaying his passion deliberately so that it becomes even more apparent.

In the trainer's room, Ed Kachur is putting an ice pack on the injured shoulder of Steve Adams. Adams winces in pain as Kachur secures the bag with tape. He needs help putting on his pads and jersey, but he will still play the second half, all of it, both offense and defense.

The Dukes play better in the second half and go on to win their sixth consecutive game. The final score is 22-0; it is their fifth shutout. In the locker room after the game, Janusek is subdued as he talks to reporters. "We have no excuses about the condition of the field," he says. "We coached for this weather."

The Dukes will finish the regular season with an 8-1 record, the second best in their conference. Their only loss, to archrival Serra Catholic by a score of 25-0, will produce another outburst from Janusek. After the game, he will tell his players, "I hate you all. I'll never forgive you for what you've done to me." Still, the Dukes will make the WPIAL postseason playoffs; but they will lose their first game 10-0, to Western Beaver, to end their year.

Kop. Kopolovich. Michael C. Born, Duquesne, Pennsylvania, 1926. Graduated Duquesne High School, 1943. Assistant varsity football coach, Duquesne High School, 1950-63. Varsity football coach, Duquesne High School, 1963-77. Fifty-three. Balding. Czech heritage. Kop, smiling a pained smile, steps from behind his desk in his tiny, spartan office in McKeesport High School and greets his visitor with a handshake. He returns behind the desk and sits down.

"Duquesne?" he says. "I loved that town. When I was a kid I walked everywhere. Theaters. Shopping centers. The high school. I loved the high school. I played football, baseball, basketball, track, everything. It was a tradition. My father—he worked forty-four years in the mill—he played before me. But then, after the war, people started moving out. The town got smaller. I went to North Carolina State on a football scholarship, and when I got a chance, I returned to Duquesne. I wanted to give back some of the things I'd got from the town. I never wanted to leave. I was offered coaching jobs at Arizona State and California State, but I stayed. I *couldn't* leave."

While speaking, Kop is bent over a scratch pad with a pencil. He prints key words of his conversation in block letters—TRADITION, LOVED, LEAVE—and underlines them. He looks up every so often to flash his pained smile at his visitor and then continues his train of thought.

"I'm a perfectionist," he says. "I don't give too much praise, or else people let down. I never let down. In college, we had an expression, 'Root, hog, or die.' A hog has got to root for its food or it dies." He prints the word on his pad—DIES—underlines it sharply. "All that talk about my physical harshness with my players was more myth than reality. I always knew who I was picking on. Some kids you couldn't touch, or they'd quit [QUIT!!]. Even the ones I slapped across the helmet, hell, it hurt my hand more than it did them. One of my ex-players, Pat Monroe, came back from college one day and told me, 'You know, Coach, you were always less hard than we thought you'd be.'"

"A lot of people in Duquesne didn't understand me. I never went to bars. Hell, at one time there were fifty bars in Duquesne, and you could drink your way up Grand Avenue. You still can. After school, after football practice, I went right home to watch game films. People thought I was aloof. It wasn't the case. I had an interest [INTEREST]."

Kop sighs, and his shoulders slump. He shakes his head and looks up at his visitor. "The town's grown old, you know," he says. "I brought tradition back to it for a while with football, but I had to leave. There was nothing left for me there. Don't get me wrong. Duquesne was a fantastic little community once. I loved every minute of working there. Maybe the town outgrew itself. Maybe football was the only thing that kept it alive. It was hard for me to leave, and yet I'm only three miles away. For so long it was a part of my life. Fifty-one years. I'm fifty-three. Some people can outgrow a town. It used to be you were born, raised, and died in Duquesne."

Kop stands up, smiling his pained smile. He leads his visitor to the door. He has one hand on his forehead, as if to soothe a headache. As the visitor shakes his hand, Kop says, "I miss it. I don't know if I did outgrow it. But you can't look back. Looking back's a bitch."

Steve Carlton

Thin Mountain Air

(from *Philadelphia* Magazine, 1994)

Durango, Colorado, is a cold mountain community 6,506 feet above sea level. It is known for its thin air, which can make residents light-headed, disoriented. It is surrounded by the La Platta mountain range. Built into the foothills of those mountains is a domed concrete house covered with snow and dirt. No one but its owner can explain what he was seeking with that house.

"I CAME TO DURANGO in nineteen eighty-nine to get away from society," he says. He is a big man, six-foot-five, 225 pounds, dressed in a Western shirt, jeans, and cowboy boots. He is standing beside his truck in the thick snow that covers the land around his bunker and rests gently on the branches of the low-lying piñon trees that dot his 400 acres. It is a few days before Christmas. "I don't like it where there are too many people," he says. "I like it here because the people are spiritually tuned in." He glances sideways, out of the corner of his eyes. "They know where the lies fall."

He makes a sweeping gesture with a long arm, encompassing his bunker, his barn with its turkey, pheasants, and horses, and more than 160 fruit trees he has planted. "This is sacred land," he says. "We're self-sufficient here. There's no one around us. We grow our own food." He points to sliding glass doors that lead inside his bunker to the greenhouse off his bedroom. "We have our own well," he says. "And sixteen solar batteries for heat and electricity."

Even his telephone works on cellular microwave transmitters. That way no one can tap his wires.

"The house is built with over three hundred yards of concrete," he

says. "Three-feet-thick walls covered by another three feet of earth."
Why? He looks startled, like a huge bird. His small eyes blink once, twice,
and then he says, "So the gamma rays won't penetrate the walls."

Built under the house is a 7,000-foot storage cellar. He's stocked it with
canned foods, bottled water, weapons. "Do you know if you store guns in
PVC pipe, they can last forever underground without rusting?" he says.
He glanced sideways again. "The Revolution is definitely coming."

He believes in the Revolution, only he isn't precisely sure which of a
myriad of conspiratorial groups will begin it. Possibly, he says, it will be
started by the Skull and Bones Society of Yale University. Or maybe the
International Monetary Fund. Or the World Health Organization. There
are so many conspiracies, and so little time. Sometimes all those conspiracies confuse him and he contradicts himself. One minute he'll say
"The Russian and U.S. governments fill the air with low-frequency
sound waves meant to control us," and the next he'll say "The Elders of
Zion rule the world," and then "The British MI-Five and -Six intelligence
agencies have ruled the world since eighteen twelve," and "Twelve Jewish
bankers meeting in Switzerland rule the world" and "The world is controlled by a committee of three hundred which meets at a roundtable in
Rome." The subterfuge starts early. Like the plot by the National
Education Association to subvert American children with false teach-
ings. "Don't tell me that two plus two equals four," he once said. "How
do you know that two *is* two? That's the real question."

He believes that the last eight U.S. presidents have been guilty of trea-
son, that President Clinton "has a black son" he won't acknowledge, and
that his wife, Hillary, "is a dyke," and that the AIDS virus was created at
a secret Maryland biological warfare laboratory "to get rid of gays and
blacks, and now they have a strain of the virus that can live ten days in
the air or on a plate of food, because you know who most of the waiters
are," and finally, that most of the mass murderers in this country who
open fire indiscriminately in fast-food restaurants "are hypnotized to
kill those people and then themselves immediately afterwards," as in the
movie *The Manchurian Candidate*. He blinks once, twice, and says "Who
hypnotizes them? *They* do!"

Maybe he isn't really contradicting himself. Maybe he is just one of
those people who read into the simplest things a cosmic significance
they may or may not have. Conspiracies everywhere to explain things he
cannot fathom. The refuge of a limited mind. "The mind is its own

place," John Milton wrote in *Paradise Lost*. "And in itself can make a Heaven of Hell, a Hell of Heaven."

Steven Norman Carlton, "Lefty," discovered his first conspiracy in 1988, when he was forced to leave baseball prematurely and against his will, he says—after a twenty-four-year-major-league pitching career of such excellence that he was an almost-unanimous selection for baseball's Hall of Fame on his first try, this past January. He received 96 percent of all baseball writers' votes, the second-highest percentage ever received by a pitcher (after Tom Seaver's 98 percent) and the fifth-highest of all time.

Carlton, who pitched for the Phillies from 1972 to 1986, after seven years with the St. Louis Cardinals, has—after the Braves' Warren Spahn—the most wins of any left-handed pitcher. Carlton won 329 games and lost 244 during his career. Six times he won 20 games or more in a season, and he was voted his league's Cy Young Award a record four times. His most phenomenal season, one of the greatest seasons a pitcher has ever had, came in his first year with the Phillies: Carlton won 27 games, lost only 10 and fashioned a 1.98 ERA for a last-place team that won only 59 games all season. In other words, he earned almost half of his team's victories, the highest such percentage ever. For almost twenty years, he was the pitcher against which all others were judged.

The secrets to his success were many. Talent. An uncanny ability to reduce pitching to its simplest terms. An unorthodox yet rigorous training regimen. A fierce stubbornness, and an even fiercer arrogance. All contributed to his success on the mound and, later, to his inability to adjust to the complexities of life off the mound.

As a pitcher, Carlton knew his limitations. A mind easily baffled by intricacies. There were so many batters. Their strengths and weaknesses confused him, so he refused to go over batters' tendencies in pregame meetings. He blocked them out of his consciousness and reduced pitching to a mere game of toss between pitcher and catcher—his personal catcher, Tim McCarver. He used only two pitches: an explosive fastball and an equally explosive, biting slider. He just threw one of the two pitches to his catcher's glove. Fastball up and in; slider low and away. He worked very hard to let nothing intrude upon his concentration. Once the third baseman fired a ball that hit him in the head. He blinked, waved off the players rushing to his aid, picked up the ball, toed the rubber, and faced his next batter. His parents, Joe and Anne Carlton, claim they've never seen their son cry.

It was not always easy for him to be so singularly focused while pitching. "Concentration on the mound is a battle," he says. "Things creep into your mind. Your mind is always chattering."

To prevent any "chattering" before a start, he had the Phillies build him a $15,000 "mood behavior" room next to the clubhouse. It was soundproof, with dark blue carpet on the floor, walls, and ceiling. He'd sit there for hours in an easy chair, staring at a painting of ocean waves rushing against the shore. A disembodied voice intoned "I am courageous, calm, confident, and relaxed . . . I can control my destiny." Carlton, said teammate Dal Maxvill, lived in "a little dark room of his mind."

His training routine was just as unorthodox. He hated to run wind sprints, so instead he stuck his arm in a garbage pail filled with brown rice and rotated it forty-nine times, for the forty-nine years that Kwan Gung, a Chinese martial-arts hero, lived. By then, Lefty himself was a martial-arts expert. He performed the slow, ritualized movements in his clubhouse before each game. He also extensively read Eastern theology and philosophy. Those texts discussed the mysteries of life, the unknowable and how a man should confront them. Silence, stoicism, and simplicity.

Those tenets struck a chord in him because, increasingly, his life off the mound was becoming more complex than a game of catch. People constantly clamored for his autograph. Waitresses messed up his order in restaurants, so he tore up their menus. Reporters began to ask him questions he didn't like, or didn't understand, or maybe he just thought were trivial. They even had the effrontery to question him about his failures.

"People are always throwing variables at you," he said in disgust, and refused to talk anymore. The press called it "the Big Silence." From 1974 to 1988, Carlton wouldn't speak to the media. (It wasn't just *Daily News* sportswriter Bill Conlin's stories, as many assumed, but a series of articles, Carlton says now, that drove him to withdraw.) One sportswriter said there would come a time when Lefty would "wish he'd been a good guy when he'd had the chance." But he didn't have to be a good guy. He wasn't interested in the fame being a good guy would bring him. He wanted only to perfect his craft, which he did, and to become rich.

Over the last ten years of his career, Carlton earned close to $10 million, almost all of it in salary because he didn't want the annoyance of doing endorsements. It was demeaning, he thought, for him to hawk peoples' wares. Then again, thanks to the Big Silence, there weren't a lot of sponsors beating down his door. He already had a reputation for sullen arrogance. When he went to New York City once to discuss a contract for a book about his life, he told the editors he really didn't care about the book, that he was just doing it for the money and because his wife, Beverly, thought it was a good idea. The editors beat a hasty retreat.

Carlton didn't need a publisher's money, or a sponsor's, because he had a personal agent who promised to make him so rich that when he retired he could do nothing but fish and hunt. He had his salary checks sent directly to the agent, David Landfield, who invested them in oil and gas leases, car dealerships and Florida swampland. Since Carlton couldn't be bothered with the checks and often had no idea exactly how big they were, Landfield simply sent him a monthly allowance, as if he were a child. These monthly allotments would be all Carlton would ever see out of his $10 million. Not one of Landfield's investments for him ever made a cent. By 1983, all the money was gone.

During the nine years that Landfield worked for him, Carlton's friends tried to warn him off the agent. Bill Giles, the Phillies' owner, and Mike Schmidt, Lefty's teammate, pleaded with him to drop Landfield. But he wouldn't listen. One time, he even got in a fight with Schmidt in the clubhouse because of Landfield, and the two, formerly close friends, stopped speaking. Carlton said it was because he was loyal to Landfield, whom he trusted. Others said he was just being stubborn and arrogant because his success on the mound had led him to believe he was invincible off it. McCarver once said that "Lefty always had an irascible contempt for being human. He thinks he's superhuman."

When the truth of what Landfield had done with his money finally intruded into Carlton's psyche, it was too late. He went through the motions of suing Landfield in 1983, but by then Landfield had declared bankruptcy. Worse, Carlton never had a chance to recoup his money, because only a few years later his career was on the downswing and those big paychecks were a thing of the past. He began to lose the bite on his slider in '85, and people told him he should try to pick up another pitch. But he refused. He continued to throw the only way he knew how. Fastball up and in, slider low and away.

Between 1986 and 1988, Carlton was traded or released five times, until finally, after being cut by the Minnesota Twins, no club would sign him—even for the $100,000 league minimum. Carlton was furious. At forty-three he insisted he could still pitch. That's when he uncovered his first conspiracy.

"The Twins set me up to release me by not pitching me," he says today. "And other owners were told to keep their hands off. Other teams wouldn't even talk to me. I don't understand it." To understand it, all Carlton has to do is look at his pitching record from 1985 to 1988: sixteen wins, thirty-seven losses, and an ERA of more than five runs per game. It was a reality he didn't want to face. So, sullen and hurt, Carlton decided to punish those who had hurt him. He retreated to Durango and soon afterward began building his mountain bunker, turning his back on the game and the real world that had betrayed him.

Steve Carlton, forty-nine, dressed in a T-shirt and gym shorts, is standing on his head in the mirrored exercise room, performing his daily three hours of yoga.

"I don't even feel any weight above my neck," he says, upside down. Just then a screaming flock of children runs into the room with their female yoga instructor, who is dressed in black tights. Immediately, Carlton takes out two earplugs and sticks them in his ears. "It takes the bite off the high-end notes," he says, smiling. He is still a handsome man, his face relatively unlined. His is a typically American handsomeness, perfect features without idiosyncrasies. Except for his eyes. They are small and hazel and show very little.

"I spend my summers riding motorcycles and dirt bikes," he says. "I work around the house. It's taken us three years and we're still not finished." (It is rumored that he doesn't have the money to do so.) "In the winter I ski and read books, Eastern metaphysical stuff. All about the power within. Oneness with the universe. I want to tap into my own mind to know what God knows." He rights himself, sits cross-legged on a mat and begins contorting into another yoga postion, the ankle of his left leg somewhere behind his ear.

"You ought to try it," he says. "Yoga for three hours a day. And skiing, too." He says this with absolute conviction, as if it has never crossed his mind that there are those who do not have three hours in the morning to spare for yoga, and three more hours in the afternoon to ski.

In fact, Durango seems to be the kind of town where people have unlimited leisure time. At 10:30 on a weekday morning, the health club is packed. Durango is one of those faux-Western towns whose women dress in dirndl skirts and cowboy boots and whose men, their faces adorned with elaborately waxed 1890s handlebar mustaches, wear plaid work shirts rolled up to the elbows. It has a lot of "saloons"—not bars—with clever names like Father Murphy's, that have walls adorned with old guns, specialize in a variety of cappuccinos, and frown upon cigar smoking. Clean air is an important subject in Durango. When the town's only tobacco shop wanted to hold a cigar smoker, its two owners were afraid it would be disrupted by protesters chaining themselves to their shop door. It's a town for people who cannot countenance the idiosyncrasies of their fellow man. So they come to this clean, thin mountain air where they can breathe without being contaminated by the foulness of the rest of the world.

Carlton believes he is in better physical shape now than when he left baseball six years ago. "In a month I could be throwing in the eighties [miles per hour] and win," he says. "There's nothing wrong with me. I was labeled 'too old.' But you can still pitch in your fifties. It's not for money but for pride, proving you can perform. That's the beauty of it. Then to be cut off . . . It's disheartening. If only they let *you* tell them when you know you're done. It hurts. But I haven't looked back. No thought of what I should have done. Maybe I should have learned a circle change-up in my later years. But I didn't think I needed a change."

Most great pitchers intuit the loss of their power pitches before it actually happens. Warren Spahn, for example. He could see, in his early thirties, a time when his high, leg-kicking fastball would no longer be adequate. So he began to perfect an off-speed screwball and a slow curve. By the time Spahn lost his fastball, he had perfected his off-speed pitches, and his string of twenty-victory seasons continued unbroken into his late thirties and early forties. But Carlton was both luckier than Spahn and less fortunate. Because he did not lose his power pitches until late into his thirties, he was deluded into thinking he would never lose them and so didn't develop any off-speed pitches.

*   *   *

Carlton, lying on his back now, pulls one leg underneath himself and stretches it. "Baseball was fun," he says. "But I have no regrets. Competition is the ultimate level of insecurity, having to beat someone. I don't miss baseball. I never look back. You turn the page. Eternity lies in the here and now. If you live in the past, you accelerate the death process. Your being is your substance."

As a player, Carlton was known for his conviviality with his teammates. He spent a lot of his off-hours drinking with them, and there were hints in the press, most notably by Bill Conlin, that his drinking contributed to some of his disastrous years, such as the thirteen-and-twenty '73 season. After he left baseball, Carlton, who used to be a wine connoisseur with a million-dollar cellar, gave up drinking.

"I had nobody to go drinking with anymore," he says. "Now when I see old baseball players, I have nothing to talk to them about. All that old-time bullshit. It bores me. I live in the here and now. I'd be intellectually starved in the game today." Still, Carlton would like to get back into it. He sees himself as a pitching coach in spring training.

"I'd like to teach young pitchers the mental aspect of the game," he says. "Teach them wisdom, which is different than knowledge. Champions think a certain way. To a higher level. They create their future. The body is just a vehicle for the mind and spirit. Champions will themselves to win. They know they're gonna win. Others hope they'll win. The mind gives you what it asks for. That's its God."

Then he relates a story about a friend in Durango, who, years ago, didn't want to play on his high school basketball team because he knew it was going to have a losing season. Before the season began, the friend was hit by a car, destroying his knee.

"See," says Carlton, as if he's just proved a point. "If you have an accident, you create it in your mind. That's a fact. The mind is the conscious architect of your success. What you hold consciously in your mind becomes your reality."

If this is so, then must not Carlton have willed his own failure in the twilight of his career? When such a possibility is broached to him, he looks up, terrified. He blinks once, in shock, and a second time to banish the thought from his psyche. "Why do you ask such questions?" he says shrilly. He has so carefully crafted his philosophies that he can become completely disoriented when they are challenged. That's why

Carlton has withdrawn from the world into the security of his bunker. There he is left alone with only his thoughts, his dictums, his conspiracies, with no one to question them. Such questions strike fear in Carlton. And above all else, Steve Carlton is a fearful man.

"Fear dictates our lives," he has said. "Fear is a tremendous energy that must be banished. Fear makes our own prisons. It's instilled in us by our government and the Church. They control fear. It's the Great Lie. But don't get me started on that."

For a man who, for fifteen years, was known for his silences, Carlton now talks a lot. In fact, he can't stop himself. When he was voted into the Hall of Fame this past January, he held a press conference. At the end of its scheduled forty-five minutes, the sportswriters got up to leave. Carlton called them back to talk some more. "I don't mind," he said. "It's been a long time." When he is inducted, with Phil Rizzuto, into the Hall in late July before the assembled national press, it will be interesting to see if he will still be so loquacious.

A lot of people are suspicious of his motives for talking so much. Carlton claims, "It's all Bev's idea." He says his wife wants him to get back into the world. For years, Beverly Carlton ran interference for her husband during "the Big Silence." After Carlton won his three-hundredth game, in 1983, he surrounded himself with a police escort and fled the clubhouse to avoid reporters. He left it to Bev to talk to the press.

"Steve would like to play another ten years," she told them. "He just might. Baseball's been great to us." Then, to humanize her distant husband, she revealed a little intimacy. "Well," she said, "he likes Ukrainian food."

In Carlton's final season, when he began to rethink his silence, he said it was because "my wife convinced me that if I want to find a job after I'm through playing, having my name in the paper doesn't hurt." Even today, Bev Carlton schedules her husband's interviews. (He no longer has an agent.) When reporters show up in Durango, Carlton will feign surprise at their presence. "I didn't know you were coming," he says. When told that his wife said she confirmed the interview with him, he blinks once, twice, and says, "I didn't pay any attention." In this way, he can lay off the distasteful prospect of being interviewed on his wife. He can maintain, in his mind's eye, the lofty arrogance of the Big Silence while no longer adhering to it. ("Bev likes to read about me," he says.)

It is likely that Carlton is talking now because he needs money, looking to reassert his presence in the public's consciousness so he can do endorsements. "We'll probably do some of that stuff in the coming years," he says. It's a distasteful position his old agent put him in, and one he doesn't like to be reminded of. "It's one of life's little lessons," Carlton says of David Landfield. "I don't want to talk about it. I no longer live in the past." Then, after a moment of silence, he adds, "It all came down to trust. You're most vulnerable there. When your trust is breached, it affects you."

Most of Carlton's money for the past few years has come from his two businesses. He claims he is a sports agent but won't mention the names of his clients. (It is hard to imagine anyone, even a ballplayer, entrusting his money to a man who lost millions of his own.) The bulk of his money, a reported $100,000 or so per year, comes from autograph shows and the Home Shopping Network, where he peddles his own wares. Caps, cards, T-shirts, little plaster figurines of himself as a pitcher—all emblazoned with the number 329, his career victory total. He sells these objects by mail, too, out of a tiny, cluttered office in a nondescript, wooden building a few miles from town. A sign out front lists the building's occupants, lawyers and such. But there is no mention of Carlton's enterprise, Game Winner Sports Management, and he likes it that way. "We didn't want a sign up so people would know where we are," he says, smiling. In fact, even the occupants of the building aren't sure where "the baseball player's" office is.

"We have a toll-free number [1-800-72LEFTY]," he says. "We accept VISA and checks. Just send me a check and don't bother me."

Now as Carlton finishes with his yoga, the instructor in the black tights ushers one of the children over to him. The teacher is smiling, giggly, blushing, a vaguely attractive woman who seems to have a crush on Carlton. She leans close to him and says, "I have someone who wants to meet you." Carlton shrinks back from her even as she urges the uncomprehending child toward him. "Go ahead," she says. The child looks up at the towering man and says, "Happy birthday." Carlton blinks, confused. "I don't celebrate birthdays," he says.

At the foot of a steep, winding dirt road rutted with snow, Steve Carlton stops his truck and gets out to engage its four-wheel drive. When he gets back in and begins driving carefully up the path, he says, "I've been lucky. I've had teachers in my life. One guy began writing me letters, four or five a week, in nineteen seventy. That's the year I won twenty games with the Cardinals. He told me where the power and energy comes from.

He was a night watchman. We talked on the phone a few times and met a couple times. He was a very spiritual guy. All I knew about him was that his name was Mr. Briggs. Then he was gone as quickly as he came into my life. It was a gift."

When he reaches his bunker, at twilight, he stops and gets out. He looks out over his land and says, "There's nothing like being by yourself. I'm reclusive. I want to get in touch with myself." He glances sideways, and adds, "But society is coming." That's why he is preparing by being self-sufficient. He is not so self-sufficient, however, that he's ever mustered the courage to butcher his animals for food. But, that's a moot point now. All his chickens were killed by raccoons last winter.

It's late. Carlton has a dinner appointment. But he's not sure what time it is now, because he doesn't wear a watch. "I never know what time it is," he says. "Or what day it is. Time is stress. Pressure melts away if you don't deal with time. I don't believe in birthdays, either. Or anniversaries. I don't watch television. We don't read newspapers. We don't even have a Christmas tree. Those things hold vibrations of the past, and I exist only in the now. Bev is even more into it than I am."

He trudges through the snow to the side door of his odd, domed bunker. Inside, he puts the flat of one palm against the concrete and says, "I'm waiting for the coldness to come out of the walls." Bev is waiting for him in the living room. She is a small, sweet, nervous woman, sitting in a chair by a space heater. She used to bleach her hair blonde, but now her short cut is its natural brown. She smiles as her husband sits down across from her. She hugs herself from the cold, and then drags on a cigarette.

Their home is starkly furnished, not out of design but necessity. A few wooden tables, a bookcase filled with Carlton's Eastern metaphysical books, a patterned sofa and easy chair, hand-me-downs from their son Scott, twenty-five, a bartender in St. Louis. Their other son, Steven, twenty-seven, lives in Washington State, where he writes children's songs.

Carlton doesn't like to talk about his kids. "Why do you have to know about them?" he says plaintively. He doesn't talk much about his parents, either, whom he rarely sees or speaks to. They, it seems, are another part of Carlton's past that he has cut out of his life.

"The correspondence lacks," admits Joe Carlton, eighty-seven and blind. "We don't hear from him much. It's okay, though."

"We keep up with him in the newspapers," says Anne Carlton, who says of *her* age, "It's nobody's damned business."

The elder Carltons are sitting in the shadowed, musty living room of their small, concrete house in North Miami, where they raised their son and two daughters, Christina and Joanne. From the outside, it looks uninhabited. The drab house paint is peeling, and the yards out front and back, dotted with Joe's many fruit trees, are overgrown, rotted fruit littering the tall grass.

Inside, the furniture is old and worn, and thick dust coats the television screen. Even the many photographs and newspaper articles on the walls are faded and dusty, like old tintypes. The photos are mostly of their son in various baseball uniforms. As a teenager—gawky, with a faint, distant smile, posing with his teammates, the Lions. With the Cardinals, his hair fashionably long, back in the 'sixties. Then with the Phillies, posing with Mike Schmidt, captioned MVP AND CY YOUNG.

"No, I haven't heard from him," says Joe, a former maintenance man with Pan Am. He is sitting on an ottoman, staring straight ahead through thick glasses. "I can't see you, except as a shadow," he says, staring out the window. He is a thin man, almost gaunt, with long silvery swept-back hair. He is wearing a faded Hawaiian shirt.

"It's no special reason," says Anne, sitting in her easy chair. "He just doesn't call me anymore."

"He called when Anne's mother died, at one hundred one," says Joe. Then he begins to talk about his son as a child. How Joe used to go hunting with him in the Everglades. "We used to shoot light bulbs," he says.

"Steve was a natural-born hunter," says Anne. "Tell what kind of animals you hunted in the Everglades."

"Lions and tigers."

"Oh, you didn't. There are no lions and tigers in the Everglades. Tell what kind of animals."

Joe, confused, says, "There were lots of animals." Anne shakes her head. "Steve was always quiet," adds Joe, trying to remember. "He wasn't very talkative around the house when he was a boy." He fetches an old scrapbook and opens a page to a newspaper photograph of his son in a Phillies cap. There is a zipper where his mouth should be.

"Can I bum a cigarette off you?" Anne says to their guest. "Oh, you don't have any. Too bad."

"The last time we saw Steve was five years ago," says Joe.

"It wasn't that long ago."

"Yes, it was. Time flies."

"It was only four years."

"He never told us about his house."

"We don't even know where Durango is. I never heard of it. Have you seen his house? Really, it's built into a mountain?"

"Steve got an interest in his philosophies when he got hold of one of my books when he was in high school," says Joe.

"He doesn't believe in Christmas trees anymore?" asks Anne. "We *always* had a Christmas tree. Bev *liked* Christmas trees."

"No, we never asked him for any money," Anne continues. "He would have given it to us if we asked, though."

"He never helped us financially. I didn't need it." Joe, who is also hard of hearing, cups a hand around an ear. "What? His sons? You mean Steve's sons? No, we never hear from them, either."

"Our daughters call, though," says Anne.

"They came down for my eighty-fifth birthday," says Joe. "They gave me a surprise party. Steve didn't come."

Joe gets up and goes into a small guest room where, on a desk, dresser, and two twin beds, he has laid out mementos of his son's career. A photograph of a plaster impression of Steve's hand when he was a boy. A high school graduation photo of Steve with a flattop haircut.

"Steve doesn't collect this stuff," says Joe. "He's too busy. Here's another picture of Steve. I got pictures all over. I got another picture here, somewhere, when we took Steve to St. Augustine, where Anne is from. It's a picture of Steve in the oldest fort in America. He's behind bars." Joe rummages around for the photo, disturbing dust, but he can't find it. He leafs through one last scrapbook; on its final page is a photograph of a burial mound of skulls and bones, thousands of them, piled in a heap. Joe looks at it and says, "We took it in Cuba. See here what I wrote at the bottom: *The end.*"

There are no photographs of Joe and Anne in their son's living room. No photos of his and Bev's children. No photos of themselves when younger. No wedding photos of smiling bride and bridegroom. No photos of Carlton in a Phillies uniform or on a hunting trip. There are no keepsakes of their past. No prints on the wall. No Christmas tree, no presents nestled in cotton snow. There is nothing in that huge, high, concave, whitewashed concrete room except the few pieces of nondescript furniture and the space heater. Bev and her husband seem dwarfed by the cavelike room. They huddle around the space heater like a twentieth-century version of the clan in the movie *Quest for Fire*. Mere survival seems their only joy, their only beauty, except for the view through the sliding-glass living room doors of the La Plata mountain range, all white and purple and rose in the setting sun, which Beverly has turned her back on.

Bev tries to make small talk as she drags on her cigarette. Curiously, her husband no longer hates cigarette smoke as he once did as a ballplayer, when he claimed he could taste it on his wineglass if someone in the room was smoking. Of course, in those days he didn't eat red meat either because of the blood. His thinking has changed now, he has said, because he realizes "that the juice of anything is its blood, that the juice of a carrot is the carrot's blood."

Bev is talking about the time she and other Phillies' wives met Ted Turner. "Oh, yes," she says, "he kept putting his hands on the behinds of the wives."

"He was crude and vulgar," says Carlton. "What's wrong with America?" He shakes his head in disgust and begins a long monologue on the unfairness of the American government, primarily because it won't allow its citizens to walk around armed. Bev listens patiently smiling her thin smile, her head nodding like a small bird sipping water. Her husband is right. She is a lot like him. Frightened. When it is time to meet their guests for dinner, Carlton stands up. Bev remains seated, hugging herself against the cold.

"Oh, I'm not going to dinner," she says without explanation. "Just Steve."

It's confusing to their guest, until he remembers Carlton's words: "Bev wants me to get out into the world," Carlton had said. Which is what she is doing now: sending him out into that fearful world in order to make a living for them. It's something she knows he has to do on his own if they are going to survive, like a mother bundling her tiny child off to school for the first time. Meanwhile she sits at home in their stark bunker huddled close to the space heater for warmth, worrying about him out there, alone and scared, in the real world he shunned for so many years.

Bobby Hurley

A Ridiculous Will

(2005)

For MOST OF US, death will not announce itself with a blare of trumpets or a roar of cannons. It will come silently, on the soft paws of a cat. It will insinuate itself, rubbing against our ankle in the midst of an ordinary moment. An uneventful dinner. A drive home from work. A sofa pushed across a floor. A slight bend to retrieve a morning news-paper tossed into a bush. And then, a faint cry, an exhale of breath, a muffled slump.

Death came for Bobby Hurley on the night of December 12, 1993, when he was twenty-two years old. He had just finished work at 10 p.m. He left Arco Arena, home of the Sacramento Kings of the NBA, and walked toward his SUV, a gold Toyota 4Runner, in the parking lot. He was distracted because he hadn't played well that night in his team's 112-102 loss to the L.A. Clippers. Hurley was the Kings' rookie point guard. He had been drafted in the first round of the NBA summer draft and given a seventeen million, six-year contract shortly after he left Duke University, where he had been a two-time All-American. He was arguably the greatest point guard in the history of collegiate basketball. He set a record for the most assists in a collegiate career (1,076). He guided Duke to a 119-26 record and two national championships during his four years there, after which his number 11 uniform jersey was retired. Now great things were expected of him in the NBA. One NBA coach described Hurley as "a gift, a blessing to the league" because of his unselfish ability to pass off to better-shooting teammates. Which was also part of his problem as an NBA player. After only twenty games in the NBA, it was clear that there were gaps in his game, ones that had not been revealed in college. He was too slightly built at six feet, 160 pounds to muscle his bigger, stronger opponents off his drives. Then there was his jump shot, or rather his lack of an efficient jump shot. His father, Bob Hurley, Sr., a renowned high school coach in New Jersey, said of his son's game, "In college, he could explode to the basket and either get the ball to an open man or finish himself. But the pros have much better shot blockers . . . so it makes sense (for him) to pull up and shoot whenever possible." The problem was that Hurley wasn't hitting his jump shot. He was shooting only 37 percent from the field, so his opponents played him loose, preventing him from passing to his better shooting teammates because they didn't respect his jumper. All of this was making Hurley anxious, impatient. He had always been a driven soul. His younger brother, Dan, said, "His talent wasn't that ridiculous, but his will and desire were totally ridiculous." But Hurley was having trouble asserting his "ridiculous" will on his bigger, stronger opponents in the NBA. For the first time, it must have begun to dawn on him that maybe will was not enough.

Hurley was thinking of all these things when he got in his SUV and drove out of the parking lot. He forgot to fasten his seat belt as he wondered if he would ever fulfill his potential. He stopped at a stop sign on Del Paso Road at the intersection of Del Paso and El Centro, the cross street. Both two-lane country roads were dark and deserted. They were surrounded by open fields barely visible in the darkness. Hurley was anxious to get back to his apartment, to relax, have something to eat, replay that night's game in his head to see just what he was missing on the court.

Dan Wiseland, a thirty-seven-year-old house painter, was also anxious to get home after work. He was driving his 1970 Buick station wagon, loaded with paint cans, north on El Centro at a legal speed of around 55 mph. He wasn't drunk, and he wasn't under the influence of drugs. But in his desire to get home, like Hurley, he had forgotten to turn on his wagon's headlights.

Hurley glanced down El Centro, saw no lights, and eased his SUV through the stop sign, turned left, and four hours later, he says, "I was pronounced dead at the hospital."

Garry St. Jean, the Sacramento coach at the time, said of Hurley, "Every young player's dream is ahead of him." Although Hurley didn't die that night, a testament to his "ridiculous will," for all intents and purposes, his dream did, which is how he ended up where he is today on a humid, misty, early morning at Calder Race Track in Hallandale Beach, Florida.

Hurley, now thirty-four, dressed in a Hawaiian shirt and baggy shorts, is standing at the rail in front of the deserted grandstand, watching race horses gallop around the track. Pigeons, doves and blackbirds peck at the infield grass as the horses gallop past the finish line. It's quiet at the track at 7:30 A.M., peaceful, amid the sounds of chirping birds, the muffled thumping of horse hooves against the dirt, their snorting breath, and the whispered voices of Hurley and his trainer, Joe Choenese, as they discuss Hurley's latest purchase, a two-year-old filly named Reason to Rejoice. Hurley's basketball glory is only a distant memory to others—though not him—where he now lives in South Florida, "flying under the radar," he says. In South Florida, basketball is an afterthought. Football—the NFL's Miami Dolphins and the University of Miami Hurricanes—is king, along with thoroughbred horse racing. In South Florida, Bobby Hurley is known as the owner and breeder of thoroughbred race horses under the banner of his two stables, Devil Eleven and Derby Dreams. His most famous horse is Songandaprayer, who competed in the Kentucky Derby in 2001 and, more importantly, changed Bobby Hurley's life.

"She's had problems at the starting gate," says Choenese, in a hushed, reverential voice. Hurley nods, turns toward the track as Reason to Rejoice comes galloping by.

When Reason's rider takes her back to the stables, Hurley and Choenese get in a golf cart and putter after her. They putter down a sidewalk, past another golf cart, turn a corner and almost collide with a second golf cart. Hurley grabs his seat as Choenese maneuvers his cart around the other one without hitting.

"That was a close call," says Choenese.

"But we made it," says Hurley.

Hurley is standing by Reason's stall, which smells of hay and dung. He watches Reason's hot walker walk her around the stable. Reason is jet black, with that stiff-legged gait of thoroughbreds, as if their legs were in splints, until a rider gets up and their legs become limber as they prance off.

"I love these times at the track," says Hurley. "The sun coming up, a cup of coffee, the horses, the silence. It's so peaceful. Everyone talks softly so as not to spook them." For many of his first twenty-eight years, Hurley worked in stifling arenas amid the screams of his 20,000 fans.

"She won her second start," says Hurley. "I usually never buy a horse I don't inspect personally, but this time I went on the recommendation of my trainer, John Dowd." Reason walks stiff-leggedly by, stops to dip her head into a bucket, drinks, then totters on around the stable. Hurley stares after her. "I love the athleticism and beauty of horses," he says. "And racing is never so intense that it isn't enjoyable." He means, in contrast to basketball, which, for him, was always intense but not always enjoyable. "Basketball put so much pressure on me to perform," he says. *He* put so much pressure on *himself* to perform. "But as a horse owner I'm just a spectator. I have no control. I feel helpless. I mean, I can't talk to her, ask her how she feels." He pauses, then adds, "But I'm lucky to have found horses as my passion. I'll let horses take me as far as I can go." He looks down at the dirt. "But nothing will ever fulfill me like basketball did. I'm still dealing with not playing." He looks up. "*I* was the guy with the ball in his hands. *I* controlled what happened."

Hurley still has those skinny little boy's legs and the long, horsey, small-eyed face. But his brown hair is now tinged with gray. He's lost his gym-rat pallor. He has a pink, Irish tan. He pats his stomach. "I've gained thirty pounds," he says. "I don't have to run sprints anymore. I use a golf cart. It's funny, but at Sacramento, they always wanted me to put on weight."

After the accident that ended his dream, his mother, Chris, his father, Bob, Sr., and his brother, Dan, all described him as a "diminished" person with an ineffable "sadness" about him. But today that sadness is not evident. Hurley is easygoing, not so ridiculously intense as he was as a basketball player. When he does talk about his lost career, it is less with sadness than with a kind of wistfulness of things long past. "Nothing will ever put me in the Hoosier Dome again," he says, "but hey, you have to grow up." He laughs. "I have no complaints. I'm happy. Except I can't play basketball anymore. Aw, I'll never let it go. I'm too immature."

Hurley grew up a city kid, in a row house in a blue collar neighborhood of Jersey City, New Jersey. His father was a probation officer and already a famous basketball coach at little St. Anthony's parochial high school, a home for students who couldn't afford a flashier prep school. Hurley, Sr., turned St. Anthony's into a national power. Over many years, he won 847 games, lost only 97, won 22 state championships and two

USA Today National Championships. He was so famous for his intensity as a coach—screaming at referees and his players while St. Anthony's nuns in the stands made believe they didn't hear his profanities—that a book, *The Miracle of St. Anthony's*, was written about him.

When Hurley, Jr., was still a baby, his father took him in a stroller to his practices and games. Hurley, Jr.'s earliest memories as a child are of the fans screaming while he lay in a stroller off the court.

"I had no choice," says Hurley. "I was gonna be a basketball player. When I was old enough I went to the roughest black neighborhoods to play. They respected my game." (One of his Sacramento teammates said of his game, "He plays like a black kid.") "That's where I picked up my instinctive game," Hurley says. "But I'd never be the player I was without the fundamentals and work ethic my father taught me."

Hurley played for his father at St. Anthony's, guiding his teams to a 115-3, four-year record, and a 32-0 record and a National Championship in his senior year. But not without conflicts. "It wasn't easy playing for my father," he says. "He'd go out of his way not to show favoritism. I ran so many punishment windsprints that I felt like a was running the marathon."

After high school, Hurley thought he'd enroll at Seton Hall until he made a visit to Duke in North Carolina. He liked the laid-back southern atmosphere at Duke, in contrast to the hyper Northeastern attitude in New Jersey. "It was culture shock," he says. "I talked faster and they talked slower. I learned what barbecue was. But it was a good experience for me. I grew up."

By the time he reached the Kings in '93, Hurley was being hailed as the reinvention of sliced bread. Sliced white bread. The new white hope in a predominantly black game. Still, his best friend on the Kings was the black man he had been hired to replace as point guard, the veteran Spud Webb. When Webb was asked if he was annoyed at this interloper into his game, a pasty-faced neophyte who arrived with so much fanfare, a sneaker contract, a bit part in a movie, and his own diary in a local newspaper, Webb said he couldn't be envious of Hurley "because he's so nice."

On the night of December 12, 1993, Mike Batham, a forty-six-year-old engineer from Youba City, had watched the Kings game and was driving home south on El Centro at 10:40 P.M. when a car came toward him with no lights on. Batham swerved to avoid the car, then moments later he heard "a crunching sound" and saw sparks in his rearview mirror. He turned his car around and sped back to what was now a crash scene.

Both Hurley's crumpled car and Weiland's wagon were in a ditch. Weiland was trapped inside his wagon, but Hurley had been thrown from his SUV. He was on his knees, face down, over a puddle of water. When Batham reached the scene it was so dark he couldn't see Hurley, until he heard a muffled plea, "Help me." Then he saw Hurley just as he fell face down into the water. Batham pulled him up into a sitting position so he wouldn't drown and cradled Hurley's head in his lap. Hurley said, "Am I gonna die?" Batham said, "No," but he wasn't so sure. Blood was pouring from Hurley's ear.

A few minutes later an off-duty police officer and his wife arrived, and then Hurley's teammate, Mike Peplowski. Peplowski called for an ambulance, then got a jacket from his car and wrapped it around Hurley. Hurley stammered, "Pep, what happened?" Then, "My back hurts." Peplowski said, "We'll take care of it." Then he took out his rosary and began to pray because, he said, "Death was very present." Hurley's breath had a foul stench Peplowski remembered from a deer he once gutted.

Ten minutes later an ambulance arrived and Hurley was put on a stretcher. He remembers the stretcher, and the pain in his back, and turning left onto El Centro, but that is all. While Hurley was being transported to a hospital Weiland was still trapped in his wagon waiting for an emergency crew with the jaws of life that would extract him.

At the precise moment of the accident, Dr. William Blaisdell and his wife were in a plane landing at nearby Sacramento Airport. Blaisdell looked out his window and saw the flash of lights below he knew to be a crash. When his plane landed he was summoned to the hospital to operate on Bobby Hurley. The first doctor to examine Hurley at the hospital was Dr. Russell Sawyer. He diagnosed, among Hurley's many injuries, two collapsed lungs, five broken ribs, a fractured left shoulder blade, a torn ACL in his right knee, a compression fracture of the lower back, multiple lacerations, a broken right fibula, and, most severely, a windpipe stem leading from the trachea to the left lung that had been torn away. A torn stem results in death 90 percent of the time. Often, the diagnosis of such an injury is missed in patients, but as luck would have it, Sawyer had recently read a chapter in a book about such an injury. That chapter had been written by Dr. William Blaisdell.

After eight hours of surgery, including the essential reattachment of Hurley's windpipe ("The most massive injury I've ever seen of someone who lived," said Blaisdell), Hurley was loaded up with morphine and put in intensive care. A few days later he could wiggle his toes and Hurley knew he was not paralyzed. "I knew I'd walk again," he said, and he knew he'd also play basketball again, for no other reason than his ridiculous will would insist on it. Like any competitive athlete, he set goals for himself. To get out of bed on his own. To walk to the bathroom alone. He felt dizzy, weak, nauseous, but still he forced himself to achieve his small goals. Finally, he was walking the hospital corridors on his own.

After he was released from the hospital, Hurley returned home to Jersey City to rehabilitate under his father's care. His weight was down to 140 pounds; he could not raise his left arm above his left shoulder, but still he began to rehab. Within weeks he was running a treadmill, then running a twelve minute mile, then dribbling up and down a court under his father's watchful eyes. He tried to shoot a basketball but he couldn't raise his left arm. He shot foul shots instead. At night, he took pain killers, Percoset and Vicodin, until one night it dawned on him that he was taking them not for pain but because he was addicted to them. "I realized I didn't need them," he says, "so I walked back and forth all night to cleanse my body of that stuff. It took me two weeks. By then I had set my long term goal. To get back in uniform for the next season."

While he was recuperating in New Jersey, Hurley spent his free time at Monmouth and Freehold racetracks watching thoroughbreds run. He had always been fascinated by horses as superb athletes ever since he was ten years old and his babysitters would take him to the track. His visits to the track now were momentary respites from the psychological anguish he was still suffering after the accident.

He didn't like to drive anymore. When a driver cut him off, he had to stop his car, his hands quivering. He woke from sleep with his body shaking from the memory of the crash. He would have cold sweats and uncontrollable tears. *Why me?* he asked himself. But as his body healed, he began to feel normal again. "I felt like a different person," he says. "I wasn't so uptight. I changed mentally. I wanted to experience other things than basketball. I had a desire to have children. (He had met his future wife, Leslie, while he was recuperating in Jersey City.) I found myself less focused on basketball. I no longer had time to feel sorry for myself."

The greatest change in Hurley's psyche was that he felt, after his accident, a profound sense of loss. He felt as if the person he had been *had* died and another person had been born in his place. It is the same sense of loss and rebirth felt by most people who have confronted death and survived. It changed them, just as that young soldier wounded in battle was changed in Ernest Hemingway's short story, "In Another Country."

Hurley returned to the Kings the following year, '94, where he received an outpouring of support and respect from his fans and players and the media for his courageous comeback. He returned to the Kings because that's what he had been conditioned to do all his life, play basketball. "My comfort zone was on the basketball court," he says. It was a reflexive action, knee jerk, from a young man who admitted he was "no longer focused on basketball. I felt normal now. I didn't want to be a one-dimensional person." The cheers didn't last long. They quickly turned to boos when Hurley's game was seen to be even more diminished than it had been in his rookie season. He was still too weak to shoulder off stronger opponents on his drives. His jump shot was even more inadequate than it had been a year ago. His still injured left shoulder "changed my shooting mechanics, but I didn't tell anyone," he says. Now, he was shooting even less than 30 percent from the floor, the lowest-rated shooter in the NBA. And his most obvious flaw was found in what had been his greatest strength. He had kept his basketball instincts, only he couldn't execute them. He could see his open teammates, but he couldn't get them the ball.

"When you play at your best," he says, "the game develops in slow motion." Now, for the first time in Hurley's life, his beloved game was being played at a pace too fast for him. "My mind was just not on basketball," he says. "Something didn't want me to do it."

Hurley remained in the NBA for five more years, primarily because the Kings didn't want to cut him and eat his huge bonus. His playing time diminished with his lack of success. He began to "pout" on the bench or when he was put into hopelessly lost games in a mop-up role. Sometimes, three and four games would pass without him even getting in a game. Sacramento fans and the media, which once cheered his arrival and his comeback, now began to mutter that Bobby Hurley was never that good before or after his accident.

Bobby Hurley left basketball in 1999, but not of his own accord. He was released by Vancouver, which had acquired him from the Kings.

He said of his career, "I didn't live up to my expectations," but he was-n't ready to give up at the age of twenty-eight. He began to play semi-pro basketball in the Jersey Shore League and help out his father as an assistant coach with St. Anthony's. "I was tough to live with at the time," he said. "No one wanted me. But I felt if I don't play basketball, something's missing." He got an offer to play in the Italian basketball league and was prepared to accept it when he tore up his ACL in a Shore League game. "Crazy things always happened to me," he says. "I always felt I was fighting my way out of a hole. I was never the total package." Even though he says he hadn't gotten over his lost career, he decided to become a college coach, another knee jerk reaction. He applied for a job at Columbia University and was turned down. It was a feeble attempt on his part, even he admits. Most college coaches have to begin their careers as assistants and work their way up. Hurley tried to jump right into the college ranks as a head coach because, he says, "I thought my family bloodlines would carry me." He laughs now, but he didn't then, 2001. He acted reflexively again, becoming a scout for the Philadelphia 76ers, "to see if scouting would inspire me." But it didn't. He lasted only a year with the 76ers, and then, in 2003, his career in basketball was over.

Hurley is driving home from Calder Race Track in the midst of rush hour traffic at 9:30 A.M. The sun has broken through the clouds and it is already hot in South Florida. Hurley guides his big, black Mercedes 600 sedan slowly down Hallandale Beach Boulevard. He changes lanes cautiously, a habit left over from his accident. Finally, frustrated with the traffic, he pulls off to a side street and maneuvers his big Mercedes through a black ghetto. Men drinking from brown paper bags stare at the car. Hurley turns right down a narrow street bordered my dilapi-dated trailer homes. Then he is across Federal Highway heading toward his home in the gated community of Harbor Island, a complex of faux Mediterranean townhomes off the Intracoastal Waterway. Before he reaches his home, however, he stops at 7-Eleven to pick up a racing form.

Hurley is sitting at his dining room table in his townhouse. There are sliding glass doors behind him that look out onto a swimming pool landscaped with palm trees and tropical plants on a sunny, late morn-ing. Hurley has traveled a long way from his native Jersey City. It was an

arduous psychic transformation from the driven and obsessed basketball player with an athlete's ocular block, to the laid-back South
Floridian horse breeder and racer in a Hawaiian shirt. He has distanced
himself from the more mercurial pleasures and pains of his competitive
life, and embraced the smaller pleasures of everyday life. His children
(Bobby, two, Sydney, seven, Cameron, nine) his wife, Leslie, a weekend
trip to Disney World, his mornings at the track with the sun coming up
in the east over the pale blue-green waters of the Atlantic. His father
once said, when he was offered college coaching jobs around the country, "I'll never leave the concrete of New Jersey." His son says, with obvious awe, "It's funny where life leads you. I've got two horses that might
run in the Derby this season."

When Hurley started going to tracks in New Jersey during his rehab,
he was approached by a trainer, John Dowd, who asked him if he wanted
to buy into a race horse. "I wrote out a check for twenty thousand dollars for twenty-five percent of the horse," says Hurley, "But I backed out
at the last minute." He laughs. "That horse earned over seven hundred
thousand dollars in his career." But still his appetite had been whetted
for horses. He began to do research—about the Derby, bloodlines, con-
formation, which pedigrees mixed well together. "Dowd was my mentor," he says. "But I had a natural sense of what an athlete is like. How
they should move. Some guys take notes about horses, but I'm either
grabbed by a horse or I move on. I can see which one's an athlete. But
the mystery is, does he have the will? I can't talk to him to find out what's
inside him. That levels the playing field."

Hurley began buying horses in '99 because, he says, "I loved horses
and the drama of a race. It's like before and after a basketball game."
Hurley treated each race of his horses like a basketball game, too, which
was considered gauche behavior by his fellow owners. He remembers the
first race one of his horses ever won. He was in the owners' box at a track.
All the other owners wore jackets and ties. Hurley and Jack Goldthorpe,
his partner in Derby Dreams, were more casually dressed. As their horse
rounded the far turn, Hurley and Goldthorpe were screaming so loudly,
gesturing with their arms, that Goldthorpe almost knocked over a table.
Hurley looked around. Every other owner was silent.

"Owners are characters," says Hurley. "They come from all walks of life.
Cowboys. The prince of Dubai." He grins. "A basketball player from New
Jersey. The only thing we have in common is a sense of competition."

In his first few years as an owner, Hurley felt he was just "dabbling" in horses while searching for something else, another passion like basketball. His price range was between $25,000 and $75,000 a horse. Then, at an auction in 2000, Hurley saw a bay colt with a white blaze on his face. He was a big horse, sixteen hands high, very muscular. "Oh, he was a grand horse," says Hurley. "I felt an immediate attachment to him. On the track he moved with such ease, without a whip, that his rider just had to hang on. When he was standing still, he had this attitude, very classy, his head up, like 'I'm the man.' He was smart and he had human qualities, a presence. Oh, he was a special type of athlete. It was the first and only time I ever connected with an animal. I fell in love with him."

Songandaprayer was the son of Unbridled Song and the grandson of Unbridled, the 1990 Kentucky Derby winner. When Song came on the auction block, Dowd told Hurley he had to buy him. Hurley felt strongly he had to, too. "But it was my money," he says. "The bidding went to seven hundred thousand and I was still in it. When it hit nine seventy-five I said I'd stop at a million, no higher." When the hammer was dropped on Song, for a sale price of $1 million, Hurley was handed his sales ticket to sign. His hand shook as he signed his name. Then he called his wife, Leslie. He told her what a great horse he had just bought, and how . . . She asked him how much. He said, "One million." There was a light pause on the line, then Leslie's voice, "You've lost your mind," and then *click, buzzzz.*

"A couple of weeks later I got her on board," says Hurley, smiling. "Why Song? Until then I didn't feel I belonged in racing. But I wanted to be at a high level. Song gave me instant credibility. I knew now I was in for the long haul."

In his first six races, Song finished first three times, winning almost $400,000. But he was a speed horse who had trouble going long distances. Still, Hurley was so enamored of his big colt that he entered him in the 2001 Derby. Song finished twelfth in that Derby and was never the same horse again. "He developed physical problems," said Hurley. Often, when Song was recuperating from one problem or another, Hurley would go to his office next to Song's stall. "He knew my voice," says Hurley. "His ears would go back and his eyes would light up. He'd stick his head out of his stall for his treats, peppermint candies." Finally, Hurley put Song out to stud, and Song immediately began generating income for Hurley, $10,000 a breeding, with often up to 173 breedings a year. Song more than helped Hurley make up for the $3 million he's spent buying horses over the past six years and his annual $500,000 in expenses, maintaining forty horses, six of them in training.

"I'd rather sell a horse for a quick profit than gamble on taking him to a race," says Hurley. "I sold one of Song's babies for two hundred fifty thousand. He's the number one juvenile sire in the country now. He generates income beyond my expectations."

Hurley is more cautious as a thoroughbred owner than he ever was as a basketball player. He sees himself as sort of like a basketball team's general manager. "As an owner," he says, "it's my job to pick out the right athlete and send him to my coach to make a team. I like to know what's going on, but I let trainers do what they've been doing their whole lives. I mean, I never liked it when someone told *me* how to shoot."

Hurley is still working on his jump shot. Recently, he found an outdoor court near his house. He goes there to shoot jump shots. He leads a fastbreak just as he did for Duke, except that he leads it alone under the pale blue Florida sky and a blazing sun surrounded by palm trees. He tosses himself a pass, begins to streak down the court, dribbles behind his back, and then either pulls up for a jump shot at the foul line or finishes the drive to the hoop. "There's no one there," he says. "No pick-up games. That's good because I'm too proud to let some kids get the best of me. I knew what I had at my best. I was on track to do something special, but I didn't get it done." He looks up with a beatific smile and adds, "I used to love to throw a creative pass, you know, the kind a coach would take you out of the game for. It didn't matter whether it was in front of sixty thousand people or in an empty gym. It was the pass that mattered."

Just then, his wife, Leslie, comes in with their son, Bobby. Hurley takes his son in his arms. Leslie stands over him, smiling. She is a slim, pretty woman, who has still not lost her Jersey City accent. "What did I say when he bought a horse for a million dollars?" she says. "I hung up."

When Leslie first met her husband when he was rehabbing in New Jersey after his accident, she says there was "a sadness" about him, "but horse racing replaced it. It filled a void for him. Horses are the best thing that ever happened to him. He throws himself into them like he throws himself into everything. He does nothing half-assed." Then she adds, "But it was Songandaprayer that really changed Bobby. He's so awesome. When Song was recovering from a surgery, Bobby was there for him everyday. Bobby didn't want to rush him back onto the track like he rushed himself back into basketball."

Every so often, when she can find a babysitter, Leslie will go with Hurley to the outdoor court and watch him go through his drills. "I rebound his shots and throw him a pass," she says. "He gets on me if I make a bad pass or don't hustle enough after a ball. There are no courtesies on the court with Bobby. There I'm not his wife anymore. My job is just to chase down the ball and get it to him. He may have put the NBA behind him, but he'll never put basketball behind him."

Renée Richards

Renée's Retreat

(from *Special Reports,* 1987)

Rᴇɴéᴇ ʀɪᴄʜᴀʀᴅs, at fifty-four, lives the quiet life of a Victorian spinster with her personal secretary, Arlene; her two Airedale dogs, Elizabeth and Barrett; her cats, especially Ray the Shma; her two parakeets; and her abundant flowers in a log cabin on a hill surrounded by woods and overlooking a clear lake in Upstate New York.

Renée sits in an easy chair facing the big stone fireplace in the living room and languidly strokes Ray the Shma while Arlene, behind her, fixes their early evening drinks. Renée puckers her lips and holds Ray against her cheek. She has thin lips, small eyes, the high-cheekboned Slavic cast of her Russian-Jewish ancestors, and thinning reddish hair. Ray squirms in her big hands, leaps away. Renée stands up—a big woman, almost six-two, 185 pounds, in a tennis dress and sneakers—and begins to drift, uneasily, about the room. She moves like a big cat, stalking, trying, despite her bulk, to move lightly on her feet as if by an act of her will. She stoops to touch a magazine. Reaches to arrange some flowers. Stops to coo at her parakeets in their cage. She sits again. Flicks the television on, then off. Drifts off again across the room. Picks up a tennis ball. Goes outside to the deck where Barrett is waiting anxiously. Renée fires the ball into the woods in her southpaw's motion. Barrett chases it. Renée returns to the living room, begins to point out the various photographs decorating the walls. Renée at Wimbledon. Renée with Martina. Renée at the French Open. Renée's mother. Her father. "My son," she says. He is seventeen, with thick, black eyelashes and swept-back black hair. He looks like a combination of Montgomery Clift and Elvis, only more troubled than even those two troubled men.

"His looks are his problem," Renée says. "The girls." Her son has dropped out of high school. He lives on the streets of New York. Once Renée found him wandering the beach at Negril. "He's trying to find himself," she says. "We keep a room for him here. He just shows up. He grew pot behind the walls. Arlene knew." She smiles a thin smile. "Parents are the last to know. His room is down here."

Renée moves down a narrow hallway in that willfully languid way of hers. Her life has been an act of will. Her creation. The rustic cabin. The pets. The flowers. The photographs. An occasional guest for drinks and dinner. The quiet domesticity of an aging woman. A peaceful life, but hard earned. Not necessarily *happy*, but not *sad*, either. Content, maybe. Tinged with only a faint melancholia.

"Here it is," she says. "My son Andy's room." It's a boy's room: Posters on the wall—Jimi Hendrix, Jim Morrison, a naked woman. A weight lifting machine. Sneakers. A desk. There is a photograph pinned above the desk at precisely eye level so that whoever is sitting there can stare directly into the eyes of the thin, prim man in that photograph. Dr. Richard Raskind, a succesful ophthalmologist and amateur men's tennis player—Andy's father—before he underwent a transsexual operation in his late thirties to become Renée Richards.

"In the old days when I was a man I was known for being very tough under pressure, very aggressive on a tennis court," says Renée. She is sitting on her deck overlooking the lake, having a drink at twilight. "You had to carry my opponents off on a stretcher. I remember one guy—the most obnoxious human being I ever met—accused me of cheating. I went up to the net and said, 'You accuse me of cheating once more and I'm gonna break this racquet over your fucking head.'" She smiles at the remembrance of that scene. Her macho threat. Even now, she is proud of that threat. "I needed tennis at that point in my life," she says. "The order of it was good for me."

Richard Raskind always turned to tennis for psychic comfort at times of emotional turmoil in his life: When he had conflicts with his domineering mother, who dressed him as a girl when he was a child. When he had conflicts with his emasculated father, who never had the will to win the club tennis tournaments he entered. When he, Richard, in his thirties, had an overwhelming compulsion to become a woman. Richard always associated tennis with a kind of order missing from his life. The game was fathomable in a way his life wasn't. It defined his maleness. When he played tennis it brought out his macho aggressiveness and pushed down into his subconscious his desire to become a woman. Finally, there came a point in his life when even tennis could not repress his urge to become a woman, and so, in his late thirties, he underwent a transsexual operation and became Renée Richards, a female ophthalmologist and a female tennis player.

"As a woman on the tennis tour, I was always less aggressive than the other women I played," says Renée. She absentmindedly strokes Barrett lying beside her. "I mean, Chrissie was a killer! I'd get into tie-breakers with her or Martina and I'd always lose. I think it was a desire not to be aggressive. I wasn't conscious of it, but maybe it was because I was experimenting with a new role. Chrissie and Martina, of course, had no problems with it. Then, too, maybe I subconsciously knew that if I came into women's tennis and won, they'd kick me out. So I didn't win. I became a sort of resident pro on the women's tour. I was forty-three and my career was over as a player. Maybe if I'd been more competitive I wouldn't have played that role. A coach I had at the time, a man, said to me, "Shit, Renée, if I had you twenty-five years ago I could have made you the best in the world. Man or woman!"

As a woman taking regular doses of female hormones, Renée had lost much of the speed and strength she had as a man. Also, the things that fed Richard's ego were different from the things that fed Renée's ego. For instance, she took great pleasure in Ilie Nastase telling her she was prettier than some of the women on the tour. Which was all she wanted. To fit in.

"Dick had been a star," she said once, "Renée only wanted to play first-string." That was not the attitude of the other women on the tour, however. When Renée teamed with Billy Jean King in a doubles match one tournament, she tried to bow out in the middle of the match because she had a fever. Billy Jean wouldn't let her. Renée whined and complained after almost every point. Billy Jean grew furious. "My temperature must be at least a hundred and one!" said Renée. Billy Jean glared at her and said, "Listen! I won Wimbledon with a temperature of hundred and three. Now, let's go!"

After they won that doubles match, Billy Jean turned to the crowd and screamed, "This is the last time I'm ever playing with a Jewish American Princess!"

Renée smiles over that moment now, on her deck overlooking the lake. In a way it was a triumph for her. Jewish American *Princess!*

"The attitude of boys and girls in tennis is identical today," she says. "It's the age. Stereotypes no longer apply. Girls want to win, be pros, be the best, just like boys. They're not hung up on being ladies on the court. I see the killer instinct in young girls all the time on the court. They just revert back to the usual social roles off it. Goolagong can win Wimbledon and then step off the court and nurture her baby. Women have aggression. They just keep it under wraps in daily life. I mean, they can't punch each other out! They kill with a look, or a word. Look at Steffi Graf. She has never said a word to anyone in the locker room. She's cold and dispassionate and she's the best in the game."

Once, when Renée was coaching Martina Navratilova for the French Open, she ran into an example of female aggression in the form of Andrea Jaeger. Martina beat Jaeger for the title, and afterwards Jaeger held a press conference in which she said Martina won because Renée was giving her signals from the stands. Martina's reaction was to break down and cry. Renée's reaction was more macho. She stormed into the press tent and told the press, "Martina doesn't need me to beat Andrea Jaeger, who never won anything in her life."

Renée, still fuming, even now, says, "Here was this...this *brat* destroying Martina's victory. If a man was in that situation, he would have said, "Listen, you sonuvabitch...." Renée falls silent, regains her feminine composure, then says, "The expression of aggression is hormonal. The result of testosterone. The predatory male. McEnroe needs to display his aggression to win. But even *he* turns it off off the court or else he'd be constantly getting his face mashed. Sometimes that aggression works against men. The most talented boy I ever saw on a tennis court couldn't control his aggression. I'd get a pro to hit with him and the kid would pick a fight with the guy. I'd yell at him, 'You jerk, this guy does me a favor and you punch him out!' The boy never made it."

Women have this male aggression to a degree, Renée says, but they control it better on the court, which is to their advantage. They use it in subtle ways to help them compete. Renée points, as proof, to her young protégé, Patty Murren, a sixteen-year-old Connecticut high school student. "She's a killer," Renée says.

Patty doesn't look like a killer. She is so small and slight for her age that she looks barely bigger than the racquet she wields. She has a pixie haircut and braces on her teeth. She is quiet around adults, respectful but not timid. Her relationship with Renée is slightly combative, both on the court and off it.

"You didn't run after that ball!" Renée shouts during practice.

"It was out of my reach," Patty says.

"No, it wasn't."

"Yes, it was."

A few strokes later, Renée says, "Your backhand sucks. If you can forget how to hit your backhand in practice, what are you gonna do in a tournament?"

Blithely, Patty says, "I won't forget in a tournament." And then, "Can I drive home after practice?"

Renée has been teaching Patty how to drive. She stops the car by the side of a country road, gets out, and exchanges seats with Patty. Patty adjusts the driver's seat forward but still looks lost behind the big steering wheel. She checks every detail Renée has taught her. The emergency brake, the gear shift, etc., etc., and then eases out into traffic. She picks up speed. "You're going too fast," Renée says. Without looking at her, Patty says, matter-of-factly, "No, I'm not."

On those occasions when Renée doesn't let Patty drive, Patty does not pout. She acts as if nothing bothers her until after Renée has driven past a gas station. Then she tells Renée she has to go to the bathroom.

"Arlene says it's Patty's way of manipulating me," says Renée. "You know, control. I don't know. I don't like to self-analyze anymore. I used to over-intellectualize. I'm much happier now."

Patty is Renée's first and only student since she left tennis almost eight years ago, when she returned to her ophthalmology practice in New York City and for all intents and purposes disappeared from public view, apart from the occasional interview with a tennis publication.

"I got in trouble a few months ago," says Renée. "I told a reporter for a tennis magazine that it was ridiculous for Martina to think she could be number one again. At her age, she could still win some major tournaments if she didn't try to play every tournament. That was a piggish attitude. Naturally, the headlines read: "Renée Calls Martina Piggish!" Martina's still mad at me, but she'll get over it."

Martina is Renée's closest friend from her tennis days, and her first student. They are a lot alike: Open, generous, giving, direct, and unashamedly outspoken. "I *had* to say it!" Renée says of her comments about Martina being piggish. It was Renée who taught Martina how to win on clay and, ironically, how to play effectively while suffering from menstrual cramps.

"Women retain water, get irritable, and sluggish," says Renée. "They can't concentrate. I taught Martina to be aware of that irritability and to play through it by an act of will."

The most important thing Renée taught Martina about competition was something most male athletes learn very early in their careers. "It's something Terry Bradshaw used to say," says Renée. "You don't win the Super Bowl by having an overwhelming performance. You win by playing your regular game. Martina used to try to win Wimbledon by playing one hundred ten percent of her game. I told her she couldn't play one hundred ten percent. All she had to do was play seventy percent of her game to win. Whatever level of competitor you are it will show through in tight situations without trying harder. When competitors break down in tight situations it's not mental, it's just the flaws in their technique showing through. Psychology in sports is for mediocrity if you don't have good technique."

As a coach of a game she calls "unnatural," Renée says there are four things a good player must have to be successful: speed, flexibility, proper mechanics, and strength. Men have the advantage in speed, strength, and flexibility, but women have the advantage in mechanics because they are easier to teach than men. "Women follow instructions better than men," says Renée, because they know they are at a physical disadvantage in the game. They develop better mechanics because they can't rely on physically overwhelming opponents the way men can. That's also why women in tennis are paying more attention to physical training than men. "Men can serve one hundred fifteen m.p.h., and women barely ninety-five m.p.h.," says Renée, "so men rely on their natural strength more and don't pay attention to their mechanics. Women are doing a lot more physical conditioning today because they are aware their strength can be improved. Still, they don't want to make themselves look like gorillas, although some of them *are* beginning to take steroids. That's one of the things that's never been told about women in tennis. Compare photographs of Gabriella Sabatini at fifteen and nineteen. It's not a normal progression."

Renée prefers to coach women, she says, because it's easier to make a woman a good tennis player than it is a man. There are many more talented male athletes than there are women, so the degree of competition is greater. "From a selfish standpoint," says Renée, "you get more return with a girl like Patty. She has fewer good women to compete with."

Boys and girls gravitate to sports as children because they're fun, says Renée. They like the feel of expending energy. Then, in high school, it becomes more difficult for girls to continue in sports, and easier for boys. Successful male athletes in high school are rewarded more. They are seen as more masculine: the high school football hero is besieged by pretty girls. Sports do just the opposite for high school girls. They don't enhance their femininity, but detract from it in boys' eyes. They have to fight the attitude that sports for girls is unfeminine. Patty's older sister, for example, refuses to play tennis seriously because she's afraid boys won't ask her out. Because sports are such an uphill battle for young girls, they have to be even more committed to them than boys do. They have to, like Patty, have an even greater will to win than boys their age have.

"I get a tremendous satisfaction in Patty's progress," says Renée. "It gives me a kick. That's why I've come back to tennis. I missed the action, the teaching. I'm going to open a tennis camp here in the fall. It's not because I feel frustrated I didn't do more in my career, because I might not have been good enough. Oh, I'm a little frustrated. I regret having gone public about my operation. I became a hated person by people who didn't even know me. I was scarred. I decided to let my celebrity die down until I could just be a coach. My life is more structured now. I'm happier."

Patty is playing a practice game against an eighteen-year-old Austrian boy named Christian Rabl on a neighbor's clay court under a relentless summer sun and Renée's relentless eyes. Renée is sitting on a bench under the shade of a tree, watching.

"Watch," says Renée, *sotto voce*, without taking her eyes off the court. "Christian will win every game. He's too strong. Patty can never be as strong as a man or as some girl on steroids. It's unfair. I would never coach a girl on steroids."

Patty and Christian seem evenly matched. Patty is one of the best female players her age in this country, while Christian, a handsome, blonde, muscular boy, is only a good male player in his native country. They volley for long moments under the hot sun until finally Patty, losing her patience, tries to put the ball away on a difficult shot. It's out.

"She's always trying to hit a winner," Renée says. "She doesn't have the patience to volley fifty balls with him, but he does. He always hits just one more ball than her. He won't let her win a game if he can help it. Not even to be a gentleman."

As the match progresses, with Christian winning game after game, it is obvious that each game means as much to Patty as it does to Christian. There is nothing polite about this match, no friendly bantering across the net, just two willful players trying to beat one another. For years, Renée says, it was thought that only men lost self-esteem when they lost a tennis match, but that women didn't because they had other roles to fall back on. "That's no longer true," says Renée. "As a tennis champion, Chrissie suffers the same loss of esteem and ego as McEnroe when she loses. She can't fall back on another role anymore than McEnroe can. She can't rationalize, 'Oh, well, I lost but I'm still loved.'"

Patty finally wins a game from Christian on a difficult shot. "Great shot!" calls Renée. "Like a violinist." Christian smiles and says to Patty, in his Viennese accent, "Yes, it vhas a vunderful shot, Patty." Patty says nothing, shows no emotion. Renée says, "Christian is secure enough in his self-esteem, so machismo doesn't interfere."

While the game goes on, Renée's neighbor, Doug, stops by to watch. It is his court the two are playing on. He often lets Renée use his clay court to hold her practice sessions, even when it is not convenient for him. But it's no use trying to deny Renée, he says, because she's tenacious. "Renée gets what she wants," he says.

"How's the court?" Doug asks Renée.

"A little lumpy," Renée says.

"I rolled it this morning."

"It's fine."

It's hard for him to roll the court to Renée's satisfaction now that he's divorced, Doug says. "I have to fit it in between shopping, decorating, and dating again," he says with a smile. Renée does not respond. Her eyes are glued to the court.

Just then, Christian hits a ball to the baseline. Patty calls it out. Christian shouts, "No! No! It vhas in!" Then he catches himself. "I'm sorry. If you say, it vhas out."

"All right," Patty says. "Take the point."

"No! No! If you say, it is out."

"I don't want it," Patty says.

"I can't continue playing like zhis," Christian says.

"She's just being a crybaby, Christian," says Renée. "She's trying to work on you psychologically."

"For vhat?" Christian says in disgust.

"Forget it," Patty says, as she prepares to serve. "I don't want the point." Christian walks to the net. "You must take it," he says. "I can't play like zhis. It's your call. It vhas on the line but if you say it vhas out, it vhas out." Christian's face is red with humiliation. He is so disturbed he refuses to play another point. Patty just looks at him coolly and refuses to budge. Finally, Renée convinces them to play the point over. They do, grudgingly, and when Christian gets a chance to hit a winner by Patty, he deliberately mis-hits it right to her so she can score the point.

"I was wrong," says Renée. "Christian is gentleman enough to let Patty win a few games."

A few games later, Patty hits a shot to the baseline. Christian lets it go.

"Was that in?" Patty asks. Christian hesitates a long moment. He wants to say the ball is out, but Patty has so intimidated him that he is afraid to. His face turns red again. "I think it vhas good," he says.

"Are you *sure*?" Patty says sarcastically.

Christian nods and hangs his head.

When the match is finally over, Christian and Patty, drenched with sweat, go over to Renée. Christian says to Renée, "Patty is an exceptional player for a girl. I am just an ordinary player in Austria." He looks at Patty. "I must apologize. It vhas my fault, that point. I vhas not being a gentleman."

Patty, unflustered, glosses over Christian's apology and begins to beg Renée to let her attend a tennis camp in Virginia. "*Please!*" she begs.

"I won't be able to watch your stroke while you're there," Renée says.

"I won't forget my stroke."

"What's in it for him?" Renée says of the camp instructor.

"I don't know," Patty says. "It'll just be fun."

"We'll think about it."

"Oh, *please!*"

It's twilight of the same evening. Patty, Christian, and Renée are swimming at the lake below the cabin while Arlene sits on a deck chair, watching from shore. Every once in a while, Arlene will stand up and throw a tennis ball into the water. Barrett races after it, dives in, and returns it to

Arlene. She has been with Renée for over five years now. Arlene is a short, pretty, dark woman of Jewish–Puerto Rican heritage. She works as Renée's secretary at her Park Avenue office, and at the cabin she cooks and cleans for Renée. Tonight she will make hamburgers for everyone on the barbecue grill. But for the moment, she is relaxing with a drink at twilight.

Christian and Patty are no longer competitors now. They are just two teenagers in bathing suits floating on a raft on a lake.

"They seem to be hitting it off pretty good," says Arlene.

Renée, in a one-piece bathing suit, is floating on her back near shore. Every so often she glances at the two teenagers floating farther and farther away from shore. She follows them with her eyes like a mother hen. This is the favorite part of her day, after tennis. A swim. Drinks. Dinner with friends. Some good tennis talk. A pleasant life. She holds on to it tenaciously. She insists that her friends stay for dinner, and then she insists they stay the night in that quiet, controlled, willful way of hers.

Barrett, sopping wet, drops a tennis ball at Arlene's feet. Arlene picks it up and throws it into the lake. Elizabeth and Barrett race to the lake, but only Barrett leaps into the water after the ball. Elizabeth stays on the shore and barks at him.

"She thinks it's a stupid game," Arlene says of Elizabeth. "She just can't understand why Barrett insists on playing it. Elizabeth is much more timid than Barrett. He's very friendly around strangers. Especially men. He loves men. It's too bad he came along too late."

Blaire Ashley Pancake

The Curious Childhood of an Eleven-Year-Old Beauty Queen

(from *Life*, 1994)

It's EIGHT A.M. The lobby of the Riverfront Hilton in Little Rock, Arkansas, is crowded with pretty young girls. Their faces are elaborately made up—lipstick, mascara, false eyelashes; their hair is in curlers. The girls are not playing or giggling. They are just standing there.

These girls are some of the one hundred contestants, ranging from infants to twenty-one-year-olds, who will compete this afternoon in the second annual America's Queen of Queens beauty pageant. They want to be named Baby Queen, Toddler Queen, or Empress Queen—and win the cash prize that goes with each title. The overall winner, Grand Supreme Queen, will get $5,000.

In room 2046, Dr. Bruce Pancake, a Chattanooga plastic surgeon; his wife, Debbie, a former Miss Chattanooga runner-up; and Tony Calantog, their twenty-three-year-old "pageant coordinator," are preparing the Pancakes' eldest daughter, Blaire Ashley, for the event. Blaire started entering contests when she was five. Now, six years later, she has competed in more than one hundred beauty pageants—and won 90 percent of them. It's a costly hobby: Entrance fees for national contests range from $250 to $800, and that doesn't include the elaborate gowns, voice lessons, drama lessons, Tony's $40-per-hour fee, or traveling expenses. Blaire's prizes range from hair dryers to television sets to a red Ford Festiva to, last year, $12,000 in cash. "I like the cold cash," says Blaire's mom, Debbie. Blaire likes the crowns. "I fell in love with this one crown," says Blaire. "God! I wanted that crown." But, she says, she sympathizes with girls not as wealthy as she, girls for whom a crown is not enough. "I feel sorry for them," she says. "They have to win a car because they don't have one. Their parents yell at them. One girl dieted so much she fainted onstage."

Child beauty pageants—three thousand or so a year—take place mostly in smaller southern cities but are spreading rapidly: more than 1.5 million contestants vie for the money, cars, trips to Disney World, and, most importantly, the experiences that will take them one step closer to becoming Miss America. There is even a magazine—*Babette's Pageant and Talent Gazette*—to fuel their dreams. The cover features recent pageant winners wearing crowns and sashes. One section announces innovations like pageants for children missing an arm or with cerebral palsy. Ads pitch banners, robes, crowns, trophies, costumes, and the services of makeup experts and pageant coaches. Articles advise little girls on the importance of eye contact and offer tricks for overcoming puffiness and dark circles. But the real problems are saved for the Letters page. "The kids end up victims," according to one mother; another writes, "There is more to life than pageants." Perhaps, but for some girls and for some girls' families, pageants are the past, present, and future.

Blaire Pancake's bedroom at home looks like Cinderella's—after she married the prince. It is filled with crowns, tiaras, batons, and trophies, all glittering with rhinestones, that make her old Little League trophy look shabby. She has a bulb-lined makeup mirror and two walk-in closets overstuffed with evening gowns just perfect for a miniature adult. (When Blaire was crowned Little Miss Hollywood Babes Superstar, she had a dress named after her. The Blaire is tulle-skirted and sequined in a herringbone pattern.)

Blaire doesn't play organized sports anymore, though she skis occasionally with her family, and she's just started to make time for a sleepover or two. (School is no problem: Blaire gets A's.) "Pageants are my only interest," she says. "They're all I want to do, I love what I'm doing. I want to become Miss America." Which is why there are no posters of Blaire's favorite rock stars in her room. No posters of a fantasy heartthrob. Blaire's room is a shrine to her own fantasy.

Room 2046 of the Riverfront Hilton is something else altogether, a shambles of toys, clothes, rumpled beds, potato chips, Pop Tarts, curling irons, makeup, cans of Coke. The Pancakes have brought three of their four daughters along. Alexis, one, also a pageant winner, is home with a sitter. While their mother, Debbie, hides in the bathroom—where she will stay until she is totally made up—and Tony prepares Blaire, Bruce plays with Elise, three, Miss Southern Charm 1993, and Erin, eight, who used to win pageants until she discovered art and sports.

"When Erin quit, we were sick!" Debbie calls out from the bathroom.

"White-blonde is the perfect look," says Bruce, dreamily fingering Erin's hair.

Bruce says, "I'm a plastic surgeon only from the neck up. I enjoy the beauty of the face. No doubt that's why I'm so involved with Blaire." Bruce is captivated by his daughter's beauty but prefers it enhanced: He apologizes to strangers when she is not wearing makeup. Some parents have accused Bruce of enhancing Blaire's looks with surgery.

Debbie, from the bathroom: "They can be ugly."

"It's ridiculous to operate on children," adds Bruce. "But if Blaire wanted me to do something when she's older, I'd consider it."

This contest has the Pancakes worried. Blaire will be competing against twelve-year-olds, some of whom, according to Bruce, "have the breast development of women." Blaire is tall and thin, like a stick figure, but this talk of breasts does not seem to bother her. She sits in a chair, dressed in a nightshirt, her hair in curlers, and watches cartoons on TV while Tony fusses over her. Blaire is used to hearing adults talk about the tools of competition. Like the fake tooth she'll wear today to hide the missing baby tooth.

When Tony begins gluing on Blaire's fake nails, she holds out her hands, limp-wristed, like the delicate wings of a bird. Finished, Tony dabs makeup on Blaire's eyelids, which flutter shut, then open. "Now Maybelline Great Lash," says Tony. "All the models use it." Bruce looks over. "New makeup! Oh, perfect!" he says. Finally, smiling, Tony holds up a lipstick. "Lasting Kiss," he says. "We can kiss collars and napkins, and it won't come off." He turns, puckers his lips and blows a kiss across the room.

At fourteen, Tony Calantog weighed 250 pounds. He went on to play offensive and defensive tackle on his Pensacola, Florida, high school football team. His teammates called him Otho, after the interior decorator in *Beetlejuice*. But Tony preferred to decorate the faces of little girls. Word of Tony's expertise in makeup, dance, modeling, dressmaking, and fashion coordinating soon spread throughout the child beauty pageant subculture.

"I saw Blaire five years ago in a Jacksonville pageant," Tony says. "I didn't think much of her. Come on! She wore blue eye shadow!" Bruce asked him to help redesign Blaire. After he did, Tony says, "she became glamorous. She had a certain look, and beautiful hair."

"Some parents said it was hair extensions," calls out Debbie.

"Blaire loves the stage," says Tony. "She totally turns on. She becomes . . . Blaire! A total package. It's who she is."

"She comes alive," adds Bruce. "She has that sparkle of spontaneity judges look for."

"I love pageants," Blaire interjects, speaking in a precise, adult voice. "Except when I have to do two back-to-back. Then I have to tell my father I can't take it anymore. I need a break. Pageants are easy for me, except for doing my hair. I'm very tender-headed. Oh, and the interviews. I try to make the judges like me. If I don't win, I try harder to make them like me the next time."

"In our first pageant we had no talent," Debbie says.

"She, not we, honey," says Bruce.

"Now Blaire looks the judges in the eye," boasts Debbie, still in the bathroom. "She smiles, turns on that charm that makes them look at her. That's talent."

"We try not to enter too many pageants where the interview is important," says Tony.

"We put Blaire in a package deal," says Debbie. "Clothes, beauty, talent, because she's got a blah personality, like me."

"Oh, honey," says Bruce.

Blaire is oblivious.

When Tony begins combing out Blaire's hair, so thick with curls it almost obscures her face, Debbie emerges from her lair.

"Hi!" she says. "I'm the mom." Her face is heavily made up, her blond hair stiffly curled. She is wearing a black velvet pantsuit trimmed with gold brocade. Debbie has a doctorate in pharmacy, which comes in handy whenever Blaire is sick, like now. She has had the flu and was coughing and nauseated until Debbie gave her Dimetapp and an antibiotic. Today Blaire is feeling better. She is eating grapes, grasped delicately between her red fake fingernails. She eats each grape in three bites, with her front teeth, her lips curled back so as not to muss her lipstick.

Debbie looks at Blaire's hair and frowns. "It's too full."

Tony says, "It'll fall."

Debbie says, "The main thing is to frame the face." There is a knock on the door. Room service with a package.

Tony cries out, "Oh, my shoes! My shoes!" He rips open a box and takes out a pair of shiny silver heels.

"Cinderella's slippers," says Bruce.

Blaire puts them on. "They're too big," she says, without expression.

"Just watch out for the cracks in the stage," says Debbie.

Tony holds up a black rhinestoned cocktail dress and stares at it in the mirror. "I couldn't wait!" he says. The dress is for the talent competition, in which Blaire will sing "On My Own" from *Les Misérables* as one of her numbers. Blaire usually wears coral ("her best color," says Tony), as she will in the western-wear, sportswear and formalwear competitions, which are really exercises in modeling. (The girls walk up and down a runway, posing, hands on hips, a little turn here and there.) Tony and Debbie make most of Blaire's costumes. When she outgrows one, they sell it, often at a profit because of Blaire's winning reputation. Everyone wants an original Blaire.

Blaire unself-consciously strips down to her panties, a seasoned performer in a crowded dressing room. Tony helps her pull on her pantyhose, then her black dress. Blaire grabs a cordless microphone. ("You should have heard her before voice lessons," Tony says.)

While Blaire performs in front of the mirror, Tony stands behind her, pantomiming her act. He spreads his arms at the finale and bows, mouthing silently but with great exaggeration, "Thank you!" Behind them, Erin faces the wall, drawing furiously. Elise, meanwhile, is holding up a bruised finger to her mother. Debbie looks at it and says, "Did you cry? No. Good. Don't ever make a scene." Bruce stares lovingly at Blaire.

The ballroom at the Riverfront Hilton is packed with parents, many of them overweight women in sweat suits or jeans, and their beer-bellied husbands in long-haul trucker caps. Bruce, Debbie, Erin, and Elise, all wearing badges on their chests with Blaire's photograph on them, are standing against the back wall, trying to be inconspicuous. Some of the parents have complained that the Pancakes get too much attention.

Blaire is waiting in line with about twenty other girls. She stares, without expression, at the floor while Tony fusses with her hair. A few places behind her stands Ariel Murray, her main competition. Ariel has already won three cars, and last August she defeated Blaire in an Atlanta pageant. "Blaire won Miss Photogenic," says Debbie. "And we were missing teeth."

When Blaire goes on, it is a seasoned performer who stalks the stage, belting out "New York! New York!" moderately well, except for the high notes. For the first time in hours, Blaire is truly alive. She bows and leaves the stage. As Blaire and her mother walk back to the hotel room, Debbie says, "If you had held the mike closer, you would have been more dynamic. But you wouldn't. Ariel did it."

Back in room 2046, Blaire wraps herself in her mother's white satin kimono. Outside, little girls race down the hall, squealing. But Blaire has work to do.

DEBBIE: "What's your favorite color?"

BLAIRE: "Coral."

DEBBIE: "Say 'Because it looks good on me.'"

BRUCE: "If you could be anyone in the world, who would you be?"

BLAIRE: "Myself, so I can obtain my goals."

BRUCE: "What's your secret weapon?"

BLAIRE: "When people have problems, I try to help them."

BRUCE: "You mean, help your sisters?"

BLAIRE: "Aw, yeah, help my sisters."

DEBBIE: "Don't say 'Aw.'"

BRUCE: "If you went to the moon, who would you take with you?"

BLAIRE: "My mom, because she never goes anywhere."

BRUCE: "If you could be like anyone, who would you be like?"

BLAIRE: "Leanza Cornett, because she was Miss America."

BRUCE: "When you look in the mirror, what do you see?"

BLAIRE: "Myself. I like what I see."

Debbie gets down on her knees and begins rubbing moisturizer into Blaire's legs because she will be wearing shorts for the interview. "If you cough, say 'Excuse me,'" Debbie says. Blaire holds out her arms, and Debbie rubs moisturizer into them.

"If they ask what the smell is," says Tony, "say 'Wings.'" He throws out his arms. "Tra-la!"

Tony takes Blaire to the interview, which is conducted in private, and Bruce goes out for some fast food. With them gone, Debbie expresses her true fears: "You got to watch out for them Louisiana girls. They pull 'em out of the swamps. They're dumb but gorgeous."

When Blaire returns, she says she thinks she did well. "It's not hard for me to talk to adults," she explains in her precise voice. "I like to spend time with adults, even though I have to act older because they expect more from me." Blaire, who has given up a child's spontaneity, shows so little offstage emotion because she's so busy editing herself with adults.

On Sunday morning, the third day of the pageant, all the girls, in their gowns, and their parents assemble in the ballroom. When last year's Grand Supreme Queen gives up her crown, the pageant organizer, a short, bald man, begins to cry. Then the winners in each group are announced. When Blaire's name is not called for her group, the Pancakes turn to leave. But the pageant organizer urges them to stay. Finally, after each of the group winners has been introduced, the name of the Grand Supreme Queen is called out: "Blaire Ashley Pancake!" Her parents scream with joy as Blaire takes the stage to receive her crown and her five $1,000 stacks of $1 bills. The huge piles weigh heavy in her hands, like bricks. Blaire stands there for only a moment, smiling, looking slight and a little bit lost, before she leaves the stage.

On the nine-hour ride back to Chattanooga, Bruce, Debbie, and Tony are still too excited to sleep. Tony says, "I feel great. I did everything correct." Debbie says, "My parents think we go overboard with pageants." Blaire says nothing. She is asleep, clutching her crown in her hands.

O. J. Simpson

The Outcast

(from *The New Yorker*, 2001)

O. J. IS TALKING. He has been talking for nine hours. I have been listening to him since seven o'clock in the morning: his baritone voice reverberating like bass from a boom box, his girlish giggle, a manic tic, so at odds with what he is saying. He insists on physical contact: his hand patting my thigh, his finger tapping my shoulder, his face inclining intimately toward mine—his huge, dark, handsome face, with slashing cheekbones, a jaw as big as the bottom half of a rugby ball, and the eager smile of a man who has spent his life trying to convince people he wants to please them.

O. J. talks obsessively, as if he fears silence and the room for thought that accompanies it. His rubbery features rearrange themselves to show the proper emotion, the one that corresponds with his words. His brow furrows and his eyes narrow to show worry. His eyebrows rise to perfect arcs to show disbelief and wonder. His eyelashes flutter like a humming-bird's wings to show humility. His eyes grow wide and unblinking to show innocence and sincerity. His lips peel apart like an open wound and he bares his teeth to show humor and bonhomie. Watching O. J. rearrange his features to show emotions is hypnotizing. It's like watching in disbelief the cartoonish attempts of a bad actor working very hard to portray emotions and thoughts and intimacies he doesn't feel because he has no insight into the character he's playing. This is a new character for O. J.: a flesh and blood human being. A man tormented by a tragedy O. J. does not feel. A man unburdening himself of the most intimate truths of his heart which, for O. J., are neither intimate nor true. O. J. doesn't really understand this new role he is trying to play, and, even if he did, he's ill-equipped to play it. He's used to playing only the persona he created over the years just as John Wayne only played the Duke. O. J. has been playing O. J. for so long, on the football field, in the broadcasting booth, in TV commercials, and in films, that it is all second nature to him. So he rearranges his features into an O. J. frown, an O. J. grin, an O. J. look of innocence, which are meant to convey the emotions he doesn't feel. His face glistens with sweat, not under the weight of his faux emotions, which are effortless, but under the weight of his endless monologues, which are exhausting. His monologues bury the simplest of questions under a mountain of words so that the answer to those questions can never be excavated. His words are meant to bury doubt, or, at the very least, to refuse to give it voice. So he talks and talks and talks, his features rearranging themselves, his booming voice riding roughshod over every other voice until it is stilled and only his voice can be heard.

When O. J. Simpson was a football running back at USC, and later in the NFL, he used to defeat tacklers with his merciless will. "I let them push me around for three quarters," he says of the tacklers. "They kept hitting me until they were exhausted by the fourth quarter. Then I worked harder because I was in better shape and I never quit. Ha! Ha! Ha! Fatigue makes cowards of us all. Check it out! I'll bet you'll find that the yards I gained in the fourth quarter of my games was equal to what I gained in the first three quarters combined."

I can see those tacklers in my mind's eye. Battered, bruised, exhausted, drained of will in the fourth quarter. And still O. J. is coming at them, his head lowered like a bull, his shoulders hunched, his spindly legs churning, his feet pounding the frozen earth, his hot breath almost upon them. They square themselves for the moment of impact, remember the pain, take an almost imperceptible step to one side, make a feeble swipe at him, and let him go. *Fuck it.* I know how they felt. Now, at four o'clock on a sunny South Florida afternoon, as O. J. drives me back to my car in his black Lincoln Navigator, he is still coming at me, still talking, relentless, determined to impose his will on me. Fuck it! Let him talk. I hold up my tape recorder toward his face, turn my head away and rest it against the passenger door window. I close my eyes and try to doze off with his voice booming in my ear and his finger poking my shoulder.

"The press created this guy who was hurting because his wife left him," he is saying. "That's bullshit! It was Nicole who wanted to come back to *me* after the divorce. She stalked *me*! Trust me. She'd come over to my house with cookies and a tape of our wedding and begin to cry, 'Please, O. J.! I wanna come home!' But I wasn't interested. Finally, I told her I'd try it for a year, for the kids. I set up some conditions. I told her she couldn't stay with me. She had to stay in a hotel down the street. But after a year it didn't work out. I had always put Nicole on a pedestal and when she left and tried to come back I couldn't put her back on the pedestal. I was always fighting her ass about drugs. That nine-one-one tape when she called the police, that was about her druggy friends being around my kids. But I'm the bad guy. They said I punched her. Hell, if I punched her she'd have more than just a bruise. Am I supposed to be responsible for every bruise on her face? Ha! Ha! I just threw her outta the room. Nicole attacked *me!* The only other time we ever had a physical beef was on New Year's Eve in nineteen eighty-nine. We were just wrestling. Ha! Ha! And oh yeah, that one other time when they said I took a bat to her car. I was just bouncing the bat off her tire. She said, 'If you hit that hubcap you'll pay.' So I hit it and said, 'I'll pay for that. I pay for everything else.' And then they said I did a number on that car, that I dented the roof. The car was a fucking *convertible!* Ha! Ha! Ha!"

He turns the corner and drives down a residential street. Housewives in spandex shorts are jogging on the sidewalk. O. J. glances at them and says, "Still, I loved the way Nicole looked. If I saw her walking on that sidewalk right now I'd pull over and hit on her. Ha! Ha! Ha! If she had a different head. But from the same tribe, that German blood. She was a terrific mother, too. I felt if she had lived and I had died she woulda been a better father to our kids than I am a mother."

At fifty-three, O. J. Simpson has reached an enviable place in his life. He lives in a world without doubt or shame or guilt. He has a perfect solipsism. He refers to Nicole's murder as "my ordeal." He talks about the pain it has caused him. O. J. has always seen the world only through his eyes, and he has convinced himself that what he sees is the only truth. But still he is not at peace. Now, in the fourth quarter of his life, he will not rest until he batters everyone who doubts him into submission in the only way he knows how, by coming at them again and again and again, until they are exhausted, defeated, not by his truth, but by his will. In his mind's eye, truth was always relative. Will was objective. It was his will, not his talent, that made O. J. Simpson one of the greatest football players ever to play the game. (His coach at USC, John McKay, once said, "Simpson was not only the greatest player I ever had—he was the greatest player anyone ever had.") It was his will, not his talent, that made him America's most beloved black athlete. ("When I was a kid growing up in San Francisco," says O. J., "Willie Mays was the single biggest influence on my life. I saw how he made white people happy. That moment, I wanted to be like Willie Mays.") It was his will, not his talent, that made him wealthy as America's first black pitchman, for Chevrolet and Hertz ("Hertz executives told me I was colorless to the American people," says O. J.) and as an actor in a host of forgettable movies in which he played an Amos-and-Andy-like buffoon that tainted his athletic glory. ("During my ordeal," O. J. says, "Marcia Clark referred to me as an actor who shouldn't be believed. It was the first time in my life I was considered a great actor. Ha! Ha!")

It was always his will. It defeated everyone. His indomitable will brought him everything he ever wanted in life—fame, fortune, adulation, Nicole, acquittal. (Before she was murdered, Nicole Simpson told a friend that if her husband did ever kill her he'd probably "'O. J.' his way out of it.") Today, O. J. Simpson has no doubt that his indomitable will will bring him what he wants now, what he insists on getting now, what, in his mind's eye, he deserves—vindication—and with it a return to fame and wealth and adulation.

Yale Galanter has a plan. Actually, he refers to it as his "grand plan."

"O. J. Simpson is the most misunderstood person on the planet," he says. "and I want people to get to know the real O. J. How giving he is. What a great family man, father, and neighbor he is. I want the media idea of him to change. I don't expect to convert everybody, but I envision one day when O. J. will again be a celebrity spokesman in the mainstream of commerce."

O. J. named Galanter his exclusive media spokesperson in March 2001 because (according to a press release) of the many statements made about Simpson that have been "unauthorized . . . creating false media stories." Galanter was recommended to O. J. by his civil lawyers after O. J. was arrested on December 4, 2000, in Kendall, Florida, south of Miami, for a "road rage" incident. O. J. was accused of cutting off another driver with his Navigator, stopping his car, confronting the other driver, and ripping off his sunglasses. The felony and misdemeanor charges are scheduled to be heard in a South Florida courtroom in the summer.

Galanter expects to return O. J. to his pre-ordeal days when he was revered, not only by the American public, but also by many of the people he worked with at Hertz and NBC Sports and on the sets of the *Naked Gun* movies. "He was the single most popular employee we had," said an NBC Sports executive, one who, according to former NBC sportscaster Will McDonough, "had more charisma than any person I ever met." And Jim Spence, who hired O. J. for ABC's Monday Night Football telecasts in 1983, said, "I never saw him not in a good mood." Galanter himself shares these opinions of his client: "My first impression of O. J.," he says, "was that he was extremely charismatic and humble. Within two months we liked each other. There was a lot in O. J.'s life that needed direction so we both decided that I would give his career a new direction.

"O. J. was an American hero," Galanter says. "And in a blink of an eye all his champagne and caviar dreams were taken away from him. I believe the public would like to see him back on top. Americans are very forgiving. They forgave Marv Albert and Frank Gifford. Not that I think O. J. did anything that needs to be forgiven. I never thought he did it. The system said he was not guilty, but he's still paying a penalty. I think he should get his life back. People adore him. Personally, I am humbled that O. J. put his trust in me. My parents are walking on cloud nine because O. J. picked me to be his spokesman."

Galanter is forty-four, a Miami–Fort Lauderdale criminal defense attorney who prides himself on his ability "to take either side of a case." He has not one, but two advertisements for his firm, Galanter and Cohn, in the Fort Lauderdale telephone directory. One reads: "Criminal and DUI. 24 hours, 7 days. Free Immediate Consultation." The add states that the firm specializes in license suspensions, traffic offenses, and speeding violations. Galanter says he has a lot of "high profile clients," such as W. W. F. wrestler Terry Szopinski; Khaled Abu Hamdeh, a Liberty City convenience store owner accused of murder; and Scott Campbell, the motorist whose car forced eighty-five-year-old Tillie Tooter's car into an Alligator Alley canal.

"But there's celebrity and then there's O. J.," says Galanter. "He's the most spoken-about human in the world. I want to control what the media says about him."

O. J. picked him to be his spokesman, Galanter says, "Because O. J. liked the way I looked on TV. Everybody wants to interview me now.

'Hard Copy.' MSNBC. 'The Today Show.' '48 Hours.' Much of my time now is taken up with interview requests, faxes, setting up parameters, and legal stuff. I couldn't get this type of experience with anyone other than O. J. This is it for me. I don't know how any lawyer can top this on his resumé."

Although Galanter has practiced law in South Florida for almost twenty years, he is not very well known among other criminal defense lawyers. Roy Black, the dean of South Florida criminal defense lawyers, says, "I've heard his name before, but I wouldn't say he's a prominent defense attorney. I figure he jumped on this case for the publicity value."

Richard Sharpstein, a criminal defense attorney in Miami for twenty-six years, describes Galanter as a "qualified attorney" who is "unrated" in the Martindale-Hubbell directory of South Florida attorneys.

"He's a nice guy," says Sharpstein. "With a small practice. I wouldn't put him in over his head in certain cases. As far as I can remember this is his most prominent case. He's impressed with stars. But TV interviews are bullshit after a while. I guess Yale thinks he's expanding his horizon, [but] most ethical criminal defense lawyers wouldn't be interested in O. J. A criminal defense lawyer should have no interest in remaking a client's career. That's ridiculous. We're not a p.r. firm. And as for Yale's plan to rehabilitate O. J.—good luck! Maybe next he can take on Yasir Arafat, Saddam Hussein, and Slobodan Milosevic. They're in dire need of rehabilitation in the public's eye, too."

Galanter's attempt to take his client's life in, as he puts it, a "new direction" is at odds with his client's seeming inability to stop his life from spiraling downhill in its old direction. O. J. has been constantly in trouble since shortly before he moved from L.A. to Pinecrest, south of Miami, ten months ago, despite Galanter's protestations that his client is "a terrific father and family man" who drives his children (Sydney, fifteen, Justin, thirteen) to and from school each day, and is in bed by eight o'clock almost every evening. (Presumably, those are not the evenings when O. J. has been seen slipping through the side door of the strip club Lipstik, so he can party with strippers late into the night.)

In addition to his "road rage" incident, O. J. has been involved in four other incidents that required the police. All of them were the result of his stormy relationship with a twenty-five-year-old former cosmetologist, Christie Prody, who sells perfume at a kiosk in the Dolphins Mall. In October, 1999, just before O. J. moved from L.A. to South Florida, he flew to Prody's South Florida home and called police to report that a female friend was "loaded out of her mind" on drugs and driving around in her Mustang. In September 2000, Prody called police to report that O. J. had burglarized her home. When confronted by the police, O. J. claimed he had just entered Prody's home to do his laundry. In October 2000, police were called to the Wyndham Hotel in Miami to quell a disturbance. When they arrived they found O. J. and Prody in a violent argument, which resulted in Prody being thrown out of the hotel for physically assaulting "the victim," O. J. Simpson. That same month, Prody sold a story to the *National Enquirer* for $50,000 in which she detailed her stormy, five-year relationship with O. J. Among those details were two abortions, O. J.'s obsession with Nicole's murder, and numerous public brawls fueled by the frequent marathon cocaine binges that often left O. J. unable to get out of bed in the morning. And then, in February 2001, O. J. was reported to be trying to sell a sex tape he made with Prody and "a surgically enhanced model" to an L.A. photographer for $1.5 million.

All of this may explain why Galanter is so desperate to control what the media writes about his client, who, he insists, is a victim of his own celebrity. "Everything that happens to O. J. is news," says Galanter, "and everything the media writes is inaccurate. You'll see. Wait 'til you meet him. You'll love him."

I am sitting at the juice bar at Wild Oats market in Kendall at 7 A.M. when O. J. comes hobbling in on his bad knees. He is wearing a gray dress shirt outside his black slacks. He hobbles toward me, hunched over, his big head bobbing up and down like the heads of those toy dogs people put by windshields of their cars. He sits down, smiling, and orders his morning health food drink of leafy vegetables and garlic which reminds him of the time he had to kiss Leslie Uggams for a Hertz commercial. "With all that garlic on my breath," he says, grinning. "But it helps my arthritis so I can play golf again, although I didn't play much golf when I moved to South Florida five months ago because I didn't want to leave my kids alone and besides I didn't think I needed golf anymore. I was still in a bunker mentality from my ordeal and I was bored exercising, burnt out after all those years. Ha! Ha! Ha! Nicole, my wife, used to say 'All you do is support your personal trainer, hanging out with him, drinking coffee, and reading the paper.' Ha! Ha! Ha!"

I put my pen and notebook away and take out my tape recorder. O. J. is still talking.

"But now I have a need to get back on the golf course," he is saying, "because my life is a little more stable now and everybody here in Florida has been terrific. My neighbors bring over food for me and the kids, and every weekend my house is filled with my daughter's girlfriends until about 9:30 p.m. when the boys show up, you know, standing around with their hands stuffed in their pockets. Ha! Ha! Ha! Now I feel I can go out more, to play golf and go to the store because people in Florida are more accepting. Everyone in Florida's got a history."

South Florida has always been a place for people with "a history." It's where people go when things get bad. They don't *move* to South Florida the way people *move* to other places, to set up mirror images of their former lives. People *flee* to South Florida, on the run from a bad check, a bad wife, a bad rap, a bad life that is driving them mad. So they flee to this honky-tonk, transient place in the sun they call "paradise," because here they can create a new life, a new persona ("a terrific father and family man," as Yale puts it), a new history that may or may not have much in common with their old history. Everyone is new in South Florida, which is why everyone is so accepting of everyone else. Everyone in Miami, for example, accepted Chris Paciello when he moved from Staten Island, New York to Miami Beach in the '90s and created his new persona as a nightclub impresario who dated Madonna and the model Niki Taylor. Then he was arrested a few years ago for murder and bank robbery, crimes he committed in the '80s in Staten Island when he was known as Christian Ludwigsen, a Mafia thug, and no one in Miami was *really* shocked.

Yale Galanter arrives. He walks toward us, smiling, dressed in a blue oxford-cloth buttondown-collar shirt, gray slacks, and black tasseled loafers. He's a good-looking man with short, dark hair and the kind of chiseled profile—straight nose, jutting jaw—found on coins.

He sits down with us and says, "Look at this, O. J." He holds up a giveaway local newspaper and, smiling his amiable smile, points to a photograph of him and his wife at a charity function. "I know it's only a . . ."

"But I still love L.A.," O. J. says. "L.A. is my home. It's still the best place to be, the weather, the golf, my friends. I miss it. I had a nice life in L.A., even after my ordeal. I only went to restaurants I felt comfortable in. Once someone keyed my car. But . . . ha! ha! ha! . . . when I was incarcerated I read the Koran, which said everyone goes through some ordeal, everyone's persecuted and overcomes it. I still had my regular friends who wanted me to play golf at the Riviera Country Club but I didn't want to bring any controversy there so I played public courses instead. One time a helicopter followed us on the fairway and I hid under a tree. Ha! Ha! Ha! And another time this big ol' guy yells out to me, 'You're a murderer!' I said, 'You've got a right to your opinion.' He says, 'You better watch out, there are snipers on this course.' I said, 'I hope they can't shoot straight.' Then he calls me an asshole, and I threw my clubs down and came up on him fast looking for leverage so I can fuck him up a little bit, my face real close to his, spittin' in his face while I'm screamin' at him, 'You call me a mother fuckin' murderer, I got to live with that, but 'asshole,' come on let's get it on.' He backs down. Ha! Ha! Ha! And now I'm a hero to all the little old ladies on the course who thought I handled it great. Another time I was on the course and a guy yells out, 'Juice, when you were masturbating in jail were you thinking of Nicole?' Ha! Ha! Ha!"

There were other incidents in L.A., too. Patrons who left a restaurant when O. J. showed up, waitresses who refused to wait on him, flight attendants who argued to determine who had to serve him, audience members at a TV talk show who walked out when O. J. appeared. And then there were the friends who dropped him.

"They were the friends who always had a problem," says O. J. "They dogged me, they needed a ticket to the game, and I helped them and then they abandoned me. Even the ones who didn't, I know twenty percent of them think I did it. So I became a recluse in L.A. I didn't leave Rockingham, and my friends like A.C. Cowlings used to hang there with me because there was all that traffic, fifteen to twenty girls a night throwing their panties over the wall. Ha! Ha! Ha! And then my daughter's private school wouldn't accept her anymore."

"Is that why you moved to Florida?" I say.

"See! See! That's another misconception." O. J. taps me on the shoulder, his grinning face close to mine. "I was *planning* on moving to Florida after my divorce 'cause it was easier to get from Florida to New York for my NBC work than it was from L.A., and besides I could play golf with my friends in Boca Raton but then, after my ordeal, I was a single parent and I had to find a school for my kids and I found one whose principal said 'Any school should be proud to take your kids,' and he had a lot of famous people's kids in his school, Gloria Estefan's kids, and Governor Bush's kid went there, so I moved farther south for my kids."

"O. J. is a wonderful father," says Yale.

After O. J. finishes his drink we go to the checkout line. The woman in line in front of us looks at us for a second, then turns away as if from a horrible accident. I pay for O. J.'s drink.

"Thanks," he says. "I ain't got any money anymore. Ha! Ha! Ha!"

The woman at the cash register says to us all, "How ya doin'?"

O. J. says, "Tryin' to stay outta trouble. Ha! Ha! Ha!"

The woman says, "Ya can't stay outta trouble in this town."

We drive across the street in O. J.'s Navigator to Roasters and Toasters deli in a strip mall. O. J. says, "I like to eat breakfast here, hanging out with judges and lawyers."

The deli is crowded and noisy with people eating breakfast, talking, the clatter of dishes. As we walk to our table they look up, go silent, then turn away quickly before they make eye contact with O. J. We sit down and order. O. J. sits with his back to the wall, facing the other patrons. The wall across from him is decorated with badly drawn caricatures of famous people, Danny Glover, President Clinton, Cher, Harry Belafonte, as if the restaurant fancied itself a South Florida version of the Carnegie Deli.

O. J. looks around the crowded dining room. "I never sit with my back to the room," he says.

"Like Yasir Arafat," I say. "Never sleep in the same. . . ."

"I am a guy who considers himself alert," he goes on. "For one and a half years after I got out I had a body guard. I felt so vulnerable for so long. Now I use my athlete's peripheral vision in case I feel bad vibes." He tosses a headfake toward a couple eating at a table in the center of the room. "I felt bad vibes from them when we sat down. But they're just embarrassed because they don't know how to come over and ask me for an autograph."

The waitress comes with our food and we begin eating. O. J. eats hunched over, his face low to the plate, but his eyes looking up through his brows, flitting around the room expectantly.

"I worry when I go out to eat with a writer," he says. "I'm afraid someone will come up to me. If it's someone I know I'll kick their ass. Ha! Ha! Ha! I haven't had a fight in my adult life."

"I've never heard a single person say anything derogatory to O. J.," says Yale.

Before I can ask him a question, O. J. begins talking. I hold my tape recorder close to his face and eat with my other hand. This is a new experience for me, interviewing someone I don't even have to pose questions to.

"I didn't picture my life like this," he is saying. "I thought I'd retire at fifty with enough money on my own terms. It's hard to retire this way. But I did it for my kids."

"O. J. is a devoted single parent," says Yale.

"As a father I was just a disciplinarian and now I'm everything to my kids. People ask me what's the hardest thing for me now and I tell them that I was always a great dad but now I'm a horrible mom. I don't cook. Ha! Ha! Ha! Women are from Mars, men are from Venus. A man's natural instinct is to solve problems. Like when Jason said Sydney did a lot of things and I never caught her. I said, 'That's why I love her. She's smart enough not to get caught.' Ha! Ha! Ha! But she's at that point where teenaged girls hate their mom. She's her mom all over again, she's got those German genes. Her grandmother, my wife, now my daughter. Ha! Ha! Ha! Those bitches'll wear you out."

While O. J. is talking, the other patrons glance over at him with a thin, curious smile on their faces and then quickly look away when he looks up. They lean closer to each other over the table now and whisper.

"Another benefit of moving to Florida," O. J. is saying, "is one that I didn't even know before I moved here. They got a funny law in this state, the Head of Household Law, which says as the head of the household my salary is protected from garnishment. Ha! Ha! Ha! I don't have to turn anything over to the Goldmans." (O. J. is referring to the $35 million judgment levied against him for the murders of Nicole and Ron Goldman in his civil trial.) "They have to find it and get a court order for me to send them money. Ha! Ha! Ha! It's a cat and mouse game." O. J.'s new $650,000 house is also safe from judgment in Florida.

O. J. looks up. A woman is standing at our table. She is in her seventies, with a bouffant puff of lacquered, pinkish-blonde hair, heavy makeup, and the kind of gaudy jewelry and clothes worn by older women in South Florida who have a difficult time forgetting the beauty of their youth.

"I just wanted to say I wish everyone would leave you alone," says the woman in a faintly indecipherable European accent.

"Well, thank you," O. J. says, grinning. The woman spreads out her arms. O. J. stands up and hugs her over our table. They kiss each other on the cheek.

"Can I get your autograph?" the woman says.

"Certainly." The woman hands him her card. There is a photograph on it of a beautiful, much younger woman with the name, Rossette. O. J. signs her card and hands it back to her. She looks at his signature lovingly, and then she leaves.

O. J. sits down and says, "People in Florida are constantly giving me hugs to show me emotional support. Before people just wanted my autograph: 'Sign this for my son.' I never got hugs before. Now the public shows me so much love. Women are my biggest defenders. Ha! Ha! Ha! It's that bad boy syndrome. Before I was everybody's American hero, now I'm a bad boy and girls chase *me*. But if a girl wants to be with me I tell them they have to be number three behind my kids. . ."

"Being a father comes first with O. J.," says Yale.

"I mean, I like gorgeous girls but I can't walk naked around my house or in the pool with a friend because of my kids . . ."

"When you say the word O. J.," says Yale, "a lot of words come to mind but not family man."

Just before we leave, the deli's cook comes out of the kitchen and sits down with us. His name is Pedro. He's a burly, unshaven man wearing a Yankees' baseball cap and a cook's smock.

"I seen you come in, Juice, and I thought I'd say hi."

O. J. introduces me as a writer doing a profile of him.

Pedro turns his attention to me and says, "Me and Juice are good buddies. He had Thanksgiving dinner with my family, and Christmas dinner. You can't get closer than that. He loves my son and I love his son."

Pedro looks at O. J. lovingly, the way ordinary people do when they can't believe their good fortune to be in the presence of celebrity. Their eyes glaze over, washing away everything human about the object of their lust except that object's celebrity.

I pay the bill and we walk through the crowded deli. Before O. J. gets to the door people stop him and say hello. He smiles and shakes their hands like a politician working a room. These are the same people who tried to avoid eye contact with O. J. when he first entered. But now, after they have digested his presence, have had time to compose themselves, have decided, after all, they are in the presence of a celebrity, not a man, they go up to him, smiling, with their hands outstretched.

We are driving south, toward Mount Sinai hospital, where O. J. is scheduled to comfort some patients as he often does in his spare time, according to Yale. "Pedro is one of my new friends," says O. J. "I got more in common with guys like him I play golf with on public courses than I do with my old friends in L.A." (He's referring to the doctors and lawyers and actors and athletes he used to play golf with at the exclusive Riviera Country Club where his membership was termed "Inactive.") "My new friends don't believe the stories about me having to leave restaurants. They're basically good people. When I get something negative it makes them unhappy because there's something in their life that sees me as an easy target. Subconsciously, people cheer for the underdog. They wanted me to be innocent. What that old lady say? 'Why don't they leave you alone?'"

Most of O. J.'s new friends in paradise are what some celebrities might call "the little people." O. J. is nothing if not adaptable. He is a chameleon who has Christmas dinner with Pedro and plays golf on public courses and sends his children off each weekend to quinces and bar mitzvahs. It doesn't seem to bother him that he has lost his celebrity friends, like Marcus Allen and Ahmad Rashaad, as long as he has someone, anyone, a satellite, to listen to his endless monologues and jokes, and to worship him. He is still worshipped, only by different people than before his ordeal. And despite his ordeal, O. J. is curiously without anger. He certainly has none of the righteous anger one would expect of a man whose life has been ruined by false accusations that he murdered the mother of his children and an innocent bystander. He seems only relieved that he hasn't lost the basic structure of his life—golf, friends, women—even if that structure has been diminished. He is still the beloved, amiable O. J., only to a different group of people. He is even amiable to people who call him a "murderer" because, as he says, "They have a right to their opinion," and, almost unbelievably, he is even amiable to the very police officers who testified against him at his murder trial.

"I was in this golf shop in L.A. after my ordeal," he is saying as he pulls his Navigator off the highway and approaches Mount Sinai. "Fuhrman's partner was there, a detective named Phillips. I didn't get pissed off. I said, 'Hello, Mr. Phillips.' He said, 'Hello, Mr. Simpson.' I said, 'I didn't know you played golf.' He said, 'I'm not very good.' We laughed. I didn't hold any grudges against him."

Yale, O. J., and I are standing outside a hospital room at Mount Sinai with Pat Stauber, a registered nurse and a licensed clinical social worker. Pat is tall, slim, attractive with straight, black hair and an earnest demeanor.

"I'm sorry," she says to Yale. "This is all I could arrange on such short notice. I wanted O. J. to visit this boy coming out of a coma but I couldn't arrange it."

O. J. laughs. "When I played in Buffalo," he says, "I used to visit these kids with inoperable cancer. The newspaper ran a story about all the kids I visited before they died. Then I had to visit another kid with cancer who was a huge O. J. fan. The minute I arrived the kid flipped out. He said, 'If O. J. is here I must be dying.' Ha! Ha! Ha! That blew me outta the water. I went ten years without visiting anyone terminal."

O. J. goes into the hospital room. Through the open doorway I can see him talking to an old man in a wheelchair with a breathing tube in his mouth and I.V.'s in his veins. O. J. sits on the man's bed and talks softly to him while they watch a golf match on T.V. O. J. points to the screen, taps the man on the shoulder, and says something. The old man can't speak. He just nods.

Outside the room, Pat says, "After O. J. visits some of our boys they tell me, 'I gotta get better 'cause O. J. was here.' O. J. affects the patients in a spiritual way. It's very moving. Even the nurses are excited having someone as famous as O. J. visit the hospital."

When O. J. comes out of the room fifteen minutes later, he says, "The guy was totally alert, he just couldn't talk, so I talked about sports."

Pat says, "Thanks."

O. J. says, "Like I got anything else to do."

Suddenly, as if on cue, nurses appear around O. J. Pat introduces them to O. J. They look up at him with big smiles on their faces. He charms them in that athlete's way that passes for humility, his head lowered, talking up through his eyebrows.

"O. J.'s a very humble guy," Yale says to me, *sotto voce*.

After the visit we drive Pat to Miami Airport. Along the way, the conversation turns toward the subject of prejudice against Jews.

"I worked in the bereavement center for Holocaust survivors," Pat says, sitting in the front seat beside O. J. Yale is sitting with me in the back seat.

"The most racially restrictive clubs are still golf clubs," says O. J. "The last bastion. I played at a club in Alabama the PGA said was racist. I was the first black. At the Sherwood C.C. in L.A., too. They were pushing to have a black member. The Regency Club in Westwood approached me, too."

"When I was growing up in Philly," says Yale, "all the clubs were restricted for Jews and blacks, so my father started a club just for Jews."

"People don't realize it," says Pat, "but Miami Beach was restrictive until the 'eighties. I live on Sunset Island and the original deed said no Jews and no blacks."

"I felt uncomfortable at Wingfoot," says O. J. "And the L.A.C.C. wouldn't take actors. I said, 'Evidently you haven't seen my movies.' Ha! Ha! Ha! Jews built a club south of it and struck oil. Each of its original members receives eighty thousand dollars a year."

"The Holocaust is the end result of hatred," says Pat.

We park amid the cars and limousines at the curb in front of the departure terminal. We all get out and help Pat with her bags. When people on the sidewalk notice O. J., they flock to him. He poses for photographs with his arms around a blonde girl and an Asian girl, both of whom are beaming. Then he poses for another photo with a Latin woman whose husband snaps her picture. She thanks O. J. with a hug and a kiss on the cheek.

Yale whispers something to Pat. She comes over to me and says, "I just want to tell you that this man has an incredible love for people. People need to know that side of him."

After Pat disappears into the terminal, we get into O. J.'s Navigator and drive out of the airport. O. J. says, "I told ya. I used to get asked for autographs, now I get hugs. When I got out of incarceration I needed to sign autographs for the public. I was flattered. Before, I thought it was something I had to do. Not that I ever felt I needed fame. Maybe I did, I don't know. Fame has always been there in abundance for me. When I went to Vegas for the De La Hoya fight my friends said, 'You gotta leave, O. J. You're getting all the play.'" (People who were at that fight remember it differently. Phil Gori, from Fort Lauderdale, says, "When they announced O. J.'s name, everyone booed.")

As he drives out of the Miami airport onto the highway heading towards the Calusa Public Golf Course, O. J. tells me that at an Evander Holyfield fight in Vegas he met Kobe Tai, the porn actress. "This was just after that story that tried to put me and Christie in a porn film. Kobe said, 'Hey, Juice, come and join us.' Now, I have all five porn channels, and I know all the Vivid girls"—Vivid is a porn distributor—"I said, 'Any other time I'd love to, Kobe, but no way I'm takin' a picture with you now.' Ha! Ha! Ha! The tabloids were saying I was the reigning King of Porn, that I had sex with two girls four times in two-and-a-half hours. If I could do that I'd *be* in a porn film. A guy, fifty-three. But I ain't need no Viagra yet. Thank God it's still there. Ha! Ha! Ha! You know, they say guys with a really big dick need so much blood to make it hard, they pass out." O. J. puts his hand to his brow and flutters his eyes. "At times I feel a little light-headed myself. Ha! Ha! Ha! I met this girl once and she tells me she only dates guys with ten inches. I said, 'Baby, I ain't cuttin' off two inches for no one.' Ha! Ha! Ha!"

I ask O. J. why he bothered to play golf at clubs that didn't want blacks. He says, "I didn't know no black golf courses. All this stuff about O. J. lived in a white world is bullshit. White people invented that. I'm aware of racial pressures. When I was a commercial spokesman I felt I couldn't screw up because I didn't want to let people down. I was opening doors for black athletes. What I did set the tone. Blacks were judged by me. Now blacks say I'm a whipping boy for affirmative action. Listen, once I lived next door to Cyndi Garvey and her cop boyfriend. When he beat her up one night she came running to my house for protection. But it wasn't in the paper the next morning because she was white. When Nicole was murdered I told my lawyer of course I'm a suspect. . . ."

"It's perception versus fact," says Yale.

"If I was white or Jewish they'd be looking for somebody else. No one wants to focus on who did it. Why don't they nail Faye Resnick's drug friends?"

"If I tried this case today," says Yale, "no way O. J. wouldn't be acquitted."

"I know the majority of Americans think I did it," says O. J. "But, hey, look at Michael Jackson, and Puff Daddy, and Pee-wee Herman. Look what they did to this guy. I could care less what he did in a porn theater. But I respect his perseverance. And the McMartins. I though they did it, too." O. J. has become something of a crime buff after his ordeal. He follows the cases of other wrongfully accused defendants who were eventually acquitted, as if to prove some point only he is privy to.

O. J. parks his Navigator in the all-but-deserted parking lot of the Calusa Public Golf Course in Kendall. There is a neat line of empty golf carts in front of the clubhouse, a low, nondescript brick building. We get out and Yale and O. J. begin putting on their golf shoes.

"In L.A., you go to a club, put your name on a list and have to wait hours," says O. J. "Here, it's empty. Hurricane Andrew blew down most of the palm trees. They let it run down. The only reason I go here is to look at it for some friends trying to buy it. Hell, I ain't got no money. Ha! Ha! Ha!"

Which isn't entirely true. O. J. receives about $250,000 a year from a pension fund, which he adamantly insists is not from the NFL.

"That's bullshit!" he says. "I couldn't put gas in this car with the seventeen hundred a month I get from the NFL. That's a subtle way of not giving me credit for starting my own pension fund in my twenties when I started making money."

Two men come out of the clubhouse and meet us at the golf carts. O. J. introduces me to Steve Lee, a music distributor from Jamaica, and Delvon Campbell, also from Jamaica. Stevie, who is part-Asian, part-black, has coffee-colored skin. He is a shy man dressed in golf shorts. Delvon is as dark as a purple plum. He is dressed in a black silk shirt, black dress slacks, black dress shoes, and lots of gold jewelry that glistens in the afternoon sun.

"Hi, mon, how ye be doin'?" says Delvon to O. J., in his lilting Jamaican accent.

O. J. shakes his head. "I have no idea what Delvon is saying. Ha! Ha! Ha!"

They all throw their bags of clubs in the golf carts and we putter off in a line to the first tee. O. J. and Yale are in the lead cart, talking. Stevie is behind them, alone. Delvon and I bring up the rear.

"O. J. has been a friend of mine since I met him at a golf tournament in the Bahamas six years ago," says Delvon. He hands me his card. He's a talent scout for E-models, owned by the model Kim Alexis. "I scout for models," he says. "I'm always looking for new talent, new faces. Comes in handy with O. J., mon."

We stop our carts at the first tee. O. J. is lining up his drive. He hunches over, biting his lower lip, and begins his backswing. His knees begin to buckle and he is forced to abort the arc of his stiff, backswing. He lunges at the ball with his driver like an angry gardener hacking at a plant. The ball bounces up the fairway for about one hundred fifty yards and stops. O. J. can barely walk on his arthritic knees that were injured so often during his playing days.

Yale and Stevie tee off after O. J. Delvon is not playing today. Yale and O. J. and Stevie get in their carts and putter after their balls. Delvon and I follow. The fairway rough is barren of trees and exposed to the hot afternoon sun. The fairway itself is so rough, with patches of dirt and clumps of dried grass, that Delvon and I bounce along in our cart, our heads bobbing as we talk.

"O. J. and me, we're tight, mon," says Delvon. "Like brothers. No way I believe O. J. had something to do with that murder. I helped O. J. find his house here, and the school for his kids." On the first day O. J. drove his children to their new school he held a press conference outside the school under a sweltering sun. As O. J. pleaded with the assembled reporters to leave his children alone, Delvon stood beside him and mopped his sweaty brow with a handkerchief.

"I negotiate O. J.'s calendar," says Delvon. "And pick up his kids from school. O. J. helps me out financially because I'm not working, I'm just trying to make ends meet."

Being a talent scout is only Delvon's part-time job. His full-time job is as a steward at the American Airlines first class lounge in Miami Airport. He has not worked in months, however, ever since he slipped and fell in the Admiral's Club, serving drinks.

"I had surgery on my knee," says Delvon. "I have a hard time walking. I sued the airline and we're in mediation now."

O. J. and the others reach the green in four strokes. "O. J.'s short game is best," says Delvon. Stevie holes his putt. Delvon says out loud, "Stevie been doin' his homework, mon." O. J., lining up his putt, glares at Delvon. Then he strokes the ball. It bounces over the green that is as rough as a pebbled driveway and stops three feet from the hole. Delvon calls out, "Mon, that's criminal."

After O. J. and Yale sink their putts, we motor toward the second tee and a fairway that is as dry as a moonscape. O. J. calls out, "Man, there can't be no life out here but gators."

O. J., Yale, and Stevie play along like this in silence, hole after hole, in a desultory, joyless game that O. J. told me was "my passion. I once played fifty-four holes in a day." He loves golf, he told me, because on a golf course he can "get away from things." On a golf course, with friends, either his former celebrity friends or his new friends, "the little people," he can be himself instead of that exhaustingly amiable O. J. he forces himself to be in the public eye.

Every so often, Delvon limps onto the fairway to hit a shot. After one such shot that landed a few feet from the hole, Delvon says, "A *big* hitter, mon. Some days better than others."

O. J. glares at him and says, "Every time Delvon hits a good shot he does a goddamned autopsy on it. A post mortem." He drives his fairway shot into the sand trap.

Delvon and I park behind O. J. as he tries to hit out of the sand trap. His first shot digs up a spray of sand but moves the ball only a few feet ahead in the sand. As O. J. tries again to hit his ball out of the sand trap, he calls over his shoulder to me.

"You oughtta learn to play this game," says O. J.

"You mean, like you?"

O. J. turns from his shot toward me. He is hunched over, his lips slightly parted, his face as blank as a bull's. His eyes begin to roll back into their sockets until he is looking up at me through his furrowed brows with only the whites of his eyes. Without saying a word, he turns back to his shot.

O. J.'s game begins to improve by the sixth hole just as dark clouds appear overhead, blotting out the sun.

"It looks like rain, mon," Delvin calls from our cart as O. J. prepares to tee off. "We best be gettin' back to the clubhouse."

"I'm weak, I'm crippled, and I'm old," says O. J. "But I'm gettin' my game back now. I ain't goin' nowhere."

"Oh, mon, don't be beggin' for shots," says Delvon.

O. J. drives his best ball of the day down the center of the fairway as raindrops begin to fall.

"We goin' back, mon," says Delvon. "Don't be stupid. Them's big drops."

But O. J., Yale, and Stevie are already motoring after their balls as the rain begins to fall heavily now. Delvon turns our cart around and we begin to motor toward the clubhouse. I look back over my shoulder and see O. J., hunched over in the rain, lining up his shot under dark clouds.

While Delvon and I are waiting in the pro shop for the other three to come in, Delvon says, "Do you need a picture of me, mon? For the story?"

"Not right now," I say.

A few minutes later, O. J., Yale, and Stevie, all dripping wet, come into the clubhouse.

"You shoulda stayed out there," O. J. says to me, grinning now. "I had my best hole."

"I'd seen enough," I said.

We leave the pro shop and walk down a narrow hallway, past offices, toward the dining room. O. J. pokes his head through the door of one office and charms two Latin girls working behind desks.

"Hey, there, Ginny," he says to one girl. Then he sings, "Ginny, Ginny,

Ginny, won't you come along with me." Ginny blushes. O. J. laughs and says, "Aw, I feel bad beatin' up on these women."

The bar and dining room of the Calusa Public Golf Club are quiet, except for a table of older women in golf clothes having lunch by the window, a bartender polishing glasses, and the club pro sitting by the bar, nursing a Coke.

The club pro turns around and smiles at O. J. "Hey, Juice."

O. J. says, "I'm almost ready to child abuse you on the golf course." The pro smiles. "Then you can call me Mr. Man."

We all sit down at a round table in the center of the room. O. J. tosses a headfake toward the club pro, and says, "That boy as henpecked as you can get." He makes a clucking sound like a chicken, then shakes his head. "Some wives are high maintenance. I got one friend, though, with a low maintenance wife. As low maintenance as a wife can be. Ha! Ha! Ha!"

We order drinks and lunch and then turn our attention to the golf match on the T.V. suspended from the ceiling.

"Look at that Tiger Woods," says O. J. "How does he get so close to the pin?"

Yale answers his cell phone. A friend of Yale's is in L.A., and he asks Yale about restaurants. "Here, let me put O. J. on."

O. J. takes the cell phone and says, "You wanna go to The Ivy at the Shore, or maybe Chinois, or Schwarzenegger's place, Schatzi's." He listens for a moment, then says, "It's like Coconut Grove. That's where my wife grew up. Nicole."

When our drinks come I light up a cigar. O. J. looks over at the older women with a grin, and says, "Those old women gonna be sayin' something about your masculinity now. Ha! Ha! Ha! You know, in L.A. the best dressed golfers are always old women. Prada. Sharp."

"O. J., did you see that Johnnie came to Florida the other day?" says Yale.

"Yeah," says O. J.

Yale is referring to Johnnie Cochran, O. J.'s former lawyer, who is now representing a fourteen-year-old black South Florida boy named Lionel Tate. Tate is accused of murdering a much younger black girl while his mother was sleeping.

"Did you see Johnnie?" says Yale.

"No. He just stayed long enough to have his picture taken with Tate. Ha! Ha! Ha!"

Yale shakes his head. "Tate's lawyers are doing it all wrong."

"I wish Johnny would just focus on the life sentence and not make it a racial thing," says O. J. The Tate boy is being tried as an adult, which means if he's convicted he faces life in prison.

By the time our food comes, the golf match on the TV is over and a woman is reading the news on CNN. O. J. looks up at her and says, "Man, she got old quick. When you think the last time that woman got laid?" He shakes his head. "You see where Kathie Lee left Regis and his viewers went up? That's interesting. I mean, I like Frank"—Frank Gifford, Kathie Lee's husband, and an NFL Hall of Famer like O. J.— "but holding her kiddies up all the time, you can't be doin' that. And then she acted so shocked over Frank havin' sex with that stewardess. I know Frank my whole life. I remember seein' this article in *Redbook* that said Kathie Lee was the sexiest woman in America. I said, 'Oh, my God!' It's embarassin' her talkin' about how good Frank is in bed. Maybe she wasn't that good." He shrugs. "Who knows? You never know in this world what rings your bell. Now that Heather Graham girl is fine. And that Jennifer Love Hewitt, that girl got booty for days. And Jennifer Lopez, that baby got back, too. But I don't think she's goin' back to Puff Daddy. Her career is too high."

The CNN entertainment reporter is now reading a news story about the breakup of the Meg Ryan-Russell Crowe love affair. O. J. watches it with interest until the report is over. Then he says, "You think if Crowe and Quaid ever met, they'd fight?" he shakes his head. "As a man, you gotta punch the man that fucked your wife."

After lunch, Yale, O. J., and I go outside to his Navigator. It's stopped raining and the hot South Florida sun is burning off the puddles in the parking lot. Yale and O. J. take off their golf shoes outside the car and put on their loafers. I ask O. J. about his friendship with Delvon. He gives me a pained look.

"Aw, he ain't really my friend."

Yale opens the back door to get in, and water splashes on the crotch of his pants. O. J. laughs and says, "Look! The man came on himself."

It is late afternoon, now, and O. J. is driving me back to my car. He is still talking. . . .

"For the last few years, I wasn't really looking for work," he is saying. "I got an offer to be a TV spokesman in Europe, an 'Inside Edition' type of thing, but I'd have to be there eight days a month and I can't leave my kids."

"O. J. is a wonderful father," says Yale from the backseat.

"Now, I'm getting' active again. I got Yale to help me."

"We've been approached by a corporation for O. J. to be a spokesman and a member of the board. We turned it down to wait for the tide to turn more."

"This is the first time I'm really ready to take advantage of offers. Yesterday a guy wanted me to be the director of a youth program. A year ago, I'd have said, 'In the future.' But basically the future's here. Another company wanted to make me president, but I can't get into that now. Ha! Ha! Ha!"

When O. J. finally stops talking, I ask him a question. "After all you've gone through," I say, "do you ever feel that no matter how hard you try you can never get it right?"

"I thought I had got it right," O. J. says in a soft voice. "I'm not prone to get depressed but sometimes . . . the weight on me reaches a point and I just wanna go home and. . . ." His cell phone rings. He answers it and listens for a moment. Then he says, "I ain't no advice to the lovelorn," and hangs up. "Christie," he says.

"Your girlfriend?" I say.

O. J. gives me that pained look again. "Aw, man, she ain't my girl-friend. She's just, you know. . . ." He makes a thrusting motion with his hips. "Ha! Ha! Ha! Find me a girl owns a golf course and will pay all my bills and I'm pretty sure I'm in love with her."

O. J. and Christie Prody have had a tumultuous relationship ever since they met in L.A. five years ago. They have publicized fights, then make up, then fight again, make up, leave, follow each other, the whole cycle repeating itself endlessly like a prime-time soap opera out of *Groundhog Day*. They seem joined at the hip, not out of love, but out of some neurotic, psychic need that is different for both. When they were together in L.A. a few years ago, O. J. treated Christie like "a pest," said a friend of his. Cathy Bellmore, Christie's mother, told me, "O. J. wanted to get rid of her so she went to Florida without him." Once she was gone, O. J. wanted her back. He harassed her from L.A. He called her on the phone repeatedly at 6 A.M. to make sure she hadn't stayed out all night. When he heard that she was "partying" with ex-baseball player Pedro Guerrero, he hopped a flight from L.A. to Florida and confronted Christie. During the ensuing argument, Christie fled her house in her white Mustang. O. J. called the police and told them he was worried about a friend of his who was on a drug binge. It wasn't worry, said his friends, it was simply that O. J. was unable to give up even a girlfriend he was bored with because he considered her his private property.

Finally, six months ago, O. J. moved to Florida, close to Christie's home. Soon there were more fights, more calls to the police, more breakups, reconciliations, until finally Christie tried to break free of O. J.'s hold over her by spilling their most intimate secrets (sex, drugs, abortions) to the *National Enquirer*. O. J. responded by telling Hollywoodgossip.com that Christie was "harassing" him, "stalking" him, because he had broken up with her over "her substance abuse problem." That's essentially the same thing O. J. told me about Nicole. The similarities between the two women's relationships with O. J. are so striking they prompted Bellmore to tell the *Enquirer* that she feared for her daughter's life. A friend of O. J.'s discounted such a threat, saying, "O. J. was really in love with Nicole but he doesn't care enough about Christie to kill her." Ironically, Christie herself has no fear of physical harm from O. J. and admits that in most of their fights she is the physical aggressor. This is a different O. J. from the one his friends knew with Nicole. "I knew he beat Nicole," said a sports agent. "It was common knowledge." An NBC Sports employee said everyone at NBC knew O. J. was a "man who used to beat his wife." Even O. J. admitted that "you put a man and a woman in the same house, day in and day out, and from time to time someone gets slapped." In another interview, O. J. said he admired Jim Brown, the former football player turned actor, because "actors have an air about them athletes don't. He's that tough guy beating up on everybody, throwing women out windows . . . but really, he's a good guy."

Even Christie's betrayal of their private life to the *Enquirer* was not enough to break O. J.'s hold on her. Soon after the story came out, they were having dinner again at a Miami restaurant and for all intents and purposes their relationship was back to square one. Christie said, "I love O. J., but sometimes he drives me crazy. Isn't that just like a man? They try to make you think you're crazy. They choose to do it."

I had a chance to witness their symbiotic relationship first hand one night at dinner at the North Miami Beach steakhouse, The Palm, a restaurant Yale insisted we dine at because "O. J. feels comfortable there."

My wife, Susan, and I arrived first. We had a drink at the bar, which was separated from the dining room by a half wall. Most of the diners were older Miami Beach couples who looked as if they had been extras in the dining room scenes in the movie *Dirty Dancing*. One woman was gnawing on a T-bone steak she held in her hands.

We sat at the bar for a few minutes and studied the cartoonish charicatures on the wall above the bar mirror. Mr. Silverman. Dick Kimble. Joe DiMaia. Grace Palmer. Mike Trager. Jim Kiick, the retired Miami Dolphin fullback, was the only name I recognized.

Yale and his wife, Elyse, arrived a few minutes later. Yale had described Elyse to me as "a magnificent creature." I told her he was right. She looked at me, then Yale. While we waited for O. J. and Christie, Susan and Elyse chatted and Yale talked about Christie.

Yale said Christie liked to go out at night. "Christie will wear you out until three a.m.," he said. "Wait'll you see her. If you and I ever walked into a restaurant with her, our stock would go up."

O. J. and Christie arrived an hour late and joined us at the bar. Christie wore a very low-cut black dress that exposed most of her breasts. She was an attractive woman with the rounded features of a tomboy, not the sharp features of a fashion model. She had short, lank, reddish-sandy hair that she had once dyed blonde because, as O. J. told me, "what woman doesn't want to be a blonde at one time." Even with blonde hair, however, it was a stretch to call Christie a "Nicole lookalike," as the tabloids had christened her.

O. J. apologized for being late. He looked at the three women, who were talking, to make sure they weren't watching him, then he made a grinning, thrusting gesture with his hips.

We were seated at a round table at the far corner of the dining room, barely noticed by the other diners. We ordered food and drinks and then I turned to Christy, who was sitting beside me. But before I could ask her a question, O. J. began to talk as he always did. Cathy Bellmore told me that on the few occasions she'd had dinner with O. J., "nobody got in a word. It was exhausting. He tires you out constantly talking about himself."

O. J. was talking about the time, when he was a teenager, "I sold dope to this white chick I was trying to make and then after we smoked some pot I thought I'll never become an athlete now so I ran home all the way to get the pot out of my system. Ha! Ha! Ha!" Then he began another story.

I turned to Christie and said, "What's the attraction between you two? There's such an age difference."

Christie smiled at me, a false, frightened smile, and then her cheek twitched and she glanced at O. J. He was smiling, talking. She turned back to me, and said, "I'm a mature twenty-five-year-old, and he's an immature old guy who likes to play golf. That's a game for retired guys who want to escape reality." She looked at O. J. "O. J.'s into denial. He loved L.A. I hated L.A. It corrupts your soul." She gestured again toward O. J. with that involuntary facial twitch. "I loved growing up in Minnesota. It was wonderful."

O. J. stopped talking and glared at Christie. "Yeah, that's why you couldn't wait to leave." Christie said nothing. O. J. turned toward me, grinning lasciviously, and said, "You're into Christie, huh?" He raised his eyebrows. "Did you ever fool around on your wife?"

"No."

"Come on. You're lying. Everybody fools around."

"I don't."

"Sure you do, you just won't admit it. Everybody fools around and lies about it. Look at Clinton. He was a great liar. Deny. Deny. Deny." He threw back his head and laughed.

Christie sat there for the rest of the night, picking at her food, not speaking. When I called her a few days later, she said, "I'm sorry. I was very uncomfortable. I'm a very sarcastic person and O. J. told me to watch what I say with a writer." Then she began to talk freely about her life: a smart, instinctive, undisciplined woman burdened by the psychic wounds left by her father, who deserted her and her mother when Christie was a child in Minneapolis.

"My mother got breast cancer a few years later and I helped her recover," she said. "My grandmother had it, too. I'm terrified I'll get it. I was always close to my mother after that. She's my best friend in the world."

Christie worked at her mother's telemarketing firm from the age of fourteen, and then, when she graduated from high school, she went to the University of Minnesota where she majored in psychology. "Go figure," she said, laughing. "Look what happened to me." She worked her way through college as a waitress and a barmaid, "But I never drank or did drugs," she said. Then at nineteen she fulfilled a dream she'd had since ten, and moved to L.A. It was shortly after O. J.'s trial. One day, on a lark, she drove by O. J.'s house at Rockingham. "Like everybody else," she said, "I thought he did it."

She saw O. J. outside riding an electric bicycle and called to him, "Hi, O. J.!" He came over to her and they talked for hours. She gave him her telephone number and that night he called her and asked her out. They have been going together, on and off, ever since.

"He was charming and charismatic," she said, "and kinda intriguing. I always like older guys. I got enough problems myself, so why hang out with young people. O. J. forgets I have a typical twenty-five-year-old's problems. I have my whole life ahead of me. But I live for today and don't worry about five years from now." She laughs. "I might not be here. In all honesty, I don't know what he saw in me. I was very convenient, I guess. He hid me for two years. I led a double life. It was very hard not to tell anyone. When I did, I had to defend him all the time. It got frustrating. I was dating the most publicized guy, and that's not the easiest thing to do when you're a private person. I don't like being in the public eye. And my dreams of L.A. were not what I thought they'd be. It wasn't the real world. Actors who drove Mercedes and lived in a one-room apartment. So I went to Florida. I didn't know if O. J. would follow me or not."

Although Christie said she no longer believed O. J. murdered Nicole, she did stand by everything she said about him in her *National Enquirer* exposé. "I was angry," she said. "I was going through a hard time in my life in Florida. I felt let down by O. J. I had given up my life for him and had nothing to show for it. He told me there was no room in his life for a wife, or more kids. I want kids. And then someone offered me fifty thousand dollars to tell the truth. So I did it. I don't deny our drug use or anything I said in it. As for the porno tape, that never happened. O. J.'s agent, Mike Gilbert, knew someone who would pay ten million and he tried to set it up with some girl who'd hit on us both. But nothing happened. There is no porno tape." She laughed. "Not yet, anyway."

O. J. is driving me back to my car late in the afternoon. I am holding my tape recorder toward his face while I rest my head on the passenger door window and try to doze. But it is impossible. O. J. is still talking, still jabbing his finger into my shoulder.

"The thing I'm most proud of," he is saying, "is that the girls I dated were offered two hundred fifty thousand dollars by the tabloids and not one single one of them said anything bad about me. I expected the cops to lie. They were told not to investigate the case because no one in L.A. wanted to hear it. And the media. They let me down the most. They got lazy and relied on police tips instead of investigating. They sold the story that was gullible. During my trial the truth was known but no one would write it. It's a much better story if I'm guilty. They didn't want to catch who did it. They didn't look at anybody but me. I was set up. They tried to pin it on me."

O. J. stops his Navigator at a red light across the street from the Wild Oats parking lot where I left my car. He says, "I wonder if I've run into this person who killed Nicole? Have I talked to them?" He glances in his rearview mirror before turning the corner, and says, "Do I see them every day?"

Frank Klein

The Fan

(from *Newsday Sunday Magazine*, 1980)

Whenever I am walking through town and I see Frank Klein walking toward me or about to pull his battered Volkswagen over to the curb and call out my name, I turn into the nearest store and wait—flattened behind the lingerie racks in Merle Norman Cosmetics—until he passes. Usually, however, he sees me before I see him. He leans across the passenger seat of his car, which is always littered with cigarette ashes and the sports sections of Connecticut newspapers, and begins telling me, in that breathless way of his, the way of a young boy—Frank is almost fifty-two—about the latest area college baseball pitching phenom. It is always a pitcher.

"Pat, what do you think about Catto?" he says.

"I don't know," I say. "What about him?"

He looks, incredulous, at me. "He was drafted! In the third round by the Reds! What do you think? Does he have a shot? Come on, Pat. You should know. You were a pitcher."

I try to control myself. I tell Frank I don't know. I have never seen Keith Catto, a former Fairfield University star, throw a baseball. *I* have not thrown a baseball in a game in over twenty years. I no longer even *think* of myself as a pitcher, as ever having *been* a pitcher (a lie). And then, before Frank can regroup, I flee to my office, leaving Frank Klein to peer, bewildered, through his rearview mirror at my hasty retreat.

Sitting in my office, flushed, I curse my rudeness. And I curse Frank Klein for eliciting that rudeness. For reminding me of that which I have worked so diligently, albeit unsuccessfully, at forgetting: my failed career. Just when I think I have exorcised the demon of my failure, when I can finally read the major league boxscores filled with names of players I had known in the minor leagues without thinking of them as they were then, in the late fifties, but as they are now, managers like Joe Torre, aging pitchers like Phil Niekro, just then, at peace finally, up pops Frank Klein like some prophetic jack-in-the-box.

But why does he upset me so? He means no harm. He is a pleasant enough man. I have known him, on and off, for years. I first met Frank when I was a twenty-two-year-old sportswriter working the six-to-2 A.M. shift on a Bridgeport newspaper. He would appear at midnight, bearing gifts of coffee for me and my grumpy boss, along with one of his interminable press releases. My boss, a big bear of a man, would be hunched over some copy paper, his face low to the desk, trying to avoid eye contract with Frank. He would reach up with his hand without taking his eyes from the copy paper and accept Frank's coffee. He mumbled thanks but still refused to look up, as if the sight of Frank's beseeching eyes would force even him, old Stonehenge heart, to use all four pages of a press release for which we had space for only two paragraphs.

Now, my editor was not averse to accepting small gratuities. On my first day on the job he informed me that one of my duties was to read the race results from the Big A to a voice I was to know only as Clyde. After each race I would call a certain number and this voice would answer, a voice like a gravel parking lot. "Hello, Dis is Clydt," the voice would say. I read the results and the phone clicked dead. At the end of my first week there was a box of Topstone cigars on my desk. I assumed this was some kind of a mistake, so I buried the cigars in my bottom drawer. The next week there was another box. And so on and so on until I finally asked my boss about them. Without looking up from his copy paper, he grumbled, "A gift from Clyde." So I began to smoke them, a free gift, I thought, which has grown over these twenty years into an expensive habit I have yet to break. I eventually found out who Clyde was one night, when I played on a semi-pro basketball team coached by my editor and funded, I discovered, by one Bernie Massassaria of the Savoy Athletic Club. The editor introduced me to our benefactor, a roly-poly little man in a rumpled sharkskin suit who resembled Nikita Khrushchev. As soon as Bernie spoke I knew he was Clydt. He sat comically in the stands, watching us play without removing his pork pie hat the entire game. I learned later from other writers on the staff that Bernie paid our boss a gratuity of about one hundred dollars a week for those results, which I read. Which is why, I guess, Frank Klein's meager payola of coffee was insufficient for the editor. Besides, I'm sure Frank meant his coffee as a kindness and not as payola. Anyway, my boss would grumble thanks to Frank and then wave him and his press release to my desk. Frank would stand over me, stuttering a few words about some local pitcher while I slashed away at his copy. Finally, no longer able to bear the pain, he fled.

I also used to see Frank at a lot of local semi-pro baseball games played usually at twilight on a weekday. These were not the American Legion games of young prospects with high stirrups, played in the cool suburbs before a polite crowd of parents and major-league scouts. These were City League games, played after work in the heat before a crowd of blacks and Puerto Ricans and old men sipping from bottles in paper bags, and even older men, who stood in the shade of the only tree and criticized the players on the field while reminiscing about their playing days with the White Eagles and the Rosebud A.C. I remember when I got released by the Braves in the early sixties, I was too afraid—I should say too embarrassed—to show my face around town for weeks. When I finally got up the nerve to leave my house, I went down to that park to watch one of those city games. The old timers were there under the tree. A cluster of wizened and bent magpies. Little old ladies, really. With nothing to do but carp. I stood behind them, unnoticed for a few moments, and watched the game in progress. I heard my name mentioned by one of the old men.

"Jordan's back," he said.

"Figures," said another. "He never had the guts."

I ran from the park with tears in my eyes and did not return for almost a year. By then, I had come to grips with my failure, at least to the extent that I could go to those games where I was once a star.

The players in those games were in their late twenties or thirties or forties, had once been prospects, had maybe even gone away to play in the minors before getting released. Some were even in their fifties, like Al Bike and Rufus Baker, a trim black man, and some had even gone as high as the major leagues, like Tom Casagrande. A huge man with thick, freckled arms dusted with orange hairs. "The Big House," his name meant in Italian, and, to me, as a kid, he was big as a house: 6-3, 250 pounds. A smooth-throwing southpaw with a Whitey Ford motion. But with more stuff than Whitey. Tom had played a few years with the

Phillies, with Robin Roberts, before he drifted back to the minor leagues
and then, even farther back, to the Senior City League. Tom was the star
of the league then, a businessman, unlike the other players who were
prospects now only for membership in the Bricklayers Guild, the league
from which they rushed to the park only minutes before game time.
Those players changed into their uniforms in their cars and took the
field without warming up—they had no careers to protect—looking so
odd with their chalky white hands dusted with lime.

I could always spot Frank at these games because he never stood with
the wise guys, the carping old men, but rather stood off to the side, listening to the chatter of the wives and girlfriends of the players. Frank
was always with the women. The girlfriends changed over the years,
became wives, brought *their* sons to the games, to whose girlfriends, one
day, Frank Klein would be listening.

But Frank never changed. Never aged. He was always a slim little man
with thick eyeglasses, slicked-back hair, and the pleased, sheepish look of
a young boy talking to older women. He shuffled his feet, looked down
at the dirt, stuffed his hands deep into the pockets of his baggy pants
with their shiny seat. His shoulders were hunched up around his ears as
if to protect against an imaginary chill. As the women chatted on,
Frank's head would bob up and down like the heads of those toy dogs in
the rear windows of so many of the cars parked at those games.

Years later, when I started writing for magazines, Frank began sending me clippings from Connecticut newspapers about various area players. He never suggested I write a story about those players, or that he had
had anything to do with their successes and so deserved recognition. He
simply attached a cryptic note that read: "Pat, thought this might interest you! Frank."

What did he want?

I have tried to guess what Frank Klein wanted all these years, and still
I could come up with nothing. In fact, the more I have thought about
Frank, a man I have known for over twenty years, the more I realized I
did not know him at all.

Frank Klein is a bachelor of German-Hungarian descent. He lives with
his tiny, eighty-year-old mother in a small, immaculate house in the
Hungarian section of Fairfield, Connecticut, where he grew up. He rises
before the sun each morning. So as not to disturb his widowed mother,

he goes downstairs to his partially finished basement to smoke a cigarette, to listen to music (Peter Nero), and to work. He has set up a folding chair, a card table, a small lamp, and a portable typewriter at one end
of the basement. There, each morning, he bangs out press releases for his
life's avocation—the Connecticut Collegiate Summer Baseball League.
He is the league's founder (1964), its director, and its sole executive officer. In short, Frank Klein *is* the CCSBL. It is his brainchild. A sort of
minor-league Cape Cod League for college-aged and older players, who
for various reasons—a lack of talent, the need to hold a summer job—
cannot afford to play on the Cape each summer with the College All-
Americans but who still want to play baseball after their collegiate
seasons are ended.

"My players maybe don't have the potential to be high draft choices
like those at the Cape," Frank says. "They play for the love of the game."

Frank began his league when he was the sports coordinator at an
exclusive country club in Darien. "I was making more money than I
could spend," he says. "I was bored. I was a bachelor with no family, no
responsibilities, nothing but a great interest in baseball. Not major
league baseball, gee, I don't think I went to a game at Yankee Stadium or
Shea in years, even though I always had free passes. I could never relate
to those games like I could to amateur games."

When Frank decided to organize his league in 1964, he sent out letters to all the major league baseball clubs to see if they would be interested in making a financial contribution. All of the teams responded
affirmatively, so Frank took money out of his own pocket and started
the league. Originally, there were four towns represented—Hartford,
Waterbury, New Haven, and Bridgeport. Today, there are twelve towns.

"I wanted the kids to enjoy it," says Frank, "so I rented air-condi-
tioned buses for them, got the best umpires, the best uniforms, everything, and then, at the end of the season, only the Cardinals sent me a
check. For twenty-five dollars. I lost over four thousand dollars of my
own money. But nowadays, between the teams' sponsors and the contributions I get from former players, fans, and most of the major league
clubs, I only lose a few hundred dollars a year."

One recent summer morning, I arrived at Frank's house at 5:30. It was
well after the hour he wakes each day. He was nervous at my being there
and he had awakened this morning even earlier than usual, about 4 A.M.,

and gone downstairs to his basement to arrange things for my coming. On his basement floor he had laid out for me, in neat stacks, his baseball memorabilia. There were piles of old CCSBL releases, the same ones I probably slashed to bits when I was a young reporter. There were letters from friends and fans and former players. There were envelopes adorned with the bright insignias of dozens of major league teams. There was a yellowed program from the 1925 World Series between the Washington Senators and the Pittsburgh Pirates. That program revealed a glimpse of baseball as it was played in a simpler time, by simpler men. On the inside cover there is a brown-tinted photograph of Judge Kennesaw Mountain Landis, who was then the commissioner of baseball. He is a stern-looking man, with a gaunt, stretched-out face the shape of a trowel. He is wearing a high, starched collar, a frock coat, and his hair—thick and tousled like a boy's—is pure white. There is nothing soft or corporate-looking about Landis, as there is today about so many of the game's executives who seem never to have played the game they control. Landis looks like an ascetic. A prophet for the game he loved.

Inside the program are advertisements for Worumbo overcoats worn by every member of the Senators, who look like a lineup for the St. Valentine's Day Massacre. For Clark C. Griffith's oil company, with a testimonial from Walter Johnson ("It's the delivery that counts"). And finally for Mike Martin's liniment. Martin, who bears a striking resemblance to W.C. Fields, especially around his nose, which looks like a light bulb, was the Senators' trainer. His liniment promises to relieve colds, aches, pains, stiff muscles, swollen joints, cold feet, lameness, rheumatism, lumbago, neuralgia, and neuritis—all for the modest sum of fifty cents for two ounces.

That program is not Frank's prized memento, however. He has other such programs. What he treasures most is a yellowed newspaper clipping of his briefly famous "Uncle Spike." In late September 1934, John "Spike" Merena was called up from the minor leagues by the Boston Red Sox to pitch against the mighty New York Yankees of Babe Ruth and Lou Gehrig. Spike Merena hurled a four-hit shutout. It was the highlight of a brief career that ended the following spring when Merena came down with a sore arm.

Frank takes a great and vicarious pleasure in his uncle's accomplishment—Frank's life seems geared primarily to vicarious pleasures—for several reasons. It was *his* uncle's accomplishment. It was the accomplishment of a *local* athlete. And, quite simply, it was an accomplishment in the game he loves—baseball. His affection for the game is that of a young boy. It is an attitude most baseball players had when they were young boys but somehow lost along the way. Frank is devoted to baseball as a game to play rather than as a game that brings rewards.

"My Uncle Spike gave me the game ball after his shutout," says Frank. "It was autographed by Babe Ruth. I was only five years old at the time so I used the ball in a pick-up game in the street. Eventually I lost it. I guess it would be worth a lot of money today, huh?" He smiles sheepishly at me, as if he is about to say something that embarrasses him. "If I was a kid today, playing the game, I'd probably do the same thing," he says.

Frank has retained this childlike attitude toward baseball on into his adult years. He can both love the game and still keep it in its place, as a game to be enjoyed, because he never wanted anything from it. Other than to play it, nurture it, and watch it be played by others. Even though he failed at the game, as do most, he was never hurt by the game, never felt any reason to lash back at the game in anger. To turn his back on the game as I did for years, until finally I made my peace with a game that I had always felt betrayed me. I had been a star! A bonus baby! I expected *so* much from the game! Wanted so much. I never thought, until now, sitting with Frank Klein in his basement, of giving to the game that had been so good to me . . . But not as good to me as I had dreamed.

"I never was disappointed my own career wasn't like Uncle Spike's," he says, "although I did play a few weeks of pro ball in the Northern League in nineteen fifty. I was an infielder with the Bennington Vermont Generals. One of my teammates was Bobby Winkles, who went on to become a major league manager." Frank reaches down among his papers on the floor produces a pink slip of paper—his Generals' player contract. He was paid the princely sum of $180 per month. "I only lasted a month," he says, with a sheepish grin. "Then they found out about me. I was flashier than I was consistent. My best shot was a soft liner over second. After I was released I went home and never even *thought* about becoming a professional baseball player again."

At six o'clock in the morning, Frank and I get into his Volkswagen and drive to the corner newsstand where he buys as many Connecticut newspapers as he can. Leaving the newsstand, he slips out the sports section from each paper, as is his custom, and drops the other sections into a garbage pail. Then he drives over to Fairfield University, where he parks his car and begins walking through the campus. We pass the Fairfield U. baseball diamond where many of the CCSBL games are played during the summer. Then we walk down a side street toward the home of one of his friends. Both men work for the Fairfield Department of Education. "Special Ed," says Frank. Each morning and afternoon both men drive retarded teenagers back and forth from their homes to their schools.

"I don't like to refer to them as 'retarded,'" says Frank. "I call them 'special kids.'" Frank also performs a similar task with physically handicapped youths. "Wheelchair kids," he calls them.

Before Frank and I reach his friend's house, he meets us halfway in an orange school bus. He swings open the door and we get in. He greets Frank with news of last night's Yankee game. He is in his early fifties, a good-looking man with an actor's resonant voice.

Frank sits behind the driver and I sit on the opposite side near the door. As we approach the home of the first student, Frank asks me to move to the seat behind the one I'm sitting in. "It's her special seat," he says. I nod, get up, and move. The bus stops, the door swings open, and from far down a long driveway, the figure of a girl moves toward us. She is carrying books under one arm. She moves so languidly that from a distance she appears almost to be floating toward us. She is a pretty girl of about seventeen. She is wearing jeans and boys' high-top black sneakers that are partially unlaced. Before she gets on Frank tells me that her name is Janice (not her real name) and that for a long time he had had trouble understanding her.

"She used to tell tales," he says. He seems unable to use the word 'lies' when talking about her. "Nothing serious," he adds, "just exaggerations. Like if one of the other kids' parents went to Washington D.C., then she'd tell us that her parents went to Europe and came back the same day. So, you see, I knew it couldn't be true." Those stories bothered him, he says, so he set about eliminating them. Now, he proudly states, she no longer tells 'tales.'

Janice gets on the bus to greetings from Frank and his friend, the driver. She sits in her special seat next to the door and puts her foot on Frank's knee. "My laces are untied, Frank," she says in a lilting voice.

Smiling, he says, "Of course, Janice," and ties them.

We are driving up a long hill, shaded on either side by maple trees that spill over the road like a covered bridge. The houses on either side of the road are stately old colonials, mansions, really, many with horse barns and riding stables and, far off, beyond the houses, corrals. The bus turns into a long, winding driveway that leads finally to a reproduction of a French Normandy farmhouse. Waiting at the door is a dark-skinned boy with curly black hair and a thin ascetic-looking man, a younger Judge Landis, with aristocratic features. Thinning, gray, swept-back hair, ruddy cheeks, an aquiline nose. The tall man has his arm around the boy's shoulders. The man is wearing gray slacks and a crew-neck sweater. Peeking beneath the sleeves of his sweater and the cuffs of his pants are his pajamas. He is wearing slippers. His eyes are almost gray. They are distant, distracted, as if, even at this moment, as he leads his son toward the bus and calls out a cheery, "Hello," he is also turning over and over again in some far recess of his brain an unsolvable problem he will never escape.

The boy, Brian (not his real name), gets on the bus and sits in the seat behind Frank. I look over at him. He seems not even aware that I am there. A stranger. Frank leans back over his seat and begins talking to the boy about baseball. The boy's head is slack against his chest, and he seems not to be listening. Suddenly, he lifts his head and smiles. "Do you know I got an award in school yesterday, Frank?" Frank says, no, he didn't know, and asks what the award was. "For the most politest," Brian says, and then his head drops to his chest again and he becomes preoccupied with turning the cuff of his sweater sleeve over and over. The door closes with a vacuumlike *whoosh* and the tall man steps back and waves goodbye. He is smiling, and as the bus moves away, the man calls out, "God bless."

"He was in World War Two," Frank says. "He was a hero. I think he got the Silver Cross and the Bronze Star and some others, too." The man is still waving to us as we make our way down the winding driveway.

At the next and final stop, the bus again makes its way down a long driveway to a sprawling ranch-type house. Frank gets out this time and goes to the front door to greet a teenaged girl wearing horn-rimmed glasses. Her name is Ruth (again, not her real name) and she is sometimes afflicted with seizures, possibly brought on by nervousness. Frank always meets her at the door to comfort her. She slips her arm inside his, as if he were her beau, and they walk slowly toward the bus. From the house, a woman's disembodied voice calls out sweetly, "Have a nice day, dear."

When they arrive at the high school, Frank gets out and waits for the two girls. Each girl slides her arm inside one of Frank's arms and they walk on either side of him to the front door of the high school. Their heads incline toward his shoulder, as if for comfort. Brian straggles behind them. Suddenly, alert, he rushes ahead and opens the door for them. Frank and his girls thank him with an exaggerated, almost formal, politeness, and pass through. They move down the corridor, the object of students' stares—Frank, both sheepish and proud, his shoulders hunched up, looking like the father of not one but two brides. Brian, distracted again, trails them sluggishly.

It is 9 A.M., of the same day. Frank and I are sitting on deck chairs in his backyard. Frank is opening his mail. Already the sun is very hot. Frank is wearing a golf sweater over a Ban-Lon shirt. He does not seem to mind the heat. I am beginning to sweat. I am also getting sick. It is a combination of the heat, something I ate last night, and the pressure I felt while riding on that bus with Frank and those "special" teenagers. I was extremely conscious of those teenagers, of their "specialness" in a way that has drained me. They lived in a world I would never know. Frank was relaxed on that bus. Unlike me, he did not seem to be thinking of how to act or what to say. He was simply himself, in a way most people can never be, not even Brian's father, when confronted by such "special" youths.

Frank opens an envelope with the orange-and-black insignia of the Baltimore Orioles on the upper left hand corner. He takes such great pleasure in these colorful major league envelopes. Inside this one is a check for ten dollars from Thomas A. Giordano, director of scouting.

"Dear Frank: It is my pleasure once again to participate in your booster program hoping that in some small way it will tend to serve in a positive way. You have done a truly outstanding job over the years in keeping the CCSBL not only in operation but in damn good shape. I have only the highest respect and regard for you as a man and as an administrator. Best wishes for a successful year."

Frank hands the letter to me with an embarrassed smile. Then he opens another. It is from a girl who was once a scorekeeper for the CCSBL. She now works for a bank. She has enclosed a check for twenty dollars, along with a note printed on pink paper.

"I'm still wildly in love with the grand old game, Frank. I'm glad to see the league is doing well." He hands me that note, too.

"I try to keep in touch with everyone who was ever associated with the league," says Frank. "At Christmas time, I send them my spring press release. Those who remember send me a little note, maybe a check for five dollars. Sometimes I find myself writing to a player's wife I never met. Maybe I haven't seen her husband in years, since before he got married, even though I may have corresponded during that time. I got such a letter recently. The wife wrote me because her husband still didn't know when to quit, she said. He'd broken his arm in a baseball game and she had to substitute for him as a letter writer."

Finished with his mail, Frank turns to his newspapers. He goes immediately to the back of each sports section to peruse each town's local baseball news. As he reads, he comments to me on each town's coverage of the CCSBL. Frank has a droning voice. Like the buzz of bees. He speaks softly, almost inaudibly, as if shy, or maybe as if imparting a precious secret. His voice and the heat and my upset stomach are making me even sicker. I take a deep breath and look around the yard. His mother, wearing a curly yellow wig and a shapeless shift, is at the far end of the yard, bent over her garden. She has brought out Frank's dog. The dog has no name, or rather many names. Frank calls him whatever name he feels like on a particular day. Sometimes he just calls him Dog. Today, he calls him Casey, after Casey Stengel. The dog is tethered to a clothesline, a small, insane mongrel, and he is racing back and forth along the clothesline, leaping madly into the air, almost strangling himself on his tether while yapping shrilly. I lean over in my chair and cradle my head in my hands. The heat and the dog and my stomach and the incessant droning of Frank's voice are getting to be too much for me. But Frank does not even notice. Or maybe he does. He begins talking more quickly, now, as if to get it all in before I bolt.

"A 'good town' is one that runs CCSBL boxscores," Frank says. "Along with a small story of the weekend's games. A 'bad town' is one that doesn't. Whenever I see an article I think might interest someone, I cut it out and send it to them." Today, Frank has found an article about John Caneira, a Naugatuck native who pitched briefly in the major leagues for the California Angels. Caneira quit baseball at twenty-six rather than return to the minor leagues after a 2-2 major league season in the late seventies. He got a job with the Travelers Insurance Company in Hartford. This pleases Frank.

"It was a wise move," Frank says. While he is speaking Casey comes running down the clothesline toward us. He leaps into the air a few feet short of us and is yanked back by his tether. He is yapping insanely, frothing at the mouth, his tongue hanging almost to the ground. I stare at the dog in disbelief, but Frank seems not even to notice him. He goes on, "He's probably making more money now than he did in four years in the minors."

I look at him. "Who?"

"John Caneira," he says. "Besides, he's got a wife and family to consider."

It is 5:30 P.M. of the same day and it is still hot. Frank and I are sitting in his Volkswagen in the parking lot behind the left-centerfield fence of the Roger Ludlow High School baseball diamond. The field is deserted—a CCSBL game is scheduled for 5:45 P.M.—and completely exposed to the sun. There is no shade anywhere. Each team's dugout is merely a bench along the baselines.

The car is so hot that I have opened the passenger side door and am sitting half inside, half outside the car. My elbows are on my knees, my head cradled in my hands. I am moaning softly to myself. I am soaked with sweat. Frank, sitting beside me in his golf sweater, is oblivious to the heat. He is smoking cigarette after cigarette and he is talking in his droning voice about his father, who was once a talented baseball player, but he was also a heavy drinker.

"He was never violent or anything," Franks says, staring at the field. "He just mostly left me on my own. There were no backyard catches, if you know what I mean. Fathers didn't come into the picture much in those days. He was a pretty fair baker, though. A pastry baker. But he always lost jobs because of his drinking. The one time I most remember his drinking was the day I was to graduate from college. There was no way he could even attend that event. Definitely not. The last fifteen or so years of his life he was in an institution."

While he is talking Frank keeps his eyes glued to the deserted field. He seems to be looking for something. I ask him what. He says, "I always get here early to see how things develop. I park beyond the outfield fence so no one can see me and I can get a true picture of what's happening. I want to see things run smoothly. I look for punctuality in the players, managers, and umpires. I look to see how many players each team has. I like to see the visiting team with at least twelve. I look to see if the field is chalked or if someone's doing it only a few minutes before game time. That would disappoint me. See, this field is already chalked.

"I also like to see the teams have roofed dugouts to protect them from the heat. And the fans should have shade, too. See, there's no shade for anyone." He shakes his head. "There's not even a refreshment stand. My favorite park is over in Stratford—Longbrook Park. It's a casual park and yet it's structured, too. The refreshment stand is always open, even though the guy who runs it doesn't make much money out of it, I'm sure. Their stands are shaded, too, by trees. It's an atmosphere conducive to baseball."

Frank glances at his watch, and as he does, a car pulls up behind the homeplate screen. A few players in uniforms get out, along with their girlfriends. Soon, other cars arrive and the diamond is filled with players warming up only minutes before the game is scheduled to begin.

The girlfriends sprawl on a grassy rise along the first base foul line. They are wearing shorts and halter tops and they lie back in the grass to take the sun. Every so often one of the players jogs over to one of the girls, takes a quick drag on her cigarette, and jobs back to his warm-ups.

"It's really not that late," Frank says. "I have a habit of setting my watch five minutes fast. These twilight games are rough. You can't expect them to start on time. Most of these kids rush over from work. They just about get here to warm up. For some of the older players you have to realize their jobs are more important than this game. I encourage teams to have a few older players among their college kids. They'll do the jawing with the umpires so as to protect the kids. It keeps the umpires awake. The older guys will also do things the younger kids shouldn't, like maybe pitch in both ends of a double-header because their team maybe got a little overanxious and scheduled more games than they could comfortably handle. I try to discourage that."

When his watch reads 5:50, Frank can no longer hide his apprehension. The umpires have yet to appear. It is his great fear that one day everything will be set for a CCSBL game—the players on the field, the coaches at home plate with the line-up cards, the fans sprawled in the stands—and no umpire. It is Frank's recurring nightmare. But it is not to become a reality today. The umpires arrive and the game begins only a few minutes late.

"It *is* a Friday night game," Frank says. "After all, the traffic is terrible." Frank relaxes considerably after the first pitch is thrown. He no longer seems interested in the action on the field, far removed from us in the parking lot beyond the outfield fence. After one inning he starts the car and prepares to leave. When I ask him why, he says, "I rarely stay for more than one inning. The idea is to organize everything and then let the kids play the game. That's why I do it, that's where I get my satisfaction from."

Frank begins to pull out of the deserted parking lot. No one has seen him arrive. No one sees him leaving. As he is about to pull out into traffic, he looks at me with a funny, embarrassed smile, and says, "You know, people think I'm nuts. Really, they do. But someone has to do these things."

Rick Ankiel

A Mound of Troubles

(from the *New York Times Magazine*, 2001)

"WE REALLY ARE NORMAL PEOPLE," says Denise Ankiel. She means herself. A mother of three grown children, she's a secretary for a bottled-water company in Fort Pierce, Fla. Her ex-husband is in prison and, as spring training arrives this week, her younger son, Rick Ankiel, Jr., is preparing to face the demons that transformed him last season from one of baseball's greatest phenoms into one of its most extraordinary enigmas.

Rick Ankiel is a pitcher of such immense talent that one baseball executive described him as simply, "one of the best left-handers I've ever seen." In 1997, *USA Today* named him the High School Player of the Year. Shortly after that, he signed with the Cardinals for a $2.5 million bonus, the fifth highest ever given to an amateur. In 1999, *USA Today* and *Baseball America* named him the Minor League Player of the Year, and by the summer of 2000, his first full season with the Cardinals, he was arguably the team's best pitcher, with an 11-7 won-lost record. He went 4-0, with a 1.97 earned run average, over the last month of the season and was picked by his manager, Tony LaRussa, to start the first game of the National League division series against the Atlanta Braves.

Before that first playoff game, Rick Ankiel, twenty-one, was being compared with another Cardinal left-hander, Steve Carlton, who is in the Hall of Fame. Like Carlton, Ankiel has a smooth, seemingly effortless delivery, an exploding fastball and a sharp curveball. Carlton, however, was widely seen as an arrogant, ignorant, and self-absorbed man. Ankiel is a sensitive, intelligent and considerate young man. He is nothing like Carlton.

In fact, his career and his nature more closely parallel that of a more distant Cards pitcher named Max Von McDaniel. In 1957, at the age of eighteen, Von McDaniel signed with the Cardinals for a $50,000 bonus on the strength of his smooth, seemingly effortless delivery, his exploding fastball, and his sharp curveball. He was described by all who met him as a sensitive, intelligent, and religious youth. The Cardinals brought him directly from high school to the major leagues, where he won his first four games. McDaniel pitched nineteen consecutive scoreless innings, including a one-hitter, a two-hitter, and a perfect game for six innings. He finished the year at 7-5 with a 3.22 E.R.A. and—with the exception of two disastrous innings in 1958, during which he walked seven batters—never pitched again in the major leagues.

McDaniel's sudden failure had nothing to do with physical injury. What happened to him is the stuff of Greek tragedy. Despite his blinding talent, there was something in his nature that fated him to fail for reasons neither he nor anyone else has ever been able to explain.

The same thing happened to Rick Ankiel in the 2000 playoffs. In two starts and one relief appearance, first against the Braves and then against the Mets, he walked eleven batters in four innings and threw nine wild pitches, most of which sailed ten feet over the batters' heads. He broke a record for wild pitches in an inning that had stood since 1890. His once-classic delivery was riddled with the flaws of a Little Leaguer. He looked like a pitcher who, in a single moment, forgot how to pitch. Ankiel seemed to be suffering a physical and psychic breakdown reminiscent of the one McDaniel suffered in the spring of 1958.

"Oh, my gosh, the same thing happened to my brother," says Lindy McDaniel, sixty-five, who himself pitched for many years in the major leagues. "He lost his coordination and his mechanics. There was no real explanation. Some people thought it was psychological. But who knew about those things then? They sent Von down to the minors, but he couldn't get anyone out. He kept sinking further and further until he couldn't pitch anymore. It depressed him for years after he left baseball. But he couldn't talk about it."

Lindy's recollections are not entirely accurate. When Von "mysteriously lost his rhythm and control," according to a 1961 *Sporting News* article, he drifted all the way down to the lowest Class D league. But there in 1960, Von McDaniel "began to throw smoothly again." In the sleepy anonymity of the Florida State League, Von fashioned a 13-5 record. The following season, the Cards brought him to spring training amidst great expectations, but once again he lost what the *Sporting News* called "his magic touch." He would never regain it.

What happened to Rick Ankiel and Von McDaniel has befallen a number of major league pitchers over the years, most notably Herb Score of the Cleveland Indians in the 1950s, Steve Blass of the Pittsburgh Pirates in the 1970s, and Mark Wohlers of the Atlanta Braves in the 1990s. They had a lot in common: blinding, youthful talent, sudden success, thoughtful and intelligent natures. They were all nice guys, humble men who somehow never trusted their success. It came too quickly. They didn't deserve it. What if they lost it? Indeed, Von McDaniel once said that "maybe things came too easily."

Pitchers who forget to pitch seem to fear not failure but success. They don't want to face the pressure of the expectations of their success. So they rebel, self-destructing in a way that puts them beyond blame. The reason for their failure, their fear, is so deeply rooted that neither they nor anyone else can ever drag it to the surface to make them confront it. It's all a mystery. But the only way they can ever overcome their apparently inexplicable collapse is to admit that it's no mystery, that it is their fault. They are afraid.

What are they afraid of anyway? Throwing a baseball? They have been doing that since childhood. Somewhere along the way, though, they realize that it makes them special. After that, a simple act takes on mythic importance. They begin to think about it, the mystery of their gift, and they get lost. They stand on the mound, their minds filled with discordant thoughts. Sometimes they replay their pitching mechanics over and over until they begin their motion and, unbelievably, it all flies out of their heads like a bird loosed from a cage. In midmotion, they remember nothing, move as if in a dream, weightless, until they release the ball and come back to where they are—on the mound, waiting for the catcher to retrieve their latest wild pitch. Now, too late, they remember everything.

Thought is their enemy. They either remember too much or forget everything. Both cause their failure. All they really need to do is perform an enormous act of will not to think. All they really need to do is what one of Rick's minor league pitching coaches once told him: "Just throw, man. Just throw."

* * *

Rick Ankiel says he had a "Tom Sawyer kind of boyhood" in sleepy Fort Pierce. He went barefoot every day, swam in the ocean, dove off piers, fished for snook in the Indian River, and put on shoes only to play Little League baseball. He says he wasn't a very good player in Little League. "I was always the smallest kid," he says. "I was terribly shy. Maybe it was because my dad yelled at me so much. I was afraid to mess up."

Rick Ankiel, Sr. was not an easy man to grow up around. He once worked hanging drywall, then as a fishing guide, a career choice that led to his last line of work, drug smuggling. He had already been arrested fourteen times—and convicted six times—for such offenses as burglary and carrying concealed weapons, before he was arrested on drug charges. Rick stood beside his father in court last March, when he was sentenced to six years in a federal prison.

"His dad has been his coach, his friend, and his foe," says Ankiel's mother, Denise. Rick Sr. said of his son, by then in the majors, "He's been rode hard a lot of times."

Rick says: "My dad was hard on me all the time. If I swung at a bad pitch in Little League, he'd make me run wind sprints when I got home. It was always *I could've done better*. But maybe if he wasn't hard on me, I would've gone down the wrong path. He always said, 'Do what I say, not what I do.'" Rick says his father taught him his smooth delivery, his high leg kick, and slow, deliberate motion. He also taught his son "never to show emotion on the mound," Rick says, "which I always thought was strange because I wasn't like that anyway."

Like many boys, Rick pitched for his father's approval and, maybe even more important, to avoid his wrath. "I tried to argue with him sometimes," he says, "but. . ." When Rick wanted to go fishing instead of play baseball, his mother would intercede on his behalf. "If he doesn't want to play," Denise would say to her husband, "let him do what he wants." What Rick wanted to do at fourteen was quit baseball. He told his father: *I'm never going to play in the major leagues. So I'm going to do stuff with my buddies, hang out on the beach, go surfing, go fishing.*

His father was adamant. "That's not gonna work," he said. "If you love the game, good things will happen."

But Rick didn't really love the game. He liked the game the way most boys his age did, but he wasn't devoted to it. By the time he was a soph-omore in high school, he was just a decent pitcher with an 84-mile-per-hour fastball. But he was also mature beyond his years. Everyone who knew him described him as a man among boys, thanks to the toughness of his father. Even his father said, "He's a very good young man, a good person at heart, a great kid."

When Rick was a sophomore at Port St. Lucie High School, his coach, John Messina, described him as "a great kid off the field, but nothing exceptional as a pitcher." Rick's greatest attribute as a pitcher, Messina says, was that "he picked up everything in seconds. He had a mind like a computer." When it came to pitching, Rick says: "I understood things in my head before I did them physically. I picked up pitching quick. Everything else. . . ." He laughs. "Well, I was goofy. I walked like a klutz. I spilled milk at the dinner table every night."

By his junior year, Rick had grown from "a small kid" into a strapping six-footer. His fastball now cruised toward the plate at over 90 m.p.h. He struck out batters at will, once fanning fourteen of the first fifteen batters he faced. "I came out of nowhere," he says. "There were major league scouts at every game. I realized I had a chance now for a scholarship to the University of Miami or a professional contract."

His father became obsessed with his son's career. He went to every game, sat in the stands, and flashed signs to Rick indicating what pitch to throw. When Rick struck out the side, he walked off the mound, glancing to the stands for his father's approval, a nod, a smile, anything. In one game in his junior year, Rick was pitching a no-hitter when he heard his father's voice screaming, "Throw him the funk!" This was his father's word for a knuckleball. Rick threw the next batter a knuckleball, and he hit a home run.

"Boy, that ticked me off," says Rick's pitching coach then, Charlie Frazier. "He was always calling Rick's pitches. After a game, he'd tell me I called a lousy game." Rick Sr. was described by one fan as a "borderline problem. He was always arguing with the umpires, coaches, athletic directors. He was a character in town. Boisterous, a drinker, a party guy. Rick tried to play down his shortcomings, and to tell the truth, his dad did try to be a good dad to Rick. He took him fishing, things like that."

Rick's father wasn't the only one to recognize Rick's gift and try to exert control over it. His coaches, who had previously just seen him as a decent pitcher, now began to treat him like a hothouse flower. They refused to let him bat right-handed (he was a switch-hitter) because they were afraid he might get hit by a pitch on his exposed left arm.

This special treatment did not go unnoticed by Rick. It dawned on him that he had a special talent, a talent that had to be protected, a talent that he began to fear losing. Rick could see this in the eyes of others, even though he didn't feel special himself. He thought of himself as just "a normal kid" until his senior year, when he was named the best high-school pitcher in the country and realized, with a shock of recognition, that the most prized possession in his life was "my left arm." The only person in his life who didn't define Rick by his talent was his mother. "No matter what you do for your career," she told him, "what you do is just what you do. That's not who you are." Then she asked her husband, "Is he really that good?"

In 1998 and 1999, Rick sailed through the minors, never lasting more than a few months in one league before being promoted to the next level. His first year, he was 3-0 at Peoria before advancing to Prince William, where he finished 9-6, with 181 strikeouts at 126 innings. In 1999, he started the season at AA Arkansas, where he won six times without a loss, and was promoted to AAA Memphis, where he went 7-3. With that, the St. Louis sports media began clamoring for Rick's promotion to the Cardinals.

The team at first resisted, with one executive saying, "We won't rush this kid no matter what the pressure is," but then promoted Rick to the major leagues in September. Pitching in relief, he was 0-1, with one save, but he had an impressive 3.27 E.R.A. and struck out 39 batters in 33 innings. The Cardinals had no choice but to put Rick in their starting pitching rotation in 2000. They never noticed the warning signs that had appeared during his two successful minor league seasons.

Most players coming out of high school stumble in their early years in the minor leagues. Away from home for the first time in their lives, they miss the comforting routine of the only life they ever knew, their family, friends, girlfriends. But Rick loved getting away from home, being "in new places with new people," possibly because life with his father was never all that comforting. Furthermore, Rick's game never went bad. He never had to stand in a phone booth crying to his father: "I can't get anybody out! What should I do?" Rick says: "I never had a bad year. I was always moving up. It was fun."

In retrospect, admits Mike Jorgensen, the Cardinals' director of player development, this probably wasn't the best thing for Rick. "Very few pitchers go through the minor leagues without adversity," he says. "It's very difficult to make adjustments in the major leagues if you haven't had adversity in the minor leagues."

While in the minors, Rick became such a hot property that Cardinal officials insisted he be given special treatment. He was not allowed to throw more than one hundred pitches in a game. His pitching coaches were forbidden to teach him a slider, for fear it would hurt his arm. His pitching coaches, probably afraid to tamper with such a precious commodity, overlooked a few minor flaws in his motion. "If you've got a race car that's leading the Daytona five hundred, you don't bring it in for a tune up," Jorgensen says. "All we did was fine-tune a couple of things with his motion, but nothing major." Besides, Jorgensen adds, "We have a pitch count for all pitchers in the minor leagues."

Once again, though, this special treatment did not escape Rick's notice. If others thought his talent was so fragile, then maybe it was. "If it goes, what do I have to fall back on?" he says. "Really nothing. It's scary." On the rare occasions when he did falter in the minors, he received no guidance. "Every now and then I'd hit the backstop with a wild pitch," he says. "But when I asked my pitching coaches what I was doing wrong, they wouldn't say a word to me. They'd just say, 'I'm not allowed to mess with you.'"

Rick's special treatment continued into the major leagues, even during last summer's stardom. He was put on a strict pitch count because the Cardinals—and his agent, Scott Boras—didn't want to overwork his delicate young arm. In his first four major league starts, Rick averaged 101 pitches. He was taken out of two games while working on a shutout and finished the four-game stretch with a 1.50 E.R.A. Rick chafed at the pitch limit. "I want to throw more pitches, but they won't let me," he said.

In the middle of the 2000 season, Rick's parents divorced, adding another shattering element to the emotional turmoil that began with his father's imprisonment. "I can't even fathom all he has to deal with," Denise said, "the choices he has had to make at seventeen, eighteen, nineteen, and twenty. He does not have a normal twenty-year-old's life." There was no way to establish a simple cause-and-effect relationship between the emotional shocks and Rick's subsequent troubles on the mound. But one thing is clear. By the time he was twenty-one, pitching in the playoffs, Rick's career and his young life began to unravel.

During his three playoff appearances against the Braves and the Mets, Rick's pitching was pitiful to the point of embarrassment. "It was tough to watch," a fellow Cardinal pitcher, Andy Benes, said at the time. After throwing five wild pitches against the Braves, even Rick had to admit that he was, as he said, "a joke. You've got to laugh." Then he talked about the mechanical things he was doing wrong: "I wasn't keeping my left shoulder in. It was so obvious, and I didn't finish my pitches. I just need to dig deep."

Before his start against the Mets, he claimed he'd figured out what he was doing wrong. "It was mechanical, totally," he said. "I feel great." Then he went out and threw five of his first twenty pitches off the home plate screen. The Cardinals tried to play down his collapse. The pitching coach, Dave Duncan, said he just needed to go to the mound and "have a nice easy inning and probably get back on track." So the Cardinals sent Rick out to the mound in a low-pressure situation, the seventh inning of a game they were losing, 6-0, to the Mets. He walked two batters and threw two wild pitches. "For some reason," Rick said, "it just didn't click."

After his three disastrous performances, Rick called his father in prison. "You were sorry," his father said. "Are you hurt?"

Rick said, "I'm okay."

"Then what the heck were you doing?"

"I couldn't figure it out."

"Aw, you'll be all right."

Back in Florida, his high school pitching coach, Charlie Frazier, had watched Rick's self-destruction on TV. "I never saw him lose his motion like that before," says Frazier. "I saw mechanical flaws. He was throwing across his body; he was standing up in his follow-through. I asked him what his pitching coaches told him. He said, "'They don't tell me anything!'"

I am standing off to the side, watching Rick. He is sitting at a picnic table under the shade of a Banyan tree on a sunny Florida afternoon in December. He is surrounded by little boys and girls, foster children who have come to Fort Lauderdale Stadium to watch celebrity athletes and models and singers play a softball game for their benefit. After an autograph session, Rick walks back to the baseball field for the game. He is a tell, husky youth with blond tints in his short, sandy hair. He walks in that plodding, hunched-over manner of young athletes not yet used to being gawked at.

The game is played for laughs. A young woman in tight shorts runs around the infield spraying everyone with sticky string. A muscular guy in a cut-off T-shirt tackles her at third base. Rick, on the mound, tosses a softball underhand to the batter. Nick Cannon, from Nickelodeon, swings and hits a little roller to Rick's right. Rick dives at the ball a second too late and falls flat on his face. Like everyone else, Rick is playing this game for laughs, only with a difference. Rick is having fun, like a kid. The celebrities are being funny to call attention to themselves.

In the fifth inning, play is stopped with Rick at home plate. He leans on his bat and watches as two men lead a statuesque girl onto the field. She is wearing a red tube top and tiny red satin shorts. Her name is Monica or Monique or whatever. According to the P.A. announcer, she has just "signed a huge record contract." She is almost six feet tall, long legged and voluptuous. One of her male handlers gives her a microphone, and Monica or Monique or whatever begins to sing and dance behind home plate. Rick watches with an amused smile. She finishes her tuneless song standing with her legs spread and her chest thrust forward. It is an impressive performance, but she receives only polite applause.

After the game, I walk with Rick to his black Tahoe in the parking lot. He's going back to his Miami Beach hotel to get some rest before tonight's charity party at Level in South Beach. "What did you think of Monique?" he asks. I smile, shake my head. "She's only fifteen," he says, raising his eyebrows. "Can you believe it?" In the hotel, Rick sprawls on his bed in a room that looks like it was tidied up with a hand grenade. A friend from Fort Pierce, Chad, is sitting on the other bed watching a movie. Chad is short, frail-looking, with a wispy blond mustache. I ask Rick if he wants to talk. He's tired, a little irritable. "Whatever you want." I ask him about his family.

"My mom's awesome," he says. "My older brother, he doesn't do nuthin'. My sister, she's got a kid."

"What about your father?"

"Some things happen in life," he says. "You get shot down. It's his life. Everyone has problems. You deal with it."

There's an awkward silence. Finally, I ask him why he recently moved from Fort Pierce to Newport Beach, California.

"Why not?" he says. "I'm twenty-one. I'm not responsible for anyone else." Rick is reluctant to talk about the unsettling events of last summer. But others aren't. "Hell, yeah, I think all those things have got to affect him in some way," says his high school coach, Charlie Frazier. "No wonder he moved to Newport to get away from it all."

The one thing Rick hasn't been able to get away from, the thing that has preyed on him throughout his long off-season, is his meltdown during the playoffs. "Last fall was my first test with adversity," he says. "I just lost it right there on the mound. I don't know what I was thinking. I'd go blank before I'd throw the ball, and then after I'd say to myself, 'How the hell did that happen?' It was definitely weird. I mean, I'd been doing it so many times in my life, and suddenly I can't throw a ball?"

He hasn't thrown one pitch since. "I'm working out," he says. "I run, lift weights, and long-toss on the grass. But no, I haven't thrown off a mound yet. I'm trying to enjoy every day."

In the early-evening darkness, Rick, Chad, and I are walking past the shops and restaurants on Lincoln Road. Rick and Chad stop at a clothing store, Biker's Den, and go inside. I wait on the sidewalk smoking a cigar. I watch them for a few minutes, pulling clothes off racks, disappearing into dressing rooms, reappearing, until finally they bring their purchases to the cash register. Rick pulls out his gold American Express card, pays for the clothes, and they step outside.

"Whaddya think?" Chad asks. "An improvement?" He's wearing his newly bought clothes, a black jersey and baggy gray slacks that bunch up around his shoes. We hail a cab, which drops us off at the party. Rick orders a glass of red wine, and we begin talking baseball. He asked me what it was like when I pitched in the minor leagues, which I did from 1959 to 1962, when I was released at the age of twenty-one.

"Nobody counted my pitches," I say. "I pitched until I couldn't get anyone out. Sometimes I threw one hundred thirty, one hundred forty pitches in a game."

"Jeez, I wish the Cardinals would let me do that."

We talk for some time. Later, having lost track of him in the crowd and feeling tired, I leave the party and begin to walk to my car. I'm surprised to hear Rick call out. I turn. He's running toward me.

"Where you going?" he asks. I tell him I'm tired.

"I'll leave, too," he says. "I don't have to stay there."

"Thanks," I say. "But you should stay." I smile. "Maybe Monique will show up."

"Yeah, maybe." Then he shakes my hand.

"That was a nice thing to do," I say. "Buy those clothes for Chad."

He looks embarrassed. "I try to do things for him. He hasn't had any advantages."

"Call me," I say. "Maybe we'll go throw the ball around one day."

"Yeah, that would be cool."

"You gotta get back on the mound. You should always be throwing from the mound."

"I know," he says. "Soon."

"It's no big thing," I say. "You've been throwing off a mound ever since you were a kid. Just don't think about it. You've got to force yourself not to think about your motion, or it will mess you up." He looks down at the sidewalk and nods. "Just remember," I say. "The mound is where you live." He looks up and smiles.

"How do you know?" he says.

"Why do you think I'm here? What's happening to you happened to me in nineteen sixty-one. I forgot how to pitch. I've been thinking about it ever since."

"What'd you learn?" he asks.

"Not to think."

Q & A with Pat Jordan

Alex Belth: Your experiences as a failed pitching prospect are the springboard for your career as a writer. How did your experience as an athlete influence your writing?

Pat Jordan: I was very methodical when I played baseball, and that helped me in my writing. When I was in Little League I used to run wind sprints so I wouldn't get out of shape. Now, what twelve-year-old gets out of shape? But even then, I approached pitching in a very methodical way. Monday we do wind sprints, Tuesday I throw a little bit, Wednesday I shag fly balls and take batting practice, Thursday I throw hard, Saturday I pitch the game. Before I would pitch, I would literally outline the game on a piece of paper. I would put each batter up and describe how I was going to pitch to him. I drew a stick figure of the batter. I'd do, "first pitch, curve ball low and away, second pitch, fastball, up and in." I was methodical even then. Didn't mean I followed the outline. But at least I had a blueprint to begin the game. I just transferred that to a writing routine.

AB: Did anyone in your family write?

PJ: No. My father was a gambler all his life, partly because he was an orphan and had to turn to himself for approval because he had no family. When he got out of the orphanage he started hustling pool and that was his identity. Then he went from pool to dice to cards to horses to whatever. His gambling defined him. I never gambled myself. But one of the things my father said to me was, "Kid, there are three vices in the world: broads, booze, and gambling. If you are going to do it right, pick one and stick to it." When he first told me that, I was married with five kids and no money. I laughed at him and said, "Dad, I don't have room in my life for any vices, I'm running from one job to another." Forty years later, after I'd been a freelance writer for years, he told it to me again. I said, "Well, I've got a little acquaintance with the first two— broads and booze, but I still don't gamble, Dad." And he laughed at me. "You don't gamble? A freelance writer for forty years and you're telling me you don't gamble?" It was his way of saying the apple hadn't fallen far from the tree, we just gambled on different things. What he was telling me is that I gambled on myself. I never worked for anybody. I define myself by the writing that I do. I can always hustle an assignment and write it in such a way that editors like it, and I get another assign- ment. After forty years as a freelance writer it's always about the next assignment. That's how my old man did it. He'd hustle up a poker game, figuring that he could win any game he got into.

AB: Do you approach writing like he did gambling?

PJ: His attitude toward gambling was that it wasn't luck, it was his manipulation of the game—shaved dice, deal from the bottom of the deck. So in his mind, he was competing against the other guy. It was about his wits. In a way, I'm using my wits to write my stories. You can make an analogy between my old man's cons and how I manipulate a subject. The difference is that my old man's con would be about stealing people's money. My con is to get people to tell me the truth about them- selves. So I like to think that my con is on a higher level.

AB: You wrote exclusively for *Sports Illustrated* for most of the 1970s, where you quickly established a reputation for covering lesser-known figures, yet one of your seminal early pieces was on Tom Seaver, who was a big star.

PJ: Seaver is the guy who made me realize that very successful people have to acquire what I call ocular block. The ability to focus on, to the exclusion of everything else, that which is most important to their careers. Most of those obsessed stars become less as human beings because of their ocular block. Tom Seaver was the lone exception.

Although he focused his ocular block on his career, he never diminished the rest of his life. I asked Seaver, "What do you do in the mornings?" He said, "I wake up and read the box scores." I said, "Well, don't you ever read a review of a play or a movie that you want to see?" He said, "No, I read the box scores first to see who got two hits off so-and-so, so I know how to pitch him the next time I face him." He told me he didn't like to read anything extraneous that would interfere with his pitching and make him think too much about anything other than baseball, until after he pitched a successful game. Only then, on his days off, would he visit art museums and go to the theater.

AB: Athletes like Michael Jordan or Derek Jeter come to mind when you talk about ocular block.

PJ: That's exactly right. I got the idea that people other than Seaver who succeed are generally not as interesting as the ones who fail, 'cause you never think about why you succeeded. You only think about why you failed. Because of my theories on ocular block, I became the "failure" writer at *SI* and they gave all the heroes to George Plimpton. One time Plimpton did a story on Hank Aaron and wrote about "the mystical grace of Hank Aaron at bat," and he went on and on, and I said to him, "I pitched against Hank Aaron, George. You know what's mystical about him? He had quicker wrists than anybody else." So he could wait on the fastball later, he could wait on the curveball until it broke, and then hit it. I said, "That's what is mystical about him, George. It was a God-given, physical gift." But that's how George saw athletes, with a kind of golden glow about them. He wasn't an athlete and he wanted to be one.

AB: You continued to write about Seaver over the years. What about him did you find so compelling?

PJ: My fascination with him is that I should have been Seaver as a pitcher. What did he know that I didn't to become a great pitcher? Plus, he's a fun guy. He's much more fun than his public image, which is as a straight arrow. He's not a straight arrow when you get to talk to him in real life. He's caustic, smartass, lot of fun. When I finally realized why he was successful I realized that I could never be successful as a pitcher because I couldn't be like him, devoting my entire life to one thing. Even when I pitched in baseball, I had a stamp collection, I read, I had all kinds of diverse interests. If someone had said, "All you can do for the rest of your life is think about baseball," I'd go out of my mind. And I love baseball. But . . . I realized that I could have never been Seaver although I had a Seaver talent. But I was able to do what Seaver did as a pitcher as a writer. That's because being singularly focused as a writer requires you to notice everything. So it's the perfect job for me. For example, I notice the woman in the airport with the funny hat. One day, I might use it. My single focus as a writer is on everything around me. I took my diffused attention span, which always makes me look all around at everything, and found a job that it was perfect for.

AB: I've read Gay Talese say that curiosity is one of the most important qualities a journalist can have.

PJ: That's right. When you have a preconceived notion about someone— for instance, I thought Bo Belinsky was a jerk when I went to do a story on him—you *still* have to be open. After I did the piece on Bo I thought he was one of the *best* guys. I love Bo. He was as analytical as Phil Hill, but the only problem was that he wasn't bright enough to come to any conclusions. *SI* was a little taken aback because they thought I was going to write a negative story and it wasn't. I said, "Well, that's the guy I met." You're always going to have preconceptions but your question is always, "Am I right or am I wrong?" For example, I have never interviewed Martina Navratilova but I've always liked her from what I've read about her. Love to do a story on Martina Navratilova to find out if I'm right or I'm wrong. If I'm wrong, fine. If you're wrong, actually, it's exciting because you have to go 180 degrees from your original inclination and if you are right you say, "See, I'm so smart, I knew they were a good guy or good girl." I once did Ted Turner for *GQ* and found him so distasteful that I lost my objectivity. I went in expecting to find him obnoxious and when he turned out to be just that I ended up writing a mean-spirited story, and my original was worse than the one they published. But that hasn't happened often. The only other time that happened was when I did a story on David Peltzer, the guy who wrote *A Child Called It*, about being abused as a child. I found out and revealed in the *Times* that he was a fraud, he had never been abused, everything in his bio was a lie, the whole thing was fabricated to make money. The editor at the *Times* calls me up and says, "My boss wants to know why you hate this guy so much." I said, "Does it show?" He said,

"Jesus, we had to soften the story, you were so negative." But he was such a fraud. It wasn't writer's jealousy, because I'm thrilled for any serious writer who makes a million dollars even if I don't. But when I see someone being a fraud and a con artist and the rest of us are trying to do good work and *we're* not making a million dollars, while a fraud is, I feel like it's dirtying the profession. I feel like they are taking a pure thing—the ability to write truthfully—and sullying it. I get furious. Charles Frazier wrote *Cold Mountain*. He spent ten years writing it. Now, I resent the fact that his wife worked, and he could afford to take ten years to write a novel. My wife doesn't work and I can't afford to take ten years to write a novel that I haven't even sold. So I resent that. And I didn't like *Cold Mountain*. It wasn't my kind of book. I don't think writing about trees is that interesting. It's a quest story, a string of pearls, and I didn't believe any of it. However, it was a serious book. So I think that Charles Frazier deserves all the accolades and awards and money that he got for it, because it was a serious artistic effort. It didn't appeal to me, I was a little personally resentful, but I admire that he had to delay his gratifications for ten years before anyone saw his book. He had to have the personal satisfaction of knowing, "Today I wrote a great scene about a flowing stream," and live with that. I can admire guys who are not my cup of tea as writers. But I'm furious with phonies.

AB: So you don't have any agendas when you are writing.

PJ: My agenda is to be true to the subject. If you are a good guy, I'm the best man to do a story on you because I'm obsessed with capturing you as you are, including the warts. If you're not a good guy, then, one of my editors said about me as a writer, "I'd push the dresser up against the door to keep you out." Sometimes I forget that if I mention a wart or two, even on the good guys, the subject won't like it. The secret to a profile is that if you don't like the subject you bend over backwards to give them a break because your dislike will show through anyway even if you try to hide it. If you like a subject, you can be as hard on them as you want because you know that you're liking them will show through too.

AB: How do you find that you can get a subject to reveal something about his or her true nature?

PJ: First, by talking a lot about yourself, not just asking questions, to make a connection. Sometimes, I'll stage a scene too, hoping to get something. For example, I did a story for *GQ* on Traci Lords, the porn star, just when she was starting to go mainstream. For some reason, I thought that the best place to meet her for the first time would be in the coffee shop of The Four Seasons hotel in Beverly Hills, in the morning, where all the power people are going to be before they go off to do business. So I met her there and she came in dressed up like a porn star. She looked like Traci Lords on the porn boxes. Everybody's head swiveled. We sat down, and she said, "Look at them all staring at me. Fuck them, they think they're better than me. Fuck them, fuck them." Now, she didn't have to do that. She could have come in wearing a gray suit, very demure, and I might have written, "Traci Lords comes in here and nobody recognizes her in her gray suit." It's got to be real, but that doesn't mean that you can't nudge it someplace. You are trying to put the subject in an environment that will most let them be themselves in some way. You are setting up action but not instigating the action like some journalists do when they ask an outrageous question that is intended to make the subject lose their temper. I never do that. I don't ask the outrageous question. I try to ask the question that is consistent with the person's nature even though but they might not want to talk about it. The whole point is, I want them to talk about more than they are willing to talk about. Most subjects have an agenda, just like the writer. My agenda is for the subject to tell me everything, and the subject's agenda is to tell me what he wants to tell me to create a picture that he wants created. It's an inherently adversarial relationship. It's rare when it isn't adversarial, when somebody doesn't have anything to hide.

AB: Some stories, like the one you did on Whitey Herzog, come to mind as having a subject who was very forthcoming in an amiable way. Then again, your two most controversial stories—the Garveys and Steve Carlton—were forward with you as well. But there was a lot of fallout once the stories came out.

PJ: In 1980 I was watching a television program, sort of like a Jerry Springer show but not as wild as that, and they had Stormy Dent on. She was married to Bucky Dent and he had just come out with a poster, a shirtless poster of himself, selling him as a sex symbol to teenage girls. And she was furious about the idea that somebody was marketing her husband—who had agreed to it—as a sex symbol when he was married with a couple of kids. She interested me. She *was* stormy. I would have hated to have been—no, I would have *liked* to have been married to her. I called John Walsh at *Inside Sports* and said, "I've got a great idea. Why don't we do two baseball wives? One who loves being the wife of a star and one who hates it. Stormy Dent hates it, let's do her. Nancy Seaver loves it." At least I thought she did. He said, "Well, we can't have two New York guys." (Even though Seaver had left already I guess he was still considered a New York guy.) He said, "What about somebody from some other place?" So I hunted around for about a week and read about Cyndi Garvey, how she had her license plate "Cyndi" with Steve's number on it. And how she rode around L.A. and loved being Mrs. Steve Garvey. I didn't know much about Cyndi Garvey, so I decided to go out there first, do her, and then I'll come back and do Stormy. I go to L.A. and find out that she hates being Mrs. Steve Garvey. She used to love it, and now she hates it. By the time I got through doing the interviews with her, I called John Walsh and said "We don't need to do Stormy Dent because I've got one wife who went both ways, AC-DC. So we can do the metamorphosis of a baseball wife." Now, Cyndi Garvey came on to me at lunch at the Beverly Hills Hotel. Susan, my girlfriend and eventual wife, was down by the pool. There was a bar down there and she was getting hit on by an heir to the Getty fortune. He was a kid. He was trying to pick her up while Cyndi was all over me. So I found a way to mention that my girlfriend was with me, down by the pool. Being a good girl at the time, Cyndi switched gears and said, "Oh, wonderful, why don't you bring her out to the house tomorrow night when you come to interview me?" I said, "You won't mind?" She said, "Well, she shouldn't stay alone in a hotel room." She was good about it, you know? So the next night we are there sitting in the Garvey's living room. It's Cyndi and Susan and myself. Steve wasn't there. I have the tape recorder on the table. I ask Cyndi a couple of questions and she starts getting emotional about Steve and Susan jumps in with something about her ex-husband. I don't remember what exactly it was. Unfeeling, not interested in sex with her. Then, at some point in the interview, Cyndi started talking to Susan, not me. It was girl talk, back and forth. "My ex-husband did this," "Steve won't do that." Finally, toward the end of it, I turned to Cyndi and said, "You know I have this all on tape, are you sure you want me to use all of this stuff?" And she said, "You print this, it's about time the world knew." Which is on tape.

AB: And the Garveys were less than thrilled when the story came out.

PJ: I was in Toronto doing a story. I'm in the press box dining room and Peter Bavasi comes in and he's got this AP wire story. He goes, "Pat, do you have eleven-point-two million?" I said, "I got a 'fifty-seven Chevy with body rot, what are you talking about?" He shows it to me. The Garveys had just announced that they were suing Pat Jordan, *Inside Sports,* and *Newsweek* for $11.2 million. And Peter starts laughing his ass off. I swallowed hard. I thought it was the end of my career. They sued me because they were embarrassed and started losing endorsement opportunities. They made a lot of money outside of baseball. Cyndi co-hosted a morning show with Regis Philbin. As soon as they started the suit they went on all the talk shows, Jon Davidson, holding hands, how much they loved each other and how this terrible writer came, blah, blah, blah. *Newsweek* wouldn't let me defend myself and do publicity. During the inquiry the Garveys demanded my tapes. See, I didn't want to give up the tapes. But *Newsweek* told me they wouldn't indemnify me and I'd have to get my own lawyers if I didn't turn over the tapes. I couldn't afford a $500,000 lawyer. This was the first story I had ever written for them. Ultimately, I didn't mind giving them up, except I used the tapes to muse, sort of like a notebook. So the tapes didn't only have my interviews with the Garveys they also had me talking into the tapes as notes. For example, after an interview, I'd get in the car, put on the recorder and say, "This broad is not getting laid, that's her problem. Steve might carry a big bat on the field but he's not carrying a big bat at home." Something like that. I also used more colorful language. When they got the tapes, they figured that my profanity on the tapes would sway a jury against me. And they wanted to try the case in Orange County, the most conservative county in California. And Steve lives in L.A.! So why? That's where all the born again Christians and Republicans were and here you had this filthy Northeastern writer talking trash about the great hero Steve Garvey in a profane way: Guilty. Doesn't matter if I had all the quotes as they said them. The lawyer who defended me said they were the most accurate quotes he'd ever seen in a libel case. He said he couldn't believe anyone would bring up a lawsuit after they had read this. But then he told me why they did. He said, "Your comments into the tape are what they want." I had to give depositions all the time. But the case never went to court. Nobody knows that. They dropped it after the Garveys spent $450,000 in legal fees, but nobody knows it. To this day people tell me, "Oh, you're the guy who lost the Garvey lawsuit." Never went to court. Never went beyond the deposition stage. And they never intended it to. They wanted to get the publicity for suing me so they could go on the talk shows and say how happily married they were and do the whole p.r. thing. So they sustained the lawsuit for I don't know, maybe a year. They dropped it, and within a year they got divorced.

AB: Cyndi Garvey provided great material for you, but you also did a lot of descriptive writing in that piece. The Carlton story seems even more startling in terms of what he provided you.

PJ: I visited him in Durango, Colorado. The weather was horrible and my car broke down the morning I was scheduled to meet him at a local gym. I made it in time, though. Now, I knew nothing about Carlton other than he hated to talk to the press. But he was going to the Hall of Fame and he wanted to capitalize on it. He was a little odd. He told me, "I'm up here because I wanted to be secluded because of what America's becoming," or something like that. So I changed the subject and told him about a new gun I had bought. I'm into guns. For some reason, I knew that would perk him up. So I mentioned that I had gotten a Czechoslovakian military pistol, a CZ-85. He said, "Oh yeah, that's a great gun. You know you'd better bury that in PVC pipes because the UN is coming in black helicopters to confiscate all of our guns." I said, "Oh, really?" He said, "Yeah, it's a world organization that's dictated by the Elders of Zion, the twelve Jews in Switzerland who control the world." At this point, I just let him go. Now, my editor didn't want this story, he wanted Steve Carlton the Hall of Fame pitcher. So I said, "Eliot, this guy's crazy. He's the kind of guy who should not be allowed to read a book. He believes everything in the last book he read. Like the whole Elders of Zion thing. He told me he had read that in a book." Well, shit, there are other books.

AB: Have there been other occasions where a subject really hated what you had written about them?

PJ: I did Roger Clemens for the *Times* when he was with the Yankees for the first time. Clemens gave me a lot of access. He was all right. I mean, he wasn't my favorite person, but I didn't dislike him. Being with him was like being with a hyperactive fourteen year old. He has a maniacal workout routine, and I always thought it was a way of self-medicating. He was a hyper, A.D.D. kind of a guy, and exhausting himself through his workout was a way of medicating his hyperness. It was also a way of burning off calories because he loves to eat, like all ballplayers. I took him out to dinner. He chose the most expensive steak house in Houston. It was like a $400 bill. He said, "That's all right Pat, I'll get you tomorrow." He takes me to a Mexican restaurant where the tacos were like $1.98 or something. Typical ballplayer. After the story came out, I didn't think he'd send me flowers, but I didn't think he'd hate it either. He calls me up, screaming over the phone, tells me he hated the story. I said, "Did you read it? What didn't you like?" He said, "I didn't read it." I said, "If you didn't read it, how do you know that you don't like it?" He said, "Peter Gammons came up to me and told me it was a hachet job, so that's all I need." I said, "Peter Gammons?" Now, part of what I wrote in the original story is the fact that Clemens doesn't read. There are no books in his house. So I went and found a copy of Roger's *Rocket Man* book, co-authored by—? Peter Gammons. I guess Peter didn't like me stepping on his territory doing a Clemens story, so he told Clemens that he should hate it. The Yankees haven't let me back in the clubhouse to do a story since.

AB: In George Mitchell's report on the use of performance enhancing drugs [PEDs] in baseball, released two days ago, Clemens' former trainer, Brian McNamee, named Clemens as a user of steroids, notably just after he left the Boston Red Sox, when he was in his mid-thirties and his career temporarily seemed on the decline. As a former pitcher and someone how was written about PEDs, what is your initial response?

PJ: If the allegations are true, I understand how he was able to work out so maniacally during those three days I was with him. Pitchers just don't throw as hard when they are forty as they did when they were thirty. When they do, there is something unnatural about them. Nolan Ryan's secret was God. He just had a gift of nature. He was the greatest waste of talent in baseball history, but he also had one of the beautiful, effortless, fastball motions of all-time. Clemens is a grunter. He muscles the ball and doesn't have a great motion. But he's never changed. He's still throwing fastball up and in, hard-breaking pitch away. It's tough to fathom how he's continued to throw that hard, until we hear that he was possibly taking steroids.

AB: If Clemens was indeed using PEDs, do your feelings about him change?

PJ: Yes. My attitude about PEDs is the same as my attitude about what writers get paid from a magazine. I don't care what you pay me so long as it's what you pay anyone else—I want an equal playing field. If steroids are legal, and everyone can take them and some players choose not to, that's their decision. But the advantage someone gets taking PEDs illicitly over someone who follows the rules is profound, much more profound than the advantage gained from some of the forms of cheating we've had in the sport, like scuffing a baseball. People say that Clemens should apologize to his fans for cheating, but I think he should apologize to all those great players before him whom he surpassed, like Tom Seaver, whose Hall of Fame accomplishments were achieved without drugs.

AB: Why do you think PEDs became so prominent and why did the sport turn a blind eye?

PJ: There is so much money at stake now. When a guy who sits on the end of the bench makes three million a year, it's important for him to find any advantage he can to stay the last man on the bench. In the sixties, guys who were making forty thousand a year at the end of the bench would leave baseball and make thirty-two thousand. There wasn't that much discrepancy. As for the stars that take PEDs, guys who were already the greatest in their fields, it is a question of ego, of being the greatest in history. Barry Bonds and Clemens have the biggest egos of all. People were talking about Bonds as the greatest hitter ever, and Clemens as the greatest pitcher of all-time. Yet their greatest achievements came after they turned thirty-five, when players generally fade. What has made them so great is their longevity of greatness.

AB: So with Clemens and Bonds, it is classic case of hubris?

PJ: Exactly. Now, take a pitcher like Greg Maddux, who was once great, and now at forty is merely a good pitcher. I admire his effort to maintain some level of proficiency despite the loss of much of his physical abilities. Warren Spahn was the perfect example of that when I was a kid prospect with the Braves. At that time, most pitchers had a simple career arc: strong in their twenties, but by their early thirties, they'd lose their stuff. Spahn knew this was going to happen to him. He still threw heat in his early thirties, but he began to work on a change-up/screwball, a slider, a number of trick pitches. He began to incorporate them earlier than he needed to, so he never experienced a downswing in his mid-thirties, because by the time he lost his fastball, he had evolved into a new kind of pitcher, and he continued to win twenty games. A guy like Maddux, El Duque, or Tom Glavine, who couldn't give you a headache if he hit you in the head with a fastball, works within his limitations, and even finds a way to improve himself in spite of getting old. That's what sports is all about. It's about the crafty old timer, who still manages to get players out.

AB: One of the biggest changes in the sports world seems to be the kind of limited access you have today when writing about major stars. You were lucky to get the Williams sisters and Deion Sanders while they were young.

PJ: I did the Williams sisters for the *Times* before they were famous. Well, Venus was already famous, but she was famous for being famous. She was like the Paris Hilton of her day. She'd never won anything, never been in any real tournaments, but she was famous as this six-foot black tennis goddess. I went to see the two girls practice in West Palm Beach. Actually, the story was for *Men's Journal* originally. Richard Williams is a big, burly guy. But I'm a big guy too. He's got his daughters, some friends, his wife with him. And Richard shakes my hand and says, "I hope all us black folks don't scare you." I said, "Uh, not really, Richard." Richard reminds me of Reggie Jackson. A total game player. He tried to throw me off my game. I'm supposed to be scared? Like I'm some effete writer who is going to fall apart at the sight of a group of black people. I noticed Serena off practicing by herself. She was a chubby little kid. But she was very happy. I didn't think she'd turn out to be nearly as good as she became. Venus was an introvert. She struck me as not a very happy young girl. She was probably brighter than Serena and that's probably why she wasn't happy. She was also a teenager and Serena was still a kid. So I wrote the story and *Men's Journal* wouldn't publish it. They thought it was too negative. So I sent it to the *New York Times*, to my editor there, Eric Copage, who is black. He loved it and they bought it. I said to Eric, "It wasn't racist, was it?" "No," he said. "Not at all." So they ran it. Richard Williams called up, furious. This is the kind of guy he is, a pathological liar. He told the *New York Times* editor that when I presented the story to him as a *New York Times* story I said it would be a positive piece. Well,

I never told Richard I was doing it for the *New York Times*, I told him I was doing it for *Men's Journal*. He managed to forget that.

AB: By contrast, Wilt Chamberlain comes across as being forthright.

PJ: Wilt was a wonderful man, a real talker. I went to his house early because I have this theory that you should always surprise your subjects by showing up a little early to see what they are really like instead of when they are all prepared for you. So I got there like twenty minutes early and Wilt came out said, "Oh jeez, Pat, I didn't put the lights on around the pool yet. I wanted to show you how the pool looked with the lights on." And that let me know that he was such a meticulous stage-setting kind of a guy. We talked in his house. He was a great guy. I asked him about the twenty thousand women he slept with, and he said, "Aw, that was just bull-shit, but it was good for my book and all." So while we're talking I mention my wife, I tell him we have a house in the North Carolina mountains. And Wilt is both African American and Native American, Cherokee. And my wife loved the Cherokees from our days in North Carolina. So I talked about Susan. I got to Wilt's house at noon, left about five o'clock and got the ten o'clock plane, the red-eye, from L.A. to Florida. While I'm on the plane, Wilt calls Susan. Wakes her up at midnight and talks to her for two hours. I come in the next morning at six a.m. She picks me up at the air-port and says, "I haven't slept all night. I was talking to Wilt." I said, "What?" She said, "Oh, he said he had so much fun talking to you, and then you talked so much about me, he wanted to talk to me. We talked about North Carolina and his mother and his Cherokee ancestors and all." So I call up Wilt and say, "What, do you want to make Susan twenty thou-sand-and-one?" Two weeks later I'm in Miami Beach to do a story. Susan was with me, and at about ten o'clock at night we went to the China Grill to have a drink. And while we're standing at the bar, I look up and there's Wilt Chamberlain sitting at a table with three other people. Now Suzie is all dressed up in her Fort Lauderdale look, high heels, mini skirt, the whole thing, tan, blond. I tell her that Wilt loves blonds. I say, "Go by Wilt, really slow, and see what happens." So she saunters by his table, he jumps up, grabs her arm. He doesn't know who she is. He's talking to her and while he's talking to her he looks around and sees me at the bar. He bursts out laughing and says, "Son of a bitch, you're Pat's wife, Susan." I always felt that Wilt and Bill Russell were the two most misread people in the media. Bill Russell always got great press and he is a very, very unpleasant human being. And Wilt always got bad press as a goliath and he was one of the sweetest guys in the business and I always felt sorry for him.

AB: You've actually been more prolific in the last fifteen years than you were in the 1970s and most of the 1980s. Do you ever worry that you won't be able to write anymore?

PJ: I joke about how I outlive most of the magazines I've written for. *Premiere* magazine, which ran the Stallone piece and nominated it for a National Magazine Award, just went under, so I've buried another. I've gone six months between paid gigs, but I'm still writing during that time. I don't lose confidence that more work will come. I've never had what they call writers' block for two reasons. One, I have to pay bills so I can't afford to have writers' block. I force myself through it. Some of those stories were great, some weren't, but all of them were professionally done and publishable. Two, I just love to do it. It's not something I'm afraid of. I mean I am afraid when I confront the first blank piece of paper—I still use paper and a typewriter—but like Hemingway said, once you write that first simple, true declarative sentence, the rest of the novel will follow. Once I get the first sentence to a story, the story is done. It's just a matter of writing it.

AB: What is your process when given an assignment?

PJ: I don't just sit down and start writing. The first thing I do before I meet the subject is read clips, old magazine and newspaper articles. There are three things that you want to get out of reading clips. One, you want to get all of the basic information about the character you need so you don't have to ask him, "Where were you born, what school did you go to, when did you get married, how many kids do you have?" You get all that shit out of the way so it saves you from asking questions that are meaningless and waste time. Two, in reading the clips you want to find questions that have not been asked. Because most clips are superficially done, newspaper stories and even magazine stories, they never get to the heart of the matter. Very often the writers get the subject to answer a question which really should lead to three follow-up questions that they don't ask. Or if they ask it, gets cut out. The third reason to read clips is because if you read, say, three hundred pages on a person, even if they are the most bland clips, you really will get an idea about that person. You still get a feeling for that person, and you get a sense of where you can go with them, what you can ask them. So read the clips first, then come up with questions, then do the interviews, transcribe the tapes, then read the notes and clips over again until I memorize them, then start outlining on a yellow legal pad of paper, like an artist making sketches before starting a painting. I'll revise the outline again and again, just like you were taught in grammar school. Do that over and over until I find an outline I like. It's a habit left over from baseball—as far back as when I played in Little league when I used to draw those stick figures that showed me how I was going to pitch the batter. Which doesn't mean I'll stick to it, it just means it'll get me started writing. After I get the outline, I think for as long as it takes me, until I get the first line. I'll memorize my notes and clips and then spend a week walking around the house jotting notes on how I want to begin it. Once I figure out how I'm going to begin it, the story is done. Now, if I have an assignment, and it has to be done in a certain amount of time,I have to force it. It's gotta be done in six days, I don't have the luxury of wandering around the house thinking about it for six days. I come up with a very simple lead and just jump in to get it started.

AB: Your writing is marked by brutal honesty, especially when it comes to yourself. What do you see as your shortcomings or difficulties as a writer?

PJ: My biggest weakness as a writer is that I'm too orderly. There are times in non fiction when you are held hostage by all the information you have. I'm almost obsessive. It's like building the perfect car and it turns out to be a Lexus, a perfect automobile that will run forever with no sex appeal or pizzazz. Now, there are times when I don't have enough clips and notes, and I'm forced to wing it, and I'll create a sentence that's like a beautiful Alfa Romeo. It's about overcoming technique, because my technique is a comfort but it can also become an albatross. The other weakness I have is in the actual writing. I don't look for the poetic moment or poetic phrase. I like to have a "flat" style, but that doesn't mean I'm averse to a poetic sentence. There are times when I could do a little "writer's dance" but I'll miss the chance because I am so dogged about getting the story down right.

AB: Magazines don't customarily run long, ten-thousand-word stories

anymore either. How has your style adapted to fit in with the shorter profiles that are run today?

PJ: When I was with *GQ* in the late eighties and early nineties I was honing in on the idea that I really wanted to write less. By that I mean I wanted to tell less in a story, leave more out, and have the subtext tell more. My style almost took on a Western Union feel. Incomplete sentences, short sentences, because I was trying to cram in as much as possible. If I wrote a 15-word sentence and realized I had only 3,500 words for the whole piece, I'd think to myself, "How can I make this into an eight-word sentence so I can still keep the gist of what I want to say but be able to do something else with those seven leftover words?" I started working on that in the early nineties. It was also that I was getting older and I was ceasing to be the kind of emotionally big guy I had always been all of my life. I'm Italian, emotional, passionate, and my writing would be *big* sometimes. After I turned fifty, I was becoming happier, I was less angry, less hot-tempered, more disciplined, more reserved, and what happened was my personality started to change and that started to show up in my writing. My pleasures were simpler. I enjoyed being at home with my wife and the dogs, cooking dinner, watching a movie. I no longer had to be the star, in a sense. You have to remember, when I was ten years old, eleven years old, Dick Young wrote a column about me in the *Daily News*. When I was twelve, I was on television, the Little League pitcher on the Mel Allen show before the Yankee game. I had been a star all my life. Then when I became a writer, I was a star at *Sports Illustrated*, then I was a star at *GQ*. So I had always been an egocentric guy. Still am, but it's much more private now.

AB: There aren't many journalists of your generation who can still call themselves working writers. They've either retired, died, or become TV personalities. But you are still first and foremost a writer.

PJ: There is something else that my dad told me about gamblers, but it really applies to any well-balanced human being. He said, "Kid, find out what you are and be it." Which is the greatest advice a gambler's son or anybody else could have. So that's what I've spent my life doing. I wasn't just a failed pitcher—though I was that too—I was a writer. I didn't know that when I started, but that's how it turned out. Writing was never a means to an end for me, it was always the end itself.